An Illustrated
OUTLINE HISTORY
OF MANKIND

An
Outline History

IN COLLABORATION WITH

✻

HANNS GROSS, B.A.
*University of
London*

✻

ALFRED DeGRAZIA, PH.D.
*Executive Officer, Committee for Research
in Social Sciences, Stanford University*

✻

FRANK L. ESTERQUEST, PH.D.
*Chairman, Department of History
Western College*

✻

CHARLES W. PAAPE, PH.D.
*Associate Professor of History, Carnegie
Institute of Technology*

Illustrated
of MANKIND

EDITED BY

Fay-Cooper Cole, Ph.D., Sc.D., LL.D.
Former Chairman, Department of Anthropology, The University of Chicago

AND

Harris Gaylord Warren, Ph.D.
Professor of History, University of Mississippi

WITH AN INTRODUCTION BY
the Editors

CONSOLIDATED BOOK PUBLISHERS
Chicago

Library of Congress Catalog Card Number: 71-97260
International Standard Book Number: 0-8326-2401-2

Introduction

THE PUBLICATION of such a comprehensive work as *An Illustrated Outline History of Mankind* gives rise to a number of questions. Foremost among these are questions that bear upon the pursuit of historical studies and upon their application in a world increasingly dominated by technology. The other questions concern the place this particular work assumes beside the myriad books of its kind.

Probably few people living in the mid-twentieth century will deny that the individual in the Western world and in parts of Asia and Africa has become more conscious than his ancestors of events that take place in the world around him. Greatly improved means of communication and transportation—resulting in more rapid diffusion of news and more widespread travel—have expanded the horizons of man to an extent that seemed impossible to previous generations. The individual is directly or indirectly exposed to the actions of men and movements following each other at breathtaking speed. He is overwhelmed by their complexities and his seeming inability to control, influence, or comprehend them, for much is outside the scope of his previous experience or in sharp contrast to it. For instance, there is the difference in outlook between nations and in their clash of interests. This growing interrelationship demands a closer understanding of the world. With the need for understanding there comes often an eagerness among the reading public to be conversant with the wider political, social, and economic issues at stake.

The person who is prepared to accept the consequences of this involvement will want to extend his mental horizons. The intricacies of current events require from him greater knowledge and more profound study. If he is not to lose himself in a maze of complexities and confusing detail about happenings in far-off lands, he must acquire a global conspectus. His outlook will assume new breadth. But almost all of his problems owe something to the past.

To trace the origin of these problems not only contributes to a deeper understanding of other nations, communities, or individuals but also often helps both to simplify contemporary issues and to recognize them before they have become inextricably interwoven with other issues. By this kind of investigation the observer adds, so far as his thinking is concerned, the dimension of time to that of breadth. Granted that a profounder grasp of affairs does not vouchsafe a facile solution to the many difficulties besetting the modern world, yet knowledge itself increases understanding. With increased understanding comes greater interest. The man who is fortified by an informed understanding no longer feels so much at the mercy of unknown forces as does his ignorant brother, be these forces only the actions of those invested with authority.

The study of history has functions to perform that reach far beyond immediately utilitarian ends. No soul with the least imagination can remain unmoved while reading the drama of mankind as it unfolds amid the haze of early civilizations and advances in time and space to the present era, when the first tentative steps are being taken toward conquests beyond the confines of this planet. The vicissitudes of fortune, man's constant struggle against nature and his own kind, and the effort to create both materially and spiritually make man a subject worthy of an epic. Such struggles reveal his failings, his virtues, his weaknesses, his passions, his hate, and his triumphs over circumstances and material foes. Yet he so often succumbs to his own defects and follies, which indicates no assured progress, as was believed so widely prior to World War I. It is true that the technological progress made during the past century has revolutionized man's material environment and demonstrated again his inventive skill. The amenities of life have reached an unprecedented height in the more advanced societies. On the other hand, there is little doubt about the failure of public morality and the higher activities of man, both of the intellect and the spirit, to keep pace with his material creations. So often the arts of peace are neglected to his detriment. This conflict, providing at once pathos and irony, has all the elements to stir the emotions of the reader, conscious of his own role in the unfinished drama. There is a peculiar fascination in the realization that life through the ages has produced plots and situations comparable to any work of fiction. This was already acknowledged by our wise forebears, the Greeks of antiquity, who identified the composition of history with the muse Clio.

Thoughts such as these evoke some random reflections on the educative value of human experience as it is encompassed within the pages of history. Mention has been made of the facile optimism that prevailed throughout the latter part of the nineteenth century. It found its expression in a firm faith in human betterment and the ultimate perfectability of man himself, to be accompanied by the abolition of wars, cruelty, and hatred. This mood sprang from the publication in 1859 of Charles Darwin's *Origin of Species* and from the rise of the social sciences. The social scientist too eagerly adopted for his field the principles of evolution enunciated in biology—without necessarily establishing their applicability. The historian, whose craft antedates that of social scientists, was not left unaffected by the new intellectual climate and was occasionally tempted to invoke the aid of related disciplines for the interpretation of his facts. Two world wars, in addition to other manifestations of man's inhumanity to man, have destroyed the strong belief in progress and, in some instances, cast doubts on the ability of the younger branches of knowledge to provide a panacea for all ills. Disillusionment spread in the ranks of thinking people, beginning in Europe, the scene of so much violence and hate, and eventually reaching America. If such disillusionment did not always result in pessimism and nihilism, it nevertheless destroyed the belief of the majority of professional historians—there are some notable and well-publicized exceptions—in a preordained, definitive pattern of

events and currents in world history that can be ascertained to some degree of accuracy by honest research. Such convictions no longer belong to the sphere of the historian but to that of the theologian or philosopher.

With some justification the question may now be raised whether the reading of history adds anything to the lessons of life, once the functions of informing and entertaining have been considered. If amid the welter of chaos and tragedy that attended man's path through the centuries the reader is not to be left in bewilderment and even despair, there must be some rays of light. Fortunately, despite so much discouragement, there is ground for hope and moderate optimism. In one aspect the present generation is but the legatee of the past, having fallen heir to all man's ills and benefits, his failures and achievements, his intellectual and scientific attainments, and his moral and political disasters. From this point of view there is no isolation in time, for history implies continuity. The awareness that men in past millenia have survived the successive onslaughts of nature and of their own race, which sometimes seem to engulf them, can inspire a modicum of confidence. The minds and spirits of people today are oppressed by the threat of nuclear warfare and its aftermath. This is a new phenomenon in its magnitude of destructive power and in the hazards to the health of coming generations. But when it is considered in the light of each generation's resources, has not man faced and weathered disasters comparable to the one menacing the inhabitants of the mid-twentieth century? Has not the course of human history, despite wounds and sufferings, persisted? This view encourages sober thinking but avoids despair.

On the other hand there is another temptation to our generation, especially the part of it that inhabits the materially more advanced countries. It is an excessive pride in the accomplishments of modern science and technology, one manifestation of which is the feeling that the present is immeasurably superior to the past. A careful and dispassionate investigation into the past will probably dispel many illusions. Given the advantages of the present and the accumulated human experience at man's disposal, there is little reason to suppose that a past generation would not have equaled the vaunted achievements of this century. The present has probably sacrificed some of the greatness of bygone ages. Almost the whole of the ancient civilizations of Egypt, China, and India has passed away. Only fragments of the art of Greece and the engineering skill of Rome are extant, whereas Greek thought has become the preoccupation of a small minority. Even the faith and craftsmanship of medieval Europe has lost its living content for most Westerners. Yet what remains of all these achievements still arouses great admiration today. In the realm of the spirit the Western world and, through its cultural influences, many peoples of other civilizations owe an inestimable debt to Greece, Rome, and ancient Israel. We also know that the Western cultural heritage has been enriched by contact with Oriental civilizations that may have developed in isolation from the West. Hence, mindful of its debt to the past it behooves the present to curb any tendency to undue arrogance. For is not true humility—not servility—an adornment of civilized man?

At this point the reader is cautioned that hitherto in this introduction events of history have been considered from the very proper view of a continuous process. But they are also a finely knit web that has been likened to an ever-expanding seamless garb. Any attempt to divide this web by periods, geographical areas, or significant movements only tears the fabric. Within the web there is a complex chain of causes and effects that the dedicated scholar strives to locate. There is, however, another facet to the study of history. Whereas one event or one movement in history is related to various others and one man's action is affected by a series of circumstances, all of which exert some determining influence, yet every occurrence in time is in some respects unique. There is no mechanical repetition, no exactly identical concentration of predetermining factors. Each generation faces its own problems and must seek its own answers. To Leopold von Ranke, the father of modern historical writing, every generation was equidistant to God. Ultimately every man, every age, every civilization is judged on its own merit at the bar of history. The present generation, which may return a verdict on the past, also stands responsible for its actions. The individual in a society that values personal liberty cannot abdicate his responsibility on the vague pretext of some compelling historical necessity. There are totalitarian creeds whose interpretation of history rests on determinants largely outside man. In the case of Marxism it is upon processes of economics, and in that of fascism or nazism it is on the glorification of state or race. These systems set out to fit events into preconceived models. But historians uninfluenced by such preconceptions try to recapture the immediacy of past happenings with as much objectivity as human nature will allow.

Like liberty, history has been subjected to misuse. In its solemn name a stream of dogmatic pronouncements has poured forth. The greater part of these seldom bears close examination in the light of strict historical evidence. Generalizing is a weakness to which human frailty is only too easily heir. In the same manner in which the Marxist seizes selected portions of history to illustrate his ideology, others avidly borrow their texts from history for their special pleading. Clio is transformed into a Fury. Her very name is outraged. On careful consideration history has been made only a pretext for personal opinion in these instances. Such judgments frequently betray a fundamental ignorance or misreading of history and its processes. That there are lessons to be drawn from history may be demonstrable, but that the past is a reliable guide to present action is a doctrine fraught with dangers. On the aforementioned premise, that every happening in history is in some respects unique, however many superficial similarities there may be between situations, it is impossible to obtain from the past definitive and detailed directions for future courses of action. Too frequently this motive is the sole stimulus to someone's interest in history. It is an error that stems from equating the study of history with that of the exact sciences. The latter proceed according to fixed laws or conduct their experiments under controlled laboratory conditions; history deals with the unpredictable nature of men living amid the unbridled forces of nature. However, since history represents the human experience in its totality, it cannot be altogether without value. If it cannot produce the readymade solutions that man desires, it can nevertheless warn and advise.

From general considerations on the subject of history one's thoughts turn to Voltaire's *Essai sur les Moeurs*. Beginning with its publication in 1756 a new genre of historical writings sprang up, based on the assumption that true history is tantamount to the sum of all human activity. It sought to depart from the purely political aspect—the actions of governments and legislatures; diplomatic negotiations; the causes, conduct, and results of wars and of civil strife; and the evolution of law—and to study the masses in all their varied economic and social activities. It aimed at investigating the life, thought, and manners of the ruled rather than the rulers and at recording the achievements of each age according to such of its cultural manifestations as literature, art, architecture, and technology. Doubtless these so-called cultural histories have rolled back the frontiers of human knowledge and have helped to recreate the image of past epochs. An increasing number of histories have been written with the aim of tracing man's life and doings from the earliest records to the present day. Yet to cover the field exhaustively is a task that strains human powers. On the one hand our available evidence is so enormous, whereas on the other hand much of the past is still hidden from us. It has become a frequent practice that works seeking to cover universal history in its wider aspects are written by several authorities in cooperation, for the extent of the historical field is so great that few, if any, men can cover it with adequate authority. This work takes its humble place at the side of such compositions. Within the restricted frame of two volumes it is an attempt to bring to the general reader in a popular form an account of human experience. Space has inevitably imposed technical limitations on all concerned in the production. In order to preserve the continuity and general coherence of the work the political structure of history has been retained, since a general cultural history sometimes tends to deprive the reader of a sense of time and sequence. At each stage in the narrative of these two volumes some indication of the salient cultural and social characteristics of the period has been given. Western civilization, which rests upon the ancient civilizations of the Mediterranean, has penetrated the greater part of the world. It is therefore natural that greater emphasis has been laid upon it and its precursors. But there were other great cultures that flourished at various periods. Even if their impact on the whole of the human heritage is not immediately apparent or if they have exerted a powerful influence over only limited areas they have not been neglected. Accordingly China, India, and Japan find a place in these pages.

An interesting feature of this work is the collaboration that took place between professional historians and their colleagues in the social sciences. Even if one bears in mind the hazards to which history is exposed by an undiscriminating use of principles borrowed from other fields—a danger already referred to—the contribution that men of other disciplines can make to the extension of historical knowledge and insights is nonetheless significant. New minds can bring fresh light and air into chambers previously shut off from broader horizons. They also supply the historian with intellectual tools for his task that would not be available to him in another form.

Maps and illustrations have been chosen to illuminate the text and to add to the vividness of the story. They are an integral part of the work, as the title, *An Illustrated Outline History of Mankind*, suggests. Brought up to date, the book is published with the hope that readers will discover or recapture the fascination of one of the world's great stories—that of man himself. Should these two volumes whet the appetite for more information, as well they might, a short bibliography has been appended. Its purpose is to serve only as an introductory guide for further reading, and it does not claim to be an exhaustive catalog of relevant literature.

May 9, 1962.

CONTENTS

Part III: EARLY INDIA AND CHINA

Part IV: MEDIEVAL EUROPE

Part V: RENAISSANCE AND REFORMATION

Part VI: EMERGENCE OF EUROPEAN NATIONS

Part VII: EXPANSION OF THE EUROPEAN WORLD

Part VIII: DECLINE OF EMPIRES

Part IX: ENLIGHTENMENT AND REVOLUTION

Part X: THE TRIUMPH OF NATIONALISM

Part XI: GROWTH OF THE MODERN ECONOMIC ORDER

Part XII: THE UNITED STATES FROM 1815 TO 1917

Part XIII: WORLD IMPERIALISM

Part XIV: WORLD WAR I

Part XV: AFTERMATH AND RECONSTRUCTION

Part XVI: WORLD WAR II AND AFTER

History indeed is the witness of the times, the light of truth.
CICERO

History, by apprising [men] of the past, will enable them to judge of the future.
THOMAS JEFFERSON

Part I: THE ANCIENT NEAR EAST

---

1. The Land

THE SEEDBED OF CIVILIZATION

DURING untold ages the mountains, valleys, streams, and coast line of the Near East have changed innumerable times. Seas have covered the land, and mountains in turn have been pushed out of the water. New rivers have started, and volcanoes have poured out their molten lava over the surrounding land. But by the time our story begins, the Near East had taken pretty much the same shape that it bears today. The Nile flowed down from its two main sources in central Africa to the point where the White and Blue branches meet, near the city of Khartum. The same cliffs bordered the course of the Nile when it reached Upper (southern) Egypt, and the Delta had already been formed. The land was prepared for the development of civilized man.

The same was true in the other great cradle of civilization, the plains bordering the Tigris and Euphrates—in the country now called Iraq, but which is better known to us as Mesopotamia. The two rivers flowed southward from their mountain sources and watered the fields of the earliest man known in this territory.

It is because land features have played such a great part in directing the course of man's development that we devote the next few pages to a rapid visit through the Near East.

THE LAND OF THE NILE

Trade follows the highways. A glance at the map will make it quite clear that the highway in Egypt lies along the narrow thread of the Nile. As the river flows northward from Khartum it passes through the arid Nubian Desert, where vegetation is frequently re-stricted to a strip twenty feet in width. Lower down, it passes Aswan and the last of six cataracts. It is here that much of the finer stone, including granite, was quarried for the Nile temples. The valley widens to some extent as we proceed northward, but nowhere, except in the Delta, is the cultivable land more than fifteen miles wide. Relics of Egypt's oldest civilizations are found in the valley bottom near the river, many hundred feet below the cliffs that rise to the west. The Delta lies to the north of Cairo, and today the Nile has essentially two mouths, although ancient sources indicate that there have been at least seven.

We thus see Egypt as a long and winding strip of green with far-reaching deserts on both sides. There are in addition the Fayum, a relatively large fertile area southwest of Cairo, and a few oases which dot the bleak Libyan Desert which extends westward from the Nile.

The reason that Egypt, of all the countries on earth, has such a queer physical form lies in the fact that practically no rain falls except in the extreme north. The Delta partakes of the typical Mediterranean wet and dry seasons, but Upper Egypt depends for moisture on the Nile. A shower in Upper Egypt is the cause of considerable excitement, and no little wonder. The Nile, then, is the life blood of

I

The Nile not only provided the valley home of the Egyptians, but carried their commerce and fertilized their fields. (Black Star Photo)

that the bed of the river has been raised four inches every century. Temples which, when built, were well above water level are now covered during the inundation, and in the Delta the foundations of many ancient structures are perpetually wet.

Trade in Egypt developed between the different settlements, and, since these were mainly on the Nile, it was the river which became the national highway. Much of the trade was done by boat, and early in its history Egypt became conscious of this second benefit of the Nile. There were also roads which led to the Red Sea, but these never assumed the importance of the Nile which is still the artery of the country.

Early in the history of Egypt, the Mediterranean became a highway of tremendous importance. Many Egyptian products have been excavated in the island of Crete, and these of course could have traveled by ship only. Trade by sea was also carried on with the Syrian coast from whose near-by mountains came the cedar of Lebanon. This was carried back to Egypt to be made into coffins, sacred ships, and other things for which good wood was necessary.

There was likewise a land road leading to Asia which went across the barren flats of

Egypt and the season of inundation is the most important of the year. Without this constant supply of water Egypt would become a desert.

The Blue Nile, which rises in the highlands of Ethiopia, is supplied by the heavy rains which fall during the summer months. The waters arrive at Khartum about the middle of May, heavily laden with mud, and two weeks later the river at Aswan begins to rise. The Nile reaches its maximum height at these places about a hundred days later. When the waters subside, they leave an even film of mud in which the crops for the next year are sown. This process, happening over and over, is the secret of the fruitfulness of the Nile Valley and has been from the time we first see primitive Egyptians as farmers. The White Nile, which comes from the Equatorial regions of central Africa, has much less volume than the Blue Nile but is effective in keeping up the water level in Egypt during the months when the Blue branch has run practically dry.

A natural consequence of the heavy load of mud carried by the inundation is that the bed of the Nile has risen steadily. It is estimated

During the Low Water Season the Nile flows below the walls of the Temple of Isis, near Aswan, on the Island of Philae. (Paul's Photos)

northern Sinai and led in time to the rich markets of the Levant, Anatolia, Mesopotamia, and Iran.

PALESTINE AND SYRIA

Palestine and Syria are small countries and never in ancient times attained the world position of the oriental powers. Nevertheless, they have always occupied an extremely important position, lying as they do on the direct road between Egypt and her Asiatic

Life Along the River Nile. This relief from the tomb of Pahri, Eighteenth Dynasty, shows crops being harvested and loaded on ships to be transported down the Nile. (Oriental Institute of the University of Chicago)

competitors. This geographic position has been unfortunate at times, but it has never lacked importance. If Egypt, in a time of national strength, aimed at the subjugation of some of the "upstart" Asiatic countries, perhaps that of the Hittites or of Mitanni in the bend of the Euphrates, she sent her armies across the Sinai highway and then through Palestine and Syria. In other cases transport ships were sent direct to the Syrian ports— this of course at a time when the ports were under Egyptian control.

On the other hand, there were times when the situation was reversed. Assyria, Babylonia, or Persia, when at the height of their power, sought to add Egypt to their empires; but to do so they had first to conquer or pacify the land that lay between. That land was Palestine and Syria, always the corridor between the eastern and western powers. The direct route between Babylonia and Egypt lies across the Syrian Desert, but the hardships in crossing this desert have been experienced by many who will never tell their tales. The easiest and therefore the most sensible route for steady travel lay along the watercourse of the Euphrates, up into the Mitanni country, and thence across to the valley highways of Syria and Palestine. Dr. Breasted, the foremost American Orientalist of his day and the organizer of the Oriental Institute at the University of Chicago, aptly termed this route the "Fertile Crescent."

It was natural that the Syrian and Palestinian cities of the Fertile Crescent should learn much about the high civilizations to either side of them. The greatest Egyptian influence was generally felt in Palestine and southern Syria, territories nearest Egypt. Mesopotamian culture, on the other hand, permeated the life of northern Syria. But throughout Palestine and Syria there was a deep-seated knowledge of both countries.

Phoenicians have always suggested sailors to the western world, and they were that in-

During the High Water Season the Nile floods the Island of Philae and covers the temple courtyard. (Oriental Institute of the University of Chicago)

deed; but how often
does one stop to ask
why the Phoenicians
became sailors? The
answer lies, to a large
extent, in the formation
of the country occupied
by them. Phoenician
territory lay on the
Mediterranean coast
from Acre, in northern
Palestine, to the north-
ern end of this same
Levant coast, and in-
cluded the famous cities
of Tyre, Sidon, Beirut,
and Byblos. Nearness
to the sea is necessary
for a country to have a
seafaring people, but
the real reason that
the Phoenicians took so
naturally to the sea is
that they possessed no

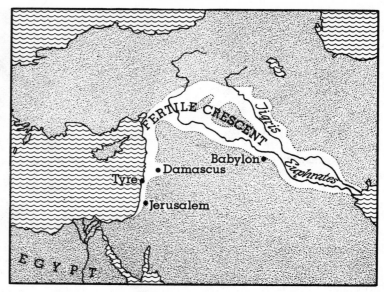

The Ancient Near East. The easiest and most traveled route between Egypt and Babylonia was named the "Fertile Crescent" by Dr. Breasted. In the midst of a desert area, it was irrigated by the Tigris and Euphrates rivers

land to develop. The several high mountain
systems come practically to the water's edge.
In spots there are a few miles of good agricultural land, but in other places the roots of
the ranges are washed by the sea. The mountains, then, acted as a barrier to development inland and naturally caused the Phoenicians to become conscious of the great body of
blue water that made them famous. In addition, the Syrian coast possesses a number of
good harbors which were put to natural use
in very early times.

Contrast this with the nature of the Palestinian coast which is practically straight and
possesses few harbor possibilities. In ancient
times the only natural harbor lay behind the
dangerous reefs of Jaffa. In consequence of
this, as well as the fact that most of the Palestine coast is flanked by a broad fertile plain,
the coast dwellers tended to remain agricultural. It is true that there were a number of
coast cities, but they lacked natural advantages. Thus, because the Syrian coast lent
itself to seafaring, the Phoenicians were encouraged to become sailors and navigators,
while the lack of harbors on the Palestinian

coast was probably a major factor in emphasizing farming.

THE LAND OF THE TWO RIVERS

In ancient times the country through which
the Tigris and Euphrates flow had taken
practically its present form. The Euphrates
rose in the mountains of Armenia and started
for the Mediterranean, but on reaching northern Syria it was deflected to the lower land
leading to the Persian Gulf. The Tigris lies to
its east and parallels it for the most part.
The two almost touch at Baghdad but do not
meet until they reach a point about two
hundred and fifty miles southeast of the City
of the Caliphs. From there they flow for
another hundred miles through the Delta and
at last empty into the Persian Gulf. The Delta
is the one land feature that has changed ap-
preciably in historic times. Five thousand years
ago the coast line was almost two hundred miles
above the present mouth of the rivers. Former
coast towns have been left high and dry by
river mud which was deposited on reaching sea
level. The rivers are still working to fill up the
head of the Persian Gulf.

The Syrian or Arabian Desert lies to the west of our territory and forms an effective barrier to direct intercourse with the countries beyond. As we have seen, the Euphrates became the important route for trade with the Mediterranean area. To the east of Mesopotamia lie the Zagros Mountains which separate it from Iran. The Zagros Range swings down from the same mountains that give rise to the Tigris and Euphrates.

Iran is essentially a high plateau, highest on the side near Mesopotamia, to which access is had through a number of valleys which drain into the Tigris. In the northern and northeastern parts of the country the land drops off to the Caspian Sea and Russian Turkestan which is flat and low.

THE LAND OF THE HITTITES

Anatolia, the home of the Hittites, is largely an upland plateau which slants gradually toward the Black Sea. In the southeast there are two high mountain ranges, the Taurus and Anti-Taurus, which have been effective all through history as barriers to approach from Syria and Mesopotamia. The famous Cilician Gates lie between these ranges and lead out to the broad Cilician Plain on the Mediterranean. The mountains continue into Armenia, southeast of the Black Sea. This territory has always been most inaccessible, and contacts with Europe have been made only with difficulty. There is a coast road around the east end of the Black Sea, and a few passes

The Euphrates River across from Hillah, Iraq, a city built of brick taken from the ruins of Babylon. (Oriental Institute of the University of Chicago)

across the Caucasus exist, but the region has been naturally sheltered.

We can thus understand that the geography of the Near East has always been important in the fashioning of its history. Mountain barriers are cultural barriers. Open and connected areas tend more naturally to form political and cultural units. We shall see further, as we go on, that the configuration of the land has been of the greatest importance in the development of the Near East.

Hittite Architects of about 850 B.C. used the backs of these two stone lions to support a palace column made of wood, an important architectural innovation. (Oriental Institute of the University of Chicago)

2. The Prehistoric Near East

A FEW years ago it would have been difficult to tell the story of the prehistoric peoples of the Near East. Today, although the picture is far from complete, we can view the main features of cultural advance during those momentous years when man ceased being a hunter and took to the soil. Excavations on sites representing the period before writing came into use have been so numerous that we can now distinguish between successive phases of that ancient world to which the better known civilizations owed their beginnings.

EGYPT BEFORE THE FIRST DYNASTY

The point at which we take up the story of man may be dated for the sake of convenience somewhere between four and five thousand years before the beginning of the Christian Era. No one knows for certain, and probably never will, because there was no writing at that time. However, dates are not everything, and furthermore there are several kinds of dates. The exact number of years represented by the prehistoric civilizations of Egypt escapes us, yet we can derive a very good idea as to which civilizations preceded others. The fact that some can be called older, or perhaps be regarded as having existed at the same time as others in a different part of the country, is a matter of considerable interest and importance.

In Stone Age times the deserts on either side of the Nile were fertile and supported wild game, for while Europe was living under glacial conditions northern Africa was having rains. But gradually these ceased and people were driven to the valley of the Nile where there always was water. Early in this period somebody made the brilliant discovery that wild grains such as wheat and barley could be cultivated, a disclosure that rocked the world of that time. Therefore, instead of subsisting chiefly on hunting and fishing, the people turned to farming for a livelihood. Where before they had been parasites they now became productive. It is quite likely that the first stages saw a thorough combination of these occupations, for it is not likely that the habits of generations were instantly dropped. But the tendency to adopt the more secure way of living offered by farming increased, and with it came the development of settled communities, the earliest of which have apparently been found. In Middle Egypt they are called Tasian because the first clear-cut evidence of this civilization came from Deir Tasa. The type of culture that existed at about the same time in Lower Egypt has been found at two places, in the Fayum and at a site in the Delta called Merimde. For this reason the northern cultures are called Fayumic and Merimdian.

Aside from farming, hunting, and fishing the Tasian folk may have made food-gathering trips to the Red Sea. At home they discovered the secret of pottery making, and, although their products were poor when compared with later pottery, it constituted a very important step forward. Before that time vessels for holding liquids were made of stone, leather, wood, or gourds. It is in Tasian times, too, that we note the earliest traces of linen, but the form of the finished costume has yet to be discovered. Paint palettes have been found which suggest that the Tasians painted their eyes and faces in a manner similar to that of the later Egyptians. It causes no surprise to learn that a people, thus advanced, wore shells and bone and ivory beads. When the Tasians died they were laid away in simple pit graves, wearing their finery and accompanied by vessels containing food and drink for the life hereafter. It was the custom in Tasian villages to compose the body of a dead person in a certain set manner, with arms and legs drawn up closely to the body.

The Tasian stage of civilization was low in comparison with that of later times, yet it was far above any which had preceded. It must represent for us that important stage when man ceased being purely a hunter. He had come in from the chase and was ready to settle on a farm watered by the bountiful Nile. Communities developed, and when that step had been taken the most important ingredient of civilization was already present. Without communities, the development of Egypt and the rest of the ancient world would have been retarded just so much longer.

At about the same time a similar development was taking place in northern Egypt. The first agricultural villages were being formed, but in a somewhat different way. The two districts were widely separated and customs varied considerably. We are not to suppose that the territory lying between was a blank as far as population is concerned, for there is little doubt that farming began along the Nile at many points at about the same time. We simply lack evidence for the unknown territories, and for that reason the differences between the cultures of Upper and Lower Egypt seem very distinct.

The type of civilization which is called Fayumic has been discovered along the edge of an ancient lake that once filled the Fayum depression. Wheat, barley, and flax were grown, and the farmers cut their grain with crude saw-toothed sickles. These people

also hunted and fished, but they had succeeded in domesticating certain animals, including the pig, cow, sheep, and goat. The men did much of their fishing with harpoons, and it was perhaps while they were thus occupied that the women made the excellent baskets that have been found. The making of pottery was an important industry, and although the vessels were crude they were an improvement over earlier ones. The people of the Fayum dressed in linen to some extent but it is likely that they used skins as well.

Merimde, which lies on the western edge of the Delta where it gives way to the desert, has produced a type of culture closely related to that which we have seen in the Fayum. These people, too, were clearly at a stage when they were giving up hunting as a major aspect of life and were taking to the cultivation of grains. Storage bins and threshing floors have been found, and even a street has been uncovered. The Merimdian people had numerous minor peculiarities that distinguish them from the other folk we have seen, but their principal difference consisted in the way they buried their dead. Here the dead were placed among the dwellings and no food or drink was placed in the graves.

One negative characteristic of these three contemporary cultures is that they show no

Predynastic Egyptian Jars and Vases. Painstakingly carved from hard stone, these vessels were often placed in graves for the use of the dead. (Oriental Institute of the University of Chicago)

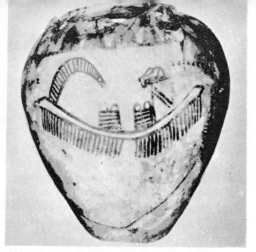

Predynastic Egyptian pottery vessel depicts a river boat being rowed down the Nile. (Oriental Institute of the University of Chicago)

traces of the use of metal; the benefits of copper were still to be discovered. It can well be said that the Tasian, Fayumic, and Merimdian civilizations represent the Neolithic stage of human development.

In the south the Tasians were followed by another people, the Badarians, so called for the town Badari where their culture is well illustrated by the excavations. These people were shorter than their predecessors, being not more than five and a quarter feet tall, and having at the same time more slender and delicately built bodies. Although the Badarians were of a different stock, they adopted Tasian culture, developing it along established lines.

Progressive steps taken by these people included the extension of trade relations. Products were brought from the Red Sea and Nubia, and fragments of cedar wood suggest that trade with Syria, which was to become so famous, had already begun. We are left in the dark on many points of interest, but one fact is clear: by Badarian times Egypt had entered the age of metals. Beaten copper beads have been found, and while not numerous they nevertheless testify to knowledge of some of the properties of copper, though it remained for a later people to discover that copper could be smelted and cast into objects of diverse form.

Passing again to the north, we find that a related civilization followed on the collapse of the Merimdian. It is called the Maadi culture

from the name of a town near Cairo where its ruins have been discovered. The Merimdian way of living was continued and improved, while copper became plentiful, much more so than in southern Egypt. At the same time trade relations were extended and included contacts with Palestine.

The southern cultures which were in existence at about the same time have been called Amratian, Gerzean, and Semainean. The Amratian followed the Badarian, and the Semainean brought the predynastic period to a close. Culture traits which had been in use in the Badarian period were continued in the next, but at the same time there was an influx of ideas which points to the introduction of North African customs. These appear to have been related in some way to the late Paleolithic culture called Capsian.

Slaves existed by Amratian times, and personal property of another sort is indicated by distinctive marks impressed on pots. Copper became more abundant, but the principle of smelting remained unknown. Merchants had greatly extended their sphere of interest, copper coming from Sinai, gold from Nubia, and wood from Syria. It is even possible that emery was imported from the far-off islands near Troy and Greece. Already the Mediterranean was giving promise of busy days to come.

There are indications of the role which religion played in the lives of the people. Dogs were often buried with their masters, as were small models of cattle and other desirable things. These suggest the Egypt of better known times when articles were placed in the grave for the use and comfort of the deceased. The models of cattle in this case surely represented real animals which were to serve the dead person in a magical way in the life hereafter. Weapons, pottery ornaments, and food were placed in the grave for the same reason. The predynastic Egyptian believed that after death he would hunt, plough his field, sail the Nile, and do all the other things that had occupied him in life.

The Amratian people were followed by the Gerzeans who continued and improved many traits already established while a number of new features made their appearance. New types of weapons, dress, and pottery, as well as different burial rites, indicate that a new strand of humanity had made its presence felt. Some of the pottery types came from Palestine while others suggest relations with the Delta. Copper remained rare, but flint work reached a state of perfection never again attained in Egypt.

It is in the Gerzean period that we see the emergence of centralized power that at length culminated in the union of the country. There had always been chieftainship of a sort, even before the stage represented by the beginning of organized villages, but in the Gerzean period we gain a fleeting glimpse of power tremendously increased. We are allowed to view the tombs of a few men which in all respects are far superior to the hundreds of other tombs known for the period. One of these was lined with mud brick which had been plastered over and then washed with a coat of yellow ochre, and on this an artist had depicted a scene which combined incidents from the chase, dances, and combat on ships. This was the tomb of a wealthy and powerful man, one distinguished in his day. His civilization may seem barbaric until we look over our shoulder at earlier times. On facing about, we dimly discern the First Dynasty rising above the horizon.

The final predynastic period, the Semainean, prepared Egypt for the coming of Menes, first historical king of united Upper and Lower Egypt. Villages grew into cities, and local chiefs assumed the grandeur of divine kingship. Tombs of the common people remained much as they had been, but the wealthy demanded burials that were finer than ever. These were of considerable size and at times were partially dug out of the rock which lay beneath the sand, and were then covered with a wooden superstructure. Stairs led down to the chambers for convenience of pallbearers and those who bore offerings. Indications are clear that wealth was being concentrated.

During this period trade relations with surrounding territories increased on both land and sea, the most interesting new "billing" being with Mesopotamia. The exact nature of this contact is not known, but that there were influences back and forth cannot be doubted, for a number of objects found in Egypt bear artistic representations characteristic of the Tigris and Euphrates regions. The stone on which they were carved is Egyptian, but the ideas are clearly eastern. The precise meaning of these things is not fully realized, but that there was communication of ideas between the valley of the Two Rivers and the Nile is apparent.

We have now reached the point in the history of Egypt when the land was divided into a number of powerful nomes, or states, each ruled by a prince. Before the end of the predynastic period these had been combined into two large kingdoms, Upper and Lower Egypt. The two vied with each other for prestige and influence, property and wealth, and each was ruled by a man whom we may now call a king. Fortunes shifted, and on a number of occasions it must have appeared that one of the kings would gain power sufficient to unite the entire country under one head. At length the inevitable happened, and about 3000 B.C. a southern king who has

Gerzean Tomb Painting. A wall decoration from the tomb of an influential man shows scenes from the hunt, dances, and fights between ships silhouetted against a background of yellow ochre. (Quibell, "Hierakonpolis" II)

A **Sumerian Frieze** of marching bulls decorated a temple of the cow-goddess near Ur about 3000 B.C. Carved from shell or limestone, the animals are mounted on a thin layer of black bitumen which was originally framed with copper strips. (University of Pennsylvania Museum)

come down in history by the name of Menes became the first historical king of Upper and Lower Egypt.

MESOPOTAMIA BEFORE THE FLOOD

While Egypt was taking her first long strides toward civilization, a comparable development was taking place in the valleys of the Tigris and Euphrates. The earliest settlements were in the north where a very respectable type of culture was evolved. The people were farmers for the most part, but they also hunted. Their pottery shows a high degree of artistic development in both form and decoration which is astonishing even to the modern eye. Trade was carried on between districts and with distant countries. Indeed, many of the essentials for the development of civilization were present in the northern part of Mesopotamia at a time which was perhaps not far from 5000 B.C. Yet it was southern Mesopotamia which went ahead to become the leader of culture and progress for several thousand years.

At the time of which we have been speaking, however, southern Mesopotamia which came to be called Sumer was still under the waters of the Persian Gulf. At this time the heavily laden rivers were carrying down mud and silt to deposit in the sea. Thus the land of Sumer was composed entirely of new land, and on these marshy flats there settled foreign people who probably came from the north or northeast.

The remains of this earliest civilization have been found and are known today as the Al Ubaid culture. As is usual in matters dealing with prehistoric material, names are given after sites which have proved typical. At Al Ubaid we find this culture fairly well represented, although other places have since yielded a more complete picture. Because the Al Ubaid people were the first ones to settle in the country, their towns and cities now lie buried at the bottom of mounds, often some distance below ground-water level. As in the valley of the Nile, the accumulation of mud and silt has caused the water to reach a higher level.

The Al Ubaid people may have been drawn to the marshes at the head of the Persian Gulf by the fresh water lagoons and swamps which were becoming a haven for wild life driven from the north by increasing aridity. These people built reed huts and cultivated their cereals. Perhaps to preserve as much ground as possible for farming they set foundations for their huts in the water. At any rate at Uruk, which is the biblical Erech, there have been found platforms of rushes set between the marsh bottom and the floor levels of huts. The huts were chiefly of reed matting plastered with clay or dung and bitumen, which is a tarlike substance found naturally in Mesopotamia. Bricks were also made by throwing clay into a mold and then drying them in the sun. Some of the houses even had doors which pivoted in a stone socket.

Rough stone hoes were used to till the fields, and cereals were harvested with saw-toothed chert or obsidian flakes set in a clay frame shaped somewhat like the jawbone of a cow. The grain itself was ground on stones. Another source of food was the date palm which to this day provides much nourishment for the inhabitants of the district.

There is evidence that these people had domesticated animals. Perhaps among the latter were cattle, sheep, and pigs; but we know of them only from the dung-plastered huts in which the people lived.

Dairy Scene, another section of the frieze on the left. Note milking being done from behind the cow, according to Sumerian custom. The four dairymen opposite the gate to the cow-yard are pouring milk through a strainer and churning it into butter

Slings and perhaps bows and arrows were used to bag game, and fish were caught in nets. Boats were an early necessity because of the marshy conditions, and as proof of their existence the archeologist has found clay models which are surprisingly like boats still used on the Euphrates.

Practically nothing is known of the physical form of the Al Ubaid population, but some idea has been gained of their habits of dress. The evidence for clothing comes from spindle whorls which were used in the preparation of thread and from painted figurines of baked clay. The latter suggest that skins as well as textiles were utilized for dress. The men wore long beards, and their long hair was put up in a bun at the back. The men's upper lips were shaved, and the women wore wigs.

Copper was probably known by the first inhabitants of the region, but has not been found until late in the Al Ubaid period. We can understand how the uses of copper might have become known earlier in Sumer than in Egypt when we recall that lower Mesopotamia possessed practically no flint or stone with which to make tools, weapons, and vessels.

The Al Ubaid people came into the country with a developed type of living and adapted themselves thoroughly to their environment. Some aspects of their culture are related to that of the highlands of Iran and Elam to the east, but the actual homeland of these people cannot yet be located with certainty. Future excavation may settle this most interesting point; meanwhile we simply know that they were foreigners who located on the newly made land at the head of the Persian Gulf.

The Al Ubaid people were succeeded in time by those known by the name of Uruk, which we have seen was the Babylonian name for the biblical city of Erech. The clearest evidence for the Uruk culture has come from that ancient city, although traces have been found generally. There are strong suggestions that a new people came in at the beginning of this period. For one thing, a completely new type of pottery with distinctive features was at this time added to the old. Transportation was entirely revolutionized through the introduction of the wheel. Furnaces of an advanced sort came into use and were employed either for baking pottery or smelting copper. It is possible that each of these innovations was invented on the spot, but there is a greater likelihood that a roving population brought them when they settled in Sumer.

It is quite clear that at this early period the necessities of the church were successfully

Uruk cylinder seal (right) and a view of the impression it makes (far right); a decorative herd feeding scene. (Berlin Museum)

met by some form of taxation to which the farmers, fishermen, and traders of the country contributed. Wealth was needed and found for the erection of huge structures in honor of the state gods. At the same time other state income was used to dig canals, thereby providing for necessary drainage and irrigation. Thus, with water drawn off, villages became cities, marshes became fields, and in the city of Erech a monumental temple was erected.

This temple was built upon a huge pile of mud, the forerunner of the ziggurat and the "Tower of Babel." The foundation platform, which consisted of lumps of mud, reached a height of about forty feet. On this rested the temple, measuring about twenty by twenty-five yards. It was built of large whitewashed mud bricks and consisted of a long central court surrounded by chambers. A stairway, down which the god might descend, led from the top of the mound. But this was not the entire temple complex, because it is likely that a larger temple existed at the foot of the ziggurat.

A tablet apparently inscribed with numbers was found in the temple atop the mound. This was, perhaps, a record of some sort kept by a servant of the temple, as was so common in later days.

The temple, of which we have spoken, fell into ruin long before the end of the Uruk period and was succeeded in turn by two others. The art of building progressed with rapid strides in this period, and we now know that vaults with true arches were being con-

Al Ubaid Vessels came from the potter's wheel about 4000 B.C. and were painted in geometric designs. (Oriental Institute of the University of Chicago)

structed. It is difficult to date this achievement with any precision, but perhaps it was not far from 3500 B.C. At a much later date the Romans borrowed this important architectural feature from the Orient.

As far as we know, it was in the Uruk period that pictographs were first employed to record ideas. However, the fact that no earlier examples exist by no means precludes the possibility that this form of expression was not older. Quite likely it was. The story of the development of cuneiform, or wedge-writing, from pictures will be told later. Now we pause to record the fact that writing had begun, but the figures represented ideas and not sounds. The numeral system was also being developed, and it is known that two types were in use. One was the sexagesimal system, which simply means that counting was based on the numbers 1 - 10 - 60 and multiples of six. The other was the decimal system, quite familiar to us, which employs 1 - 10 - 100 and multiples of ten. It was the first which later became typical of the territory and is responsible for our division of the circle into three hundred and sixty degrees, the hour into sixty minutes, and the minute into sixty seconds.

Culture was clearly progressing at a rapid rate, but we see that even greater strides

An Ancient Ziggurat is surrounded by ruins of the courtyard of a large temple at its base and is topped by another, smaller temple. (Oriental Institute of the University of Chicago)

were made in the Jemdet Nasr period which followed.

At Jemdet Nasr, a large fortress over a square block in size was found, which towered above the flat plain. A new type of brick was used in the construction of buildings in this area. They were thin, rectangular, sun-

Cuneiform Ledger from the reign of King Shulgi of Ur is account of disposal of dead cattle in 2062 B.C. (Oriental Institute of the University of Chicago)

dried mud bricks. A stairway led up to a building of considerable size. This gives one an idea of the extent to which community living had progressed. But there was progress in other matters as well.

Writing was strongly developed during the Jemdet Nasr period. The pictorial symbols which were impressed into the soft clay of tablets now had a phonetic, or sound, value. In the preceding period the pictures had stood only for ideas, but now spelling was coming in. The words seem to be early Sumerian, the language of the period following Jemdet Nasr. As regards numbers, the two systems

that we have already noticed were still in use. The sexagesimal system did not become dominant until the following period. Among the still primitive written records that have been preserved from Jemdet Nasr times, are school texts and temple accounts.

A new animal, "the ass of the mountains," was introduced to the plains of Babylonia at this time, but whether it was the true horse is still uncertain. At any rate the same term was used in historical times to designate the horse.

The artist kept stride with the times. Among other things brought to light by the excavator, is a boar carved in stone. Pottery was pleasantly decorated in color, and seal designs characteristic of the period reveal a wealth of artistic ability.

The metalsmith made many things of copper, and that metal became more plentiful than ever before; but we may believe that it still was a luxury.

During this period the Jemdet Nasr people expanded northward; perhaps the land of Sumer was becoming too crowded. The region to which some of the people went is called northern Babylonia. By about 2500 B.C. it became famous as the land of Akkad.

But what of the "Flood" of Babylonian tradition that has come to us in the story of Noah and the ark? We can only say that there must have been many floods along the lower courses of the Tigris and Euphrates, many more than have been exposed by excavation. At Ur there was a flood in the Al Ubaid period. During early historic times, at

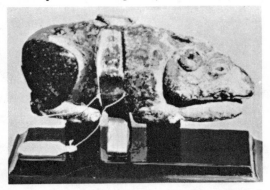

Stone Boar carved in Jemdet Nasr Period. (Bagdad Museum)

Ram Caught in a Thicket. One of the most unusual discoveries at Ur, the ram is made of shell and lapis lazuli over a wood core; the thicket is overlaid in gold. (University of Pennsylvania Museum)

Kish there was another flood of considerable proportions. Was this the overflowing of waters that loomed so large for later generations? For a number of reasons it is unlikely. The Babylonian myth tells of kings with lives of supernatural length who ruled before the flood, and Noah and his forefathers also lived lengthy lives; but in both stories those who followed existed for periods more within our understanding, and those in the Babylonian tale are to some extent historical and appear to belong to the period following 3000 B.C. It happens that there was a flooding of the ancient towns of Uruk and Shuruppak at about that time, but the difficulties persist. This flood was by no means general and did not affect many of the principal cities of the time. There remains, then, only the persistent and world-wide tradition that there was a flood of tremendous size. But floods leave records, and archaeology fails to support the tradition.

By the end of the Jemdet Nasr period, about 3000 B.C., the stage had been set for the advent of true history. All preparations had been made, as in Egypt at about the same time. Thereafter, in both countries we are able to follow developments by means of the written word.

It was the Sumerians, a people whose origin is by no means clear, who were the actors during the next scene and who accepted and improved the cultural advances that had taken place so laboriously through the centuries. Through them Babylonia was carried into the full light of history.

THE DIM PAST OF ANATOLIA

Meanwhile other regions were not dormant if not as progressive. Anatolia, which is the name given to the Turkish possessions on the great peninsula of Asia Minor, had passed out of the Stone Age directly into the Metal Age. There are some questionable Neolithic sites in this region, but recent excavation indicates that copper was used in the earliest organized villages. The city at the bottom of the ruin of Troy used copper, as did the first community at the site of Alishar in central Anatolia, east of the modern town of Yozgat. These earliest communities represent the Chalcolithic period, a term indicating that both copper and stone were in use at the same time. But Asia Minor covers an immense territory and possesses varied geographic outlooks, and we are not at all surprised to learn that there were several types

The Goddess of Vegetation, a relief on the fragment of a stone vase, dedicated by Entemena, an early ruler of Lagash, about 3000 B.C. (Berlin Museum)

of culture represented in the Chalcolithic period.

We have seen that geographic differences caused a variation between the cultures of Upper and Lower Egypt. Thus there were three main types of development in early Anatolia. The one to the west is well illustrated by the lowest city at Troy, which appears to have been related to the ancient culture of the Balkans. On the other hand, the inhabitants of the first city to be built on the site of Alishar made use of a type of pottery whose forms and decoration seem to tie it to the "Black Earth" culture of the lower Danube and southern Russia. The third culture area, which shows still other variations, is located in southeastern Anatolia and may be related to northern Syria, or to Cilicia which borders on the Mediterranean.

Excavation is being continued in Anatolia, and in time we may know the answers to many of the riddles that now cloud the picture for the period which lasted from about 3500-3000 B.C.

SUCCESSORS OF THE CAVE MAN IN PALESTINE AND SYRIA

Because of the influence of better climatic conditions men were leaving their caves even before the new Stone Age and were discovering that wild grains could be cultivated. We know this because flint sickles, which had been set in bone holders have been found in cave debris of the later Stone Age. But pottery had not been invented and the age of metals was a long way off. Grain had been added to the diet, but the essential elements of civilization had not been conceived.

It is likely that the discovery of grain cultivation led directly to the development of communities. Farming areas lay in the open fields, and the people had to be near by in order to till them. But to a man living with his family on his plot of land there were dangers that had never beset him in his cave. He was open to attack from all sides, and for this reason alone the community idea was bound to develop. In a village, man had mutual protection as well as numerous other advantages of various kinds.

The earliest village known in either Palestine or Syria is Jericho. It may have had another name at that early time—that we may never know; but it stands out today as perhaps the oldest town in the world. An agricultural people lived there soon after the close of the Stone Age, but flint and stone continued to be the principal materials from which tools and weapons were made. Pottery had not been invented, and liquids were kept in other types of vessels. We know of these people from the ruins of a number of superimposed floor levels which were found at the bottom of a deep excavation a few years ago. Before that, knowledge of the period was entirely lacking.

The whole Near Eastern world appears to have learned of the benefits of pottery at about the same time, and at Jericho, too, the invention was presently made known. This important event cannot be dated with precision, but for a number of reasons it seems likely that it happened some time between four and five thousand years before our era.

The first pottery was crude, but for certain purposes it had great advantages over stone and skin containers. The potters developed styles and gradually improved the quality of their product. Metal was still unknown, but flint and bone were put to good use.

Jericho is the only site in Palestine that has produced the type of culture of which we have been speaking, but undoubtedly there were other villages that existed at the same time. A number of cities in Palestine have been explored to the bottom and have not exposed a comparable culture, but the sites are not exhausted by any means. Ruins in the Jordan Valley, in which Jericho is situated, possibly cover the remains of villages that were known to the first towns at Jericho.

Settlement of other fertile parts of Palestine and Syria was made at last, and contacts with surrounding countries assumed importance. By Gerzean and Maadi times in Egypt trade was carried on with Palestine. Pottery with a distincitve Palestinian character has been found far afield in Upper Egypt as well as on the Syrian coast. Egypt seems also to have discovered by this time the value of cedar of

Lebanon. The world was still young as far as civilization was concerned, but trade for necessities had already assumed a position of importance in the lives of the people who lived around the Mediterranean.

The pottery vessels which have been found in Egypt probably got there by donkey pack. Perhaps they were filled with olive oil which has always been an important product of Palestine. Caravans also crossed the Sinai Desert, going east, bearing things from Egypt. Among these were pots, filled no doubt with desirable things from the valley of the Nile. Some of them had been made in Upper Egypt. The liquids and foods were consumed, but the pots remained. Moreover, their different shapes were admired by the foreigners, and so the local potters began copying the shapes that were most appreciated. The potter on the Nile reproduced vessels from Palestine, and the potter in Palestine did likewise. But the inevitable happened; neither could make a perfect copy since each shaped the clay by hand, and the product was a mixture of two distinct pottery traditions.

By a time shortly before 3000 B.C., Palestine and Syria were closely linked by excellent trade routes to both Egypt and Babylonia. We can visualize the first hardy merchants who were ready to risk much that they might become enriched. Seals and seal impressions of a distinctive Jemdet Nasr character have been found in both Syria and Palestine and testify to a relationship which must have been of real importance.

Syrian ships carried cedars to Egypt, but they also sailed to the islands of the Mediterranean, even as far as Malta. Their masters were really the first Phoenicians, but we cannot give them names. These may be gone forever because writing lay in the future.

Toward 3000 B.C. we find that considerable progress had been made on the road to civilization. Cultures had become specialized according to regions. The people of North Syria used pots that were quite distinct from those made at Byblos on the coast. The latter, in turn, were somewhat different from the pots and pans of Palestine. And within Palestine itself there were smaller regional differences. Each community, as well as each series of communities, was working things out for itself. The best was adopted by all, but each retained its own character and individuality.

The world was becoming national. Languages had already done much to further this distinction, but accumulated wealth and the widening gap of custom were also playing their parts. Soon the countries on the borders of the Mediterranean and the people of inland countries who were attracted to the sea were to become much more conscious of the national groups that lay about them. Writing, by means of which the greatest strides toward civilization have been made, played an important part in this process, and with it we enter the realm of true history.

Walls of Jericho, now in ruins, enclosed Palestine's earliest known village

3. The Beginning of Recorded History

OLD KINGDOM EGYPT

Henceforth we shall be able to speak of Egyptian history in terms of dynasties. Dynasty is simply a convenient term to designate the various royal houses in the same way that we refer today to the House of Windsor or the Hapsburg House.

Manetho, an Egyptian priest who lived around 300 B.C., wrote a history of Egypt and arranged the rulers from Menes of the First Dynasty to Alexander the Great. He stated that there had been thirty dynasties, and this has been accepted by writers of history. The latter have in addition regrouped certain dynasties on the basis of major trends in Egyptian history. Thus the first six dynasties can be conveniently examined as a whole and are given the name Old Kingdom.

It was about 3000 B.C. that Menes brought Upper and Lower Egypt together to form a united kingdom. The date is not certain by any means; perhaps it is a couple of hundred years off. But around 3000 B.C. the south conquered the north and set the machinery of centralized government into motion. The capital was at Thinis, near Abydos, and for this reason the first two dynasties which ruled from there are called the Thinite Dynasties. Eighteen kings are known to have reigned during this period which lasted two or three centuries. No sharp cultural lines can be drawn between late predynastic and dynastic Egypt. Progress continued along initiated courses, but there were no real changes. Sculpture and stonework gradually improved and led naturally to the great structures and works of art of the Pyramid Age.

The first king of the Third Dynasty was Zoser who chose Memphis, which is not far from Cairo, as his capital. He represents for us another family and tradition, that of the north, and it was he who built the first pyramid. His step pyramid, so called because it was erected in tiers, stands at Sakkarah on the edge of the desert south of the great pyramids at Gizeh. The first extensive stonework in Egypt began with Zoser who kept large numbers of men busy at the quarries. The masonry of the times shows clearly that stonework was relatively new to the Egyptian mind, for stone blocks were laid in mud-brick fashion, and wood and reed architecture was imitated. The earliest known stone columns in Egypt were erected during Zoser's reign in imitation of bundles of reeds.

Zoser had an extraordinary man as his grand vizier. Later Egyptian tradition regarded him as the inventor of hewn stone. We know that this was not the case, but it is altogether likely that he had much to do with the development of stone masonry. This man was Imhotep, and in history he is better remembered than many a king. He illustrates admirably the attitude of Egypt, from his time on, toward higher learning. His reputation as a wise man, priest, maker of proverbs, man of medicine, architect, and patron in general, only increased as time went on, and by the time of the Ptolemaic successors of Alexander he had become a full-fledged god.

The Third Dynasty lasted but ninety years or so, coming to an end about 2686 B.C. It was followed by the Fourth Dynasty group of kings whose tombs are bywords the world over as symbols of durability and power. These are the great pyramids which were built to house the earthly remains of the wealthy king-gods. Kings had long since ceased to be merely human in the eyes of their subjects. The kings of the Fourth Dynasty,

Slate Ceremonial Palette commemorates King Narmer's victory over the Libyans in unifying Egypt. (Cairo Museum)

especially Khufu who was called Cheops by the Greeks, were among the most powerful persons who ever lived. At no later time would it have been possible for a single man to order the erection of a tomb like the great pyramid.

Khufu was the second king of his dynasty, and he was followed by four others. Two of these are well remembered by their pyramids which stand next to that of Khufu. Khafre built the second pyramid at Gizeh, and Menkure the third, but these were smaller and poorer than the first although they too stand for untold wealth. Looking up the Nile from the top of the great pyramid, one can see still other pyramids, including the one built for Zoser. They stand along the edge of the valley like attentive sentinels observing the march of events. The greatest of them saw the end of the Fourth Dynasty which came to a close about 2560 B.C.

The Fifth Dynasty lasted for about 140 years and included nine kings. The royal family had changed, but Egypt prospered as before. These kings, however, lacked the complete power of those who had preceded them, for by now the nobles had attained a

higher position in the affairs of the nation. Nevertheless the Egypt of this period was able to invade foreign territory and maintain the country in a state of unity.

The last dynasty of the Old Kingdom, the sixth, lasted from 2420-2270 B.C. and included five kings. One of them, Pepi II, held the throne for over ninety years, the longest reign of any Egyptian king. Egypt prospered as a unified nation, developing commerce with Nubia and the coasts of the Mediterranean, improving the arts, and creating a considerable ethical standard. But as the country grew, so grew the necessity for greater governmental care. Districts were allotted to the favorites of the king. These became more powerful day by day and at length created themselves hereditary princes. The end of the Old Kingdom was in sight. The time came when the

King Khafre, Fourth Dynasty, carved diorite. (Metropolitan Museum of Art)

king could no longer maintain discipline and respect among the nobles. It was a matter of each man for himself and the spoils to the most clever. Finally the Sixth Dynasty came to an abrupt end, terminated by an invasion of foreigners from Asia. For 170 years Egypt was prey to these people and to ambitious Egyptian nobles who contrived to gather together a following. This period is little understood and is appropriately called a Dark Age, but out of it there again came unity which developed into the classical age called the Middle Kingdom.

EARLY EGYPTIAN WRITING

The scribal profession is as old as the transmission of ideas by writing. The first scribes drew pictures to convey the ideas that they had in mind. This stage of writing occurred long before the First Dynasty, for by that

First Pyramid at Sakkarah was built in step design by Zoser, first king of the Third Dynasty

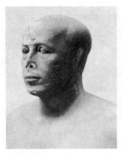

Old Kingdom Nobleman. (Museum of Fine Arts, Boston)

time the system of hieroglyphic writing had been well formulated, although it cannot be read with assurance. Pictures were quite satisfactory for certain things and gave the intended idea, but we can all appreciate the difficulty we would have if we tried to tell a story in picture form.

We might find it fairly successful thus to relate that a dog was chasing a man. Such a picture is easily drawn. Or perhaps it would not be too difficult to depict men fishing in the Nile, or others paying their respects to one of the numerous Egyptian gods. But these are action pictures. How, with the primitive equipment which we for the moment possess, could we make clear the idea that we were tired of the place where we were and wished to go home as soon as possible; or that we were undecided as to the best course to follow under the circumstances?

The Egyptian could probably have explained all these matters with the greatest fluency and surely did if he was anything like his modern descendant, but to send a written

First Dynasty Egyptian Hieroglyphics. (Cairo Museum, Photo by R. Rohrbach)

message was different. Pictures served for a while, yet these lacked complete effectiveness. At length someone whom we shall never know conceived of the idea of syllable writing. The method can be well illustrated in English. The picture of a *bee* can be placed next to the representation of a *gun*, the resultant word being *begun*. This is called phonetic, or sound, writing. Of course the *bee* and the *gun* have lost all of their true picture meaning and stand for an altogether different idea. In the same way a *bee* and a *leaf* can be combined to indicate the word *belief*. This system was continued in Egypt until all the syllable sounds in the language could be represented by pictures which had a sound value. In addition there came into being an alphabet of twenty-four letters from which our own was in time partially descended.

King Menkure and his Queen, Fourth Dynasty. (Museum of Fine Arts, Boston)

The Famous Palermo Stone. A Fifth Dynasty copy in hieroglyphics of the annals of Egyptian history, it records in each rectangle the name of a year and its events from about 3400 to 2700 B.C. Each king's name appears above the rectangle depicting his ruling years. Named for the museum where it is at present, this stone is the earliest known list of years

Thus equipped, the scribe recorded things that could never have been described with pictures. But to a busy scribe it became laborious and impractical to draw all the details of the many hieroglyphs, so he developed a system which we may compare to our handwriting. Thenceforth the capital letters, the hieroglyphs, were used mainly for monuments, public inscriptions, sacred writings, and the like, while the longhand, or hieratic, was employed for letters, documents, and state and business records.

THE EGYPTIAN CALENDAR

All early calendars possess difficulties that arise from the fact that a day does not evenly divide the lunar month or the solar year. There are roughly 365¼ days in the year and about 29½ days in the moon month. The Egyptians seem to have had a moon calendar to begin with, but they had also observed that a con-

spicuous star in the Egyptian sky, called Sirius or Sothis, appeared again over the horizon just before sunrise at about the time that the Nile began to rise. The beginning of the flood was the big event in the Egyptian year, and we can well understand why the calendar-makers chose the reappearance of Sothis to mark the first day of the year. The Egyptian year thus included the time between the days when Sothis appeared again, after having for some time been invisible, just before sunrise.

This year was divided into three seasons of four months each, one representing the inundation of the Nile, another the winter or sowing season, followed by the summer or harvest period. The months were considered to be 30 days long and twelve of these totaled 360 days. A five-day period devoted to feasting was added to these and brought the days of the year to 365.

The difficulty with this system is that the solar and star years, which are practically identical, measure roughly 365¼ days. Thus every four years Sothis rose a day later, and as a result the calendar year and the solar year fell out of gear. The Egyptians must have noticed that a discrepancy had come into the system, but they did nothing with it until much later when a day was added for Leap Year. This uncorrected error meant that New Year's Day became a day later every four years. After 1,460 years, however, it came back to the time when the Nile began to rise. This period of 1,460 years is known as a Sothic cycle.

It is known from a Latin source that the Egyptian New Year's Day coincided with the appearance of the Sothic star in 139 A.D. It is evident then that the same thing had happened in 1321 B.C., 2781 B.C., 4241 B.C., and so on, all these dates being 1,460 years apart. Now it must have been on one of these dates that the calendar came into use, but 1321 is eliminated because the calendar was definitely in use before that time. Of the remaining possibilities it seems most likely that the year 2781 B.C. marks the event, but we cannot yet be absolutely certain that the Egyptian calendar did not come into being in 4241 B.C. In any case it is over 4,500 years old and is the calendar which Julius Caesar introduced to Rome with some modifications and which with further changes has become the instrument by which we adapt our days, nights, weeks, and months.

MUMMIES

The date of the first mummification in Egypt is not known, but it seems to have been no later than the Second Dynasty, or soon after 3000 B.C. A number of tombs from that dynasty contained bodies that had been bandaged in mummy fashion. After this early period the evidence for the practice increases and continues into early Christian times when it was discontinued.

It seems likely that mummification came about through a wish to preserve the form and identity of the deceased. Details of the treatment varied from period to period and according to the wealth of the person, but the following description may be regarded as general. After death the body was sent to the embalmer's establishment where it was placed on a board. The brain was removed through one of the nostrils, after which the face was covered with a resin-like pitch. The next step involved the removal of the viscera through an incision which had been cut in the left side. All the vital organs were removed except the heart and sometimes the kidneys. The parts that had been taken out were placed in special containers. Then the body was immersed in a salt bath, only the head remaining out of the solution. This process removed the outer skin and disintegrated the fatty tissues of the body. The body was then dried and treated with spices, oils, and resin. Sometimes the brain and abdominal cavities were stuffed with linen, and a number of mummies contained onions, for what reason is not known. In other cases the legs, arms, and parts of the trunk were cut out and stuffed with linen with the probable intention of making the form more lifelike. Preliminary to wrapping the whole mummy in a linen shroud, the nostril through which the brain had been drawn was stuffed with a linen plug, and pads of the same material were placed over the eyes. After these preliminaries, the mummy was

tightly bound with yards and yards of linen bandages, and they in turn were covered with a coating of linen, glue, and plaster. This coating is usually quite colorful, for at the head of the mummy appears a painted human face, while brightly colored paintings and hieroglyphs appear on the body. It is usual to find at least a prayer for the dead inscribed on the outer casing. The body was then ready for the rites at the grave.

THE GREAT PYRAMID—ONE OF THE WONDERS OF THE ANCIENT WORLD

The Greeks regarded the pyramid tomb of Khufu as one of the seven wonders of the world, and it still remains an object for deep consideration by both the historically and mystically minded. But we need not dwell on those who see in the pyramid and its measurements the explanation of life's mysteries; our purpose is to tell what the pyramid was and what it stood for.

The Great Pyramid was a tomb built for Khufu, second king of the Fourth Dynasty, who reigned around 2650 B.C. and was one of the most powerful men who ever lived. He had at his command all the resources of the country, and it seems clear that the principal event of his time was the building of the pyramid. It was to be a structure which could be penetrated by no human being, and which would house forever the remains of the king. Herodotus, who lived in the fifth century B.C., related the Egyptian tradition that a hundred thousand men were engaged in its construction for twenty years, and we can well believe that such was the case.

The immense size of this largest of ancient stone structures will be gathered from the following figures. The area covered by the pyramid is about thirteen acres, the base being 755 feet on a side. The ground plan is practically square, and its accuracy and that of the pyramid as a whole arouses our greatest admiration for the mechanical skill of the architects of this early period. The pyramid towered to a height of 480 feet, which is equivalent to that of a modern skyscraper 48 stories high. It is composed of a solid mass of yellow limestone blocks and at the time of its completion was

"Weighing of the Conscience" from the papyrus of the great scribe, Ani. Part of a Book of the Dead, it contains magic charms for those in the next world. Anubis, the jackal-headed god, who presides over embalming, is testing the bottled heart of Ani for justness by balancing it against a feather, symbol of truth. (The Oriental Institute of the University of Chicago)

Coffin of the Roman period of Egyptian history (about 30 B.C.). Crude modeling and exaggerated detail are characteristic of the decline in the art of burial technique at this time. (Chicago Natural History Museum)

Mummies of two children of the Ptolemaic period, in the same coffin. The casket is a plain rectangular box of sycamore wood. (Chicago Natural History Museum)

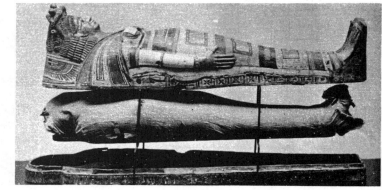

Scenes from Life adorn the interior of this Twenty-first Dynasty woman's mummy case. (Chicago Natural History Museum)

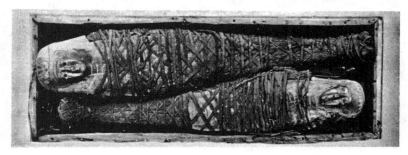

False Door for the Dead painted on the wall of the tomb of Khnumhotep, permitted this Middle Kingdom monarch to reenter the world of the living. Portrayed as the largest figure, Khnumhotep is seen on each side of the doorway snaring birds and harpooning fish assisted by his slaves. (Oriental Institute of the University of Chicago)

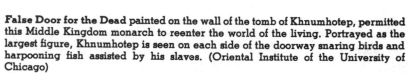

covered with an outer layer of fine white limestone. Shining in the sun, it must indeed have pleased the soul of the great king.

Not the least remarkable aspect about the pyramid was its method of construction. In that day there were no pulleys and little in the way of mechanical assistance to ease the labors of the multitudes. The lowest courses were dragged into place by brute force, while those in the courses above were hoisted by means of a sloping ramp of mud brick which had been thrown against the completed portions of the pyramid. When the building was finished, the ramp was removed. Approximately 2,300,000 limestone blocks went into the construction, and the average weight of each was two and a half tons. Considering these immense weights, it is all the more astonishing that the work was so perfectly done. Joints of only one ten-thousandth of an inch between blocks were apparently normal in the outer limestone casing.

The tomb entrance—which is in the eighteenth masonry course above the ground on the north side of the pyramid—leads to several chambers, in one of which the body of the king was placed. But for all the care and precaution taken in building the tomb it was entered by thieves, and the mummy of Khufu has never been found. It once was thought that the queen also had been buried in the pyramid, since there was more than one burial chamber. It appears, however, that Khufu, at different periods during construction of the

Great Pyramids at Gizeh. In order of age and size, Khufu (right) is first; Khafre (center) is second; Menkure (foreground) latest and smallest. (K.L.M. Dutch Airlines)

pyramid, changed his plans for the size that he wished and accordingly had it enlarged several times. This seems to account for the number of chambers and for the passages leading up to them. After Khufu had been laid away in state, stone plug blocks were dropped into place in the various passages in order to keep intruders away, and the entrance on the north side was closed with the same white limestone that covered the surface of the pyramid.

Members of the family and favored nobles built their tombs around the pyramid of their king and near the pyramid temple which had been erected just to the east facing the Nile. Food, drink, and other necessities were placed here for the use of the dead king in the afterlife. The pyramid complex was completed by a covered causeway which led from a temple at the edge of the cultivation up to the pyramid temple.

We have seen that Khufu was defeated in his principal purpose, which was to preserve

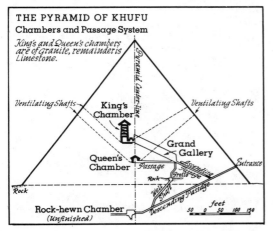

THE PYRAMID OF KHUFU
Chambers and Passage System
King's and Queen's chambers are of granite, remainder is Limestone.

Pyramid Center-line

Ventilating Shafts — King's Chamber

Ventilating Shafts

Grand Gallery

Queen's Chamber — Passage

Entrance

Ascending

Rock — Grotto

Well Shaft

Descending Passage

Rock

Rock-hewn Chamber (*Unfinished*)

feet
50 0 50 100 150

Great Sphinx symbolized pharaoh's power by portraying king with lion's body. (TWA Airlines Photo)

Others since his time have freed the monument of its quilt of sand and built walls as a preventive measure, but all to no avail. It requires constant attention to keep the Sphinx above ground. Aside from sand the colossus has suffered from natural cracking of the poor rock, and in addition has been willfully mutilated in recent times. Several hundred years ago it was used as a target by the Arabs. But the Sphinx still stands with face toward the east bearing with unchanged expression the marks of a long life.

for all time the body that had been a great and magnificent king. But his monument still stands as a symbol of his age. Untold powers and wealth lay in the hands of the king; the entire land of Egypt was dominated and made to obey the word of a single man.

THE IMMUTABLE SPHINX

The Great Sphinx, which stands in front of the second pyramid at Gizeh, exists because quarrymen for the first pyramid found a mass of limestone which they considered too poor in quality to be used. Thus the good stone on all sides was quarried away and the poor stone remained. When Khafre, builder of the second pyramid, was erecting his tomb and the temples that were associated with it, attention was called to the huge stone knob which lay to the east of the pyramid. Forthwith it was decided to shape it in the form of a sphinx with the head of a king and the body of a recumbent lion. Thus two accidents, one geologic and the other human, conspired to give the world a monument which has been little less famous than the pyramids themselves. This, too, is a huge structure, being about 66 feet high and 240 long. The ear alone is 4⅞ feet in length and the mouth 7½ feet wide.

The Sphinx, like the pyramids, stands at the edge of the desert and has always been subject to the shifting sands which tended to cover it up. The first known excavator of the Sphinx was King Thutmose IV who set up a slab (about 1420 B.C.) recording the fact.

THE MINES OF SINAI

Before the time of Menes, Egyptian expeditions had made the treacherous journey to Sinai in search of copper, turquoise, and other desirable materials which nature had imbedded in its rocks. This we know from materials which have been found in the ruined villages and towns of predynastic Egypt. From the First Dynasty on, the kings of Egypt began to leave inscriptions on the rocks of southern Sinai where the mining was carried on. The earliest inscription tells of the punishment of wild tribes that had dared to attack the king's workers.

Zoser, the first king of the Third Dynasty (about 2780 B.C.) and builder of the first

Chisel Cuttings at an Ancient Mine in Sinai. (Sir Flinders Petrie, "Researches in Sinai")

First Dynasty King smiting a native chieftain is carved in low relief on a stone found in Sinai. (Sir Flinders Petrie, "Researches in Sinai")

pyramid, also sent expeditions to the mines, as did Snefru who introduced the Fourth Dynasty (about 2686 B.C.). In fact, Snefru left in Sinai such a strong impression of his might that in later years he became a patron god who would aid and protect officials sent to the wilds in search of riches for their pharaohs.

Inscriptions were also left by Fifth and Sixth Dynasty kings and others who doubtless gained revenues from the rich rocks of Sinai. It was necessary at all times to have an adequate armed guard because of depredations by the roving Semitic natives of the country who were related to the later Hebrews and Arabs. One may doubt whether the officials, delegated to conduct the work and transport the copper and semiprecious stones back to Egypt, actually relished the honors that were be-

stowed upon them. Sinai never became quite civilized, yet it is a curious fact that by way of Sinai the alphabet was passed on to Palestine and Syria and to the Greeks and ourselves.

SHIPS TO LEBANON

Even before dynastic times there had been trade by sea with the Syrian coast, but the record comes only from materials uncovered in excavation. However, by the time of Snefru (about 2720 B.C.) we are told in so many words of such an expedition. The king sent forty ships which returned laden with cedar logs from the slopes of Lebanon, at that time blanketed with trees. Quite likely the trade in timber was carried on through Byblos where an Egyptian temple had been erected as early as the Second Dynasty. In fact, objects of the First Dynasty have been found in the ruins of Byblos.

With favorable winds, the voyage from the Delta to Byblos could be made in four days. The logs, after seasoning, were used for coffins, sacred boats, door lintels, and other objects that required good wood to be durable. Cedar of Lebanon thus brought Egypt into early contact with Byblos, which all through history appears to have been a sort of Egyptian outpost and the center of Egyptian culture in Asia.

THE END OF THE OLD KINGDOM

All dynasties come to an end, even in China. The Egyptian Sixth Dynasty had enjoyed a prosperous rule, yet weak kings had

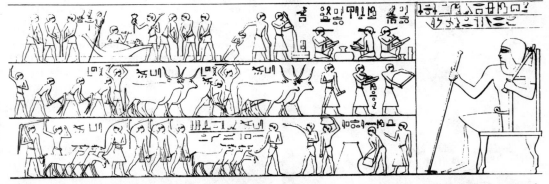

Agriculture in the Fifth Dynasty. A bas relief from the tomb of Neferbauptah shows the nobleman seated at the right supervising the plowing, sowing, and trampling of the grain. (Lepsius, "Denkmaeler")

allowed the nobles to assume ever increasing power. The tombs of this and the preceding dynasty clearly indicate the wealth and powerful position that the nobles had assumed. Influence in government matters was being split, with one noble gaining power here and another there. While some strong kings reigned during these two dynasties, they were not powerful enough to halt the trend toward a feudal state in which nobles in effect become petty kings.

This uncentralized state of affairs left Egypt prey to foreign invaders whose coming marks the end of the Sixth Dynasty as well as the end of the Old Kingdom. Very little is known about these people except that they came from Asia, presumably from North Syria. They were probably Semites who entered in small but rapidly increasing numbers into the Delta, settled there, and learned the ways of the country. In time they themselves became strong enough to make the disruption of the government completely effective. A period of chaos followed, an era of almost total darkness as far as our knowledge is concerned. In this period of almost two centuries must be placed the Seventh, Eighth, Ninth, and Tenth

Dynasties. The latter two of these covered periods of native Egyptian rule, but they were far from controlling the territory governed by the Old Kingdom dynasties. Further excavation may do much to clear up the tremendous uncertainty of this period, but until then we must pass it by for the most part and pick up the threads of Egyptian history again with the advent of the Middle Kingdom, about 2100 B.C.

THE LAND OF THE TWO RIVERS IN THE THIRD MILLENNIUM B.C.

By 3000 B.C. Mesopotamia had gone through the laborious stages which lead to civilization. Cities had grown up, and communication with distant territories had been established. But most important, the country now possessed a system of writing which came into general use when the people who are called Sumerians assumed historic control of the country.

The system of writing used in Mesopotamia began with pictures, just as in Egypt, but the Babylonians developed their script in an altogether different way. The reason for this is that the clay tablet came into early use as the object on which writing was recorded. In Egypt there was plenty of stone and papyrus, whereas these materials were lacking along the Tigris and Euphrates. Furthermore, clay is not a particularly good material on which to paint or scratch pictures for permanent use. As a result the Babylonians developed the

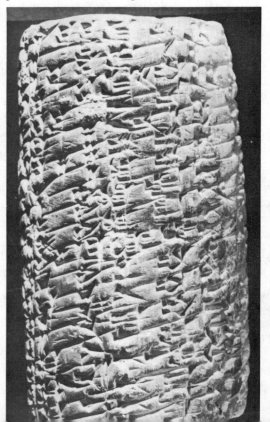

Clay Cylinder (left) from Tell Harmal, inscribed with unusual syllables, possibly a musical notation. Early pictograph writings (below) from Kish. Cuneiform tablet in its "envelope" (below right), dated about 2200 B.C. (Directorate General of Antiquities of Iraq and New York Public Library)

use of the stylus for impressing wedge-shaped characters on the soft clay tablet. In this way the original pictures were depicted in increasingly angular form until finally they became so conventionalized that the originals can be detected only with the greatest difficulty. This type of writing is called *cuneiform*, from the Latin *cuneus*, meaning "wedge."

We recall that Egyptian picture writing originally stood for ideas and not sounds. The same was true of Babylonian. But in time the necessary transition to sound recording was accomplished. In Mesopotamia, however, the signs came to stand for syllables such as *mar* or *duk*, but there was no possible way to represent the sounds *m* or *r*, *d* or *k*, or any of the other alphabetic sounds. Thus while the cuneiform system was phonetic it did not progress beyond the syllabic stage.

The Sumerians developed the cuneiform system to the point where it was convenient for recording their language. Then about 2550 B.C. their country was conquered by a group of Semitic nomads under the leadership of Sargon I. The nomads spoke a language different from that of the Sumerians, and in addition they did not know how to write. But under the influence of the civilization in which they now found themselves they adopted the Sumerian cuneiform system and began to write their Semitic language with the now established wedge system.

In later times cuneiform was borrowed by a number of different peoples speaking different languages, among them the Persians.

THE SUMERIANS

The origin of the Sumerians is still clouded in mystery. It may be that they were in the land before 3000 B.C., but not before that date do we get a full view of these people settled in their cities on the lower stretches of the Tigris and Euphrates in the land that they called Sumer.

Sumer never became a kingdom in the sense in which we understand that word. There were, on the other hand, a series of small city-states, all under the influence of a common culture, yet constantly at war with one another. Each city was ruled by a priest-king whose

Bull's Head of gold and lapis lazuli (right) and engraved shell plaque (left) decorated a harp found at Ur. (University of Pennsylvania Museum)

territory extended for some miles in all directions around the city. We might compare such a domain to a present day county with its county seat, but infinitely more powerful and independent. In those days Ur, which later became famous through association with Abraham, was among the stronger of these city-states; Lagash and Kish were others.

The Sumerians are important, less for the fact that they controlled a considerable portion of lower Mesopotamia for a number of centuries, than that their culture became the basis of later Babylonian civilization. They passed on their mode of life, their system of writing, their laws, their art, and a good part of their religious practice. Many hundred years later rituals were still being recited in Sumerian in exactly the same way that Latin is today. Sumerian became the classical language in Babylonia.

SARGON OF AKKAD AND HIS DYNASTY

It was about 2550 B.C. that a wave of Semitic people from the Syrian Desert swept into Babylonia and, under the leadership of Sargon, settled just north of the land of Sumer. They called their country Akkad, and from that time on Semites dominated the Babylonian scene. The Sumerians were soon conquered and one of their last priest-kings, Lugalzaggisi, was led through the city of

Gudea, priest-king of Lagash, about 2600 B.C. Devoted to religion and literature, he was worshiped after death, as a god. (Museum of Fine Arts, Boston)

Nippur in chains. He had carried his own conquests to the Mediterranean, and at his downfall his territories fell into the hands of Sargon. Semitic victories also took place to the east of Babylonia in the mountains and highlands bordering Persia, and before he died Sargon had welded together an empire of considerable extent.

Naram-Sin from his Victory Stella. (Louvre)

Sargon became the hero of heroes to later Babylonians, and quite naturally incidents in his life became subject for folklore. The story was told that he had been born in secret and was placed in a basket of reeds upon the river. The current carried him downstream where he was found by a peasant who brought him up as his own son. He became a gardener, and finally, through the love of the goddess Ishtar, ruler of the kingdom. From basket on the waters to ruler of his people! But where have we heard a story very much like that? Shades of Moses, and the basket and pharaoh's daughter. The ancient east had many popular tales into which past heroes were placed. The story of Romulus and Remus, the foundling founders of Rome, is but a variation of the tale of the miraculous and wonderful early days of Sargon and Moses.

Sargon was followed by other great kings and warriors who were fairly successful in keeping together the gains that had already

Woman's Headdress and ornaments, taken from the great death pit at Ur. When an Assyrian king died, servants, guards, and women were sacrificed and buried with him to serve him after death. (Oriental Institute of the University of Chicago)

been made. There were revolts, of course, but these were halted, and new territories were added to the already considerable Kingdom of Akkad. Naram-Sin, who flourished about 2550 B.C. and is generally considered to have been the son of Sargon I, was one of the greatest of Sargon's successors. So extensive was his empire that he called himself "King of the Four Quarters of the World." Some time after his death, however, the land of Akkad underwent another of the periodic uprisings of the eastern mountaineers on the borders of Babylonia.

These people, called the Guti, left their homes in the Zagros Mountains and at length took possession of the fertile lands and busy cities along the Tigris and Euphrates. Their rule began about 2400 B.C. and lasted for a century or more, after which the Sumerians, who had been subdued by Sargon, again came to the fore and established themselves for a century. But conditions were far from settled. Sumerians and Semites continued to struggle, and Elamites from the edge of Persia descended into the plain. The time was ripe for the coming of a powerful people who could establish themselves as sole rulers. At length they came, a Semitic people from up the Euphrates, who first settled at Babylon and later conquered all of Babylonia. This was the First Dynasty of Babylon, destined to give to the world the famous king, Hammurabi. Before 2000 B.C. Babylon had been a very insignificant town. Thereafter it was to assume an importance as great as any city in ancient Asia.

TRADE WITH INDIA

Many hundred miles lie between Mesopotamia and the Indus Valley in India. The land journey is difficult and the sea voyage is treacherous even today. Yet, almost five thousand years ago, trade relations between the two territories had been established. Merchants went back and forth with their goods and, as the world travelers of that day, brought back tales of the lands they had visited. A clear indication of this condition is seen in the design cut on a cylinder seal found in a house of the Akkadian period (about 2500 B.C.).

We may be perfectly sure that there was intimate knowledge of India in the western countries because this cylinder seal, which is Mesopotamian in form, was cut with a typically Indian design. The elephant and rhinoceros which form the essential part of the pattern were animals unknown in the Tigris-Euphrates region. Moreover they were depicted in a manner closely resembling Indian representations of the same animals. Consequently we are certain that people from the Land of the Two Rivers had actually gone as far afield as India. They had seen and been impressed by specimens of Indian art, perhaps they had viewed the strange animals as well,

and had brought home these ideas with them. The same thing was happening in India, for her merchants who had gone to Mesopotamia brought products and ideas characteristic of the Tigris-Euphrates back to the valley of the Indus. Excavation in prehistoric sites in India has really just begun, and in time we may know

The Elephants and Rhinoceros on this Akkadian cylinder seal are vital clues in establishing the link between India and Mesopotamia. (Oriental Institute of the University of Chicago)

much more about relations between eastern and western Asia during this early period. It is possible that such communications began much earlier than we now believe, for shipping by sea and by caravan is an old institution, almost as old as simple barter between neighboring tribes.

THE CANALS AND RIVERS OF BABYLONIA

We are accustomed to think of the Babylonians in terms of commerce, money lending, and astronomy, and in this we are right, for they had aptitude in all these matters, even in early days. But the Babylonian was essentially a farmer who earned his "daily bread" through the cultivation of wheat, barley, and millet. We have seen that Egyptian farmers were dependent on the yearly over-

This cylinder seal used by a scribe of about 2300 B.C., reveals a highly developed art, an epic folklore and a native literature of the ancient Babylonians. The design illustrates a part of the great poem of Babylonian literature known as "The Epic of Gilgamesh." Gilgamesh, the legendary ruler of pre-flood Uruk, and his friend, the satyr, Engidu are fighting with a bull and a lion. (Oriental Institute of the University of Chicago)

The Code of Hammurabi. This detail of the stele shows Shamash, the Sun God, commanding Hammurabi to establish just laws. (Oriental Institute of the University of Chicago)

flow of the Nile for water for their crops. In Babylonia the water of the rivers was just as important but had to be obtained in a different way. Because the rivers did not rise far enough out of their banks to flow over the surrounding country, it became necessary to install a vast irrigation system covering the entire land. The god Marduk was given credit for the discovery of irrigation, and its importance is shown in the royal inscriptions. From earliest times every king who has left us any mention of himself or his administration tells of constructing or repairing canals by which water might be brought from the two rivers to the fertile land. Trading may have been a strong mark of these people, but farming was the backbone of their life.

THE DYNASTY OF HAMMURABI

About the time Egyptians were recovering from the disorders that had taken place when a foreign people invaded their country, the First Dynasty of Babylon established itself in the fertile lower stretches of the Babylonian plain. These people who had come down the Euphrates to find themselves in the midst of civilization were related in language to the Semites who had entered the country with Sargon four hundred years earlier. They made the town of Babylon their capital and soon it became the greatest city of the land.

The most important name of the First Dynasty of Babylon is that of Hammurabi, and frequently one speaks of the Dynasty of Hammurabi. But he was not the founder of this line of kings, for he came to the throne a hundred years after his ancestors had swept into the land. The earlier kings made successful conquests which tended more and more to make the country Semitic, but not until late in Hammurabi's reign was the whole country unified. The Elamites and other natural enemies were conquered, and Marduk, originally an insignificant local god of the town of Babylon, became the patron god of the entire country. In later days Babylon was to be ruled by foreign dynasties, but never again did it lose its Semitic quality.

The First Dynasty of Babylon lasted for about three hundred years—until 1750 B.C.—but the peace of Hammurabi's later years was short-lived. The country was rich and naturally became the object of envy of the surrounding peoples. After his death trouble rained on the head of the son who succeeded him. Cities revolted, and in the south along the Persian Gulf an independent dynasty, known as the "Sealand Dynasty," established itself so thoroughly that it outlived the Dynasty of Hammurabi. About 1760 B.C. a raiding band of Hittites from the northwest entered the city of Babylon and sacked it, and out of the ensuing period of disorder the Kassites emerged as the ruling people about 1750 B.C.

THE LAW CODE OF HAMMURABI

Long after Hammurabi's death, a monument on which he had inscribed the laws of his country was taken from Babylon by a conquering Elamite who set it up in Susa, his capital city in the mountains on the border of Persia. It was there that the French found it during their excavations. Hammurabi is pictured on the monument as receiving the laws from the sun god Shamash, and below the relief and on all sides of the monument were cut in cuneiform the laws that governed conduct in Babylonia about 2000 B.C. The monument, a diorite monolith, is in the Louvre.

Quite wrongly these laws have been attributed to Hammurabi, and while some of them were undoubtedly developed during his reign, it is certain that most of them went back to Sumerian times. It is a case, then, of the king having gathered together the existing laws, some of which had experienced a long and complex history, and putting them together in one volume. The stone monument on which they are inscribed may properly be called a volume on law.

The Code of Hammurabi was the basis for part of the later Biblical Code of the Covenant. Its provisions were extensive and in the main were extremely humane for the times. Through them we are given a view of the everyday life of Babylonia, and, in order to gain this feeling ourselves, we shall cite a few of the more interesting provisions.

The first law said that if a man accused another of murder, but could not prove it, he himself was to be put to death. Death was the penalty for many misdemeanors. If a man stole from the temple or the palace he was to die, and the receiver of the stolen goods was to meet the same fate. The penalty for kidnapping a minor son was the same. A man who aided a slave to escape paid the same penalty. The captured thief likewise paid with his life.

There was burglary insurance in Babylonia in those days. If the thief was not captured the man who had been robbed could go before the god and swear as to his loss, and the city and governor in whose land the robbery was committed gave him full value.

All business was conducted by written contract. Even the shepherd who grazed his sheep on another man's property had to come to an agreement as to the value of the grass eaten by the animals. If a man neglected to get a receipt for money or grain owed him there was no way in which he could force the payment. Today we often hear the statement, "Put it in writing." The Babylonians four thousand years ago were keenly aware of the dangers of oral agreements, and we may believe that few of them were careless more than once.

There were barmaids who, if they gave short measure, were to be thrown into the water. If the barmaid learned that a conspiracy was being hatched in the wineshop, she was to notify the authorities or else be put to death.

An eye for an eye and a tooth for a tooth was the law of the land as we see in the following provisions: If a man destroy the eye of another man, they shall destroy his eye; if a man knock out a tooth of a man of his own rank, they shall knock out his tooth. But if a

Marduk battles Tiamat, the monster of chaos, from Ashurnasirpal II's palace at Nimrud. (Layard's "Monuments of Ninevah")

man knocked out the tooth of a common man he merely paid a fine. A man striking his superior on the cheek received sixty lashes from an oxtail whip in public. But if this same man struck a man of his own rank he paid only a fine. We see that there were grades to society and penalties were judged accordingly. If a slave hit the son of a gentleman the offender paid with the loss of an ear. On the other hand if two men got into a quarrel and one of them was hurt, the incident was closed by the other swearing that it was not intentional and then paying the physician's fee.

The physician himself must always have felt a deep sense of responsibility when he took over a case. He seems not to have been free to charge according to his whim, but received a set sum for a certain type of work. Yet, if a wealthy patient died as a result of an operation or lost the use of an eye, the surgeon paid dearly by the loss of his hand. If a slave died after an operation the surgeon was forced to substitute a slave of equal value.

There were laws on debts, marriage, bankruptcy, partnership, inheritance, adoption, and even collision of ships. These and many others make up the inscription on the black rock that Hammurabi set up in the city of Babylon about 2000 B.C. and which was carried off to Susa as a trophy of war long after the great king had died. But the laws themselves could not be stolen and many centuries later we find the Hebrews, newly come to the "Promised Land," adopting those measures which best fitted their society at the time.

31

Here was a people with trade by great caravan routes and sea. To facilitate this, they had banking houses and a system of credit. A tablet inscribed in cuneiform and bearing the proper credentials might travel hundreds of miles and be good for a shipment of goods simply on presentation. There were libraries containing thousands of tablets on diverse subjects, and works of art for those who appreciated them. Indeed, the civilization of Hammurabi's time had many qualities.

THE NO-MAN'S LAND OF PALESTINE AND SYRIA

Although there are scattered references to Palestine in the Egyptian and Babylonian records, the story of the country during the third pre-Christian millennium, that is between 3000 and 2000 B.C., must be told largely from debris turned up by the archeologist. The people were apparently of the same Mediterranean physical type that had inhabited the land during the preceding period, but important trends toward civilization are to be seen among the excavated cities of the fertile plains.

THE POTTER'S WHEEL IS INTRODUCED

Before 3000 B.C. the potter had made his jars, jugs, and bowls by hand, and had become very skillful. But it was slow work and not always perfect. Then, about five thousand years ago, a type of pottery wheel on which the plastic clay could more easily be molded and handled found its way into the country. It is likely that the idea for this device was transmitted from the north, by way of Syria. The wheel, which allowed the potter to spin the raw clay on a revolving plate and quickly work it into even shaped vessels, proved a great time saver and no doubt lowered the price of pots. Peasant folk have always been quick to save a penny, or grain and vegetables as it probably was in those days, and as a result the wheel became a fixture in this civilization. The form of the wheel is unknown except through its effect on the structure of pottery. But we know that it was of simple construction and had to be turned by hand.

Yet, simple as it was, it was nevertheless part of the "machine age" which was being ushered in. It was a very modest machine age when thought of in terms of today, yet invention was by that time many thousands of years old.

At the same time that the pottery wheel was introduced, the furnaces in which the pottery was baked were tremendously improved. They gave a greater hardness to the clay than had the old furnaces, and burned the vessels more evenly so that all parts of a pot tended to be of about the same quality. This improvement may be difficult for us to understand, but the new techniques must have been much appreciated by the women who did the cooking and needed vessels on which they could depend. These inventions, of course, did not lead to the making of unbreakable pots, and for that we may be truly thankful, for, as we have seen, the broken pots of antiquity have become the fossils by which we tell the age of buried cities.

EGYPTIAN AND MESOPOTAMIAN FORAYS

At all times Palestine and Syria have been the corridor leading to Egyptian forays on the Asiatic powers. At the same time Syria had to be controlled by Mesopotamia to keep the population of the upper Euphrates country from breaking loose over the fertile plains of Babylonia. Palestine and Syria have thus in a sense always been pawns in the great political game of empire in the Near East. We know little of the first interplay involving Palestine and Syria except that as early as the time of Lugalzaggisi, who was later conquered by Sargon, Mesopotamian armies marched to the Mediterranean. All the country between the Euphrates and the mountain of Lebanon on the coast was apparently in Sumerian hands. When the Akkadians came into power about 2550 B.C. this vast foreign territory fell prey to Sargon, for he too marched to the Mediterranean and even went as far north as Asia Minor. The details of these forays are lacking, and we can only guess as to their meaning and consequences. The bare facts, however, can be interpreted to mean that Syria was highly desirable in the eyes of Mesopotamian monarchs. If nothing else, her rich fields in the valley of the Orontes River and the cedar wooded slopes of the mountains would be most attractive.

By these incursions and the resulting settlement of some of the conquerors, the high civilization of the Tigris-Euphrates country was carried westward. Perhaps it is to these beginnings that we must trace the later cultural influence on the eastern Mediterranean states.

Egypt, too, was interested in the Levant, the coastal region of Palestine and Syria. We have seen that Byblos possessed an Egyptian temple as early as the Second Dynasty. Trade between Syria and the Nile was lucrative, and the merchants of Byblos seem always to have felt that becoming Egyptianized was well worth the price if their profits were large enough.

Thus it is not surprising to find that the Egyptian army and navy, as well as merchants, gained a knowledge of the country that lay between. Fragmentary and tantalizingly meager inscriptions tell of punitive expeditions to the region beyond Sinai. The earliest known of these occurred about 2400 B.C. when, during the reign of Pepi I, troop ships were sent to quell a revolt somewhere on the Levant coast. The troops landed and, according to the inscription, every insurgent was slain.

It is undoubtedly a fact that every powerful ruler in Egypt or Mesopotamia cast envious eyes on the narrow strip of Palestine and Syria. Perhaps more of them than we suspect played an active part in the history of this territory. The study of the history of the Near East is still young enough to cause little surprise at the discovery of long hidden documents. We have only to recall that a few years back almost nothing was known of the Hittites.

SYRIANS OVERRUN EGYPT

A number of times in her history Egypt fell prey to marauding foreigners from Asia. The first definite instance came at the end of the Old Kingdom, about 2270 B.C., when the country had already been weakened by the spread of power among the great nobles. The evidence, however, lacks many of the details that we should like to possess. The foreigners have been traced to North Syria through a peculiar type of decorated seal which they brought with them to Egypt. These seals have their counterparts in numerous specimens that have been found in Syria. But one of the mysteries regarding their movement is that such seals have never been found in contemporary deposits in Palestine. If we grant that the foreigners came from Syria, we must ask how they got to Egypt if they did not cross Palestine. It is possible that they went by sea. On the other hand it may be that evidence of their passage through Palestine still lies buried in the ruins of cities along the coast.

The invasion of these people was in any case an event of extreme importance to the history of Egypt. The advance of civilization was momentarily halted and the whole country found itself in turmoil. But out of this condition emerged the glories of the Middle Kingdom which we shall soon have occasion to view.

ON THE OTHER SIDE OF THE TAURUS

The Taurus Mountains which separate Anatolia from the region south and east have always been an effective barrier to progress of culture. Anatolia remained a cultural backwater until about 2000 B.C. when we find the first instances of writing.

The Copper Age lasted for about six hundred years, ending around 2400 B.C. There was again a distinction between east and west. The second city at Troy was related to the first, but in central Anatolia there seems to have been an incursion of new people from the northeast. Copper became plentiful, and bronze was also known.

The distinction between east and west remained during the Early Bronze period which followed. Troy's outlook was to the sea and to Europe; Central Anatolia was purely Asiatic. It is likely that another wave from the northeast entered the land during this period. Perhaps some of them were Indo-Europeans. We now approach the time when Anatolia took an important part in the political interplay of the Near East. The earliest known written records come from about 2000 B.C., at a time when Egypt and Mesopotamia could look back on a venerable written record.

AN ASSYRIAN TRADING COLONY

Later we shall hear much more of the Assyrians. Before 2000 B.C. they had established themselves in upper Mesopotamia and had formed a small kingdom on the Tigris River. But the great days of Assyria lay centuries ahead, and the greatest did not come until after the time of David and Solomon.

The excavations in Anatolia have revealed the existence of a small group of these people who left their homes on the Tigris during the twentieth century B.C. We know they were Assyrians because most of their names left us on tablets are made up of the names of the Assyrian gods Ashur and Adad and the goddess Ishtar. This is excellent evidence that the people came from the territory in which these deities were supposed to reside. The people described on the tablets were independent and had their own judges. They lived in a foreign quarter of the towns they inhabited, probably in much the same way that Christians, Jews, and Arabs long lived in separate parts of Jerusalem. The Assyrians in Anatolia were evidently transients, there to trade with Assyria's neighbors to the northwest.

When the tablets were first discovered they created much excitement not only among those interested in history but also among the nearby natives. It was not long, therefore, before forgeries began to appear in the market of antiques. Fortunately they were so badly done that nobody was deceived. In recent years authentic tablets of the same general type have come to the surface, and these with the others give clear-cut evidence that there was a considerable group of Assyrians in the country in the twentieth century B.C.

THE OLD HITTITE KINGDOM

There were two Hittite kingdoms, called the Old and the New by modern historians. A comparatively short time ago their existence was doubted by some, and nothing was known of the kings and events of the time. Now, however, we not only know for certain that there were Hittites, but much of the detail of past periods can be filled in.

The history of the Old Kingdom begins at the time of the Assyrian merchant tablets. The country had for some time existed as a series of small disunited city-states, each with its native prince. Such a situation we have seen before, and we are not surprised in the least to learn that one of these princes made plans to join some of the cities under his personal rule. He was successful to a certain extent, but much larger plums were in store for his son Anittas. Before the end of Anittas' reign a large part of central Anatolia succumbed to his might. But then darkness falls upon the scene, for there are no records for the next few decades.

At length we learn of a king named Labarnas who began a dynasty shortly before 1800 B.C., which was destined to have considerable influence on the history of the Near East. The land became a true kingdom under his rule, and was divided into provinces for tax and administrative purposes.

As far as we know it was during the reign of his successor, Hattusilis, that the Hittites first attacked North Syria and captured the city of Aleppo which at that time was one of the strongest city-states in the region.

The kingdom reached the peak of its power under Mursilis who came to the throne about 1775 B.C. He engaged in wars at home, but was also able to enter Syria as his father before him had done. And then, after subduing this region, he made his famous raid on Babylon some four hundred and fifty miles away. This happened about 1760 B.C. and proved to be the death blow to the dynasty of Hammurabi, for Babylon was sacked and plundered, and the population were made slaves. It is one of the unaccountable facts of history that the Hittites then turned homeward with their booty, leaving Babylonia to the Kassites.

A period of misfortune for the royal family and decline for the kingdom followed, and we may bring the Old Kingdom to a close about 1650 B.C. The two succeeding centuries are ones of darkness, but we are then allowed to resume the course of Hittite history with the interesting story of the New Kingdom.

4. The Time of the Patriarchs and the Judges

THE Middle Kingdom of Egypt is usually regarded as including the Eleventh, Twelfth, and Thirteenth Dynasties which lasted from about 2100 to 1700 B.C. The Eleventh represents for us the reaction against disorder and the rebuilding of the country. The Twelfth is certainly the climax of the movement and is, moreover, the classical period of Egyptian culture. This was one of the most prosperous periods in the history of Egypt. Buildings were erected in all towns of consequence, and literature and art flourished. The Thirteenth, which is less known, stands for political decline. It came to an end at a time when another foreign people, the Hyksos, found Egypt a favorable spot to end a long journey through Asia.

The origin of the Eleventh Dynasty is very obscure. We know that it arose in Thebes which before that time had been an insignificant Upper Egyptian village. Now kings by the name of Intef or Mentuhotep established a rule stronger than any since the Old Kingdom. The feudal system with local lords still prevailed, and the kings had to be extremely careful how they treated them. But neither were these kings weaklings. They had welded the various elements into an Egyptian state, and the national unity is illustrated by the revived expeditions to the mines in Egypt and Sinai, commercial ventures to the Levant, and an extensive building program at Thebes.

Amenemhet I, the first king of the Twelfth Dynasty, claimed to be related to the Intef family. He overthrew the last of the Mentuhoteps and established a strong line of kings whose names were either Amenemhet or Sesostris. Their pyramid tombs, which are smaller than the largest of the Old Kingdom, lie near the Fayum, south of Cairo. The last ruler of the dynasty which lasted from 2000 to 1788 B.C. was a woman who reigned but four years. The first Amenemhet had probably been vizier under the last king of the Eleventh Dynasty. He was a strong-willed person and carried Egypt's conquests abroad, but even he in his resulting strength was unable to subdue the powerful landed families that made up Egypt and which traced their ancestry to the Sixth Dynasty lords. In all probability it was through the aid of the strongest of these that Amenemhet became king. But all he could do with the insidious feudal system was tactfully to readjust the various provinces within their normal bounds and be content with ruling a feudal state. The limited extent of the king's political strength is clearly shown by the fact that some of the provinces had their own priestly and governmental organizations, and dated their documents from the reign of the local prince.

Amenemhet appears to have been supported by most of the south, for he deliberately founded his capital in the north near Memphis. From there, commerce developed to heights never before known in Egypt, for Egyptian ships traded with the Aegean territory, Crete, the Levant, the Red Sea, and Nubia as far as the second cataract. Military campaigns occupied a good deal of the following kings' time, and it is likely that Egypt had much more to say about conditions in Palestine and Syria than has been suspected in the past.

The vizier was a powerful individual, for he supervised all the government offices. He thus handled the taxes which were paid in kind, and had something to do with the standing army. The great military power, however, still lay with the local princes, and we see again how dependent the king was on the good will of his lords.

Amenemhet III. (Oriental Institute of the University of Chicago)

The literature of the period was of a high order, and in it we find the first works written for amusement although such had probably existed earlier. A Sinbad the Sailor tale was frequently told, as were numerous other stories of a popular nature. Much of this material is preserved to us because for the first time the schools were teaching a uniform system of writing.

In religion there was a great change and development. When the Sixth Dynasty ended the sun god Re was supreme, but now the local god of Thebes who had guided the destinies of the Middle Kingdom kings gained national status. He was Amon who in time, through a peculiar oriental way of thinking, became merged with the sun god Re. The result in the minds of Egyptians was Amon-Re, supreme god of the country of the Nile. There were many local gods as well, all related in the mythological genealogies.

Osiris rose suddenly in the religious thought

Sesostris III. (Oriental Institute of the University of Chicago)

of the people and became the universal judge after death. He was such a strong figure that his life, death, and resurrection were enacted by local theatrical groups in much the same way that the Passion Play is presented at Oberammergau in Bavaria. Even the powerful princes fell under the sway of this god and became models of benevolence. When the crops were bad they helped support the people and created work. One of these princes says in his tomb biography, "Then came great Niles, rich in grain and all things, but I did not collect the arrears of the field." This high ethical

Early Egypt.

standard was due almost entirely to Osiris. There was a definite realization that the acts of this life determined one's position after death. Osiris, in his capacity as judge of the dead, determined where the deceased were to reside, sending them either to the crocodile or lion executioners, or proclaiming them "triumphant." The latter entered the Egyptian heaven, called Yaru, where fruit was plentiful and grain grew twelve feet high.

THE PHYSICIAN AND SURGEON IN EGYPT

It has long been known that there was a large medical literature in the Near East before the rise of Greek medicine. We have seen that the Code of Hammurabi recognized

36

the rights and duties of the physician. There exist also a number of Egyptian works on medicine, which, although they contain much magic, were on the whole leading to true medical knowledge. Science, too, had its beginnings in magic.

The earliest known surgical treatise, on the other hand, shows an amazing amount of real medical knowledge. It is the Edwin Smith Surgical Papyrus, named for the man who purchased it in Luxor during the American Civil War. The papyrus was copied about 1600 B.C. from earlier sources, some of them older than the Middle Kingdom. The inscription was never finished, for what reason we do not know. It starts with the head and proceeds systematically downward like a modern textbook on anatomy. The lower part of the body is missing in the discussion of

Earliest Known Surgical Treatise. This section of the Edwin Smith Surgical Papyrus deals with the treatment of head wounds. (New York Historical Society and the Oriental Institute)

cases. The document consists of 48 cases, each of them classified by one of the three following remarks: 1) favorable, 2) uncertain, or 3) unfavorable. The last, which was expressed by the phrase "an ailment not to be treated," pertained to a group of cases which were considered by the surgeon to be hopeless.

In view of the fact that the Egyptians all but discovered circulation of the blood and the function of the heart, and came close to realizing that special parts of the brain had definite functions, we may well pay our respects to them as keen medical observers. A few cases will clarify the method followed in the Edwin Smith Surgical Papyrus.

"If thou examinest a man having a gaping, wound in his head, penetrating to the bone and perforating his skull, thou shouldst palpate his wound. Shouldst thou find him unable to look at his two shoulders and his breast,

Temple of Amon, Karnak. The Pharaohs honored their chief god with the largest columned hall ever built. (The Art Institute of Chicago)

and suffering from stiffness in his neck, thou shouldst say regarding him: 'One having a gaping wound in his head, penetrating to the bone, and perforating his skull, while he suffers with stiffness in his neck, an ailment which I will treat.' "

The treatment is then given: "Now after thou hast stitched it, thou shouldst lay fresh meat upon his wound the first day. Thou shouldst not bind it. Put him on his customary diet until the period of his injury passes by. Thou shouldst treat it afterward with grease, honey, and lint every day, until he recovers."

Another case, which was considered fatal, follows: "If thou examinest a man having a crushed vertebra in his neck and thou findest that one vertebra has fallen into the next one, while he is voiceless and cannot speak; his falling head downward has caused that one vertebra crush into the next one; and shouldst thou find that he is unconscious of his two arms and his two legs because of it, thou shouldst say concerning him: 'One having a crushed vertebra in his neck; he is unconscious of his two arms and his two legs and he is speechless. An ailment not to be treated.' "

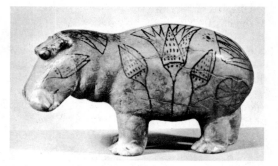

A Faience Hippopotamus is decorated with rich, blue lotus flowers, symbols of his natural habitat. (The Metropolitan Museum of Art)

EGYPTIANS KNEW MORE THAN THE TABLE OF 2'S

By the Twelfth Dynasty the Egyptians had established a system of mathematics of considerable complexity which served them in accounting, land measuring, and other practical matters. This knowledge had been built up through the centuries, for as early as the First Dynasty the system of numbers was well established. Land measures that were used later had already come into use by the Fourth Dynasty, and by the end of the Old Kingdom simple fractions of the bushel were in common use. Egyptian fractions were very cumbersome, for with the exception of 2/3 and ¾, none had a numerator higher than 1. Thus, 63/64 was written ½ + ¼ + ⅛ + 1/16 + 1/32 + 1/64.

By the time of the Twelfth Dynasty, mathematics had progressed to the point where numbers could be squared, and an understanding of the square root existed. The cube and cube root are not indicated. But the area of a rectangle and triangle could be computed with little error. The circle was conceived to be a square with sides equal to 8/9 the diameter of the circle. To obtain the area the Egyptian mathematician then multiplied 8/9 D by 8/9 D, in doing which he made an error of only about ½ of 1 per cent when compared with the true area of the circle. This formula was used to ascertain the contents of granaries which were cylindrical in form. The volume of such a granary was correctly seen to be equal to the area of the base multiplied by the height.

Egyptian mathematics grew out of practical needs such, for instance, as the laying out of the Great Pyramid, or measuring a pile of grain which lay upon the ground. Nowhere is there any indication that Egyptians were interested in theoretical problems.

THE COMING OF ARYAN-SPEAKING PEOPLES

While Egypt was approaching and passing the heights of prosperity during the Middle Kingdom, a dark cloud appeared over the horizon in Asia. The Thirteenth Dynasty, which was mainly restricted to the south, perhaps sensed little of its meaning. But the Fourteenth Dynasty, which had set itself up in the Delta soon after the end of the Twelfth Dynasty, must have seen the danger more clearly. A host of Aryan-speaking peoples were leaving their homes north or northeast of Syria and Mesopotamia and were bound southward across the mountains and toward the pleasant valleys and rich cities of civilization.

The word "Aryan" is commonly misused in everyday speech, being incorrectly understood as a racial term. Aryan is actually a linguistic expression which includes the large group of Indo-European languages both ancient and modern. Those who speak English, German, French, Italian, Rumanian, Greek or Sanskrit, among many others, speak Aryan tongues. The only people who may rightly be called Aryan are those who spoke the original Aryan language, but since that early time there has been so much interracial mixture that Aryan has lost all meaning as an expression of race.

Aryan-speaking people began drifting into Anatolia during the third millennium, and the language of the Hittites has proved to be Indo-European, whether written in cuneiform or hieroglyphic. This has been among the most astonishing discoveries made in the field of ancient history since World War I. Those who know Latin recognize many familiar forms in Hittite.

The Aryans who first entered Anatolia probably came from the northeast. Some authorities believe that the plains of southern Russia were the original home of these people

Pectoral of Senusret II. In gold inlay, eternity, shown as a kneeling man, supports the royal cartouche. (The Metropolitan Museum of Art)

who soon were to rock the Semitic world and in time take it for its very own.

There are also indications of Aryan influence in Mesopotamia, for the Kassites, who took the throne of Babylon after the Dynasty of Hammurabi had collapsed, had worshiped Aryan gods before reaching the plains. They came from the northern Zagros Mountains, but as soon as they reached civilization they were quickly absorbed by the Semites.

About the same time a related people were moving on Egypt, the Hyksos, or so-called Shepherd Kings. Their history is all too vague, yet we know that they established themselves in the Delta by about 1730 B.C. at the expense of the Fourteenth Dynasty. There they conducted their government with considerable success for a century and a half, at times drawing heavy tribute from the south where native princes did their best to keep up a semblance of kingship. The Hyksos constitute the Fifteenth and Sixteenth Dynasties.

The native Seventeenth which arose at Thebes in the south long before Hyksos rule was completed, became strong enough in time to drive the Hyksos out of Middle Egypt. A few years later, about 1580 B.C., the first king of the Eighteenth Dynasty succeeded in crushing the hated foreigners at their capital in the Delta and driving the remainder back into Palestine.

But who were the Hyksos? There are indications that some of them came from the steppes of southern Russia or Turkestan, and as such they may have spoken an Aryan tongue. The Hyksos brought the horse to

An Asiatic, in typical braid-edged shirt with tasseled hem, acts as servant in an Egyptian household. (Muller, "Egyptological Researches")

Egypt, and its name can be traced to an Indo-European origin. But there are no known Hyksos names that can be similarly traced. We may only suppose that the Indo-Europeans among the Hyksos rapidly lost their native language when they came into contact with the peoples along the Mediterranean.

There were other elements among the Hyksos, Semitic being the most prominent. And the movement which culminated in the establishment of two dynasties in Egypt may also have picked up Hittites along the way. It is plain, also, that a people from eastern Anatolia called Hurrians, whose language was unrelated to any we have here mentioned, were among the composite group that came to be known as Hyksos. These are the newest people to make themselves known from the lost cities of the Near East, for it is but a matter of a few years since the Hurrians became known and were identified with the Horites of the Bible.

The Hyksos, then, included Aryans, Semites, Hurrians, and quite possibly Hittites—a group of composite people who made a lasting impression on the minds of Egyptians for many centuries afterward. These were scattered through Syria and Palestine before destiny placed some of them on the throne of Egypt. Those who went to the land of the Nile became Egyptianized, and some of their kings took good Egyptian names. If Hyksos parents had given names in keeping with the original languages they or their ancestors had spoken, how much easier would be the problem of the Hyksos.

This is the period of Abraham and Isaac, Jacob and Joseph. Their history, as told in the Old Testament, can fit quite well into the Hyksos background. They were Semites, some of whom went down to Egypt, and the story of Joseph as vizier to the king of Egypt could hardly fit anywhere else. A Hyksos king might well have welcomed a man of Joseph's caliber, especially if he too were a Hyksos. And while there are other records of Semitic groups settling in Egypt, we can hardly fail to see that the Hyksos period would have been an exceedingly appropriate time for Jacob and his sons to migrate to the Delta. In general, then, the biblical account of the patriarchs merges into the

historical record of Egypt during this time.

Bronze had been known long before this in Anatolia and Mesopotamia, but it was the Hyksos who brought the secret of the alloy to Syria, Palestine, and Egypt. Bronze is a mixture of copper and tin, and when properly smelted produces a metal which is harder than copper and which can be cast more easily. The new metal was rapidly adopted in the countries of the eastern Mediterranean, and the perfection attained by the metalsmith is ample testimony that culture had taken another long step forward. The Hyksos are often regarded as barbarians, but this is largely an echo of the Egyptian verdict. Actually they lived in a high type of civilization which recognized the benefits of organized living. They practiced commerce by land and sea. Accounts had to be kept, and the writing that the Hyksos in Palestine used was a progressive alphabet which had just been invented at the mines in Sinai. We recall that the Egyptians also called the Greeks barbarians.

SODOM AND GOMORRAH

The story of the destruction of Sodom and Gomorrah, the most famous of the cities of the Dead Sea Plain, is known to all. The Lord promised Abraham that if ten just men could be found in the wicked city of Sodom it would be spared. But only Lot and his family qualified, and they were told to flee the city before Sodom and Gomorrah should be destroyed by brimstone and fire. They were warned, moreover, not to look back lest they be turned to salt. Lot and his wife with their two daughters then hastily left the city, but Lot's wife turned back in a moment of curiosity and was turned to salt. Many have been the stories that peculiar erosional salt formations around the Dead Sea, called the Sea of Lot by the Moslems, actually represent the remains of that venerable woman.

But what of the cities that perished? Troy and Mycenae of Greek legend have been found, as have been other cities famous in legend and history. Archeologists looking for Sodom and Gomorrah have thought at times that they lay at the north end of the Dead Sea, but now there is almost general agreement that they must have existed to the south. However, the search for the lost cities may never be successful, since it is altogether likely that they now lie beneath the rising salty waters in the shallow embayment at the lower end of the sea. Aviators claim to have seen ruins in the water, but this has never been verified. Yet we may be certain that any ancient settlements in this region were built, not upon rock, but on sinking bottom lands in a valley which still slips whenever there is an earthquake. Possibly that was the fate of Sodom and Gomorrah.

THE STORY OF THE ALPHABET

It was long believed that the Phoenicians, those famous merchants and sailors who lived in the busy seaports of the Syrian coast, had invented the alphabet. The fact is clear that the Greeks borrowed their alphabet from the Phoenicians, and after making certain modifications passed it on to the Romans. We in turn took our alphabet from the Latins. Now we know that the Phoenicians, too, at an earlier time, had borrowed this important mechanism of civilization from still another people, for, strange as it seems, the alphabet arose as a practical means of writing in the Sinai Peninsula about 1800 B.C.

Long before this the Egyptians had an alphabet of 25 signs, but in addition they used a large group of complicated hieroglyphs which stood for combinations of two or three of the simple alphabetic sounds. The Egyptians used their alphabet every day, yet never seem to have realized that they had an alphabet. Had they used it alone, their writing system would have been infinitely more simple.

SINAITIC	CANAANITE-PHOENICIAN	GREEK				LATIN			HE-BREW

Diagram Showing the Development of the Alphabet. (Martin Sprengling, Modified After Butin)

During the Twelfth Dynasty Egyptian kings sent numerous expeditions to the mines in Sinai. The natives who served the expeditions spoke a Semitic language quite different from Egyptian. One of them, perhaps a mine foreman, learned the principle of the Egyptian alphabet and applied it to his own language. He imitated Egyptian hieroglyphs but gave them a Semitic value in the same way that we might take Egyptian signs and give them arbitrary English values. Thus he regarded the head of an ox as *aleph*, and the Egyptian hieroglyph that looked like the plan of a house he called *beth*, because *beth* in his language meant house. Our unknown native of Sinai continued this process until he had a sign for every consonant in his language. It did not occur to him to formulate signs for the vowels because the scribes with whom he talked wrote only consonants. That was the way in which Egyptian was constructed, and because of that the Canaanites, Phoenicians, Hebrews, Ethiopians and others who learned of the alphabet through Sinai, never used vowels.

It was probably in the eleventh century before our era that the Greeks borrowed the Phoenician alphabet. The shapes, names, and order of letters were taken over bodily. *Aleph* became *alpha*, and *beth* was pronounced *beta*. Semitic *gimel* was changed to *gamma* in Greek, and *daleth* became *delta*. In this manner arose the word "alphabet"—*aleph-beth* to *alpha-beta*. The original meaning was ox-house.

The Greeks improved the Semitic alphabet in a number of ways. They introduced vowels by appropriating signs for Semitic sounds that did not occur in Greek. The vowels *a*, *e*, *i*, and *o* were derived in this fashion. *Upsilon* was invented and placed at the end of the Phoenician alphabet. And since there were more *s* sounds in Phoenician than in Greek some of these letters were used for peculiarly Greek sounds. In addition to all this, the Greeks invented characters for the *phi*, *chi*, *psi*, and *xi* sounds.

In this manner the original alphabet was adopted by an Aryan-speaking people and passed on to us. But credit for its invention must go to that unknown native of Sinai who about 1800 B.C. got his inspiration from Egyptian hieroglyphs.

THE EGYPTIAN EMPIRE FROM 1580 TO 1350 B.C.

About the year 1580 B.C. Ahmose drove the Hyksos from Egypt. Two hundred and twenty years later the royal family line of the Eighteenth Dynasty died in the period of weakness following the reign of Tutankhamon. But the years between were rich in accomplishment for the group of kings most of whom were named Amenhotep and Thutmose. In this family we see such varied and interesting characters as the energetic warrior, Thutmose III, and the religious zealot, Amenhotep IV, who let the empire slip from between his fingers and changed his name to Ikhnaton in honor of the god Aton whom he had chosen as his own.

The Eighteenth Dynasty is the period of Egypt's first greatness as a world empire. Conquests in Nubia and Asia by the first kings provided wealth for a great building period at home, especially at Thebes, now the political and religious capital of Egypt. The great temple of the god Amon at Karnak had been started during the Middle Kingdom, but now it received new and monumental treatment. Huge gates, called pylons, arose, and behind them were erected buildings for worship of the god of Thebes. Pylons and buildings were covered with carved reliefs and inscriptions. Many of the latter consist of religious formulae, but on others are accounts of foreign campaigns and booty and prisoners taken for the glory of Amon. Obelisks similar to the one now standing in Central Park, New York, or on the embankment in London, were quarried in one piece and brought over a hundred miles down the Nile and set up in Karnak. The state of the treasury was excellent.

QUEEN HATSHEPSUT BUILDS A TEMPLE BELOW THE CLIFFS

Egypt's ruler at the beginning of the fifteenth century was a strong-willed woman named Hatshepsut. No wars are recorded for her reign. Instead, she seems to have expended most of her efforts in a great building program and in keeping the young Thutmose III off the throne. In both of these matters she was ex-

tremely successful for a long time. Hatshepsut set up two obelisks at Karnak, and in other parts of Egypt she built temples. But the building triumph of her reign was the delightful temple of Deir el-Bahari set in a semicircular area at the foot of the awe-inspiring cliffs across the river from Karnak. Behind a spur of this cliff lies the Valley of the Kings in which the great ones of the period were buried.

Few forget their first impression of Hatshepsut's architectural gem nestling at the base of the towering cliff. Built in terraces which lead

successively toward the sanctuary cut deep into the rock at the rear, it has appealed to many Westerners as the perfect Egyptian structure. An avenue of sphinxes led to a lower court, which in turn gave way to the central court reached by means of an inclined ramp. At the back of both these courts is a series of colonnades on whose walls are depicted events of prime interest in the reign of Hatshepsut. The upper court is reached by another ramp, and at this level one arrives at the rock-cut sanctuary and a number of chapels on either side of the pillared court.

Among the reliefs on the walls we see ships bringing two obelisks from the quarries at Aswan. Another shows the process of their erection and dedication. The walls of one of the colonnades are devoted to scenes commemorating a trading expedition to the land of Punt which was somewhere on the Red Sea coast. A village of this far-off land is depicted showing beehive huts built over water in the midst of palm and incense trees. The natives required ladders to reach their homes. We see the Egyptian fleet arriving and being laden with a rich cargo of merchandise. The queen's envoy is received by the prince of Punt who loads him down with precious gifts. One learns here how

Portraits of Queen Hatshepsut show her as both man and woman. To satisfy public prejudice, the queen wore male garb and a false beard on state occasions, but her mortuary statue (right) shows her as a woman. (The Metropolitan Museum of Art)

the Puntites looked, and then the fleet returns to Egypt with its spoil which the queen dedicates to the god Amon.

Hatshepsut's temple was never completed. She was succeeded by Thutmose III whom she had been so successful in keeping away from the throne, and he in turn attempted to obliterate the memory of the woman who had been so hateful to him. At Deir el-Bahari he began to remove the name and figure of the queen which appeared many times in the reliefs on the walls. But his workmen were careless at times and left tell-tale traces. In some cases Thutmose ordered that his own name and figure be inserted. The result was confusing indeed, and the unity of the inscriptions was further disturbed when late in the Eighteenth Dynasty Amenhotep IV, the devoted adherent of the Aton, destroyed all reference to Amon. The mutilated inscriptions and reliefs were left in this condition until Ramses II (1292-1225 B.C.) restored them, but with very poor workmanship. No changes were made on the temple

until after the time of Alexander the Great when a few unimportant additions were made. After Christianity had been introduced into Egypt, a group of Coptic monks founded a monastery in the temple. The chambers that Hatshepsut had built were converted into chapels, and all representations on the walls which were considered heathen were crudely defaced.

That is the story of the temple which Hatshepsut dedicated to the god Amon. In recent years the Metropolitan Museum of New York has done much to restore it to its original state without changing any of the writing or carving left on the walls.

THUTMOSE III, THE WARRIOR-KING

We know too little of the relationship between Thutmose and Hatshepsut. For a time they were joint rulers of the country, but the queen seems to have held the upper hand. Nevertheless, Thutmose considered that his reign began in 1501 B.C., the very year that

Thutmose III attempted to obliterate Queen Hatshepsut's portrait and name from this relief in her temple. (Gaddis and Seif)

Temple Guardian Dog, carved in reign of Thutmose III, is shown fighting lion god of death. (Palestine Museum)

Hatshepsut became queen. We must, however, believe that he did not become king in fact until the queen died in 1479 B.C. At the same time her adviser and architect Senmut, disappeared most mysteriously.

Then, with the pent-up emotions of many years bursting their bounds, the new king set out on a series of devastating marches against the revolting countries of Asia which had not seen an Egyptian army for many years. The first expeditions by land across the Sinai Desert secured the territory nearest Egypt as well as the important seaports of the Syrian coast. With these well in hand, he was enabled to lead later expeditions by sea and thus save precious time for warfare with the more inland peoples. But each year his troops returned to Egypt before the heavy winter rains set in. The absence of the mass of Egyptian troops, and especially the dominating figure of the king, caused some of the more daring of the conquered to revolt, but they paid dearly when the king returned again. Thutmose made seventeen campaigns

in all during the twenty-two years that he ruled alone, and at the end of that period Egypt could fairly claim sovereignty over Palestine and Syria. Neighboring kings sent gifts as tokens of their respect for the martial king of Egypt. Among these were the kings of Assyria, Babylonia, Anatolia, and the island of Cyprus. The land of Mitanni, which lay in the great bend of the Euphrates, was conquered and although it later revolted, its rise as a nation was delayed until after the death of Thutmose. From the countries that had been subdued there was collected a yearly tribute calculated to tax the offending nations that they might realize the benefits of peace with the great country on the Nile. Tribute after all was better than appropriation by the soldiers of the king.

Thus the energetic Thutmose welded together an empire which extended from well up the Nile in Nubia to the Euphrates in Asia. Only in the reign of his son, Amenhotep II, did Egypt possess greater holdings, but the basis for this slight expansion had been provided by the tireless years of conflict during which Thutmose was the most respected and powerful man on earth.

THE BATTLE OF MEGIDDO

Thutmose ordered that the story of his wars be inscribed on the walls of the temple at Kar-

The Megiddo Pass. A modern caravan emerges from the narrow pass through which Thutmose III led his army to surprise the enemy at Megiddo. (Oriental Institute of the University of Chicago)

nak. The scribe who was probably also a priest of Amon began very well and gave a tolerably full record of the first campaign in the year 1479 B.C. But as he progressed he lost interest in the details of warfare and devoted himself mainly to recording where his majesty had gone and how much had been brought back for the temple of Amon. Of the later campaigns we learn in full measure of the horses and chariots, gold and silver vessels, and other valuables that the army had taken from the enemy. It is really only the account of the first campaign that tells something of the battles.

The Battle of Megiddo was the first engagement of the first campaign. Thutmose and his troops crossed the one hundred and sixty mile waste of the Sinai Desert in nine days and then proceeded up the coast until they reached a point opposite the pass leading to the city of Megiddo in northern Palestine. Here Thutmose called a council and asked his officers what they had in mind to do. The enemy included all the important states of northern Palestine and Syria, and their army was collected at Megiddo prepared to fight the Egyptians. There were three roads which would lead eventually to Megiddo, standing on the southwest side of the Plain of Esdraelon. Two of these were indirect; the third was narrow but led straight to Megiddo which guarded it at the other end. Thutmose listened to his officers argue for the first two, but the king characteristically said that they could do as they wished. He was going to take the direct pass and would personally lead any who wished to follow him.

Early in the morning Thutmose began the march and by about one o'clock emerged from the pass to see Megiddo looming up ahead. At this time his rear had not yet entered the heart of the narrow defile and he therefore waited until all could assemble by the brook south of the fortress. The Asiatics had lost a wonderful opportunity to destroy their foes as the latter went single file through the pass.

By the next morning Thutmose had swung a wing of his army to the west of Megiddo, and this with the wing that had remained south of the city then closed in on the Asiatic defenders, who by this time had taken a position between the Egyptians and the city. The first Egyptian charge was so effective that the enemy line broke and ran headlong for the city leaving the horses and chariots of gold and silver. The gates of the city had been closed and the demoralized enemy had to be pulled over the wall by means of clothing which was lowered for them. The ringleader, the king of Kadesh, as well as the king of Megiddo, thus saved their lives and presumably escaped through the northern gate, for we hear nothing more of their whereabouts.

After the rout the Egyptian soldiers gave themselves up to plunder. Horses and chariots, living prisoners, and hands cut from the dead were at length brought into the presence of the king. But he was grieved and seriously annoyed that his troops had stopped for booty when they might have captured the city. In rebuke he said to them, "Had ye captured this city afterward, behold, I would have given many offerings to Re this day; because every chief of every country that has revolted is within it; and because it is the capture of a thousand cities, this capture of Megiddo."

Thutmose then ordered that the city be surrounded by an enclosure of earth and cut trees. He would besiege Megiddo until it surrendered. Sentinels stood continually on guard and no foe escaped after the enclosure had been finished. After about five months the besieged city opened its gates and surrendered, and the chiefs came forward bearing gifts with which to placate the great king Thutmose.

The spoil taken from the captured city gives an idea of the wealth of Palestine and Syria at this time. Included were nine hundred and twenty-four chariots, over two thousand horses, two hundred suits of armor, five hundred bows, the beautiful tent and rich household furnishings of the king of Kadesh, besides large quantities of gold and silver. Thousands of head of cattle, as well as the harvest of the near-by fields, also fell to the Egyptians.

Megiddo had been thoroughly tamed and never again during the reign of Thutmose did northern Palestine cause him any trouble. Future revolts were centered around Kadesh in Syria, but we have seen that in the end Thutmose was ruler over all of Palestine and Syria.

It is more than likely that battles had been fought before this on the plain of Megiddo, the Armageddon of later times and the proverbial battleground of the ages. There followed others of which we know. During World War I the same pass, by which Thutmose had surprised the Asiatics, became the means by which Lord Allenby's cavalry bottled up the fleeing Turks in the historic plain, and caused their commanding officer to dash hurriedly out of Nazareth in the middle of the night clad in his pajamas.

AMENHOTEP THE MAGNIFICENT

Amenhotep III was a great grandson of Thutmose III and grandson of Amenhotep II who had advanced the boundary of the empire to Mitanni. His father had married a Mitannian princess, perhaps because he saw the inherent weakness of Egyptian control in Asia. When his father died at the early age of thirty, Amenhotep III inherited a vast empire which extended from the Euphrates to the Third Cataract of the Nile. In his earlier years as king he showed some energy, penetrating Nubia farther than any king before him. But as time went on he settled down to the life of a glamorous and exotic oriental king.

Amenhotep was early dominated by the will of his remarkable wife, Tiy, a woman of unroyal and otherwise obscure background. It is true that the king had other wives as well, among them a daughter of the king of Mitanni, but Tiy remained throughout her life a woman of tremendous will and apparently considerable charm. It was unusual enough for a royal queen to be continuously named in documents, but Tiy soon became used to such distinction.

Tiy, wife of Amenhotep III and mother of Ikhnaton, was a commoner. (Oriental Institute of the University of Chicago)

During the early part of the reign the empire was secure, and for once the troublesome states of Syria were quiet. Egyptian officials collected the taxes there and elsewhere, and Egypt became exceedingly wealthy. Under such conditions it is perhaps only natural that a king of the temperament of Amenhotep should build up a court which in its brilliance may well be compared with that of Louis XV. The finest artists in the country were engaged on a host of projects which extended far up the Nile as well as across the desert into Syria. Colossal additions were made at Karnak, and one of the finest temples in Egypt was placed in construction to the south in the present city of Luxor. The intervening mile and a half was beautified by avenues of rams cut from stone, and in addition, an artificial lake, horseshoe in shape, was dug in the precincts of Karnak. But this was just on the east side of the river.

On the opposite side near the line where vegetation gives way to desert, Amenhotep erected a large mortuary temple in front of which were placed two obelisks and the two colossi, which to the classical world of a later

The Colossi of Memnon. Seventy feet high and weighing seven hundred tons apiece, these twin portraits of Amenhotep III were cut from a single rock. (Paul's Photos)

was filled with the finest art of the empire. Tapestries hung on the walls, and the floors were painted with scenes from wild life. Wonderful vessels of gold and silver, bearing designs of exquisite workmanship, graced the tables. The front of the palace was decorated with flagstaves bearing pennants, and above the entrance was a comfortable cushioned balcony surrounded by nicely worked columns.

The riches, pouring into Egypt, also allowed Amenhotep to set aside a quarter near by for his queen. Here he excavated a lake which was approximately a mile long and over a thousand feet wide, the sluices of which he opened on the occasion of the twelfth anniversary of his coronation. It was a festive day when the king and queen sailed out together on the royal barge to the accompaniment of music from the royal band on shore.

day, were among the wonders of the earth. These immense statues of the king were originally, before the crowns fell off, almost seventy feet high, and while today they are not things of beauty they nevertheless excite our interest for their connection with the fabulous king Amenhotep and the traditions of classical times. During the Roman imperial epoch they were thought to be statues of Memnon who had slain Antilochus during the Trojan War and who in turn had been killed by Achilles. The northern colossus is the famous singing statue which in Roman times was said to have given forth musical notes at sunrise.

Between the mortuary temple and the western cliffs Amenhotep built himself and his queen a luxurious palace in bright colors. It

But trouble was brewing. While the king had been building his beautiful capital, a work which he often left for the pleasures of hunting wild cattle or lions, the Hittites had become organized sufficiently to invade Mitanni. From this time on, until they disappeared about 1200 B.C., the Hittites were to be a constant thorn

Papyrus Plants, raw material for Egypt's busy paper industry, are carried in solemn procession by the servants of Ramose. (Oriental Institute of the University of Chicago—Painting by Nina de Garis Davies)

Colonnade of Amenhotep III at Luxor. The columns symbolize papyrus stalks with open flower capitals. (Oriental Institute of the University of Chicago)

in the side of Egypt. This was the period of the New Hittite Kingdom which had emerged from the darkness of two centuries. And in the reign of Amenhotep began the long series of letters written in cuneiform, telling the king of the dangerous state of affairs in the Asiatic states controlled by Egypt. The Hittites also attacked northern Syria and thus challenged Egypt directly. The king sent troops but failed to go himself. The trouble was halted

for the time being, but Egypt's day as empire was fading. The energy of former kings was needed in such circumstances, but a rapidly aging king sat upon the throne. To add to his troubles a new element of disorder was making itself felt in Syria. The Habiru, whose relationship to the Hebrews we shall presently see, had joined in the attack on Egyptian rule in Asia, and, to cap the situation, the more powerful of the cities belonging to Egypt began fighting among themselves for increased territory.

Amenhotep's efforts to stem the tide were futile, and when he passed away in 1375 B.C. after a reign of almost thirty-six years he left a sadly disorganized situation to his son who on ascending the throne bore the name Amenhotep IV.

IKHNATON, THE HERETIC KING

Had the new king been a figure of the caliber of Thutmose III, we may say with little doubt that the course of Egyptian history would have been altogether different. Instead, he was a dreamer, completely impractical as far as statecraft was concerned. His intimate group was composed of Queen Mother Tiy, his own queen Nefretiti who may have been of Asiatic descent, and his favorite priest, the husband of his childhood nurse. Doubtless he had been strongly influenced by the life of his father's court in which the seeds of social rebellion were already to be observed. While revolt was rising he gave himself up to religious philosophy and contemplation. The search for truth was of infinitely greater importance than affairs of state.

The disk of the sun shining in the heavens became for him the essence of all that was

Painted Floor from Ikhnaton's palace shows new naturalism in the treatment of birds, animals, and foliage. (Sir Flinders Petrie. Tell El-Amarna)

Ikhnaton and Nefretiti constantly appeared in public together, contrary to Egyptian traditions. (Oriental Institute of the University of Chicago)

worthwhile, and it was soon established that the Aton should be the sole official god. We may well imagine the effect that this proclamation had on the existing priesthoods, especially that of the powerful Amon. For generations the revenues of war and peace had supported the holdings of the great god of Thebes, and had moreover been kind to that large body of men who ministered to Amon. From high priesthood down, there was immediate rebellion and deep feeling against the interloper who at a stroke had supplanted the religious structure of centuries, for we can easily see that the Aton would now have recourse to wealth that had formerly been used for the glorification of Amon.

Amenhotep built a temple to the Aton between Karnak and Luxor and, in the fury of the feud between Amon and Aton, ordered that the name of Amon be obliterated wherever it occurred. Amon had been the patron god of Egypt since the Middle Kingdom, and his name appeared widespread through the temples. Even the Amon element in the name of his father Amenhotep III was expunged, and finally the king took action on his own name which was the same. Thus Amenhotep IV became Ikhnaton, which means "Spirit of Aton."

But even this was not enough. The residence of Aton in Thebes lay in the midst of buildings and gardens associated with Amon. Ikhnaton decided that the Aton should have a city of its own, and in his sixth year we find him established three hundred miles down the river at Ikhtaton, meaning "Horizon of Aton." The ruins of this city which have been excavated are known as Tell el-Amarna. Ikhtaton lay

Royal Family Life. Ikhnaton kisses the eldest princess; his wife holds their other daughters. (Oriental Institute of the University of Chicago—Berlin Museum)

in a bay in the cliffs near the river and rapidly took on the aspects of a national capital. The court came here and worshiped the Aton for political reasons if for no others.

The town and adjacent territory were deeded to Aton by royal decree "forever and ever," and specific revenues were allotted for its upkeep. Three temples to the Aton were erected, one for Queen Mother Tiy, one for the princess Beketaton which means "Maid-servant of Aton," and the third for the king himself, while around the temples arose the palace and the estates of the nobles who had deserted Thebes. The Aton breathed his spirit into all the functions and life of the city through the dominant will of the king.

The mysterious qualities of Aton that so thoroughly molded the life of the king may perhaps be summed up in the word "truth." The old religious philosophy of many gods was not satisfactory, and here in the fourteenth century, long before the Hebrews had begun to worship one God, an Egyptian was doing that very thing. He had grasped the idea that a single power ruled not only the destinies of Egypt, but also those of Nubia and Syria and the rest of the world. The birds and beasts as

well as man owed their lives to this god's beneficence; all nature revealed the existence of the Aton. The Hymn to the Aton, which shows many parallels with the one hundred and fourth Psalm, is filled with the deep-seated thought that life and death are subject to the goodness of Aton. Some writers have advanced the hypothesis that Jewish monotheism stems from Moses' stay in Egypt, where he was influenced by the religious ideas of Ikhnaton.

The spirit of truth invaded all aspects of life in the capital. Artists depicted what they saw and forsook the traditions of the guild that had stamped the works of their predecessors. Realism became the rule and even the king, who was queer-looking physically, was depicted as he was. Convention was dropped, and in its place stood a healthy attitude toward nature. The king appeared frequently in public in the company of his wife, Nefretiti, and their daughters, and the population came to know them from personal observation. In this, another of the once treasured traditions of royalty was shattered.

Meanwhile the storm that we saw gathering in Asia grew blacker, encouraged by Ikhnaton's lack of interest in military affairs.

Temple of Amon at Karnak. The smaller temple flanked by two statues was built by Ramses III. (Oriental Institute of the University of Chicago)

EGYPT LOSES PALESTINE AND SYRIA

During the reign of Ikhnaton's father, trouble had begun in the Asiatic possessions of Egypt, and the lax attitude of the court of Aton merely made matters worse from the empire point of view. This we know from a large group of tablets written in cuneiform which were discovered in 1888 in the ruins of Ikhnaton's city. These included the letters to Amenhotep III and Ikhnaton written by the kings of Babylonia, Assyria, and Mitanni, and by Egyptian vassals in Palestine and Syria. These messages, giving as they do a detailed picture of events, constitute one of the most important bodies of ancient literature that has come to the attention of historians.

The first letters show the strongest Syrian chieftains striking out for more territory, turning a lax eye on Egypt and an intriguing eye on Anatolia where the Hittites had again come to life. Abdashirta, an Amorite chief in the valley of the Orontes, was one of these, and after a poor pretense at faith with Egypt, openly waged war with Ribaddi, the faithful vassal of Byblos. Abdashirta's principal allies were the Habiru, a roving people who came into Syria at the time of the first letters from Ribaddi. Meanwhile the Hittites had pushed down into Syria cutting off one of the larger cities. And toward the end of the period included in the letters we see Egypt's old ally, Mitanni, joining in the anti-Egyptian movement. One by one the Egyptian strongholds fell, and it was Byblos and Beirut which held out to the end. With the disappearance of Ribaddi the entire north country passed into the hands of the Amorites and Hittites.

The story of the faithful Ribaddi is one of the most interesting and touching episodes that has come down to us from the ancient world. Had he not been so staunch in the face of the inevitable overthrow of Egypt in Asia he might have saved his life. Message after message did he send to the court of Egypt, begging for troops and money with which to buy food for his starving people. The cities round about were falling rapidly before the onslaught of anti-Egyptian forces, and when they had all been captured how would it be possible for Byblos to hold out much longer? But no effective aid came from the Nile. Instead, court intrigues placed Ribaddi in a very unfavorable position in the eyes of the state department. Yet he did not desert the trust which had been placed in him, even when his family urged him to desert to the other side, or when attempts were made on his life by the people of his own city. At length the long series of complaining letters came to an end. Byblos fell, and Ribaddi probably met the same fate as other loyal vassals who had tried to preserve the name of Egypt in Asia.

In tracing the story of mass movements from the Amarna letters it is clear that the Hittites settled as far south as the Lebanons, while some of them may have continued on into Palestine. Letters from Palestinian cities complained about the Amorites and Habiru, and these cities too were soon in non-Egyptian hands. It is altogether likely that Joshua was a Habiru and that Jericho fell at this time.

A Tell El-Amarna Letter. This clay tablet written in cuneiform was part of the personal correspondence between Tushratta, King of Mitanni, and Amenhotep III. In it Tushratta announced the dispatch of gifts and also requested gold in return for his daughter whom Amenhotep had married. (British Museum)

Tutankhamon. A gold portrait mask from his mummy. (Oriental Institute of the University of Chicago)

The Egyptian empire in Asia had been squandered, but that seemed to cause Ikhnaton little concern. The court at Ikhtaton continued the life that it had chosen, and when the king died in 1358 B.C. a son-in-law stood ready to take his place, ruling from the city of the Aton.

Excavations at the Hittite capital have revealed what must surely have been a headline story in the year 1358 B.C. Ikhnaton was dead and his queen, the beautiful Nefretiti, wishing to retain the throne for herself, wrote to the Hittite king, Shuppiluliuma, asking for one of his sons in marriage. The letter read, "My husband is dead, I have no son. You are said to have many sons. If you will give me one of your sons, he shall be my husband. I fear to take one of my slaves and make him my husband." The Hittite king suspected treachery, but, when at length he became convinced that Nefretiti spoke the truth and wished to have a Hittite as king of Egypt, he sent one of his sons. By this time, however, Ikhnaton's son-in-law had become king and the Hittite prince was murdered on his way to Egypt.

Ikhnaton's son-in-law was followed shortly by a youth who, on becoming king, bore the name Tutankhaton.

TUTANKHAMON, THE BOY KING

The new king had been born and reared in the atmosphere of the new religion, and when he came to the throne as a boy of about twelve probably knew little else. His short reign of six or seven years is noteworthy principally for the fact that before its completion he changed his name to Tutankhamon, thus eliminating the Aton element that was so distasteful to the old priesthood. The total eclipse of Atonism came in the next reign when King Eye moved the capital back to Thebes.

Tutankhamon apparently made one campaign into Syria in an effort to retrieve Egypt's lost possessions, but aside from that we know little about his short reign. Tutankhamon is probably the best known of pharaohs, yet his fame rests chiefly on the discovery of his richly furnished tomb which had the good fortune to survive serious plundering. It is likely that his tomb was poor in comparison with those of Thutmose III and Amenhotep III.

The glorious line of Eighteenth Dynasty kings came to an end about 1350 B.C. with Eye

Tutankhamon and his Queen wore elaborate, pleated clothes typical of the luxury of the New Empire. (Oriental Institute of the University of Chicago)

Tutankhamon Slaying the Syrians. Chariots were decisive war machines in ancient times. Egyptian chariots were lighter than the Syrian and carried only two men, a driver and a bowman. (Daruer and Gardiner, "Ancient Egyptian Paintings," Cairo Museum)

who reigned for a very short time. For two hundred and thirty years a remarkable group of sovereigns had occupied the throne of Egypt and for almost two hundred years of that period Egypt had been supreme among the nations. The first world empire had risen to the heights and had been eclipsed. Egypt's greatest days ended with the religious revolution of Ikhnaton which failed, but the world had been given a preview of things to come. And although Egypt's best days as empire were over, there were yet good days in store. A few years after Harmhab, one of Ikhnaton's generals, had usurped the throne to begin the Nineteenth Dynasty, kings named Ramses made their appearance on the Egyptian and foreign scenes.

THE EGYPTIAN EMPIRE—
FROM 1350-1090 B.C.

When Harmhab began his career as king he restored Amon and all other Egyptian gods except the Aton to their former positions. Temples and inscriptions that had been despoiled by the heretic king were restored, while at the same time an effort was made to remove from the scene all that might recall the memory of the "criminal of Akhetaton." Ikhnaton's temple in Thebes was demolished and the stones used to build a pylon for Harmhab, and his tomb and those of his nobles were wrecked. Revenues which had been allotted to the worship of Aton "forever and ever" were appropriated for Amon who was soon to become a force greater than the king himself.

Harmhab reigned for some thirty-five years during which time he spent most of his energy in reorganizing the country and purging it of its corrupt official element. Many laws were made in an effort to eliminate bribery of judges and executives, and honest and capable men found themselves in demand. For his efforts at reform Harmhab must be given a high place in history.

During his regime Egypt appears to have made no foreign conquests, all energies being applied to conditions at home. Harmhab was succeeded by the first Ramses who, however, was an old man when he became king. After two years his scepter was passed on to his son, Seti I, and again Egypt had a warrior king of the type that had made Egypt famous in earlier days.

Seti (1313-1292 B.C.) set out in his first year to reconquer Egypt's lost lands in Asia, and he was successful to the extent of subduing Palestine and certain ports on the Phoenician coast. He collected heavy tribute including cedar logs which were floated across the Mediterranean to the Delta. After quieting the always disturbing elements in Libya the next year, he again moved into Syria with the intention of giving battle to the Hittites. The two forces met, but this was not a contest between Egypt and a weak opponent. Two first class powers were on the field, and although we know nothing about the battle itself, it is clear that the Egyptians gained nothing. The Hittite boundary remained much as it had been during Amarna times, and perhaps because he saw that the Hittites could not be dislodged, Seti then or soon after concluded a treaty with the Hittite king. Egypt, however, had recovered a portion of her Asiatic empire.

At home, Seti continued the restoration of Karnak and the repair of the damage done to Amon's monuments by Ikhnaton. The latter project, which involved the recarving of old figures and inscriptions, was carried on by the next king, Ramses II.

RAMSES THE GREAT

Ramses was not the eldest son of Seti. The rightful older brother had been brushed aside by the ambitious young Ramses who was to have one of the longest reigns in Egyptian history. Ramses ruled for sixty-seven years after his accession in 1292 B.C.

After he had consolidated public opinion, and especially the Amon priesthood, behind him, Ramses laid plans for his Asiatic campaigns. Like his predecessor Thutmose III he would gain control of several seaport towns in Syria before sending his army inland, since transportation by water was so much quicker and easier. The Hittites were still the power

Seti I with Hathor, who symbolizes woman's love as cow-goddess of the sky and mother of the sun. (Florence Museum)

Ramses II lined the court of the Temple of Amon at Luxor with these colossal portraits of himself

in northern Syria and they, being fully warned by Ramses' preparations, likewise laid their military plans. Everything pointed to a great and decisive battle between the Egyptians and Hittites. The latter brought together all the vassal kings of the now great Hittite Empire, while the Egyptians added mercenaries who were well paid for their services in the army. In the year 1288 B.C., Ramses advanced with his army of perhaps 20,000 toward Kadesh on the Orontes for what was to be the prelude to the last test between Hittite and Egyptian arms.

Surveying was a necessity in Egypt where floods erased all boundaries each season. Here surveyors of 1400 B.C., aided by note-taking scribes, measure a wheat field with rope

White Kilts, starched to a stiff point in front were worn by all classes in the Fifth Dynasty. Only the straight staff of authority distinguished a noble from a herdsman

Two Dancing Girls, above, nude except for jewelry, entertain the best male society to the music of hand claps and a double pipe. At left, a slave holds a pair of frisky horses hitched to an overseer's chariot

Harvesting the Wheat Crop (above) was an important activity in Egypt where wheat was a main source of food. At right, oxen tread out the grain; in the center, farm hands throw it in the air to separate the chaff from the wheat. A servant brings cooling drinks to the landowner, who stands sheltered in a papyrus lean-to at the left. Below, workers fill a vaulted storehouse with grain through a ceiling hole. (Oriental Institute of the University of Chicago)

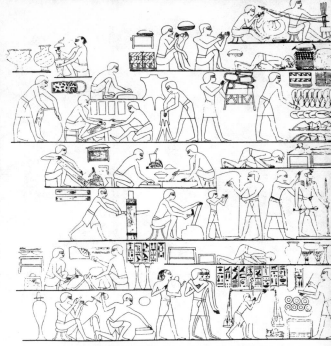

Vintagers Trod the Grapes by foot and bottled the wine in pointed jars. Bird catchers trapped wild birds in the marshes and dressed them for market

The Egyptian Middle Class contained artisans as prominent members. Above, such craftsmen as jewelers, sandal-makers, carpenters, sculptors, and metalworkers are pictured practicing their trades. At left, two women, wearing the kalasiris, a form-fitting sheath with a single shoulder strap, are buying fish and ointment jars in the market place

Bartering in the Market (above). At left, a man sells fishhooks; center, a baker exchanges his sweet cakes for sandals and a collar; at right, the merchant says "Let me see your offer" to his customer. Below, Egyptian sailors stride up the gangplanks of Queen Hatshepsut's ships, loading them with such "marvels from the country of Punt" as pure ivory, myrrh trees, the green gold of Emu, apes, and eye cosmetics. (Oriental Institute of the University of Chicago)

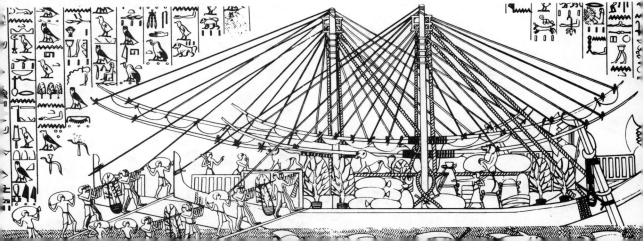

Temple of Ramses II at Abu Simbel. Here in the sandstone cliffs were carved massive 66-foot high statues of Ramses as a God. Around them are smaller statues of members of the royal family and household. (Ewing Galloway)

THE BATTLE OF KADESH

The Egyptian army approaching from the south consisted of four divisions, each named for one of the great Egyptian gods: Amon, Re, Ptah, and Sutekh. Ramses personally led the division of Amon and, anxious to get into action, pushed on faster than the other divisions could follow. When he was still some distance south of Kadesh, two Bedouins came to Ramses saying they were deserters from the Hittite army. They said that the Hittite king had retreated far to the north of Kadesh, and this Ramses believed because his own scouts had seen nothing of the enemy.

With this information, Ramses and his household troops hurried ahead. In the meantime the crafty Hittite king had marshaled his troops on the opposite side of the high city

of Kadesh, now an imposing tell, and, as Ramses approached, the Hittite at all times kept the city between himself and the unsuspecting Ramses. The two Bedouins had done their work well.

The division of Amon at length caught up with Ramses and pitched camp northwest of the city, and, while the horses were being fed and the troops were preparing their meal, a couple of Hittite spies were captured. After a merciless beating they confessed that the Hittite king and all his troops were at that very moment on the other side of the city. Ramses was alarmed and sent swift couriers to his straggling third division. Apparently the fourth division was so far behind it could not arrive on time; the second division, on the other hand, was seemingly close enough to be of assistance.

Ramses did not know that by then the Hittites had begun the battle having cut his second division in two. He first learned of this catastrophe when his routed troops dashed into his camp, followed by the Hittite chariotry. The fright of the second division was such that part of Ramses' own division also took to its heels, leaving Ramses with a mere handful of body troops, surrounded on all sides by enemy chariotry. The king was desperate and

The Battle of Kadesh, as portrayed in the Ramesseum, shows Ramses II pursuing the Hittites to the river. At the far right the half-drowned King of Aleppo is held upside down by his soldiers to resuscitate him. (Lepsius, "Denkmaeler")

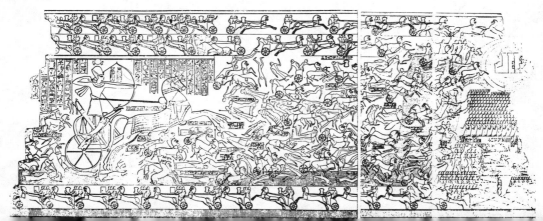

Ramses III Hunting Wild Bulls. Troops surrounded the wild herd first and drove it into a large enclosure for the convenience of the Pharaoh. (Oriental Institute of the University of Chicago)

made an attempt to break through to the south in an effort to join his missing third and fourth divisions, but he soon saw that only to the east would he have any chance for success. Thus he and his chariots charged again and again with a power born of desperation, and succeeded in beating back their foe. But Ramses owed his life to a peculiar oriental trait that we have already seen at Megiddo. The Hittite chariotry at his rear, instead of closing in on the Pharaoh, found themselves in his deserted camp and gave themselves up to the rich plunder. Ramses had obtained a fortunate breathing spell and then, quite unexpectedly, a group of Egyptian troops from the west or north attacked the booty-maddened Hittites and slew them all.

The battle, however, had only begun. The Hittite king threw in strong reserves who engaged the remnants of the now collected first and second divisions, but although the Egyptian forces were far outnumbered they held their ground until late in the afternoon of that eventful day when the third division hurried into view from the south. The Hittites were thus suddenly placed in a most unfavorable position between the two Egyptian armies and after considerable loss retreated within the walls of Kadesh.

The battle was over, and although Ramses claimed a victory he returned to Egypt without laying siege to the city. His army had been seriously crippled, and the most one can say is that the engagement was a draw.

The loss of Egyptian prestige in Asia is clearly seen from the fact that most of Palestine revolted in the next few years, and Ramses was forced to begin exactly where his father had almost thirty years before. Ramses, however, possessed considerable military ability in addition to his firm desire to reconquer the empire of his Eighteenth Dynasty predecessors. We see that in time he regained not only Palestine but also won battles in Syria, even north of Kadesh. And then, after fifteen years of campaigning, Ramses' wars with the Hittites suddenly ended.

Ramses II Captures Dapur, from the relief in the great hypostyle hall of the Ramesseum. A scaling ladder, such as the one on the right, was important military equipment in conquering walled cities

It was in the year 1272 B.C. that Ramses and Hattusilis, then the Hittite king, agreed to their famous treaty which was witnessed by a thousand gods and goddesses of the Hittites and a similar number from the country of the Nile. Each ruler swore not to invade the territory of the other, the line probably being set somewhat north of Palestine, and to come to the aid of the other should either need assistance. The treaty was apparently satisfactory to both parties since peace followed, and thirteen years later Hattusilis appeared personally in Egypt to give away his eldest daughter as the wife of Ramses.

We can readily understand one of the Hittite motives in terminating the long war. Mitanni had fallen and no longer proved a buffer to the states in Mesopotamia. In its place Assyria, the northern offspring of Babylonian culture, had risen to a threatening position. Assyria was still a youth among nations and her best days lay ahead, but power was being gathered and the Hittites were sensible of its threat.

During his long life Ramses built many edifices in Egypt, in Nubia, and in Palestine, and on their walls inscribed the valorous deeds of his wars. His personal triumph at Kadesh figured prominently as did the treaty, and both were considered by him as Egyptian victories.

When he died as a very old man, he left a deep-seated impression on his age, and during years to come Egyptian kings, most of them of far less ability, assumed the same name.

Ramses was succeeded by his son Merneptah, by this time also an old man, who after an ineffective reign of ten years was followed by three short-lived kings. The Nineteenth Dynasty ended in 1205 B.C. when a usurper from Syria captured the throne, and held it for five years. It was at the end of this period that the Twentieth Dynasty began.

RAMSES III VS. THE PHILISTINES

Ramses III was the second king of the Twentieth Dynasty and was not related to the man for whom he had been named. He had inherited a badly disrupted kingdom, for not since the earlier days of Ramses II had Egypt been a threat to Asia. Since then, a new menace to peace had appeared in the Near East.

Immigrants and peoples driven out of Crete and Greece by barbarian pressure from the north had flooded the eastern Mediterranean. Some of the Hittite allies at the battle of Kadesh probably belonged to this strain, and during the reign of Merneptah, the Sea Peoples, as they were called, raided the Delta as allies of the Libyans. Among these were a group of

Storming a Syrian Fort. Ramses III's archers protect his soldiers with a volley of arrows. (Oriental Institute of the University of Chicago)

First Known Sea Battle was fought by Egyptians and Aegeans, whose ships had goose-head prows. (Oriental Institute of the University of Chicago)

Acheans, related to the famous people of Mycenae and the besiegers of Troy.

Trade had first introduced these northerners to Egypt, Palestine, and Syria, and, drawn by business, many of them came to settle away from home. Ras Shamra, on the north Syrian coast, received many of them, to judge from Mycenaean type burial vaults discovered in excavation, and many other trading centers must have known the early Aegean peoples in person. The Mediterranean of that day was dotted with sailing vessels from numerous ports, bearing produce to the consumers' markets.

The hope of capturing some of these markets was probably responsible for certain raids that occurred around 1200 B.C., but the principal urge came from the fact that northern tribes, who later became civilized Greeks, were driving the Aegean peoples out of their homeland. The whole northern sector of the then civilized world was menaced, and before the trouble subsided the Hittite empire had disappeared. Anatolia was invaded from the Balkans by an Indo-European group called Phrygians, and thereafter the Hittites lived principally in northern Syria. Troy was destroyed at about the same time and the Etruscans left their ancestral home to settle in Italy.

The same movement drove a group of people called Philistines to Syria and Palestine, women and children forming part of the group. The Philistines came by land and sea, probably from southern Greece, and shortly afterward loomed as a threat to Egypt.

Ramses III in his eighth year (1191 B.C.) was faced with the necessity of giving battle to a coalition of Egypt-bound Philistines and related people, though Egypt was not as weak as they had supposed. The new king had gathered together a formidable army, composed in large part of mercenaries, and, somewhere along the Syrian coast, gave battle to the northern intruders. At the same time he dispatched his fleet to meet the enemy, and in both engagements he was victorious. Egypt was spared and Palestine and parts of Syria remained in her possession, but the Philistines were allowed to settle on the coast below the hills leading to Jerusalem. Here they formed a league of five strong cities—Gaza, Ascalon, Ashdod, Ekron, and Gath. The troubles that Saul and David experienced with the Philistines at a later time dated back to the period when Egypt allowed them to establish themselves on the fertile coastal plain. It is a curious fact that the Philistines who were so despised by the Hebrews are the very ones who gave Palestine its name.

Ramses III was the last great king of that name. Eight others of the same name followed him after his death (1167 B.C.), but they were inconsequential for the most part; no mining was carried on in Sinai after Ramses IV. The empire died with Ramses III who despite great energy and ability was faced with insurmountable handicaps. Thereafter Egypt slipped rapidly, a good share of the trouble lying in the increased power of the Amon priesthood. Ever since the Aton revolution had been quashed,

61

Amon had risen steadily in power until most of the revenue of the state went for the upkeep of his buildings and officials. Matters grew rapidly worse after the death of Ramses III, foreign policy was forced to one side, corruption made headway, and in 1090 B.C. the last Ramses gave way to the high priest of Amon, who became the first king of the Twenty-first Dynasty, one of the weakest native dynasties in all Egyptian history.

JOSHUA AND THE HEBREWS

The origin of the Hebrew people will continue to cause much discussion between those who read the Bible literally and others who try to fit historical evidence into the biblical narrative. Complete agreement is not always possible where two sources offer differing statements concerning a single occurrence.

The difficulties probably arose from the fact that the Bible was written late in Hebrew history, long after many of the events which it chronicles. Abraham and Isaac, Jacob and Joseph, are hazy characters at best, but we have seen that the Patriarchal period fits well into the Hyksos background. When we come down to the story of Hebrew entry into Palestine the problem is greatly aggravated.

The Bible states that the Hebrews entered at the time of the Exodus from Egypt where they had been oppressed for many years. Moses was their leader, taking them through the Red Sea and the wilderness of Sinai. Before reaching Palestine, the Promised Land, Moses died and was succeeded by Joshua who took Jericho and other cities in Palestine. There followed the long period of the Judges during which no king ruled Israel.

We can say that there is much truth in this narrative and if we had it alone there could be little to question. However, we have seen that a group of people called the Habiru were coming into Palestine in numbers around 1400 B.C. when the Aton in Egypt had diverted attention from Asia. These Habiru settled in the country and gradually took on the attributes of natives.

We know from the excavations at Jericho that the city was destroyed and deserted about 1400 B.C. This catastrophe apparently happened during the period when the Habiru were entering the country. But Joshua is so closely associated with the fall of Jericho in Hebrew tradition that it is therefore necessary to place his lifetime around 1400 B.C.

Moses on the other hand appears to be linked to a period about two hundred years later, for the Hebrews slaved in the cities of Ramses. The story, then, of Joshua following Moses seems to be a confused version of two originally different episodes. The Habiru who came from north of Palestine about 1400 B.C. bore the name Hebrew. Although there were before this time other elements in the country that contributed to the blood of the Hebrews, it was the movement of about 1400 B.C. that first began to settle Palestine with people we may call Hebrews. These were the northern tribes, first living in the hills and later taking Canaanite cities. The Moses group left Egypt about 1200 B.C. and probably entered Palestine from the south. Most modern historians believe the two groups united their blood and traditions many centuries later.

The period of the Judges thus began about 1400 B.C., which is not far from the date indicated in the Bible, and lasted for about 400 years during which time the Hebrews grew continually stronger. It was probably about the middle of the eleventh century that Barak defeated the Canaanite Sisera in the plain of Megiddo. This is also the period of Samson and Delilah and of many skirmishes between the Hebrews and their enemies in the land across the Jordan and on the Philistine plain. It was the hammer blows of the Philistines that at last aroused the Hebrew tribes to the need for union, and the period of the Judges ended when the prophet Samuel anointed Saul king of Israel.

From the desert and the hills to civilization is the story of Hebrew origins. On entering the land as widely differing groups they adopted the "tongue of Canaan" as well as much of its culture. But there persisted that element in the Hebrew makeup that in the course of time gave Israel its God. It is this trait that principally distinguishes the Hebrews from all other ancient peoples, and to this source must we trace our own religions.

5. The Last Thousand Years Before Christ

THESE WERE momentous years in the history of the world. The Egyptian Empire had come to a lingering end, but three more Oriental empires were to bloom and pass, before Europe, through the Greeks, assumed the leading role. Assyrians, Babylonians, and Persians succeeded one another in turn, and the last was the greatest. Yet before any of them reached maturity a state was formed in the highlands of Palestine, a state which at the moment it was conceived might have risen to political heights. Instead it was destined to serve a much greater purpose through the religion it gave the world.

THE HEBREWS BECOME A NATION

Saul was last of the Judges and first of the Kings of Israel. He had been anointed by Samuel and later, at Mizpah, the people had gathered to choose him king, thus making his selection unanimous. The tribes, which heretofore had fought among themselves, were brought together and a united front was presented to the Philistines who had come up into the hill country around Jerusalem. But Jerusalem itself was still in foreign hands, and not until David was made king did it become Hebrew property.

Saul and his son Jonathan were effective military leaders and by the end of the reign the Hebrew kingdom included most of the Judean hill country except Jerusalem, and perhaps extended as far north as the Plain of Esdraelon on which stood the famous stronghold of Megiddo. Saul also ruled over parts of Transjordan and must be credited with forming the foundation of the kingdom of which David was later king.

David of Bethlehem became the armor-bearer of Saul and gained renown in battle, so much so that the women of Israel began to sing, "Saul slew his thousands, but David his ten thousands." This resulted in David's banishment, for Saul wished no rival for his newly-won throne. At the same time Saul disagreed with the priests of Yahweh, as God was called by the Hebrews, and David soon found himself in their favor. But Saul hunted him through Judah, and David at length was forced to seek protection from the Philistine lord of Gath. David wished for Hebrew independence but valued his life as well.

Finally the Philistines gathered in the Plain of Esdraelon at Mt. Gilboa for one last attempt to destroy Saul and his kingdom, and on that fateful day the Hebrews were routed and Saul and Jonathan killed. Their bodies were exposed on the walls of Beth Shan and the Hebrews were, for the time being, without a leader.

David was still a Philistine vassal and had to proceed carefully, but through his earlier marriage with Saul's daughter, and what may have been several judiciously planned deaths, he became at length the sole contender for the throne of the small state. Accordingly, the elders of Israel journeyed to Hebron, far in the south of Judah, and anointed David "King of Israel and Judah."

DAVID, KING OF ISRAEL AND JUDAH

Soon after David became king, around 1000 B.C., he declared his independence of the Philistines, and wars with these people continued. Out of them grew one of the world's famous stories, that of David and Goliath, a story that is as unhistorical as it is fascinating. Far from being the hero of any such episode, David appears to have been in danger of his life, but later Hebrew romancers had no difficulty in placing Israel's hero in a more

David, by Verrochio, stands victoriously over the head of Goliath. (National Gallery of Art, Kress Collection)

favorable light. There appears to have been a Goliath of Gath, but he was slain by Elhanan of Bethlehem.

In the course of time the Philistines admitted Hebrew independence, and David was allowed to look after other matters. It was then that Jerusalem ceased being a city of the kingdom. The capture of Jerusalem was of lasting importance, for from that time on it has remained the Holy City. Making Jerusalem capital of the country was strategic from several points of view, the principal one being that it lay between Israel and Judah but was part of neither. Friction always existed between north and south, therefore a neutral capital possessed many advantages.

David conquered almost all of Palestine and held Transjordan as far south as the Gulf of Akaba which leads out to the Red Sea. Damascus, which by now was inhabited by a closely related people called Arameans, was also controlled by David as was a good part of central Syria. The kingdom under David was the largest it had ever been or was to be.

The rise of the Hebrew kingdom may be attributed in large part to the tremendous energies that David exhibited in his early years and to his wise choice of generals, but at the same time the general situation in the Near East was favorable. Egypt was in eclipse and Assyria, soon to become the ranking oriental power, had not yet felt its strength. The Hebrew kingdom was short-lived, and before David died there were signs of disintegration. His son Absalom revolted as did a number of the tribes, and harem intrigues created a situation well known in the east. The outcome was that Solomon, the son of

Bath Sheba, became king at the death of David. We shall never know for certain what it was that David said on his deathbed. The only witnesses were Bath Sheba and the priest Nathan, and Bath Sheba was the ambitious mother of Solomon.

David was a man of great ability, an able general, and an astute politician who carried Israel to its heights among the nations. His reign is important too for its effect on Hebrew religion, for at that time Yahweh, or God, became the principal god among the many that the Hebrews worshiped. David was not

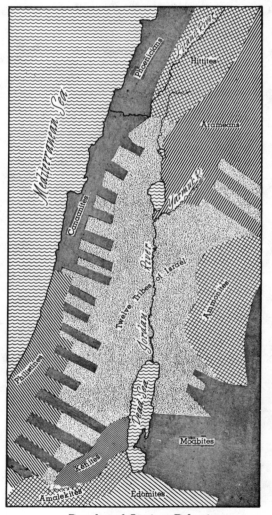

Peoples of Ancient Palestine

Tie Posts and Cribs still stand to mark the individual stalls of Solomon's stables at Megiddo. (Oriental Institute of the University of Chicago)

a monotheist but he was leading the way to the later acceptance of God as the only true god. Succeeding generations glorified David in his relations with God far beyond the evidence and among other things claimed that he had written the Psalms. David was indeed a poet of considerable attainment, but it seems improbable that he wrote many of the Psalms or that he was the author of the Twenty-third Psalm.

THE GLORIES OF SOLOMON

Solomon murdered all aspirants to the throne and thus began his "peaceful and wise" reign about 970 B.C. It was truly a reign of peace, for no military activity is recorded. But peace in the larger sense does not mean that there were no revolts. Some of these occurred early in his career as king, and soon his father's empire began to slip through his fingers.

While Solomon was not a military man he apparently knew a great deal about economics. He developed a large trade in horses, buying them from Egypt and selling them to the northern countries. During his reign the Hebrews carried on an extensive trade with the Red Sea countries. Ships went to Ophir and returned with monkeys, peacocks, and spices. Copper mines were discovered and worked in southern Palestine, and with

Solomon's other activities added greatly to the balance in the treasury. These sources of wealth, to which must of course be added taxes levied on the people, resulted in the erection of a large number of royal buildings throughout the land.

The greatest of these was the temple which Solomon erected in Jerusalem and which stood until almost four hundred years later when it was destroyed by the Babylonians. Solomon also strengthened strategic points throughout the country, building horse and chariot stables in some of them. At Megiddo alone there were accommodations for almost five hundred horses, complete with stalls, tie posts, and stone troughs for food and drink.

Solomon was remembered and glorified by later generations for his building of the temple to Yahweh, but he, like his father, worshiped more than one god. Nevertheless Yahweh had become the principal state god, and held a position in the minds of the people that may be compared to that of Amon in the Egyptian empire period. Yahweh was head of the Hebrew pantheon.

After a reign marked by great luxury for the upper classes, but untold hardship for those who made up the peasant and working groups, Solomon died. The kingdom that David amassed had largely disappeared, and, sadder yet, Solomon left to his young son Reheboam a country exceedingly close to revolt because of the heavy taxes and forced labor that had been customary for years.

Solomon's Temple in Jerusalem, a sectional reconstruction. The innermost room is the Holy of Holies where the Ark of the Covenant was placed. (D. El Osgood)

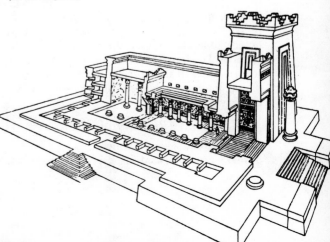

THE DIVIDED KINGDOM

The sixteen-year-old Reheboam was accepted immediately as king of Judah, but the northern tribes assembled at Shechem, wishing first to have an understanding before accepting him as their king as well. Their spokesman said, "Your father made the yoke grievous upon us, and made grievous the securing of the food for his table; now therefore lighten it upon us, and we will serve you." Reheboam's young friends were indignant, and, urged by them, Reheboam replied, "My little finger is thicker than my father's loins; my father chastised you with whips, but I will chastise with scorpions."

Thus the promising kingdom, that Saul had brought together and David had enlarged, came to the turning of the ways. Judah and Israel had always been annoying to each other, and now the northern tribes cried out, "No portion have we in David, no heritage in Jesse's son! To your tents, Oh Israel! This man is no leader or prince." With that Reheboam fled back to Jerusalem to escape the fury of the mob.

The northern tribes then made Jereboam king of Israel. He had been an official under Solomon but had fallen into disfavor and fled to Egypt. Shishak, first king of the Twenty-second Dynasty, gave him his queen's sister as wife, and at the death of Solomon, Jereboam hurried back to Palestine. Here he gathered together a force of men and when elected king of Israel he rebuilt Shechem as his capital.

Jereboam became king in 935 B.C., and from that time on there was continual friction between Judah and Israel. This situation was interrupted for a short time when in 930 B.C. Shishak invaded the country and momentarily revived the Egyptian empire. But Egypt lost power soon after his death, and, although she often in later years interfered with Palestine for political reasons, she never again as a native power attained a real footing in the country.

SAMARIA ON A HILL

A new line of kings, ushered in by Omri in 885 B.C., established its capital at Samaria. The hilltop site had not been occupied since prehistoric times, and any buildings that may then have existed had long since disappeared. The capital was thus a new and fresh city which alone would have distinguished it from other cities in the land. But other matters were to give Samaria its lasting name. Omri founded a dynasty that rose to real significance in the affairs of the time, and long afterward Assyria referred to Israel as "The House of Omri."

Shortly before Omri became king, the dominant figure in Phoenicia was a young priest of the goddess Astarte, who had usurped power and called himself "King of the Sidonians." When Omri came to the throne of Israel, an alliance was formed between the two kings similar to the one between Hiram and Solomon, and the pact was sealed when the Phoenician gave his daughter to Omri's son Ahab. This new member of the royal family of Israel was Jezebel, one of the most notorious women in the Bible, and destined to play an unwilling part in the development of Israel's religion.

Jezebel was strong-willed in everything she did. If she wished for a temple to her native god, Baal Melkart, she got it, even though Ahab's principal god was Yahweh. If she desired to have a vineyard in which her husband might plant herbs, she acquired it by trickery when it could not be bought. Ahab had offered to buy Naboth's vineyard in Jezreel, a few miles south of Nazareth, or to replace it with another and better vineyard. When Naboth refused, Jezebel contrived to have him accused of insubordination to God and the king; Naboth was dragged from the city and stoned to death. Thereupon the prophet Elijah, already Jezebel's enemy because of their differing religious points of view, told Ahab that swine and dogs would lick his blood, and dogs would feast on Jezebel. How true was this prophecy we shall presently see.

Meanwhile the Assyrian menace to the east had been crystallizing, and in 854 B.C., twenty years after Ahab had become king, the army of Shalmaneser III marched into the west. But Ahab had not been idle. Temporary

Progress in War was Assyria's chief cultural contribution. Here soldiers besiege a city. (Oriental Institute of the University of Chicago)

peace existed between Israel and Damascus, and a coalition of other Syrian powers, twelve in all, met Shalmaneser at Karkara in central Syria. Ahab was as important as any of the allies, and the ensuing battle resulted in a draw, if not a defeat for Shalmaneser. It was in any case a political victory for Ahab who had been strongly opposed in his plans by the prophets of Yahweh. But the prophetic party eventually won the day in Israel, with the result that Judaism was allowed to develop. Hebrew history is significant chiefly because of Judaism and its offspring Christianity, but if not for Ahab, who in fighting with the prophets contributed his strength at the Battle of Karkara, Israel might well have disappeared before it did. The Assyrians did not again prove a menace for over a century, and in that time religious views crystallized to the point where they could not be extinguished short of extinction of the whole people. Samaria and Israel succumbed in time, but Yahweh was by then strongly entrenched in the minds of the people.

After the Assyrian threat had been repulsed, the coalition, which so successfully had met it, broke up. Israel and Damascus again came to blows, and in one of the battles in 852 B.C. Ahab was struck by a chance arrow which pierced his coat of mail. By evening he died, and with him went the last real opposition to the prophets. Ahab had worshiped Yahweh but he had also been a patriot for Israel.

JEZEBEL AND JEHU

Ahab's son, who followed him, soon lost his foreign possessions and after a couple of years when he died he was succeeded by his brother Jehoram. Strife still existed between the royal house and the prophets, and, when Jehoram returned to Jezreel to recuperate from a wound received in battle with the Damascenes, the prophetic group plotted his downfall. Led by Elisha it decided that Israel's future lay best with a man sympathetic to Yahweh. It was thus that Jehu, senior general of the army, came to the throne of Israel.

Driving furiously toward Jezreel he was met by Jehoram and Ahaziah, king of Judah, who inquired whether all was well. Jehu directed his reply to Jehoram saying that things could hardly be well so long as Jezebel's influence remained unchecked. At this, Jehoram turned quickly to reach safety in the city but Jehu pierced him with an arrow and ordered one of his officers to throw the body onto the land that had been Naboth's vineyard. Ahaziah, too, was struck and after escaping he died in Megiddo.

Jezebel, who was in Jezreel at the time, soon learned of these events and knew that her time had also come. So quite calmly she fixed her hair and painted her eyes and then sat down at a window overlooking the gate of the

Solemn Processions decorate this bronze relief from the ruins of a palace at Balawat. (British Museum)

city. When Jehu appeared she taunted him with the murder of his master and he in a fury responded with an order that two of her eunuchs throw her out of the window. Her blood splashed on the wall and her body was trampled by the horses where it was left for the dogs. In those days the zeal of Yahweh could bring about such atrocities.

Jehu, however, was not yet content. He slew all the relatives of the house of Omri and all who had been sympathetic with Jezebel and her sons. Moreover he alienated Judah which for a short time had fought side by side with Israel. And finally when, in 842 B.C., Shalmaneser of Assyria returned for a short foray into Syria and Palestine, Jehu bowed his head to the ground in token of fealty. Jehu may have been a champion of the people, but he had no thought of defeating Assyria's desire for empire.

THE NEW PROPHETS

Israel experienced another period of prosperity under Jereboam II (785-745 B.C.) as we learn from the prophet Amos, a Judean shepherd. But Amos predicted evil for Israel because of its unjust social abuses, and Assyria was to be the agent of destruction, the agent of the Lord. He saw in Yahweh a god opposed to the bloody reforms of Elijah's followers, and this message was so strong in his heart that he journeyed northward to Israel to denounce the evils of the day. He addressed the Israelites on the subject of their expensive clothing and homes, their corrupt lives and lack of feeling for the poor. He was the first great Hebrew social reformer and did much to point the way to a higher form of religion.

A generation later there lived Hosea, an Israelite with much the same attitude toward social conditions, but he differed from Amos in believing that God still loved Israel even though it turned to other gods. Hosea also saw that Assyria would be the earthly means of Israel's downfall, and he, like Amos, protested violently against the religious setting that had been sponsored by Elijah and Elisha.

As predicted, Israel fell when the revived Assyrians returned in the latter part of the

eighth century. Tiglath Pileser III (746-728 B.C.) raised Assyria from its temporary eclipse and swept westward, and soon his country was to reach its pinnacle, even taking Egypt. But before that happened the kingdom of Israel was to pass out of existence. Shalmaneser V of Assyria in 723 B.C. captured the capital at Samaria, and many of the people of Israel were carried off as captives. Thenceforth the Hebrew scene was shifted to Jerusalem.

Amos and Hosea were followed by the prophet Isaiah who lived at the time Sargon's son Sennacherib was slashing his way through western Asia. Many of the Hebrews on

Capture of an Egyptian City. Assyrian soldiers scale the walls and carry off prisoners and spoils in this relief from the palace of Sennacherib. (British Museum)

looking at the wasted land of Palestine came to believe that Ashur, the principal god of the Assyrians, was a far greater god than Yahweh. But Isaiah addressed them on numerous occasions in the streets of Jerusalem, even as Sennacherib approached with his mighty battering rams in 701 B.C. Isaiah proclaimed that Yahweh ruled much more than simply Palestine. He ruled the entire world and Assyria was but the "rod" of Yahweh's anger for the wrongdoing of the Hebrews. In addition Isaiah predicted a great and glorious future for the Hebrews and disaster for Assyria.

His prophecy was fulfilled when Sennacherib's army, momentarily expected out-

Ashurnasirpal II, one of the great conquering kings of Assyria, is shown on a royal lion hunt in this bas relief from his palace at Kalakh (884–860 B.C.). Note characteristic exaggeration of muscles on men and animals. (British Museum)

the way of Israel. Its inhabitants were taken away as captives, but out of her new misery, the Exile, the Hebrews developed the spiritual concepts of Judaism that have been so enduring.

THE ASSYRIAN EMPIRE

For about two centuries the Assyrians played a leading role in the destiny of Palestine, but Assyrian interests were far wider than Palestine and included conquests in all directions from their homeland on the upper Tigris. Therefore let us retrace our steps and pick up the thread of history in the land of the god Ashur.

The earliest capital of Assyria was Ashur, named for the great god of a Semitic people who early in history settled in the northern part of Mesopotamia. To begin with, it was a

side the walls of Jerusalem, was suddenly afflicted with a plague from the marshes of the Nile Delta. Jerusalem was spared and many Hebrews then came to believe in the beneficence of the world God, Yahweh.

Less than a century after Jerusalem's deliverance the Hebrews saw the collapse of Assyria (612 B.C.), but the downfall of Judah was likewise not far distant. The Chaldeans of Babylon became the next masters of Palestine and the unsubmitting Hebrews, having not yet learned their lesson from Samaria and the prophets, fell finally to Nebuchadnezzar in 586 B.C.

Thus ended the kingdom that Saul had founded. Short-lived as a unified nation, it had split soon after the death of Solomon, and now, a little more than four hundred years after the anointing of Saul, Judah had gone

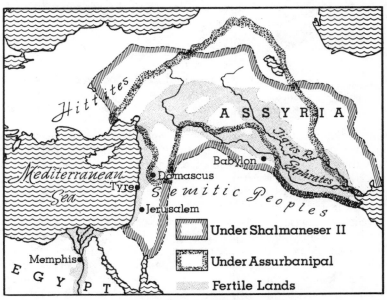

The Assyrian Empire

small city-state subject to the great powers in the south. Sargon of Akkad in the twenty-sixth century and Hammurabi in the twentieth century had controlled it, but at the same time it had received the benefits of Babylonian culture. We have noticed the small but active Assyrian trading colonies that migrated to Anatolia about 2000 B.C., but in world affairs Assyria played a minor role until the fourteenth century when her kings pushed westward, sweeping back the Hittites. It was

Royal Scribes record booty from a captured town in this relief of Tiglath Pileser III from Nimrud. (British Museum)

during the Amarna period in Egypt that Assyria first gave signs of emerging as a power. About 1100 B.C. the first Tiglath Pileser marched to the Mediterranean through the obstinate Aramean and Phoenician lands, but Assyria was not yet powerful enough to hold permanently these distant regions.

The Arameans, whose strongest city was Damascus, proved for several centuries to be a bulwark against Assyrian invasion, while at the same time their industrious merchants worked eastward, carrying with them their alphabet based on the one in-

Nebuchadnezzar had this pottery cylinder inscribed in cuneiform

vented in Sinai about 1800 B.C. The Aramaic alphabet in time displaced use of the more cumbersome cuneiform, and before its eastern march was completed it had penetrated beyond Mesopotamia and Persia into India and China.

The language spoken by the Aramaic merchants likewise gained extreme importance, finally becoming the principal language of the Near East. Many centuries later Jesus, like other Hebrews of the time, spoke Aramaic and not Hebrew, although the two are closely related.

We have seen that the strong Syrian-He-

brew coalition which included Ahab of Israel was able to stop Shalmaneser III at Karkara in 854 B.C. Nevertheless, Shalmaneser more than doubled Assyrian territory by incorporating former vassal states into the kingdom, and his grandson expanded it still farther. The former small city of Ashur was now surrounded on all sides by recently acquired territory. But Assyria's star was temporarily dimmed after the death of Shalmaneser's grandson, and for a few years the most important state in the world was Haldia whose capital lay far to the north near Lake Van. During this period the devotees of Yahweh in Israel were able to solidify their ideas of God.

It was Tiglath Pileser III (746-728 B.C.) who revived Assyria and launched it on its conquering way. The monarch laid hold of Babylon, the mother of Assyria's culture, and on the east he subdued a group of people including the Medes. Then, turning his attention to the Haldians, he met them first in northern Syria where their cities succumbed to the fury of the Assyrian king. Working southward he then invaded Palestine, and wherever he created new provinces he forestalled revolt by moving the population bodily from one part of the empire to another. Mountaineers were sent to the plains, and southerners left their homes for unfamiliar territory in the north. In each of the vacated places, others from far-off regions were sent to replace those who had been removed. Tiglath Pileser built temples in his new provinces and put in them statues of his god Ashur and himself. It is possible that the temple in Jerusalem possessed such images to the consternation of Yahweh's priests. Thus was the Assyrian empire controlled by its king and his governors.

A Guardian of the Gate, this colossal bull served to ward off enemies from the palace at Khorsabad. (Oriental Institute of the University of Chicago)

Shalmaneser V (728-722 B.C.) continued the forceful policy of his father and, four years before he died, began the siege of Samaria that ended three years later in its surrender. The prophets had spoken the truth, and Samaria's inhabitants were forced to leave for distant parts of the empire. Shalmaneser himself died the year after Israel disappeared, and the Assyrian throne was taken by his brother who bore the famous name Sargon.

SARGON AND HIS SUCCESSORS

The second world empire was given a new royal city when Sargon (722-705 B.C.) was elevated from generalship to the kingship. Not content with the older capital he chose a fresh spot, the present Khorsabad, on which to build his city, and called it Sargonburg. It was larger and more magnificent than anything Asia had ever seen, and it truly reflected the grandeur and power of the king. The ruins of this mile-square city have been investigated by archeologists, most recently by the Oriental Institute of the University of Chicago, which has discovered vast numbers of reliefs depicting events in the reign of the king. But Sargonburg was short-lived. When the king was succeeded by his son Sennacherib in 705 B.C., Sargonburg was deserted and the capital moved to Nineveh. The famous city of Sargon had been built with the riches flowing into Assyria from her foreign possessions, but as a monument to its builder it has only in recent years come to the surface and become significant.

Sargon's conquests were followed up by Sennacherib whose name was feared far and wide. All of Mesopotamia, the border of Persia, the mountains north and northwest of Assyria, Anatolia, Syria, Palestine, and the frontier of Egypt, knew his might from actual experience, and, although Jerusalem was momentarily saved by a pestilence that destroyed the Assyrian army, Hezekiah, Judah's king, realized his extreme good fortune.

Sennacherib (705-681 B.C.) had designs on Egypt and, while he never succeeded in really entering Egypt, he defeated an Egyptian army in southern Palestine. Ever since the rise of Assyrian power, Egyptian policy had been to stir up discontent among those paying taxes or tribute to the state on the Tigris. It was of the greatest necessity, therefore, that the Assyrians master this source of trouble once for all.

Assyrian Priest, costumed as a god, holds fir-cone and situta

Sennacherib had not been entirely successful in this respect, and his son Esarhaddon (681-668 B.C.) therefore proceeded to the Delta in 675 B.C. But there he was defeated in 673 B.C. in a battle with Taharka, one of Egypt's Ethiopian kings of the Twenty-fifth Dynasty. Assyrian prestige in Asia suffered to the extent that after three years Esarhaddon's army was forced to return to the Delta. This time it could not be stopped, and the Delta, from Memphis northward, was incorporated into the Assyrian provincial system.

Egypt, however, was a long way from Assyria, and this made administration of the Delta difficult. The very year that Esarhaddon died, it became necessary for his son Ashurbanipal (668-626 B.C.) to march to the Delta to punish the Ethiopians, and seven years later, when the Ethiopians made a serious effort to regain Egypt, Ashurbanipal's

Esarhaddon, in conical crown, holds kings Baal and Taharka captive. (Berlin Museum)

army drove them far up the Nile. This time the Assyrians sacked Thebes, and since then it has had no real importance.

Ashurbanipal set up an Egyptian named Psamtek as viceroy of Egypt, but, when Assyria's attention was diverted to more pressing matters near home, Egypt revolted and Psamtek became the first king of the Twenty-sixth Dynasty, ruling from 663 to 609 B.C. This was the last powerful native Egyptian dynasty, and before it fell to the Persians in 525 B.C. it had made a serious attempt to revive Egyptian culture. This was a period of close contact with Greece. Greek settlers made their homes in the Delta and mercenaries from across the sea found service in the Egyptian army. At the same time Egyptian thought returned to Greece with the trading merchants, and early Greek art came under the influence of Egyptian sculpture.

Wherever Assyrian armies went, there they left a reign of terror; and ruins and desolation replaced busy cities and growing fields. But these depredations served the purpose of building the greatest empire the world had yet seen. At Nineveh we find that art was greatly stimulated, the reliefs of Ashurbanipal being the finest in all Assyria.

Ashurbanipal was rarely with his army, having been told by a goddess to stay at home. He was highly educated for the times and even knew Sumerian, although badly. He was a patron of letters and collected a great library, the largest of the earlier Near East, much of which is now in the British Museum.

The Assyrian Navy, as depicted in the Nineveh palace of Sennacherib, included double-decked ships

But other aspects of his character were most unattractive, especially his cruelty which was excessive even for those times.

Sennacherib's Aqueduct led water from this river to Nineveh. Carved rock in center was part of conduit. (Oriental Institute of the University of Chicago)

Hunting was one of the chief pastimes of the Assyrians. Here Sargon II's retinue chases game

The Assyrian star began setting long before his reign was over. Mercenaries, always a dangerous element, filled out the army and Aramean merchants controlled trade. These internal weaknesses were aggravated by the approach of two peoples soon destined to replace Assyria. Semitic desert tribes, known to us as the Chaldeans but not to be confused with a people north of Assyria, had for some time been establishing themselves at the head of the Persian gulf, south of Babylon. Eventually these people gained sufficient power to take Babylon itself, and it was their second king, Nebuchadnezzar, who forced the Hebrews into unhappy exile. The other movement was from the eastern mountains and consisted of Indo-European peoples led by the Medes and including the Persians. These had fought against Assyria before, but now, toward the end of the seventh century, they became an irresistible force, and in 612 B.C. through the cooperation of Medes and Babylonians, the famous city of Nineveh, symbol of world might, became a heap of rubbish.

Assyrian arms had been carried to distant parts of the Near East where its terrors were long remembered. Ruled from its various capitals, Assyria for a century and a quarter had been continuously master of western Asia. The next great empire, with its seat in Babylon, followed, to be cast aside in turn after a century by Cyrus the Great and his Persian forces.

NEBUCHADNEZZAR AND THE CHALDEANS

The Chaldeans began their dynasty when Nebuchadnezzar's father revolted on the death of Ashurbanipal in 626 B.C. Twenty-two years later the son came to the throne to begin a forty-three year reign that became one of the best known in history. Nebuchadnezzar's part in the story of the capture of Jerusalem, the destruction of the temple, and the exile of the Jews attained world fame through the spread of the Bible.

Ishtar Gate, dedicated to the love goddess, was a brightly tiled portal to Babylon's Sacred Way

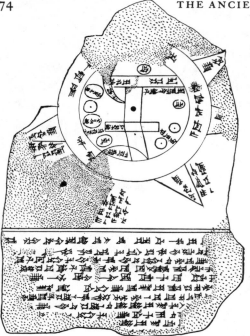

World Map 6th century B.C. The Babylonians charted the Tigris and Euphrates through the center of their world as two broken verticals. Cities, marked in cuneiform, are surrounded by two big circular seas. (British Museum)

After Assyria fell, Egypt continued the same old policy of fostering discontent among the small states that lay between her and the Tigris-Euphrates. But Nebuchadnezzar defeated an Egyptian army in northern Syria, and as part of these military measures subdued the small state of Judah. The capture of Jerusalem and the deportation of Hebrews to Babylon figured less in the world news of the day than the fact that Egypt had been halted. Judah, after all, was an extremely small state.

Nebuchadnezzar was a busy warrior, bringing a large portion of the old Assyrian

empire under his control. The revenues that thus poured into his treasury allowed him to rebuild Babylon on lines of splendor and beauty previously unknown. Temples were erected to the deities that had long been at home in Babylonia, and the gateway of the city he dedicated to the goddess Ishtar, the patroness of love. His huge imperial palace and government offices lay beyond the gate, and overlooking it, on the roof of the palace, was a series of gardens filled with luxurious plants. These were the mysterious Hanging Gardens of Babylon which so intrigued the Greeks and caused them to include the gardens among the Seven Wonders of the World. Here among the palms and ferns on his roof the great king would chat with his intimates or in solitude consider matters nearest to his heart. Little remains of the glories of Babylon except heaps of tumbled mud-brick out of which the buildings were made, but the colorful Ishtar Gate and the tales of Hebrew and Greek have given us a very adequate picture of Nebuchadnezzar's Babylon. The old world was a colorful world and Babylon will always remain one of the greatest cities of that age.

Ram Weight was used to establish the value of unstamped metal ingots that Babylonians used in place of money. (Yale University Art Gallery)

The Chaldeans made great progress in the study of astronomy through an effort to discover the future in the stars. This art we call "astrology." Much information had been systematically collected by the Babylonians and from it we have here the beginning of astronomy. The groups of stars which now

Marching Bulls, in low relief on the Ishtar Gate, were made of specially designed bricks, each of which were cast in a separate mold. This type of ceramic mural originated in Babylonia and spread to Persia

Babylonian Dragon from the Ishtar Gate. (Oriental Institute of the University of Chicago)

bear the name "Twelve Signs of the Zodiac" were mapped out for the first time, and the planets Mercury, Venus, Mars, Jupiter, and Saturn were known. Since these planets were thought to have special powers over the lives of men, they were named for the five leading gods and goddesses. We refer to these planets by their Roman names, but the Romans had adopted the Babylonian terms and simply translated them into their equivalents in Rome. Thus the planet of Ishtar, the goddess of love, became Venus, and that of the god Marduk was changed to Jupiter.

Chaldean power and civilization reached their height during the reign of Nebuchadnezzar, yet when he died in 562 B.C. Babylon's days were numbered. The exiled Jews of that city now looked to the east for their deliverer, and in 539 B.C. he came. He was Cyrus the Great.

THE PERSIAN WORLD EMPIRE

When Shalmaneser III of Assyria in 835 B.C. returned from an expedition to the northeast he carried with him tribute from the Medes and Persians. This is the first time that these Iranians appear in history and we see that they were far from their later home. After a century and a half the Persians opposed Sennacherib at a point much farther south. When Cyrus took Babylon the center of the Persian world was near Persepolis. Thus for three hundred years those Indo-European speaking people had moved steadily southward.

At the time of the downfall of Nineveh, the Medes had been the leading group among the newcomers to Persia, and thereafter expansion was made in the name of Media. But in 559 B.C. when Cyrus became king of the Persians, then only vassals of the Medes, he laid plans to take over the throne of Media as well. This he succeeded in doing in 550 B.C., and thenceforth his great energies laid the foundation of an empire that was to reach far east toward China, and west to include Egypt, Babylonia, Assyria, Palestine, Syria, and Asia Minor. Even Greece was included in the plans of empire. Thus the last oriental empire was the greatest, exceeding by far even the large area encompassed by the Assyrians at their height.

When Cyrus made the Medes his vassals, he as king inherited a tremendous territory that included not only that occupied by the Aryans on the highlands of Persia, but also a large portion of Assyria and Asia Minor as far west as the Halys River. But across this river ruled a powerful king noted in legend for his extreme wealth. This was King Croesus of Lydia, a proud king, who refused to surrender to Cyrus' approaching army. Yet nothing could stop the king of the Persians, and Croesus' kingdom with its access to the Greek seas became part of the fast-growing Aryan empire.

Cyrus then turned his attention to the east. Babylonia was still unconquered but her king was more intent on religion than on matters of state, and Cyrus could afford to ignore him for a few more years. Therefore he pushed on to far central Asia, subduing tribes as

Royal Stairway at Persepolis was crisply chiselled with reliefs of animals, a favorite Persian motif. (Oriental Institute of the University of Chicago)

distant as the Jaxartes River which flows into the Aral Sea. Having in these operations enlarged the Persian empire to previously unknown proportions, the much-feared conqueror returned to his native land, only to start out almost immediately for Babylon, the most famous city of the time.

With little effort Cyrus defeated Belshazzar, the crown prince, and captured Babylon in 539 B.C. Thus came into his possession not only Babylonia itself but also its foreign

allowed the Jews wishing to return to Jerusalem to do so, there to rebuild the temple destroyed by Nebuchadnezzar.

Many, but not all, returned and took with them the religious conceptions which are included in Judaism, the religion of the Jews. During the exile Ezekiel and a great teacher whose name is unknown developed the view that Yahweh was the Creator and only God of the universe, and that hardship and affliction were necessary to make a people useful to the

New Year's Gifts for the Persian emperor included two prize rams from Cilician envoys. The Persepolis reliefs record presents from twenty-three subject nations, guarded by terminal winged bulls (at right). (Oriental Institute of the University of Chicago)

holdings including Syria and Palestine and the part of Assyria not already held.

It was in 550 B.C. that Cyrus had revolted from the Medes. A little more than a decade later this extraordinary man had, at the head of his peasant soldiery, created the greatest empire that the world had seen. Moreover, Cyrus was the first great Aryan conqueror of whom we know, and through his efforts the Semites, long the lords of western Asia, lost control until the coming of the Arabs a thousand years later.

Cyrus was very human to those he had subdued. King Croesus of Lydia lost his kingdom, but once pacified he was made an official in the old land of the Medes. Persian policy was to leave the conquered content, and it is therefore not surprising that Cyrus

world. God had prepared those in exile for a greater service, and they would eventually be liberated and allowed to return to their land. But kingship was not revived, for Jewish thought now saw that kings were but the tools of God. It was then that the old Hebrew state became a Jewish religious organization. Instead of a king there was a high priest in Jerusalem.

The Jewish leaders now set about restoring the city and the temple, and collecting the sayings and writings of the prophets and others whose history we now read in the Old Testament. As the service in the temple developed, there came into being the remarkable group of religious songs known as the Book of Psalms. Many of the Psalms were written during the Persian period, while some

Ahura-Mazda, "Lord of Wisdom", ·watches over Darius I while the king hunts lions from his chariot. (Oriental Institute of the University of Chicago)

may be as early as the time of David. Thereafter Israel's greatness was to lie in her religion and in the fact that Christianity's great teacher was a Jew.

CAMBYSES MARCHES TO EGYPT

Cyrus was killed 529 B.C. while in battle east of the Caspian Sea, and was succeeded by his son Cambyses. Why Cyrus had never tried to incorporate Egypt into his realm is not known for certain, although it is probable that he was much too busy in other sectors. At any rate Cambyses soon set out with that purpose in mind. Having marched his army across southwestern Asia he passed over the desert from Gaza and engaged the Egyptians near the mouth of the present-day Suez Canal. The power of Egypt was gone, and Cambyses annexed the country of the Twenty-sixth Dynasty with ease in 525 B.C. Then with the ambition and madness of a world conqueror he decided on the capture of Carthage, even then a very important city on the north African coast. He planned to attack it by land and sea, but the Phoenician fleet from Tyre refused to fight against a city that had been founded by its ancestors and in which blood kin now dwelt. Cambyses was thus forced to concentrate on a land force which was to cross the treacherous desert west of Egypt. Fifty thousand men were selected and they reached several of the oases in safety, but after that nothing was ever heard of them again. It was as though they had been swallowed by some superhuman fury, and indeed it is probable that a great sandstorm was the means of keeping the conquering Persians away from Carthage. Nevertheless, Cambyses had taken Egypt and thereafter until Alexander came out of Greece the country remained under Persian control except for short periods of revolt.

THE PERSIANS INVADE GREECE

Cambyses died while returning from Egypt and after some typical oriental difficulty over title to the throne, it passed finally in 521 B.C. to Darius, a distant relative of the dead king. Darius was not only an excellent general but an able administrator, and after a few years the unwieldy empire attained a semblance of calm. It was then (512 B.C.)

Silver Tablet from the Persepolis audience room reads: "Darius the Great King, the King of Kings, the King of the Lands, Vistepa's son, the Achaemid, speaks Darius the King: 'This is the Empire which I possess from the Sacae, who are beyond Sagdia, as far as the Kush, from Indus as far as the Sparda, which Ahura-Mazda has granted to me, who is the greatest of gods; may Ahura-Mazda protect myself and my house.'" The terms show Darius' empire extended from Afghanistan to Ethiopia and from India to Greece. (Oriental Institute of the University of Chicago)

Tomb of Darius I, hewn from the side of a mountain, was carved to simulate the facade of a palace. (Oriental Institute of the University of Chicago)

that further conquests were begun. Darius marched westward over his vast domain to cross the narrow waters of the Bosphorus that separate Asia from Europe. The principal result of this expedition was to take Thrace, in doing which he clearly threatened the rising Greek states. About the same time a Persian army entered the Indus valley in northwestern India.

Greece, however, was Darius' main objective because various Greek cities consistently aided the Ionian trouble makers on the Aegean coast of Persian Asia Minor. Matters came to a head in 492 B.C. when Darius led his army into Thrace, but the

difficulties were great and in addition the fleet was wrecked while rounding a promontory. Accordingly the advance was abandoned in favor of a direct attack by water.

It was in 490 B.C. that the Persian army landed in the Bay of Marathon twenty-six miles northeast of Athens, intent on punishing that city for aid it had given the Ionian revolters. The Athenian forces were far outnumbered but through the strategy employed by their commander, Miltiades, the Persians were badly defeated, the survivors fleeing to their ships. News of the victory was carried to Athens by a dispatch runner named Phidippedes who covered the twenty-six miles at his greatest speed and arrived crying, "Rejoice! We conquer!" only to fall dead. His feat was commemorated by the Greeks in their Olympic games and the marathon races of today measure twenty-six miles, the distance run by Phidippedes.

Darius realized that a stronger land and sea force was necessary and returned to his beautiful palace at Persepolis with plans for a return engagement. Three years later all was in readiness when the king died, and left the fate of Greece as well as that of Persia in the hands of his son Xerxes.

Athens became convinced after Marathon that its navy had to be strengthened if it was

Darius I and Xerxes were portrayed on the portico relief of the Treasury at Persepolis. King Darius is seated; behind him stands Xerxes. Courtiers and guards watch as a dignitary makes a sign of obeisance. (Oriental Institute of the University of Chicago)

Persians of the time of Darius and Xerxes deemed it indecent to bare more than the face

Thrace and followed the seacoast down into Greece, the fleet adopting a parallel course just offshore.

By this time Athens had induced Sparta to come to her aid, and with a small force the Spartan king, Leonidas, held the important pass of Thermopylae against the approaching Persians until a flank movement caught him in the rear. The Persians then proceeded unimpeded toward a deserted Athens which they promptly burned.

In the meantime the Persian fleet had skirmished with the Greek ships but the action was indecisive. Far more potent was the effect of a storm which destroyed two hundred Asiatic vessels. The Greek ships withdrew southward and came to anchor in the Bay of Salamis just west of Athens prepared to fight the approaching flotilla.

Xerxes was on the heights above the bay as the action began and before long he must have sensed its end. When the day was over, he had seen his ships, far outnumbering those of the Athenians, suffer almost complete annihilation. Salamis had been a brilliant Greek victory, and the worried Persian survivors and their king turned quickly for home.

An army of about fifty thousand was left to winter in Thessaly, and the following year the Persians advanced once more through

to ward off the Persians when they returned. The entire Phoenician coast with its well-trained sailors was subject to Persia and constituted an ominous threat, should its fleet be sent to Athens. This was actually part of Xerxes' plan, and in the summer of 480 B.C. the Persian army crossed the Hellespont into

Slender, Fluted Columns, used on a grand scale, were the most creative contribution of Persian architecture. Seventy-two columns originally supported the roof on this audience hall of Darius and Xerxes. (Oriental Institute of the University of Chicago)

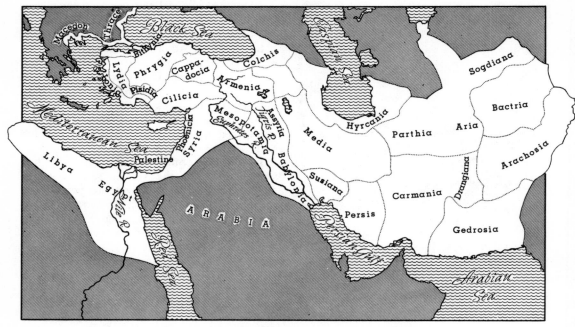

The Persian Empire at its Greatest Extent (about 500 B.C.)

Attica, but at Plataea they met their final defeat. Thus ended Persia's bid for supremacy in Europe. The Athenians hastened to occupy the northern side of the Hellespont and their fleet drove the remaining Phoenician ships from the Ionian coast. While there continued to be trouble on the Graeco-Persian frontier, never again did a Persian army set foot in Greece.

For another century and a half Persia remained mistress of Asia but many were the signs that foretold her doom. Revolts were continuous and palace intrigues weakened the kingship. At length a Darius, the third of his name and the last king of the Persian empire, came to the throne in 336 B.C. The same year a young warrior named Alexander became king in Macedonia, several hundred miles north of Athens. The story of Alexander's great expedition into Asia that resulted in the destruction of the Persian Empire and the partition of its territories among Alexander's successors is told in Part II of this work, in the chapter entitled, "Alexander the Great and the Hellenistic Age."

THE MACCABEAN REVOLT

During the early part of the second century B.C. the Seleucids, descendants of one of Alexander's generals, controlled Palestine, and King Antiochus Epiphanes (175-164 B.C.) made himself most objectionable to the Jews for a number of reasons but chiefly through his efforts to force them to worship Greek gods. An edict was issued ordering the erection of pagan altars throughout Palestine and officers were provided to see that the Jews obeyed. There followed the movement known as the Maccabean revolt which began when Mattathias, a priest, slew a Jew who was willing to forsake Yahweh for pagan gods. Mattathias and his five sons then fled to the mountains to organize their followers for the fight against Syria. The old priest soon died, but he had nominated his son Judas Maccabeus to carry on the fight to preserve the traditional Jewish religion in Palestine.

The military genius of Judas defeated the Seleucid armies and the Jews regained their

The Temple of Jerusalem was built on this site. The space is now occupied by the Haram esh-Sharif, or "Noble Sanctuary," a large platform extending to thirty-five acres. (Black Star)

end. Temple practices were restored and guaranteed by Syria whereupon many of the Jews withdrew from the struggle. But Judas had visions of a politically free Palestine as well and the war continued. Judas was killed, yet his aim was accomplished by Simon, the last surviving son of Mattathias, who negotiated a treaty of independence in 142 B.C., a little over twenty years after his father had made his bold break.

For a short time Israel had her own kings, Simon becoming the first of the Hasmonean Dynasty. During his administration the country prospered, but he and two of his sons were murdered by Ptolemy who wished to regain Palestine for Egypt. The third son, John Hyrcanus (135-105 B.C.), at length succeeded in establishing himself as head of the state and Palestine was enlarged to a size it had not enjoyed since before the Exile. How-

The Sheep-gate on the north side of Jerusalem was identified through descriptions of the reconstruction of the city fortifications in the book of Nehemiah. Here Jesus healed the bedridden man on the Sabbath

ever, internal troubles between the peaceful Pharisees and the warlike Sadducees, together with disturbing elements from outside, finally caused Rome to intervene and take matters in hand. Pompey besieged Jerusalem in 63 B.C. and reduced the Jews to vassalage.

HEROD THE GREAT TO THE FALL OF JERUSALEM

Then as always Palestine lay between contending nations, and it was in the interests of Rome that this small country remain peaceful and friendly if possible. Parthia had become the principal power east of the Euphrates, and Julius Caesar before his death had planned a campaign against her. Thus it was that Herod, an Edomite from the southern end of the Dead Sea, became king of Judea with Roman sanction, but was forced to flee to Rome when the Parthians penetrated Palestine. Not until 37 B.C. did he return to Jerusalem, there to rebuild the temple and contend with the factions that split the Jewish people. Some were pro-Roman; others pro-Parthian. The Pharisees were content with any kind of rule as long as they could live as they wished.

In his thirty-third year as king Herod the Great died and it was in that year or earlier that Christ was born. The year of Herod's death was 4 B.C. It was not until the sixth century after Christ had lived his fruitful life that his birth was made a starting point in chronology. Soon afterwards it was adopted by the church in Rome and came into popular use in the tenth century.

Not long after Herod's death Judea became a Roman province administered by procurators sent from Rome. The best known of these is Pontius Pilate who presided at the trial of Jesus. Herod's descendants maintained a semblance of power in Palestine, but the Jews would not be reconciled to Roman rule. At length, unwise and criminal actions on the part of the procurators thoroughly inflamed the already dissatisfied religious zealots, and open rebellion took place in 66 A.D. and the death struggle with Rome began.

Murders and massacres by the infuriated and momentarily successful Jews finally brought Vespasian, one of Nero's ablest generals, to quell the rebellion. Approaching Jerusalem from the north Vespasian subdued one section of the country after another until he controlled all outlying fortresses except those at Masada and Herodium. At that point he was proclaimed emperor by his troops and yielded his former position to his son Titus who then advanced on Jerusalem.

Meanwhile the people of the city had been quarreling and annihilating themselves instead of conserving all strength and coming to a common purpose for the approaching siege. Various factions among the Jews continued to fight for control in a useless and hopeless strife that greatly reduced their numbers. And then, just before Passover in 70 A.D., Titus appeared.

For five months Titus attacked the city, breaking through one wall after another, meanwhile sending frequent messages to the inflamed Jews inside to surrender. Finally his engines of war proved too strong and the Roman soldiers poured through the last breach, and soon, despite all efforts of Titus, the temple, the glory of Jerusalem and the Jews, was in flames. Yet at this intense moment the Jews still quarreled in another part of the city.

With Jerusalem laid waste, the Romans had only to subdue the remaining minor fortresses. The last to fall was Masada, far to the south overlooking the Dead Sea. When its fanatic defenders realized that it too must fall they decided that death with their ideals was better than life under the Romans. Therefore according to plan the women and children were killed first, followed by the men, until there remained one lone survivor in the midst of almost a thousand bodies. True to the pact he likewise plunged a sword through his own body after setting fire to the palace. The Romans entered and learned of the desperate deed from two women who had hidden in a cave with five children.

The Jewish state was no more, but centuries of philosophy had made Judaism impregnable. Nations came and went but Judaism survived its long travels, and became part of the heritage of Western civilization.

6. The Cretan Background of Greek History

THE LARGER ORIENTAL BACKGROUND

THE CULTURES OF THE MODERN WESTERN WORLD have been carried back traditionally in a direct line to the accomplishments recorded for ancient Greece and Rome. However, it has become increasingly clear within the last decades of scientific research and investigation that Western culture not only is deeply indebted to its Greek and Roman predecessors, but also to an older, yet brilliant, pre-Grecian culture, which developed on the island of Crete.

The spectacular deciphering of a number of ancient oriental languages within the last century, and the astounding archeological discoveries during the same period, have recovered millenniums of early history, formerly entirely unknown. Now, before our astonished eyes, peoples and civilizations of which we never have dreamed move slowly and significantly across the stage of history. The Sumerians, Elamites, Babylonians, Assyrians, Egyptians, Hittites, Syrians, Hebrews, Hurrians, Medes, and Persians are but some of the more significant groups of this early Near Eastern history.

Beyond the borders of the Near East there were other related cultures extending eastward into India. Just how great a debt the Occident owes to the Orient for the origins of its civilizations it is impossible to ascertain at the present stage of our knowledge; nor are we particularly interested in tracing the general developments of this older oriental world. It is sufficient that we are conscious of its existence and importance as we now turn to a brief survey of the civilization of Crete, the immediate cultural predecessor of the later Classical World.

In the eastern Mediterranean Sea, close to Greece and Asia Minor, lies the island of Crete, an obvious stepping stone between Europe and Western Asia. To the north of Crete in the Aegean Sea, in that practically enclosed stretch of water between Greece and Asia Minor, are hundreds of smaller islands which came to share the earlier Cretan culture. Hence, the term "Aegean Culture" also is applied to the cultures of this entire area, which apparently were centered in Crete. The climate enjoyed by the people of this area was mild and sunny. Crete had fertile valleys and plains which induced her development along agricultural lines, and her geographical location developed also in the people of Crete certain commercial and industrial interests, which for centuries made her the significant commercial and cultural center of this area.

EXCAVATION

Later Greek mythology was rich in legend reaching back far beyond written history to a preceding glorious heroic age. Tales of Minos, and his beautiful daughter, Ariadne, of Theseus, and the Minotaur, are definite reflections of impressive past ages, but they are not history. The recovery of the early history of Crete and related areas is the accomplishment of modern archeology.

Heinrich Schliemann is the romantic figure whose fervent interest and ambitions began the spectacular and unbelievably rich investigations of the ancient city of Troy and of the Greek city of Tiryns, both reflecting the culture which was centered in Crete. Here, the brilliant work of Sir Arthur Evans, begun in the early twentieth century, revealed a civilization which immediately became significant for an understanding of Greek history. The continued work of Evans, as well as that of other archeologists working in these areas, has added immeasurably to our information concerning the early history of man in these areas. Since Cretan writing, as preserved on thousands of tablets, has not yet been deciphered, Crete's political history is accordingly vague. The general material and cultural history of these people is well and richly illustrated, however, thanks to the archeological materials recovered.

NEOLITHIC CULTURE
(BEFORE 3000 B.C.)

Near Knossus, the later capital of Crete,

twenty-four feet of Neolithic deposits indicate that Crete experienced a long Neolithic, or New Stone Age, development. The materials here recovered are comparable to Neolithic materials recovered elsewhere in the Near East and in Europe. These people used stone axes, hammers and knives, and made crude pottery which they ornamented with primitive geometric designs. Their early huts were of wattle, daubed with clay, in round or oval shapes; houses with stone walls and several rooms appeared much later. Spindle and bobbin weights indicate the beginning of spinning and weaving in this period. Small boats had made their appearance.

The early Cretan belonged to the Mediterranean race, relatively short and slender, and fairly dark-skinned, similar in type to the early historical Egyptian. The mixing of races, however, began at an early time in Crete as it did elsewhere in the Near East. While relations were established with the neighboring islands and settlements along the Asiatic coast, the closer and more important contacts at this time may have been with

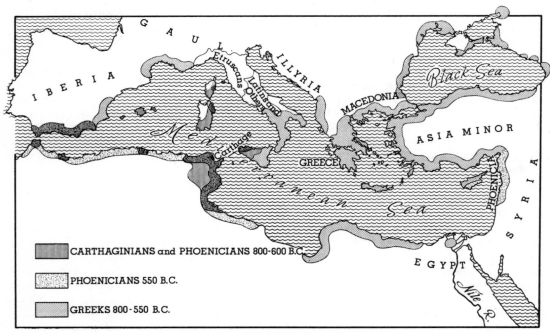

CARTHAGINIANS and PHOENICIANS 800-600 B.C.

PHOENICIANS 550 B.C.

GREEKS 800-550 B.C.

The Ancient Mediterranean World

Egypt. The undeciphered writing of the Cretans apparently is a partial imitation of some of the Egyptian signs. Copper and early technical advances came from Egypt, but the suggestions of actual control or invasion by Egypt in this period, or later periods, cannot be proven.

The periods of succeeding history in Crete have been designated as the *Minoan*, after the traditional, important King Minos. The excavators have distinguished the Early, Middle and Late Minoan Ages, and for purposes of further identification and classification have redivided each of these ages into three periods.

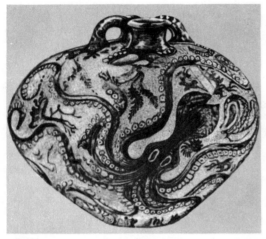

Octopus Vase, Crete's Golden Age about 1500 B.C. (National Museum, Athens)

The last age of Cretan-Minoan culture, which centered on the Greek mainland at Mycenae and Tiryns, is conveniently designated as *Mycenaean.*

THE EARLY MINOAN AGE
(c. 3400-2100 B.C.)

The early period of Cretan civilization, known as the Early Minoan Age, began with a culture which was practically Neolithic; it continued into the Copper Age and ended with the beginning of the Bronze Age. Pottery likewise began with the crude geometric wares which developed slowly into more complicated wares, including spouted vases with polychrome decoration. Relations

Cretan Flying Fish. This fragment of a fresco was found in a small house of about 2000 B.C. Marine motifs were popular among the seagoing Cretans

with Egypt had brought the potter's wheel, as well as the use of copper and certain other cultural advancements. The crude huts of the primitive period slowly developed into substantial houses, in the construction of which both stone and brick were used.

THE MIDDLE MINOAN AGE
(2100-1580 B.C.)

Toward the end of the third millennium B.C., Crete came decidedly to the front. This rather marked cultural advance ushers in the Middle Minoan Age, the period of Cretan greatness which apparently was centered at Knossus and Phaestus, where there arose impressive royal palaces with elaborate halls, long corridors, grand stairways, massive colonnades, surprisingly modern drainage systems, and fresco wall decorations depicting both human life and the natural forms of the immediate environment. As the palaces became magnificent, so also the private houses improved in size and structure. Artists and artisans produced remarkably fine works. The potter's wheel, introduced during the previous period, helped the potter to manufacture the famed "Kamares" ware early in the second millennium B.C. This ware, which often has been compared in its eggshell thinness of walls with the best of present-day Haviland china, was decorated in a brilliant harmony of white, crimson, orange, and yellow. From the original pictographic, or hieroglyphic, script, there had developed a linear writing containing about a hundred signs and adapted to writing on clay tablets. Many hundreds of these undeciphered tablets, possibly important government archives, have

Cretan Throne in council room of palace at Knossus was offset by gay frescoes of mythical griffins. (Brown Brothers)

been recovered by the excavators at Knossus.

Shortly before this new script appears, the palaces of Knossus and Phaestus experienced disaster, indicated to the archeologist by a covering layer of ashes. Possibly an earthquake, as well as a revolution, brought about a new dynasty about 1750 B.C., which rebuilt the destroyed areas in a more elaborate manner. The already expansive civilization became even more flourishing. The political power of the state under its king seems to have expanded at this time when invasion and decline occurred in Egypt under the Hyksos. The evidence points to elaborate and increased military and naval equipment. Industry and commerce flourished, and artistic advance toward a new naturalism is noticeable in the several fields of graphic art represented in these early periods.

THE LATE MINOAN AGE
(1580-1400 B.C.)

This cultural swing upward continued in the Late Minoan Age with further elaborate building in the capital cities. The peak may have been reached shortly before this new age began, and when that cultural peak had been reached, and even before, the inevitable decline set in. Creation of new forms and new expressions of cultural expansion are everywhere lacking during this period. The colorful and expressive art of the Middle Minoan Age now becomes merely excessively decorative and baroque.

There seems to be sufficient evidence for a continuing of Cretan development, along the lines already designated above, until shortly after 1500 B.C., when destruction again swept over the cities of Crete. Out of this collapse, only Knossus arose, possibly to become for the first time the supreme ruler over all Crete. Royal control becomes evident in the many discernible phases of Cretan life. There even appears an apparently new royal script, a further development of the linear writing already noted, while the art of this period reflects, with a definite tone, a royal age. Into this late period of Cretan history belong Minos and the empire which is reflected in the early Greek myths which appeared in written form much later. It also is in this period that Cretan imperialism brought its broad cultural outlines to the Grecian Peninsula, and established them in lower Greece, where their transplanted forms comprised the Mycenaean culture, which was significant during the thirteenth and fourteenth centuries B.C.

About 1400 B.C., the entire island of Crete was plundered and ravished. Knossus was sacked and burned, never to rise again. Other island cities suffered the same fate. Crete as a political power ceased to exist. All evidence

Second palace at Knossus. Cretan columns taper from wide, cushion-like capitals to narrow bases

Cupbearer has pinched waist typical of Cretan men. Metal belt may have been riveted on in youth. (The Metropolitan Museum of Art)

points to an invasion of peoples from the mainland, peoples who had in part absorbed something of Cretan culture before they turned upon their teacher and destroyed her. Before we turn our attention to this Greek mainland, we pause to gain an appreciation of certain cultural developments of Cretan civilization, and to note some of the more general cultural contributions which Crete made to later Greece.

CRETAN SOCIAL AND POLITICAL ORGANIZATION

For an appreciation of Cretan social and political developments, one unfortunately is dependent wholly upon a combination of the very uncertain evidence contained in the later Greek myths and epics and the Cretan archeological remains. It seems, however, that Cretan social organization began with the primitive family and clan, and then developed into a town community which was governed by a prince or king. What democratic elements originally had existed vanished during the centuries when centralized authority expanded until an absolute king ruled over a kingdom which extended beyond the borders of Crete. Greek tradition correctly recognized an absolute, all-powerful monarch in this earlier civilization.

The unwalled Cretan cities are evidence that the Cretan rulers must have built and employed a powerful and dominant navy. Within the state, there had been developed a complex, centralized administrative system, as evinced by the material remains of the huge palaces and buildings of state, with their many rooms and storage places. Classes of Cretan society—the wealthy, the proletariat, and the poverty-stricken—all can be identified. Detailed information concerning the colorful clothes worn, especially by the women, is furnished by many fresco paintings, plaques, and statuettes. Women seem to have occupied a much freer position in Cretan society than they did in the later Greek society, and various portrayals show them participating in sports and in the active business and industrial life.

CRETAN INDUSTRY

Quite naturally, the original economy of Crete was agricultural, with varied grains, fruits, and vegetables abundant in a fertile land. Flocks and herds also may be included in the early economy of Crete. However, Cretan pre-eminence was built upon her industry and commerce. In the cities, there grew up industrial quarters where artists and artisans labored to create the products which made Crete famous. Certainly, some of these workers were under direct state control. Potters, stonemasons, carpenters, metalworkers, equipped with tools that appear surprisingly modern, excelled in their respective crafts.

Jewelry-making had become a fine art in Crete. Gold and silver were wrought into exquisite repoussée patterns in cups, or spun into thin beads, employed in contrasting inlays and used for unnumbered ornamental and decorative purposes. Trade extended not only over the island itself, but covered the eastern Mediterranean and Aegean Seas. Cretan

Snake Goddess. Two gold snakes coil around arms of this carved ivory deity. (Museum of Fine Arts, Boston)

Boxing, and Bull Leaping, an acrobatic game, were among the popular sports of Crete in the late Minoan period about 1580–1504 B.C. (Original in Candia Museum)

sailors and Cretan ships were equal or superior to any on the seas during the centuries of Cretan expansion. Even in far away Sicily, Italy, and Spain, there are material evidences of relations with early Crete. Exports from Crete were chiefly manufactured products, but included oil and wine, while the imports seem to have been comprised primarily of base and precious metals so necessary for any civilization.

CRETAN ART

The distinctly artistic trend, which appears in the later Greek peoples, may be linked to the Cretan civilization which we now are considering. If Cretan art is judged upon the basis of our personal, rather arbitrary standards, it probably comes nearer to pleasing us than does the art of any of the other civilizations of the ancient Near East. The Cretans achieved a naturalness and harmoniousness of composition and use of color which has an immediate appeal for one reared in Western traditions.

Cretan art does not interest itself in the colossal, nor is it formalized and stylized as is so much of oriental art. Small figures in stone, ivory, and metal often are the Cretan's artistic gems. His mural painting is superbly done; only the actual scene itself, or a good color plate reproduction, can convey the real beauty of some of these elaborate fresco scenes from the palace of Knossus. The Cretan's subjects show a wide variety, including human beings, animals, flowers, plants and marine subjects characteristic of the sea which so closely surrounds Crete.

Brief statements relative to the variety of the colorful jewelry already have been made, as well as a brief recognition of the unexcelled pottery which these early craftsmen produced. Certainly, the Cretan appreciated the elements of the beautiful, which he managed to develop to a high degree in his culture, and undoubtedly some of these highly artistic accomplishments were transmitted to the Greeks.

CRETAN RELIGION

Cretan religion was as complex as was her civilization, and embraced a number of divergent elements. Gods and spirits were recognized and grouped in categories. A female divinity, very similar in appearance to the Great Mother Goddess, the Fertility Goddess, known in India, Asia Minor, Syria, Palestine and elsewhere in the Near East, was the most important deity. The male god, often associated with the goddess as her husband or son, was considered distinctly inferior. Linked to the goddess and the god were various sacred symbols, such as the pillar and the double axe, and certain sacred animals and birds, such as the lion, bull, snake, and dove. These sacred objects and animals are reflections of diverse, earlier elements in Cretan religion which may point toward fetishism and totemism. The cross, as a sacred symbol, and the sacred number "three," appearing commonly in Cretan Minoan religion, arouse our curiosity. Cretan

Huge, Knobbed Jars in the east storeroom of the palace at Knossus originally held grain, oil, or wine. (Macmillan & Co., Ltd.)

Partridge Fresco, reconstructed from fragments found at Knossus

religious rituals apparently were performed in the open air on altars, or in small shrines within the private houses. Elaborate temples are conspicuous by their absence. Festivals, ceremonies, magical rites, and amulets were all parts of this complicated religion.

Cretan religion also concerned itself with the problems of life after death, and accordingly gave the dead a ritual burial in fine coffins and in cut rock tombs, though the burial customs differed from one culture period to another. In death, the deceased was given elaborate equipment in the way of clothing and all the necessities which the individual had used in life; even figurines of his servants were included, perhaps as an assurance that even after death he would have their customary attentions. Out of some of these tombs come many of the finest objects of Cretan craftsmanship. Final sacrifices were performed at the time of the sealing of the grave, and both food and drink were supplied periodically to the dead. Obviously, these people believed in a life after death, but the details of that belief are still unknown to us.

Cretan Sarcophagus (detail), showing food being brought for dead. (The Metropolitan Museum of Art)

CRETAN INFLUENCE ON GREEK CULTURE

When the Greek invaders swept over the eastern Mediterranean world, Crete also was overrun and her glorious civilization perished. Yet, even though these invaders destroyed much and absorbed the remaining peoples, the culture of Crete was not destroyed in its entirety. Its influences had spread through the eastern Mediterranean area and had become part of the cultures of the peoples there.

In Greece, where our present interest lies, we have noted the relation between the spirit of the Cretan art and the Grecian artistic interests. In religion, the emphasis of the Mother Goddess carried over to the Greeks. Grecian athletics, music, and dances have their Minoan background of sports, notably bull leaping, boxing, theaters, and musical instruments. The chief Grecian festivals have their origins in the pre-Greek ages. A relationship exists between the technical and industrial development of the Cretan-Mycenaean world and those of later Greece, despite the centuries of disorder and decay which lie in between. With a broad appreciation of Cretan culture, we now direct our attention to the mainland of Greece.

7. The First Stages of Greek Development

IMPORTANT FACTORS IN GREEK CULTURE

THE history of ancient Crete, which has been summarized in the preceding pages, constitutes an early chapter of the captivating "Story of Man." As one turns from this intriguing and highly significant epoch of man's development to the next, one must turn to consider the peoples of areas farther west, who have received relatively little attention in the foregoing narrative. Greece and Rome, respectively, became the next centers of civilization. Just how great a debt the classical cultures of Greece and Rome owe to their oriental predecessors cannot be ascertained at the present stage of our knowledge; certainly, the debt is a very great one.

One should recall, particularly in connection with the cultures of Greece, the apt statement that "geography is latent history." Certainly, the physical features of any given area are related significantly to the development of the history of that area. We have seen that the Egyptians and Babylonians had need of cooperation between the several communities for the very regulation of the river waters and canal systems. Greece, however, was divided by natural barriers—islands, harbors, and mountains—into many distinct sections which practically precluded any unity among the several groups, thus giving rise to a strong individualism. The Greeks were dependent upon their own resources in securing a meager living from a land never too fertile. Fruits, vegetables, and grains all needed attention if the yield was to be at all satisfactory. The sea, which was near at hand in every part of Greece, provided a convenient means of intercourse and travel, with the better harbors on the east and thus facing the Aegean Islands and the Orient. The lands of Greece were rich in building stones, including the best of marbles; gold, silver, copper and iron were found in limited quantities; but tin, essential for the making of bronze, was missing entirely. A more vigorous climate than that experienced by most of her oriental neighbors helped to create the daring spirit characteristic of her people; and the colorful, varied, and inspiring scenery of the country may well have added a dignity to the virile spirit of the Greeks as graphically portrayed by the later artists and poets.

Greece had long centuries of Stone Age development, which were relatively crude, giving little promise of developing into something significant in terms of world culture. As we already have seen, an important and brilliant culture had been developed to the south of the Greek mainland, on the island of Crete and the neighboring Aegean Islands. This Cretan culture, an oriental culture which retained some native features, had developed and flourished for a number of centuries without having any appreciable influence upon the people of the Greek mainland, lying less than a hundred miles to the northwest. Then, shortly after 1500 B.C., Cretan culture—transplanted as Mycenaean culture—began its short but significant development on the mainland, especially in the Peloponnesus, and on the plain of Argos at Mycenae and Tiryns.

MYCENAEAN CULTURE

Mycenae, the traditional city of Agamemnon, the hero who led the Greek forces against the Trojans, now rose to prominence with mighty walls and impregnable fortifications. The massive Lion-Gate at Mycenae remained, until the excavator uncovered it, a symbol of power. Tiryns today has walls which in some places are fifty-seven feet thick. In central Greece, Orchomenos came to be an influential center of the Mycenaean culture, the culture which spread rapidly over Greece to the adjoining islands of the Aegean Sea and the coast of Asia Minor during the fourteenth century B.C.

For the relatively brief span of its existence, Mycenaean civilization was prosperous and productive. Industry and trade flourished. Artisans and artists continued the Cretan traditions. The royal graves at Mycenae contained a wealth of materials— rings, buckles, bracelets, crowns, face masks, cups, toilet equipment—all of yellow gold, and many other artistic objects which constitute mute evidence of the richness of the culture. From the tomb at Vaphio come the two superbly wrought

Perseus, legendary king of Tiryns

cups with hammered reliefs, artistic creations which are practically in a class by themselves. It was a golden age, but here also decline set in amid the splendor. Creativeness seems to have vanished, and writing was much more rare than in Crete. The emphasis upon fortifications and weapons was indicative of the impending catastrophe. Invaders had been pushing for centuries into Greece; they brought not only destruction and chaos, but also a new age.

INDO-EUROPEAN INVADERS

Northern Greece, for the present, is the center of our interest rather than the Mycenaean area of southern Greece, subject to the influences from Crete. Into the broad area of northern Greece, the cultural influence from the eastern Mediterranean penetrated but slowly. However, the traders gradually brought a few of the products of higher cul-

Gate of Lions at Mycenae, built about 1200 B.C., is the entrance to the royal grave circle. Carved center column is a cult object

tures to the backward natives along the water routes of the north. Perhaps most significant was the introduction of the simple uses of copper, which reached southern Europe about 3000 B.C., though it did not come to be used commonly for tools and weapons before 2000 B.C. The discovery of tin in Bohemia, at the end of the third millennium B.C., gave impetus to the development of a bronze culture which spread widely in Europe.

Such was the general stage of European cultural advance when certain significant movements of peoples were noticeable in southern Europe, extending through the Balkan states eastward into southern Russia. While larger numbers of Indo-Europeans were moving into western Asia, related tribes were moving westward around the Black Sea and then south toward Greece proper. The earliest groups, migrating with their families and transporting their possessions in crude horse-drawn carts, moved into northern Greece around 2000 B.C. Unable to write, possessing few elements of culture, but having developed and acquired good weapons, they moved into the outskirts of the cultured eastern Mediterranean world, under the influence of which they were to go forth toward the creation of a civilization and culture grander and more refined than any that had ever preceded it.

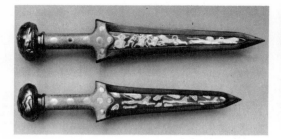

Damascened Daggers show Mycenaean lion hunt. Elongated animals fit perfectly into design of blade. (The Metropolitan Museum of Art)

Vaphio Cup, made of hammered gold, depicts bull hunting. Here the trapper hobbles a captured bull. (The Metropolitan Museum of Art)

Small tribes and groups of tribes continued their penetration of Greece, sometimes amid fierce conflict and sometimes incurring little opposition as they selected the sites for their new homes. It is reasonable to believe that by 1500 B.C. the Indo-European groups had taken over most of Greece, but their migration and settlement certainly had modified their racial characteristics. In fact, history knows of no pure races. The newcomers, mixed and blended with the natives, were continually joined by new invaders; and this blending of diverse racial stocks through a number of centuries ultimately produced the people known to us as the classical Greeks. Perhaps partly because the Indo-Europeans were the dominant people, their language became the common tongue, even though many place names did remain current and a few of the words of the older culture were taken over by the newcomers. Aeolians,

Boar Hunt, from a fresco found at Tiryns. Dressed in a short tunic, a hunter restrains his eager dog. (The Metropolitan Museum of Art)

Arcadians, Ionians, and Achaeans are numbered among the early tribes inhabiting Greece.

As ever more groups pressed into the Greek mainland, some of the more adventurous pushed out to the islands. As Achaean chieftains, they had settled in the fortresses of Tiryns and Mycenae. As already noted, Crete was raided about 1400 B.C., and the great city of Knossus fell before the rapacious newcomers. Cretan civilization never recovered. The old and wearied Orient also was to feel the fresh invaders' strength; the coasts of Asia Minor, Syria, Palestine, and Egypt were plundered during the thirteenth and twelfth centuries. The Achaean chieftains accomplished the destruction of the ancient city of Troy; other Indo-European warriors brought about the fall of the Hittite Empire in central Asia Minor, and almost destroyed the Empire in Egypt. The Aegean territories, renowned in Homer's immortal epic, definitely came to be under Indo-European control.

However, still one more wave of invaders was to flow over this peninsula, now become Greek, before a measure of peace was to be restored. Again from the north, but primarily along the western coast, these Indo-European invaders, the Dorians, moved in during the twelfth and eleventh centuries. Chaos followed: Tiryns and Mycenae were burned, and with them were lost important cultural advances which were not to be equaled by the Greeks for centuries to come. However, by 1000 B.C., the Dorian movement of peoples had spent itself and Greece was now settled by the *Greeks*.

Because of the insufficient archeological materials and the uncertain tales and legends of later authors, the history of this early period is difficult to reconstruct. Centuries of migration and conflict, of destruction and neglect by the new settlers of the cultural advances made by the preceding inhabitants, characterized the several migrations of the Indo-Europeans as they moved in upon a native stock which in all probability comprised a part of the large Mediterranean group. Out of this admixture of peoples came the classical Greek peoples; and while the opening of the first millennium B.C. saw the end of invasions from outside, peace was not to be the lot of these Greeks, whose particular characteristics were forged in the heat of strife. The next four hundred years also were years of conflict, from which emerged the several city-states, whose history was to be the history of Greece itself.

It is possible to relate with some certainty how the Greek peoples lived and organized their tribes after they settled in the country. Our information is supplied partly from the attempts of later historians to reconstruct their past, partly from the surviving elements of their cultural development as retained in later political institutions, and partly from their customs, interests, and prejudices as depicted in the Homeric poems.

Long after these people had taken possession of Greece, they remained seminomadic, tending flocks and herds. The basis of their social organization was the family, with its patriarch or chief. As the numbers of the new settlers increased, families came to be grouped as tribes, which created the possibility for the more powerful chief to assume the importance of a *king*, who was the leader in times of war, judge of all the members of the tribe, and the high priest for all ceremonial rites. A *council* of old men, often jealous of the king's position and power, consulted with the king in matters of tribal policy. In these councils, one sees the origins of the ruling bodies of later aristocracies. Sometimes an *assembly*, of all weapon-bearing men of the tribe, was held either for a feast or in order to get an expression of their opinion upon some important proposition, such as the waging of a war. In this gathering of the *assembly* lay the germ of democracy, which was to grow and ripen at a later time. However, the tendency of the time was to ignore the influence of the large assembly and to emphasize the interests of the aristocracy.

The Greek nomads, or wanderers, slowly became Greek farmers; but naturally the old interests and customs did not change quickly, and for a long time herds comprised the most valuable possessions. But as these nomads settled in communities, villages grew up. Nor was it long before certain ones of these small villages experienced a more rapid growth than others, thus becoming cities which incorporated the smaller villages of the immediate, surrounding territory. This development was perhaps the most significant in governmental arrangement ever made by the Greek, for his entire political life came to be centered in the *city-state*.

Originally, each city-state was independent, concerning itself with the regulation of the affairs of its citizens, developing laws to control their endeavors and relationships, and establishing formal relations with other groups within, or even outside of, Greece. The government of such a city rested with its king and council. If the king was powerful and wealthy, he erected for himself a fortified castle, often known as a citadel or acropolis. If the city prospered, it surrounded itself with a wall for protection from its neighbors who might envy its prosperity and attempt to plunder it. Thus, quite slowly, Greece and her islands became organized along the lines of small independent cities, generally based upon family or tribal relationships, by turn friendly and hostile to neighboring cities, and developing a distinct culture.

COMMERCE AND CULTURE

It also should be noted that important cultural influences were coming into Greece from the outside during this period of the development of the city-states, influences which helped and directed the slowly forming Greek culture. Iron technology, developed by the Hittites shortly before the destruction of their empire by the Indo-Europeans, had become familiar to the Greeks by 1000 B.C. The col-

Historical and Mythological Map of Ancient Greece

1. Birthplace of Aristotle, 384 B.C.
2. Polygnotus, famous Greek painter, born here fifth century B.C.
3. The empire of Alexander perished in this battle 155 years after his death.
4. From this summit Poseidon surveyed the plain of Troy.
5. At near by Libethrum, Orpheus lived.

6. Mt. Olympus, home of the gods.
7. The most ancient oracle in Greece, dedicated to Zeus.
8. The Aloidae attempted to pile Mt. Pelion upon Mt. Ossa to storm heaven itself.
9. Home of Scyllis who dived to the bottom of every sea and taught his daughter Cyana to dive.

These two helped wreck Xerxes' fleet off Mt. Pelion by loosening the anchors from below.
10. Darius' expedition of 492 B.C. ended by the wreck of his fleet in a storm off this point.
11. Leander swam the Hellespont nightly to visit Hero.
12. Anaxagoras (exiled from Athens), died here, 428 B.C.

13. Xerxes' bridge of boats over the Hellespont.

14. Hellespont named for Helle who fell from the ram with golden fleece and was drowned.

15. Burial mound of Achilles honored by Alexander as first act of his invasion of Asia.

16. Thymbra, 546 B.C.; Cyrus defeated Croesus in a "model" battle here which influenced tactics of Scipio and Napoleon.

17. Hephaestus, god of fire, fell here when hurled down from Olympus. The Argonauts found here only women who had murdered all their husbands.

18. The Greeks withdrew here to induce the Trojans to receive the wooden horse.

19. After Plato's death, Aristotle taught here and married Hermias' adopted daughter.

20. Home of Arion, lyric poet.

21. Birthplace of Theophrastus, successor to Aristotle.

22. Here was the cave of the centaur, Chiron, who taught Asclepius, god of medicine, and other heroes.

23. Home of Achilles.

24. Octavian's victory over fleet of Antony and Cleopatra, 31 B.C.

25. Sappho, because of her unrequited love for Phaon, is said to have leaped into the sea from this rock.

26. Poisoned by blood of Nessus, Heracles came here to die on a great pyre.

27. Thermopylae; heroic defense of Leonidas with 300 Spartans against the army of Xerxes, 480 B.C.

28. Poseidon lived here in the depths of the sea.

29. Achilles sent by his mother to court of Lycomedes disguised as a maiden to prevent his going to Trojan War. Lycomedes treacherously killed Theseus whose bones were returned to Athens by Cimon, 469 B.C.

30. Home of Corycian nymphs. Landing place of Deucalion, the Greek Noah.

31. Theban sphinx.

32. Celebrated as birthplace of Odysseus.

33. Heracles fought Achelous, the river god, for possession of Deianira.

34. Destroyed Pisa near Olympia to maintain its control of the olympics. All contestants forced to train here one month. School of Phaedo.

35. Oracle of Apollo.

36. Oracle of Trophonius.

37. Home of the Muses.

38. Spartan power ended with victory of Epaminondas, 371 B.C.

39. Heracles destroyed Erymanthian boar.

40. Tomb of Alcmaeon.

41. Apelles, who painted Alexander the Great, studied here.

42. Actaeon changed to stag by Artemis and killed by own dogs.

43. Marathon, 490 B.C.

44. Home of Thespis, father of Greek tragedy.

45. Glaucus of Chios invented iron-welding, seventh century B.C. Birthplace of Theopompus. Claims of Chios and Smyrna to Homer seem most plausible.

46. Under Polycrates the Samian navy ruled the waves, sixth century B.C. Birthplace of Pythagoras and Epicurus, and according to tradition, of Hera.

47. Helen landed after fall of Troy.

48. A Cean law prohibited a citizen prolonging his life beyond 60.

49. Here Odysseus found his mares.

50. Birthplace of Hermes.

51. Home of Perseus and Andromeda. Heracles brought up here.

52. Xenophon wrote "Anabasis" here.

53. Of all cities on earth Lycosura is oldest. The rest of mankind learned to build cities on its model—"Pausanias."

54. Home of Polybius and of Philopoemen, last hero of ancient Greece.

55. Here Heracles slew the Hydra.

56. Tegea—one of the oldest Greek cities. Women of Tegea assisting in battle routed Spartans (by surprise attack).

57. Home of Theseus. Legend of Hippolytus.

58. Demosthenes took poison in Temple of Poseidon and died 322 B.C.

59. Therapnae, near Sparta, famed in mythology as birthplace of Dioscuri.

60. 292 Spartans taken prisoners by Athenians who had always regarded a Spartan surrender as inconceivable, 425 B.C.

61. Founded by Lacedaemon, son of Zeus, who married Sparta and named the city for her.

62. On the island of Cranaei, Paris first embraced Helen after carrying her off.

63. Perseus turned Polydectes and his court to stone with the head of the Gorgon, Medusa. Roman emperors exiled state criminals here.

64. Parian chronicle, now among Arundel marbles at Oxford, found here, 1627.

65. Smallest but most famous of Cyclades, Delos drifted about until moored by Zeus for the birthplace of Apollo and Artemis. Became seat of worship of Apollo. Sacked by Menophanes, 87 B.C.

66. Famous gold and silver mines.

67. Famous Parian marble quarries.

68. Here Dionysus found Ariadne asleep on the shore.

69. Invaded 416 B.C. by Athenians who killed all adult males, sold the women and children as slaves, and planted an Athenian colony.

70. Returning from Troy, Odysseus met with violent winds here. Driven before them for nine days, he arrived at the land of lotus eaters.

71. According to some traditions, Aphrodite here emerged from the sea.

72. Originated from clod of earth, given to Argonauts by Triton. Cyrene in Africa colonized from here by Battus, 631 B.C.

73. Knossus, first large city of Europe. 80,000 estimated population in 15th century B.C. Palace of Minos was first real architecture in northern Mediterranean. Daedalus built the labyrinth here where Theseus slew the Minotaur.

74. In a cave here the infant Zeus was hidden from Cronus and tended by the Curetes.

75. Crete, center of great Aegean civilization that flourished here 2000 to 1400 B.C. A brilliant chapter of history uncovered by the spades of Sir Arthur Evans, and other 20th century investigators.

76. Zeus, taking the form of a bull, brought Europa here from Phoenicia. She became the mother of Minos. Gortyna's famous legal code, longest existing Greek inscription, was found here (in a mill stream).

Glorification of Homer. The relief was probably dedicated by a poet who had won a contest, and had derived his inspiration from Homer. Zeus and the Muses are shown upon a mountainside at the top. Below is Apollo in a cave. On the right is the poet. In the lowest row, Homer is enthroned between figures of the Iliad and Odyssey and is being crowned by Time and the World. Myth, History, Poetry, Tragedy, and Comedy make an offering before him. (British Museum)

dazzling merchandise, the Phoenicians brought to the Greeks that most significant contribution, the alphabet.

A millennium earlier, the Semitic people in the Sinaitic Peninsula, south of Palestine, had adapted from the Egyptian hieroglyphic writing twenty-two signs or letters. This entirely new system of writing spread rapidly among the Semitic peoples, and within a very few centuries came to be used widely among the Phoenicians. Somewhere around 1000 B.C., this alphabet was introduced to the Greeks. All of the Phoenician letters were consonants, an awkward arrangement which the Greeks changed by introducing vowels. Also, with the alphabet came an Egyptian writing material called papyrus, which served as paper, and pen and ink.

HOMER—BARD OF THE GREEKS

As the activities, interests, and tastes of the Greeks expanded, wealth in material possessions came at least to a few, who soon became concerned with adequate means by which to protect such wealth. Armies and armor acquired a greater importance. The conflicts that followed, along with other consequences, as they became expressed in attitudes, desires, social relationships, tastes, interests, and endeavors, came not only to be described in poetry but also depicted on vases and household articles. Most significant of this early period are the epic poems attributed to Homer, whom tradition places somewhere between 900 and 850 B.C. We read in Homer's *Iliad* that the Trojan prince Paris, son of King Priam, visited Greece, abducted Helen, the wife of Menelaus, and returned with his beautiful captive to Troy. Menelaus was the brother of Agamemnon, powerful king of Mycenae, who immediately gained support from most of the princes of Greece for an expedition to recover Helen and avenge the wrong. The Greeks gathered their fleets and with Agamemnon at their head sailed for Troy, where they besieged the city for nine years. Included in the group were Achilles of the vulnerable heel and Odysseus, king of distant Ithaca, whose travels after the fall of Troy formed the substance of Homer's *Odyssey*.

lapse of the Cretan and Egyptian empires had given the trade of the Mediterranean to the Phoenicians, who were located in a strategic area on the Syrian coast. As soon after the Indo-European invasion as some semblance of order had been established in Greek lands, the ambitious Phoenician merchants sailed into Greek waters, bringing the varied products of older civilizations. Thus, the Greeks came to wear colorful, woven robes, decorate their persons with jewelry of silver and gold, anoint themselves with perfumes and fill their crude dwellings with accouterments strange to their interests and modes of living. Along with

The Gods descend from Olympus to battle for Troy, in a scene from the Iliad

Thetis entreating Jupiter to honor Achilles

The Reunion of Andromache and Hector

Diomed casting his spear against Mars

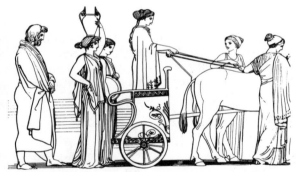

Nausicäa leading Ulysses into the city

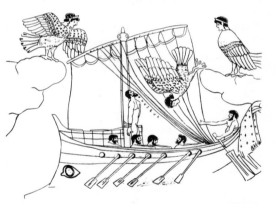

Bound to the mast, Ulysses resists the Sirens

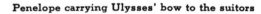

Penelope carrying Ulysses' bow to the suitors

Ulysses killing Penelope's suitors. (Drawings by John Flaxman)

The Elopement of Helen in the chariot of Paris. Paris wears the charioteer's lappeted cap and trousers. (Metropolitan Museum of Art)

Priam also had his allies and the war continued with no real result until the tenth year when the Greeks pretended to sail away. Then occurred the renowned incident of the wooden horse. The Trojans dragged it into the city and at night Greeks who had been hidden inside opened the gates of Troy to their returning comrades. Troy was demolished, the war was over, and Helen was restored to her husband.

It seems certain that Homer drew, for his materials, from a number of older tales and legends; yet he managed to combine them with such masterful skill that these two poems came to be very significant factors in the develop-

ment of Greek culture and civilization. They came to comprise the "bible" of the Greeks, dictating the patterns and boundaries of much of their imaginative thought, the values to be most highly esteemed by respected members of the tribe, and the conduct to be expected of the aristocracy of the city-states. Thus, Homer cast the mold for all the Greek gods, who largely were patterned after those of the incoming Indo-Europeans. The Greek gods differed from men only in their superior stature, accomplishments, pleasures, dwelling places, and lives of ease; they needed sleep, suffered pain, made mistakes, indulged in hatreds, and gave unabashed expression to their lusts and desires. And because these altogether human gods were a little superior to man, and more capable than he was, they constituted the ideals of the Greeks and at the same time encouraged a certain dignity among the Greeks in the face of inevitable failure to achieve the imagined human perfection exemplified by them.

CENTRALIZATION AND TYRANNY

Along with the expansion of trade, increasing exploitation of the natural resources of defenseless peoples, and growth of military power, the strongest city-states gradually absorbed their weaker neighbors. This absorp-

At a Council on Mount Olympus the gods decide that war shall continue between Greece and Troy. Jupiter sits upon a golden throne, while Hebe (holding the pitcher) serves nectar in cups of gold. (Drawing by John Flaxman)

Jason and the Argonauts, who sailed with him in the ship, Argo, to Colchis in search of the golden fleece, an amulet thought to possess magic powers

tion followed the natural geographical divisions of the country, as determined by the sea, mountains and rivers.Within the Peloponnesus, the southern portion of Greece proper, the topographical features of the country led to the creation of two major city-states. The first to rise was Argos in the north, while Sparta in the south gradually absorbed her neighbors and built a small kingdom. In the Attic Peninsula, to the north, Athens gradually came to control the entire area. Farther north, the Boeotian League was formed with Thebes as the center. The city-state principle remained operative in all these newly-created states.

Simultaneously with the struggle of the city-states for more power, territory, and wealth, came the increased and unified efforts of the common people for more equitable rights and a more satisfactory living. This struggle, beginning in the eighth century B.C., continued until some semblance of democracy was realized throughout the major part of Greece. Opposition to this demand of the people by the king, his council of equals, and the nobles had grown with the increase of wealth and expansion of power. They had used their more fortunate positions to build up large estates, frequently at the expense of the poor peasant, who saw himself slipping into a more desperate situation with the ultimate prospect of soon losing his small farm and becoming a day laborer or slave. The original assembly of free men had degenerated until it no longer had any sig-

nificance. Thus it came about that the office of the king had disappeared gradually by 650 B.C. In some cases, the king's removal was violent; however, in most states, his powers were taken from him gradually by the nobles, who apportioned such powers among the individuals of their own class. Sparta invented the interesting innovation of two kings. In neither situation, however, was the popular unrest appeased, and the Greeks soon knew that the nobles could be as offensive and abusive as the kings.

COMMERCE AND COLONIZATION

These oppressive internal conditions induced many Greeks to seek new homes outside of Greece proper. Greeks not only had learned the Phoenician alphabet, but also they

Lady of Elche, found in Spain, shows Spanish and Phoenician influences on Greek art. (Art Institute of Chicago)

had learned readily the techniques of a trader and set sail upon the Aegean, Mediterranean, and Black seas. Trading posts had been established and regular traffic begun. To the oppressed and impoverished Greek peasants and small merchants, the broad expanses of fertile, unoccupied, or thinly settled lands near these trading posts seemed highly desirable.

From 750 to 600 B.C., a steady stream of Greeks poured out to the several areas of Greek trade. The Black Sea shore line was dotted with colonies. The coast of Asia Minor, already strongly Greek, became solidly Greek. The islands of the eastern Mediterranean, Egypt, and northern Africa received large numbers of colonists. In the western Mediterranean, Greek colonists became a most significant factor in the development of a new culture, that of the later Roman state. Greeks settled in southern Italy, occupied most of Sicily, and established substantial settlements on the coasts of Spain and France.

For a time, the colonization movement alleviated the pressure within Greece. They removed thousands of people and relieved the overcrowded farms, while the needs of the Greek colonists brought an increase of manufacturing and commerce to the cities of Greece proper. The colonies opened new markets for the homeland, comprising both themselves and the new territories which they exploited, with the important result that raw products and especially grain, so sorely needed, came to Greece in unprecedented quantities and variety.

Athens, the future leader of Greece, became commercially important much later than many of the other Greek city-states. The land belonging to Athens, known as Attica, was not particularly fertile, with the result that Athens had little to export. Finally, however, Athens did develop pottery-making into a fine art, and her wares have been found scattered over the

Called "the owl," this four drachma piece was used as money in 6th century Athens

Mediterranean world. In her vases, Athens exported olive oil and wine, and her ships in return brought the several raw materials and foodstuffs she desired. Soon Athens began to surpass most of her rivals in trade and industry.

Expanding foreign trade created a keen interest in shipbuilding. The shipyards began to produce much larger, sail-driven ships, so large that they no longer could be drawn up on the beach but required harbors where they might be anchored. Then a large merchant marine necessitated a navy to protect it, and warships with decks and oar benches constructed in three superimposed tiers set a new style for ships of combat.

Also, another useful invention was brought to the Greeks as the result of an expanding commerce. From Lydia in Asia Minor, coined money was introduced into Greece shortly after 700 B.C. While the Babylonians and Assyrians had used metals, often stamped or cast into definite pieces, many centuries before this time, they never had grasped the full possibility of this technique, and thus the credit for the invention of coinage generally is given to the Lydians. The Greek traders quickly appreciated the benefits to commerce of a piece of precious metal stamped by the state with weight and value, and the coin which came to be most popular in Athens was the silver *drachma*, a coin not quite as valuable as an American quarter in actual silver content, yet because of an entirely different relation between silver and commodities, a *drachma* might buy a sheep, or five such coins could be traded for an ox.

BENEVOLENT "TYRANTS"

With actual money in use, wealth needed no longer to be counted in actual possessions of land and cattle. Moneyed wealth came into being, and brought complicated problems of finance and business. Gradually, a new class of men appeared in the structure of Greek society, the well-to-do business men, who formed a middle class between the nobles and the peasants. But this new social development did not aid the peasant. On the contrary, it seemed only to push him farther into poverty and increase his ultimate burdens. The peasant farmowner seemed doomed to extinction, and he either sank into apathy or began to threaten revolt. However, this state of affairs brought to the fore a number of men, generally of noble birth, who championed the peasants' cause, and thus gaining their support seized control of the state. These rulers, who were called "tyrants" merely because they had obtained extra-legal power in this manner, and not necessarily with any odium implied by the name, were well liked generally, and exerted themselves in behalf of more equitable rights for the peasants. Those few "tyrants" who were hated were soon assassinated. However, the "tyrants" generally interested themselves in improving their cities and often patronized the arts.

8. Development and Decline of the Greek City-States

As our narrative approaches the year 600 B. C., the chronicle of events becomes more precise and more consistently connected. With more available facts, our history becomes both more accurate and more complicated. However, it is quite possible to gain a satisfactory appreciation of Greek history for the next several hundred years by focusing one's attention upon the two important rival states, Sparta and Athens.

Each state claimed to represent a different branch of the Greek racial stock: Sparta was Dorian while Athens was Ionian. As time went on, each asserted leadership over different parts of Greece, Sparta in the Peloponnesus and Athens both in central Greece and the Aegean Islands. The rivalry thus begun led to that prolonged and bitter struggle known in history as the Peloponnesian War.

During the period which followed the Dorian invasion of the Peloponnesus, a small district in the southern part of the peninsula under Dorian control came to be known as Sparta. Surrounded by pre-Dorian peoples, partly independent and partly under Spartan rule, the recent arrivals began the creation of a state which admitted to full citizenship only the limited few who belonged to the tribe. Spartan citizens were forbidden even to intermarry with other classes or tribes. Then, below the Spartan citizens, and yet living within the communities, were the *perioeci*, the mixed population of workmen: artisans and traders who were neither citizens nor slaves, but free men heavily taxed. Below the *perioeci* were the mass of people, enslaved by the dominant Spartans, who were called *helots*, and composed mostly of serfs working the farms for their Spartan masters. These serfs, or *helots*, were the most downtrodden of all the Greeks and frequently revolted.

After long years of bitter struggle, the small Spartan state conquered her immediate neighbor, Messenia, and then gradually increased her power and possessions. Before 500 B.C., Sparta forced the remaining states of the Peloponnesus into a league dominated and utilized chiefly for her own interests and gain. Then, realizing that she was hopelessly outnumbered by her subjects, Sparta turned to a rigorous policy of military training; she deserted all personal interests and became a military encampment with a secret police to aid in the continuance of her rule over unwilling peoples. In government also, she followed unusual lines suggested by her particular military and political needs. Sparta had inherited, possibly from an early union of two tribal groups, two kings who were leaders in war and the priests in charge of the religious ceremonies. Judicial and legislative power resided in the council of twenty-eight elders chosen for life from among the nobles. The assembly of citizens approved or disapproved the propositions of the council. Five *Ephors*, administrative officials originally of minor importance, came into actual control of the state in the sixth century B.C.

With such an emphasis upon the military interests of the state, the entire cultural development of Sparta was retarded. Through seeming necessity, trade and manufacture were discouraged, since all able men were needed for the militia. Thus, Sparta measured wealth in terms of land and serfs, long after a money economy was established elsewhere in Greece. Her foreign relationships outside the Peloponnesus were relatively few, and were restricted primarily because of her narrow view, concerned largely with the preservation of things

Gods at Presentation of Veil to Athena, from Parthenon frieze depicting the birth of the goddess. (Art Institute of Chicago)

as they were. While Spartan courage and discipline have become proverbial, one is not attracted particularly by Sparta's rather barren civilization which had such a one-sided emphasis.

ATHENIAN DEMOCRACY AND TYRANNY

The political development of Athens, down to about 600 B.C., had followed pretty much the normal lines already described. Her executive officers, three in number, performed the functions of priest, judge, and military leader, respectively. As elsewhere, a council exercised most of the actual power, while an assembly of citizens had only a nominal voice in elections and state policies.

The poverty of the masses and the general unrest brought about various social disturbances which resulted in the codification of Athenian law by Draco about 625 B.C. While rather harsh, it did fix a standard by which decisions were to be rendered; on the other hand, it made no effort to relieve the economic pressure or reform the constitution. These problems were faced some few years later, by Solon, who was elected one of the officers of

the state and entrusted with the problems of adjusting the lot of the poor and oppressed peasants. The reforms which he instituted fall naturally into two categories: economic and political. In order to relieve the economic pressure, he cancelled the debt of the enslaved peasants and declared future enslavement for debt to be illegal. He further limited the amount of land which might be held by a noble, forbade the spending of exorbitant amounts for funerals, prohibited the export of all home products except olive oil, and finally made definite provisions for the encouragement of trades and professions. Solon's political reforms aimed at a more just balance of power between the nobility and the growing middle class; and while he increased the number of citizens eligible to sit in the Assembly, the right to hold office was reserved only for the wealthier, higher classes of citizens. A new council of four hundred was created to assist the Assembly in its business. A new code of laws was developed and popular courts established for a better administration of justice. Aside from these significant accomplishments, Solon also was instrumental in arousing his people to a consciousness of the need and value of sea power.

Patroness of Athens, Athena wears the aegis adorned with a Medusa head. (Art Institute of Chicago)

The Athenian Democracy, despite the beneficial accomplishments of Solon, was not yet to attain success. During Solon's absence, one of the able Athenian aristocrats managed to acquire power and local support sufficient to install himself as "tyrant" of Athens about 570 B.C. Pisistratus ruled with energy and good sense. He quickly saw that Athens needed a dependable supply of grain, such as came from the Black Sea region, and that, by furthering Athenian control in the Hellespont, the assur-

The Acropolis of Athens, as it looks today. Center is the Erechtheum; right the Parthenon

ance of this grain supply would be achieved. He exploited the silver mines of Attica and reached out to the gold mines of Thrace. At home, he encouraged agriculture and especially the cultivation of olive trees, by making state loans to small farmers. Artisans and craftsmen from other cities were welcomed to Athens, and his encouragement of building and support of the local festivals raised him in popular esteem. By the time of his death, Pisistratus had laid the foundations upon which much of the later greatness of Athens was to be built. His sons, despite their good intentions and abilities, did not win Athenian support. One was assassinated, and the other finally was obliged to flee. Thus, shortly before 500 B.C., Athens was freed from her tyrants.

The popular cause of the peasants was taken up by another noble, Clisthenes. His rather complicated reforms included a reorganization of the voting system, and a weakening of the formerly supreme powers of the old council of the nobles. He gained for the people the right to banish, by vote once a year, any person from the state for a period of ten years, a power which at a later time was not always used wisely.

Already during the latter part of the tyranny, Sparta had intervened in Athenian affairs, and during the following years the rivalry and disputes between these two states, both Greek, yet in so many ways very different, continued to increase until the great conflict broke out between them. Athens, with the reforms of

Tower of the Winds, Athens. Each of the eight sides faces the points of the compass and the frieze represents each of the eight principal winds

Solon and Clisthenes, had taken significant steps toward real democracy. However, before we can follow the fortunes of Athens in this direction, it is necessary to review briefly the Graeco-Persian conflicts, so important in the growth of western civilization.

RISE OF THE PERSIAN EMPIRE

While the Greeks were developing slowly and painfully their unique civilization in the West, a related Indo-European people had pushed its way around the distant Caspian Sea. These hordes were the Persians who, through a series of remarkable campaigns, made themselves masters of the entire oriental world before the close of the sixth century B.C. In the process of their rapid expansion, they absorbed

the Lydian Empire in Asia Minor and took over the political control of the coast, which was dotted with independent or semi-independent Greek cities. In many ways, these Greek cities had surpassed those of the mainland in wealth, culture, and accomplishments. Out of this Asia Minor territory came such great figures as Thales, student of astronomy, mathematics, and philosophy; Pythagoras, mathematician, scientist, and philosopher; Hecataeus the historian; Alcaeus and Sappho, renowned for their love lyrics.

These flourishing Asia Minor centers of Greek life suddenly were made subject to the Persian king, who crossed over to Europe and, in his insatiable desire for more conquests and lands, fought against the Scythians in the region of the Danube River. Darius' failure to achieve real success in this campaign, together with the intrigue and support coming from the Greek mainland, induced the Greeks of Asia Minor, the Ionians as they were called, to revolt in 499 B.C. During the futile five-year struggle, the Athenians sent twenty ships to aid the Ionians. When the revolt had been quelled, Darius the great Persian king saw in the Athenian help an excuse for further conquest and expansion of his empire so as to include also Greece.

GREEK VICTORY AT MARATHON

To this end, his first invasion of Greece was undertaken in 492 by both land and sea. The Persian fleet followed along the shore line from the Hellespont, by the way of Thrace, down to Greece. However, the fleet was wrecked just off Mt. Athos, and had to return for repairs; because of this, the land force also was withdrawn. Two years later, the Persian fleet, enlarged and carrying an army in transport ships, sailed across the Aegean and landed in Attica, at the Bay of Marathon, only a few miles from Athens. Prior to this, Persian aggression in Asia Minor and the earlier advance into Greece had caused considerable confusion and excitement among the several Greek states, which now wavered between desertion to the Persian cause, flight, or cooperative effort against the invaders. Athens, almost entirely deserted by the rest of the Greek

"The Discus Thrower" of the 5th century B. C.

states, faced the Persian army on the plain of Marathon and gained a real victory against overwhelming odds. Then, when the commander of the Persian transport troops sailed around the Attic Peninsula and appeared before the port of Athens, he found it useless to attempt to land, for the victorious Athenians were already encamped beside the city. Accordingly, the Persians retired; the courage and stout hearts of the Athenians had gained a victory long to be recounted in song and literature. More significant, they thus had achieved a new spirit which was to help lift Athens, and Greece with her, to new heights of culture.

The Persians had withdrawn, but had not relinquished their projected conquest and subjugation of Greece. The death of Darius and the accession of Xerxes gave a brief respite to the Greeks. The ten years between 490 and 480 were years of conflict and jealousy within Greece, severely handicapping the preparation for the inevitable conflict with Persia by a failure to agree upon any definite plan. However, when the Persian engineers began cutting a canal behind the Mt. Athos promontory, so that the next Persian fleet might be spared the dangers of the open waters off the point,

Themistocles, the new Athenian leader, was able to persuade the Athenians to build a great fleet of one hundred and eighty fighting ships. It was planned that with this fleet the Persians might be attacked, and if defeated the land forces could then be cut off from supplies. Also, a land battle was to be avoided while the Persian army was to be delayed as long as possible in the northern passes which could be defended with relatively few men. However, the attempt to enlist all the Greek states for this campaign failed; Sparta could be induced to cooperate only upon the basis that she be given command.

The Marathon Race in the Olympic games honored Phidippedes, who ran to Athens to announce the victory at Marathon, then dropped dead

THERMOPYLAE AND THE END OF PERSIAN MENACE

In the summer of 480, the Persian army and fleet moved slowly down upon upper Greece; the first resistance was encountered at the pass of Thermopylae where the Spartan king Leonidas was in command.

The Spartans fought courageously until taken from the rear by picked Persian troops, but the supporting Persian ships were destroyed and driven back by a storm before the Greek navy could engage them in battle. The main army of the Spartans and their allies held the Isthmus of Corinth, the only point where a real defensive stand might yet be made. Themistocles removed the Athenian citizens to the little islands of Salamis and Aegina and the

shores of Argolis, and Athens was taken and plundered by the advancing Persians. Nonetheless, Themistocles had managed to hold together the irresolute Greek leaders, while Xerxes was induced to attack by means of a false message that the Greek fleet was preparing to slip out of the bay. But the Greek ships had taken up positions in the narrow waters between the island of Salamis and the Attic mainland, where the lack of space seriously handicapped the Persian maneuvers. All day the battle continued, and when night came the most impressive Asiatic fleet ever assembled had been destroyed. Xerxes, who personally had conducted the campaign, withdrew in haste to Asia Minor, while his army went into winter quarters in Thessaly.

The next spring, 479, the Persian advance into Greece was checked by the united armies of Athens, Sparta and allies at Plataea in Boeotia, where the Greeks again achieved a decisive victory. Then a final victory of the Greek over the Persian fleet, off the coast of Asia Minor, restored Greek prestige on the mainland and once more opened the Hellespont to the Athenians. No Persian army ever again appeared in Greece. These invasions and victories had a profound effect upon Greek culture, and, with the danger of foreign conquest past, Greece was to have opportunity to express her increased pride in developments of cultural and political significance.

Battle of Salamis. The swordlike ram of a Persian ship is advancing on a fifty-oared Greek galley

ATHENIAN EXPANSION—THE DELIAN LEAGUE

The Hellenic federation formed against Persia might logically have developed into a great Greek state. Sparta, nominally the leader in the war against Persia, logically should have been the leader in the new Greece, but Sparta failed woefully. Her very political and social organization, as described in a preceding section, made her a poor leader for a progressive Greece. Her jealousy of Athens immediately after the final defeat of the Persians gave the rival city a chance to step in as the leader of the Greeks in the formation of a new defensive league, and the Spartan refusal to cooperate made the Athenian fleet mistress of the Aegean. Under Themistocles, Athens first expanded the navy, fortified the city and its seaport, and then in 478 B.C. persuaded the Ionian cities and many Aegean Islands to become members of this new defensive league, with its treasury located on the island of Delos in the Temple of Apollo. The wealthier members of the league contributed ships, while others paid fixed sums of money. Then Athens, who had command of the fleet and collected the money, soon began to transform the league into an Athenian Empire. Athens, strong and ambitious, supplanted Persian influence in the Aegean. Sparta watched this development with increasing jealousy.

Pericles

During the next half-century, under the leadership of three great statesmen, Themistocles, Cimon, and Pericles, Athens became the most powerful and prosperous state in Greece. The Aegean cities at first were happy to have a champion and protector in Athens; later they began to resent the control and autocracy which Athens exercised over them. When some of these cities wished to withdraw from the league, Athens forced them to remain members and waged offensive war against them; and in 454, when the treasury and congress of the Delian League were removed to Athens, a number of these allied members began to look for a new champion to free them from the yoke of the Athenian bondage.

ATHENIAN DEMOCRACY

While Athens was creating this empire, several important developments were taking place within the city itself.

Themistocles, the hero of the later Persian struggles and creator of the new Athens, somehow lost favor with the citizens over matters of policy and was banished in 471 B.C. In his anti-Spartan policy, he had become involved with the pro-Persian party. Cimon, another hero of the Persian conflicts, favored alliance and peace with Sparta. This proposal ultimately served to bring about his downfall, and he too was exiled, just ten years after the dismissal of Themistocles. Then, a new political leader, Pericles, pushed his way to the fore in the Athenian political situation. Pericles, friend of the people and champion of democracy, exercised tremendous power in Athens during the next thirty years. His influence was so great that the Periclean Age often is considered the most significant in Greek history.

Democracy expanded in several ways. The old council of nobles was stripped of its political powers. Citizen juries, acting as courts of appeal, were enlarged. Pay was instituted for state officials and for jurymen. The higher officers of the government, with a single exception, were not elected, but chosen by lot. The ten generals, who were leaders of the political state as well as military commanders, were still elected. The chairman of this board of generals was the most powerful man in the state; yet, in order to hold his position, he had to retain the confidence of the assembly of the citizens. Thus, at times, a good orator achieved more general support than did a poor public speaker who otherwise was an abler man.

Athenian democracy was truly unique in the ancient world. Her citizens were more self-reliant and independent than any preceding or contemporary people. Athenian citizens recognized fully that with privileges also go duties and services to the state in one capacity or

British Museum, London

The Central Hall in the Temple of Amon-Ra at Karnak, Egypt. Amon-Ra was the Egyptian creator of the universe. The temple was founded in the 12th Dynasty.

Three Lions

The Great Sphinx at Giza, near Cairo. The Sphinx has a lion's body and a man's head. It is about 75 feet high and over 160 feet long. It is about 5,000 years old.

Vatican Library, Rome

Assyrian Palaces near Nineveh. This city on the Tigris River was the capital of the Assyrian Empire. It reached its zenith as the leader of the ancient world under Esarhaddon (681-668 B. C.) and his son Ashurbanipal (668-625 B. C.). This picture shows an artist's conception of some of the famous palaces of the ancient city.

G. BAUERNFEIND: Associated Galleries Ltd.

The Wailing Wall in Jerusalem (Old City). This wall is all that remains of a great Hebrew temple. Built by King Herod in the 1st century A. D. on the site of Solomon's Temple, it was destroyed by Titus A. D. 70. This section was part of the western wall; it measures about 160 feet long by 60 feet high. It is a Jewish holy place.

Death of Socrates, 399 B.C. Socrates' ideas were highly controversial in his day. His enemies brought him to trial for introducing new gods and "corrupting" the youth of Athens. Rather than give up his ideas or go into exile, he chose to accept the death penalty, which consisted of drinking a cup of poison hemlock.

Achilles Discovered on Scyros. The Greek hero had been disguised as a girl and sent to the island of Scyros to prevent him from being killed in the Trojan War. A prophet had foretold his death. He betrayed himself when he showed too great an interest in, and knowledge of, weapons of war. The story is in Homer's *Iliad*.

GIUSEPPE SCIUTI: Three Lions

The Roman Forum. An indoor scene in one of the great Roman forums, or marketplaces, about the 3d century B.C. The citizens are contributing goods and other belongings to pay the cost of the Second Punic War (218-201 B.C.). Hannibal, the Carthaginian general had invaded Italy. The Romans won the war.

C. ADEMOLIO: Three Lions

The Circus Maximus was used by the Romans for chariot races, games, and public shows. During Julius Caesar's time it was enlarged to hold over 350,000 people.

THOMAS COUTURE: Three Lions

The Decadence of Rome. Roman civilization and culture declined after the 3d century A. D. Government disintegrated, and barbarian tribes invaded the empire.

Greek Vase Painting is a very important source of today's knowledge of Greek life. All phases of activity were depicted, even the pottery factory (above). Top left, a music lesson on the lyre; top right, the departure of a four horse chariot; right, a woodsman. (British Museum, the Metropolitan Museum of Art)

Reconstructions of life in ancient Greece were drawn in great numbers during the 19th century, when interest in the classical period reached a high peak due to archeological discoveries. Left, a female acrobat performs a sword dance and another stirs liquid with her foot; bottom left, a Greek family at dinner. Right, Greek slave girls drawing water at a village fountain; bottom right, the flower market at Athens

another. However, one should not overlook the fact that there were definite limitations to Athenian democracy. Within the Athenian state, the great majority of people were not citizens, and accordingly were not given all the rights and privileges listed above. Citizens of full privileges did not include women. Neither was citizenship granted to the large groups of slaves and freemen, who generally were traders and artisans, many of whom were of foreign extraction and denied citizenship on that basis. However, within her citizen ranks, there was an equality and cooperation such as the world had not seen before. Thus, to the layman, the particular ideal theories of democracy appear to comprise the greatest contribution that Greece has made to Western civilization.

CONFLICT BETWEEN ATHENS AND SPARTA

Athenian imperialism in the Aegean brought her wealth and power in a measure far beyond that of any other Greek state. Her industries were greatly expanded and her trade increased. The city of Athens not only was embellished artistically through lavish expenditures of state funds, but also it was connected, by means of a fortifying wall, with her seaport. Thus, if Athens remained mistress of the sea, it would seem that no power could attack her successfully.

Sparta, the strongest military power in Greece, had not changed materially with the passing years. She had weathered successfully the internal disturbances and revolt, and had managed to retain her political and military systems almost intact. Neither had her social and economic patterns of life been changed. But Pericles, in the interest of expanding Athenian power, had made alliances on the Greek mainland, particularly with Megara, Thessaly, and Euboea. Also, an understanding, if not an alliance, was negotiated with Argos, the close neighbor of Sparta. Sparta retaliated by arranging similar alliances with other Greek states, especially the important city of Thebes, leader of the Boeotians, and Corinth, the commercial rival of Athens. During these years, Greece slowly was lining up in two opposing camps, and conflict between them was inevitable.

Actually, the conflict began shortly before Pericles came into prominence. The first Peloponnesian War (459-446 B.C.) began when Athens attacked Thebes, and ruined her industry and trade by blockading her ports. The little island of Aegina, which had enjoyed commercial success and allied herself with Sparta, was attacked likewise and annexed to the Athenian Empire. After fifteen years of struggle during which little was gained by either contender, a formal peace was established, with the provision that it was to endure for thirty years. Yet, while an exhausted Greece formally declared peace, there was little hope that the bitter rivalries and opposing policies would permit that peace to be maintained. During the war thus ended, several members of the Delian League had made futile attempts to free themselves from Athenian domination.

The commercial rivalry between Athens and Thebes was in itself a sufficient cause for reopening the war—fully as sufficient as the

Mourning Athena shows Athen's protectress grieving over the ravages of the Peloponnesian War

enmity between Athens and Sparta. Nevertheless, the second Peloponnesian War (431-421 B.C.) began with a formal declaration of war by the Spartan League. Subsequently, the strategy adopted by the Athenians was the withdrawal of Athens as a military power, in order that all her energies might be concentrated on a fleet which would protect Athenian interests in the Aegean, assure an adequate food supply, and be available to harass the movements of the enemy troops. Attica was deserted and all the people gathered within the walls of Athens and her port, Piraeus. A terrible plague that swept through the crowded city killed thousands of people and demoralized most of the living. Pericles, the guiding personality of the Athenians, died during the third year of the war. His successors were not at all skillful in the management of the war, and, after several reverses formal peace once again was negotiated in the year 421, this time to last for fifty years.

DESTRUCTION OF ATHENIAN POWER

The fifty-years' treaty gave no more promise of peace than had the negotiations for thirty years of peace. Even though Athens and Sparta seemed to have reached a working agreement, various new lines of conflict were being formed under the encouragement of Thebes and those cities which had commercial interests opposed to those of Athens. Under inferior leaders, such as Nicias and the brilliant but unreliable Alcibiades, Athens soon was embroiled in new conflicts. The large and prosperous Greek settlements in the west also were drawn into the conflict. Under Alcibiades, a large Athenian force moved to Sicily and attacked the important city of Syracuse. But Alcibiades was accused of mutilating certain sacred images just before he made his sudden expedition to Syracuse. When he was recalled to Athens to stand trial, he deserted to Sparta. Then, in 413 B.C., the blunders of Nicias, who was left in command, resulted in the capture of the entire Athenian force, comprising possibly about 40,000 men and 240 ships.

Athens, with her ships and men gone, was doomed. The long years of warfare had brought all kinds of hardships. The discouraged and desperate Athenians, attempting a political *coup*, established a new government upon an oligarchical principle, and the subsequent counter-revolution only added to the miseries of the already wretched state. Alcibiades was even recalled, only to be banished again; and the tragic, hopeless struggle ended only when the last Athenian fleet was surprised and captured near the Hellespont in 405 B.C. Her empire destroyed, her fleets captured and her people starving within the city walls, Athens only could surrender to the commander of the Spartan fleet which was blockading the port. The terms dictated by the Spartans were severe. The harbor walls and those connecting the port to Athens were to be torn down; all but twelve ships were to be turned over to Sparta, the Delian League— which was the Athenian Empire—was to be broken up; and Athens was to join the Spartan League as a subject ally. This final Spartan victory, however, had been achieved through the aid of the Persians, and so once again the shadow of the Persian Empire came to rest ominously upon war-torn Greece.

While the victors in the struggle thus ended insisted that liberty had been restored in Greece, the next century of Greek history is colored largely by the continuation of these rivalries and subsequent struggles which led to the final destruction of the Greek states. However, prior to this final disintegration, the Greeks, and especially the Athenians, had attained to many cultural accomplishments.

CULTURE IN THE AGE OF PERICLES

We have noted, in passing, the gradual cultural development which the Greeks underwent during the centuries following their arrival in Greece. It was noted also that the Greek cities along the coast of Asia Minor were the cultural leaders of Greece, at least down to the sixth century. But with the rise of Athenian power came the supremacy of Athenian culture, which perhaps drew to a large degree upon the scholars and craftsmen of Ionia. The foundations of Athenian culture certainly were laid before Pericles, but to him does belong the credit for making Athens the center of Greek intellectual and cultural

The Doric Order, first architectural style developed by the Greeks, culminated in the design of the Parthenon, 447–438 B.C. (T.W.A. Airline Photo)

The Ionic Order, a later style with slender flutings and more delicate lines, was used in the Temple of Nike Apteros at the gateway to the Acropolis

life. Pericles called Athens "the school of Greece," and justly so.

After the third Peloponnesian War Athens, sacked and ravished by the invaders, was rebuilt slowly. Some of the more beautiful buildings of the ancient world were erected of fine marble, especially on the Acropolis, the old citadel hill. Here arose the famous Parthenon with its simple Dorian columns, the Winged Victory Temple with its beautiful Ionian columns, and other structures the ruins of which still inspire the visitor. The several temples were decorated with reliefs and statues executed by some of the greatest

of the world's sculptors: Phidias, famed for his statues of Athena and Zeus, and Praxiteles, renowned for his "Hermes" and "The Satyr." This interest in the beautiful and the pleasing was carried by the Greeks into all phases of their daily life. In his small home, the Greek lived without many desirable conveniences, but often surrounded by abundant and beautiful furnishings.

Education was a matter largely of social discussions and private tutoring. Those in charge of teaching were men whose sophistication intrigued the inquisitive youth, rather than offered a safe guaranty of knowledge

Paeonius' Nike, found in fragments, was reconstructed through the study of Roman copies

Greek Originals, such as this statue of Hermes with the infant Dionysus by Praxiteles, are rare

which became the obsession of the leisured Athenians during this period. The arts, philosophy, and embryonic sciences flourished during this Periclean Age as never before. While early Greek history has been recorded in various literary sources, it is only from this Periclean Age that we have preserved for us the great historical contributions made by Herodotus, commonly called the "father of history"; Thucydides, who gave an unusually fair account of the wars between Athens and Sparta; and Xenophon, who efficiently concerned himself with both Persian and Greek history. The Greek drama, which had its origin in the rites of ceremonial festivals, was raised to a high degree of refinement during this cultural period. Aeschylus, Sophocles, Euripides, and Aristophanes are immortal figures in the field of world literature.

Greek philosophy did not have its beginning in Athens, but now it became highly elaborated. The Sophists, interested primarily in rhetoric and grammar, taught that truth and reality could not be ascertained, and that appearances must be accepted. Their expressed doubts concerning the nature and value of the gods brought them into a certain disrepute. Of wider fame is Socrates, whose teaching is known to us through his pupils Plato and Xenophon. Plato and Socrates are names which will not be forgotten as long as Western culture endures.

The foundations for a new intellectual age were being laid by inquiries in the realms of astronomy, mathematics, geography, zoology, and medicine. Hippocrates, a famous phy-

Plato and Aristotle from the "School of Athens" by Raphael. Aristotle was the elder philosopher's pupil for 20 years. Both carry books that gave them fame: Plato, the "Timaeus", and Aristotle, the "Ethics"

sician of this age, although not from Athens, made the daring statement that "every illness has a natural cause," a statement which has come to be appreciated only in the modern age. While civil strife was carrying Greece to political extinction, the cultural life of

Herodotus

Socrates

Euripides

Sophocles

Greek Sculpture was votive, commemorative or architectural in purpose. Left, the "Apollo Belvedere," a Hellenistic cult statue. Center, a victorious charioteer, late Archaic. Right, a caryatid building support

 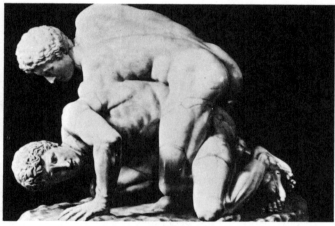

The Classic Style, as in this head of Hera, was restrained and placid

Hellenistic Style, as in "The Wrestlers," exaggerated movement, tried to imitate emotion, and ignored sculptural concepts

Bas Reliefs, 5th Century B.C. Right, boy playing lyre. (Museum of Fine Arts, Boston) Center, woman wearing chiton caught down on shoulders to form sleeves. Left, Athena and Hercules holding firmament while Atlas brings the golden apples captured from the garden of the Hesperides

Venus de Milo, Hellenistic Period

these small states flourished with a brilliance almost beyond comprehension. During these years of struggle lived men whose names are associated with some of the great cultural accomplishments of mankind.

FINAL INTERSTATE CONFLICTS

When Athens had been crushed and disarmed by Sparta in 404 B.C., the leadership of the Greek world was usurped by her conqueror. The Greek cities soon realized that they merely had exchanged a bad master for one that was even worse. Sparta ruled by force, established garrisons in many of the Greek cities, and entrusted the actual government to a few nobles who ruled in a manner that often was cruel and tyrannical. Less than ten years after the Athenian surrender, a new combination of Greek states was formed to oppose the arrogant administration of the Spartans. Thebes, Corinth, Argos, and Athens turned against Sparta and accepted aid from Persia who still was interested in getting a

hold in Greece. Thebes and Athens quickly won victories over Sparta. With a Persian fleet, an Athenian admiral defeated the Spartan navy. Athens rebuilt her walls, recovered some of her possessions, and formed new alliances. Then Persia came to fear Athens and quickly swung her support to Sparta. As a result, Persia was able to dictate a peace treaty to the Greeks, known as the King's Peace (387 B.C.), which recognized Asia Minor as part of the realm of Persian influence and retained Sparta as the one to enforce the peace among the Greek states.

In the succeeding years, Sparta came to be hated more cordially than Athens ever had been. Athens and Thebes again took the lead in organizing the states against Sparta. Theban and Athenian victories on land and sea brought a general peace conference in 371 B.C. Sparta might still have retained leadership over the confederacy of Greek states had she granted equal rights to every state. Sparta's refusal to recognize Thebes as the head of the Boeotian state caused a war in which Sparta was decisively defeated by the great Theban general and statesman, Epaminondas. The long invincible Spartan army existed no longer, and Spartan leadership, narrow, selfish, and autocratic, was ended.

For a brief span of years, it seemed that a third great power had arisen in Greece. Thebes formed a confederacy in northern Greece, overran Thessaly, and even invaded distant Macedonia. Attempts to control the Peloponnesus, and to humiliate Sparta further brought about the fall of Thebes when her famous commander, Epaminondas, fell in battle against Sparta in 362 B.C. Exhausted Athens tried to rise from the depths to which she had fallen and rebuild the Aegean Empire; but the centuries of struggle had taken their toll, and, before Athens could accomplish much of importance, Macedonia from the north of Greece began her meteoric career. The several Greek states which might have led in the formation of a federation had wasted their energies and resources in mutually destructive conflict. A spirit of individualism and self-determination prevented the formation of a Greek national state.

9. Alexander the Great and the Hellenistic Age

PHILIP OF MACEDON

ABOVE Thessaly lay Macedonia, an area in which cultural development had been much retarded. Macedonian people were predominantly of Indo-European stock, certainly related to the Greeks, but whose Indo-European speech was not understood by classical Greeks. Greek culture had made itself felt in Macedonia, but its influence was limited to the few, so that by the middle of the fourth century B.C. the country was still barbarous.

Philip became king of Macedonia in 359 B.C. He had a Greek education, was a good general and a fair diplomat. After establishing a strong, permanent army of professional soldiers, both infantry and cavalry, he began his career as empire builder. In the hills of Macedonia there were hardy peasants and nobles for his army; in the captured gold mines of Mt. Pangaeus was the necessary wealth. His early conquests were northward and eastward in areas unknown to the Greeks. Along the coast line, however, he soon came into contact with the Greek colonies. In keeping with his expansion program, Philip of Macedon gradually extended his influence southward into Thessaly and northern Greece.

Two parties then arose in Greece: one favorable toward Philip and ready to accept his friendship, and the other bitterly hostile to him. To this latter group belonged the orator Demosthenes, some of whose finest speeches were denunciations of Philip. But Philip's army and gold were irresistible, and after a series of conflicts, which terminated in the battle at Chaeronea in 338 B.C., the last armed Greek resistance was crushed. At the Congress of Corinth in the same year, Philip organized a Pan-Hellenic League with himself at its head. The following year, he announced to the league an expedition to avenge all the injuries which Greece had suffered at the hands of Persia. Two years of preparation followed; and then, in 336 B.C., on the eve of the projected Persian War, Philip was stabbed by his enemies during the celebrations in honor of his daughter's wedding.

ALEXANDER THE GREAT

The heir to the throne was his son Alexander, a young man of twenty who had been educated by the Greek philosopher, Aristotle. The young prince thus became an ardent admirer of Greek genius and culture. General revolt of the league members immediately confronted the young king, but within a few months his decisive actions, prominent among which was the thorough destruction of the revolting Theban state, proclaimed to the world that a great son had succeeded a great father.

The complete annihilation of the revolting Thebans taught the rest of Greece to accept and obey their new master. He declared himself the avenger of Greece, and two years after his ascension to power he followed his father's plans and crossed the Hellespont into Asia Minor, which was not at all an unknown territory. Many of the Greeks had been in the service of the Persian kings at various times in the past decades. Also, the famous expedition, in which Xenophon had participated at the end of the fifth century, had demonstrated the obvious superiority of the Greek soldiers over the forces of the great king of Persia. Alexander advanced with courage. His compact and well trained army numbered about 35,000 men, of whom by far the majority were his own Macedonian troops. In Asia Minor, Alexander dramatically stopped at Troy and worshiped at the shrine of Athena, thus linking himself to the romantic sentiments of the Greek people.

CONQUEST OF THE PERSIAN EMPIRE

Meanwhile, Darius III, destined to be the last king of the Persian Empire, had made what

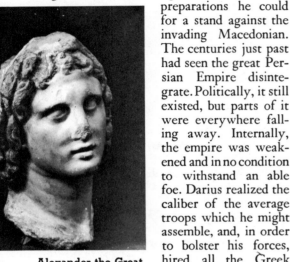

Alexander the Great

preparations he could for a stand against the invading Macedonian. The centuries just past had seen the great Persian Empire disintegrate. Politically, it still existed, but parts of it were everywhere falling away. Internally, the empire was weakened and in no condition to withstand an able foe. Darius realized the caliber of the average troops which he might assemble, and, in order to bolster his forces, hired all the Greek mercenary troops he could find to fight the invading Greeks and Macedonians.

In rapid succession, Alexander achieved victory after victory. In Asia Minor in 334, the battle of Granicus gave him the surrounding portions of the Persian Empire, while the Greek cities welcomed him as a deliverer. At Issus in 333, he routed the Persian army in north Syria under the personal command of Darius, who then in vain offered Alexander half of his realm. Tyre, the impregnable city of Syria, was besieged and taken. Egypt opened her gates to the invincible commander, and at a remote desert shrine, to the west of Egypt, Alexander worshiped the god Zeus-Amon. The Persian fleet, which had operated in the eastern Mediterranean, was now cut off from its base of supplies since the entire coast line was controlled by Alexander. For nearly two years, Darius III had been collecting his armies for what proved to be the last desperate stand against the Macedonian. After the Egyptian campaign, Alexander marched back through Palestine, Syria, and then eastward into the heart of the Persian Empire, into the territory where once had flourished the ancient Assyrian Empire. The Tigris and Euphrates rivers were crossed, and finally, near Arbela in 331 B.C., Alexander again faced the king of the Persians. The Macedonians, well armed and disciplined although greatly outnumbered, crushed the Persian army and drove them off the battlefield in flight.

MASTER OF THE WORLD

The Persian Empire no longer existed; it now belonged by right of conquest, not to the Greeks, but to Alexander. Babylon, the famed city of an earlier civilization, received the new master and opened to him her treasuries which contained gold and silver stores which were beyond the imagination of the Greeks. But Alexander pushed on, first into the heart of the original Persia, a mountainous territory to the east of Babylonia. Other capitals of the empire—Susa, Persepolis, Ecbatana—received the conqueror with added treasures. Persepolis, with stately structures built by some of the great Persian kings, was sacked and burned; and Darius III, fleeing eastward to the Caspian Sea provinces, was murdered by his own attendants in the year following the disaster at Arbela. Thus, no longer was there a Persian claimant for the throne.

During the next five years, Alexander advanced into the distant eastern provinces and beyond. He crossed the Oxus and Jaxartes rivers, then turned southward across the Indus River and into India, a march accomplished amid difficulties and struggles such as no army ever experienced before. Finally, his troops induced him to turn back, and so down the Indus River the great conqueror moved until he reached the Indian Ocean. He then turned westward again and marched back through the arid wastes, while the fleet which he had ordered built also sailed back to Babylonia. The magnitude of this campaign can be appreciated only by following its

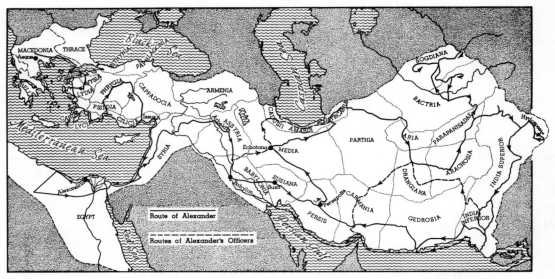

Alexander's conquests extended the influence of Hellenism into Africa and Asia

route on a map, and Alexander's accomplishments can be described only in superlative terms. In his long march, he had set up Greek colonies at strategic locations, and in various ways he revealed the fact that he was interested in merging the Greek and the oriental cultures. Upon his return to Babylon, he began the reorganization of the state so as to give a share of power to the Orientals as well as to the Greeks. He married a Bactrian princess, and encouraged his soldiers to marry native women.

Alexander's plans for further conquests were not certain. He was interested in Arabia and also in the western Mediterranean lands; but the twelve years just past had wrought deep changes in him. Hardships and the strain of conquest had accentuated his quick temper and his irritability. His best friends, for the most part, had been alienated; one he even had killed in a fit of rage. His successes, coupled with his training and his background, seemed to have induced Alexander to consider himself as divine and as an oriental monarch, for of course he would be deified by his subjects. These aspects of his character, as well as his imperious orders, caused unrest and revolt in Greece. But, while in the midst of reorganization plans for the empire and

preparation for an Arabian campaign, Alexander suddenly fell ill with fever and died in the year 323 B.C. He was thirty-three years old at the time, and, although he was still a young man, his was one of the most influential lives in the history of the world. It may be said of Alexander that he made history. Through him, the developing Hellenistic civilization spread throughout the ancient world, and his deeds set in motion influences which altered the course of events long after his time.

DIVISION OF ALEXANDER'S EMPIRE

Alexander's sudden death left the vast empire without a master. A son, born after the conqueror's death, was killed in 310 B.C. After a generation of struggle between Alexander's generals for possession of the empire, it was divided into three parts, with one of his generals, or their successors, at the head of each. Egypt became the kingdom of Ptolemy, one of Alexander's officers. Most of the Asiatic provinces were administered by Seleucus, another officer who saw service under Alexander. Macedonian Europe passed finally into the hands of Antigonus Gonatas, the grandson of another of Alexander's generals.

Ptolemy began a dynasty of rulers who

Ptolemy II, the thoroughly Egyptianized son of one of Alexander's generals, presenting offerings to Anquet, goddess of the fertilizing waters of the Nile

held Egypt for nearly three centuries. Recognizing his dependency upon Greek mercenary troops, he wisely built a fleet for the control of the eastern Mediterranean. Ptolemy did not create a Greek form of state in Egypt; rather, he installed himself as the successor of the ancient Egyptian Pharaohs, and became an absolute, deified monarch. While often at war with her Seleucid neighbors, Egypt retained her autonomy until she became a Roman province at the end of the first century B.C.

Seleucus inherited the bulk of the old Alexandrian empire, extending from the Mediterranean coast eastward to the boundaries of India. The Seleucid Empire, as it is commonly called, never achieved the unity which was characteristic of Egypt. The strong Egyptian navy prevented the Seleucids from enjoying the economic prosperity which otherwise might have been theirs, though the Seleucid capital, Antioch, in upper Syria, did become a commercial rival of Alexandria, the capital of Egypt. The internal disturbances, as

well as the continued attacks from the East, gradually brought about the disintegration of the Seleucid Empire, so that its western provinces were absorbed by Rome when her armies appeared in the East; and the eastern provinces gradually became incorporated in the new nationalistic states which began to rise in this area as early as the third century B.C.

Antigonus Gonatas, who inherited Macedonia and Greece, had the least attractive portion of the Alexandrian Empire. He and his successors faced the continued pressure of the new northern invaders, and within Greece there was the constant threat of some new revolt in an attempt to establish autonomy. Although Antigonus successfully contested Egyptian naval supremacy, he never did bring economic prosperity back to Greece. Trade and industry had found new centers in Alexandria, Antioch, and Rhodes. The incessant wars had drained Greece of wealth and manpower, while the variety of new opportunities offered by the now open world drew still more thousands out of Greece. Greek armies had disintegrated; Greek ships were lacking; and protective federations, like the Aetolian

The Rosetta Stone, a record from Ptolemy V's reign, was written in Egyptian and Greek, and formed the key to the translation of hieroglyphics. (British Museum)

Sarcophagus of Alexander, battle scene. Poly-
chromed figures still retain original, colorful paint

and Achaean leagues, could neither free Greece nor bring back prosperity. Greece and Macedonia both succumbed to Roman control within a few centuries.

CULTURE IN THE HELLENISTIC AGE

The three centuries following Alexander are known as the Hellenistic Age, the age during which Greek civilization made itself felt throughout that portion of the Orient conquered by Alexander. Greek rulers and traders carried their culture into all Mediterranean lands, and far beyond the Mediterranean. Greek became the accepted language of business, art, science, and government. However, the Hellenistic cultures which developed in this period drew heavily from their oriental backgrounds. Out of this fusion there developed a new and striking culture which was broader, more brilliant, and more significant for a greater number of peoples than either the Greek or the oriental cultures before it.

This fact may be illustrated clearly by a few examples of the accomplishments of this new culture. Pergamum in Asia Minor developed under Athenian influence and became renowned for its magnificent sculpture depicting the struggle between Pergamum and the invading Gauls. Also at this site, a remarkable marble sarcophagus depicted in relief the scenes from the life of Alexander. Alexandria in Egypt, the greatest city of the age partly because of the patronage of the Ptolemaic

High Relief from "Battle of Gods and Giants" frieze on altar of Zeus and Athena at Pergamum shows Hellenistic emphasis on violent movement in sculptural representations

Alexander, from the so-called Alexander sarcophagus, a coffin carved for a follower of the conqueror

kings, and partly through commerce and industry, contained public and private buildings which were built and decorated on a scale surpassing anything which Greece ever was capable of producing. A lighthouse guided ships into her spacious harbors. Her famous "Museum," an institution supported by the government for purposes of scientific research, contained a world-famous library of half a million rolls. Here Euclid organized his geometrical theorems; Eratosthenes computed the size of the earth to within fifty miles of its actual diameter and laid the basis for the scientific study of geography; and Aristarchus, an astronomer, discovered the revolutions of the planets around the sun. The physicians who studied at the "Museum" identified the nervous system, linked it with the brain as the center of the entire system, and even traced the optic nerve from the eye to the brain. Greek dictionaries were compiled for the first time in connection with the library of this great institution.

Syracuse in Sicily was also an important cultural and intellectual center during the Hellenistic Age. Here the scientist Archimedes carried on such exacting researches as

Victory of Samothrace. The goddess stands on the prow of a ship; her clinging drapery wind-swept into the restless folds characteristic of Hellenistic art

to give him recognition as the discoverer of the principles of the lever and specific gravity.

HELLENISTIC PHILOSOPHY AND RELIGION

There also were important philosophical advances during this age. Aristotle, one of the most renowned of the Greek philosophers, established his Lyceum in Athens where he and his students investigated a number of fields of study. They compiled information relative to the several natural sciences, and

Aristotle, a statue in the Palazzo Spada, Rome

wrote treatises on logic, ethics, psychology, drama, government, and other subjects of popular concern. In Athens, a school of philosophy new to the Western world at that time, Stoicism, taught that duty was the highest virtue, that fortitude and indifference to pleasure and pain were the desired accomplishments, and that brotherly consideration was the fundamental rule of living. Also, the Epicurean School, founded by Epicurus in Athens but later moved to Africa, set forth a doctrine of highly refined living, based upon three premises: First, the body is not immortal, hence there was no need to give thought to what might happen after death. Second, if the gods really were gods, they must be happy, and if they were happy they must of necessity be wholly unconcerned with the disturbing and bewildering affairs of mankind; thus there was no need of concerning oneself about the gods. And third, since there was nothing to hope for after death, nor was there any assistance or guidance to be had from the gods, it was possible to endure pain and enjoy pleasures, of which the highest were to be found in beautiful, dignified, and refined human relationships. Nevertheless, the philosophy of Epicurus was a system only

for highly cultured people, and it soon was perverted by the masses so as to refer to a quest for the mere emotional pleasures of the passing moment.

Also characteristic of this Hellenistic Age was the unusual expansion of the salvation religions, known as the Mystery Religions. While the causes of the unprecedented popularity of these cults are both manifold and complex, several of the factors conducive to this development may be noted briefly. The Greek, Persian, and Egyptian high gods fell into disfavor as these empires fell. Further, the peoples of the Mediterranean world were both mixed and mobile during this period, having been forcefully moved from their native habitat by the wars and invited to travel as order was established under Alexander. Thus, the people not only were away from their family gods, which were closely attached to the home soil, but also they were strangers in strange lands, needing companionship which could be had only by overriding racial and political differences, which the Mystery Religions did by considering all communicants as brothers. And finally, and more important perhaps, was the fact that the Mystery Religions offered an easy and certain salvation to people who were living in a precarious and dangerous age. The Alexandrian conquests were influential to a great extent in increasing the popularity of these mystery cults.

Epicurus

These achievements in science, philosophy, and religion gave an indication of the possibilities of Hellenistic culture. But while this fusion of Hellenic and oriental elements was going forward, significant events were occurring in the Italian peninsula. A new military giant was growing to maturity, unnoticed and unheralded. This newcomer was Rome, destined to rule over a greater Mediterranean world.

10. Roman Origins and Early Conquests

INFLUENCE OF GEOGRAPHY

WHILE we have been following the course of Greek history and the history of the eastern Mediterranean area, we have permitted the retarded western region to drop more or less out of our consideration. The most important land in the western Mediterranean area in early times was Italy.

Here, as in studying Greece, some appreciation of the geography of the country is necessary for an understanding of the history. On the north, Italy is protected to a large extent by the Alps, which acted as a barrier against the barbarians of central Europe. In the western portion of Italy are large fertile plains which extended to the sea; along the eastern coast and running from north to south are the Apennine Mountains which make the eastern part of Italy almost inaccessible. These mountains divided the people of Italy, not into many city-states as in Greece, but into two classes: the poor, backward hill peoples, and the wealthy plainsmen.

Throughout Italy's coastal length of over two thousand miles, there are remarkably few deep bays and good harbors; and those that do exist are located generally on the southern and western coasts. Geographically, Italy and Rome looked west. This fact probably was instrumental in causing the Romans to turn their early attention to Spain, Gaul, and Britain. The island of Sicily served as a stepping stone to Africa and brought Rome into contact with the Orient. Two other islands near by, Sardinia and Corsica, have always trailed Italy culturally, perhaps because the rugged and mountainous character of their lands definitely limited economic growth. When Italy had been welded into a single state, its central position greatly facilitated the extension of domination over the whole of the Mediterranean area.

Important metals such as iron, copper, tin, gold, and silver were found in limited quantities in Italy and the near-by islands. Building materials, including a variety of stones and timber in abundance, were present. The climate, like that of other Mediterranean lands, was characterized by a moderate temperature and an absence of extremes of heat or cold. On the whole, Italy was endowed naturally with many of the essentials required for the development of a significant civilization, and early became an attraction to hordes of wanderers.

PREHISTORIC ITALY

Paleolithic, or Old Stone Age, implements found in several parts of Italy indicate that early man had been attracted to the area which was destined to be the home of a great civilization. Paleolithic man buried his dead in shallow trenches, and with him his crude stone axes and scrapers; he apparently had not yet developed pottery and lived as a hunter finding shelter in natural caves.

The Neolithic, or New Stone Age, which brings with it new types of implements, blends easily into the succeeding Copper Age. Aside from improved tools, man now constructed huts and lived in villages. The burial customs showed few significant changes aside from the increasingly elaborate tombs. Pottery and weaving appeared, as did herding and agriculture—all significant developments. Boats, also important in the progress of civilization, were introduced at this time. Italy and Sicily show relations with the Aegean and Balkan cultures during this period, and northern Italy reveals connections with areas in central Europe and Spain. The general physical type of these men was that characteristic of the Mediterranean race, which we already have encountered in the eastern Mediterranean area. Already in the prehistoric era, migrations of peoples from neighboring territories to the east from across the Adriatic Sea, had occurred.

INVADERS DURING THE BRONZE AGE
(2000-1000 B.C.)

Invaders from the north side of the Alps pushed their way into Italy about 2000 B.C. Their culture was related to that which then

existed in Switzerland and the upper Danube Basin. They are known as lake dwellers because they commonly built their houses on piles in lakes and rivers, probably to secure protection. In succeeding centuries, there gradually moved southward other invaders who are called the *terremare* people. Their distinguishing practice was the cremation of their dead and the burying of the ashes in jars. Possibly, the *terremare* people were related to the Pile-village groups. However, this second

Bronze Wolf Head recovered from Lake Nemi

group certainly represents the western Indo-European invaders whom we already have met coming into Greece at approximately the same time. As in Greece, these invaders came into Italy in successive waves. They became the historic Italic or Italian tribes who later gave their language to all Italy. They brought with them their distinctive customs and a sound bronze technology devoted specifically to materials used in warfare. The appearance of more Illyrian invaders during the second millennium further complicates the study of conditions in Italy during this period.

ETRUSCANS, PHOENICIANS, GREEKS

Possibly a new Indo-European invasion occurred around 1000 B.C.; certainly, there were definite movements and various changes

within the Italic peninsula during the tenth century B.C. The Etruscans, invaders from the Aegean Sea area, settled on the Italian west coast to the north of the Tiber River during the early part of the tenth century. They brought their own customs, traditions, and in many ways a superior culture; it was

Etruscan Button of gold, 6th century B.C. (Metropolitan Museum of Art)

this culture which left a permanent stamp on the later Roman civilization, giving a particular character to Roman art, architecture, and sports. The arch is an Etruscan contribution, and the gladiatorial combats of later Rome had their origin in this Etruscan culture.

The Phoenicians, whose early commercial activities had brought a cultural stimulation to the Greeks, also were significant in the west. Carthage in northern Africa was founded as a Phoenician colony, in the ninth century, and from here these famed traders rapidly established colonies and trading posts at strategic points on the Mediterranean Sea, including the islands of Sicily and Sardinia

Bronze Mirror of 5th century B.C. with story of Odysseus' attack on Circe incised on back. (Metropolitan Museum of Art)

which were near the Italian mainland. Trade relations with the Etruscans made the Phoenicians important for the early culture of Italy, while their enterprises in the western Med-

Demareteion, silver coin of Syracuse. (British Museum)

iterranean territories made them potentially dangerous politically.

The Greeks began to make their influence felt in Italy by the seventh century. One of the first Greek cities on the peninsula was Cumae, and it was from this settlement, ancient as Rome itself, that Greek influences spread northward. But competition from the Etruscans and the Phoenicians prevented the Greeks from settling the entire peninsula.

While Etruscan political control had ingrained portions of the Etruscan culture into the developing life of the Roman people, the Greeks exerted an even stronger influence. Traders brought their culture with them, and the Greek alphabet was adapted by the Romans to their Latin tongue. Even though the Romans remained essentially an agrarian people until the third century, eventually the Greek system of coinage was accepted, and Rome began to issue copper and bronze coins in the fourth century. Greek religion likewise was imported and adjusted to the Roman people with a definite emphasis on ritual. Literature, science, and philosophy all came west with the Greeks. However, one must not think that this transplanting of Greek culture was accomplished suddenly, nor even before the sixth century. The process continued almost as long as the Roman state existed. Romans never possessed the Greek appreciation of the harmonious and the beautiful, nor had they the imagination of their predecessors. Likewise in realms of science, the Romans could make no contribution. Their genius was devoted to the fields of war and government.

THE LATIN LEAGUE

The Italian people thus, in the early centuries of the first millennium, found themselves surrounded by these various new invaders. At first the Italians occupied the center of the peninsula, but later separated into two main divisions. The so-called highlanders took the central and eastern portions. The Latins, or lowlanders, dwelt in the west. Because of close association with the Etruscans, the Latins came to be more thoroughly civilized than the highlanders. Slowly their settlements grew into cities, and these became city-states. Although these city-states were independent, they were bound together by the necessity of defending themselves against the Etruscans and their foes. Early in the first millennium they formed what is known as the Latin League. One of the cities in this confederation was Rome.

Originally a settlement on the Palatine Hill, populated by shepherds, farmers, and traders, Rome grew into a city when another settlement on Quirinal Hill was incorporated. The low land between the Palatine and the Quirinal became the Forum. Soon the surrounding hills were settled and they, too, were added to Rome. Later the Wall of Servius was built around all these settlements.

Rome's advantages were many, not the least of which was the defensibility of its location. Pirates could not strike it from the sea. Seven hills fortified it against the Etrus-

Palatine Hill, where according to legend Romulus traced the boundaries of the first city of Rome, was later the residence of Mark Antony and Cicero. (T.W.A. Airline Photo)

The Forum, once the civic center of Rome. (T.W.A. Airline Photo)

cans. The Tiber, Italy's largest navigable river, made trade easy. In addition, Rome was in the center of Italy—a fortunate position for an ambitious state.

THE LEGEND OF ROMULUS

According to legend, Romulus became the first king of Rome in the following manner. Rhea, beloved of Mars, the god of war, gave birth by him to two sons, Romulus and Remus. As a result of a plot against her father, Numitor, king of Alba Longa, Rhea was separated from her godlike sons, and they were set adrift in a basket on the Tiber.

However, no harm came to them. They were nursed by a shewolf during their infancy and later adopted by a shepherd. When they grew to manhood, it was made known to them that they were the rightful princes of the kingdom. They set out to claim their heritage. They are said to have built Rome, beginning at that point on the banks of the Tiber where, having been cast ashore, they were at the mercy of the she-wolf. Later, in a fit of anger, Romulus slew Remus and ruled as the first king of Rome.

THE EARLY MONARCHY

The amusing little story of Romulus and Remus, however, is not history; nor is 753 B.C., the traditional date for the founding of Rome, at all acceptable. Actual archeological investigations have revealed Bronze Age settlements extending back to approximately the twelfth century B.C. The small Latin city, which existed on the site of Rome, was suddenly captured by the Etruscan invaders—always feared by the Latins—who then established a small Etruscan state about the middle of the eighth century B.C. Echoes of this period are preserved only more or less accurately in the later Roman accounts of the Seven Kings of Rome.

A monarchy certainly was established in Rome under the Etruscan rulers, who gradually extended their power over the other Latin peoples inhabiting the surrounding territories. Alba Longa, once the leading Latin city, disappeared under Etruscan aggression. Later tradition correctly assigns several building projects and new techniques in the crafts to this period of Etruscan control, during which Roman culture became essentially Etruscan, even though Latin speech and Latin consciousness remained. Then, around 500 B.C., the Etruscan tyranny provoked dormant Latin patriotism to active opposition, and in the ensuing revolt, the Etruscan king and his retinue were driven into exile. Thus, there was ushered in a new era of Roman history.

THE EARLY REPUBLIC

When the Roman people, in cooperation with the nobles, expelled the last king and formed a nominal republic with major powers residing in the nobility, the Roman state comprised only a few hundred square miles south of the Tiber River. Etruscan attacks from the north, which followed immediately, were repulsed only with difficulty and the loss of some territory. War also was waged with other Latin cities in the immediate neighborhood, but with them a treaty was concluded which remained in force for nearly one hundred and fifty years. An offensive and defensive alliance was concluded on an entirely equal basis, and a partial exchange of citizenship was arranged, which was aimed particularly at better commercial relations.

This warfare, which gave birth to the infant state of Rome, was to characterize Roman history in succeeding centuries. With her newly acquired Latin allies, wars were waged against the Aequi and the Volsci, tribes to the south of Rome. More significant for Rome was the prolonged conflict with Veii, a strong Etruscan city a few miles to the north. This

Etruscan Musicians performing in honor of the dead, fresco from Tomb of Triclinium, 5th century B.C.

city probably was both the political and economic rival of Rome, and it was not until the beginning of the fourth century, nearly a hundred years later, that Rome, after an eleven-year siege, managed to capture and destroy the city. The conquest of Veii nearly doubled the territory of Rome which immediately settled colonies in this newly acquired territory and absorbed what native peoples remained there.

Hardly had Veii been overcome when a new and greater threat to Roman existence appeared in the form of the invasion of the barbarous Gauls. These invaders had pushed into the Po Valley, in northern Italy, where they overran the country and settled on the northeastern borders of Italy. In a sudden thrust southward across the Apennines, they appeared in Roman territory and defeated the Roman army. Panic-stricken and seriously doubting the adequacy of their defenses, the Romans deserted their city (387 B.C.) leaving only a garrison in the citadel. The city was sacked and occupied by the Gauls for some months; then, upon a ransom payment of gold, the Gauls left and returned to the extreme northern sections of Italy.

The Romans at once occupied and rebuilt their city, and soon after provided it with more adequate defenses in the form of a new stone wall. For some years, the Gauls ceased their raids into Roman territory, but in 368 and 348, two more invasions indicated to the Romans that the Gauls still were a serious danger to the Roman state. In 334, Gauls and Romans concluded formal peace which lasted for the remainder of the century.

ROMAN CONQUEST OF CENTRAL ITALY

The Gallic invasion and sack of Rome encouraged her foes to resume their warfare against the ambitious city, but the Aequi, Volsci, and Etruscans each met with defeat. Rome now seemed to realize that if she were to continue to exist, she must build herself into a greater power. Among the problems which she had faced for some decades was her relationship with the Latin tribes, who although allied still tried to hinder or break

The Appian Way in Roman Times. Carefully planned for military purposes, it was begun in 312 B.C. Tombs flanked the sides of the road for the first three miles

with her. Accordingly in two years of conflict with her former allies, Rome subdued the Latin tribes and incorporated them into the Roman state (338-336 B.C.), while at the same time a close alliance was concluded with the Campanian peoples.

New hostilities over territorial problems very soon broke out in central southern Italy with the Samnites, a strong, fierce Italic tribe. Rome lost several battles, but despite her defeats carried on. The Samnites managed to enlist the aid of the old foes of Rome, the Etruscans and the Gauls. When this powerful combination was met by Rome on the battlefield of Sentinum in 295 B.C. and decisively beaten, all danger to Rome from this quarter was past, and she stood as the leading power in the Italian peninsula. The Samnites were forced to become subject allies to Rome by 290 B.C.

During the next ten years, intensive Roman campaigning ended with defeat for the Gauls. Rome appropriated a part of their territory, while the several Etruscan cities with their allies were subdued and incorporated in the Roman state as allies. Rome was mistress of all central and northern Italy. Only southern Italy still remained independent.

CONQUEST OF SOUTHERN ITALY

Southern Italy and Sicily for the most part had been held for centuries by the Greeks, and had in part shared the conflicts as well as the cultural advances of Greece. As their mother states had failed, so also these Italian Greeks failed to unite into a Greek state of large proportion. Tarentum and Syracuse were two of the more significant cities of this area. Already during the last half of the fourth century, kings from Epirus, a Greek state across the lower Adriatic Sea, and from Sparta fell fighting in behalf of the Italian Greeks.

These several cities became embroiled in war with Rome in 280 B.C., and called in King Pyrrhus of Epirus, who came over with nearly twenty-five thousand well equipped troops and a number of war elephants, new to western warfare. Pyrrhus achieved two hard-fought victories over Roman arms and was about to negotiate an advantageous peace when Carthage, the Phoenician power which had grown up in North Africa, became afraid of the success of Pyrrhus and sent her fleet to support Rome. Rome promptly refused to make peace with the Greeks in Italy as long as their foreign champion remained on Italian soil. However, Pyrrhus continued his spectacular career and next campaigned in Sicily with great success against the Carthaginians. Lack of support from the Greeks, who apparently feared him as a new master, caused his return to Italy and ultimately his withdrawal to Epirus. The disunited Greek cities were then reduced and added to the Roman alliance. By 265 B.C., the entire Italian peninsula acknowledged the supremacy of Rome.

The Appian Way Today. Constructed of hewn stones laid on cement according to sound engineering principles, the road is still in use. (T.W.A. Airline Photo)

NATURE OF ROMAN DOMINATION

As we review Roman expansion from the beginning of the fifth century, it is obvious that her earlier wars were defensive; it also is obvious that when the last Greek city had surrendered, her wars, if still defensive, had assumed all the color of an aggressive offensive. Her conquests eliminated undesirable rivals, provided territory into which her excess population might expand, and did not ignore plunder and booty. By 265, the Italian population included three distinct political groups: the Roman citizens, Latin allies, and federate allies. Roman citizens, including peoples outside of Rome, might enjoy full rights; on the other hand, they might be deprived of the right to hold office or vote.

Some of the Latin groups had citizenship, and their cities were called municipalities. Latin allies included some of the old Latin groups as well as Roman colonies founded throughout Italy at strategic points. They were bound closely by blood and interests to Rome. Federate allies or Italian allies included the larger group of Italian people.

Approximately one hundred and fifty communities were bound to Rome by special treaty, and most of the treaties demanded military aid and the relinquishment of individual diplomatic relations. Apart from the various duties which might be stipulated, these communities were locally autonomous.

Thus, we see that while Rome controlled Italy, there was by no means a single state or a united people. Formally, Italy was united by alliance; practically, there was being created a Roman empire on Italian soil.

CONSTITUTIONAL DEVELOPMENT

Upon the overthrow of the monarchy, the Romans set up a republican form of government, wherein the chief executive office was filled by popular election. At the head of the state were two annually elected magistrates, called consuls, of equal power. In times of special need, a single dictator might be given full power for a period of six months. A senate composed of 300 nobles, or patricians as they were called in Rome, assisted the consuls, holding their offices for life and having the power to veto or to pass the laws proposed by the general assembly of the people. Thus, the power was not actually with the people, but with the senatorial body of nobles. Traditionally, the Roman people were organized into three tribes, but by the end of the third century, these had been expanded to thirty-five tribes. The high priesthood became a public office at an early time, and accordingly religion remained under the direction of the state.

From these general bases, the constitutional development of Rome proceeded along two lines. There was a gradual change in the magistracy by the creation of new offices with functions adapted to the needs of a progressive, expanding community. Again, there was a long struggle between the patricians and the plebeians or common people, resulting from the desire of the latter to place themselves in a position of political, legal, and social equality with the former.

By the end of the fifth century, the expanding state already had added magistrates whose names only can be enumerated here: quaestors, aediles, censors, praetors, and tribunes. In the fourth century, still more distinctions arose, most significant of which is the appearance of promagistrates who, like the proconsuls, might serve a second year or longer. This device was necessary because there was a provision that the same office could not be held by an individual until ten years had elapsed. By the close of the fourth century, the Roman magistracy had attained the form which it preserved until the end of the Republic. Early Roman officials had strength, and gained the respect of the public for their authority.

PROGRESS TOWARD DEMOCRACY

The struggle between patrician and plebeian is comparable in certain respects to the early popular struggles in Greece against the nobles, only in Italy the struggle was much prolonged. Economic and social problems also contributed to the conflict in Rome, quite as they had in Greece. Attempts at an establishment of a tyranny also were found in fifth-century Rome. Then followed a long series of constitutional changes and additions which tended to grant the people more power, recognition and protection. Early in the fifth century, the people gained the right to elect tribunes, who had the right to veto any of the acts by the consuls, Senate, or even the Assembly. Likewise, their efforts brought about the codification of the law, while a second, more democratic assembly was developed. Theoretical social equality was attained by legalizing marriage between patrician and plebeian.

By 300 B.C., all offices were thrown open to the plebeians. With the opening of the higher offices also came the privilege of belonging to the Senate, the aristocratic stronghold, for it was an early established custom that certain higher officials upon the conclusion of their service automatically became members of the Senate. Finally, the Senate lost its power of veto over the popular Assembly, and the people found themselves in control of the state.

The struggle of the orders left its mark upon the Roman constitution and left a certain amount of duality in the offices of the state. But despite the above changes, Rome remained an aristocratic state, for the new office holders became the new nobility and, by control of the elections, kept the offices rather well among themselves. In this aristocracy, the Senate remained the controlling body because of its permanence and because the officials would later become senators and thus could not afford to offend the Senate. It was under the able leadership of the Senate that Rome had her steady rise to power.

MILITARY ORGANIZATION

Upon the history of no people has the character of its military institutions exercised a deeper effect than upon that of Rome. The Roman military system rested upon the universal obligation of the male citizen to render military service. Early organization of the army probably followed the Homeric type with nobles in chariots and attending common folk. Due to Etruscan influence, a long, closed phalanx had been developed as the basic formation. Definite improvements in the military organization were made in the fourth century. At that time pay was introduced and the legionary formation developed. The legion contained about 4,000 men divided into smaller units for flexibility of movement in broken country. The throwing of the javelin also was adopted and the cavalry was strengthened. The frequency of the Roman wars automatically brought about a universal military training; and Roman army discipline was vastly superior to that of nearly all peoples she met on the field of battle. The insistence upon fortified camps was another definite advantage which Roman military technique included. In military matters at least, Rome could face the future with confidence.

11. Roman World Domination

ROME AND CARTHAGE

THE origins of Carthage, already noted in an earlier section of this volume, go back to the Phoenician colonial expansion early in the first millennium B.C. For centuries, there was no basis for conflict between Carthage and Rome, even though they were relatively close together. Carthage was a commercial, trading city, while Rome definitely was agrarian and interested narrowly in the problems of Italy. Carthage gradually created a colonial empire based on commercial interests; the coast line of North Africa was hers; she exploited southern Spain and occupied part of Sicily. Carthage, a nominal democracy, actually was governed by a wealthy aristocracy. Her trading activities naturally had built up a navy, but, lacking a citizen army, she employed such mercenary troops as she needed. This was the power which Rome was to challenge for the control of the western Mediterranean world.

With Roman control of Italy came the gradual growth of commerce which eventually would bring her into direct conflict with Carthage; and with Roman expansion southward also came contacts and relations with the several groups of people in Sicily. Rome logically looked to Sicily as the next area into which to expand, although Carthaginian traders and settlers had long been there.

THE STRUGGLE FOR THE WEST

The First Punic War (264-241 B.C.), as the struggle which now began is known, opened with Roman troops coming into Sicily to engage in a local dispute in which Carthage was on the opposing side. Roman successes induced her to build a fleet, and on the sea she also achieved the first victory off the coast of Sicily; but an African invasion was decisively repulsed near Carthage. Then Rome suffered the loss of most of her fleet in a storm, with the consequence that the Carthaginian war-ships plundered the coasts of Italy. The Roman treasury was empty, but by private subscription money was raised for a new fleet of 200 ships which finally forced the Carthaginians to sue for peace despite the successes of their great general, Hamilcar Barca. Rome imposed a hard peace. Sicily and the surrounding islands became Roman, and an indemnity of about three and a half million dollars was to be paid by Carthage. As an aftermath of the war, the mercenaries of Carthage revolted and almost destroyed her; Rome meanwhile annexed the neighboring islands of Sardinia and Corsica.

In the interlude, for it was obvious that the Carthaginian-Roman struggle was not concluded, Rome faced problems in the northwest, and was drawn into conflicts on this frontier. Across the Adriatic, above the state of Epirus, a loosely organized, semibarbarous people formed the state of Illyria. Illyrian piracy against the Italian cities induced Rome to send an expedition to punish them. Illyrian warfare brought Rome into conflict with Macedonia, the remnant of what once had been the Hellenistic kingdom of Macedonia and Greece. Here, too, Roman arms were victorious. While these campaigns were being carried out, a new Gallic invasion swept over the Alps into northern Italy. In a desperate battle, Rome annihilated the invader and once more secured her northern frontier, adding to the territory under her control provinces extending to the Alps.

The Second Punic War (218-201 B.C.) began in Spain where Carthage had recouped her

Triumphal arch built by Romans in Africa. (Acme)

paigns in North Africa forced Carthage to recall Hannibal from Italy. The final struggle between the exhausted rivals took place at Zama, near Carthage, and the great Hannibal was defeated by Scipio. Rome had become the greatest power in the ancient world. Rome took Spain, where she created two provinces, imposed an indemnity of nearly twelve million dollars on Carthage, appropriated all but ten of the Carthaginian war ships, and made her a dependent ally.

losses of the first war by the creation of a great colonial empire, exceedingly wealthy and powerful. It would seem that the actual occasion for the war was created by the great Carthaginian general, Hannibal, an able and trusted leader though still a young man. Over a frontier dispute, Hannibal with a well trained and well equipped army left Spain, crossed northward over the Alps during the winter and suddenly appeared in Italy. Hannibal knew and employed military techniques far superior to those employed by any Roman commander. In three battles in northern Italy, Roman armies were routed, cut up, and almost annihilated.

After three years of preparation by Rome, a supreme effort at Cannae ended in a prolonged slaughter of Roman troops. The Romans were panic-stricken by this brilliant commander who seemed invincible, but they refused to give up. Fortified Rome could not be taken, but practically all the rest of Italy was under the control of the invader. Some of the Roman allies deserted, while Hannibal negotiated an alliance with Macedonia; and though Rome had to arm her boys and slaves, the war went on. After ten years in Italy, Hannibal appealed to Carthage for more troops with which to finish the war, but his brother, marching from Spain to his aid, was met by a Roman army en route, defeated, and killed.

ROME VICTORIOUS

Now Rome began an aggressive policy under the able general, Scipio. His conquests in Spain deprived Carthage of revenues and help from this most important source, and his cam-

Scipio Africanus

Despite all her reverses, Carthage continued to prosper commercially. Rome could not forget how desperate had been her struggles for victory, and Roman merchants quickly begrudged Carthage what trade and industry she could develop. When Carthage defended herself against the aggressions of the Numidians of North Africa, Rome declared that she had violated her treaty arrangements and after a three-year war, captured and destroyed Carthage (146 B.C.). Thus Rome made certain that she would have no rival in the West.

ROME AND THE EAST

In the first half of the second century B.C., Rome attained the same dominant position in the eastern Mediterranean that she had won in the West as the results of the First and Second Punic Wars. Roman entry into, and conquest

The ruins of Carthage. (I. N. Robins)

of, the complex Hellenistic world was aided materially by the conflicts which had arisen everywhere between and within the several states. The prospect that Macedonia and the Seleucid power would conquer Egypt, as well as the Macedonian aid recently given Hannibal, induced Rome to intervene by sending an ultimatum to Philip V of Macedonia in 200 B.C. Three years later, Macedonia was crushed by Roman legions, forced to pay indemnity, give autonomy to Greece, and accept an alliance with Rome.

Roma

The war with Macedonia brought Rome into conflict with Antiochus the Great, the Seleucid ruler who controlled the larger part of the old Alexandrian Empire. Though Hannibal was at the court of Antiochus and freely offered his advice, Rome achieved a decisive victory in Asia Minor at Magnesia in 190 B.C. Peace terms demanded that eastern Asia Minor be turned into small independent states, that all but ten war vessels be surrendered, and that an indemnity of eighteen million dollars, the largest yet, be paid to Rome.

These early operations did not result in direct Roman control, but the traditional Hellenic political restlessness, and attempts at expansion by the greater powers, continued to draw Rome back into the eastern Mediterranean area. Harsh measures finally were adopted in Greece, as symbolized by the destruction of Corinth in 146 B.C. By this time Macedonia, through continued aggression, had brought additional Roman armies upon her and had been reduced to a Roman province with a Roman governor. Rome interfered in Egyptian affairs to save Egypt from Seleucid aggression, and continued her policy of ordering Asia Minor to suit herself, although no Roman provinces were created there until 133 B.C., when the kingdom of Pergamum was

willed to the Roman people. Long before the close of the second century, there was little doubt that Rome was the real mistress of the eastern Mediterranean, even though she did not nominally control the local political states.

The last half of the second century was characterized by a variety of conflicts and revolts on the wide-flung, three-continent frontier, as Spain, Gaul, Macedonia, Greece, and Asia continued to struggle ineffectively against Roman imperialism. However, before we follow the political expansion of Rome, it is necessary to understand some of the internal problems which Rome was facing.

IMPERIAL GOVERNMENT

The constitutional government of Rome, as has been pointed out, experienced few changes after its earlier adjustments. Until the social struggles late in the second century, the Senate exercised practically unchallenged control over the government of the Roman state. Outside of Rome, the acquisition of vast territory demanded the organization of the state along new lines. Most of the conquered states came to be organized as provinces, each under a Roman governor who, with an army to support him, possessed almost unlimited power. He had complete control over the taxes, so that the terms of these governors often came to be periods of looting and robbery. Even the efforts of the Senate to control them proved inadequate. Roman business men also swarmed into the provinces and helped to loot the provincials.

CULTURAL DECAY

In Italy, there arose a wealthy class of merchants and government officials, and quickly the old Roman simplicity of living gave way to a luxury which probably never had been equaled. The plunder of war was brought back and installed in Roman homes. From Greece

Roman Vase, with sculptured relief. (Metropolitan Museum of Art)

came hundreds and thousands of objects of art. Elaborate houses demanded many servants, and these too the wars furnished as thousands of slaves were poured into Rome.

Greek thought and expression had a tremendous effect upon the Roman culture, especially during the last centuries before the Christian Era. Greek art objects were abundant in Rome; Greek literature became well known, and Greek theaters and Hellenistic buildings appeared in Italy. Wealthy Romans hired Greek tutors for their children, which shows how completely the Roman aristocracy was under the influence of Hellenistic culture; and inevitably the art and literature which began to appear in Rome reflected its Greek background.

With luxury came decay. The seriousness and the sternness of old Rome passed. Gladiatorial combats in arenas and chariot races became the popular forms of amusement for the people. Corruption in the provincial administration was matched by the bribery and dishonesty which appeared at home in governmental officialdom.

Outside of commercial Rome, the wealthy landowner became yet wealthier and absorbed the lands of the poor peasant about him until the small farm almost disappeared in Italy, and one large estate joined the next. The thousands of slaves employed on these estates were ill-treated and desperate. Revolts, some of them serious, broke out in various parts of Sicily

and Italy. The free landowner of the small farm was either forced to sell to the wealthy noble, or war called him from his farm, which would be usurped during his absence. Dispossessed, unhappy men began to drift into Rome where they came to constitute a serious social problem. It became evident that Rome either must reorganize herself into a more efficient imperial state or perish, for beyond her

Greek Temples at Paestum, Italy (6th century B.C.), were part of Hellenic culture that influenced Romans

borders in central and northern Europe new hordes of barbarians now were organizing to press upon the southern areas of culture.

THE GRACCHI—CHAMPIONS OF THE PEOPLE

The changes in Roman society and in the political state showed evil aspects which had to be corrected if a measure of peace was to prevail. The dispossessed farmers who drifted

Crowds of about 50,000 Romans filled the Colosseum to watch athletic games and chariot races

about the city should be restored to the land. Honest and efficient government needed to be restored. The restricted Roman citizenship only led to discontentment and trouble, even among the closest of Rome's allies. And some solution of the growing problems connected with slavery also needed to be found.

The people found a champion in Tiberius Gracchus, grandson of the great Scipio, the conqueror of Hannibal. Tiberius advocated citizenship for all Italians, and a land law which limited the amount that one person could hold, and provided for the redistribution of public land. While he managed to pass his law, he was killed by a mob of senators in the disturbances that followed (133 B.C.), and a new age of revolution and civil war was introduced. Ten years later, a younger brother, Caius Gracchus, was elected tribune of the people, and attempted to put through even broader reforms which also aimed at the curtailment of senatorial power. In order to secure his measures, he too attempted to usurp more power than was constitutional, and subsequently suffered the same fate as had his brother. What benefits had been achieved soon

were undone; the eloquence of the Gracchi seemed only to hasten civil war, while the newly voiced idea that one man could be above the Constitution, and force be used to secure power soon produced an evil fruit.

MILITARY MASTERS OF ROME

The people had been taught to look for leaders in their struggle for privileges and justice. Senatorial corruption in the management of the war in Africa resulted in the popular election of Marius as commander in the African war, even though the Senate had the right to designate by lot the consul who was to conduct the war. The people had overruled the Senate. After the successful completion of the African war, Marius illegally was elected consul five years in succession because of his important victories against the German invaders who were crossing the northern borders of Roman territory (106-100 B.C.).

However, the unconstitutional assignment of power caused disturbances in Rome. A Roman army was required to quell a revolt of Sicilian slaves, and a two-year rebellion of the Italian allies, who demanded citizenship, was ended only when this condition was met. Certainly, Rome was in the midst of an internal upheaval. Sulla, who had gained a reputation by the subjugation of the Italian allies, somehow aroused the distrust of the democratic popular party. The management of the Asiatic war was voted to the old, popular favorite, Marius, even though he was without an army at the time. Sulla at once occupied Rome, restored senatorial supremacy, and had himself appointed commander for the war against the ambitious Mithridates, King of Pontus in Asia Minor. When Sulla had left for the East Marius immediately invaded Rome and restored popular control amid frightful massacres of the senatorial party. Then, having concluded a victorious campaign in Asia Minor, Sulla returned and speedily defeated the various armed forces of the popular party, retook Rome, wreaked an even bloodier vengeance on his foes than that which Marius had dealt the Sullan supporters, and restored supreme authority to the Senate. But his retirement did not bring peace to Rome, for new leaders sought both power and wealth.

While these various struggles were taking place at home, the developments in the East

Julius Caesar, general and statesman

were drawing Rome into even wider conflicts with the several native states in Asia Minor and the rest of the Near East. Pompey, who had gained success in Spain, gained further renown when, by a masterful sweep of the Mediterranean, he destroyed strong pirate bands that were preying on commerce and plundering the Italian coasts. Next, he was given command of the Asiatic forces; he won important victories in Asia Minor, crushing the remnant of the Seleucid Empire, creating new provinces, and returning to Rome as her greatest hero—an unusual hero, for he disbanded his army and then requested approval of his acts and rewards for his troops (62 B.C.).

JULIUS CAESAR'S RISE TO FAME

Meanwhile new figures had appeared in Rome. Cicero, whose oratorical ability has

Roman Bath, Somersetshire, England. (Ewing Galloway)

Roman Amphitheater, Nimes, France. (French National Tourist Office)

Cleopatra, queen of Egypt, 69–30 B.C.

come to be proverbial, distinguished himself in handling the affairs of state as consul. Julius Caesar, a nephew of Marius, had pushed himself into a position of power through the aid of the wealthy Crassus. When Pompey appeared in Rome without his army, he quickly realized that he needed support if he was to secure the demands he had made. So an alliance for personal gain, called the First Triumvirate, was arranged between Pompey, Caesar, and Crassus. As a result, Caesar was elected consul in 59 B.C., and in the next year was appointed proconsul, or governor, of Gaul (France). Caesar felt that he needed military success for a career in the Roman state. In eight years of campaigning in Gaul, Caesar became a skillful military commander, conquered and organized the territory up to the Rhine and the English Channel, and even invaded Britain. For later

European history, these conquests are of great significance, for they began the transmission of classical culture to the West.

ACROSS THE RUBICON TO POWER

The prestige and ability of Caesar as popular leader aroused fear in senatorial ranks, and when his return was imminent, Pompey was offered a command for the defense of the Senate, while Caesar was ordered to disband his army and return to Rome. Immediately, Caesar crossed the Rubicon River into Italy. As Pompey had no time to organize opposition, he fled. Caesar then had himself elected consul in Rome and proceeded against the "enemies" of the state. Pompey held the eastern provinces as well as Spain, so that Caesar faced a difficult situation even though he controlled Rome. By a swift thrust into Spain, the opposition there was isolated and forced to surrender; a few months later, Caesar landed on the coast of Epirus, and on the field of Pharsalus in Thessaly, Pompey was crushingly defeated. His forces surrendered and Pompey fled to Egypt, only to be murdered before Caesar arrived. In Egypt, Caesar found Cleopatra, the last of the Ptolemies, on the throne.

Amphitheater, built in 27 B.C., Switzerland. (Swiss Federal Railroad)

Roman Arena, Arles, France. (French National Tourist Office)

The charms of this remarkable woman held even the great Caesar from the immediate conclusion of his civil wars. He tarried for the winter under the guise of ordering Egyptian affairs. The following year, Caesar crushed the final opposition against him, which had been organized in Africa (46 B.C.). A revolt in Spain occurred a little later, but Caesar now was undisputed master of the Roman state. A monarchy or dictatorship in Rome had seemed inevitable decades before it occurred. The corruption of the people and the government, the need of honest government for the provinces, and the need of better defense against the dangers of the frontiers had not been adjusted under either popular or senatorial rule; possibly a centralized government directed by one person might be the solution. Rome had had earlier dictators, appointed to meet some extraordinary crisis, but they had governed for limited periods of time, in accordance with constitutional provisions.

Caesar used his extraordinary powers along broad fronts to adjust the social, economic and political problems of the state. A few of his projected reforms were as follows: Unemployment was to be reduced by public work and by enforcement of the law that one-third of the labor on landed estates should be free. Debtors might escape imprisonment by turning over their assets to their creditors. To relieve the pressure in Rome and to Romanize the Empire, colonization projects were encouraged. More roads were planned. The corrupt provincial system of government was to be reorganized. Broader citizenship and a more representative Senate were to be achieved. The Egyptian calendar, which had many advantages over the old Roman system, was introduced.

It is apparent that Caesar intended to establish himself as the permanent head of the great empire Rome had created, despite the fact that he retained various republican titles and forms. Thus, a Republican opposition, led by Brutus and Cassius, caused the assassination of Caesar in 44 B.C. Democracy, however, had fled from Rome and only more civil war resulted, while an obviously great and able man had been removed from a state which sorely needed guidance. A few years later Rome deified the tyrant she now cut down.

The Roman Empire at its greatest extent, and its final division

12. The Last Five Centuries of the Roman Empire

OCTAVIUS—SUCCESSOR TO CAESAR

CONFUSION followed the murder of Caesar, but various leaders and factions soon became discernible. Mark Antony, renowned for his funeral oration over Caesar, gathered the remnants of the Caesarian party under his control. Lepidus, another supporter of Caesar, set about bringing order to Spain. The third person who came to the fore at this time was Octavius, a young man of eighteen, nephew and chief heir of Caesar.

When Octavius appeared in Italy he was given scant recognition either by the opposition or by the friends of Caesar; but in the following year the Second Triumvirate was formed by this seemingly insignificant youth, Antony, and Lepidus. With the defeat of Brutus and Cassius at Philippi on the border of Macedonia and Thrace (42 B.C.), the Caesarian party had complete power and by agreement divided the provinces into three general spheres of control for the three successors of Caesar.

Mark Antony

Brutus

During the next ten years, Octavius gradually strengthened his position and managed to remove Lepidus, the third member of the coalition, from military power by assigning him to a religious position, that of *pontifex maximus*. Antony, in control of the eastern provinces, was unsuccessful in his campaigns against the Parthians, the new nationalistic power which had grown up south of the Caspian Sea and had expanded westward until conflict with Rome had arisen. Antony also had fallen under the charms of Cleopatra and it was reported that they planned to establish themselves together with their children as rulers of the Roman world. Octavius, obviously interested in sole power, forced war upon Cleopatra and Antony. In a great sea battle at Actium, off the west coast of Greece, Antony was decisively defeated (31 B.C.). Pursued into Egypt the following year by the relentless Octavius, Antony and Cleopatra committed suicide. Egypt became a Roman province and Octavius stood alone as the political head of the Roman Empire.

PEACE, REFORM AND PROSPERITY

When Octavius returned to Italy there was no resistance, and it seemed as though at last the people were ready to accept a ruler for the Empire. In 27 B.C., Octavius offered to relinquish all powers, but the Senate officially gave him control of the army and the frontier provinces. He also was made tribune and the titles of Augustus and Princeps were conferred upon him. While Augustus, as he now was called, preserved the republican forms and recognized the Senate, he came to be the absolute ruler of the Empire. The popular Assembly disappeared. The reorganization of the provinces, while providing no more political recognition of her citizens, did provide better administration with more permanent, paid officials. The plundering of the natives, the custom of the past century and a half, was reduced. Linked to the provincial reorganization was the problem of adequate frontier defense and often the problem of defining just where that border had best be maintained. A large standing army of professional soldiers was imperative, and during the next century this army was increased to over two hundred thousand men. With the coming of "Imperial Peace," the war-torn Mediterranean world now had its first prolonged peace in many centuries. While legions held her borders, commerce, trade, and industry flourished.

Rome, the Empire's capital, received a building impetus partly through state building and partly through private endeavor. Augustus built a palace, finished a basilica begun by Caesar, and also erected a forum and a theater. Impressive colonnades, columns, and arches were commonly used in structures of the age. Painting and interior decoration of homes were emphasized beyond that of the finest age in Greece. Yet, the best Rome could do was either to plunder the original Greek model or to copy it.

Cicero

In science, Rome seemed entirely dependent upon Greek and Hellenistic civilization. Cicero, just before the Empire period, had written beautiful rhetorical prose. Keen interest in literature during the Augustan Age not only produced students of classical Greek but also created a genuine Latin literature. Horace and

The Emperor Augustus addressing his army

Virgil created Roman poetry; Livy wrote Roman history; and Strabo, a Greek living in Rome, produced a geography. In the middle of the second century of the Christian Era, Ptolemy, a great astronomer and geographer, lived and worked in Alexandria, Egypt; but this is taking us beyond the early Empire period.

THE SUCCESSORS OF AUGUSTUS

Forty-one years after he had been appointed head of the Roman state, Augustus died. Estimates of his abilities in the several fields of government have differed, yet he did take a confused, warring world, and he changed it into an ordered, peaceful empire. His organization and the precedents which he established helped to hold classical civilization together for a few more centuries. Throughout his long reign, Augustus had been concerned with the succession of power, for he knew that without central authority internal disorders would break out. During the last years of his life, he had associated his stepson, Tiberius, with him in the government; thus upon the death of Augustus, the succession was accomplished without trouble.

Roman Sarcophagus. Greek style and Greek story of Achilles are copied in high relief decorating sides

The next four rulers, related by blood or adoption to Augustus, are known as the Julio–Claudian line (14-68 A.D.). Tiberius, a trained soldier and able administrator, followed the policies of Augustus to the best of his ability. Mutinies in the army and plots in Rome were handled ably. When his successor,

Claudian Aqueduct, finished 50 A.D., carried water for 44 miles to Rome. (T.W.A. Airline Photo)

Claudius

Caligula, wasted the reserves saved by Tiberius and attempted to establish an absolute monarchy in which he insisted that all subjects recognize his deification, officers of his own imperial guards put him to death.

These same guards elevated Claudius, a member of the ruling family, but one who had been given no particular recognition, to the rank of Imperator. Soldiers elevated a new emperor, and a new precedent had been set. In general, Claudius followed the steps of the first emperor. The conquest of lower Britain was accomplished in several campaigns and the new province of Thrace was formed. The census taken during the reign of Claudius revealed almost six million Romans, nearly a million more than in the time of Augustus. At Rome, Claudius was interested in furthering building and improvements. Despite his abilities, Claudius was too much under the influence of certain freedmen whom he employed in governmental service, as well as of various relatives—including four wives.

NERO—INFAMOUS TYRANT

Nero, the last of the Augustan line, owed his throne to the intrigues of his mother. Nero had been educated by the philosopher Seneca, who served as his chief counselor for five years. But Nero poisoned his half-brother and his mother, who had made him emperor; later his wife suffered the same fate. This series of murders left him free to follow his own evil nature in such a career of vice and cruelty that his name has gone down in history as one of the blackest.

In the conviction that he was an artist, he appeared publicly as a singer and musician, both in Rome and in Greece. He tried to arouse a greater interest in Greek culture among the Romans. A terrible fire in Rome, lasting six days, ruined the greater part of the city. Subsequently, Nero was accused of having caused the fire so that he might rebuild the city more splendidly, and it was gossiped that while he

Nero

watched the city burn he recited poetry on the destruction of Troy, accompanying his verse with the lyre. The city was rebuilt more beautifully, but a scapegoat had to be found; so the Christians in Rome were blamed and death resulted for many.

The extravagances, the cruelties and excesses of Nero alienated men throughout the Empire. In the East, the expansion of a powerful Parthian king caused Roman reverses there; Britain, only recently brought under Roman

Nero persecuting the Christians. Crucifixion was the most ignoble of death sentences, since it was illegal to punish even Roman freedmen by this method

control, revolted; conspiracy flared in Rome and in the closer provinces; provincial governors with armies moved toward Rome. The Senate voted the death of Nero, who dramatically committed suicide (68 A.D.).

MILITARY EMPERORS

Upon Nero's death four claimants were nominated by the various military forces of the Empire, and only after a year of bloodshed did Vespasian, an able general, who at the time was carrying on a war against the Jews, attain the throne. Under Vespasian, another period of peace began for the Empire, a period of great prosperity. The chief problem of the Empire during this period was that of protecting the frontiers. On the south, the great Sahara formed a good barrier, and on the west, the ocean. But on the long northern frontier were German barbarians ever anxious to penetrate farther south, and on the east, the Euphrates River boundary, the Parthian Empire remained as a serious threat to Roman tranquillity.

Vespasian and his sons, Titus and Domitian, were essentially military commanders, natu rally not of the Augustan clan. They held their positions for twenty-seven years after 69 A.D., partly at least because of the support of the army, ignoring the Senate with the result

Arch of Titus commemorates Jerusalem's capture, 70 A.D. Relief depicts a triumphal chariot entering the city. (Fritz Henle)

that at last Domitian incurred its hatred. Their interests were primarily the preservation of the various frontiers, and that duty they performed well. Only on the lower Danube River, the Dacian peoples apparently could neither be defeated permanently nor adjusted. When senatorial conspiracy removed Domitian and elevated the senator Nerva to the throne, this danger spot on the frontier became more threatening, for Nerva was no soldier.

Trajan capturing a wild boar during an imperial hunt, a detail from the Arch of Constantine

TRAJAN AND HADRIAN

Fortunately for Rome, the death of Nerva in less than two years returned the power to a military commander, who assumed office, not in Rome, but in Cologne near the frontier. Trajan, a native of Spain, spent his reign (98-117 A.D.) in defending the borders of the Empire. He realized that if the Empire was to be at peace the Dacians must be crushed. Bridging the Danube with boats and hewing his way through dense forests, Trajan defeated the Dacian warriors, captured their strongholds and ultimately their capital. He erected a massive stone bridge over the Danube and Dacia became a new Roman province with Roman colonists.

Hadrian

Having so brilliantly settled the Dacian problem, Trajan next turned to the eastern frontier where Parthian aggression again caused unrest in the areas under Roman control. Trajan overran Armenia, Assyria, and Babylonia, and reached the Persian Gulf, only to be recalled by a serious revolt in Mesopotamia. Shortly thereafter, revolts in Africa and Britain called him still farther away from the lands he had hoped to conquer, but which immediately were reoccupied by the enemy. Before his death, he secured the succession of Hadrian, a tried soldier, who also became a vigorous administrator (117-138 A.D.). Hadrian wisely did not attempt to expand the Roman border on the east, but kept the boundary at the Euphrates River. He strengthened the Danube defense line up to the Rhine by the completion of a fortified wall. A similar wall was constructed along the northern boundary of Roman Britain. Hadrian interested himself extensively in Greek culture, while in the government of the state he instituted intelligent judicial and administrative reforms.

MARCUS AURELIUS

Antoninus Pius (138-161 A.D.), the elected successor of Hadrian, managed to hold during a long reign the lines of the frontiers as they had been established, while he gave his chief energies to judicial reforms. His successor, Marcus Aurelius (161-180 A.D.) was by nature a student and a devout follower of the Stoic philosophy. His *Meditations* bear testimony to the true nobility of his character, and he spent his reign in valiantly defending the frontiers. From campaigns to reestablish Roman authority in the East where the Parthians

Marcus Aurelius with toga over head sacrifices before the Temple of Jupiter Capitolinus. Flute is played to drown out ill-omened sounds

were again pressing forward, the soldiers brought the plague back with them and its empire-wide ravages caused widespread depopulation.

Hard-fought battles and costly victories checked the barbarian invaders on the Danubian and German borders, after the enemy had broken through the frontier defenses for the

Antoninus Pius. (Metropolitan Museum of Art)

first time in two centuries and penetrated into upper Italy. Some of the invaders were even permitted to settle within the frontier under the impression that they would help defend it against their kinsmen. Marcus Aurelius was a great and a good ruler, but no ruler could stop the processes of decay and decline which had begun throughout the Roman world. Commodus (180-192 A.D.), an ignoble son of a noble father, hastened the evil day by his vicious self-centered and cruel reign during which problems of state were commonly ignored. Following two centuries of relative peace and prosperity, there now came almost a full century of revolution, decline, and anarchy, which produced a very different Roman world.

ROMAN CIVILIZATION

We have had a glimpse of the culture which flourished in Rome under Augustus and the early Empire. That culture underwent significant changes, and it is only appropriate that we note those developments before the final chapter in Roman history is considered.

Although the fiction of senatorial partner-

Roman Upper Class Life. Professional philosophers were often hired to lecture to the family (top left), but Roman wives spent many more hours at their toilette, while their husbands conducted business in the city, walking over the narrow streets on convenient stepping stones (center). Refreshments could be bought in the city's shops (bottom right), but the day's climax was dinner at the 10th hour or 4 P.M.

Caracalla's Baths. The Roman entered a warm ante-room, then progressed through a hot bath, a cold bath, and an oil rub down to complete his daily bath

Roman Amusements. Chariot races (above) were a favorite entertainment among the Romans, who wagered recklessly on the drivers. The successful driver, although of low social standing, was feted by all. Less popular was the theater (below) where the two hour performances were given during the day because of lack of lighting. Bakers (bottom left) ground the grain as well as baked the bread and made flat, round loaves marked with radiating lines

143

ship with the emperor existed, the administration of the Empire was in the hands of the emperor. With the passing of time, there was built up in the Empire a large civil service composed of all types and classes, who were paid by the government and who were rewarded for efficient service by advancement.

In the provinces, tremendous changes had taken place since the good old days of wholesale looting. When Augustus attained to power, there were probably thirteen provinces; a century and a half later, there were forty-five. While these provinces fell into different categories, their administrations ultimately came to be very similar. Governors still held supreme and almost absolute power, but now there were significant checks and safeguards. It was no longer difficult to bring a governor to trial in Rome for abuse of power and for dishonesty. Taxation was carefully controlled by law and regulated by the census rolls. Direct and indirect taxes went into governmental treasuries and not into the pockets of governors.

Within the provinces, the local cities or municipalities enjoyed a relative autonomy in regard to local affairs, once taxes were paid. The two centuries of internal security brought a teeming, prosperous activity with complicated industrial organization to these provincial cities, be they in western Spain or in eastern Asia Minor. As early as the second century, however, financial troubles in the municipalities augured evil for the future, since the life of Rome was linked with that of her provinces. Excessive taxation and the steady drain of manpower were causing havoc.

ALL ROADS LEAD TO ROME

Rome, the imperial center, still continued to increase the number of elaborate buildings and to beautify the city further. Underneath the veneer of wealth, however, were the increasing masses of impoverished people whose demands for food and amusement were a serious burden on the state. The practice of freeing slaves, who then gradually became absorbed into the free population, gave Rome a mixture of race probably attained nowhere else in antiquity. The concentration of population stimulated commerce and industry. Both capital and labor could be found abundantly in Rome. Italy became a manufacturing center and imported her food and raw products. The peak of Italian industrial life was reached early in the second century of our era, but decline and collapse followed in the third century. Behind political decline were the state demands for men and money; behind economic decline were the problems of production and distribution, the decay of agriculture, and the creation of new industrial centers in the provinces.

While there was probably a larger educated public in Rome than ever before, and more imported objects of art from Greece, more libraries, and more entertainment, there was a definite decline in intellectual life. Originality had departed; and the old appeared only in poorer dress. Censorship exercised by some of the emperors restrained the writing of honest history. Among the few men in the entire Roman world who produced worthwhile literary materials during this long period were Tacitus, known for his historical writings; the Greek Plutarch, renowned for his remarkable series of biographies of the greater men of Greece and Rome; and Pliny, famed for his "Natural History" which however, offered only encyclopedic knowledge and not new contributions.

In the area of classical culture, Rome failed to produce anything comparable to that of the Greek world, yet at the same time, Rome's conquests had hastened the decline of other states which had shown aptitude in cultural fields. The disorders of the third century dealt a fatal blow to the material basis of the classical civilization and cultural collapse followed rapidly.

COLLAPSE OF OLDER RELIGIONS

The religious transformation of the Roman world was as significant for future ages as its political transformation. Throughout the empire, there was diffused a group of oriental religions, originating in the eastern Mediterranean. As the Greek gods had vanished, so Roman gods, their partial descendants, also lost their significance as the Roman world expanded. In Rome too, men turned to philos-

Mars

ophy, particularly to Stoicism and Epicureanism. Many more turned to the Mystery Religions which had swung into popular favor during the early Hellenistic Age. The reasons why people turned to them in the West are practically identical with those already enumerated in our section on Hellenistic Culture.

The cult of Isis from Egypt and the cult of Mithra from Persia found hundreds of thousands of converts throughout the empire. Judaism, carried throughout the empire by dispersed Jews, did not have the popular appeal which Christianity had with its teachings of brotherhood and love, its utter lack of class distinction, and its assurances of a blissful future existence. Having its roots within Palestine, it often was associated in the first decades with Judaism. It soon separated itself, even in the popular mind, from the Hebrew religion and flourished in spite of intensive persecution. By the end of the second century of peace, it was rapidly outstripping the other religions of the Empire.

A CENTURY OF DECLINE
(182-285 A.D.)

The economic decline beginning in the second century has been noted. Linked with it was the definite drop in population as a result of wars, plague, and a decreasing birth rate. All these factors weakened the army, the bulwark of the Empire, for both men and pay were lacking. The inability of the state either to secure hereditary succession for her emperors, or to devise a legal method of electing them, repeatedly had thrown the Empire into disorder and civil war.

When Commodus, the unworthy successor of Marcus Aurelius, had been assassinated, various contenders sought the throne. After four years of civil war, the rough but able general, Septimus Severus secured it. He established a military monarchy (197 A.D.) which functioned satisfactorily under his forceful administration. Spending several years restoring order in Britain, he rebuilt the wall of Hadrian. He was concerned primarily with military problems. This interest in and emphasis upon the army brought incompetent men into government positions. The five rulers who followed Severus were unworthy and incapable of coping with the problems of empire defense. Their weaknesses were all the more dangerous because of the rise of a new dynasty in the East, the Sasanids, who inherited Parthian pretensions to a great empire and pushed westward with fresh energy and zeal. When the last Severus, Severus Alexander, was murdered by a mutiny of his own soldiers on the Rhine frontier in 235 A.D., a half century of greater confusion and anarchy had begun.

During this half century, twenty-six emperors were recognized and of these only one escaped violent death. In addition, there were various usurpers and claimants who did not make good their ambitions. There was little order as plundering soldiers swept through the Empire. Life and property were nowhere safe; robbery and murder were everyday occur-

Soldiers of Septimus Severus sacrificing to the gods of Palmyra and Dura. (Oriental Institute of the University of Chicago)

council. The emperor assumed the gorgeous dress and golden symbols of the oriental kings, and was recognized as the sun god incarnate. For purposes of administration, the Empire was divided between two emperors; each of whom chose a Caesar as heir apparent and assistant in keeping the frontiers. There was to remain, however, the fiction of one empire. Provinces were reduced in size to prevent rebellion, and the powers of governors were reduced and shared with military officials. The legions also were broken up into smaller regiments to lessen the influence of the army in politics.

The scarcity of money forced the state to accept grain and products for taxes, and induced it to legislate on problems of private business. The famous Edict of Prices, in 301 A.D., attempted to fix prices for each commodity and every form of labor and professional service. This law could not be enforced, however, even though it threatened the death penalty. Men might no longer leave their occupations or professions, lest the government lose by such procedure. Everywhere oriental despotism was appearing, and liberty disappearing. Diocletian's persecution of Christians seems to have been motivated not because of religious convictions, but along the lines of further government control in the lives of its citizens. Diocletian's plan for securing an orderly succession of rulers for the Empire failed because it did not take into consideration the ambitions of generals and the loyalty of soldiers to their commanders. For the same reasons the scheme of subordinate emperors instituted by him failed.

rences. Private business was ruined and the nation became bankrupt. The civilization of the classical world was actually in the process of disintegration. The several barbarous tribes on the long northern frontier began breaking through and overrunning Greece, Italy, Gaul, and Spain; some even crossed to Africa. The plague, sweeping in from the East, again raged for fifteen years in the Empire. The state itself, lacking all central authority, was threatening to fall into its constituent parts. Roman prestige had fallen low when a Sasanian work of art could show Valerian, a Roman emperor who had been taken captive, kneeling before the great Persian king.

When it looked as though the empire were ready to collapse, Aurelian became emperor (270-275 A.D.), and began the restoration of order. His rivals defeated, he cleared Italy and the Danube region of barbarian invaders, built a massive wall around Rome, and then restored order in the East and in Gaul. Ten years after he died, Diocletian continued the restoration of the Empire and opened the last significant phase of Roman history.

DIOCLETIAN AND REORGANIZATION

Diocletian (284-305 A.D.), once having restored order, remade the Roman Empire into an oriental monarchy with himself as its absolute ruler. The Senate became merely a city

CONSTANTINE AND CHRISTIANITY

Out of the struggles for the throne following Diocletian, Constantine, later called the Great, emerged victorious as sole emperor, though he retained the other forms of administration inaugurated by Diocletian. In 330 A.D., he formally dedicated Constantinople as the new capital for the Empire. Conveniently located between Europe and Asia, at the entry to the Black Sea, Constantinople was also nearer the more dangerous frontiers and centrally located for trade. This transfer of the capital to the East actually meant the separation of the Empire into two parts, although nominally one Roman Empire continued.

As already indicated in a preceding section, Christianity was expanding steadily despite opposition and persecution. By the opening of the fourth century, it had developed a complicated church system and constituted very definitely the largest religious group within the state. In the famous Edict of Milan (313 A.D.), toleration was proclaimed, and Christianity placed on an equal basis with other cults of the state. Constantine's formal acceptance of Christianity shortly before his death, raised the church to an unusual position of favor and influence. Despite reverses suffered in succeeding years, the church continued to grow until it expanded beyond the Empire limits, driving out other religious beliefs and ultimately becoming the foremost religion of Europe. The barbarians who continued in ever larger numbers to press against the Empire, ultimately accepted Christianity and also incorporated into their cultures remnants of classical civilization.

The sons and successors of Constantine again revived the military struggles for sole power within the state, while the state suffered further economic decline and invasions from without. Julian, an able soldier and forceful administrator of the middle fourth century, made a last attempt to check Christianity and to substitute for it a type of philosophic paganism. His efforts were in vain: the pagan cults had lost their appeal for the masses; and the only converts were those who sought to curry imperial favor. His efforts on the Rhine frontier where he checked the Germanic invasion were more successful. In the East, the forces of the Sasanid Empire were attacked unsuccessfully and Julian fell mortally wounded.

THE LAST INTERLUDE

The last half of the fourth century saw the increased pressures of Germanic peoples on the long northern frontier. A new element had been injected into an already complicated situation by the westward thrust of the Huns, a nomadic people of Mongolian origin, whose fierce onslaughts drove the West Goths, a Germanic tribe on the lower Danube, to beg admission into the Empire for protection. This was granted, but Roman administrative dishonesty resulted in Gothic insurrection and in the Goths overrunning the entire Balkan Peninsula.

In this crisis, Rome still found a champion who might check the inevitable deluge for a few years. Theodosius the Great (378-395 A.D.) managed to defeat the Goths and confine them to the Danube areas under nominal Roman rule. His quelling of revolts in various western provinces, as well as his championing of Christianity, won for him the title of "Great." But already ecclesiastical power had become so strong that Ambrose, a Roman bishop, insisted upon and obtained a public apology from the emperor who had offended the church.

Upon the death of Theodosius, the division of the Empire into Eastern and Western

Arch of Constantine was built to honor battle of Milvian Bridge, which made Constantine sole emperor. (T.W.A. Airline Photo)

became more apparent. The administrations of the two areas now were completely distinct; even the succession of rulers in the two sections was independent. The Western Empire came to be under the nominal control of military dictators, who could no longer maintain order in the state. In the east, the struggle for existence was more successful. The old Hellenic civilization, in a revived form, managed to organize its defenses against the barbarians and at the same time to develop an adequate internal administration and ultimately create a distinct civilization in the Byzantine Empire.

BARBARIAN TRIUMPH OVER ROMAN GLORY

The fifth century A.D. opened with widespread raids into the Western Empire by West Gothic tribes. Under the leadership of Alaric, they captured Rome in 410 A.D. and spent three days in wholesale looting of the imperial city. A nominal Roman emperor was helpless and the entire western Mediterranean cultural area was overrun. Alaric's successor even took as wife a Roman emperor's captive sister. Italy was plundered; Gaul and Spain were invaded. Here, however, another Germanic tribe, the Vandals, had preceded them in campaigns of pillage and destruction. Gradually, the Vandals were pushed into Spain and, by 430 A.D., under continued pressure removed to North Africa, where about ten years later they received Roman recognition as an independent kingdom.

Roman feebleness and the Eastern Empire's lack of cooperation permitted the Vandals to create a powerful navy, for a time in actual control of the Mediterranean Sea. Their territory included all of Roman North Africa, Corsica, Sardinia, a fortress in Sicily and the Balearic Islands. In Gaul and Spain, the Goths began the creation of their own state, despite the invasion of new tribes, such as the Burgundians and some of the Franks.

In eastern Britain the Saxons, Angles, and Jutes were firmly established by the middle of the fifth century and Rome had lost complete control there. The feeble western emperors finally resorted to the ancient Roman device of alliance in the hope of maintaining some control in the areas of their former Empire.

To add to the general confusion caused by the advance of the German tribes, the Huns, who first had pushed the West Goths into the Roman Empire seventy-five years earlier, now advanced farther into western Europe creating terror in their relentless advance. Attila, the Hun chieftain whose name is still linked with the concept of ferocity and brutality, united various Hun tribes and moved with a great army into Gaul. In desperation, the Germanic peoples joined Rome and turned the invading savages back after a tremendous struggle (451 A.D.). Attila next invaded Italy, but famine and disease among his own troops, as well as the appeal of the Roman bishop and the arrival of troops from the Eastern Empire, induced him to withdraw. His death in the following year brought about the collapse of organized Hun power.

"FALL" OF THE ROMAN EMPIRE

The year 476 A.D. has commonly been taken as the date of the "Fall" of the Roman Empire of the West and the beginning of the Middle Ages. That date is quite appropriate because in that year the last of the weak and inefficient rulers at Rome, who still pretended to have power over an empire which no longer existed, was removed by Odoacer, a German commander of mercenary troops. Odoacer, with the support of his German troops, proclaimed himself king. The barbarians had acquired full control. The Roman Empire was no longer.

Many have been the inquiries and studies aimed at an explanation of why Rome fell. After following her republican and imperial career, various suggestions make their appearance. The uncontrollable and unpredictable movements of peoples outside the Empire, internal economic decay covering wide categories, social change and disintegration, political and military developments—these are some of the factors which enter into any study of Roman decline. As Western civilization again took on new life in later centuries, significant elements of the classical life were recovered and became inextricably bound into the culture which is ours today.

13. The Pageant of India

EARLY INDIA

THE GEOGRAPHIC CHARACTERISTICS of India have at all times been of the greatest importance in the history of this great subcontinent. To the north lie the highest mountains in the world, the Himalayas, always effective in preventing mass movements of people from that direction. South of this forbidding ridge lie the broad plains of the Indus and Ganges valleys. This, the territory called Hindustan, extends southward to the mountains feeding the Narbada River. To the south of these ranges is the plateau called the Deccan, bounded near the coast of the Arabian Sea by the mountains called Western Ghats and on the east by the lesser Eastern Ghats. The rivers of the Deccan, rising in the Western Ghats, flow eastward through valleys in the Eastern Ghats and drop down into the third great geographic division of India, the Carnatic, which stretches to the southernmost point of the great peninsula opposite Ceylon.

These three geographic divisions continually played a part in the settlement of races and peoples, but one feature of the land not yet mentioned was the most important. Often in the past had India been invaded by foreigners who entered by the one natural gateway, aside from the sea, which leads into the country. This was on the northwest where the Himalaya ranges tail off into the Hindu Kush, which, although extremely high themselves, nevertheless are deeply cut in certain places. Through these passes, the most famous of which is the Khyber Pass, and over the still lower territory between them and the sea, have poured many armies, peoples, and influences, perhaps more than we shall ever know.

Recent excavation in the Indus Valley has revealed the nature of civilizations that lived there more than five thousand years ago. The height to which these civilizations had risen, compared to Egypt and Mesopotamia, then beginning their historic careers, is most astonishing, for it had long been considered that India was backward indeed before the coming of the Aryans. These impressions had been gained from the hymns of the Rigveda, the Hindu Bible, which indicated that the despised people the Aryans found on coming to India were far from being their equals. We may hardly doubt now that the Indus Valley, and probably other parts of India as well, had attained an excellence in many traits of civilization concerning which the Aryans knew nothing when they first became inhabitants of India. Perhaps the Aryans brought with them little more than their energy and a language which seems to have a tendency toward developing mentality.

In many respects the early civilization that has recently been discovered in northwestern India approximated those we have seen in Egypt and Mesopotamia. Grains were cultivated and numerous domesticated animals lived in the settlements. Among these animals were the humped zebu, buffalo, short-horned bull, elephant, camel, sheep, pig, and dog. Oxen probably pulled the wheeled vehicles

Pre Aryan Seal from the Indus Valley portrays bull under pictograph script. (Govt. of India Info. Services)

Action Toy of terra cotta from Indus Valley. (Govt. of India Info. Services)

for horses were apparently unknown.

The introduction of writing must always be regarded as among the major achievements of any civilization and we see that here, too, the Indus Valley was not behind Egypt and Mesopotamia. About 300 signs of the old Indus script have been found inscribed on seals and other objects dug up in the ruins of this pre-Aryan civilization. Unfortunately the writing cannot be read, but eventually scholars may find the solution. The point to be made at present is that phonetic writing had been developed in India some five thousand years ago.

There were among the Indus people clever metalsmiths, sculptors, and jewelers, some of whose fine products have been fortunately preserved by the protective debris of ages. Cotton for textiles was used during this period, probably for the first time in the history of the world. The people themselves lived in commodious and comfortable houses, a strange contrast with most of the existing civilizations of that age; in addition there were ample provisions for bathing and for town drainage.

We know of the prehistoric peoples of India principally through excavations in and near the Indus Valley, but there is good reason to believe that a related civilization extended widely in all directions. Already it is known that strong trade relations existed between the Indus and Tigris-Euphrates regions. It is likely that the more accessible parts of India came also within the sphere of influence of the high culture that has been disclosed on the Indus, but this we shall not know until proper investigation is made in the territory east of the Indus.

Perhaps eventually the earlier history of India may become known from its writings. Excavation is still young in that great subcontinent and many inscriptions may lie waiting for a fortunate discoverer. We recall that Egyptian and Mesopotamian writing, through which the vital history of the Near East has

Sacred Tank with six-foot-high drain was built in Mohenjo-daro, India about 2900 B.C. as part of a well-planned town with hundreds of houses and shops made of burnt brick laid in mud or gypsum mortar. (Gov. of India Info. Services)

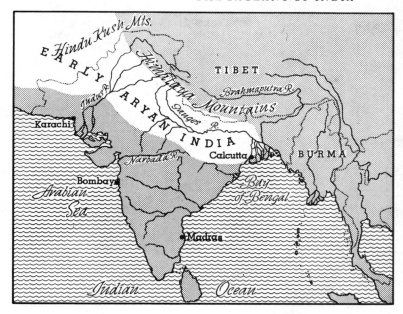

Early Aryan India. (After W. W. Romig)

in Sanskrit the hymns and epics that tell of their entry and settlement of the land.

The Dravidians were forced southward where today their descendants may still be seen. Living first in the Indus Valley as simple farmers and shepherds, the Aryans gradually spread eastward into the valley of the Ganges and its tributaries. From early writings we learn that the people worshiped and sacrificed to forces of nature such as the sun, rain, and sky, and had gods and goddesses with the names Indra, Chandra, Varuna, Savita, and so on, some of them identical with Persian deities. The conception of transmigration, or future life in other forms, seems to have come in, if it had not already existed. The caste system

been recovered, was unread until a century or so ago.

THE COMING OF THE ARYANS

It was some time after 1400 B.C. that the Aryans crossed the mountainous northwestern frontier of India and settled around the Indus. The early civilization of which we have spoken had by then disappeared and the people who confronted the Aryans were called Dravidians. The original home of the newcomers is not known for certain, perhaps it was on the plains of Southern Russia or Turkestan. They formed part of the great Indo-European family several of whose members we have already noticed. In the west the Italic tribes that formed Rome and the Greeks of the classical period, in the east the Medes and Persians as well as others, all were descended in speech out of the same root from which sprouted the Aryan tongue of India. The new people lived many centuries in the country before writing

Shiva, here portrayed as the cosmic dancer, was worshiped by pre-Aryans in the fourth millennium B.C. (William Rockhill Nelson Gallery of Art)

Father of Hindu Trinity, four-faced Brahma looks toward the four winds. (Museum of Fine Arts, Boston)

was being developed during this period, but in a much simpler form than at present. From two hereditary groups, the priestly and the noble, there developed three main castes, each of which excluded any of the conquered peoples who formed a fourth class.

The priests were the teachers and perpetuators of the Vedic tradition and came to be called Brahmans from the four-faced god Brahma. The noble class included warriors, while the commoners consisted of the large body of workers, herdsmen, farmers, and merchants. This social system developed until now we see a multitude of castes, each of them exclusive as regards marriage and way of living.

BUDDHA

During the middle of the sixth century B.C., at about the time that Cyrus the Great revolted from the Medes and launched Persia on the road to empire, a child was born to noble parents near the foot of the jungle-covered Nepal Hills. In time this child came to be known as Gautama Buddha, founder of a religion that is still of tremendous world importance, although not in India itself.

Growing to manhood he was unable to find contentment in life and after a great deal of thought left his wife and newborn child, to adopt the ways of a recluse in search of wisdom. Presently, still not finding the truths he was after, he became an ascetic, fasting, doing without sleep, and physically tormenting himself in a way common to many an Indian today. In his much weakened state he tried to pierce life's problems, his fame spreading meanwhile, but all to no avail. One day in his weakened condition still trying to discover a remedy for the ills of the world, he fell unconscious from exhaustion. On recovering he realized that his method of seeking the truth would never be successful. To think well one had to have a healthy body, and he accordingly demanded food of his companions. They were horrified and deserted him in his heresy. Alone he wandered, wrestling with his conflicting problem, when finally the religion he was to preach dawned on him.

Krishna, greatest reincarnation of Vishnu, depicted as a godly lover, awaiting his mistress, Radha, in a walled orchard. (Museum of Fine Arts, Boston)

Buddha, in the pose of meditation, from Taxila

Buddha taught the extinction of desire and selfishness, and kindness to all living creatures. He traced the troubles of life to personal greed, envy and desire. If one wished to be truly happy and serene one must forget one's self and live for others. Through this ideal way of life one would obtain Nirvana, a state of peaceful bliss. If not in this life, then in a succession of lives, the perfect goal could be attained.

This of course was a direct blow to the caste system and in so many words he made his point clear. As the four streams that flow into the Ganges lose their names as soon as they mingle their waters in the holy river, so all who believe in Buddha cease to be Brahmans, nobles, commoners, and low caste.

Buddha gained disciples who spread his teachings, at times with misunderstanding, until the new religion became a real force in India and was adopted by royal families. As is natural with many a religious founder, Buddha came in time to be given a supernatural birth and ultimately the distinction of being a god, although at no time did Buddha claim divinity. Monasteries were founded and the lower castes especially found pleasant the new religion of equality. As Buddhism grew and kings embraced the faith, missionaries were sent to surrounding countries, and eventually it reached Turkestan, Manchuria, Tibet, China, Japan, and the countries east of India, where still it is of the greatest importance. Missions even visited the Near East. In India, however, the Brahmans had never ceased to preach the Hindu faith, and growing stronger through the centuries they and the caste system finally prevailed over Buddhism, although embodying some of its better points. By the eleventh century A.D. Buddhism was practically extinct in India, and the religion that had been founded by an Aryan was thereafter practiced for the most part out-

Revelation Under the Bo-Tree. According to tradition, Buddha received enlightenment while meditating under a fig tree. (Metropolitan Museum of Art)

The Worship of Buddha's Ashes is depicted in this frieze, part of a pediment fragment from a mammoth stone Buddha. (Art Institute of Chicago)

Bardi Das, Jain temple of white marble in Calcutta has courtyard filled with statues of Jain saints. (Canadian Pacific Railway)

side of India by Mongolian peoples. Thenceforth India's principal religion, except for a period under the Moghuls and Mohammedans, was Hinduism, with its many gods, sacred cows, holy rivers and pools, and supremacy of the Brahmans and the caste system.

It is not known exactly when Buddhism reached China, but many believe that it happened about the time of Christ. Buddhism spread east, west, north, and south of the region of its birth, even penetrating the forests of Cambodia beyond Burma and Siam. At Angkor Thom one may still see the ruins of the old royal city of the Khmers whose civilization flourished 900-1200 A.D., while less than a mile away stands the temple of Angkor Vat, that stately and exotic structure devoted to worship of Buddha, the god.

In connection with Buddhism we should mention another religion with which it had points in common. Jainism can be traced to about 800 B.C. at which time its followers vowed not to injure life, not to steal, to be truthful, and to possess no property. The Jain sect gained influence during Buddha's lifetime through the efforts and reforms of a man named Jina, who in fact was Buddha's teacher for a time and whose name was ever after attached to this set of beliefs. The Jains are important for the part they played in history, for their sumptuous temples, and the fact that they still persist in India. Kindness was the chief virtue of Jainism as with Buddhism but it lacked the breadth of the latter.

THE PERSIANS AND GREEKS IN INDIA

By the time Buddha was a young man, various Aryan kingdoms had been formed in northern India, the most important being Kosala and Magadha. Across the Hindu Kush Mountains, Persian armies marched over the eastern Iranian plateau, soon enlarging the empire founded by Cyrus. Cyrus himself may have reached the Indus country, but nothing is certain regarding the entry of Persian troops until the time of his second successor, Darius the Great. It was probably soon after 520

Greco-Buddhist Reliefs from Gandhara depict sea gods of the Greek type and a Corinthian column. (Metropolitan Museum of Art)

Buddhist Shrine in Rangoon, Burma. (Canadian Pacific Railway)

B.C. that the Persians gained a foothold in the land of their blood and speech brothers in the northwestern part of India. This became a province of the greatest importance to the court at Persepolis, about one-third of all Asiatic tribute coming from it alone. The Indus Valley remained under Persian control during the reign of Darius' son, Xerxes, who had Indian infantry and cavalry in the army which he led into Greece in 480 B.C. The evidence concerning Persian influence in India is extremely scant for the following period, but Darius III, the last king of his dynasty, called for Indian troops when he made his last stand at Arbela against the army of Alexander the Great.

With Alexander we reach firmer ground, for his conquests were fairly well recorded. After taking Persia and the immense territory that had formed the northern and eastern parts of the Persian empire he crossed the mountains into India. After reaching the Hyphasis River (now called the Bias), Alexander was persuaded to give up any further advances into India, and turned back toward Susa, in Persia. We shall not go into detail here, however, on Alexander's great campaigns in the East, for they are described in Part II, Chapter 9.

THE MAURYA DYNASTY

Greek rule in India was doomed the moment Alexander turned for the long march to Susa. Soon there was a general revolt against the garrisons he had left behind and within a year or so northern India had a new ruler. He was Chandragupta, the earliest great Indian conqueror of whom we know. The founder of the Maurya Dynasty, named for his mother or grandmother, gathered his forces, and perhaps after taking the territory over which Alexander had so recently passed, proceeded to annex the Ganges Valley as well, which at that time was in the hands of the Nanda Dynasty. Chandragupta had acted in the name of liberty but he was soon better known for his tyranny. One district after another bowed to his fierce power and eventually his realm extended from the Bay of Bengal to the Arabian Sea, and the Himalaya and Hindu Kush Mountains to the Narbada River at the edge of the Deccan. It is possible that he invaded the Deccan itself. The size of Chandragupta's kingdom was reflected by his army which is said to have numbered 30,000 cavalry, 9,000 elephants, 600,000 infantry, and a host of chariots.

Seleucus, the general who inherited most of the Asiatic portion of Alexander's empire,

"Descent from the Ganges," a 7th century relief at Mamallapuram, was laboriously cut from solid rock. (Berko)

advanced hopefully with an army into the Indus country about 305 B.C. to meet Chandragupta, and although some are of the opinion that Seleucus met serious defeat, the essential facts of the case are unknown. The available details indicate that a peaceful solution may have been reached, for, while Chandragupta gained new territories to the northwest, Seleucus with 500 elephants marched away to the more important wars in Asia Minor. The fact, too, that Seleucus gave a daughter in marriage to Chandragupta suggests that enmity between the two kings was not at the breaking point. However, Greek political influence was thereafter a thing of the past.

From the accounts of writers, including Seleucus' ambassador to the Indian court, we learn much regarding the country, government, and life of the time. India possessed a high civilization, one which could meet the western cultures on terms of understanding and equality. Numerous foreigners traveled on peaceful missions to Chandragupta's capital, thus testifying to the intercourse that connected east and west. From these writers we hear of the royal palace which stood in a park, beautifully landscaped with fish ponds, trees, and shrubs. The gilded pillars were decked with golden vines and silver birds. All the luxuries of the age made Chandragupta's court a marvel of the day, as brilliant as that of a modern rajah. When the king traveled far from his capital he mounted an elephant covered with gold trappings. The court was often entertained by combat between bulls, rams, elephants, rhinoceroses, and even men. On other occasions the king and his intimate circle enjoyed the spectacle of a curious kind of race in which mixed teams of horses competed with speedy oxen drawing a vehicle. The course was over three miles long and provided much tension and anxiety for the observers who bet on the outcome.

The government was efficiently organized, a war office and civil administration taking care of routine matters. Taxes were collected under close supervision and a bureau of vital statistics recorded births and deaths. Irrigation was closely watched so that all might get their share of water, and of course be taxed accordingly. Roads were much improved during Chandragupta's reign, the longest one connecting the capital with the northwest frontier. This was probably built for military reasons as much as for any other purpose.

The penal code of the times was very strict indeed and demanded death for crimes such as robbery. Third-degree methods for obtaining confessions were legal and freely used. The law recognized eighteen kinds of torture, including seven methods of whipping. In some cases it was legal to submit a prisoner to all eighteen varieties.

Chandragupta had been king for twenty-four years when he either abdicated or died in 298 B.C. The Jain sect has a tradition that he abdicated in order to become a Jain ascetic. In any case his son, Bindusara, succeeded him and although practically nothing is known of his twenty-five year reign it is probable that Bindusara extended the Maurya Empire into the Deccan as far south as the Pennar River, a hundred miles or so north of Madras.

ASOKA AND THE BUDDHISTS

Chandragupta's grandson, Asoka, inherited the Maurya Empire when he came to the throne about 273 B.C. The following years were ones of vital significance to the history of India, and Asoka thereby takes his place among the distinctive monarchs of the world.

Asoka was king for forty years, but his deeds during the early part of the reign are unknown. In his thirteenth year he set out to add to his already large empire the kingdom of Kalinga on the coast of the Bay of Bengal. This war, possibly the only one in which Asoka participated, was bloody and ended in untold suffering for the people of Kalinga. Remorse for his actions set in almost immediately, and under the influence of Buddhism Asoka foreswore war and adopted the precepts of kindness that Buddha had preached several centuries before.

The Buddhists were only one sect among many when Asoka became king, and in fact there were many sects within Buddhism itself. Therefore one of the first things Asoka did was to bring the elders together to decide on

Shiva. The drum held in the left hand symbolizes creative sound. (Museum of Fine Arts, Boston)

Cambodian Balustrade Terminal from Angkor Thom, 10th century A.D. (Toledo Museum of Art)

Hindu Shrine in a cave temple on the Island of Elephanta. (Canadian Pacific Railway Company)

Altar to a Jina in the white marble, Jainist temple of Dilvarra on Mount Abu. (Asia)

Frieze from Sanchi Gate narrates the story of Buddha's life. (Berko, Pictures)

Sanchi Gate leads to sacred Buddhist relic mound, oldest Indian edifice. (Gov. of India Info. Services)

the official form of Buddhism. Long before he died it became the state religion and had traveled to other countries as well. Thus while Buddha had the original revelation, it was Asoka who gave Buddhism the necessary vitality and prestige to place it among the world religions.

Asoka devoted his entire later life to propagation of the faith. Formerly a Brahmanical Hindu he now became a zealous Buddhist monk. He made a pilgrimage to the scenes of Buddha's birth, life, and death, and endowed them liberally.

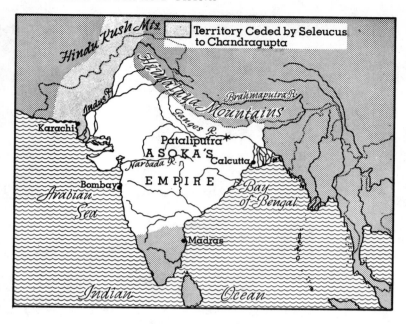

Asoka's Empire. (After W. W. Romig)

The monk-emperor issued many edicts on ethical and moral behavior, some of which carved on stone have been found.

The Buddhism preached by Asoka insisted on the sanctity of all animal life. Belief in rebirth was the basis of this edict, for even an insect might once have been a god. Perhaps it was on the way to being one again. All animal life was sacred, at times more hallowed than human life, for one could be put to death for killing an animal. On fifty-six days of the year it was a crime attended by capital punishment to slay animals for food. As part of this attitude toward living things the royal hunt which had been an important function in the life of his grandfather was abolished. Instead, Asoka substituted acts of piety and dissemination of his faith.

Reverence, truthfulness, and toleration he preached with undying zeal. Toleration to other religions formed part of his creed, but in practice they were seriously impeded, for sacrifice was definitely restricted, even though regarded as essential by some of the sects.

While much attention was directed to animals it must not be understood that the Buddhism of Asoka neglected man. It was the human misery he had caused in Kalinga that proved the turning point in his life, and numerous later acts proved his feeling and sympathy for the sufferings of men. Medical treatment of the sick was provided not only in his empire but in the neighboring independent kingdoms.

Asoka Inscription of about 250 B.C. is one of thirty-five extant religious edicts issued by the king. (Gov. of India Info. Services)

Lion capital from sandstone Asoka edict column

We see that Asoka had growing plans and ambitions for Buddhism, and before the middle of his reign he organized a large system of foreign missions. Ministers of the faith were dispatched to the surrounding countries and even reached the Mediterranean and Aegean. Egypt, Syria, Asia Minor, and Greece were visited by these holy deputies in an effort to spread the benefits of what Asoka believed to be the only right and true religion. Whatever their adventures may have been, for that information may be lost forever, they left the seeds of their faith in widespread places, and some writers have suspected that Buddha's views contributed to the more orthodox forms of Christianity.

From his throne, but as a man of human feelings, Asoka taught reverence, truth, and sympathy. At the same time through a long reign he successfully administered a vast empire. For these reasons and the fact that through him Buddhism became a world force Asoka must be counted among the immortals of history.

THE CENTURIES AFTER ASOKA

After his death about 232 B.C. Asoka was followed by several ephemeral kings who lacked the ability of their gifted predecessors. Perhaps, too, the Brahmans whose privileges had been seriously curtailed by Asoka now threw their weight into an attempt to overthrow the Mauryas. In any case the dynasty ended about 185 B.C. and the history of the country for several centuries thereafter was one of struggle between local dynasts and eastern Asiatic invaders from the northwest. Of these the most important were the Kushanas who established a large empire in the first and second centuries A.D. which consisted of northwestern India, Afghanistan, and Turkestan. Of the Kushan rulers the most famous was Kanishka, about 120 A.D., who as a vigorous patron of Buddhism ranks second to Asoka alone. Following the Kushan period, the country broke up into small states reunited for a brief period by the Gupta Dynasty in the fourth and fifth centuries, and again by Harsha, the last important native ruler, in the seventh century.

Mohammedans from the west, and Tartars and Moghuls from Turkestan, all played their parts before European aggressors again made their appearance on the Indian scene. Then by sea came Portuguese Vasco da Gama in 1502 to bombard Calicut on the southwest coast. Europe had just emerged from the Dark Ages and once more trade with India assumed importance. For a century the Portuguese controlled the trade of the east, and then came the Dutch, French, and English, the last eventually winning India through formation of the East India Company.

Indian Noblewoman of the 18th century playing with a pet gazelle. (Freer Gallery of Art)

14. China and Its Dynasties

THE NAME AND THE LAND

We CANNOT be sure of the origin of the name China. It is usually believed, however, that the name was derived from the Kingdom of Ch'in (pronounced Chin) which in the days of the Ch'in Dynasty (255–206 B.C.) brought the loosely knit Chinese states together as an empire. It is said that Malay sea traders made the name known to India and the west.

In the medieval period China became known to Europeans as Cathay. It was thus that Marco Polo, the Venetian traveler, referred to it. Russians still do call it Kitai. The term Cathay owes its origin to the Khitans, a formidable group of Tartars from eastern Asia who were well known to eastern Europe in medieval times.

The Chinese of today think of their country in terms of north and south. This is not a political division but rather one based on different ways of living. The principal difference between the two is that the north lives on millet, maize and wheat, while the south lives on rice. Of course, other foods are eaten as well.

By concrete geographical distinction China is further divided into groups of provinces in the same way that we set off New England or the Pacific Coast with their various states from the rest of the country. The Chinese groups of provinces are located as follows:

1) On the Upper Yellow River (Hwang Ho)
2) On the Lower Yellow River
3) On the Upper Yangtze River
4) On the Middle Yangtze River
5) On the Lower Yangtze River
6) On the South Coast

In the first of these groups, in the north, we find the Chinese at the dawn of history. The province of *Kansu*, a highland with great variety in scenery, has always been associated with adventure, and has been called the "Wild West of China." *Shensi* is made up largely of rich, rolling plains and is famous for its opium-smoking population. *Shansi*, still another province of the Upper Yellow River district, is rugged for the most part and is noted, even far inland in Asia, for ability of its merchants.

The second group includes *Honan*, in the northern part of which evidence of early Chinese culture has been found. The people of *Honan* are strong of body and character but generally slow of mind. Peiping, the capital of China until 1928, lies in the province of *Hopei* which is called the "Metropolitan Province" by foreigners. *Shantung*, in this same group, extends to the coast and is noted as the birthplace of the great sages, Lao Tzu, Confucius, and Mencius. To the present day the scholarly tradition persists in *Shantung*. The people of this province are regarded as being the finest physical specimens of North China, and it is of interest to recall that during World War I *Shantung* coolies were in great demand in the war area of France.

To reach the third group of provinces we travel south and west to the headwaters of the great Yangtze River, to the borders of Tibet and China. The land is extremely rugged for the most part and as a result we meet one magnificent scene after another. Due to the nature of the country some of the agriculture is done by terracing. Desirable mineral resources will some day make this area of extreme importance. Influences from India in the past have entered China by way of the Upper Yangtze Valley.

Proceeding down the river we enter the fourth group of provinces which constitute the lake region of China. Here tea and rice are grown, but the territory is rapidly gaining greater importance for its commercial enterprises. At the junction of the Han and Yangtze rivers three large cities have developed in recent years. They are Hankow, Wuchang, and Hanyang.

The Lower Yangtze group, our fifth, brings us at length to the sea, many hundreds of miles from the headwaters of the river. Tea and rice are important·products of this area, but it is more significant for its industries. Shanghai, symbol of the coming of the industrial west to China, is situated on a small tributary near the mouth of the great river. It is not an old city, dating only from the middle of the nineteenth century.

The sixth group of provinces, on the South Coast, is cut off from the rest of China by high mountain ranges and it is not surprising that noticeable differences of language and physique characterize the area. The South Coast has excellent harbors, and the people have always looked to the sea. It is in this area that we find Canton, from which about ninety-five per cent of the Chinese in America have come. Hong Kong lies a little over fifty miles to the east of Canton. It was an uninhabited island until the British transformed it into one of the world's greatest ports.

The population of China is pretty much an unknown quantity and has been the subject of considerable guesswork. Recent estimates range between 270,000,000 and 500,000,000. The true figure is probably something more than 400,000,000, or approximately one-fifth of the total population of the world.

This, then, is the China whose earlier history we are about to investigate. When did Chinese civilization begin and when did it take on the form in which it is known to us today?

THE ERA OF MYTHOLOGY AND LEGEND

At the present time China's known history goes back no farther than about 1500 B.C. but in view of recent progress in the field of archeology it is quite probable that this figure will in time be increased. In the past few years archeology has produced a very respectable outline of the Shang Dynasty (1766-1122 B.C.) which before that had been shrouded in the mists of legend. Preceding the Shang Dynasty we learn from Chinese annals of an extremely long history. It is called history, but mythology is surely a more appropriate term. All peoples on earth have their creation stories.

According to the Chinese Genesis the first man had an unknown beginning. He simply came into being and immediately understood the wonders of Heaven and Earth. When he came into the world, order was made out of chaos. He is pictured working with chisel and mallet on huge pieces of granite floating in space. From this mass the sun, the moon, and stars emerged, and heaven and earth took their present form under the guidance of his knowing hand. And then, when his work was done, he died.

But the earth continued to develop. The original man's head was changed to mountains,

The Yang and Yin Symbol represents the balance of the forces in nature—negative and positive, male and female, dark and light. Later, the dragon and phoenix became associated with this dualism, the dragon with Yang and the phoenix with Yin, and hence became symbols of the emperor and empress respectively

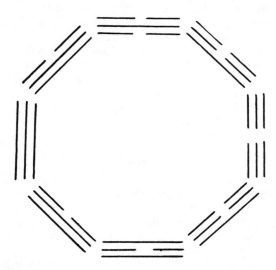

The Pa Kua Symbol, an eight-sided diagram composed of opposite pairs of broken and full lines. According to tradition it was invented by Wen, father of Wu Wang, the founder of the Chou Dynasty. Originally used in divination, the design is now merely decorative or protective in function

his breath became wind and clouds, and his voice turned into thunder. His veins became the rivers and his sinews hill and dale. The fields were fashioned from his flesh. His beard became stars, and his skin and hair were turned into herbs and trees. His teeth, bones, and marrow became metals, rocks, and precious stones, and his sweat was turned to rain. Finally, the insects that had been attracted to his body became the Chinese people.

There follows a long period treated in much the same mythological manner with one culture hero following another. Among these are Huang-ti, Yao, and Shun, names which play a significant part in the classical writings. About 2205 B.C., according to the chroniclers, there began the Hsia Dynasty which immediately precedes the Dynasty of Shang with which we may begin to view Chinese history with some assurance.

THE ORACLE BONES OF SHANG

From time to time in the past ancient bones with inscriptions on them have been dug up by ploughing in the fields of northern *Honan* prov-

ince, not far from the Yellow River. We now know that the inscriptions on these bones are part of the royal records of the later part of the Shang Dynasty which according to tradition extended from 1766 to 1122 B.C. These writings are the oldest records known from far eastern Asia.

We possess these inscribed bones with their wealth of information for the reason that the royal court employed fortune-tellers, or diviners, to question the ancestors and gods whether certain actions should be taken or not. The fortune-teller, or diviner, asked a question, one of importance to the well-being of the state or the people. Then he heated the bone which was usually the shoulder blade or leg bone of a cow, or might in other cases be the shell of a turtle. The heat developed a T shaped crack, and it was from the details of this crack that the diviner decided what answer was being given by the spirits. Fortunately for us the question was sometimes written next to the crack. We may guess that this was done mainly when following events proved that the diviner had been correct. These inscriptions are not completely understood, but the study of the writing has progressed to such a point that the main idea of most inscriptions can be grasped.

ORIGINS OF THE SHANG PEOPLE

By the time we reach the period of the Shang Dynasty (about 1766 B.C.) we may be sure that we are in the midst of Chinese surroundings, primitive it is true, but Chinese

Oracle Bones of the Shang Dynasty record in the earliest known form of Chinese writing ancient prophecies and their consequences

Shang Wine-Beaker was used in the ritual of early Shang religion. (Raeburn Rohrbach Photo)

settled. Clearer evidence is needed.

Other elements are clearly foreign to the territory in which the Shangs lived: for instance, bronze, an alloy of copper and tin, which is far superior in many ways to pure copper. The idea probably came from the west, perhaps carried slowly over the central reaches of Asia from the Near East where it had been known as early as 3000 B.C. Rice, too, appears to have been brought into North China from the outside, this time from the south. It is clear that no cultural progress is possible without knowledge of the outside world.

HOW THE SHANGS LIVED

With continued digging in China we shall some day know much more than at present regarding the lives and occupations of the Shang people. But we know a great deal about these things already. We know, for instance, that the poor and probably the slaves lived in underground mud hovels. But others lived in complicated houses very much like Chinese houses of the present day. They were built on a platform of beaten earth. Today this platform is faced with brick. Excavation has

Royal Shang Tomb was an inverted pyramid dug into the ground and approached by steps

nevertheless. And that brings up the question regarding the origins of the Shang people. One fact alone might appear to go a long way toward solving this problem. Bronze was introduced into China from the outside during the Shang period, and one might suppose that a foreign group had been responsible and had in fact set itself up as the Shang Dynasty. But we observe a most interesting state of affairs in the nature of certain Shang bronzes. These include sacrificial vessels which, detail for detail, copy the form of earlier pottery vessels. One supposes that we have here a case of the immutability or conservatism of religion, since we are dealing with religious vessels. Still other elements in Shang culture appear to go back to an earlier beginning and argue for a connection between the peoples of the two periods. But perhaps a more important point to be made just now is that the question is not shown that the ground plans of Shang houses have their counterpart in present Chinese architecture. Remains of wooden pillars have been found. One of the pictographs on the oracle bones represents a large building and seems to show us the type of roof that was used. Even then the gable seems to have been the favored style.

Among occupations of the people we may be sure that farming was the most prominent. The rich soil and level land of the Yellow River Valley must then have yielded bountiful harvests. We know that in Shang times wheat and millet were grown extensively. In the Neolithic period only millet seems to have been cultivated. It is still the important food of North China, rice being eaten only by the wealthier people.

The Shang people also raised domesticated animals, or hunted and trapped for meat and skins for clothing. One of the methods of hunting was to set the grass on fire in order to get the animals into the open. From the rubbish heaps that have been dug and from the oracle bones we learn a great deal about the animals known to the Shang people. The rubbish contains a great many things of interest, among them animal bones tossed out by the housewives of long ago. When these are collected and studied by experts we shall have another valuable instrument for the understanding of Shang life.

A number of animals had become domesticated by this time. Very important among this group were the horse, two types of dog,

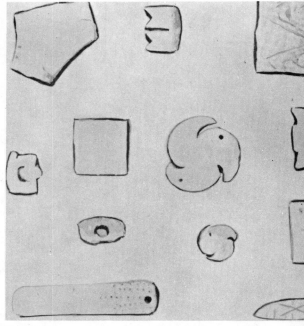

Shang Handicraft, decorative objects in bone, stone and mother of pearl. (Raeburn Rohrbach Photo)

cattle, sheep, and goats. The horse became a natural draft animal, but for this purpose it is quite likely that cattle, oxen, and water buffalo were also used. Other animals that had probably yielded to domestication by Shang times are the pig and possibly one kind of deer. Once in a while elephant bones are found and it has been suggested that elephants were sometimes tamed. This is based on the

Tomb Guardians, these two limestone statues stood at the gates of a royal grave of the Shang period. At far left is a mystical, carnivorous animal. The bird is an owl and may symbolize a deity of the powerful thunder cult

Symbol of Strength to the Shang people, was the elephant. When made into a ritual vessel, this animal was thought to safeguard religious food offerings. The raised decorations are also designed to avert evil. (Freer Gallery of Art)

form of one of the pictographs on the oracle bones which seems to show a hand leading an elephant by its trunk. The rubbish piles of Shang have even yielded monkey bones.

Animals which seem clearly not to have been tamed include the bear, tiger, and panther, and the badger, tapir, and hare. These are

Bronze Dagger-Axes of the Shang Dynasty are more primitive than the ritual vessels of the same period

surely trophies of the hunt which on certain occasions became state affairs and seem always to have called for conference with the gods. Of birds which were known to the people of Shang and which have been identified in the remains we may mention the pheasant and the chicken. The latter seems to have been introduced to North China about the time of the Shang Dynasty.

The dog and pig had been the most important meat animals in the Neolithic Age and in the following period both continued to

be important foods. The pig, however, appears to have had a more important position in the menus of the time. We know that the dog was sacrificed as well as eaten.

It is quite certain that the early Chinese did not use milk or other dairy products, for nowhere in the literature is there a hint that conditions as regards this aspect of things were any different than they are today. Nobody seems to know the answer, but the Chinese, Koreans, Japanese, Indochinese and Malayans use no dairy products. On the other hand Mongols, Turks, and Tibetans seem always to have used them.

There are many things we cannot be sure of as regards Shang civilization. For instance, was irrigation practiced? Silk may have been made in Shang times. There is no doubt that the silk industry began in China. To this all traditions are agreed, the only question being, when? Certain traditions place it before the Shang Dynasty. It is known that royal and noble families were keenly interested in the development of silk but the secret was closely guarded. However, Japan finally gained knowledge of the process around 300 A.D. India received its knowledge of the silk process, it is said, through a Chinese princess who illicitly carried silk moth eggs and the seed of a mulberry tree hidden in her headdress.

The money of the period consisted of a type of shell called the cowry. The qualities which made this shell useful as a monetary unit were its durability, its lightness, and the fact that it was by no means numerous. Metal coins did not make their appearance in China

Shang Ceremonial Tripod is decorated in relief with a large, meandering ogre, called "the glutton." (Art Institute of Chicago)

until the period following Shang.

The arts and crafts of the period were of a high order. One has only to view a typical group of Shang bronzes to realize that the metalsmith of the day had standards hard to approach at the present time. Chinese scholars interested in such matters have compared Shang work with some of the best of the European Renaissance. It is certain that the Shang craftsmen had at their command an ability that can only create wonder in our eyes. Sculpture was done in stone as well as bronze, and wood and bone were mediums for carving. The pottery of the period was either wheel or hand made, but in both cases presents an interesting product. The beginnings of glazing must be traced back to the Shang period. Painting, too, had made a start, for polychrome designs have been found on remnants of walls.

SHANG SCRIBES

It is most likely that there was widespread knowledge of reading and writing in Shang times. As in Egypt and Mesopotamia it was the scribe who carried on the serious business of transmitting messages. And because of this we are able to look at Chinese writing at a time when it still looked much like pictographic writing. As with the other great systems of early writing, that of the Chinese grew out of primitive pictures representing well known objects of the time. But we have seen the difficulties the people of the Near East had with this type of expression. Actions and ideas were at times impossible to express by picture and so the written language began to develop and accommodate itself to the needs of easy written expression. Shang writing employed pictures but it was a long step beyond simple picture writing. The basis of later Chinese characters had already been established in Shang times. We see this from the inscriptions on the oracle bones. Of course, many characters have since been added. There are around 2,500 Shang characters. Modern dictionaries have something like 50,000, or twenty times as many. Grammar and style have also changed considerably since Shang times but by then the foundation for later development had been laid.

Contrary to general belief, writing by brush came into use during the Shang period as can be seen from the oracle bones. Prior to this discovery it was held that the brush had been invented in Ch'in times, late in the third century B.C.

SHANG RELIGION

The three great religions of present China were not known in Shang times. These are Confucianism, Taoism, and Buddhism. But it is an interesting fact that ancestor-worship, something that was very characteristic of Shang religion, is connected with each of these. The ancestor became a force to be seriously considered the moment he died. One's measure of success depended on offerings and sacrifices to the spirits of the dead. It is for this reason that objects of many kinds were placed at the graves.

But we get our best idea of Shang thoughts on supernatural beings from the written records of divination. The ancient Chinese appealed to the spirits for information on all manner of things. We may read the record on the oracle bones. For instance, questions were asked regarding sacrifices. To what spirits were they to be made? Sometimes the sacrifice involved a captured enemy. If the event called for an animal sacrifice it was necessary to find out what animal would be best suited to the purpose and, just as important, the color of the animal. At times the spirits were told of wars that were going on, or of serious illness in the group. Probably the spirits knew what to do under the circumstances. If a person were to undertake a journey it would be well for him to find out what day would be most propitious, or whether it might not be advisable to break the journey and spend some time at an intermediate point. Advice was sought with regard to hunting and fishing. What was the appropriate time and where was the best place? At the bend of the river? The spirits knew all of the answers.

War was of course a serious thing and the spirits were freely consulted. First of all, was it advisable to go to war? And if so, how many men should be taken? Or would it be better to remain on the defensive?

The weather was of as great interest then as now. Questions were asked about rain, snow, wind, and fog. Would there be good weather for a special occasion planned for the future? The farmer wished to know whether the coming year would be good for millet.

Illness and recovery were naturally matters of almost daily interest to the people of Shang and their gods no doubt found much of their time occupied in considering the answers. A particularly common request to the gods was whether the coming week would be lucky or not. All these questions and more were forwarded to the spirits by the diviners who read the answers in the details of the T-shaped crack that developed on bones that had been plunged into fire.

In time to come we will undoubtedly be much better informed as to the history of the Shang Dynasty, but the curtain has already been lifted. We have seen on the Shang stage the beginnings of that quality called Chinese civilization.

THE CHOU DYNASTY

The Chou (pronounced Jo) Dynasty was the longest in China's long history. It is traditionally dated from 1122 to 249 B.C. It will help us to comprehend more fully the length of this period if we realize that about the same length of time is marked by the interval between the conquest of England by William and our own time. Much happens over such a period, and China of Chou times was no exception. It was a period of tremendous changes and within its limits falls the Chinese classical period. The great literary works and the names best known to the western world fall within this period. Confucius, Mencius, and Lao Tzu all lived and made their contributions to Chinese thought during the Chou period. The area of the empire was greatly extended during this era, and in its early years there occurred the first of a number of attempts at state socialism. Metal coins apparently came into use early in Chou times, and the plough, according to tradition, was introduced late in the period.

The origins of the Chou line are rather misty but it seems that a confederacy of western Chinese, led by the Chous, defeated the Shangs and captured their lands about 1122 B.C. The Chous themselves appear to have sprung from the same general Neolithic stock of North China which had produced the Shangs. But they were barbarians when they left their homes about 350 miles southwest

Miniature Bronze Bells were used as tokens of barter in the Chou Dynasty, about 500–250 B.C. (Chicago Natural History Museum)

Wooden Dancing Girl of the late Chou Dynasty. (Seattle Art Museum)

of the Shang capital and came into Shang territory on the Yellow River. There it was that they learned to write and painstakingly assume other phases of Shang culture that were superior to their own. The Chous borrowed divination, the system of writing, certain phrases, dating, architecture and some religious elements. Even some king's names were the same as those of the Shang Dynasty. And like many other barbaric people in other parts of the world, the Chous required a genealogy when they came to power. The solution was found in short order, for it was soon being told that the Chous were descended from one of the earliest rulers of ancient China. The genealogy of Rome was manufactured in the same way, and with as little basis. But in both cases self-respect was satisfied.

We have mentioned cultural elements that the Chous borrowed. We are not to believe as a result that the Chous were dependent for everything. They developed these traits along very original lines, and before the dynasty came to a lingering end the culture of China had been greatly enriched.

THE MARTIAL KING—CONQUEROR OF SHANG

According to tradition the war between Shang and Chou went back to the time of the grandfather of the Martial King, the first Chou ruler. The Chou objective for at least two generations was thus the subjugation of Shang. Essential details are lacking and those we have may be regarded to some extent as myth. But we may accept as fact the defeat of Shang. The Martial King (Wu Wang) is said to have assembled a large army and decisively defeated the defending armies of Shang. The last of the Shang kings is said to have fled to his favorite resting place, a pleasure pavilion, where in his despair he dressed himself in all his finery and set fire to the building and was consumed with it. Shortly thereafter the Martial King made his way to the burned building and discovered the corpse, whereupon he shot three arrows into it. The final act of this scene which symbolizes the transfer of power from Shang to Chou was the cutting off of the head and setting it upon the new king's banner as a trophy. The Martial King had at last achieved an aim treasured by his grandfather.

Just how much territory had been conquered by the new people is unknown. It seems unlikely that it extended down the Yellow River

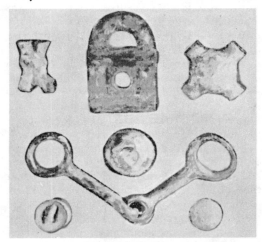

Bit and Bridle Equipment of the Chou Dynasty. (Raeburn Rohrbach Photo)

to the sea. But the area was undoubtedly large and presented a real problem in government. The solution adopted was to parcel out different territories to relatives and allies. Thus the new governing system grew into a full-fledged feudal order, as much so as that of medieval Europe. The local lords gave revenue (taxes), troops, and allegiance to the Martial King, but aside from these obligations they were kings themselves in their own territories. But this was too ideal a state of affairs; trouble always brews in such circumstances. In a feudal state personal ambition has ever been the cornerstone of unrest and war.

THE DUKE OF CHOU—BROTHER AND UNCLE OF KINGS

On the death of the Martial King the throne passed to a son who was still very young. The solution then, as in many a similar circumstance in European history, was to set up a regency until the young king attained maturity. The Duke of Chou, younger brother of the old king and uncle of the new one, kept this office for seven years. He was such an unusual man that it will be worth while to look closely at his character and accomplishments. Indeed it is likely that without him Chinese thought and institutions would not be what they are. He was a great

Bronze Ritual Cauldron with four handles and a wide mouth, Chou Dynasty. (Freer Gallery of Art)

humanist and had vast influence in standardizing custom. He is regarded by some as the most remarkable man in Chinese history. He was possessed of an intellect, energy, and force of character unique in any one person. Some Chinese have considered him greater than Confucius as a molder of thought, and Confucius himself regarded him as the inspirational source of his philosophy.

The duke held the empire together when it seemed on the verge of falling apart. At a time when many forces were working against the unity for which he stood, his will and strength of purpose served the country well. Two of his own brothers attempted to resurrect the old Shang Dynasty, but the duke put one to death and exiled the other. Ultimately the young king reached maturity and assumed control, but the duke remained as aid and adviser. At this time the capital was moved eastward near the modern city of Loyang which is about 150 miles southwest of the old Shang capital. Other cities were also built and the duke had a large share of responsibility in their erection.

Interesting and no doubt characteristic stories have been told about this remarkable man. It is said, for instance, that the duke was so zealous in the accomplishment of his duties that he would see interviewers while taking his bath. No time should be wasted. Another tale relates that when his brother, the Martial King, was ill on a certain occasion the duke beseeched the spirits of his ancestors to take his life instead. The recovery of the king naturally proved the powers of the duke's prayers, and the fact that the spirits were on the side of the duke.

THE KINGS AND THE NOBLES

Early in the history of the Chou Dynasty it appears to have been relatively easy to keep the various nobles under control, although we have seen that at the death of the Martial King certain factions schemed for power. First of all, many of the Chou subjects were newly conquered and would readily have revolted against the nobles had they broken faith with the king. Then, too, the king could play off one or more nobles against another. For instance, if one of his vassals attempted to break away, the king could readily get aid from others by promising them any conquered territory. Thus in the early days of the dynasty the people and the king were able to keep the nobles under control.

Mongolian Boy of the late Chou Dynasty. (Museum of Fine Arts Boston)

Chou Wine Vessel. (Art Institute of Chicago)

Bronze Po or Bell. (Art Institute of Chicago)

But many factors enter into such a situation and it was not long before the Chou kings had their hands full. A few generations served to establish the nobles in their own territories and their subjects came to regard them as rightful rulers. With the spirit of independence thus growing and armies and wealth increasing it is little wonder that the king soon ceased receiving his accustomed revenues. Trouble naturally followed, and for many years the ambitions of local nobles directed the course of Chinese history.

The test of kingship in a state such as we see here lies in the character of the king. In a feudal system revolt will surely follow on the accession of a king unmindful of his duties to his people. Such a man was King Li who ascended the throne about 878 B.C. about the time that Samaria was being built in Israel. Li became a cruel tyrant and oppressor, and refused to listen to the wise counsel of his minister. Inevitable revolt took place and the king ended his days in exile. The prestige of the House of Chou was at low ebb, and al-

though its passing was still some time in the future the end was in sight. In Chinese annals the Chou Dynasty lasted until 249 B.C. but its real end as a dynastic power came with the death of Yu in 771.

After that the Chou line became as one of its former vassals, a small state struggling for a place in the sun. None of the states was powerful enough to make a lasting union of the scattered dukedoms, but it was in this setting that there developed much of China's philosophical thought. In this latter part of the disrupted Chou period there lived a man whose effect on later China was to be of the greatest magnitude. That man was Confucius.

CHINA'S GREAT SAGES—LAO TZU, CONFUCIUS, AND MENCIUS

To comprehend fully the significance of Confucius it will be well to look first at another great philosopher, Lao Tzu, who was born about fifty years before Confucius.

Lao Tzu, whose name was later Latinized as Laocius by the Jesuits, was the first great

Lao Tzu. (Chicago Natural History Museum)

Confucius. (Chicago Natural History Museum)

religious teacher of China. He was born about 604 B.C. a few years after the fall of Nineveh. Lao Tzu is very much a legendary figure and some believe him to be entirely mythical. However, he may have been a person of flesh and blood notwithstanding the fact that he enters Chinese history mysteriously and passes out in the same way. He is supposed to have been keeper of the archives of the city of Loyang, but did not take his duties very seriously. For some unknown reason he decided to leave China. Coming to the gateway at the western pass he was asked by the gatekeeper for a writing. Lao Tzu complied, according to the story, and left with the keeper the famous *Classic of the Way.*

The religion advocated by Lao Tzu is called Taoism, that is the Way-ism. It is in most ways quite opposed to the teachings of Confucius. In general it may be said to advocate a harmony with Nature, and this is to be done by linking life to the Tao, or the Way. A definition of Taoism is very difficult to give since even Chinese scholars are disagreed as to the real meaning of the Way. Regarding a definition Lao Tzu himself said, "Those who know do not tell; those who tell

do not know." In a later generation Confucius studied the Tao, for twenty years in fact, but was unable to comprehend it.

One of Lao Tzu's principles was that good should be returned for evil, but this, interestingly enough, was not supported by the practical Confucius who said that evil and wrongdoing should be punished.

Lao Tzu had disciples, the foremost being Chuang Tzu. That he had learned well his lesson from the master may be seen in the following story. One day Chuang Tzu was fishing in the river when two officials went out to ask him to take charge of the administration of the Ch'u state. Chuang continued fishing and did not even turn his head, but said, "I have heard that in Ch'u there is a sacred tortoise which has been dead now some three thousand years, and that the Prince keeps this tortoise carefully enclosed in a chest on the altar of his ancestral temple. Now, would this tortoise rather be dead, and have its remains venerated, or be alive and wagging its tail in the mud?" "It would

"Confucius at the Apricot Altar," a 17th century painting by Kano Tanyu, showing the philosopher with Yen Hwui and Tsenp-Ts'au, two of his favorite disciples. His followers often sat reverently at his side, watching his every movement and taking down his sayings. (Museum of Fine Arts, Boston)

rather be alive," answered the two officials, "and wagging its tail in the mud." At that Chuang cried, "Begone! I too will wag my tail in the mud."

Taoism has had three major periods of development. In the time of Lao Tzu and his disciples it was sincere philosophy. During the Ch'in Dynasty, that following Chou, it became for a short while the state religion. After that it deteriorated and became little more than the practice of magic under the influence of the Taoist priests. At present Taoism is devoted largely to a search for the secrets of the "Philosopher's Stone" and the "Elixir of Life."

K'UNG TZU WHO WAS CALLED CONFUCIUS

Confucius, whose Chinese name was K'ung Tzu, was born in 551 B.C. about fifty years after the birth of Lao Tzu. Confucius represents the characteristic Chinese philosophy and today, over two thousand years after his time, a large portion of the people of the earth continue to be profoundly influenced by the workings of his mind.

Confucius lived during a very confused period in China's history and tried to save society by returning to the ways of old. He emphasized ethics, moral education, and ceremonies, and preached the return to the virtue of the Golden Age of Yao and Shun. He said that the educated people, by their example, should lead China to new glories. This, of course, was not a new idea, and in fact Confucius never claimed to be the founder of a set of religious views. He was rather a coordinator of older teachings. He was a very democratic man and is perhaps best remembered by the Christian West as the author of the Golden Rule, phrased by him in a negative form: "What you do not like when done to yourself, do not do to others."

Confucius appears to have been a very stern and righteous man. As a father he was the same, apparently always acting with great reserve. A story, hard to credit, is told of his son who was asked by a disciple of the sage, "Have you learned any lessons from your father different from those received by us?" The reply was that Confucius had asked him only two questions, "Have you read the *Odes?*" and "Have you studied the Rules of Propriety?"

Confucius had strong moral characteristics and was a great teacher of righteousness. Early in his career, at a time when he had a government position as minister of crime, he was influential in bringing about certain reforms. For instance, he brought to justice those who watered their sheep to make them heavier before bringing them to market. It is said that during his time the spirit of honesty was so prevalent that lost jewels were left untouched on the highway.

The teachings of Confucius which have so profoundly affected China and its neighbors are included in the so-called *Confucian Classics*. This series comprises several works and is sometimes called the Old and New Testament of Confucianism. The sage had many followers who created a greater interest in his teachings after he was dead than they had enjoyed during his life. There was a brief period of persecution under the short-lived Ch'in Dynasty, but with the coming of the Hans (206 B.C.) the Confucian principle that government is for the good of the people and should always be based on justice was finally victorious.

Confucianism owes much to the sage Meng Tzu whose latinized name was Mencius. He lived several centuries after Confucius but was nevertheless one of his principal disciples. Much of his thought was original but he is best known as the interpreter and popularizer of the teachings of Confucius. He taught that in matters of government the people came first, then the gods, and finally the emperor. As a result he believed that the people had a right to rebel when the government consistently disregarded their best interests. The democracy of Confucianism is here most apparent.

After about 350 B.C. it must have been clear to most Chinese that little headway could be made against the growing power of the state of Ch'in, and it was actually less than a century later that this state took over the destinies of China for a short but very significant period.

THE CH'IN DYNASTY

The Ch'in Dynasty lasted from 249 to 206 B.C., a relatively short period for an important Chinese dynasty. As we have seen, the Ch'in state was growing steadily in power during the last century of the Chou Dynasty. When Chou rule finally collapsed, it was Ch'in, of all the Chinese states, that was recognized as the rightful leader of the country. However, it was not to be that the chief of the Ch'ins was to enjoy for long the power he had earned. He had already ruled his own Ch'in state for fifty years when he found himself sole ruler of China. The old man died shortly and was followed by his son who reigned only three days.

The most important ruler of this dynasty was the fourth who, after gaining complete control, assumed the splendid sounding title of "First Emperor of the Ch'in Dynasty." He was an extremely forceful person and merits the further distinction of probably being China's greatest general and political genius. The emperor's name and state were held in high regard and it is perhaps from the name of his dynasty, Ch'in, that the name "China" was derived, for we are assured that the First Emperor was the man who really brought all the states together. By 221 B.C., after a series of very deliberate campaigns, there was but one master of China.

There can be no doubt that the emperor was a despot since even his son protested and was banished for his pains, and the Chinese today show no particular reverence to the grave or the memory of the Chinese Napoleon.

It is easily understood that Confucianism, with its democratic principles, was hardly to the liking of the First Emperor. As a result he decreed that except for works on agriculture, medicine, and divination, all the Confucian books were to be destroyed. The First Emperor was so successful in his attempt to remove Confucianism from the scene that when the Han Dynasty came into power several years later it was with the greatest difficulty that the classics were gathered together again. It is said that a descendant of Confucius, a member of the ninth generation, had hidden copies of the works of his ancestor in the walls of his house.

At the time that the books were burned an attempt was also made to stamp out the followers of the sage. On one occasion it is said that four hundred and sixty of them were put to death in such a cruel manner that the son of the emperor again protested.

At the same time the emperor was heartily devoted to the teachings of Taoism. Perhaps its magic qualities, which embodied the hope of knowing the secret of life, had made a strong appeal to the monarch. He was personally fearful of death and sent expeditions in search of the "Elixir of Life." One of these expeditions is said by tradition to have reached Japan. It has also been suggested that his Taoist leaning was a natural course to take in view of his strong feeling against the dominant Confucian philosophy. It is a fact at any rate that Taoism flourished during the Ch'in period.

THE GREAT WALL OF CHINA

There had been earlier ramparts and sec-

The Ch'in Empire. (After W. W. Romig)

The Great Wall of China. (H. Armstrong Roberts)

tional walls along the long northern frontier of China, but credit must be given to the First Emperor for building the mighty wall as it is known today. About 214 B.C. he united into one mighty rampart the sections that then existed in order to keep out the northern hordes who from time immemorial had regarded China as choice prey. The Great Wall winds in and out, over mountain and stream, for about 1,500 miles. It starts at the sea opposite Peiping at Shan-hai-kuan and travels inland almost to the Gobi Desert. It is faced with either brick or granite and is filled with earth. The wall has an average height of twenty feet and the roadway which runs on top is fifteen feet wide. As a means of additional protection there are fortified towers at every hundred yards.

The Great Wall which remains as one of the more spectacular monuments of the Ch'in Age is truly a great engineering feat. But it will be remembered also as a monument to the unremitting power behind the name of the First Emperor, for the lower classes, criminals, merchants, and even Confucian scholars, were driven into the ranks of the corvée.

END OF THE CH'IN DYNASTY

The First Emperor had raised a mighty empire, the greatest that the Far East (or the Near West as some think it should be called) had yet seen. The feudal system had been largely dissolved and government was centralized. But in this case the government was no stronger than the man and when the Emperor died, Ch'in's days were numbered. A son became the Second Emperor but the title was an empty one. The new king reigned but three years before he was murdered, and during that time the magnificent tomb of his father, in which several hundred maidens had been interred alive, had been sacked by one of the generals of the army. Thus Ch'in passed, giving way to strife between several of the army factions.

HAN—THE FIRST GREAT NATIONAL DYNASTY

The Han Dynasty (206 B.C.-220 A.D.) made such an impression on later times that to this day Chinese sometimes call themselves "Sons of Han." But the establishment of the house was not easy. There were several years of intense struggle after the breakdown of the Ch'in line. At length, however, Liu Pang emerged the victor and became the founder of the first great national dynasty. This was in 202 B.C. but he dated his reign to 206, thus including the period of internal disorder. For a while feudalism with all its dangers to government seemed on the verge of returning, but after about a century the hereditary nobles were removed from office. In their stead were placed officials who had proved their worth by examination. This was a true civil service, and although its origin probably went back to Chou times, it was the Hans who really adopted and developed the system. The basis on which the officials were selected was by examination in the Confucian classics which by this time had been revived from their short-lived banishment during the Ch'in Dynasty. In later Chinese history we see that the civil service was greatly enlarged.

During the Han Dynasty China's interests expanded westward. The most famous of Han sovereigns was Wu Ti who reigned for fifty-four years (140-87 B.C.). He successfully fought the Huns and his troops penetrated deep into central Asia. Among the more notable figures of this period was Chang Ch'ien who explored extensively and brought back valuable information regarding the countries west of China. At the time of its greatest expansion the Han empire extended to the Aral and Caspian seas.

After a territory had been subdued it followed naturally that trade would flow more easily than before. Soon Chinese products were finding their way over the thousands of miles of midland Asia into the Hellenistic world, and Mediterranean goods were being sent in return. Trade between China

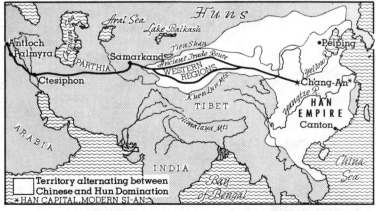

The Han Empire at its greatest extent. (After W. W. Romig)

and Rome is claimed to have begun at the time Marc Antony was governor of Egypt. Soon Roman writers—Horace, Virgil, Pliny the elder and others—were telling about this trade with the Far East. The products which were brought from China included silks, furs, and iron. The long overland route lay through Turkestan to Ctesiphon whose arch still stands by the Tigris. From there the caravans might either go across country to Palmyra and Syria, or turn southward to the Persian Gulf to meet ships which would take the goods around the Arabian Peninsula to Egypt. Still another route from China to the west lay over the passes of the Hindu Kush Mountains to the mouth of the Indus River, at which point the transfer was made to ships.

Pagodas, near Peiking. (Fritz Henle, Black Star)

A Chinese Buddha. (Art Institute of Chicago)

BUDDHISM IN CHINA

It was through such contacts with foreign countries that Buddhism found its way into China. No one knows for sure exactly when it was introduced except that it came during Han times. Many, however, believe that the Indian faith reached China about the time of Christ, and several stories are told of the event. From these it may be gathered that it was not pure Buddhism, but rather a modified Central Asiatic form, that came into the region protected by the Great Wall. And once in China it was changed still further to accord with the family traditions of the Chinese. Thus a third religion joined the two other great ones.

Chinese Buddhism today has traveled a

Paper Making in the Orient. At left, bamboo is being gathered. At right, the cooked bamboo pulp is being transferred from the mold to a felt blanket for further drying. (Drawings from Dard Hunter)

long way in both time and manner from the Buddhism founded by Gautama in India. The best of the mysticism of the Taoists was added to the Buddhist foundation and created a new article of faith. The influence of Buddhism on China has been extremely important in many respects. Art and architecture were enriched. The pagoda may be traced to such influence, and for simplification in such fundamental matters as speech and writing the Chinese owe a great debt to the Sanskrit world.

PAPER

The manufacture of real paper can be traced to 105 A.D. when Ts'ai Lun, a studious official, made the discovery. Before his time documents had been written on bamboo boards or on a near-paper made of silk. The latter appeared in the third century before our era. But silk was expensive and bamboo was heavy. Ts'ai Lun devoted himself to the problem and

Chinese Ink Cake of the Ming Dynasty. (Cleveland Museum of Art)

presently conceived the idea of using the inner part of bark, pieces of hemp, old rags and fishing nets. He announced his invention to the emperor in the year 105 from which time paper has been in general use in China.

It should not be understood that all the substances with which Ts'ai Lun experimented were mixed together. Each was kept separate and pounded into pulp to form hemp paper, bark paper, rag paper, and so on.

The use of paper remained exclusively eastern Asiatic until about the middle of the eighth century when it is said that the Arabs at Samarkand were attacked by the Chinese. The attack was a failure and during the flight certain Chinese experts in the art of papermaking were captured. From these the Arabs learned the process, and developed it, and ultimately passed their information on to Europe.

Brush and ink, contrary to general belief, were invented long before paper, in Shang times in fact. This is an archeological fact which contradicts one of the basic traditions of Chinese invention.

HAN AND HUN

We have seen that the rulers of the early part of the Han Dynasty were successful in beating back the forays of the Hun marauders

Wild Ass Finial, Han. (City Art Museum, St. Louis)

on the northwest frontier. But about the middle of the four hundred year period the Huns came on with added fury, so much so that it was considered necessary to move the Han capital eastward. As a result one speaks of the western Han and eastern Han dynasties. In the latter part of the period even the Great Wall proved to have little effect on the determined attacks of the barbarians who were related to the Huns who later made such a lasting impression by their forays into Europe.

Han Vase of Bronze. (Art Institute of Chicago)

Perhaps part of China's inability to cope with the foreigners lay in the fact that there was constant civil strife between weak emperors and upstart generals. It is true that to have been called general in those days was greater than being called emperor. Certainly the generals had more power. It was one of these who about the beginning of the third century A.D. captured the capital and ended the dynasty by disposing of the Emperor.

THE INTERMEDIATE PERIOD

After the fall of the Han Dynasty, there were approximately three and one half centuries during which no state was able to hold power for more than a short period. The first phase is known as the Age of Romance and is remembered in the *Story of the Three Kingdoms*. There followed a period when invaders from the north beat their way into the country. The Chinese in the south organized to some extent in an effort to thrust back the barbarians, and as a result the period has been called the age of the northern and southern dynasties.

During these centuries civilization was greatly modified. The invaders brought with

Chinese Buddhist Stele. (Art Institute of Chicago)

ichaeans. The Nestorians, who were a Christian sect from western Asia, came as missionaries and church builders. Persians came to China seeking aid against the Arab conquest. Simultaneously the Japanese learned much that was to raise their country out of barbarism.

After a brilliant period of progress in the arts, including poetry and music and the development of block printing, the T'ang Dynasty weakened and came to an end. This dynasty is known as one in which the earliest known

Kuan-yin, Goddess of Mercy. (Museum of Fine Arts, Boston)

them non-Chinese traits, while at the same time they absorbed much that was thoroughly Chinese in nature. Buddhism became very popular and Chinese pilgrims visited the sacred shrines in India. The real growth of Buddhism in China can be traced to the last years of this intermediate period. It was during those years and the century or two following that Buddhism reached its peak as an influence in the life of China.

Due to the numerous military ventures that took place during the intermediate period a complicated code of chivalry sprang up. It was this age also that supplied later China with many of the romantic figures that we know from fiction and drama.

THE SUI AND THE T'ANG

The country was brought under control again by the Sui who ruled for about thirty years (589-618 A.D.). The T'ang (618-907 A.D.) followed and for a while China was the greatest and largest empire on earth. T'ang armies marched to Korea, Turkistan, Tibet, and northwest India. China attained its peak in cultural achievement during the period of what was perhaps the greatest native dynasty. Chinese still call themselves "Sons of T'ang" as they do "Sons of Han." The capital was the converging point of philosophers, scholars, and religious leaders of many faiths. At the same time the country was opened to foreigners, among them Moslems, Nestorians, and Man-

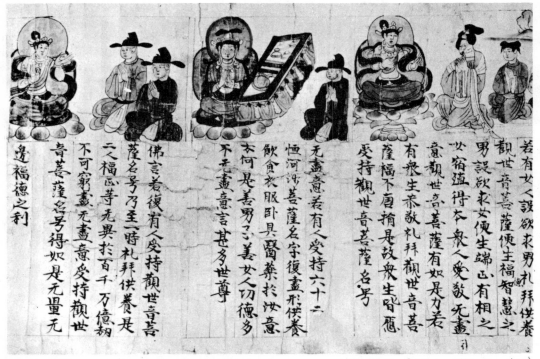

The Lotus Sutra, a T'ang copy of one of the most popular of Buddhist scriptures. Chapter 25 is devoted to the miracles of Kuan-yin, who became a favorite deity in the 8th century. (Bibliothèque Nationale)

printed book appeared, as well as the one which first saw printed money. Unfortunately religious strife toward the close of the T'ang rule (907 A.D.) caused the destruction of most of the dynasty's art works.

From that year to 960 there was much disorder in the country. Various factions fought among themselves for power, and five of them were strong enough for short periods to be granted dynastic distinction.

THE SUNG DYNASTY

The Sung Dynasty, a period especially glorified by achievements in literature, philos-

Ceremonial House. (Museum of Fine Arts, Boston)

T'ang Polo Player. (Museum of Fine Arts, Boston)

Sung Kuan-yin of wood. (Art Institute of Chicago)

izers, led his Mongols into North China early in the thirteenth century, and by 1214 most of the territory north of the Yellow River was in his hands. At the time of his death in 1227 still more territory had been added. Alliances between Mongols and Sung were effective for a time, but this brotherhood was most unnatural. By the year 1280 we see the last of the Sung monarchs throwing himself into the sea at the time Kublai Khan, grandson of Genghiz, became emperor of all China.

THE DYNASTY OF KUBLAI KHAN

The Mongol Dynasty, for all its fame in history, lasted less than ninety years. It was founded, as we have seen, by Kublai Khan, the

ophy, and the famous socialistic experiment of Wang An-shih, existed for over three hundred years (960-1280 A.D.). It began well but soon felt the pressure of the frontier barbarians. These included the K'itans, the Chin Tartars, and the Mongols. Genghiz Khan, one of the world's foremost fighters and military organ-

Portrait of Kublai Khan, from a Chinese engraving

Silk Workers of the Sung Dynasty, from a painting by the Emperor Hui Tsung. Designed to be unrolled from right to left, the scroll shows the silk being beaten, wound and ironed. (Museum of Fine Arts, Boston)

Weeding the Rice Field, part of a series of 15th century drawings depicting rice and silk production

Young Rice Plants, a few inches high, are transplanted by hand from half-liquid mud to water

Human Treadmills pump water to the terraced fields. Below, grain is removed by beating the stalks on rods, then tossed in air to winnow out husks and chaff

Stacking Sheaves is done after the rice field has been drained. Below, dry rice is stored in the barn, after it has been threshed

Silk Production, China's most ancient industry, is based on the harvesting of the mulberry orchards

Silk Worms are fed only tender, fresh leaves

Silk Farmers keep the cocoons warm with the heat of their own bodies. Below, weavers set up a loom to produce floral patterns in the silk

Silk Thread is prepared by unwinding the cocoon

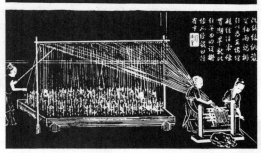

Twisting the Silk into warp threads, above. Below, grading finished silk according to quality

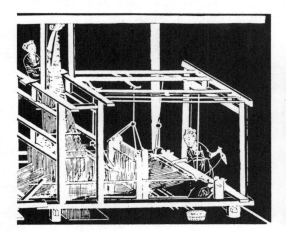

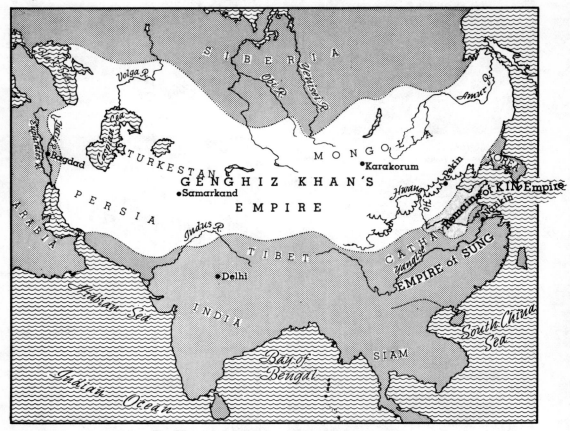

The Mongol dominions at their greatest extent

hero of Coleridge's celebrated poem. He was in all respects as able a soldier as his grandfather had predicted. The capital was by this time near Peiping and from there he ruled not only China, but most of the sprawling Mongol empire which extended across Asia to Mesopotamia and into Europe. Military expeditions were sent also into Japan, Cambodia, Burma, and Java, but these added no glory to the name of the brilliant Kublai.

Mongol power reached its peak under Kublai Khan, and the tremendous extension of influence was a great boon to trade. Consequently there was steady travel by both ship and caravan between Europe and Cathay, as China was then called in Europe. Missionary and merchant met on the high road of Asia. Among the merchants were three Venetians named

Polo. Marco Polo spent many years in the service of Kublai and on returning to Venice wrote the memoirs that have made him famous and helped stir European interest in the East.

The Mongol Dynasty was no exception to the rule that Chinese dynasties based upon forced military power are short-lived. In fact it collapsed about ninety years after having begun so auspiciously. When this happened the outlying districts lost their protection and the trade routes became unsafe. For a while China lost contact with the west.

THE MING DYNASTY

The Ming Dynasty (1368-1644 A.D.) was purely Chinese. Although it was brilliant in many respects, not much originality can be claimed for it. The third ruler moved the cap-

Kuan-yin, as the child-bestowing goddess, white jade. (Parke-Bernet)

ital to Peiping, and the palaces and temples which are so much admired by the tourist were largely the work of this emperor. The Ming rulers sent expeditions to Java, Ceylon, and even as far as the Persian Gulf. Korea was also invaded. But with the weakening of the Ming line the Japanese entered Korea and sailed as pirates up and down the Chinese coast.

As has already been mentioned, China of the Ming period was not particularly creative, even though architecture and glazed pottery had considerable charm. The China of that day was wealthy, but lacked abilities observed in earlier days.

During the Ming Dynasty Europeans began again to interest themselves in China. The Portuguese, in the sixteenth century, sailed to India, Malacca, China, and Japan; and Spanish ships landed in the Philippines, thus establishing a control that lasted until the Spanish-American War in 1898. The Jesuits soon followed and after some difficult years established themselves in China. Some of them were so highly regarded for their knowledge of astronomy and mathematics that they were put in charge of the government bureau of astronomy in Peiping. During the following (Manchu) period they were given more duties.

THE MANCHUS

The Manchu Dynasty carries China into the midst of present-day relations with the rest of the world. It lasted from 1644 to 1912. The Manchus were a small Tartar tribe northeast of China who easily pushed aside the weakened Ming Dynasty. They were conquerors, these Golden Tartars, but they accepted Chinese customs. Moreover, the native Chinese were eligible for office, except in their own provinces. This was the Manchu method for preventing revolt. At the same time no official was allowed to remain in one place long enough to gain a real following.

By 1700 the Manchu Empire included not only China, but Manchuria, Mongolia, Tibet, and Turkestan. A few years later Cochin China and Korea were paying tribute.

The principal events of the Manchu Dynasty were connected with adjustment to European influence and affairs. As we have seen, the Jesuits were in the country before Manchu times. Missionaries of other orders followed, with the result that Europe learned a great deal about the glamour, the life, and especially the opportunities existing in the land of China.

During the nineteenth century increased European trade interest in China caused serious trouble and a number of grave skirmishes took

Manchu Civil Officer. (Seattle Art Museum)

place. China was subdued and practically came to believe that she was destined to serve the interests of the world. The complete downfall of the Manchus came with revolution in 1911 and since 1912 the country has had a republican form of government. The later history of China is told in chapters 84 and 88.

TIBET, THE MOUNTAIN KINGDOM

Tibet and especially its capital, Lhasa, have always spelled romance and adventure. Naturally rugged and inaccessible, the country has become even more difficult to enter because of the development of anti-European feeling. Tibet lies across the Himalayas from India and is the highest country in the world, being on the average over three miles above sea level, while its very lowest valleys are almost as high as Pikes Peak. To get into the country by any one of the passes one must climb to a height of at least three miles. The population, largely herders, is widely scattered through the mountains and has been estimated at about 3,000,000 people. Nobody knows the area of the country, and little is certain as to the natural resources of this mysterious land. But gold is to be found in most of the river beds.

The Tibetan name for the country sounds something like *Bhöt*, and it was through a strange misunderstanding that our name for the country came into being. In the early days travelers went cross-country to China and India by way of the high plateau—the *Tö-bhöt*. They couldn't pronounce it correctly but they did their best, and the result was "Tibet." Thus an original misunderstanding to which was added mispronunciation produced a term which must seem queer to Tibetans.

LHASA—THE FORBIDDEN CITY

Few Europeans have seen Lhasa with its picturesque Potala—the early seventeenth century fortress-palace of the Dalai Lama built on a rocky hill—and the city houses stretching out below. The Dalai Lama is the spiritual and political ruler of these secluded mountain folk whose religion is a modified form of Buddhism developed through many centuries. Many have tried to reach the forbidden city but few have succeeded. However, in earlier days antagonism toward foreigners was not as strong as at present.

The first Englishman to enter Tibet came in 1774, just before the American Revolution, but he did not reach Lhasa. However, another of his countrymen visited the famous city in the early part of the last century and stayed five months, apparently on good terms. Shortly afterward yet another Englishman is said to have resided in Lhasa for twelve years disguised as a Moslem. Effective exclusion of Europeans dates back only about a century. Nevertheless, the lure of adventure and the hope of gaining a new understanding of this strange country have prompted many others to make the attempt. Of these, some were killed, others saw extensive portions of the outlying districts of Tibet, but Lhasa, the goal of all, has been seen by few.

Sloping Stairways lead up steep Potala Hill to the 17th century fortress-palace of the Dalai Lama

15. Meaning of the "Middle Ages"

AN INTERLUDE BETWEEN TWO ERAS

VIEWED from the vantage point of later centuries, the Middle Ages appear as an interlude beween the fall of the Roman Empire and the growth of the modern world. The Middle Ages extended over a period of approximately one thousand years, from the fifth to the fifteenth centuries.

It is impossible to assign arbitrary dates for the beginning and the end of a period, movement, or age. For example, the "fall of Rome" is frequently mentioned as though it occurred definitely in 476. When did Rome start to fall and when did Rome lie prostrate before the barbarians? As a matter of fact, that phenomenon which is known in history as the "fall of Rome" had its origins long before 476.

For purposes of writing, however, it is sometimes necessary that certain dates be used so that the author and reader may conveniently outline the vast historical material. Therefore, one finds that often the dates 476 and 1500 are used to denote the chronological space covered by the Middle Ages. Realizing that such dates are artificial limits because they are conventionally used to describe the duration of the Middle Ages, we begin our story with the so-called "fall of Rome" in 476 and carry it to somewhere near the beginning of the sixteenth century.

As with dates, so with names. One is forced to label a period with a title that is at best vague. Persons in the so-called Middle Ages never thought of themselves as belonging to the "Middle Ages" because they were living in the *present*, just as we do today. Later historians have named this period the "Middle Ages" because it occurs between ancient times and modern times. But a thousand years from now

all of these terms may be relative, for what is modern in our day may be the "Middle Ages" to some future age. But again, because this term has become the conventional way of describing our period, we shall call those thousand years the Middle Ages.

MIDDLE AGES—DARK OR BRILLIANT?

It is of great importance to note that in recent historical works the Middle Ages have been viewed in an entirely different manner than heretofore. Formerly, historians and students alike looked upon this period as one of deep darkness in a spiritual, intellectual, and cultural sense. With our growing knowledge of what really existed in these times, based upon the evidences of exhaustive research, we have had to revise our opinions and acknowledge that the Middle Ages were productive of some of the greatest geniuses and institutions of all ages.

It was our ignorance *about* the Middle Ages and not the prevalence of ignorance *in* the Middle Ages that accounts for this popular misconception. Practically all of our supposedly modern theories in the fields of government, education, and even religion were current in some form in these "dark ages." As we shall see later, the Middle Ages preserved most of the classical culture which we have enjoyed and are enjoying today. Some of the most glorious buildings of all times were patiently erected by medieval genius. The various national languages were first employed in the fables, sermons, hymns, and poems of the Middle Ages.

A FUSION OF CULTURE

Before beginning the actual narrative of the Middle Ages, it would be well to consider briefly those elements which were fused into the cultural, social, economic, and political life of the Middle Ages. First of all, it should be remembered that everywhere in Western Europe were scattered the decaying foundations of the once magnificent Roman Empire.

Enough Roman law survived to be incorporated bit by bit into the crude law systems of the barbarians. Certain features of Roman government, especially local government, were adapted by the newcomers. The Latin tongue in its popular usage became the basis for the language of the kingdoms founded by the barbarians—French, Spanish, Italian, Portuguese, and Rumanian. Even the sturdy Anglo-Saxon language of our English forefathers has been diluted by the latinized language of the Norman conquerors. Roman names clung to places and persons and things; Roman dress and social customs were admired and then adopted by the Germanic folk. The Church indirectly preserved the Latin language in its services and used it as the medium of teaching and writing. This Roman or classical element, then, was inescapable; it was never absent from the foundation of medieval society.

THE ALL-PERVADING CHURCH

In a like manner the Christian Church was an integral part of the medieval structure. It was perhaps the greatest single agency for introducing and preserving civilization during the early Middle Ages. Most of the learned men of the times were to be found in the service of the Church. Certainly, whatever education was to be had was obtainable only through the medium of the church schools. Music and the arts were employed in those early medieval centuries mainly by the Church. The clergy and especially the monks were the most active agents in civilizing the untutored barbarians. The Church set up standards of morality and good conduct in a lawless period and tried to punish the undisciplined members of a community by various spiritual means.

The Church represented the most reliable and comforting institution in times which were frequently chaotic and dangerous. Being international and universal, the Church through its broad contacts with other parts of the world, especially with Rome and the Near East, proved the best agent for spreading ideas and culture even of a purely secular nature. No matter what the individuals in their sundry positions may have done to disgrace their office, the teachings of the Christian Church remained as a steady and ennobling guide for all the folk within medieval society.

BARBARIANS AS CIVILIZERS

The barbarians themselves, however, had something to contribute to medieval life. They brought with them a potential capacity for absorbing and amplifying what they found. They found a decadent Roman society that was slowly rotting away, and they infused into this dying society all of their unspoiled vigor and vitality. No matter what we may believe concerning "racial purity" and its desirability, nevertheless we must admit that these Germanic tribes brought racial elements into anemic stocks which revived them and started them on the road to still greater civilization.

It was desirable at least in part that the barbarians destroy the decadent feature of Roman society before they began to adopt that social pattern in their own individual way. If the barbarians had merely copied Roman customs and institutions, they would have produced only a worthless imitation of the old Roman system, probably using the worst elements of the former civilization. When it is duly considered how these primitive folk within the space of a few centuries built up a new society out of their native talents, the contributions of the Christian Church, and the decaying remnants of the Roman social order, then we begin to realize their tremendous capacity for civilization and the magnitude of their service to future generations.

16. The Germanic Kingdoms

BARBARIAN FOUNDATIONS

OUR modern European states owe their birth to the whims of certain barbarian tribes which entered the old Roman Empire and circled about until they found just the land they desired. These folk from the German forests moved in the fourth and fifth centuries as a heavy tidal wave sweeping all obstacles before them. As a rule they were fairly decent in their behavior toward the older inhabitants, seizing only those things which they needed for sustenance and plundering only when angered by stubborn people. Usually the former Roman citizens were permitted to continue in their previous customs and were granted the right of being judged by Roman law.

The barbarians had been converted to the Arian form of Christianity, the heresy which had originated in Alexandria during the fourth century and which held that Jesus was the Son of God but not equal to Him. By the efforts of such famous missionaries as Ulfilas, who translated the Bible into the earliest known form of the German language, the barbarians were introduced to Christianity but remained broad-minded in their religious policies. In general they allowed the orthodox Christians of the West, who were in communion with the Bishop of Rome, to practice their faith undisturbed, and even permitted the orthodox clergy to win converts from their Arian fold.

Thus the infiltration of the barbarians was as peaceful as could be expected from a great mass of uncultured people who for the first time, in many instances, were beholding the wonders of the civilized world and in their childlike way wanted to possess them. These folk from the northern forests began to adapt themselves to their new environment quickly, settled down next to the older Roman populations, saw the advantages of certain Roman ways of doing things, and soon started to intermarry with this older population. Just what proportion of these new national groups was composed of the blood of the former Roman group and what of the new barbarian infusion, is beyond the guess of the historian. But from the studies of places and personal names, language modifications, physical characteristics, and other anthropological information, we can conclude that the proportion of Germanic blood must have been considerable.

FOREFATHER OF THE ITALIANS

The East Goths, or Ostrogoths as they are frequently called, were the tribe that settled in Italy and most quickly absorbed Roman civilization. The intelligent, though probably illiterate, leader of the Ostrogoths, Theodoric by name (493-526), had an active appreciation of the values to be salvaged from the previous Roman system of government. He continued the old administrative offices of the Roman government and tried to uphold the enforcement of Roman law. He permitted the Roman Senate to function, and in general tried his best to copy the actions and attitudes of the former Roman rulers. Despite the fact that he could have ignored the ruler of the Eastern Roman Empire, he always maintained the utmost respect for that office. Likewise he was very gracious to the Roman clergy, although he was an Arian.

Theodoric's reign is memorable in the annals of these half-barbaric states because of his unusual personal qualities. His tact in handling institutions which had existed over a long period of time and which had proved their worth; his toleration in religious matters; and

Theodoric's Palace at Ravenna is depicted in this 6th century mosaic in the nave of the basilica, Sant' Apollinare Nuovo. Christian saints carrying crowns flank the palace; above, are prophets and apostles

his ability to find talented secretaries of state—all these qualities made Theodoric a distinguished ruler for such uncertain times.

Two names are closely associated with his reign that should be familiar to everyone interested in the history of culture. One of these is Cassiodorus, a secretary of Theodoric, who was influential in guiding Theodoric along the paths of wise government. The letters written by Cassiodorus are a mine of information

Boethius, Roman statesman and philosopher

about this whole obscure period. The other great name is that of Boethius (480-525). This great scholar rendered invaluable service to the Middle Ages and all times by his translations and abridgments of the Greek writings of Aristotle, and of famous mathematicians and scientists like Euclid and Archimedes.

Theodoric in his later years, however, grew suspicious of intrigue, and the unfortunate Boethius was one of his victims. While in prison, Boethius wrote what has been considered the last great outpouring of classical Roman genius, *The Consolation of Philosophy*, which is read and admired even in our sophisticated age.

OTHER DESPOILERS OF ROME

Closely allied to the Ostrogoths was another Germanic tribe, known as the Visigoths or West Goths. These people also had poured into Italy with the general barbarian invasions, but then had moved farther west into what is now the south of France and down into the Iberian Peninsula, the region occupied by modern Spain and Portugal. Like the Ostrogoths, they were fortunate in having a capable monarch in the person of Euric. This king kept his people well in hand and tried to follow Roman models in making his laws. Although the Visigoths tended toward a rapid intermarriage with the native population, they never achieved the higher type of civilization which prevailed in Italy. The Visigothic kingdom never proved to be long-enduring and fell easy prey to almost any group of invaders.

"The Planetary Systems," a woodcut from the German edition of Boethius' Consolation of Philosophy

Another Germanic tribe had settled for a while in Spain and then had passed on to the coast of North Africa. They were the Vandals. This tribe has given its name to our language in such forms as "vandalism," because they were noted throughout the world as the most destructive and ruthless of the invaders. Their importance was due mainly to the ambitions and activity of their restless king, Gaiseric. He set up an absolute monarchy on the coast of North Africa and then proceeded to terrorize the Mediterranean. His ships harried the coasts of most of the nations which lay along the Mediterranean; he and his men became a byword for pillaging and destruction.

However, like so many one-man powers, as soon as he died his kingdom began to disintegrate and the danger from the Vandals grew less and less. Life in North Africa diluted their primitive vigor so that in 534 the great Roman general Belisarius was able to defeat them easily. As a matter of fact, these Vandals were probably no worse than any other barbarian group, but the popular opinion of the time and the bitter feelings of the Roman clergy have associated the name of Vandal with all that is uncivilized.

About the middle of the fifth century the Burgundians settled in the valley of the upper Rhone River. These peoples were rather late in the barbarian contest of grabbing lands. They seem to have been quite peaceful and willing to assume Roman culture. Because of their relatively settled life, they soon turned to

Belisarius, renowned for his mercy as a conqueror, was often portrayed as a kindly, blind beggar

WANDERINGS OF THE GERMANIC PEOPLES

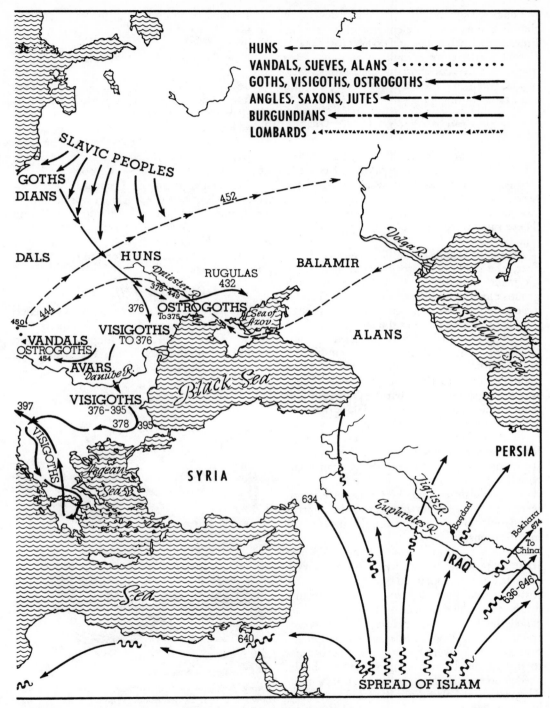

HUNS ←----←----←----←----←----←

VANDALS, SUEVES, ALANS ◄·······◄

GOTHS, VISIGOTHS, OSTROGOTHS ◄——————

ANGLES, SAXONS, JUTES ◄—·—·—·—·—·◄

BURGUNDIANS ◄—··—··—··—··—◄

LOMBARDS ▴▾▴▾▴▾▴▾▴▾▴▾◄▾▴▾▴▾▴▾◄▴▾▴▾▴▾

SLAVIC PEOPLES

GOTHS
DIANS

DALS HUNS

452

RUGULAS
432

Dniester R.
375-449

BALAMIR

Volga R.

444

376 OSTROGOTHS
To 375

Sea of
Azov

Caspian Sea

450

VISIGOTHS
TO 376

ALANS

VANDALS
OSTROGOTHS
454

AVARS
Danube R.

Black Sea

397

VISIGOTHS
376-395

378 395

PERSIA

VISIGOTHS

Aegean
Sea

SYRIA

634

Tigris R.

Euphrates R.

Bagdad

Bokhara 674

To
China

IRAQ

636-646

Sea

640

SPREAD OF ISLAM

DURING THE LAST YEARS OF THE ROMAN EMPIRE

the cultured pursuits of leisure and developed the first noteworthy elements of Germanic literature in their songs and epics. How far this Burgundian attempt at civilization might have gone is a story cut short by the Franks, who, in 534, conquered them and absorbed them into the Frankish kingdom.

ANGLO-SAXON INVASION OF ENGLAND

Up in the northern part of Europe a different kind of invasion had been taking place. The Angles, Saxons, and Jutes were said to have harried the coasts of Britain ever since the Roman troops had been withdrawn in 407. These raids were made largely for the sake of plunder.

About the middle of the fifth century, however, the traditional story has it that these Germans first began to colonize in small groups along the seashore and rivers. Then by a slow and almost imperceptible process they gradually filtered all over the island so that by 600 much of the island was governed by their chieftains. The Germans simply shoved the older British or Celtic inhabitants into the highlands or onto the smaller islands. There was some intermarriage, but the Germanic element swallowed up all other racial ingredients.

The Angles, Saxons, and Jutes went right on living as they had lived back in the German forests, and completely ignored whatever institutions and improvements the Roman occupation of Britain had established. Hence, Roman civilization and the Christian religion were utterly wiped out and were to be reintroduced only after a long struggle and radical modifications.

In 568 a group of latecomers marched into Italy supposedly at the invitation of Narses who had been appointed ruler of Italy by Justinian and then deposed after Justinian's death by jealous officials. This group was called the Lombards, or Longobards, on account of their long beards and unkempt appearance. They were the last of the barbarians to invade the Roman Empire, and probably needed no special urging on the part of Narses. They had heard already of the fabulous luxury of the Italian cities. Their cruel and able king

was Alboin who quickly reduced all of Italy to his command except Rome, Ravenna, and Sicily.

Thus the Lombards threw off the yoke of the Eastern Roman Emperor and left to his jurisdiction only Ravenna and the southern tip of Italy. The popes clung to what is known as the Papal States, the territory that immediately surrounded Rome. The Lombard conquests, therefore, may be said to have brought completely to an end the power of the Eastern Roman Empire in Western Europe.

The danger from the Lombards was considerably lessened when Alboin was slain by a rival, and when the Lombards started to set up rival states and quarreled among themselves. In Italy, the Lombards had proved stronger than both the Roman emperor and the previous Ostrogothic invaders.

CLOVIS AND THE FRANKS

The most important of all the Germanic tribes that took up residence within the framework of the old Roman Empire were the Franks. Their history is obscure before the

Frank Archers used the crossbow, drawing its stiff bowstring taut by windlass. When the trigger was released, the arrow was projected with great force

At the Baptism of Clovis, according to legend, a white dove brought a vial of holy oil from heaven

The story of Clovis' dramatic conversion to the Roman Church because Jesus Christ gave him victory over some enemies may have been a later invention; but the fact that Clovis did join that communion and did reap great benefits for the Frankish realm is beyond dispute. Of course it is not to be imagined that his conversion in any way affected the private life or public conduct of Clovis, for he went on living as he always had lived.

The most remarkable achievement of Clovis' reign was the compilation of the Salic law. This code of laws explained the procedure of the Franks in settling their legal difficulties, and by so doing sheds much light on the customs of these peoples. Two main procedures appear: first, compurgation, which was the method of bringing in oath-helpers to swear to one's innocence; second, the ordeals, whereby the accused person was subjected to certain tests of endurance, such as walking through fire, and his guilt or innocence was established by the outcome. In order to avoid feuds, these laws decreed a graduated scale of money payments, called *wergeld*, by which the offending party could offer compensation to the clan of the slain or injured person; the payment depended upon the rank of the person involved and the extent of the damage inflicted.

time of Clovis, who came into kingship about 486. He proved to be a worthy king of these wild pagans—they were the only invaders who had not been converted by the Christians—who won their battles by ferocious fighting and invincible zeal. They had preserved their primitive and warlike habits without succumbing to the temptations of Roman civilization.

Clovis soon made himself master of all the Franks by fair means or foul; he wisely removed all kinsmen who might profit by his death. Then he led his united Franks against the other Germanic tribes who had settled in what we call modern France, subduing them in short order. The former Roman cities, heretofore unconquered, fell before him.

In 496 Clovis made the wisest decision of his whole career. He joined the orthodox Roman Church, and thus became the first of the barbarian rulers to gain the good grace and help of that already powerful institution. Henceforth the Roman bishop and the whole Western Church looked to the Franks for support and at the same time gave them material and spiritual aid. No longer was the papacy dependent upon the Eastern emperor.

After Pillage of Soissons, Clovis was beseeched by St. Remi to restore a sacred vase. The episode is legendary, but shows deference of king to clergy

"DO-NOTHING" KINGS

The ruling family or dynasty founded by Clovis was called the Merovingian. When Clovis died in 511, his sons divided his realm and began at once to quarrel among themselves. His youngest and cruelest son, Lothair, finally gained control of the whole kingdom of Clovis and ruled it as a bloody tyrant until 561. His sons again divided the realm into the territories called Austrasia, Neustria, and Burgundy. There followed several unfortunate reigns, each worse than the preceding, often having a relentless woman like Brunhilde or Fredegunde plunging the land into unbelievable internal strife.

Because these Merovingian kings were for the most part worthless and incapable rulers, the administration of the Frankish kingdom gradually slipped into the able hands of the mayors of the palace who often were the king's chief officials. The duty of defending the realm fell into the hands of the great dukes and border margraves. Thus the Merovingian kings served no function in the government and were called "do-nothing" kings.

In 687 Pepin, son of a family that acted as mayors of the palace for Austrasia, defeated the mayor of the Neustrian palace and the Burgundians. He virtually then ruled the whole Frankish realm, and proceeded to conquer and add more land to the kingdom. It was his son Charles Martel who finished the task of replacing the Merovingian kings by the Carolingian line in the person of his grandson Charles the Great, usually called Charlemagne.

Charles Martel dictated all the policies of the kingdom to the weak Merovingian rulers. He earned the right to rule, for it was he who kept order among the disorderly nobles, reduced the neighboring powers who hoped to take advantage of the civil strife, and saved Europe from the heavy hand of the Moslems by utterly defeating the Saracens at Tours in 732. It was no wonder then that the Franks looked with confidence to this brilliant leader and were prepared to depose their useless Merovingian king within a short time.

Charles Martel, eldest son of Pepin, receiving the news of his father's death in 714

17. Papacy and Church in the Early Middle Ages

CIVIL AND RELIGIOUS POWERS OF THE PAPACY

THE IMPACT of the Roman Church on the Middle Ages is one of the most important and exciting studies which medieval history offers. In a way the Church forms the background of the whole medieval picture. There is no period of medieval history which can be studied independently of the Western Church.

By the fifth century the Roman Church emerged as the dominant spiritual power in the West. Just how the Roman bishop gained his supremacy is a matter of some debate. We shall examine a few of the apparent reasons for this circumstance.

First of all, the bishop of Rome became an important person when he assumed the secular control of government in Rome and outlying districts. The machinery of the old Roman Empire had collapsed; the secular rulers were no longer able to govern the city of Rome, and barbarian hordes from the north destroyed the civil administrative system. In the ensuing chaos the popes, who were often very capable men, gradually assumed the right to regulate the civil life of the Romans. Their government was effective and usually just; therefore, in time the people came to look to the popes as their protectors. The Eastern emperors were quite willing to let the popes manage Roman affairs so long as the popes would be loyal to the court of Constantinople.

Furthermore, the popes occupied the city which had for centuries been the center of Roman life and culture and government; their bishopric naturally would be looked upon as the most important and most dignified in the West. Thus the bishop of Rome had the prestige of centuries to back his claim for leadership in the Latin Church.

Another factor was the distance from the Roman emperor of the East, who resided in Constantinople. Had the emperor held his court in Rome, the popes very likely never would have been permitted to acquire so much civil or even religious power. The patriarch of Constantinople, who was recognized as the religious head of the Eastern or Greek Orthodox Church, was always under the eye of the emperor who allowed him no direct civil powers and who often interfered in purely ecclesiastical matters. The popes were far enough away from the emperor to do almost as they pleased, especially in times of danger, for example, when the new Germanic kingdoms usurped the lands of the emperor in Italy. The emperors had to use the popes as deputies and therefore had to make concessions to the spiritual jurisdiction of the popes as far as the West was concerned.

HEIRS OF ST. PETER

The reason advanced by the Roman Church itself for its right to control the churches of the West was the Petrine Theory. In brief this theory claimed that St. Peter, who was the Prince of Apostles and singled out by Christ to govern His Church, according to Matthew 16: 18-19, was the first bishop of Rome. Therefore, all the successors of Peter in the Roman See were especially endowed by the Holy Ghost with the favors and preeminence that had originally belonged to Peter through Christ's commission. They held that for this reason all Christians should hearken to the bishop of Rome who was the prince of all bishops and who took the place among the clergy that Peter had enjoyed among the apostles. Neither the New Testament nor any other early historical sources mention Peter as bishop of Rome; the evidence quoted by the popes comes from a later period. Moreover, the early Roman bishops were quite obscure men, and these claims did not arise until very capable bishops appeared in Rome. The Church in the East never knew and never accepted this Petrine Theory, although it readily acknowledged the pope as head of the Western Church.

Rome since about the middle of the second century seems to have been considered by her sister churches in the West as the center of orthodoxy in Latin Christendom. The various local churches one by one had to yield to Roman jurisdiction, either through political pressure or through emergencies such as dangerous heresies. The Church of Rome and her decisions came to be held as the best defense against the poisonous assaults of heretics.

Probably as important as any of the aforementioned reasons is the fact that in the fifth and sixth centuries there arose great bishops who advanced the Roman cause through their personality and ability. Leo the Great (440-461) made an emphatic statement about the powers inherent in the bishopric of Rome as to jurisdiction over all Western churches. Gregory the Great (590-604) is counted among the most distinguished pontiffs who ever reigned. He was a great statesman who was recognized as such by secular rulers, and he was a deeply pious man who carefully shepherded his flock. He was very active in the missionary program of the Church, always threw his influence in behalf of the election of good churchmen, and probably saved the Church from destruction by the Lombards.

CHURCH GOVERNMENT

Although the bishop of Rome stood at the head of the Western Church, he had to have officials to rule the Church locally. The Roman Church in its administration followed the outline of the Roman Empire. It kept the divisions of the provinces and dioceses; at the head of the former was an archbishop, and of the latter, a bishop. Archbishops and bishops formed the hierarchy or ruling group within the Church. All clergy above and below the rank of bishop were supposed to hold office by virtue of the doctrine of Apostolic Succession.

This doctrine taught that all clergymen who were in valid Holy Orders, and who were authorized to administer the sacraments, had to receive their ordination at the hands of a bishop whose jurisdiction could be traced back to one of the Apostles. This doctrine was formulated to protect the Church from heretics and unauthorized persons.

The parish priests managed the local congregations and made their reports to the bishop in charge of their diocese. Deacons and subdeacons were appointed to assist the parish priest. There were several other minor offices which a person seeking an ecclesiastical career might have to begin by filling.

Thus we have a church system which by the fifth century was rather carefully worked out. From the humble acolyte to the mighty bishop of Rome there existed a rising scale of power and responsibility; each person on the scale being responsible to the one next highest; at the peak was the pope, responsible only to God. It was the most completely organized institution in the history of the world.

MONASTICISM

As a whole the Roman clergy came to be divided into two main classifications: secular clergy and regular clergy. The secular clergymen were those who were not bound by the *regula* or "rule" as were the regular or monastic clergy. The secular clergy were the ordinary priests and members of the hierarchy who performed their tasks out in the world. The regular clergy, as we have already suggested, were those who took a vow to live according to some "rule" which usually confined them to a life of contemplation and retirement. These men were called monks.

It has been the special work of the monastic order to be the silent but indispensable army of the Roman Church. In its quiet way monasticism really won and preserved the Middle Ages for the papacy. The Western Church, however, was not the original home of monasticism. Monks originated in the deserts of Egypt under the auspices of the Eastern Church, with its emphasis on the contemplative aspects of religion. At first a few hermits decided to live in a community rather than in complete isolation. As the group grew, it was necessary to formulate some regulations so that the spiritual and physical routine of the community could function at its best.

St. Benedict of Nursia (c. 480-550) was the founder of Western monasticism. Born of noble Italian lineage, he had planned a secular career. But the type of life he encountered at Rome sickened him and so he decided to withdraw to a quiet place and become a hermit. His reputation as a holy person, however, would not allow him any privacy; soon others joined themselves to Benedict. Ultimately he moved to Monte Cassino where he founded a famous community, still in existence.

The rule which he drew up for his followers has become the model for all subsequent orders. Benedict did not draft an impossible and fantastic set of rules, but tried to make them as practical as possible. He wanted to fit his regulations to a community of average human beings. Thus he produced his famous Benedictine Rule, which is very sane and humane, avoiding the extremes characteristic of the Eastern communities and some later Roman orders. The basic principles he laid down were few and simple: all Benedictines were to surrender their earthly possessions and lead a life of poverty within the community. They were to remain unmarried and lead a life of exemplary chastity; they were to render absolute obedience to their superiors. These regulations are found in every Western order.

Benedict wisely saw that to maintain a balanced religious life his monks should lead a well-rounded schedule of activities. Monks had to attend divine worship as a group several times a day. Other hours were allowed for private devotions. Each friar had to perform a certain amount of manual labor. Sufficient time was given for reading and study. At least eight hours were allotted for sleep. This well regulated life did not permit any idleness, that sin of sins whose effects Benedict understood and feared. And he was very careful about giving his monks a sensible diet; the rations seem very generous—at both meals there were two hot dishes, vegetables, fruits, as well as a pound of bread a day. Meat was forbidden, except to invalids, but wine was generously supplied.

The monastic system furthermore had to preserve some form of government and discipline. Therefore, not everyone who applied at the monastery could be admitted. Every applicant had to serve a period of time as a novice so that he and the community could decide whether he might fittingly become a monk. If he proved acceptable, he made a solemn vow to observe the rules of the order.

At the head of the monastery was the abbot who had absolute command over the persons and activities within its walls. Later in the history of monasticism, priors were heads of the individual monasteries and abbots were appointed to supervise a number of priors. The abbot was chosen by all the members of the religious community, in what was probably the most democratic procedure in the Roman Church.

SOCIAL POWER OF THE CHURCH

The position of the Church in the early Middle Ages was one of extreme importance. Socially it had the power to regulate conduct. If an individual's actions were counter to the precepts of the Church, he could be cut off from all relationship with members of the Church and with its clergy throughout the world. This drastic disciplinary measure, known as excommunication, enabled the Church to coerce individuals to mend their ways, for anyone who died outside the fold was considered eternally lost.

In Rome the Church had at her disposal the appointment of civic officials, and she gave these offices to persons who were faithful members. Through their influence with kings and men in high places, ecclesiastical authorities could request favors for needy and pious members, and on the other hand could keep undesirable persons out of office. When it became the fashion to be a Christian, and the whole social structure became Christian at least in name, the Church naturally became the most influential force in medieval society. When we consider that the Church not only controlled men in this life through fear of damnation in the next, but also controlled whatever education was to be had, we begin to realize how extensive was its might.

18. The Eastern Empire and Islam

THE REIGN OF JUSTINIAN

DURING the period in Western Europe when civilization and all that it implies in matters of education, culture, and good government was fighting for existence, the Eastern Empire was continuing its heritage from the classical world and adding to that body of knowledge. The Eastern Roman Empire was fortunate in having such an excellent machinery of government headed by energetic rulers who could successfully combat the barbarian invasions. Moreover, the center of the Eastern world, Byzantium or Constantinople, preserved the civilization of antiquity without a break. Accordingly, the Eastern Empire has a different story and a different culture to offer the historian.

During the early Middle Ages the most outstanding ruler in the East was Justinian. By sheer ability he made himself co-ruler with his uncle in 527. Soon he became sole monarch and proceeded to put into effect his own ideas of government and culture which were obviously patterned after the old Roman standards. But he planned first of all to restore the outlines of the old Roman Empire and to com-

bine the Eastern and Western realms once more under the leadership of a single Roman emperor. Just how much of his ambitions may have been the work of his wife Theodora is uncertain. She had been an actress of questionable reputation, but she became pious after her marriage and proved a wise empress and wife for Justinian. It was her heroic and clever action that prevented Justinian's resignation from the imperial throne, and her advice which quelled the riots of 532.

Justinian's reign was to be characterized by a constant struggle with invaders on all sides of his empire. He had to buy off Persia on the east because he realized he could not hope to carry on a war successfully so far from his home base. In the west he contended with the Ostrogoths, Vandals, Franks, and Visigoths.

Justinian and Theodora are shown in the mosaics of San Vitale, Ravenna, presenting gifts at the consecration of the church. On the emperor's left is the archbishop, Maximian. (Metropolitan Museum of Art)

These barbarians, now settled in the Western Roman Empire, were so divided among themselves that he felt that the opportune moment had come to reconquer those states. So he sent his famous general, Belisarius, to North Africa to subdue the Vandals, a task which was accomplished by 534. Then Belisarius turned his attention to the reconquest of Italy from the Ostrogoths. In 536 he seized Rome and Naples without a struggle; but not until 552 was Italy purged of the Gothic chieftains by another great general, Narses. Even the coast of Spain and the Mediterranean islands fell into Justinian's hands. Except for the outlying provinces, almost the whole outline of the old Roman Empire had been restored. Justinian was truly a Roman Emperor.

But Justinian's main contribution to the world lay in the field of law; in this he was a true son of old Rome. At his order, a compilation was made of all the laws for the past thousand years. This work, the *Corpus Iuris Civilis*, is the basis of the laws still used in Europe, South America, and parts of North America. It is divided into four parts: the "Codex," containing the imperial Roman laws; the "Digest," giving the opinions of the jurists; the "Institutiones," a sort of legal textbook; and the "Novellae," new constitutions added during the reign of Justinian and later. Justinian's *Corpus Iuris Civilis* forms the greatest legal work in existence.

Captive Goths, bearded and shaggy, contrast sharply with the clean-shaven Romans

SUCCESSORS OF JUSTINIAN

The attention of Justinian's successors, Justinus II (565-578), Tiberius (578-582), and Maurice (582-602), all of them able administrators, was taken up with meeting the Slavic invasions; but in spite of their ability, the empire was steadily going down-hill. Maurice was not able to make headway against the barbarians; and owing to his harsh and niggardly treatment of his army, a rebellion broke out against him, which resulted in his murder in 602. The revolt was led by Phocas, a centurion in Maurice's army. Phocas was then raised by the army to the imperial throne but proved much more incapable than Maurice. He was deserted by his own troops, and Heraclius, in 610, took over the empire, then almost in the throes of dissolution.

HERACLIUS AND THE PERSIANS

For twelve years Heraclius strove to reorganize the army and the finances of the empire, without much apparent success. Against the Persians he could not hold his own, till the blasphemous insolence of the Persian king, after his capture of Jerusalem, roused the empire to a holy war. After a prolonged struggle with the barbarian Avars on his northern boundary, Heraclius was able in 622 to take the field against Persia; and in six campaigns he crushed its power, and in 628 concluded a peace which restored the empire to its former boundaries. But his victory did not secure him rest. The Saracens quickly overran Syria and Egypt; and in 641 Alexandria alone of Egyptian territory remained in Roman hands.

THE EMPIRE'S FIGHT AGAINST THE MOHAMMEDANS

After the death (641) of Heraclius things became worse, although, after 27 years' war, the empire received a valuable respite, by the civil war among the Mohammedans due to the contest for the califate. This respite enabled Constans II (641-668) to reorganize the administration of the empire practically on a war basis.

In 673 the now united Saracens launched a fleet and an army against the capital itself, and

Santa Sophia, built by Justinian in 532. Its richly colored interior glows with gold ground mosaics of glass, deeply veined marbles, and decorative carving. Its spaciousness was created by the use of a pendentive dome, a structural technique developed by Byzantine architects. The church has been a mosque since 1453

for four years strove in vain to capture it. But this success against the Arabs was short-lived, and for a quarter of a century anarchy prevailed, and the empire lost most of its provinces in Asia to the Saracens, and in Europe to the Bulgarians, and was only saved from complete destruction by the energy and ability of Leo the Isaurian, one of the generals in the East, who in 717 seized the throne. The same year Constantinople had to endure another siege by the Saracens; but they were repulsed with heavy loss, and, so far as danger to Europe was concerned, their power was broken.

THE CONTROVERSY OVER IMAGES

The eighth century was marked by a controversy regarding image worship. It was begun by Leo the Isaurian, whose severe edicts against the use of images in church worship were supported by his friends, but roused the fierce opposition of the bishops and monks. The policy of most of his successors until nearly the ninth century was similar. The bishops of the European provinces were alienated, and the controversy helped bring about the separation of Italy from the Byzantine

Empire. Meanwhile Crete and Sicily were lost to the Saracens, and the theological controversy was not brought to a close till the Council of Nice in 842 decided against the iconoclasts. So long as the Asiatic provinces supplied the emperors the controversy continued, and was not really ended till a European line, in the person of Basil the Macedonian (867-886), ascended the throne.

THE MACEDONIAN DYNASTY

The dynasty founded by Basil continued, with some short interruptions, till 1056. It ruled over an empire which was now solely an empire of the East. Down to 800 the West had, through the popes, acknowledged nominal dependence on the East; but when, in 800, Pope Leo III crowned Charlemagne as Roman emperor, the division of East and West was firmly and permanently completed.

The 80 years which followed the death of Basil in 886 are the most uneventful in the history of the empire. A period of military glory under the successful general Nicephorus Phocas, who became emperor in 963, revived the memory of earlier days; but nothing of decisive importance occurred. Isaac I (1057-59) founded the Comnenian Dynasty which ruled to 1185.

WARFARE WITH THE SELJUK TURKS

A new and more formidable enemy was gathering strength in the East while the dribble of incompetent emperors continued through the 11th century. The Seljuk Turks had made themselves masters of Asia, and in the 11th century became the most powerful of the Mohammedan powers. This made them the foremost aggressors against Christendom, and especially the Eastern empire. They conquered Armenia, invaded Syria and Palestine, and established themselves in Asia Minor, where they founded the kingdom called Roum, extending from Mount Taurus to the Bosporus. The forces of the empire, which should have been employed against the Seljuk Turks, were wasted in almost continuous civil wars; and after the defeat of the Emperor Romanus by the Seljuk chief Alp Arslan at Manzikert in 1071, no serious effort was made to check the advance of the enemy. The Turks had reached the Hellespont, when the First Crusade gave a much-needed relief. The Byzantine Empire was too exhausted to make vigorous resistance, and would have fallen if the Latin and Teutonic Christians had not come to its relief. The enemy was driven back 200 miles, and was so badly beaten by the crusaders that for a hundred years he acted mainly on the defensive, and the empire recovered many of its richest Asiatic provinces.

THE LATIN EMPIRE AND THE PALEOLOGI

The welter of obscure and incompetent emperors continued during the 12th century, and the empire began the 13th century with a Latin occupation (1204) by French and Venetian adventurers diverted from the Fourth Crusade by the wily policy of Venice—an occupation which lasted for nearly 60 years, long enough to inflict irreparable injury upon the empire, which never recovered from the anarchy of this time. The feudal ideas of those adventurers, chief of whom was Baldwin, Count of Flanders, were rejected by most of the Asiatic provinces; and in these a succession of usurpers kept alive the idea of the empire till, in 1261, the Latins were driven out by Michael VIII, the founder of a new dynasty, the Paleologi, who ruled to 1282 with some energy and wisdom over a realm greatly shrunken in its European limits.

In the interval the commercial importance of Constantinople, on which the prosperity of the empire had largely depended, had been reduced by the opening up, as a consequence of the crusades, of new avenues of trade with the East. Trading supremacy was transferred to the Italian cities, and much of the little energy that remained in the empire was dissipated in the fruitless struggle with Venice and Genoa.

FINAL STRUGGLE WITH THE TURKS

The restoration of the empire was, however, followed by renewed activity on the part of the Turks; and the Western allies whom the weakness of Andronicus II (1282-1328) called in did more damage to the empire than to the infidel. In the meantime the Turks—now the Ottoman or Osmanli Turks—deprived the empire of all its Asiatic possessions except a narrow strip opposite Constantinople (1333). In the civil war the usurper John Cantacuzenus (1341-55) called in the Turks to his aid, and in preserving his own cause destroyed the

Last Stronghold of Greek Culture. Byzantium produced this Hellenic David and Goliath dish in silver during the 6th century. (Metropolitan Museum of Art)

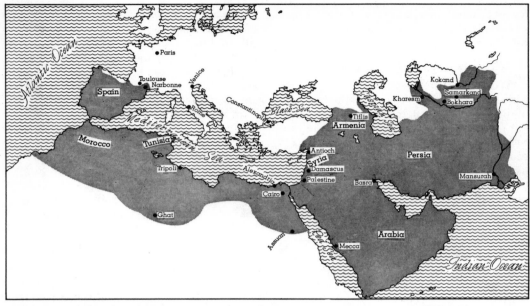

Map of the Islamic World shows extent of Mohammedanism at its peak, 750 A.D.

empire at which he had aimed. Thereafter it was a matter of years only. In 1354 the Turks made their first permanent settlement in Europe by the capture of Gallipoli. In 1365 Adrianople was taken by Murad, but the capital remained for yet a century the sole remnant of the Eastern empire. For a moment in 1402 there was a prospect of relief, when the Tartar hordes under Tamerlane burst into Asia Minor, and the emperor of the East recovered, during the civil war which followed the defeat of the Turkish Bayazid at Angora (Ankara), some of his ancient realms. But little use was made of the opportunity, and by 1444 Constantinople was again the limits of the empire. In 1452 came the final siege, and after a heroic defense the city was captured by Mohammed II on May 29, 1453.

INFLUENCE OF THE BYZANTINE EMPIRE

The verdict of history has become more favorable to the Byzantine Empire. For centuries it remained the bulwark of Christianity against the Saracens and then against the Turks. It kept alive the tradition of classical learning during the dark ages in Western Europe, and it bequeathed to Eastern Europe a treasury of ideas and attainment in art, architecture, and religious thought which has profoundly influenced the life of its governments and peoples.

THE PROPHET OF ALLAH

Out of the shadows of the Near East arose an empire that rivaled the Eastern Roman Empire at its height. In the desert lands of Arabia there appeared a lad who was destined to be called the prophet of millions of Mohammedans. Mohammed was born about the year 570, and from childhood on was afflicted by strange seizures. He soon began to receive commands from heaven to preach. His preaching, however, won few converts, for his message had nothing new or exceptional about it except that he called himself the greatest prophet of God. When he preached against prevailing idolatry in Mecca, he had to flee to Medina; this occurred in 622, the year from which Moslems reckon all their dates. His personality was so well liked by the people of Medina that he soon converted them.

When he had enough converts he decided to punish Mecca, the city which had rejected

The Kaaba, a dark, cubic building in the court of the Great Mosque at Mecca, is the center to which Moslems turn in prayer. In it lies the Black Stone, said to have been given to Abraham by Gabriel. (Ewing Galloway)

him. In 630 Mecca was captured. He set up the Black Stone in the Kaaba as a spot of pilgrimage for all faithful Mohammedans. During these years he had his holy prophetic words written down in the Koran. This bible of the Moslems he declared to be necessary as a guide for holy living. Because the Koran consists of fragmentary bits written down by his disciples, it is a rather confused and obscure document in many places. The religious concepts are a mixture of Christian and Jewish doctrines and customs, with the addition of elements from some of the oriental cults and Arabian superstitions.

Mohammed died in 632, and immediately his followers and relatives began quarrels which eventually split Mohammedanism into sects as numerous as those of Christianity. The fights at first centered about which version was the authentic copy of his words. Othman (644-656) made one form authoritative and destroyed all others; but that form is by no means the best, for there is no unity or chronology to guide the reader through its contents.

The definite doctrines taught by Mohammed are few in number. He insists upon a thorough monotheism, that is, the worship of only one God. Consequently, Mohammedans call the Christian doctrine of the Trinity polytheism, the worship of many gods. There are a Day of Judgment, Resurrection, and a heaven in which the faithful will be very happy in every physical sense. Heaven is best achieved by dying in the fight to spread Mohammedan-

ism. One must pray five times a day, facing in the direction of Mecca. Prayer, alms-giving, fasting, and pilgrimages are four necessary duties. Fasts are observed for the month of Ramadan; every believer should make at least one pilgrimage to Mecca. Wine, gambling, and pork are forbidden.

The religion of Mohammed was one that could be taught very quickly and was readily acceptable to most of the Arabs and Near Eastern people who had a warlike disposition. It was a religion which took small notice of racial or national differences. Therefore it was admirably suited to the situation in the Near East during the eighth century.

Illuminated Koran, designed with geometric and floral patterns, shows the effect of the Islamic law against representing human and animal figures. (Oriental Institute of the University of Chicago)

THE SPREAD OF MOSLEM POWER

Under the fanatical Arab leaders the Mohammedans began to conquer the outlying provinces of the Persian and the Eastern Empires. By 650 they conquered the whole of Egypt, Syria, and the large islands in the Eastern Mediterranean. Persia also fell before them. The world seemed to be theirs.

Then civil wars broke out. Ali, the son-in-law of Mohammed, claimed jurisdiction over the Mohammedan world, but this was contested by the widow of the prophet, Aisha or Aisheh, who led a revolt from the back of a camel. The Ommiads also opposed Ali who held Persia and Mesopotamia, while they held the caliphate of Damascus. The Ommiads soon conquered Arabia, and then started a campaign to reduce North Africa. This was accomplished by 710. The Berber population here had been aggrieved at all the former governments; therefore they welcomed the Moslems and accepted their faith in place of the Christian religion.

From North Africa, Spain is a short step. The Visigothic kingdom in Spain was so fragile that a single blow from the Moslem general, Tarik, was enough to destroy it completely (711). Soon the whole Spanish peninsula was overrun with Arabs and Berbers. But the Mohammedans were not to be satisfied with Spain, for they pressed into the Frankish kingdom and wandered as far north as Tours where they were stopped by Charles Martel. However, the Arabs continued to raid the southern part of Gaul up to the time of Charlemagne.

Arabian civilization in Spain reached a peak which it did not attain elsewhere. The Moslems founded universities and taught the Greek classics which the Latin West did not discover until the late Middle Ages. Sciences flourished as well as the intricate studies of mathematics. Their Moorish architecture has been admired down to the present. The cultured and flourishing civilization of these Spanish Moslems has been attested by even the most hostile medieval Christian writers.

Court of the Lions in the Alhambra, a Moslem palace built by Moors in Granada, Spain. (Anderson)

19. The Carolingian Renaissance

RISE OF THE CAROLINGIAN HOUSE

UNDER THE chapter dealing with emergent Germanic kingdoms, the rise of the early Frankish monarchy was described. In connection with that rise the ancestors of Charlemagne played an important part. Charles Martel left his entrenched position to his son Pepin who helped consolidate the influence of the Carolingian family with the papacy and the Frankish lords. Pepin was so successful that, when some of the Frankish bishops visited the pope in 751, the pontiff declared that the Merovingian family had forfeited its rights to rule and that the person who was exercising the real royal power, namely Pepin, should be the king. This declaration was all that the Franks were awaiting; immediately they assembled, deposed and sent to a monastery the last Merovingian king, and elected Pepin as their new king.

Of course Pepin was under obligation to the papacy for this good fortune. He had to render some military aid to the pope against the troublesome Lombards. For this service, the pope anointed Pepin as king and declared excommunicate any Frank who did not recognize Pepin as the lawful and anointed ruler of all the Franks. Thus the Carolingian line received a tremendous moral prestige which the popes had never offered the Merovingian family, nor for that matter to any other monarch before that time. However, Pepin did the papacy a great favor also; in 756 he presented to the pope the keys of the Italian cities which he had captured from the Lombards. This act was called the Donation of Pepin and furnished the papacy with a good reason for claiming the right to govern what came to be called the States of the Church or the Papal States.

CHARLEMAGNE AND HIS EMPIRE

On King Pepin's death, Charlemagne divided the Frankish realm with his brother, as was the custom with the Franks. When the brother died in 771, Charlemagne lost no time in seizing all of his brother's share and driving the widow and her family off to Lombardy. Then he engaged immediately in a war to put down the revolting Aquitanians. No sooner had he subdued them than the pope appealed to him to rescue Pepin's Donation from the Lombards who resented Charlemagne's treatment of his brother's widow. The Lombards also were angry with Charlemagne for repudiating his wife, who was a Lombard princess. The Lombard conquests and these family quarrels gave Charlemagne a good excuse for invading Italy. Charlemagne soon was victorious and became king of the Lombards. The pope persuaded him to confirm the Donation of Pepin. Actually, however, Charlemagne kept the real control of Italy in his own hands.

Next, Charlemagne became involved in a lengthy war with the strong Saxon tribes; this war continued off and on for thirty years, because the Saxons were never really conquered. In this instance, Charlemagne made use of the Church and her monks; he encouraged the sending of Christian missionaries into the Saxon forests, probably not so much to convert the pagans as to bind them through religion and education to the Frankish realm.

It has been estimated that Charles spent about forty years in steady warfare. Memorable at least in literary records was the famous expedition into Spain, during which campaign his rear, commanded by Roland, was attacked and annihilated by the Gascons. His biographer Einhard described his military activities as taking place from Hungary and Dalmatia to

Spain and north Germany. The extent of Charlemagne's realm and all of the problems which were contained within its borders taxed even the ability and strength of this incredible man. The various wars conducted against organized enemies were difficult enough, but the constant matching of wits and arms against the intrigues within his wide-flung territories was almost a superhuman task. Bavaria was one such problem; so was Aquitania. The barbarians also were a vexation. The Avars, an Asiatic horde, required attention along the Danube lest they become bold enough to attack Charles's German duchies.

Charlemagne wisely depended to a great extent upon the establishment of border marches, counties lying on the edge of his Frankish conquests, which acted as buffer states against any external attacks. Over these marches he set certain reliable nobles. The armies stationed in the marches could be quickly moved about so as to head off any serious invasion; and, if the enemy did penetrate into the marches, such a hostile force was still quite a distance from the core of the Frankish kingdom, and there was time to rush reinforcements.

The Pilgrimage to Jerusalem is a Charlemagne legend created in the 10th century to authenticate the St. Denis relics supposedly donated by the king

From 778 to his death in 814, Charlemagne seems to have had dreams of an international system in which he would play a dominant role. There was some talk of his marriage to a Greek princess, an alliance which would cement West and East; at least Charles and the Eastern emperor courted each other's good will. More significant was his relationship with the Moslem caliph of Bagdad, Haroun-al-Rashid, who solicited the Frankish Christians to aid the Abbasid caliphate against the rebellious Ommiad caliph of Cordova. Letters and gifts were exchanged, and the Caliph Haroun-al-Rashid was said to have given Charlemagne and the Franks some sort of protectorate over Jerusalem and its holy places. Whether or not this be true, the fact that the story was widely circulated indicates the tremendous impression Charles made upon international affairs.

A NEW "ROMAN" EMPIRE

The papacy with characteristic insight into the main tendency of world affairs recognized the prestige of Charlemagne and carefully studied how his power might be turned to the service of the Church. The papacy realized that its traditional dependence upon the Eastern Roman emperor was leading the Western Church nowhere. Therefore, if a suitable and dependable Western monarch could be found to supplant the place that the Eastern Roman emperor nominally filled, why not use such a person? It was to the advantage of the papacy to create and bless that sort of new secular defender of the Church. Since the papacy had fared so well with all of the Carolingian family and since Charles himself had proved helpful against the enemies of the Roman Church, why not elevate Charles to a position where he could be expected to aid the Church in exchange for her favors?

Pope Leo III fled from Rome in 799 to escape the threats of certain Roman nobles. He put himself under the protection of Charles, who re-established him upon the papal chair and cleared him of the accusations that had been leveled against him. Two days later, on Christmas Day, 800, after mass, the pope placed the imperial crown upon Charles's head as he was kneeling in prayer, and proclaimed

The Coronation of Charlemagne by Leo III took place in St. Peter's, Rome. The Roman people acclaimed the new emperor in the set form used to welcome patricians, proving that the crowning was not a surprise

him "Emperor of the Romans." The contemporary writers tried to make this momentous event appear as something spontaneous on the part of Charlemagne, and claimed that he was surprised into receiving this great honor. Considering the temper of Charles, the pope would not have dared to thrust this crown upon him without previous consultation and permission.

The significance of Charlemagne's coronation cannot be over-estimated. Charles and his heirs were assumed to be forever under the obligation of acting as the secular arm of the papacy. This situation proved as embarrassing as often as it proved advantageous. The coronation of a Western Roman emperor completely broke all feeling of dependence which the Roman Church had felt toward the Eastern Roman emperor. And the title of "Emperor of the Romans," "Holy Roman Emperor" as he came to be called, remained a sore spot in the side of Europe until Napoleon cut it away a thousand years later.

CAROLINGIAN GOVERNMENT

But the reign of Charlemagne is notable for more than its imperial power and its series of wars and intrigues. It marked a sudden spurt of intellectual and cultural activity such as had not occurred since the beginning of the barbarian invasions. And the whole course of his royal career is noted for its good government.

Charles was an absolute monarch, ruling without dictation from, or reference to, any person or group. He did not reject the advice of great men, however, but sought to use capable counselors for the good of the kingdom. Although a despot in many ways, Charles always kept well within the limits of the old Frankish laws applying to the rights of kings. He maintained a well-regulated household, which also served as his royal court. The chamberlain acted as manager of the palace and royal treasurer. The seneschal watched over the king's food and estates; the butler had charge of the royal cellar and vineyards; the constable or marshal controlled the army; and the chaplain conducted religious services for the king and his household.

The larger provinces were governed by dukes or counts whose titles and positions had become fixed during Merovingian times. The Margraves, whose frontier marches have already been discussed, were Charles's most useful subordinates. The great number of

minor nobles were in turn dependent upon
these dukes and counts as these latter were
upon Charlemagne. Thus Charles controlled
a secular hierarchy which was based upon an
ascending scale of responsibility, each person
in the governmental system owing obedience
to the person just above him. To maintain a
thorough check upon the great nobles,
Charlemagne devised the plan of sending out
missi dominici as his personal agents to report
on conditions within the empire. These
missi, composed of both lay and ecclesiastical
persons, were authorized to hear and examine
complaints concerning the miscarriages of
justice; if they were unable to settle the
matters locally, then the case was to be referred to Charles himself. In this way local
and national injustices were remedied. Even
the churchmen could not evade the watchful
eye of the *missi* who could report clergy
whose lives were scandalous.

To aid the cause of justice which had been
much neglected during the dark Merovingian
days, Charles issued capitularies, or ordi-
nances, which covered a multitude of matters
connected with the welfare of the state and
church. In the local courts, which still administered justice according to the local laws,
Charlemagne had the counts appoint regular
boards of judges. The laws requiring military
service at one's own expense for three

Charlemagne's Chapel in the cathedral at Aachen.
The body of the emperor was reputedly found seated
in this marble chair when his tomb was opened

Europe at the height of Charlemagne's power

months a year were amended to apply only to
persons possessing certain amounts of land.
Poorer landowners could group together and
support one of their number in military
service. To raise cavalry Charles exacted a
number of mounted men from each large
estate. This practice led directly to establishing the feudal order.

Charles realized the value of having a large
royal income so as to be independent of any
person or institution. He owned many villas
or estates which yielded considerable income
as well as supplied his large household with
the necessary stores. Charlemagne's management of the estates was very economical, for
he knew where every product went, how many
buildings he possessed on every farm, how
many tools were listed, and so forth. He did
not have to expend much for the maintenance
of the army and the judicial system, because all
persons serving in either capacity had to
pay their own way. Royal properties and the
public works were taken care of by direct
levies. The old Roman systems of taxation
had disappeared and Charles did not revive
them, but instead he collected revenues
through indirect taxes. The mighty nobles of
the land were subject to the exaction of gifts.
In these different ways Charles contrived to
acquire wealth without having to spend very
much of his own or of the royal income.

CAROLINGIAN CULTURE

The church owes much to the zeal of Charles in promoting missions and educational work under the auspices of the bishops. He insisted that the clergy be able to speak the Latin of the mass correctly and be able to read the Latin Bible. The conduct of clergymen was regulated and their usefulness to the social order was broadened by establishing schools in the larger towns. Several church edifices were erected at the command of Charles. The monasteries likewise fell under the all-embracing program; Charles signified his choice of abbot; he ordered monks to follow up his conquests so as to bring the new group into Christian society. Monasteries were erected all over the Carolingian empire.

Education was favored as it had not been since classical times. Although Charlemagne had little formal education—he never learned to write—he had a keen appreciation of the value of an education. Consequently he imported from England Alcuin, the leading scholar of his day, and set him up as head of the palace school whose pupils consisted of Charlemagne's children and those of the great nobles. Charles established other schools throughout his realm, especially in cathedral towns and in connection with monasteries. The curriculum was simple, but it was better

Ivory Diptych, a product of the Carolingian Renaissance, depicts the entry of Christ into Jerusalem. This is a portion of a leaf on which several scenes are carved. Ivory workers reached a high degree of skill during Charlemagne's reign. (British Museum)

than any schooling since the decay of classical education. The courses consisted of Latin grammar and literature, mathematics, astronomy, and some music. In addition to these more elementary schools, he founded the Academy, in which Alcuin, Paul the Deacon, Theodolf of Orleans, Angilbert, Peter, Paulinus, and Einhard, all of whom were among the foremost scholars of that time, were active members. These members tried to imitate the glorious writers of the classical ages. In general the attempts of Charlemagne to revive interest in solid learning merit the title of the Carolingian Renaissance.

BREAKDOWN OF CHARLEMAGNE'S EMPIRE

It is unfortunate for the history of education and culture that the institutions and foundations of Charlemagne were to disappear soon after his death in 814, plunging Western Europe into her most benighted period. Before his death Charles had already anticipated some division of his empire because he had the pope anoint two of his sons kings of Italy and Aquitania respectively. He was spared the trouble of dividing the realm because all the sons except Louis died. But Louis was a person whose temperament was far different from that of Charles. He was pious and easy-going, although quite capable of decisive action on occasion. The vast empire had proved a difficult problem for a superman like Charles, and so it was to be expected that at Charles's death the empire would suffer change.

First of all, the nobles felt that with Charlemagne's strong hand removed from their midst they could act independently of the crown. In this way the rise of the powerful local baron who dominated the Middle Ages can be accounted for. Anarchy and decentralization of government followed the path of the insolent nobles whom Louis and his sons could not check.

Family troubles added to the complex situation. Louis' two marriages brought him grief because the children of the first marriage resented the children of the second. The empire was scandalized by the plots and revolutions hatched by the disgruntled sons. Whenever a member of the family died, it was the signal for fresh troubles to break out such as Charlemagne would never have endured. Louis sought to heal the jealousies of the family by giving the oldest son, Lothair, the kingdom of Italy and the imperial title; Pepin

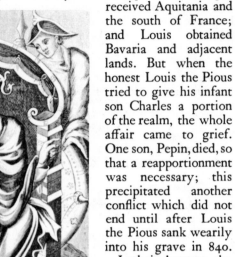

received Aquitania and the south of France; and Louis obtained Bavaria and adjacent lands. But when the honest Louis the Pious tried to give his infant son Charles a portion of the realm, the whole affair came to grief. One son, Pepin, died, so that a reapportionment was necessary; this precipitated another conflict which did not end until after Louis the Pious sank wearily into his grave in 840.

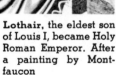

Lothair, the eldest son of Louis I, became Holy Roman Emperor. After a painting by Mont-faucon

Lothair became the Holy Roman Emperor, but soon found that all of his brothers had, in jealousy, united against him. No settlement could be reached before 843, when the Treaty of Verdun was drawn up. Lothair was forced to recognize the rights of his brothers: Charles the Bald was to rule what is approximately modern France, and Louis the German held all the Germanic lands. Lothair governed the central section which ran from the Low Countries down through Burgundy and the kingdom of Italy. Thus was the great empire of Charlemagne hacked to pieces. This division weakened all three new kingdoms and left the door open to barbarian invasions and to the growth of the feudal nobility. No longer was the chief power of the individual kingdom centralized in the hands of the king. No longer did the king control the wealth and military resources of his territories. Each of Charlemagne's grandsons was too weak to prevent rebellions within his state, which led

to the establishment of many petty kingdoms and independent duchies and baronies.

Charles the Bald died in 877 and was succeeded by a son and two grandsons who survived him only until 844. The Franks then invited Charles the Fat, son of Louis the German, to be their king, probably because he had also secured the Italian throne and the imperial crown. Charles the Fat thus became the last ruler of the united realms. But by 887 he was deposed because he was so incompetent in resisting the Vikings; in his stead Count Odo ruled, and in the Germanic kingdom Arnulf, an illegitimate Carolingian, was chosen. In Italy the kingdom broke up into two separate petty kingdoms and several independent smaller states.

TROUBLES FROM OUTSIDE

The new barbarian invasions, however, hastened the process of decay. The fierce Vikings from the Scandinavian lands swooped down upon the unprotected coasts of the western portion of the Frankish empire and plundered, burned, and murdered. Gradually they pressed farther inland and attacked some of the large cities like Paris. Only the courageous leadership of Count Odo of Paris saved the city from ruin. Slowly the Norsemen began to settle along the coasts and set up permanent habitations; their colonies along the mouth of the Seine formed the nucleus of the later duchy of Normandy.

On the eastern borders of Charlemagne's old empire a wild horde of Asiatic nomads called Hungarians broke through and settled along the Danube. These Hungarians or Magyars pushed into the heart of the Germanic kingdom and by 925 penetrated the Burgundian territories. Added to these difficulties were the renewed attacks of the Moslems in the Mediterranean. They shut off all Western commerce through their raids, attacked Rome itself, and captured all of the island ports in the Mediterranean. Thus was Europe hemmed in from all sides and her economic and cultural life so hampered that all of the advances made by Charlemagne were lost in the chaos of the next two hundred years.

20. The Feudal System

HOW FEUDALISM BEGAN

THERE have been many widely different views as to what constitutes feudalism. For the point of view to be followed in this chapter, feudalism may be briefly defined as the social and economic system which is found operating in Europe, and most perfectly in France, during the eleventh century. Of course the roots of feudalism go back several centuries, and the system in part has survived right down to modern times. But feudalism was working most effectively during the eleventh and twelfth centuries and had its fullest scope in France. Therefore this chapter concerns itself primarily with eleventh century French feudalism.

The elements that composed feudal society emerged very gradually out of the conditions of the early Middle Ages. It was not a social order thrust upon the people, but rather it grew out of the demand for just that type of society. The conditions which gave rise to the feudal order will now be dealt with in detail.

One element, at least, went back to the later days of the Roman Empire. During those uncertain times of the fifth century the small farmer felt the need of protection; for this reason began the custom of placing one's possessions and family under the care of some powerful landowner. This action was called *patrocinium;* some farmers availed themselves of this procedure so as to avoid the burdensome taxes. Of course the landowner who guaranteed protection and patronage (*patrocinium*) demanded that the title of the lands under his care be transferred to his name. The former owner was allowed full use of his farm for the rest of his life, but after his death the patron took over complete possession of it.

Another late Roman custom was that of the *precarium.* Whenever great landowners held more property than their slaves and tenants could adequately farm, they might heed the prayer (*precarium*) of some unfortunate person for the use of a bit of land. Private arrangements were agreed upon, usually with the provision that the owner could dispossess the "precarious tenant" at any time. Thus the *precarium* and the *patrocinium* became the accepted way for bankrupt and homeless men to maintain themselves in a changing order. Naturally persons under this system came to look to the landowner as their lord upon whom they were absolutely dependent.

There was also a Germanic element that entered into the establishment of the feudal order. This was the institution known as the *comitatus,* which was the band of followers, surrounding the German chief, who were bound to him by the closest of personal ties. They fought with him in battle and he in turn furnished them with food, shelter, weapons, and a share in the booty. This idea of personal service in return for certain "gifts" from one's lord was one of the most characteristic elements in feudalism.

Grants of immunity—exemption from the king's jurisdiction—were Germanic customs. These grants were almost exclusively bestowed upon church property and seldom given to laymen, although some of the more influential and wealthy lords usurped private jurisdiction over their large estates. Later on, these usurped privileges were confirmed by the Frankish kings and called *potestates.* The regular grant of immunity, however, forbade secular officials to enter the property of any abbot or bishop who held such a grant. The kings had willingly issued these grants because the church property thus protected was directly under royal supervision; and the church officials were more willing to have a remote king act as their patron than to have some greedy local baron invading their lands.

As a further evidence that the individual no longer looked to the state for protection but instead relied upon some more powerful neighbor to protect him, the practice of "commendation" appeared. By commendation, one could promise to hand over himself and his services for life to some guardian who would promise to feed and clothe and maintain him in a decent manner. The services to be rendered were not to be those of manual labor, but honorable duties such as fighting, acting as companion, and so forth. If either party wished to withdraw from the agreement, he had to pay the other person the sum stated in the contract. Commendation, then, differs completely from *patrocinium* in that the former preserves a person's dignity and position, while the latter implies taking on an inferior status.

As land was concentrated into fewer hands, it was no longer necessary to hand out small parcels for just a short period of time. It became customary for the lord to grant the lands for a lifetime or even longer. Such arrangements came to be known as benefices. The person who received the benefice was permitted to make full use of the land, but had to make a certain payment for the grant. This system proved so good that many persons readily handed over their property and received it back as a benefice.

The political and social conditions of the period following the death of Charlemagne were such that these various customs just described were modified and combined to form the basis of the feudal order. The weakness of the national government, the renewed invasions by the barbarians, and the rise to power of local nobles who seized authority wherever possible, have already been discussed. These conditions and the prefeudal customs outlined above helped bring about the fully developed feudal order. Development of armored cavalry and stone castles contributed to it, and there was a close relationship between trade routes and castle building.

HOW MEN BECAME VASSALS

The main feature of the fully developed feudal order was the fief. The fief was the grant of property made by the owner or liege lord to the holder of the fief, or vassal. The property was not given outright, but the use of it was given under certain definite terms to the vassal, who could pass it on to his heirs, provided that the contract was fulfilled by both parties. This hereditary transmission of the fief distinguished it from the benefice which was only for the duration of the life of the original vassal. In return for the full use of the fief the vassal had to render to the lord certain knightly services which will be described below. The fief did not have to be of land only, but it could consist of a monopoly of an office, tolls, mills, or even a sum of money.

This system became so widespread that it was said that there was no man in France who did not have a lord. Nearly all the land was in fief; no one could escape the feudal order. The system also became increasingly complex, for the lord who granted a fief to some vassal might in turn become a vassal to another lord. Thus most of the larger landowners were both lords and vassals. The difficulties in such an arrangement will be easily seen when the various services which vassals owed to lords are discussed. And, furthermore, one could be the vassal of more than one lord. The problem then would be which lord to serve when both quarreled. It is therefore worth noting that the feudal system was not as simple as it appears at first glance.

The act by which a vassal received a fief from the lord was called fealty. The ceremony consisted in having the vassal kneel bareheaded and unarmed before the lord, place his hands within the hands of the lord, and swear to be the lord's man (Latin, *homo*) for life. This was the act of homage, or becoming a lord's man. The lord kissed the vassal and formally accepted his allegiance. The vassal then swore the oath of fealty on the Bible or some relic; after which the lord invested him with the fief, usually by some symbolic means, and the contract was made.

Act of Fealty. The future vassal knelt, placed his hands in those of his lord and offered him homage. The lord then presented him a token of investiture

The feudal contract required certain obligations on the part of both the lord and the vassal. As has already been mentioned, the lord gave some sort of fief; he was also supposed to aid his vassal by arms if necessary whenever the vassal was unjustly attacked. The lord was available for advice and friendly counsel.

HOW VASSALS SUPPORTED THEIR LORDS

The vassal, however, had many more duties to his lord in return for the fief. His main service consisted of military aid. He was expected to give the lord so many days a year, usually forty, at his own expense and using his own equipment. If he were needed over the specified period, the lord had to assume his support. Frequently the vassal had to spend a fixed amount of time every year in castle-ward, that is, guarding the lord's castle. In case a man was vassal to two lords at war with each other, the vassal could be excused from coming to the aid of either lord.

The lord could require what is known as court service whereby the vassal could be called upon to sit in a trial and help the lord render a decision. Or the vassal could be summoned simply to give advice to the lord on private matters. If the vassal had a lawsuit, he had to submit it to his lord's court and allow the fellow-vassals to decide the case.

There were special "aids" which most feudal contracts required. The vassal usually had to make some sort of money payment at the time he was invested with the fief, although, theoretically at least, this was not part of the contract. Often annual payments were expected. In the early days of feudalism all sorts of special "aids" were demanded so that the lords imposed some very unjust dues. In time, however, these extra fees came to be fixed by custom. These three main "aids" were: payment when the lord's eldest son was knighted, when the lord's eldest daughter was married, and when the lord had to be ransomed. During the Crusades, the vassals sometimes had to help equip the lord for the journey.

The lord also had the right of purveyance, that is, he and his court could expect to receive food, lodging, and entertainment from vassals. Theoretically, the lord could bring his court for an unlimited stay; but, because certain lords took unfair advantage of this privilege and tried to save themselves from expending money to support their courts by long visits to the castles of their vassals, strict regulations were made concerning how often a lord might visit and how many followers he might bring. This was the only way to save the vassals from complete economic ruin.

Relief was another source of income for the lord. The relief was a payment in money or produce that was due whenever there was a new holder of the fief or a new lord. Since the feudal contract was essentially a personal arrangement between two individuals, it was necessary to renew that contract all over again when a new lord or vassal appeared. The relief was a heavy expense, because it usually required that the fief pay the equivalent of one year's income; if there were several deaths and consequently new holders in either the lord's or the vassal's family, the vassal found the fief rather costly. The whole tendency was to change the relief into a fixed money payment, assessing the fief on the basis of so much for each "knight's fee." A knight's fee was counted as being that part of a fief which would support an armed knight. The larger and richer the fief, the more knight's fees could be required as relief.

The lord had some other well-paying privileges. If the heir to a fief was not of age, the lord could assume wardship or guardianship over him and the fief. But when the heir became of age, the fief had to be restored upon payment of the usual relief. Meanwhile however, the lord had full use of the fief and its income, although he had to support the heir and the family in a decent manner. The matter of marriage always complicated the feudal relationship. If the heir was a daughter, her marriage would result in the loss of the fief to an outsider. Therefore, the lord felt that it was highly important to him to know whom the heiress might marry. Special contracts and fees were required in order to protect the lord's rights in the fief.

KING AND CHURCH UNDER FEUDALISM

The feudal system applied to more than the lands of the great and lesser nobility. The king, according to the theory of the system, was considered as the head of the feudal society. The king held certain lands of his own called the royal demesne; but the king could also be a vassal if he were to hold a fief from one of his subjects. As the Middle Ages wore on, the kings tended to free themselves from any relationship that would make them vassals, and tried to control as much land as possible so as to build up their independent royal demesne.

Nor did the Church escape the feudal order. Many bishops and abbots, in order to increase the lands necessary to build up the power of their monasteries or dioceses, accepted fiefs and became vassals to secular lords. These clergymen were required to render the same feudal duties as laymen; the bishops often went to war in shining armor to fulfill their feudal contracts, and many of them were excellent fighters. The famous old French epic, the *Song of Roland*, depicts the part that the feudal Church played in one of the wars conducted by Charlemagne. On the other hand, the Church often handed out her own lands in fief to some noble so that the Church would not be without defenders in case of trouble with neighbors. Thus the Church maintained her own private army in the feudal society which necessitated armed protection for every institution.

Under Feudal System, serfs paid rent in kind. They had to receive the lord's permission to hunt or fish

SERFS

Up to this point no mention has been made of the class which did the real work of providing a living for feudal society. Members of this class, who were bound to the soil, transferred with the land, and forced to remain on a given plot so long as the lord or vassal wished, were known as serfs. The serf was the actual property of the person who held the land. He possessed no civil rights nor could he demand justice in the courts of the lord. His condition in life was little better than that of a slave. Because serfs were necessary to do all the hard work in feudal society the lords could not be too harsh lest the serfs perish. But the serf in general was allowed only enough to keep him and his family, who were also serfs, alive and able to work. They had to live in places hardly fit for good animals.

The serf was required to pay the master a fixed rent at particular times of the year. This rent was paid in produce, and was set so high that there was very little left over to support his own family. Not only was the produce of his plot of ground taken from him, but also some of the fowls and animals and dairy products were demanded by the lord of his steward.

Besides these regular payments, the serf owed certain free work to his master. This was called *corvée*. The serf was supposed to work for no pay certain days out of the week, with extra days during the period of sowing and harvesting. Since his own little field needed attention at these same times, often his sowing was delayed and thus his crop would be small; or, if the master's harvest

required a lot of work, then his own harvest might suffer. Therefore, the wife and children of the serf frequently had to do a man's work to save the crop lest they starve to death. The *corvée* also included doing all the local road work and bridge building; sometimes the serfs had to go off a long distance to some other property of the master and remain there for a long time mending roads. The most vexing *corvée* was that of military service because the serf never knew how soon he might return; of course, the serfs were not drafted for fighting unless it became absolutely necessary, since they were untrained warriors and were necessary for maintaining the productivity of the manor.

Some serfs were used for other than agricultural purposes. If a serf were a good toolsmith or knew how to run the water mill, he could be relieved of working in the fields. Other serfs were used as domestic servants, as cooks, bakers, scullery maids, and so forth. Some folk existed on even a lower plane than the serf; these were the cotters who worked no land for the master, but merely had a small hut and a little garden in return for doing odd jobs around the manor. A few persons were better off than serfs; these were the free peasants or villeins. They owed certain fixed services to the local lord for protection, but they could buy, sell, and leave their land. These were, however, very few in number.

As the feudal system became more rigid, the serfs were exploited to even greater degrees. A series of extraordinary payments crept in. If a son were to become a priest, obviously he would represent a lost worker to

Castle of Pierrefonds was built in the 14th century. Castles, although drafty and poorly illuminated, were far superior to the homes in which the serfs lived

the master; or if a daughter were to marry outside of the manor, she too would be lost. In such cases the permission of the master had to be received, and that usually meant an extra payment of some sort. When the serf died, the lord found an excuse to seize all movable property, especially the animals. The heir to the serf had some extra fees to pay in addition. Frequently a sort of yearly head tax, called *chevage*, was levied.

Since the serf was bound to the lord's land, he had to use the lord's mills, ovens, and wine press. The use of this equipment required him to pay a certain percentage of his flour, bread, and wine to the master. The master also held a monopoly of all the fish and game on his manor; these could be caught only with his permission. The woods were reserved for the lord's use, although twigs and small timber could be taken by the serf. Standing timber, however, could be cut only by special permit. The lord controlled the markets on the manor and exacted market fees known as *banalities*.

Group of Villeins receives instructions from lord of manor before going into fields for the day's work

All legal cases arising on the manor had to be tried in the lord's manorial court so that a goodly profit went into the lord's pocket from the fees and fines. Any violation of the many little rules that regulated the life of the manor cost the poor serf a fine. A special sort of tax was often levied yearly, the tallage, which was arbitrarily fixed and collected by the master.

All of these various instances of what the lord of the manor could exact from his serfs reveal how profitable the great estates were and why this manorial system in feudal society was the backbone of their economic life.

LIFE IN A FEUDAL MANOR

The organization of the manor or estate upon which the serf lived under the eye of the master, was an important institution in the feudal system. The manor was a large estate upon which were built a manor house or castle, the barns, and the huts of the serfs. The lands consisted of the fields under culti-

Serfs Tilled the Soil by methods used since the Romans. A few standard crops were sown and harvested

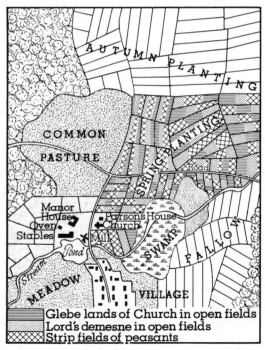

Feudal Manor was divided among the villagers in scattered strips so that each had his share of good and poor land. Three-field system preserved fertility

vation, the meadows and pastures, and the woodlands. Thus the manor was equipped by nature to be self-sufficient. Practically all the necessities of life could be found on the manor. Only metals for the smithy, salt, and fancy clothes had to be brought in from outside. This was a fortunate situation because the commercial life of the period was such that it could never have supplied a heavy demand for imported articles. Feudal society was so isolated that it had to be self-sufficient.

The agricultural system on the manor was unprogressive. The serf tilled the soil just as it had been tilled by the old Romans. A few standard crops like wheat, rye, barley, or oats were sown. The plowing was done usually by oxen and a small iron blade. Hence work was slow and hard. Because it was difficult to work all alone, some free persons would combine and work what is known as the "open field." A common fund took care of the oxen, tools, and materials. Each was supposed to contribute an equal amount of labor. In order to give everyone a fair share, each villager or villein was allotted his ground in scattered strips so that no one person received all the good or poor land. Because these strips were not fenced off, this system came to be called the open-field system. Often these strips were redivided every year so that each man would have worked several kinds of soils.

Since their knowledge of fertilization was limited, and since the supply of manure was not sufficient to take care of all of the land, the villagers resorted to the three-field system. It was the only way they knew to prevent exhaustion of fertility. The whole field was divided into three parts; one-third was left fallow, one-third was planted with a spring crop, and one-third with a fall crop. The next year the fallow plot was planted and one of the other thirds left fallow, and so on. In this way the soil of Europe was preserved until the discovery of chemicals and of new crops which would replace the nitrogen necessary to plants.

The villagers also divided the meadows, pastures, and woods. Each peasant was allowed so much hay, the right to graze so many cattle, and the use of a limited amount of wood. In this way the free peasants managed to conserve their property so that they could live above the starvation level.

The life of the feudal noble, while it did not include the ease and comforts which the ordinary man knows today, was a much easier

Karlstein Castle, built high on a hill near Prague, overlooks the village and surrounding countryside

and more pleasant life than that of any serf or free peasant. In the first place, he lived in a large castle, which, although far from sanitary and comfortable, was luxurious compared to the dwelling of a serf. The master and his family always had enough food to eat and wood to burn. They had, furthermore, whatever cultural advantages their crude society had to offer. The traveling troubadours stopped with them and sang the song of

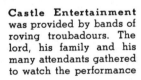

Castle Entertainment was provided by bands of roving troubadours. The lord, his family and his many attendants gathered to watch the performance

In Colorful Ceremony, helmets and banners of the contestants were ranged around a cloister. The judges distributed these in the presence of the ladies whose knights were taking part in the tournament

Entrance of a Knight into the lists was part of the pageantry of the tournaments. Trumpeters riding ahead sounded the arrival of the combatants

Young Knight in center is being prepared for combat by his sponsors. In the background a servant holds the horse which the knight will mount

A Friendly Tourney. Although various safeguards were taken to protect participants against injury, jousting was a rough sport exacting many casualties

The Tilt, a board fence separating the contestants. insured the greatest possible safety in tournaments. A knight, riding on one side of the tilt, had to hold his lance at an angle to his opponent

Dismounted Knights in full armor engage in single combat. Note narrowness of the eye-slits in the helmets

Degradation of a Knight involved stripping him of his helmet, sword, and spurs. Such cases were rare

the heroes and of courtly love. The chaplain of the manor was at hand to instruct the boys of the castle in the fundamentals of medieval learning. Some luxuries like clothes and armor and furniture were brought in from the outside world; and these nobles were the only ones who could travel away from the manor. The banquets they held reveal that they enjoyed plenty of food and drink.

"WHEN KNIGHTHOOD WAS IN FLOWER"

Inseparably linked with the feudal order was the institution of chivalry and knighthood. Chivalry was essentially the preparation of the young boy for a career of fighting. Since there was little formal education, this knightly training was his most important schooling. The young boy of noble birth was sent off to a neighbor's court to be a page, in which station he was supposed to learn how to behave in polite society and to become versed in knightly etiquette. In his teens, he would continue his knightly exercises of riding, dueling, and jousting. Then he could become a squire, or knight's assistant. Finally he would be ready to ride to battle and to prove himself a man.

When he had demonstrated his fitness to be a real knight, the young man was prepared for the ceremony of dubbing, or the formal investiture with arms. He spent the previous night in a watch before the altar of the parish church; then in the morning he attended

mass, was dressed in a white robe, and his sword was blessed by the priest. Some older knight performed the ceremony either by giving the candidate a blow with his fist upon the neck, or by striking his shoulders with the broad side of the sword. The youth was now a man and a knight.

The ideals which were set before the knight were high. The Church tried to impress her teaching upon the ceremony of knighting. The knight should scorn any unfair actions and be brave, loyal, and gallant. But all of his knightly duties were necessary only in connection with people from his own station in life. He did not have to be courteous to a serf nor gentlemanly to a peasant's wife. Chivalry pertained to the upper classes exclusively.

Because warfare was not constant and because all of their education was built along the lines of fighting, the knights had to occupy their leisure time and their energy in games that would test their skill. Therefore the tournament was popular because it gave them a chance to exercise their ability and keep them in training for war. The tournament and joust were very exciting and dangerous, but were beloved even by the gentle ladies who gave their gloves and hearts to the victors.

WHAT FEUDALISM ACCOMPLISHED

Now we have seen all sides of feudal life—the sweaty toil of the serf and the pleasures of the knights. We might ask whether it was an effective system. The answer would be that it was the system that naturally grew out of the conditions in the early Middle Ages and therefore was probably the best system for that particular time. It was by no means as perfect a system as some writers have represented, for it flourished in a lawless age and encouraged bloody strife. Feudalism had no means of settling all the problems it raised. Despite its complex system of contracts, persons ignored the duties imposed by the contracts and, if they were powerful enough, they suffered no punishment. In summary, it may be said of the feudal system, then, is that it served a necessary function for quite a long time, and, when it was no longer useful, it was discarded, never to arise again in Europe.

21. The Holy Roman Empire and the Papacy

LAST OF THE CAROLINGIANS

WHEN the last Carolingian heir of legitimate birth, Charles the Fat, was removed from the office of king, the united kingdoms of France and Germany separated in 887 and each proceeded to choose a ruler. The German nobles assembled and declared the throne vacant; they then exercised their ancient right of election and, as we have seen, chose Arnulf, a grandson of Louis the German.

Arnulf proved to be a wise choice, for he was capable of defending Germany from the attacks of her barbarian foes. First he had to subdue the roving Danes who invaded the Empire in 891; he led the German troops against the Danish fort at Louvain and by his personal bravery won a telling victory over them. Then he turned his attention to the eastern borders where the Moravians led by Sviatopluk were raiding the German provinces. In 892 he attacked them without much success; but Sviatopluk opportunely died and his Moravian kingdom gradually faded away. Meanwhile the Hungarians whom Arnulf had hired as mercenaries continued to fight the Moravians, and then turned upon Arnulf and the Germans whose towns they plundered for the next fifty years.

Because he had brought some peace to the north, a disappointed claimant for the Italian throne invited Arnulf to invade Italy. Arnulf was pleased by the idea of wearing the imperial crown of Charlemagne; so he went to Italy and finally pushed his way into Rome where Pope Formosus crowned him emperor. This was really an empty title for him because he had to leave Italy at once for his health; and as soon as he departed, the Italians threw off his rule.

Arnulf died in 899 and his son, Louis the Child, became king. The young boy was under the careful regency of Archbishop Hatto of Mainz. But this churchman could not keep order among the quarrelsome nobles, and to make matters worse the Wends, Danes, and Hungarians swooped over the German borders and terrorized the realm. Each great duke of Bavaria, Swabia, Franconia, Saxony, and Lorraine hoped to seize the leadership for himself; and the great German archbishops along the Rhine tried to protect the church properties against the dukes by playing one against the other.

The reign of Louis the Child is not very remarkable. When he died in 911, last of the German Carolingians, the nobles assembled and elected Duke Conrad of Franconia as king. But his was an empty title, because he had no power except in his own duchy; and, while the other great dukes recognized him as king, the Saxon duke was in constant warfare with him. Conrad died in 918, wearied from his brief and futile reign. The Carolingian line was ended.

OTTO, GREATEST OF THE SAXON KINGS

The German nobles convened again to elect a ruler, this time choosing their most powerful member whom Conrad had not been able to subdue, Henry the Fowler, Duke of Saxony. Strong enough to command peace in Germany, he proceeded at once to prove his might by forcing the dukes of Bavaria, Swabia, and Lorraine to recognize his title. Now he could give his full attention to the Hungarians; realizing that he did not have a chance to wipe them out completely, he wisely made a treaty which secured a truce for nine years.

A 10th Century Repast. Each person cut his food with a dagger and ate it with his fingers; he washed down the quantities of food with many drinks of wine

He spent these years preparing his kingdom for a decisive war with the Hungarians, and in 933 he utterly defeated them. By the time of his death in 936 he had advanced the cause of centralization of power among the duchies.

It was Henry's son, Otto the Great (936-973), who completed what his father tried to accomplish. But he did not achieve greatness without working hard. To begin with, his mother favored a younger son for the kingship, and his older illegitimate brother sought the help of disappointed nobles to start a revolt. So the first five years of Otto's reign were full of rebellions, all of which he stamped out. By 941 Otto realized that it was necessary to crush the great dukes in order to bring peace to his realm. Therefore he followed a policy of destroying the old ducal families and substituting his relatives as the rulers. He made his brother Henry Duke of Bavaria; he married his daughter to Conrad the Red whom he placed over Lorraine. One son married the Swabian heiress and received that duchy. To cement international relations, he married off members of his family to the two leaders in the French realm; he himself took Queen Adelaide of Italy as his wife; and then he found a Greek princess for his heir. Thus he found that alliances based on marriage were useful.

Otto inherited the old trouble of the restless Hungarians and Slavs. The Hungarians, who had become very bold because of their raids into the heart of France and Italy, were defeated in 955 along the Lech. Otto turned against the Slavs after this victory. Although he could not crush them as he had the Hungarians, he overawed them and transplanted many of them onto German territory.

OTTO AS HOLY ROMAN EMPEROR

Otto had an opportunity to intervene in Italian affairs when Queen Adelaide of Italy whom he afterward married, appealed for help. By 951 he rescued her from the Italian nobles; but before he could conquer Italy he had to hurry home to put down rebellions. These civil wars lasted about ten years, during which time he had to fight members of his treacherous and ungrateful family, some of the leading archbishops, and the Hungarians. He was able to return to Italy in 961 at the invitation of the pope, from whom he received the imperial crown in 962.

As Holy Roman Emperor, Otto confirmed the Donation of Pepin and Charlemagne, and demanded that, for the good of the Church, popes should be canonically elected, that is, according to Canon (Church) Law. The pope-

Early Reign of Otto I was marked by uprisings. Otto defeated his brother Thanckmar in battle and then slew him as he sought sanctuary

elect should furthermore take an oath before his consecration. In this way Otto hoped to eliminate bad popes. To insure what he thought would be better conditions in the German Church, he appointed his brother Archbishop of Cologne and one of his sons Archbishop of Mainz. He set up bishoprics among the conquered Slavs and extended the institutions of the Church in his own realm.

Despite all that Otto had tried to do for the Church, Pope John XII, abandoning himself to an unholy life, plotted against him. Otto returned to Italy and held a synod to try the pope, who ran off and refused to attend the trial. Therefore the synod elected a new pope under the auspices of the Emperor. For several decades the emperors were to have the most influence in the choice of popes. But all of these Italian affairs were to prove troublesome and even fatal to German rulers.

Otto must be given full measure of credit for his attempts to unite and pacify Germany, destroy the menace of the barbarians, and purify the Church. If he unwisely neglected his interests in Germany to make expeditions into Italy, he did so under the idea that he was aiding his native country. His promotion of letters and learning in Germany deserves high praise in itself.

A PERIOD OF PETTY POLITICS

Otto II, son of Otto the Great and Queen Adelaide, was made king in 973. This boy of eighteen nursed the ambition to complete the conquest of Italy. But first he had to put down rebellions led by the Bavarian duke and the Bohemian king, and then one in Lorraine. At last, in 980, he marched south, but the Moslems wiped out his army and he died of fever in 983 before he could accomplish the conquest of southern Italy.

This unfortunate young king was followed by his infant son, Otto III, whose mother acted as regent. At once the deposed Bavarian duke and the French king hoped to use this chance to further their own ends. In 994 Otto assumed the throne. He was fortunate in having been tutored by perhaps the most learned man in Europe, Gerbert, an Aquitanian who had studied in Spain. Otto's high esteem se-

Otto III, after a 10th century painting

cured for Gerbert the various positions of Archbishop of Rheims, Archbishop of Ravenna, and finally the papal chair as Sylvester II.

Otto's interest in Church matters prompted him to acquire the papacy for his cousin Bruno, who became Pope Gregory V. This election reversed the usual policy of electing popes from Rome and the vicinity; for the next two and one-half centuries popes were chosen more widely from the whole Western Church. Thus the intrigue and influence of the local Roman nobility was checked. Gregory repaid his cousin by crowning him Holy Roman Emperor. When Gregory died Otto used his influence to win the papal office for his tutor Gerbert, who was chosen pope as Sylvester II. Both the emperor and the pope tried to find a perfect balance between church and state. But neither the German nor Italian subjects of Otto appreciated his semi-Byzantine ambitions. Only his death in 1002 saved him from ruin.

Otto's death brought three candidates before the German nobles, who heretofore had permitted the Saxon family to assume the German throne; but now they insisted upon exercising their electoral rights because Otto had died without heirs. The choice fell upon Duke Henry of Bavaria, who became King Henry II (1002-1024). Henry had won the election mainly through Church intrigue; therefore he had to reward the Church with favors, especially immunities. His reign of 22 years was rather peaceful, and his gifts to the Church so magnificent that he was made St. Henry.

His successor was Conrad II (1024-1039) who was elected to the German throne also through the aid of the Church. But Conrad was not so easy-going and sought to curb the enormous powers which the Church had secured in the previous reign. He began a system of checking both the great lay and ecclesiastical lords by recognizing the hereditary rights of the lesser nobles. Then he established some exempt abbeys so as to offset the mighty bishops. He also used the towns in his plans, granting them privileges so that they could act independently of the nobles. Finally he forced the Bavarians and Swabians to make his son Henry their duke. Through a promise made to Henry II, Conrad forced the king of Burgundy to make him his heir; thus Burgundy was added to the German realm, in 1033.

When Henry III ascended the throne he found himself in a more secure position than his father had been. The German duchies were his, and the kingdoms of Burgundy, Carinthia and Bohemia, Poland and Hungary were his vassals. The German ruler now appeared as a mighty person in European affairs. If Italy could be managed somehow, then the German ruler would be thoroughly entrenched.

REFORMATION WITHIN THE CHURCH

The fatal interest in Italian politics was renewed by urgent conditions in the papacy. Ever since the tenth century the papacy had been losing prestige; some very unworthy popes had taken the office through intrigue, bribery, and even murder. Worst of all were the conditions in the Church at large. The monastic houses were no longer models of industry and religious zeal, but were often filled with lazy, dissolute monks. Furthermore, church discipline was in a sad state. The priests were too busy with secular activities to shepherd their parishes; they were frequently married and passed on church property and offices to their children; they could buy church offices for themselves and their relatives. The whole Church threatened to be submerged in the rising tide of worldliness.

But once more the monastic system proved the savior of the Church. The abbeys belonging to the Congregation of Cluny, founded in 910, became the centers of reform agitation. Abbot Odilo of Cluny (994-1049) and his Cluniac monks carried their reforming zeal throughout Europe and preached fearlessly to pope and king. The eloquence of the Cluniac preachers was unforgettable, and when the time was ripe it bore fruit.

When Henry III was called to Italy he was already a champion of church reform, even going so far as to allow the churchmen of his realm an unusual amount of independence of royal authority. At the synod of Pavia in 1046 he promised to suppress the practice of simony, that is, the selling of church offices, a promise which cost him considerable revenue. In Sutri he called a council to weigh the claims of the three rival popes. Two of the popes appeared and were deposed for simony, and the third refused to come but was deposed anyway. Henry, as a patrician of Rome, and the Roman nobles chose a German bishop as Pope Clement II. He died shortly, possibly from poison. Henry's second appointee also served but a short time before going to his reward. Finally, a French bishop was chosen who, as Leo IX, did manage to live for a few years.

Leo IX was an ardent reformer of the papacy and the Church. He decided to call a council at Rheims where he was to consecrate a church. This action displeased the French king so much, because he had not been consulted first as was the custom, that he called all of his nobles and bishops to attend a royal assembly on the same day. The bishops were in a predicament: they could not afford to offend either king or pope. When only one-third of the unhappy bishops attended the pope's council, the absentees were excommunicated. Leo's council was able to flout royal power and to declare simony cause for removal from office because the French king was weak and Henry III was such a devoted reformer of the Church.

THE QUESTION OF INVESTITURE

The cordial relations built up with the papacy died with Henry III in 1056. His son Henry IV (1056-1106) proved a disappointment to the papacy. The boy was shunted around in his youth from one party to another; his education was neglected, and he grew up rather undisciplined. Antagonism concerning the way he handled the Saxon duchy, together with the opposition of German lay and ecclesiastical lords, threatened to cost him his throne. So Henry appealed to Pope Gregory VII, a reformer who was greatly influenced by the Cluniac movement. Gregory had arrived at the papal chair by a violation of the canons of the Church which he in 1059 had helped to formulate. Pope Nicholas II had placed the papal elections in the hands of the College of Cardinals, leaving to the Roman clergy and people only the power to ratify the selection.

Despite the fact that Gregory had been elected by acclamation of the Roman people and clergy, he was a sincere reformer, intent upon ridding the Church of all abuses immediately if possible. He angered the German clergy by trying to remove all married priests and bishops; he excommunicated all married clergymen, and cut off their incomes whereever possible. Then in 1075, realizing that the German king could do nothing to prevent him, he forbade any further lay investiture, threatening excommunication to all who disobeyed. Lay investiture was the practice of having lay rulers bestow the temporal signs and lands of a bishopric or abbey; it should be clearly understood that bishops did the actual consecration of the candidates.

Gregory sent his declaration on lay investiture to Henry in 1075 just as the latter was rejoicing over his defeat of the Saxons. The letter, undiplomatic as it was, made Henry very angry and inspired him to reply with heated words. Then Henry persuaded some of the German bishops to write a letter against Gregory, denouncing him as unworthy of the papal office. Gregory's response was to excommunicate Henry and to appeal to the bishops and nobles of Germany who had little love for Henry. These leaders assembled in 1076 and decided to give Henry one year in which to make his peace with the pope.

POLITICAL REPENTANCE AT CANOSSA

Henry was a good politician and knew when he was beaten. Therefore he took advantage of the offer from his nobles and planned how he might force the hand of the pope. Henry eluded his guard and hurried to the pope, who was proceeding to Germany to consult with the nobles. Finding Gregory at Canossa, the penitent monarch stood outside the castle barefooted in the snow for three days begging forgiveness. The pope was neatly trapped because he really wanted to depose Henry, and yet as a priest of God he had to grant forgiveness to a repentant sinner. Once Henry was absolved, he hastened back to Germany.

Many have considered Henry's conduct at Canossa a deep personal humiliation; but it really was one of the cleverest political moves ever made. Henry felt no true repentance and was perfectly willing to make the pretense if that would reinstate him once more in Germany. Then he could bide his time and revenge himself upon the nobility and the pope. His plans worked out in just this manner. After the excommunication had been lifted, the German people rallied to him rapidly. He defeated the antiking Rudolph whom his opponents had elected. In 1080 Gregory again excommunicated Henry, but this time nobody seemed to care, not even the bishops who supported Henry against the pope. An antipope was now set up to oppose Gregory.

TOO MANY POPES AND KINGS

Thus two sets of popes and kings started a bloody civil war in Germany and Italy. After Henry defeated Rudolph, who died in battle, he descended upon Italy and laid siege to Rome. The Roman nobles supported Henry and helped him to be crowned emperor by the antipope. Gregory died the next year (1085) in Salerno, still declaring that he was the true pope. The final years of Henry's life were not much happier; his family turned against him, and he was forced to give up his throne to his son, who became Henry V.

Henry V, who ruled from 1106 to 1125, was no better friend of the papacy than his father. He interfered quite regularly in Church elections and was threatened with excommunication. However, he decided to attack the pope, Paschal II, at once; and the pope, having no aid, had to agree to a compromise; namely, that the Church should surrender her fiefs in Germany if the bishops and abbots should not have to be vassals. Henry readily agreed, and the pope promised to crown him emperor. But the Roman mob was so angry that they broke up the coronation. Henry seized the pope and cardinals and released them only when they gave him full right to invest.

THE CONCORDAT OF WORMS

In this way one of the most sensible compromises thus far suggested was brought to an unfortunate end. The clergy advised Paschal to reject this agreement, which he did; and he excommunicated Henry in addition, in the year 1112. The quarrel continued until 1122 without either side gaining very much. Finally, the Concordat of Worms was drawn up in 1122, which provided that the German king should yield on the right of investing bishops and abbots with the symbols of their office (the ring and the staff); that the Church elections should be free, but were to be held in the presence of the king who might decide disputed elections.

This Concordat did not settle the problem for it left many loopholes, as the following years revealed. Neither the pope nor the king received the settlement he wished. But certain definite changes did occur after this investiture struggle. The papal elections were no longer decided by the German kings; the German dukes gained more power at the expense of the king and the Church; cities became more independent; and persons awoke to the fact that the venerable institutions within their state were open to criticism and reform.

Cathedral of Saints Peter and Paul in Worms. In this city in 1122 was drawn up the Concordat of Worms which reduced the influence of the German king in the affairs of the church and paved the way for reform

22. England and the Norman Conquest

SEVEN EARLY KINGDOMS

WHEN the Germanic invaders had succeeded in wresting most of what is now England from the native Celts, they did not immediately found a unified kingdom. They were themselves divided among three main tribes, the Angles, the Saxons,

and the Jutes, which were further subdivided into seven great tribes, or kingdoms. The Jutes, the least numerous, settled in the kingdom of Kent in the southeast. Around them were the kingdoms of Essex, Sussex, and Wessex, composed of Saxons, and to the north were the Angles in the kingdoms of Mercia, East Anglia, and Northumbria. The tribes themselves were probably loose organizations and not in any sense like our modern kingdoms. Thus the most important development in pre-Norman England is the gradual growth of a unified monarchy and of institutions which were to be the basis of the later English government.

It is unnecessary here to follow through the somewhat confused history of the constant wars between the kingdoms which resulted in the supremacy of now one, now another. Such supremacies were temporary and were based upon the personalities and military force of individual kings. Seldom did their gains last longer than the life of a strong king, or at most the life of his son. It is important, however, to point out that between the invasion of the Germanic peoples and the coming of the Danes, a partial and rather unstable unification was accomplished by the warring of the tribes.

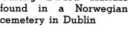

Viking Sword Handle found in a Norwegian cemetery in Dublin

When the Anglo-Saxons first came to the shores of Britain, they were pagan and still worshiped the Norse gods of which Woden and Thor are most familiar. The first to bring Christianity to the English was Augustine, who was sent from Rome by Pope Gregory the Great in 597 to convert them. So successful was he that within a few years the new religion had spread throughout Kent and parts of the kingdoms which then happened to be under the domination of Kent. Some years later when Mercia, still heathen, came to dominate, Christianity suffered a reversal; but it was reinstated by the Scots, who had been Christianized during the Roman regime and had never given up the faith.

St. Augustine was sent to England in 597 to introduce Christianity

Gradually the Christian communities spread, so that during an interval of peace, a council was held at Whitby in the year 664 to give some organization to the scattered churches. The main question at the council was whether the form of Christianity practiced by the Scots should be followed, or the form brought in by Augustine. The latter won out, and, since this was the form practiced by most of western Europe, the decision meant that the English church would be brought into harmony with the ideas of church government which were being practiced on the Continent. A few years later the new archbishop of Canterbury carried through these ideas, and organized the clergy in orthodox fashion.

COMING OF THE DANES

When the Christianization of the Anglo-Saxons had been completed, a new heathen people appeared on the stage of British history. These heathens were the Danes, a Nordic people who came to England from Denmark, Norway, and Sweden, for much the same reason that the Angles and Saxons had come earlier—love of plunder, adventure, and conquest. The first arrived on the shores of England shortly before the end of the eighth century, intent only upon raids for plunder. At first the raids were made only occasionally, but about the middle of the ninth century whole armies of Danes began to arrive, bent not upon plunder but upon conquest and settlement in permanent homes. Northumbria was soon conquered (865), Mercia offered more resistance, but East Anglia and Essex fell to the Danes in 870. The invading armies then turned toward Wessex, the last stronghold of resistance.

It was fortunate for the Anglo-Saxons and for Wessex that the king of that country happened to be one of the greatest of the Anglo-Saxon rulers, King Alfred, with whom every schoolboy is familiar through the myths and legends that surround his name. Alfred proved his military ability by reorganizing his fighting forces and, after a series of hard campaigns and reverses, he won a decisive victory over the Danes. He forced them to a treaty by which their leader agreed to accept Christianity, withdraw from Wessex, and keep the peace. By a subsequent treaty (885) a line was drawn from just east of London up to Bedford and then diagonally across England to Chester. North of this line the Danes were to be left in possession, and the territory was known as the Danelaw; south of it Alfred, by right of his success against the Danes, was sole master. This unification of a fairly large block of territory under one king for purposes of defense against foreign invasion, was to be the foundation on which Alfred's son and three grandsons built a single kingdom in England by slowly reconquering the Danelaw. Besides thus providing a basis for political unity, Alfred deserves a claim to greatness by the way he governed his kingdom and by his efforts to promote learning, religion, and new industrial arts inside his realm.

When the last of Alfred's grandsons had succeeded in conquering all the Danelaw (954), there was at last a real king in England. The royal powers were still fairly weak, however, and the kingdom itself was in a bad condition. The ravages of constant warfare had not only prevented economic development from taking place, but brought about a degeneration in the intellectual and moral atmosphere. The monasteries, which, in the time just after the conversion of the country to Christianity, had flourished and contributed much to the development of agricultural resources and had been centers of learning as well as examples of a saintly life, were nearly blotted out as a result of the Danish invasions. Alfred's attempts at reform, while praiseworthy, did not bear much fruit. There was need of peace and a strong ruler.

Alfred the Great, one of England's greatest rulers, defeated the Danes. (Ewing Galloway)

Edgar the Peaceful, who ruled from 959-975, gave his kingdom the two things it needed most. There were no wars at all in his reign, and his able adviser, Dunstan, carried through a monastic revival that accomplished splendid results. But all the good of this reign was swept away in the next. The successor, Ethelred, was soon known as "the Redeless," meaning "without foresight or judgment." The nobles, who had grown very rich and powerful, got out of hand and quarreled among themselves constantly. Dunstan's reforms were gradually undone. Worst of all the Danes renewed their invasions and found the English defense weak and disorganized. The Danes who had remained in the Danelaw as settlers after Alfred's descendants had reconquered it, went to the assistance of the new invaders. Everywhere they were successful, and Ethelred was forced to flee to Normandy in France. For a time his son, Edmund Ironside, was successful against the Danes, but his death left the English without a leader, and in 1017 they acknowledged the Danish leader, Canute, as their king.

DANISH RULE

From 1017 to 1035 Canute ruled England and ruled it well. He tried to be an English king and not a conqueror. He maintained the old laws and customs, supported the Church and kept law and order inside the realm. Since he was also king of Denmark by hereditary right and king of Norway by right of conquest, Canute in reality was head of a huge empire of which England was only a part and was a person of great importance in the Europe of his day. But again a strong reign was followed by a comparatively weak one. After the death of both of Canute's two sons (1042) the crown passed to the last son of Ethelred, Edward the Confessor, who had been raised at the court of his uncle, the Duke of Normandy. Edward was not able to control the barons, and for most of his reign was forced to submit to the domination of the house of Godwin, whose head was the powerful Earl of Wessex. Since this reign leads up to the Norman conquest, it will be discussed in more detail later; but it is necessary to say here that throughout the reign there were constant internal troubles and a further deterioration of the moral and intellectual tone.

ANGLO-SAXON POLITICAL ORGANIZATION

Before considering the Norman conquest, which brought many changes to England, we must stop a moment to speak of the institutions of the Anglo-Saxons. In the first place the whole structure of their society was built upon agriculture. The mass of the population lived in small, almost self-sufficient villages and tilled the surrounding soil. From the first there also were nobles who claimed certain honors and privileges by right of their position. Originally these so-called "earls" may have gained their rank by being the military companions of the king, but gradually their rank came to be the result more of wealth and land than of military prowess. They did constitute the main part of the army, and were known as thegns.

The mass of the people originally were independent men who tilled their own land; but basic features of feudalism soon appeared for the same reasons that caused it to develop in Europe. Therefore, we rightly expect to find its forms also similar. There were great divergences in the system, however, and many communities were still free. The part which once had been the Danelaw in particular retained many local customs in regard to land holdings, as did the remote parts of the kingdom to the north and west. Not until Norman times did feudalism assume a definite form.

Canute and His Courtiers. Canute, king of Denmark and Norway, was accepted as ruler of England in 1017

The king was a hereditary monarch whose own will was practically law within certain restricted limits. He was bound only to consult the witan, or council of the wise; and, since in practice he chose those who sat in the witan from among the great nobles and ecclesiastical officials, it was not apt to offer much resistance.

On the other hand, war, the Church, and the maintenance of order were about the only things that came within his jurisdiction. He could tax his subjects for special emergencies, as in the case when Danegeld was levied to buy peace from the invaders. This Danegeld came to be raised for other purposes, but was the only tax which the king could impose. In each local division, known as the shires, the king had two representatives, the earl and the sheriff. The earl, who was always a noble, held an important social position. His main duties were to summon and preside over the local militia and preside over the local public meeting. The sheriff was an official with a lower social status whose business it was to maintain the peace and look after the king's revenues, which came not from taxes but from his vast estates scattered all over the kingdom.

Besides the king's officials in each shire or county, there was a popular assembly called the moot. All the freemen may once have been expected to come; but by the end of this period only the great landowners actually did. It met twice a year and was a court that could decide both civil and criminal cases, declare local custom, and transact all sorts of business for the county. Each county was divided into hundreds, which also had a moot with similar powers to which the common man actually came. The king's reeve, a word meaning simply "official," presided, but the local men transacted the business.

The powers of these popular courts to declare custom was very important, for at that time all law was held to be custom. Only occasionally were new laws made. Most of the decrees of the witan were held to be merely clarification of existing law or custom, and not new law. The king and the assemblies were not supposed to change the fundamental law, and his powers were mainly executive. It was an age, however, not only of custom but of force, and a strong king was apt to make many changes without opposition. On the other hand, when the king was weak, the great nobles and the witan were apt to control things.

EARLY NORMAN INFLUENCES

The reign of Edward the Confessor prepared the way for the Norman conquest. In the first place, Edward had been raised at the court of the Duke of Normandy, and hence was familiar with Norman institutions and ways. It was only natural that he should attempt to introduce them into England. He brought over several of his Norman friends to fill high places at the court. The Anglo-Saxon barons resented this and under the leadership of the Godwin family finally forced the king to dismiss the Normans and accept the domination of the house of Godwin. Among those dismissed was the Norman archbishop of Canterbury who, in spite of papal disapproval, was replaced by Stigand, one of Godwin's supporters. The pope withheld from Stigand the *pallium*, the emblem of papal approval of the appointment of an archbishop, but the house of Godwin supported Stigand and thus incurred the opposition of the papacy at a time when the pope was beginning to exercise considerable influence in European affairs.

The Norman ideas which Edward wished to import along with his Norman friends were the ideas current in the northwest of Europe. As we have already seen, in spite of several noble attempts at reform the religious and intellectual tide in England was still at low ebb. During the eleventh century English learning was declining, and immorality was widespread among the clergy. On the continent, however, and especially in Normandy, there was at this time a great intellectual renaissance and moral revival. The importation of these ideas and the contact with the continent which would bring it about were begun in Edward's reign. Furthermore, Edward's inability to control his barons and the generally creaky condition of the Anglo-Saxon monarchy constituted a situation that, to a strong ruler like William of Normandy, could almost be considered an invitation.

Harold Takes Oath to support William's claims to England; later Harold himself claimed the kingdom

WILLIAM—CONQUEROR OF ENGLAND

When Edward died at the beginning of 1066, Harold, the son of Godwin, was Earl of Wessex, chief adviser of the king, and the strongest man politically in England. The dead king left no heirs, and the succession was immediately claimed by both Harold and William, Duke of Normandy, who was long known to have ambitions for the English throne. Neither was descended from the royal Anglo-Saxon family, though William was a first cousin of Edward's, but each claimed that the dead king had designated him as the heir.

Harold was chosen king by the witan, but William declared that Harold was a perjurer for he had previously sworn to support William's claim to the English throne. However, the oath had been a forced one, exacted when Harold had been shipwrecked and seized on the Normandy coast. William immediately prepared for armed invasion. The pope, who was still enraged over the treatment of the Norman archbishop through the influence of the Godwin family, lent his support to William and sent him a consecrated banner, thus making the invasion something of a crusade. This appeal, together with the prospect of possible spoils, attracted to William many barons from Flanders, Spain, and Italy who owed him no allegiance.

Harold also made preparations, enlisting many of the English barons. Before meeting William, however, he had to deal with an attack by his brother and the king of Norway, who wished to re-establish the Danish supremacy. After defeating their army, Harold hurried southward and met William with his army on a hill near Hastings. The result of the battle was that Harold fell mortally wounded, his forces were defeated and William could advance toward London. As he neared the city, almost without opposition, the witan offered him the crown. On Christmas Day, 1066, he was crowned.

But King William was not yet master of England. There were several uprisings in the west and north. He suppressed them slowly without much difficulty, building fortifications along the route. The opposition came mainly from the great barons who wished to rule the country themselves, and who would lose many large estates from the conquest. The mass of the people, who were mainly tenants, were not dispossessed, but merely experienced a change of lord. This is one reason that the conquest was accomplished with such ease and why it was permanent. The people welcomed the law and order which the conqueror established. Those who were sincerely religious had supported William from the beginning. Finally, and most important of all, there was no feeling in the eleventh century comparable to the modern nationalism. This lack of national consciousness explains the ease with which Canute held England with a comparatively small garrison of soldiers as well as it explains William's easy success.

Arrival of Normans at Pevensey for invasion of England, from The Bayeux Tapestry

ENGLAND UNDER WILLIAM THE CONQUEROR

William adopted a policy of keeping as much as he could of the old Anglo-Saxon law and tradition. He did, however, bring in certain innovations. Most important of these was the institution of feudalism. He had himself recognized as the sole owner of land in the kingdom. Then he gave out large estates to his followers on definite promises of personal adherence and military support with a set number of armed knights. These retainers let out the land to others, and the serfs remained as the tillers of the soil with new masters. There had been something of the same system under the Anglo-Saxon regime. What was new was the definite nature of the contracts that bound man to man.

William strengthened the monarchy considerably. He kept all of the prerogatives of the

Norman knights push on to Hastings, another scene from The Bayeux Tapestry

old English kings and combined them with his rights as a feudal lord. Thus he could call upon the lords for the military service they owed him for their land, and also he could call out the fyrd, or old Anglo-Saxon national army composed of all freemen. He continued to levy the Danegeld while deriving certain income from his feudal vassals. He kept the administrative officers that the Saxon kings had used, and instituted new ones as well. In local government he followed the same policy. The old shire-moots and hundred-moots were allowed to continue side by side with the new courts which the feudal system gave to the lord as a right over his vassals. The thoroughness of William's administrative system is shown by the compilation of the Domesday Book, a detailed inquiry into the size, resources, and inhabitants of all the estates and lands in England. It was compiled for the purpose of a new and heavier assessment of the Danegeld, but contains much information which would be useful to a ruler in other respects.

The Church settlement which William imposed needs to be summarized in view of its importance in later times. As we have seen, he owed much of his success to the pope. Consequently, together with the new archbishop of Canterbury, Lanfranc, he began the reorganization of the English Church. Norman clergy were put in vacancies. The disciplinary

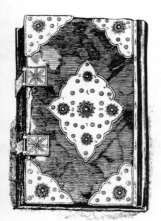

Binding of Domesday Book and chest in which the volume was kept. This great survey of England was made by William the Conqueror. (Lib. of Congress)

measures of the church were strictly enforced. Monasticism was revived and many new monasteries were built. Instead of an ordinary lay council an ecclesiastical council was set up to legislate for the Church. The bishops were given rights of jurisdiction over certain ecclesiastical cases, thus removing certain matters from the courts of the hundred and the shire. All of these measures tended to strengthen the power of the Church. But William was conscious that the Church might get out of hand and dictate to the lay government, including the king. Therefore, he provided that no pope could be acknowledged and no papal letters or legates sent into the kingdom without his consent. He retained the right to veto acts of ecclesiastical councils and decreed that none of his tenants-in-chief and officials could be excommunicated without royal consent. William was strong enough to enforce these rules and keep the church in a subordinate position. Some of his weaker successors were less successful in asserting their authority and the privileges of the Church were a constant source of friction.

The language spoken in England underwent important changes as a result of the Norman invasion. Before the conquest the common people used a language purely Germanic in origin. A few words remained from Celtic times, and yet a smaller number might be traced directly to the Danes who spoke a Germanic tongue similar to Anglo-Saxon. But the Normans brought French with them. It became the language of the court and of polite society, although the common people continued to use their familiar idiom. Nevertheless, so many French words were introduced that the language was modified considerably.

Perhaps the principal result of the Norman invasion was the imposition of order upon the prevailing loose and vague practices. Everywhere the conquerors built a social structure which was more complicated and more clearly defined than the Anglo-Saxon institutions which formed the foundations of their work. The Normans established a strong legal system under monarchial supremacy. They infused a vigorous, quickening spirit into the stream of English development.

Alfred the Great, King of England. Alfred was proclaimed king in A.D. 871. He defeated the Danes in the north, but England was not united under one crown until the reign of Edgar (959-975). Alfred was a great scholar and administrator. He reorganized the defenses of his kingdom, and encouraged schools.

The Emperor Charlemagne inspecting construction of the cathedral at Aachen, or Aix-la-Chapelle. The cathedral was begun under his direction in A.D. 796, and consecrated by Pope Leo III in 805. There Charlemagne was buried. Many emperors were also crowned here. The cathedral was damaged during World War II.

Richard the Lion-Hearted, King of England. He defeated Sultan Saladin at Arsuf during the Third Crusade (1189-1192). The capture of the city of Acre during this crusade by Philip II, king of France, and Richard the Lion-Hearted, after a two-year siege, resulted in the establishment of a bulwark for the Christians in the East.

King John Signing the Magna Charta. The great charter became the basis of English parliamentary government. It was exacted from John by feudal barons who sought to reassert their feudal rights or freedoms. Later these rights were extended to all Englishmen. The charter was signed at Runnymede, June 15, 1215.

Queen Philippa and the Burghers of Calais. During the Hundred Years' War between England and France, the English besieged and captured Calais. Edward III demanded the lives of six citizens in return for sparing the city. His queen, Philippa, and son, Edward the Black Prince, interceded and saved the citizens.

CHARLES LENEPVEU: Three Lions

Joan of Arc Burned at the Stake. Joan, a peasant girl, born in Domrémy, inspired by visions from God, went to King Charles VII and obtained an army to free France from English domination. Inspired by her courage, the French defeated the English. Joan was captured, tried, and burned by the English in 1431.

23. Feudal France

LAST OF THE FRENCH CAROLINGIANS

WHEN Charles the Fat could no longer protect the French realm against the attacks of the Vikings nor maintain a steady government, the French nobles asserted their right to choose another king. Their choice fell upon Count Odo of Paris who had all the qualities of a king. Although Odo's brother Robert held the counties of Paris, Blois, Touraine, and Anjou, there were still many strong nobles who disliked the present regime and plotted to put the son of Louis the Stammerer, Charles the Simple, on the throne. So when the archbishop of Rheims crowned Charles in 893, the discontented nobility flocked to Charles's banner and requested Arnulf to help set up the rightful heir to the throne. The rebellion that followed caused Odo to surrender a part of the realm to Charles and to promise him the crown.

Charles the Simple came to the throne in 898 with the consent of all the nobles, even that of Count Robert who still was the most powerful man in France. France was glad of some peace within her borders, for the Northmen were hammering at her doors. After the Northmen had been temporarily defeated at Chartres, Charles made a treaty with them whereby they were to become Christians and to confine their presence to the country around Rouen. This territory came to be known as Normandy. Once having settled down, the Northmen, or Normans as they were now called, built towns and founded churches.

Charles's activities on behalf of France further prove that the title "Simple" hardly applies to a man capable of pacifying the Northmen and adding Lorraine to the French crown. He aided the nobles of Lorraine in throwing off the German yoke of Conrad and settled down to enjoy himself in that duchy. Soon a rebellion arose and in 922 Count Robert was chosen king. In the main battle that followed, Robert was killed. His son Hugh

was proposed as successor, but he declined and suggested his brother-in-law, Duke Rudolph of Burgundy, who was elected king. Charles was betrayed into the hands of the rebels who held him until his death eight years afterward. His family escaped to England with his heir. Rudolph (923-936) had many enemies and difficulties facing his reign. In the first place, Lorraine fell back into German hands. Then the rebellious Normans had to be defeated and made vassals again. The Hungarians raced over the borders and terrified France. And his nobles never gave him their full cooperation.

When Rudolph died, Count Hugh of the Robertian House was influential in placing three Carolingians on the throne. The third one was Louis (936-954), son of Charles the Simple, who was called "D'Outre Mer" because he had been recalled from his exile across the sea in England. Louis never trusted the intentions of Hugh, and after a while open warfare broke out during which Louis was captured. Through the aid of Otto the Great, his brother-in-law, Louis was restored to the throne.

Louis died soon afterward and was followed by his son Lothair (954-986), who was elected without trouble, probably because Hugh was acting as regent. Lothair had to be pro-German in his policies because he owed so much to the support of Otto; in the matter of filling Church offices he was obliged to nominate Germans. This irked him; so, when Otto II became king, Lothair tried to capture Lorraine. Otto II promptly invaded France. An agreement was made to oust Lothair and elect Hugh Capet,

King Robert II was a student of theology and music. Here he is composing sequences and responses in Latin

son of Count Hugh the Great. Lothair died before the plots of his churchmen to make Hugh king could be realized. His son ruled only about a year. With him the Carolingian line comes to a quiet end.

It is interesting to pause for a minute to think why the Carolingian rulers were so ineffective. First of all, they had practically no lands of their own which would yield them an income large enough to support a large private army. They had given away too much in fiefs over which they had later lost control; and they had allowed aggressive nobles to seize privileges and to keep them; they had not exacted the revenues the early Carolingians had demanded; the system of immunities robbed them of the court fines. Even coinage had slipped out of their weak hands. There was no royal army recruited; but, instead, each lord was free to guard his own district. This made for confusion during the barbarian invasions.

It would take a strong hand to hold the course of France straight.

EARLY CAPETIANS

The Capetian line, which assumed royal leadership in 987 in the person of Hugh Capet, gave the needed guidance to the French monarchy. Hugh Capet had the qualifications that were necessary to make a good feudal monarch. He was the duke of the Ile de France as well as count of several other French districts. Thus he had a large independent income with which he could buy needed support. His family, moreover, were powerful rulers; his brother ruled Burgundy, and his sisters had married the dukes of Normandy and Aquitania. The Church, furthermore, had been won over to his side.

The remnant of the Carolingian line offered only a minor difficulty to the accession of a Capetian monarch. This was the Duke of Lorraine, who was looked upon unfavorably because he was a German duke. Since the French nobles and clergy had little love for a German duke, they asserted their elective rights at the assembly at Senlis, insisting that the French monarchy was elective and not hereditary. By using this theory the French avoided giving the throne to a foreigner who really had the hereditary right to be French king. So Hugh was elected in 987.

Several Capetian kings followed in rapid order. Hugh reigned from 987 to 996, but apparently accomplished little more than keeping the pro-Carolingian group from gaining headway. But his son Robert II (996-1031), a person of pleasing appearance and courtly ways, was far more colorful. Robert's main interests seem to have been cultural, for he was a serious pupil of the great Gerbert, later Pope Sylvester; theology and music were especially dear to him. Nevertheless, he was not lacking in military ability, as is readily seen from his expedition into the country of Burgundy. Robert had always been supposed to be a pious son of the Church, but it soon became apparent that he could fall from grace. For financial reasons and those of state he had been married off to a woman old enough to be his mother, Countess Susanne of Flanders, who was the widow of the Count of Flanders. He endured her a year and then threw her aside for a married woman who was several years older than he, the mother of five children, and the wife of Count Odo of Chartres, Tours, and Blois.

Her husband died shortly afterward, and the marriage might have been arranged by the Church by means of an annulment of Robert's marriage to Susanne. But Robert had acted as the godfather to one of Count Odo's children; therefore, church law forbade the marriage on grounds of incest. Robert married Bertha with the sanction of the local bishop. Finally the Church forced him to give Bertha up and to marry another woman, but he always felt attached to Bertha because she was the mother of his heir.

Bertha's child was King Henry (1031-1060) who did little during his long reign. For most of it he maintained peace with his powerful Norman vassals. He reached out toward international relations with far-away European countries, and in fact married a Russian grand duchess. Their son was Philip I (1060-1108) whose name denotes Byzantine influence of his Russian mother. Perhaps the traits he inherited from his mother unfitted him to rule easily in the static society of feudal France. At any rate, he quarreled with the papacy and with his Norman vassals. But he did help to preserve the Capetian family on the royal throne.

CAPETIAN COUNTIES AND DUCHIES

These first four Capetians began to show the same weaknesses that their Carolingian predecessors had revealed after the time of Charlemagne. From their extensive lands they had to hand out many fiefs in order to win friends against the Carolingian faction; and, as their land melted away, their strength also ebbed. Moreover, the Capetian holdings were now scattered all over France in small bits. Several of the nobles were lords over more land than the king; this was always a dangerous situation. The various vassals acted independently of the king and lived like little kings on their own domains. Only Philip recognized the value of rebuilding the royal domain.

It would have been hard for any family to rule France in the feudal age so long as there existed all these great fiefs. Burgundy which lay as a bone of contention between Germany and France, was pulled to one side or the other. In the south, Aquitaine was fertile ground for the growth of rebellions because of its remoteness and its racial character. Brittany, in the northwest, was a backward duchy. The duchy of Normandy will be discussed in another connection.

Then there were some great counties whose power was equal to that of the duchies. The county of Flanders was always the most important because it was the greatest commercial and industrial center during the Middle Ages. Near the center of France were the counties of Blois and Champagne; and Anjou was also important through its rich agricultural holdings. The counties of Toulouse and Barcelona were almost independent in their actions because they were so distant and had, as inhabitants, peoples whose background and race were different from those of the northern French. They spoke a French dialect; and in Barcelona, of course, Spanish was the language.

Added to the number of these great secular powers were the lands of the Church whose abbots, bishops, and archbishops were the equivalent in strength and resources to any count or duke. Some of these clergymen held regular counties as fiefs from the monarch because the kings had used this method to check the might of the lay nobles. For example, the bishops of Laon and Châlons were also counts. Since no one ever inherited or divided Church properties, the Church gradually through the centuries came to hold vast amounts of land. The nobles had, at least, to provide for their children and were forced to split the property.

NORMAN DEFIANCE AND EXPANSION

The most mighty of the French vassals in feudal times was of course the duke of Normandy. The Normans were the best fighters and the most ambitious people in Europe. Economically they were in the most favorable position in France since they held the Seine River. Their government was steady in the hands of

Robert the Devil, father of William the Conqueror, died in 1035 on his way home from a pilgrimage to Jerusalem. He had aided Henry I

France and forced him into humiliating agreements. Philip I was wise enough to do no more than torment the Norman dukes until William bribed him to stay out of Norman affairs.

Meanwhile, ambitions moved the Normans to attack some of the southern European states. Their attacks proved most successful in Sicily and South Italy, where they set up the foundation of the Norman kingdom of the Two Sicilies. This adventure was a fortunate outlet for their excess energies and drew off from Normandy and England some of the restless Normans who wanted to increase their means and secure land. Men like Tancred d'Hauteville and Robert Guiscard made themselves feared throughout Italy. Pope Leo IX led an army to dislodge them but was defeated and captured by the Norman host. The popes soon came to understand the Normans and to realize what useful allies they would make; from that time on the papacy and the Italian Normans became fast friends.

the absolute dukes, who intermarried into the great French families. In general they cooperated with the French monarchs; Robert the Devil aided Henry I against his relatives and, in return, asked Henry to protect and recognize his illegitimate son, later known as William the Conqueror, as heir to the duchy of Normandy. Henry fought the wars for William which enabled the boy to hold onto his duchy.

But when William grew to manhood, the French king found the Norman duke too strong; therefore, he encouraged rebellions in Normandy. William married the Countess of Flanders and eventually conquered England. He was able to defy the rule of Henry I of

THE PEACE OF GOD

It was necessary, therefore, that the French monarchy get along as best it could with such valiant warriors. If the Normans and the other great vassals could be handled diplomatically, then the French monarchy would remain in the hands of the Capetians. The Capetians set about to combine the idea of a divinely anointed kingship with their feudal powers over all French lords. The Capetians were more successful than preceding families because the kings always had sons to follow them, and consequently there was no hereditary break which would give the vassals a chance to set up a new ruling family.

The Capetians used the Church as much as possible in order to avoid giving the feudal lords any more powers. Of course their ambitions did bring them into some conflicts with the papacy. Hugh Capet battled with the pope over deposing of the archbishop of Rheims whom Hugh removed for treason and replaced with Gerbert. He succeeded in defying the

William the Conqueror reviews his troops. This powerful Duke of Normandy attained such power that he defied the rule of his former protector, Henry I

papacy. Robert was allowed by the pope to pick his own bishops so as to avoid all similar struggles. His marriage to Bertha, already referred to, caused the pope to excommunicate him and to force him into repentance.

In general it may be said that the Capetians were more willing to enforce the reforms within the Church than were the German rulers. Thus the French escaped all the dreadful results of the investiture struggle which tore Germany apart during the eleventh century. The Capetians aided the Cluniac monks in their program of reforms, and were the first to extend the peaceful policy of the Roman Church. The French clergy started the Peace of God which tried to enforce the following program: peaceful clergy were not to be attacked; animals were not to be carried off; peasants, women, children, and peaceful merchants were not to be molested; churches and Church property should not be violated; and all employees of the Church were to be safeguarded.

In order to make the Peace of God more effective, the Truce of God was instituted by the Church. There was to be no fighting from Friday to Monday out of respect to the days of Christ's death and resurrection; certain holy days and seasons were to be observed, as Advent (including Christmas), Epiphany, Lent, Whitsuntide, and certain of the important saints' days. If fighting could be eliminated on all these days, then there would be only a small fraction of the year in which to quarrel. Unfortunately for feudal society, even the Church could not enforce such an idealistic program. But the papacy was indebted to the French kings for their whole-hearted support of these policies.

The Capetians had nothing to lose by upholding the reforms of the Church directed at the disobedient clergy who were guilty of simony as the selling of Church offices was called, or of violating the vows of celibacy. The Capetians feared married priests and bishops who could bequeath property to heirs. Philip seems to have been the only Capetian to defy the reform policy by openly selling Church positions; but he finally repented after the pope excommunicated him.

24. The Crusades

THE BREAK IN THE CHURCH

TOWARD THE MIDDLE of the eleventh century occurred one of the most important events in the history of the Christian Church up to that point, namely, the schism or split between the Eastern and the Western Churches. This unfortunate situation had been developing for a number of centuries. The Eastern or the Greek Church by its geography and cultural background was quite different in its forms and attitudes from the Western or Latin Church. The Greek language had always been used in the Eastern service. Indeed, it was used in the earliest services in the Roman Church. The liturgy was very ancient, probably having been composed by the Apostles themselves who ministered in the Greek tongue. The main theological beliefs, such as the Apostles' Creed and the Nicene Creed, had been drawn up first in the East, because the Greeks enjoyed making carefully drawn distinctions. In fact, most of the doctrinal statements relating to the fundamentals of the Christian faith had been made by the Greek doctors of the East.

The West depended upon the Eastern Church for most of its ecclesiastical literature, translating it into Latin. Even the Christian Bible was in Greek, as were the early hymns. The Greek mind, since ancient times, was occupied with philosophy; the Greeks, therefore, combined their theological studies with their philosophy in such a way that the line between them was often obscured. Thus their whole mental outlook was different from the formalized practical approach of the Western Church which was satisfied with a brief doctrinal statement. The western Europeans distrusted the subtle Greek arguments which they did not fully understand.

Because the Greek Church had arisen in those places where the Gospel had been first preached by the Apostles and the early Church Fathers, it was proud of its ancient and distinctive way of doing things. Customs of all sorts were different in the East from what they were in the West: the Greek clergy wore different, and probably older, types of vestments in the liturgy; their long and involved liturgy took three hours to perform; they used leavened bread in the Eucharist; they permitted the marriage of the clergy, as was the apostolic custom; the priests let their beards grow; and there were other minor variations which the West found it hard to reconcile with their way of doing things.

In the early centuries when the bishops of Rome were obscure, the Roman Church was content to let the Greek Church do as it always had done. But after the fifth century, Rome began to adopt another attitude toward the Eastern Church; through the Eastern emperors Rome tried to have both Churches conform to Roman standards of what was orthodox. These attempts were ignored as impudent in the East. The emperors tried to please the Roman bishops as much as possible because the latter acted as their agents in Italy and generally had the most influence over western states. But the emperors never recognized the Roman Church as head of all Christendom; the universal opinion in the East was that Rome was the apostolic see in the West only and therefore the head of the Western Church.

CAUSES OF THE SCHISM

Rome and the East came into conflict in a serious way during the eighth century when the Eastern Church was involved in the Iconoclastic Controversy. This dispute concerned itself with the use of icons or holy pictures in the churches; one party wanted to abolish them because the Mohammedans were accusing the Christians of idolatry (and, indeed, there were many extravagant uses of these icons together with much superstition), and the other party fought to retain them. The latter party won out, probably because the weight of the Roman bishop was on their side. The pope had excommunicated all who had opposed the use of images. But the controversy left hard feelings against Rome for her interference.

The next issue arose over the *filioque* clause in the Apostles' Creed which the Latin Church had inserted in the interest of a more orthodox confession. The Greeks, who had originally formulated the Creed, resented the Roman attempts at improvement. This clause refers to the procession of the Holy Ghost both from the Father "and the Son," as the Roman Church amended it. The Greeks insisted that the early Church and the Gospels taught that the Holy Ghost proceeds only from the Father. This may now seem quibbling, but it was then a passionate matter of dispute between the two Churches.

There were other causes of disagreement. The Greek missionaries had converted the Slavs to the Christian faith in the ninth century. This had been largely the work of SS. Cyril and Methodius, who had also translated the Bible into the Slavic tongue and created a written language for these peoples. Then the Roman Church, under the patronage of the German rulers, seized the mission fields from the Greek Christians and introduced Roman Christianity; this was true of Bohemia, Poland, and Hungary. The Southern Slavs and Bulgars were, in general, preserved for the Eastern Church.

It was little wonder then that the East and West were ready for a schism in 1054. The Roman Church no longer was dependent upon the Eastern emperors, and it had a champion in the form of the Italian Normans; therefore, it could defy the emperor and condemn his state church. The patriarch of Constantinople and the pope excommunicated each other; this schism has lasted until our present day.

THE MENACE OF THE SELJUK TURKS

At this time the Moslems of the Near East again forced their way into the Christian world. Since the eighth-century conquests of the Mohammedans, the Moslem world had settled down to a routine of civil wars, with an occasional expedition against the Eastern Empire. Much of the early fanaticism disappeared, and in a short while the Moslem world was doing business with Christians; they found it profitable to allow Christian pilgrimages to Jerusalem and other holy places.

Except for the brief persecution and destruction of shrines under Haken about the year 1010, the Christian pilgrims from Europe were allowed to pass unmolested through Moslem territory. Minor frictions would, of course, be natural; but, in general, Christians probably were treated more kindly than Moslems traveling in Europe would have been. When certain pilgrimages were attacked by irresponsible Beduins, the Moslem officials pursued and tried to punish such bandits because the pilgrim traffic was a good source of income to the government.

But the coming of the Seljuk Turks in 1071 and their capture of Jerusalem aroused all Europe. Many wild tales of their atrocities were circulated. The rumor got around that the Turks were closing the Holy Places to pilgrims and slaughtering the Christians. There was no foundation to these stories, because pilgrims went to the sacred spots just as always; but the people in Europe believed these falsehoods, and the accounts seemed real to them. Thus the Seljuk Turk came to be looked upon as a wild beast from whom the Holy City must be rescued.

The theory, sometimes advanced, that pilgrimages began to be armed in order to ward off attacks, is utterly without proof. There is no evidence that pilgrims ever went armed; in the case of the Great German Pilgrimage of 1064, when some seven thousand pilgrims traveled together, they defended themselves only with stones and sticks found at hand. Therefore the Crusades were not, as they have been frequently called, "armed pilgrimages."

CAUSES OF THE FIRST CRUSADE

The causes of the First Crusade are not easy to determine. Probably the basic cause was the matter mentioned above; namely, that stories of mistreatment of pilgrims and the desecration of the Holy Sepulcher were widely circulated and believed. This emotional attitude probably prepared the Western Christians for the stirring appeal made by Pope Urban II at Clermont.

The next reason is that the idea of a crusade had been simmering in the plans of the papacy since 1073 when Michael VII, East Roman Emperor, requested Pope Gregory VII to do something to stop the Turks. The papacy saw in the crusading idea a chance to recapture its dominant position in European affairs, for the papacy would naturally lead such an expedition. The Church could make this a religious war and promise certain spiritual advantages to all who participated. Furthermore, the papacy saw a way to direct the warlike spirit of the feudal period into activities less dangerous to itself; the Peace and Truce of God had not worked as well as the Church had hoped. Now warriors could be appealed to on both military and religious grounds.

The Church also hoped that the Latin princes would set up states in the Near East which would be excellent centers from which Western clergymen could proselytize the Greeks. The Church hoped that, in return for the military aid of the West secured through the activity of the papacy, the Greek emperor would force the Eastern Church to submit to the pope.

The cause usually given as having started the immediate crusading movement is the famous appeal of the Emperor Alexius. This appeal is supposed to have come in the form of a letter to the Roman pope, Urban II. Modern scholars have been inclined to consider it a later forgery to cover the results of Western intrigue in the Eastern Empire. At any rate, the appeal rests upon the evidence of just one document; furthermore the Greek emperor had no immediate cause to fear the Turks, for he had long been holding

Pope Urban II at the Council of Clermont. Here his impassioned plea, promising worldly and spiritual rewards, opened the campaign for the First Crusade

his own against them. The emperor would not have invited Western interference in his realm when he had already had so much trouble with the Normans and the French adventurers. He had no intention, nor was he able, to turn the Greek Church over to the pope; and certainly he had no desire to divide his kingdom with the Western princes after he had saved it from the Moslems by his own efforts. For all these reasons it would seem that Alexius was not appealing to the West. When the Crusaders arrived at Constantinople, he was angry and gave no indication that he had ever invited them.

The immediate cause of the Crusade was the Council of Clermont, summoned by Pope Urban II in 1095. In a council held at Piacenza, Italy, he had already tested the temper of Europe toward a crusade. It seems that all the details were worked out beforehand and that the effect produced at the Council of Clermont was not as spontaneous as it was made to seem. The famous speech of Urban was not enough to get a crusade started, because it took another year to send the Crusaders on their way. Probably the tour of France, made by the pope, and the result of the ardent preaching by special orators and the local clergy had much more effect.

Peter the Hermit has often been credited with giving the needed impetus to start the

Peter the Hermit gives Urban II the message of Simeon, patriarch of Jerusalem. The fiery preaching of Peter was a great factor in the First Crusade

Crusaders on the March in the Holy Land. The men suffered much distress from hunger and thirst; the loss of their horses forced many to proceed on foot

Crusade. He was a picturesque, emotional preacher whose influence has been greatly exaggerated. He was no organizer and his preaching had nothing to do with the formation of the main body of the First Crusade. The group that followed him was comparatively small and totally unequipped to go on a Crusade; its ill-organized company broke up in the Byzantine Empire amid much strife.

THE FIRST CRUSADE

Several small groups of Crusaders, who had more faith than practical sense, started out half-prepared and came to grief in the Near East where their zeal proved to be insufficient protection. The regular Crusaders needed much prodding to send them on their way; some of the rulers had to be pressed into service. In the main, the kings did not participate; aristocratic but landless younger sons of noble families and the lesser nobles, who had little to lose and much to gain by starting a fresh career in the East, were the most willing Crusaders.

The leaders of the First Crusade were unusual men. Bohemond, a Sicilian Norman, was the best military leader, and he was ably seconded by his nephew, Tancred. Robert II, Count of Flanders, was also an excellent soldier with much experience. Count Raymond of Toulouse led one of the best crusad-ing armies, and he had spent years fighting the Moslems in Spain. Duke Robert of Normandy was himself not much of a military commander, but the army of Normans which accompanied him was renowned for its valor. The man with the highest ideals and most piety was Godfrey of Bouillon, Duke of Lower Lorraine; his brothers Baldwin and Eustace were useful military aides. So, although no monarchs led the First Crusade, the Crusaders were not without brilliant and illustrious leaders who were to prove themselves the equals of kings.

In 1096 the huge army of Crusaders slowly moved eastward. It traveled along three main routes: down through Italy and thence by boat to Constantinople; across Hungary and Bulgaria to the same city; and down the Dalmatian coast and across the Balkan Peninsula. All the forces met at Constantinople, much to the dismay and discomfort of Alexius. He did his best, however, to provide food and ships for this vast army, and asked in return that the chiefs keep their men from pillaging and molesting the Greek people, but the Crusaders were a disorderly lot who would not be restrained.

The Crusaders were greedy and demanded more supplies than Alexius could give; and they grew resentful that he was not more enthusiastic about their presence. Alexius re-

Priests Exhort the Crusaders. Large numbers of priests accompanied the fighting men on the Crusades

quired an oath of fealty of all the Crusaders who planned to set up states on Asia Minor territory. He was right, according to the feudal system; if he were to furnish food and ships and supplies, the least he deserved was an oath that the Crusaders would behave as allies and not enemies. The Crusaders finally agreed and made Alexius promise that he also would lead an army personally against the Turks.

Crusaders, right, clash with Turkish forces in the Battle of Nicopolis (Bulgaria), in 1396

The First Crusade moved across the Hellespont and captured Nicaea. The garrison surrendered to the emperor rather than to the Crusaders, and the Westerners were angry because Alexius let the Moslems depart in peace. Another battle ensued at Dorylaeum, in which the Crusaders had the victory. On the way to besiege Antioch, Baldwin left the army to carve out the county of Edessa for himself. After a long siege Antioch was taken; but then the Crusaders in turn were besieged by a great Moslem army. The Greek emperor could not come to their aid because he was busy fighting the Turks elsewhere. It was the miracle of finding the Holy Lance, which supposedly had pierced the side of Christ, that gave the Crusaders courage to sally out and defeat the Turks. Many of the Crusaders, however, claimed that the lance was a fake relic.

Now the Crusaders decided to throw off any allegiance to Alexius because he had not come to their aid as he had promised. They said that the feudal contract was broken because he had failed to live up to his part. Therefore they were free to do as they pleased. Bohemund then seized Antioch as his own principality and refused homage to Alexius.

CHRISTIANITY CAPTURES JERUSALEM

The army arrived at Jerusalem on June 7, 1099, and waited until July 15 before making a serious attempt to capture it. When the Holy City fell that day, the Crusaders let go their pent-up feelings and slaughtered every Moslem to be found.

Disregarding any ecclesiastical advice, now that the papal legate had died, the nobles assembled in feudal fashion and elected the most pious leader among them, Godfrey of Bouillon. He would not accept the title of king in the city where Christ had suffered death, but instead chose to be known as the "Defender of the Holy Sepulcher." When Godfrey died the next year, his brother Baldwin was summoned to rule the Holy City. He did not have the religious scruples of his brother and assumed the title of King of Jerusalem.

Godfrey of Bouillon, known as the "Defender of the Holy Sepulcher"

By now the Western nobles had set up Latin states all along the Asia Minor and Palestine coast, but they had not penetrated very far inland. The Mohammedans still hemmed them in from all sides. But neither Moslems nor Christians were able to dislodge the other; therefore, they had to develop a certain amount of toleration toward one another. Good friendships arose in this way between both parties.

The Latin nobles had to employ Moslems to work for them because there were not enough Christians to carry on extensive works. The Western people came to enjoy the luxury and refinements of the East; they adopted Eastern ways of living and appreciated oriental foods and Mohammedan science and medicine.

This intermingling broke up the crusading movement and caused splits between various Latin leaders in the East. The Italians were more interested in maintaining good commercial relationships with the Moslems than in fighting them. The rulers of the four Latin states were never able to form a united plan of action; these states were the kingdom of Jerusalem, county of Edessa, county of Tripoli, and the principality of Antioch.

THE SECOND CRUSADE

But the Moslems learned the advantage of union before the Western nobles in the Near East could make up their minds. By 1144 the county of Edessa fell into the hands of the Moslems again. This event shocked even Europe into activity; and the pope, in great alarm lest the gains in the East be lost, requested St. Bernard to preach a Second Crusade. Bernard's zeal induced the French king, Louis VII, and the reluctant German king, Conrad III, to undertake the Crusade.

So in 1147 both of these rulers started out, losing most of their followers before they got to Jerusalem.

At Jerusalem they decided to attack Damascus, but poor leadership and treachery made their expedition a hopeless one. The Second Crusade thus ended without accomplishing anything except revealing individual greed and ineffectiveness. The Latin kings were left without much support; they were blind to the growing Moslem unity under the brilliant Saladin. The various factions in Jerusalem could never agree upon what should be done. Guy of Lusignan favored a war policy and Raymond of Tripoli tried to keep a truce with Saladin. But Reginald of Chatillon broke the truce by seizing a caravan.

Saladin decided that the time had come to punish what he considered Christian treach-

The Wealth of the East was a constant source of astonishment to the Crusaders from Western Europe

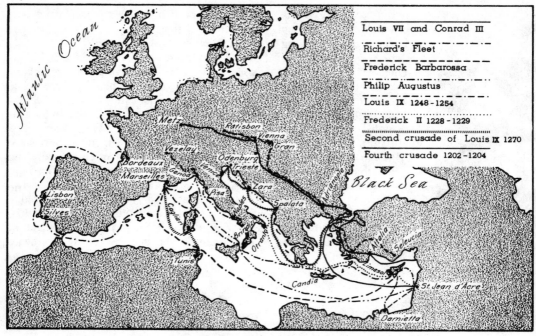

Routes taken by the Crusaders from Europe to the Holy Land

ery, and so he launched a war against all the Christian states. The Christians united but would not listen to good military advice. Consequently, Saladin won a great victory over them, swept down on the Christian cities, and ultimately captured Jerusalem in 1187.

THE THIRD CRUSADE

The capture of Jerusalem led to the organization of the Third Crusade. This is the most romantic of all Crusades, for most of the European monarchs participated in a magnificent style. Frederic Barbarossa of Germany, Henry II and Richard the Lion-Hearted of England, and Philip Augustus of France were the moving spirits. Frederic was a diplomatic genius who tried to save the expedition all the trouble he could before it started; besides enjoining strict discipline on all the members, he tried to persuade the Greek emperor and the sultan of Iconium to unite against Saladin. The emperor had already made a treaty with Saladin, but he was neutral enough to let the Crusaders pass through his territory.

The French and English slowly proceeded to the siege of Acre, which was enlivened by the quarrels between the two nationalities. After two years the Christians finally captured the town in 1191. Philip, however, became angry and deserted the Crusade. Richard after a while made peace with Saladin and returned to his kingdom. This agreement, made in 1192, was that Christian pilgrims could enter Jerusalem freely. Beyond that concession the whole Crusade was a failure.

THE FOURTH CRUSADE—
A COMMERCIAL ENTERPRISE

The Fourth Crusade can hardly be called a crusade. In 1201 another zealous group gathered at Venice where they had been promised transportation by the Venetians; but the crafty Venetians, knowing that the poor Crusaders had no money, refused to help them unless they attacked her commercial rival across the Adriatic, the city of Zara. The pope forbade this expedition against a Christian city, but the Venetians and Crusaders ignored him. Then the Venetians

Richard the Lion-Hearted objects to the banner of Leopold of Austria being placed next to his own. Such squabbles foreshadowed the Crusades' failure

decided to divert the Crusade against Constantinople, which was the great Eastern commercial power. Using one of the pretenders to the Greek throne as an excuse, the Crusaders sailed away to Constantinople, where they captured the city amid one of the most disgusting scenes in the history of civilization. Priceless art objects of the ages were wantonly destroyed; the city was set on fire; and all valuables were plundered. The churches were violated beyond description.

The outcome of this Crusade was the setting up of a Latin Empire of the East with the Count of Flanders as emperor, and with a Latin patriarch instead of a Greek. Venice received all the business concessions.

There were other crusades and semi-crusades which cannot be separately distinguished. All of them were useless, but they show how long the crusading spirit lasted. One of the most pathetic movements was the so-called Children's Crusade which arose about 1212 and which hoped by faith alone to rout the infidels; the Italian seaport merchants managed to kidnap a number of them and sell them as slaves to the Turks whom they were going to convert. St. Louis, king of France, also tried an expedition against Egypt, but failed to accomplish anything.

SOME RESULTS OF THE CRUSADES

By 1291 the Christians lost their last possessions in the East. Territorially, then, these movements were distinct failures; nor were the religious purposes realized. Perhaps the most important result of these invasions of the East was the influence they exerted upon Western civilization. Trade routes between the East and the West were developed rapidly in order to satisfy the European taste for oriental products. Stories of the crusaders circulated freely among the more "sensible" people who stayed at home, and so aroused the desire to see more of the world. It would be difficult to determine to what extent the Crusades were responsible for the remarkable explorations which were begun by Prince Henry the Navigator in the fifteenth century. But we may be fairly certain that European life, manners, and attitudes were by no means left unchanged as a result of the crusading movement.

Count of Flanders grants a charter of peace to the town of Cambrai. The clothes show eastern influence

25. The Church Triumphant

THE SECRET OF PAPAL AUTHORITY

By the twelfth century the Church of the West had fully developed its system of doctrine and government. Her power over the individual Christian in Western Europe was undisputed except by occasional heretics who were too few to harm the Church. The whole social structure was built so that everybody was assumed to belong to the Church just as he belonged to the state. The Church also was powerful in medieval life because it was the richest institution having accumulated wealth for centuries without having passed it on to various heirs.

The secret of the Church's power lay, however, in the religious concept of the medieval mind which believed that the pope was the spokesman of God and the direct apostolic descendant of St. Peter, to whom Christ gave all spiritual power. The pope held in his hands the keys to eternal life and damnation. If a person were to be saved from damnation, he had to be within the Church; and the pope was the Church. Therefore, the average man in the Middle Ages took care that he would not die outside the fold of the Church.

The popes wielded two very powerful weapons which were based upon the assumption that they held the keys to salvation. One was the interdict, by which a city or nation could be laid under the ban of the Church and all religious services and the sacraments suspended from public performance. This weapon usually forced the country or city to yield quickly to the Church for fear that the citizens would die unabsolved. No prince could stand out against the pressure of the devout populace who feared the Church more than they feared him. The other weapon was the use of excommunication, by which the individual was cut off from the consolations of the Church and all the faithful were forbidden to associate with him.

THE SACRAMENTS

What were these sacraments that the Western Christians felt were necessary for salvation? A sacrament is an outward and visible sign of an inward and invisible grace, instituted by Christ. The Church was undecided for many centuries just how many sacraments there really were; some said two and others said twenty. But in the middle of the twelfth century, Peter Lombard wrote his *Sentences* in which he argued so well for the number seven that his reckoning was accepted by the Latin Church as the standard number.

The first sacrament necessary for salvation was that of baptism. Through baptism all the sins inherited through Adam's fall were washed away. Baptism was required of all believers.

When the child who had been baptized came to the age at which he was supposed to be able to think religiously for himself, he could receive the anointing of the forehead and the breath of the bishop as a sign that he had received the sacrament of confirmation. Now he was ready to participate in the full rights of Church membership.

The sacrament of penance is divided into several parts. The sinner must heartily repent of his sins and resolve never to commit them again before he is ready to confess his sinful ways to the priest. If the priest is assured that the person is repentant, then he pronounces the absolution or cleansing of the soul from the deadly guilt. All sins must be

"Christ Giving the Keys to St. Peter," a painting of the symbolical transfer of all spiritual power to Peter, who was recognized as the Church's first pope

confessed since a soul is damned which dies unconfessed of mortal sin.

As part of the system of penance the priest might impose certain punishments upon the confessed person, such as extra prayers, going on pilgrimages, and giving up certain pleasures so that he could escape some of the temporal punishment otherwise to be endured here or in purgatory. The practice grew up that, when persons could not undertake pilgrimages or perform other arduous penances, the priest might in his discretion change the penance into a gift of money for some pious cause.

When the Christian was gravely ill or dying, the priest was called to administer the sacrament of extreme unction. This was done to wash away all carnal sins and give hope of Heaven to the soul. The ceremony consisted of anointing the several parts of the body with holy oil.

Marriage was not a sacrament that was necessary to salvation, for indeed the clergy, monks, and nuns were unmarried. The Church set a high value on celibacy and held that it was better than the married state. Nevertheless, since men married and the human race had to be preserved, marriage was held to be a sacrament which all contracting parties had to receive from a priest to be validly married. No divorce was permitted; but, since an influential person sometimes insisted on changing mates, annulment of the existing marriage could be arranged if some grounds could be found.

Ordination, likewise, was a sacrament that everyone need not have. The candidate was presented to the bishop, who alone could impart this sacrament which gave the priest the right to perform the Mass. The bishops were the officials of the Church through whom the Apostolic Succession was transmitted to all the ministers of Christ. Once the ordination was given, nothing could erase its indelible character, not even heresy or desertion of one's post.

The great sacrament performed by the priest, however, was the Holy Eucharist or Lord's Supper. By the twelfth century the idea was firmly rooted that the essence of the sacrament was the mystical change that took place in the substances of bread and wine, transforming them completely into the Body and Blood of Christ. The theory was that Christ had instituted this sacrament as a perpetual, bloodless sacrifice to offer up daily to God in propitiation for the sins of the living and the dead. This change of elements was called transubstantiation, and the doctrine of the Real Presence of Christ was associated with it.

Therefore this performance of the daily sacrifice of the Mass was considered the heart of the Roman worship. Persons flocked to the Church to adore Christ in the Reserved Host, as the consecrated wafer was called. Many persons left special funds for the priest to say Mass for their departed souls. Thus it is rightly considered as the most important feature of the Roman cult.

CHURCH GOVERNMENT

The monarchial form of church government became rigidly established during the high Middle Ages. The pope stood at the head as the absolute ruler from whom there was no appeal. He proclaimed all laws; no person or council could issue laws relating to church matters without his consent. Furthermore, he might set aside any previous laws, except those of God Himself, as the Ten Commandments, and he could issue dispensations from all human regulations. Thus he might free a person from his vows as a priest, or let a king marry a near relative. As chief lawgiver and dispenser he had the right to try all cases appealed to his court.

The practice of having the pope pass on all candidates for higher offices had grown steadily. He could decide the fitness of the person and judge disputed elections; usually he received a fee for granting permission to assume the *pallium*, the woolen scarf worn by archbishops. Since the middle of the eleventh century the popes claimed the right to remove or transfer any bishop. Because he could not attend to every detail of his office, he allowed the *Curia* or papal courts to do some of the work for him.

Under the pope were the archbishops, each of whom controlled a province. They could summon provincial synods with the pope's consent to decide purely local matters. They could take cases appealed from a bishop's court.

The bishop as head of a diocese was about the most important person locally in medieval society. He ordained all clergy, confirmed the children; consecrated churches; and anointed kings. He was the busiest man in the Middle Ages, for he was not only a church officer but also a secular lord who had to govern a city or even a county. He was elected by the cathedral chapter or by the priests attached immediately to the cathedral church. But kings or popes could and did choose candidates.

On the parish priest devolved the hard work of doing all the thousand unseen, unappreciated, and unrewarded acts that kept the main body of the Church alive throughout the Middle Ages. The priest was the least well provided of all the clergy, for his living often depended upon the local lord who held the lands. The manner in which many of these priests managed to keep alive is a great mystery.

The remarkable fact about the medieval church was that in an essentially aristocratic society the Church was a democratic institution. Any intelligent boy, no matter how lowly his origin, had a chance to enter the service of the Church and to rise to the top, even to the papal chair, as did Gerbert (Sylvester II). Despite its shortcomings, the Church did stand as the most charitable and humane institution in the Middle Ages.

MONASTICISM

Since the days when St. Benedict had organized Western monasticism, the movement had spread over all Europe. The Benedictine order was the only one to claim the attention of serious-minded men who wanted to leave the vain pleasures of the world and to seek salvation within monastic walls.

In the eleventh century the Cluniac system, which had been founded in the ninth century, had already influenced the religious life of Europe. The Cluniacs were especially interested in furthering the work of reforming the Church; they supported the popes in all their efforts to eradicate married priests, simony, and inefficient clergy. They placed greater stress upon discipline than did the Benedictines.

In the eleventh century the order of Camaldoli was founded by persons who wanted rigid discipline; these monks lived in separate cells like hermits. The order of Vallambrosa started a new practice. They not only took in monks, but also admitted lay brothers who from lack of education were not fit for the regular monastic duties, but who had pious spirits. The lay brothers assumed most of the menial labor so that the monks could have leisure to study.

Near the end of the eleventh century the Carthusians were founded in the neighborhood of Grenoble, France. They were the most severe of all orders; they hoped by their severity to preserve their order from falling into the sinful luxury which crept into the others. Conversation was prohibited except when absolutely necessary. Their clothes were very poor, and they wore hair shirts next to their bodies. They fasted almost all the time and subsisted on the plainest food. This order is

A Templar in Travel Dress. The Templars were an order which combined the military and the religious

able to boast that it has never had to be reformed because it never was deformed.

The Cistercians, an outgrowth of the Benedictines, were organized in 1092. This order received its great fame mainly through its most illustrious monk, St. Bernard. It, too, was very ascetic. All its monasteries and monks were directly under the direction of the abbot of Citeaux. Every action of every monk was strictly regulated. In order to avoid worldly sins the Cistercians built their

Hospitalers' Fortress in Syria. This group was first organized to assist needy pilgrims, but later became primarily a military order

monasteries in deserted and unfruitful districts. But they became famous for the diligence with which they turned their desert into a garden. Gradually they acquired the wealth which they wished to avoid, and, following the inevitable course of medieval monasticism, with wealth came laxity. A great contribution of the Cistercians to medieval women was the establishment, following the lead of the Benedictines, of a charitable order of Cistercian nuns.

Two new orders appeared which opened their doors to both men and women. In 1096 Robert of Arbrissel founded a joint order at Fontevrault. It became famous as a refuge for the poor of both sexes. St. Norbert started the order known as the Premonstratensians. He was a wandering reformer who preached against the evils of the time, especially in Germany where the investiture struggle was ruining the land. He claimed that the Virgin had pointed out Prémontré as the place to begin a reforming order.

During the Crusades some orders were founded which combined the military and the religious. Among these were the Templars and the Hospitalers. They originally planned to protect pilgrims on their way to Jerusalem. The Templars used the Temple of Solomon as their headquarters. It was rather aristocratic, for only nobles could belong to its first class; clergymen acted as chaplains; and freemen might act as squires or servants. The Hospitalers, or Knights of St. John, were devoted to caring for needy pilgrims. Both of

the orders took monastic vows but had great freedom of movement, especially in fighting the infidel.

Because not all secular priests who had to serve the world in regular parishes could have the benefits of monasticism, a plan was arranged whereby clergy who lived together in a cathedral chapter or in connection with a large church could lead a monastic life. These men were called the secular canons; they observed the monastic life in so far as possible, in their regular parish work.

The whole monastic movement of the eleventh and twelfth centuries was an attempt to reform the corrupted Church from within; if one monastic group failed, another stricter order arose to carry on the work. Each order tried to outdo the other in strictness; but, since all monks were mere men subject to the weaknesses of the flesh, many failed to achieve the perfect monastic life.

HERESY AND THE FRIARS

That not everyone in the Middle Ages conformed to the dogma of the Roman Church is evident from the number of heresies which arose during that period. Sometimes heresy was confined to one person who had little influence; he would in that case be dealt with by the local authorities under the direction of the Church. But the followers of a heretic often became numerous and had to be met with strenuous methods.

At various places and mostly in individual cases, the old Donatistic heresy of the first centuries of Christianity reappeared. This heresy denied the worth of a sacrament performed by an evil priest. Other individuals, like Eon of Brittany, Peter of Bruys, Henry of Lausanne, and Tanchelm of Antwerp, were persons who became locally famous for attacking the moral condition of the Church.

Arnold of Brescia was a religious rebel who founded the Arnoldists in Rome about 1145. He advocated a return to the simple life of the earlier Church and preached against wicked popes who misled their flock. But his heretical teaching was cut short; to gain the pope's favor, Frederick Barbarossa had Arnold captured and burned.

St. Dominic, the founder of the Dominican order of Friars. (National Gallery of Art, Kress Collection)

There were, however, large and persistent groups of heretics who stubbornly held out against the local Church powers and required the efforts of the whole Church to suppress. The Waldensians, followers of Peter Waldo of Lyons, were such troublesome heretics that the Church had to use strong methods to root them out. Peter had read the Bible in translation and become convinced that he should lead a better life. He went around to the common people, preaching the good news that he found in the Bible. Many joined his pious society and twice sought permission from the pope to form an order. The popes refused, but the Waldensians went right on preaching. They lived good lives, better than their orthodox neighbors; but they committed the sin of denying papal and priestly authority. They also denied the value of Masses and prayers for the dead.

The Albigenses in the south of France were much more heretical, for they were Manichaeans; that is, they believed in the coexistence of good and evil. The south of

St. Francis of Assisi, founder of the Franciscan order. First organized as a lay order, the Franciscans sought to relieve distress produced by urban living

France was always tolerant in religious matters, and the feudal disorder prevented any strong steps to stop this heresy. They led such good lives that even orthodox clergymen were impressed. Their numbers grew rapidly, partly because they taught that only the leaders were expected to be perfect; others should have faith and try to lead a good life, and they could be saved if they received the last rites from the "perfect." They denied hell and purgatory; they preached against the wealth of the Church.

Strappado or Vertical Rack, a method of torture used to force heretics to confess in the Inquisition

Such successful heretics were dangerous; so Innocent III preached a crusade against the heretics and Count Raymond for tolerating them. This meant that any prince in the faith could help himself to Raymond's lands. In 1209 the crusade descended upon the county of Toulouse and eventually captured it for the king of France; heretics and orthodox alike perished in the bloody massacres.

The Church now saw that the best way to combat these heresies was to catch them before they developed. Thus the Church set up the institution of the Inquisition to handle cases of heresy locally. The government gave its co-operation for reasons of state. A board of clergymen was appointed to hear cases and accusations. Often persons received little chance to defend themselves. If the person was found guilty and would not renounce his heresy, he could be handed over to the civil officers to be executed; the Church never did the executing. In the thirteenth century, St. Dominic's friars, the Dominicans, were used to prevent and check heresy by their preaching; they also served on the board of the Inquisition. They were very learned and zealous, and were quite successful in checking the spread of heresy.

The Franciscans of Friars Minor were recognized in 1215. They were very effective in laboring among the wretched poor whom the Church had neglected and who were a

Franciscan Monastery at Assisi. St. Francis was born in the small town at the base of the hill. This monastery is one of the most famous religious institutions in all Europe. (Ewing Galloway—Burton Holmes)

fertile field for the spread of heresy. The Franciscans were very poor and humble in the beginning and thus won the love and confidence of the lower classes. Both the Franciscans and the Dominicans spread all over the globe, each doing a different kind of work and each winning many converts among the unbelievers.

EXTENSION OF TEMPORAL POWER

In the political sphere the Church reached her period of greatest power. In the person of Innocent III she stood out above any king and made monarchs tremble at her word. During his papacy, from 1198 to 1216, he rebuilt the prestige of the Holy See, which had withered away because of the failure of the Crusades and because of the imperial power which flaunted papal admonitions.

Innocent set about bringing the states of the Church directly under his control and enlisted the Italian cities against the German kings. In German affairs he threw his weight on the side of the Guelphs and opposed the Ghibellines. He set up Otto as king and removed him when he disobeyed. In France he laid an interdict upon the kingdom until Philip Augustus took back his first wife. He excommunicated and deposed John of England, and finally restored him only when John became his vassal. King Sancho of Portugal

and Peter of Aragon made their lands fiefs of the pope; Alphonse of Leon had to give up his wife, who was his cousin; the king of Hungary gave his country to the pope and ruled as a vassal; and the monarchs of Poland, Denmark, and Bohemia were obedient servants of the papacy.

Never had the papacy been so triumphant and never had a pope wielded so much power. At Innocent's Fourth Lateran Council of 1215, all of Western Europe and the Latin kingdoms of the East were represented. This council passed all the reforms that the Church had been needing for many decades. With the death of Innocent III the Church lost forever her vast spiritual and political empire, which no monarch, lay or spiritual, has ever equaled.

King John surrendering his crown. Excommunicated and deposed by Innocent III, he regained his throne by becoming the pope's vassal

26. Medieval Culture

MEDIEVAL EDUCATION

Education in the middle ages was a child of the Roman classical schools which survived in part, at least, the collapse of the Roman Empire. In the lower schools of the Roman system the elements of reading, grammar, arithmetic, and music were taught; in the higher schools, which prepared young men for the professions or public life, such subjects as oratory, rhetoric, literature, astronomy, law, and philosophy were emphasized. Although classical schools disappeared during the fifth century, their influence was felt in the curriculum and text books adopted by the schools of the early Middle Ages.

During the fifth and sixth centuries the schools quietly passed into church control. It was during these two centuries that Christian grammarians set the pattern for the curriculum of the High Middle Ages when the medieval university was developed. Martianus Capella defined the seven liberal arts as grammar, rhetoric, logic, arithmetic, geometry, astronomy, and music. Boethius (c. 480-524) called the first three the *trivium* and the last four the *quadrivium*. Cassiodorus passed this system and division on to the monasteries which spread it throughout Europe.

By the time the sixth century closed, education was so expensive that it came to be limited to those who were preparing for the priesthood, and the secular schools practically died out. In order to preserve their warlike qualities the Germanic invaders forbade their people to attend schools. By the seventh century, schools were episcopal and monastic. The so-called court schools of the Merovingian palaces offered little more than a combination of military and athletic training with some incidental study in law and grammar.

The episcopal and monastic schools changed the ideal as well as the content of education. If the papacy had not been so powerful, education might have continued in the classical mold; but the Church insisted upon the primary importance of theological and biblical studies. Sermons and the lives of saints became the usual text books for the ordinary schools, and this material was often in questionable Latin.

Education during the Carolingian Renaissance has already been discussed. It suffices to say that Charlemagne used the existing monastery schools and founded some cathedral schools, borrowing scholars from the famous Irish and English monasteries, and financing their educational work. He himself became the patron of learning in his own court where he assembled some of the most learned men of his time.

With the collapse of Charlemagne's Empire, his great efforts on behalf of education almost vanished. At a few great monasteries, like those at Fulda or St. Gall, the monks kept an "inner" school for boys preparing to be monks and an "outer" school for those who expected to be priests. General secular education, such as Charlemagne urged, was neglected.

THE SCHOOLMEN

Here and there from the ninth to the eleventh centuries arose a man who has become important in the history of education; but no really great name is encountered before that of Anselm (died 1109). He is the father of Scholasticism, the method which came to dominate education until the late Middle Ages. Stated briefly, the Scholastic method is this: we believe in order that we might know. In other words, faith precedes reason; the Christian takes certain fundamental premises on faith and proceeds to prove or substantiate his faith by reason. Then the Scholastics use the Aristotelian method of the logical syllogism to make all sorts of deductions. Naturally, if everyone will take the first premise on faith, the logical steps that follow will inevitably prove the truth of the conclusion.

The Scholastic method became the regular way of defending Christian doctrine throughout the later Middle Ages, and is even used today in modern Neo-Scholasticism. Schoolmen like Anselm worked out the most subtle rational argument to prove those doctrines which they had already accepted by faith. The *Cur Deus Homo* by Anselm is the most outstanding example of the Scholastic method.

Although the universities had not yet been born, some of the greatest intellectual battles of all ages were being fought during the eleventh and twelfth centuries by eminent theologians. The question of transubstantiation and predestination had been wrangled back and forth, until the Church, fearing the results of free debate, settled the argument by setting up a rigid doctrine which all the faithful must accept. The most widely debated subject was that of Realism versus Nominalism. The Realists maintained that ideas were real and had substance and that universals could exist apart from individual objects. The Nominalists, on the other hand, declared that universals are merely convenient names and had no reality. The orthodox clergy and teachers held that the Nominalists were almost heretical and endangered such doctrines as that of the Trinity and the Eucharist.

This controversy proved to be the most intellectually stimulating event that had happened since classical times. These new ideas threatened to upset the static theological life of the Middle Ages. All the constituted powers were on the side of Realism because that system would prove that all the powers that now existed were ordained by God; while the intellectual radicals found an outlet for their rationalism in the more liberal

Abelard teaching at the University of Paris. This teacher stressed the use of reason to attain faith

system of Nominalism which could question the right of the Church to establish doctrines for which there was no rational proof.

Abelard (1079-1142), with brilliance and daring in his book *Sic et Non*, used the disagreement of the Church Fathers to show that in order to have faith a person had to use his reason to know what to believe. He stressed honest doubt as the best way to arrive at an intelligent faith. By his charming personality and ready wit he made people doubt and then laugh at older methods. His popularity was so great that Realists like St. Bernard called upon the Church to silence him. But Abelard was no heretic; he simply wanted to make the theological method free from absurd arguments.

THE UNIVERSITIES

The fact that prominent teachers could attract students from faraway countries, and that students gathered in those places where certain subjects were taught by men who were authorities, may account for the rise of medieval universities. The exact cause of their growth is still obscure. Some say that universities first arose in Italy because the classical tradition of learning was still strong there, and because the growth of trade and commerce in that area of the Mediterranean created a demand for the study of law. Therefore, the University of Bologna was founded in 1158 as a center of this all-important study of law. The University of Paris, which emphasized theol-

Rector of Prague University and four scholars from different nations studying at that university

The teachers were clergymen and the teachings were subject to church control. The popes required candidates for degrees to be certified by a bishop. Later on the Franciscans and Dominicans came to dominate most of the professorships. Theology was always the main study.

The better universities had a number of "faculties" or departments: arts, theology, canon and civil law, and medicine. The teaching staff was composed of masters of arts who formed a closed society which could admit or reject members. The curriculum was that established by Martianus in the fifth century; the trivium and quadrivium with the addition of some of Aristotle's scientific works. This curriculum would lead to the Bachelor of Arts degree, and required four or five years. Three or four more years were required for the Master of Arts, which demanded more specialized study in the higher branches of theology, philosophy, and other subjects. The Doctor's degree was not given before a person was thirty-five, and then only after about eight years of additional study.

ogy and philosophy, was established around the year 1200 as an outgrowth of the cathedral school. Within a comparatively short time universities were set up at Salerno, Oxford, Cambridge, Heidelberg, and in many other centers.

The word university, or *universitas*, means an association of teachers and students grouped together for the purpose of study. The students organized themselves into "nations" to distinguish whether they were Normans, Bavarians, Lombards, Flemish, or of some other nationality. Each "nation"

Seal of the University of Paris, which was established during the 12th century

chose a councilor, and these councilors in turn elected a rector. Some universities were run by the students who hired the masters or teachers and paid them. At other universities, like that of Paris, the masters organized and managed all school affairs.

It must be remembered, however, that the university was born under church influence.

University of Oxford Seal. University College, the first college at Oxford, was founded in 1249

ARABIAN PRESERVATION OF GREEK THOUGHT

Several intellectual currents brought further knowledge into the medieval university. Although the university was a Christian foundation, it could not escape the influence of Arabian learning which made the Moslem universities in Spain so famous. After the Moslems settled down to a civilized routine, they eagerly translated into Arabic the great works of classical Greece, especially those of Aristotle. It is largely to these translations that we owe the survival and introduction of the magnificent Greek culture and intellect into Western Europe. The many Jewish scholars in Spain helped to edit and translate these Arabic works into Latin.

Thus Aristotle came from the original Greek through Arabic, then Hebrew, and finally Latin translations. The new body of ideas was so revolutionary that the Church banned the study of Aristotle as heretical. It took the genius of St. Thomas Aquinas (died 1274) to prove to the satisfaction of the

Church that this new and dangerous body of classical ideas and methods could be combined with and used to defend the Christian faith. He demonstrated that there were two kinds of knowledge, that of revelation from Scripture and the Church, and that which came from reason and experience. His job was to reconcile these two kinds of knowledge.

St. Thomas Aquinas in the Summa reconciled the knowledge of the Church with that of experience

His Scholastic method was so successful in the *Summa* that the Church has declared his Christian-Aristotelian arguments its official standard of doctrine.

Some famous men toward the end of the Middle Ages attacked the Scholastic method. Roger Bacon (c. 1214-1294) condemned the use of deductive reasoning and the Scholastic reliance on tradition. Duns Scotus (c. 1265-1308), one of the keenest opponents of Thomism, taught that the will was superior to the intellect, and that God was beyond abstract reasoning. William of Occam (c. 1280?-1349) shifted attention from universal abstract ideas to concrete individual things. Occam's "razor," the adage that things are not to be multiplied needlessly, cut away a good deal of the stubble of formalism and, some think, some of the flesh on the face of philosophy. By making morality dependent on faith, not on reason, he tended to separate science and religion. By the early 15th century, Scholasticism was in disrepute, not to reach wide favor until its revival in the Neo-Scholastic movement which began in 1880.

Roger Bacon was among the great scholars who opposed scholasticism. (Brown Bros.)

SCIENCE IN THE MIDDLE AGES

Medieval science grew out of classical pseudo-science and medieval magical practices. The earlier Middle Ages had been quite content to depend upon the amazing *compendia* or encyclopedias of scientific misinformation which had been made by the Romans or early medieval Christians. These books were full of such nonsense as that of unicorns and dragons, or strange plants which if picked at full moon would have magical effects.

There was no real effort made to correct all this false information about the physical world so long as the Church was the absolute guardian of all knowledge. There was no place for the practice of pure science in a curriculum loaded with theological studies. Therefore, science fell into the hands of misguided men or deliberate charlatans who spent their time trying to turn lead into gold or trying to find the elixir of life.

Not until the body of Greek knowledge plus the experiments of the Arabs and Jews, came into the West through Moslem Spain was there any attempt to study science by a scientific method. The Arabs were the foremost physicians of the Middle Ages because they not only knew all that the Greeks had discovered, but they also had learned much by experimenting in anatomy and the effects of medicines. They knew much about the science of optics, the study of the eye, and they were skilled surgeons.

In some of the mathematical sciences they were able not only to transmit Greek mathematics, but they helped to simplify arithmetic by the use of the so-called Arabic numerals—probably borrowed from India—instead of the awkward Roman numerals. They gave the West algebra and other advanced calculations and transmitted geometry from the Greeks. Their astronomy was vastly superior to any Western European study of that subject. They calculated longitudes, and corrected the geography and maps of the older scholars. Their chemistry was free from much of the magical element which discredited Western science.

When all of these scientific data began to cross the Pyrenees in the Latin translations made by the Jew, the Church was alarmed. Study of physical phenomena, which had been ignored or incorrectly reported by Church Fathers, threatened to upset the infallible authority of the Church on matters pertaining to the construction of the world and the universe. But her fears were quieted when good monks were able to use the scientific materials to help substantiate the teachings of the Church.

Although medieval science can boast of such names as Roger Bacon, Grosseteste, and Abelard of Bath, it never became the predominant study it is today. Probably the greatest reason for this lag is to be found in the medieval mind itself. It had been trained to accept knowledge on faith, while science demands a curious, skeptical, inquiring mind. This attitude took many generations to develop; in the medieval period we see its first glimmerings. Another factor preventing scientific development was the lack of apparatus. Today, as the result of hundreds of improvements in technology, we have delicate measuring instruments and complicated equipment to enable us to experiment and to check our results. Those few inquiring minds in the Middle Ages who held correct scientific ideas were unable to prove them because of the lack of instruments.

VERNACULAR LANGUAGES

By the High Middle Ages, all of the Romance and Teutonic languages had become fixed in forms which do not differ greatly from our modern European languages. The vernacular, or everyday Latin of the Classical period, had been corrupted into a number of dialects which later became French, Spanish, Portuguese, and Italian.

Many new words came in through the German barbarians. And often, when there was no old Latin term to express some newer idea, the medieval writer just invented one. Thus, the classical Latin had no word for "to baptize," therefore the Church coined the verb "baptizare." Also, many words became so corrupted in pronunciation by the thick-tongued barbarians that their formal form bears almost no resemblance to the original Latin.

Through the use of Latin in the Church and the study of good Latin classics in the schools, the medieval Latin was always being revised in the direction of better grammatical constructions. School boys were consciously taught to imitate the pure Latin style; however no medieval author ever attained pure Latin style or vocabulary.

MEDIEVAL LITERATURE

Aside from the classical Latin texts used for teaching purposes, the most familiar medieval Latin literature is the annal or chronicle. These works are the histories of the Middle Ages written in the form of brief accounts under each year. The Latin Vulgate Bible, written in fairly good Latin, was read eagerly by the clergymen until the late Middle Ages. Sermons and the lives of saints were very popular. Latin hymns and sacred poetry sprang up; these were unlike classical verse because they had rhyme and the accent fell on the ordinary accent of the word. The poetry was not always sacred, because the students sang some naughty songs in Latin. In fact, a great deal of Latin literature in the Middle Ages was not religious in subject matter.

But there was also vernacular literature, that is, literature written in the ordinary man's language. Latin was the language of the Church and scholars; but the common man spoke only his native tongue—French, German, English, or some other. The Germans at least had a folk literature that was handed down orally from perhaps the third or fourth century. The folk literature was made up of legends and songs about some national hero or about the tribal gods.

Other vernacular literature came from classical sources which had been translated and modified into stories with mixed classical and vernacular contents. Many of our fables and fairy tales represent such a mixture. The Bible furnished the basis for many folk tales, often being translated into long, rhymed metrical verse. In the eleventh century a great

harvest of songs and ballads appeared, carried from court to court by troubadours or minne-singers. Along with these arose some medieval epics like the *Song of Roland* and the King

Arthur cycles. The modern novel had its origin back in the medieval allegories and novelettes, such as the *Romance of the Rose* (about 1250) and *Aucassin et Nicolette*.

Short stories, called *fabliaux*, were the popular reading in the later Middle Ages. Very pleasing to the public were the mystery and miracle plays which were presented to huge audiences. The drama was originally under the auspices of the Church, but it soon graduated into secular hands. In the beginning the subject matter was largely biblical or the lives of saints; but it soon came to represent the actions of the common man.

Medieval literature thus combines elements of classical literature with certain native traditions. On this basis our great body of modern literature has been built.

MEDIEVAL ARCHITECTURE

The greatest contribution of medieval art was that of architecture. Perhaps no greater monuments to the genius of man have been erected than the medieval churches, both Romanesque and Gothic. Medieval architecture and its accompanying arts were distinctly inspired by the Church.

Romanesque architecture has a venerable ancestry which stretches back into dim Roman and Greek styles. The early Christians adapted the secular Roman buildings for their Basilicas. This basilica design was then copied in the glorious Byzantine churches of which St: Sophia in Constantinople is the greatest example. When church building revived in the West during the eleventh century, the Byzantine models were perhaps unconsciously followed.

The Romanesque church was constructed of stone instead of wood. It had huge, thick walls with few windows. The most characteristic feature was the rounded arch used in the doorways and windows. The heavy walls were given extra support by buttresses. The Romanesque church was built usually in the form of a cross, often with a dome over the transepts, and two towers in front. Inside, the effect was one of heavy magnificence, because the large amount of wall space left room for frescoes and mosaics in brilliant

Medieval Architecture. Byzantine: Mosque of St. Sophia in Istanbul, above. Romanesque: Abbaye aux Hommes in Caen, above right. Ornate Gothic: Great Milan cathedral, below. English Gothic: Canterbury Cathedral, right. French Gothic: Reims Cathedral, bottom left, Notre Dame Cathedral in Amiens, bottom right. (Ewing Galloway, British Information Services)

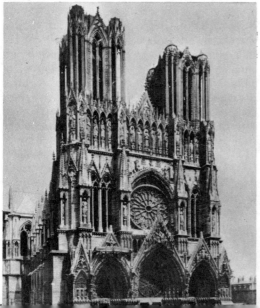

English Stained Glass of the 15th century. This is a window from Beauchamp Chapel in Warwick. The secret of these stained glass windows has been lost

Gargoyle, above, on the battlements of Notre Dame Cathedral in Paris. Choir of Canterbury Cathedral, below, is notable for fine ornamentation and use of arches. (Paul's Photos, British Information Services)

colors. Statuary of a polychrome sort added to the colorful effect.

Contrasted with the Romanesque, the Gothic architecture which originated in the late twelfth and thirteenth centuries, seems severe and a trifle cold. Because Gothic is located mostly in northern Europe, where light is needed, it became necessary to cut away as much of the stone wall as possible. It was discovered that a great part of the wall could be cut away and support given by flying buttresses. The pointed arch and the high-pitched roof became the distinctive features. Inside, the groined vault was used. By these means, an effect of great height could be achieved, giving the building an appearance of being light and airy.

Perhaps the main glory of the Gothic church is its decoration. Aside from the abundance of fine and detailed carving, including the gargoyles—those queer figures of men and animals which decorated the gutter spouts,—the chief beauty lay in the stained glass windows whose secrets of color and pattern have died out of modern art. All the symbolism of the Gothic church is a study in itself.

The contrasted feelings inspired by these two forms have been aptly expressed in these words: "The Romanesque brings the glory of heaven down to earth, while the Gothic reaches fingers of frozen prayer to heaven."

27. The Medieval Towns

THE RISE OF THE MEDIEVAL TOWN

THE CITY HAS BECOME THE SYMBOL and the scene for modern civilization. For this reason, the growth of towns in the later Middle Ages has a significance which is hard to overemphasize. Western civilization is primarily an urban phenomenon, and modern metropolitan life had its beginning in the early medieval towns.

Large cities were not an innovation of the Middle Ages. Practically every ancient culture went through a stage when life was centered in the cities, and archeologists are still busy uncovering ancient buried cities from the debris that has covered them during the ages. Even during and after the decline of the Roman Empire, cities continued to exist although largely reduced to insignificance. Life in these cities had reverted to an agrarian stage, and cultural activities virtually disappeared. Yet, throughout the Middle Ages two large cities flourished in southern Europe, both the product of a foreign civilization. One was Constantinople, the capital of the Byzantine Empire; the other was the great center of Moorish culture in Spain, the city of Cordova. These were huge metropolises, each containing a population of more than five hundred thousand.

After the eleventh century the beginning of an urban movement may be discerned. Italy was the scene of the earliest development of towns. Here it was that the lively contact with distant lands, as well as the stimulus of the Crusades, influenced the life of the Italian people. The growth of trade with the East and the resulting prosperity greatly fostered aggregations of people which proved favorable for the development of commerce. Furthermore, Italy was a fertile country with a pleasing climate, and centrally located between the East and northern Europe. In Italy, where feudalism had never become strong, the towns usually sprang out of the old Roman settlements. Northern Europe soon followed with a great number of flourishing towns, especially commercial centers which prospered on the profitable herring fisheries in the North Sea and the Baltic. Towns were built at strategic locations on the sea coast, on rivers, or, for protection, on hills. In northern countries most towns received their populations from the medieval manors. While here, as in Italy, numerous towns developed from centers colonized by Romans, we must note that especially in the north the urban movement was an original, local force, and not a re-awakening of Roman cities. Climate, resources, native industries, and in some cases historical background, were some of the factors involved in the formation of new urban centers.

FROM MANOR TO TOWN

Throughout the Middle Ages the manor was the center of feudal social life. It was practically an independent unit which required little contact with the outside world. A self-sufficient community, then, it subsisted with a fair degree of prosperity on such agricultural and industrial pursuits as would supply its own needs. The first indications of the medieval urban movement were the settlements of a few traders and merchants outside of the feudal castle. The nobles were eager to acquire the textiles, ornaments, and other luxuries from foreign lands, so they frequently encouraged the merchants in their new settlements. They were able to obtain

A Manorial Chamber of the 14th century. The huge fireplace was the heating system. The bedchamber was closed off from the rest of the room by curtains

privileges and exemptions from feudal obligations in consideration of certain money payments. These arbitrary commercial communities were usually walled and their inhabitants were called burghers from the name of their settlement, the burg. It was not long until they attempted to obtain complete independence from the overlord, and their early struggles were often unsuccessful. But gradually a more rigid organization, substituting compulsory memberships, under oath of loyalty, for the early voluntary membership, and the need for common defense made a definite, strong community out of the early primitive settlements. They were soon able to achieve virtual freedom from the lord and founded the *commune*, the smallest politically independent unit.

The strife for freedom usually involved numerous battles with the old authorities. Not only the lay lords, but also the Church and royal or imperial authority, opposed the movement for autonomy. Yet the desire for money often moved the nobility to grant charters which guaranteed the burgs protection from arbitrary and outrageous exactions.

The early burgs soon developed into medieval towns. They grew because of a natural increase in population as well as the influx of escaped serfs who automatically were granted freedom after having resided in the town for one year. With this small aggregation of citizens and a certain amount of industry and commerce as a start, the cities were now ready to develop in their own particular environment and according to their individual character.

CRAFT AND MERCHANT GUILDS

The heart of the social and municipal life of the medieval town was the guild. Each worker in a certain craft or profession was a member of his particular craft guild. There were guilds for barbers, carpenters, cobblers, butchers, scribes, lawyers; every vocation in life was represented by a guild. Membership was compulsory, and adherence to guild regulations was rigidly enforced. Their main purpose was to insure satisfactory living conditions by enjoying a monopoly of the craft. They further saw to it that there was a continuous supply of workers in a particular type of work, and established certain standards of quality to which their members must conform. It was their endeavor to give apprentices a thorough training and to produce good work at fair prices. This policy, while protecting the customer at first, later degenerated into an unsocial monopolization which often outrageously exploited patrons and purchasers.

The control of the guild was in the hands of the masters. They admitted to their workshops a number of apprentices who worked for the master in return for the privilege of learning the craft. Having served his apprenticeship, the beginning craftsman received a small donation from his master and started out on the road as a journeyman. He now worked for various masters and received daily wages, whereas while an apprentice he received no pay. Upon completion of a certain masterpiece and other qualifications, such as the possession of a certain amount of capital, a journeyman became a master. Apprentices and journeymen had their room and board at the house of the master. To a journeyman it was therefore often desirable to enter the employ of a master who showed signs of old age or weakness, so that when the latter died, the journeyman might succeed to the business by marrying the widow. While new members were at first freely admitted into the guild, there developed

Officer of the Mint stamps out coins. The right to coin money was held by many lords, who often debased the coins to increase the profit to themselves

Goldsmith's Workshop. Etienne Delaulne, 16th century Parisian, made this engraving of his shop

Papermaking was introduced into Spain by the Moors in the 12th century; by 1400 paper was widely used in western Europe. It was made by hand

16th Century Printing Shop. Apprentice at the right is applying inking ball to the form; pressman is at left, and in the background are typesetters

Bookbinder's Workshop. Even after the introduction of paper and the invention of printing, bookmaking remained the work of craftsmen

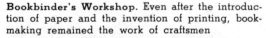

At the Gunsmith's. Small arms were important to all. Ornate scrollwork done by hand was considered one of the most important features of a weapon

later a tendency to exclude everyone except the members of the masters' families. The qualifications for journeymen to become masters were made more difficult; standards and fees were raised, greater capital was necessary. Consequently, journeymen were reduced to the status of mere wage earners, and an unwholesome relationship between employers and employees developed.

The guilds not only entertained economic aims, but also were very socially-minded bodies. They emphasized the equality of guild members, and no one was to suffer injustices at the hands of other members. When a member was ill or in distress, he was visited by appointed members who brought him gifts and nourishment. Members would attend baptisms, marriages, and funerals in one another's families, and give mutual help in difficulties, such as debts or imprisonment.

Besides the craft guilds, there existed merchant guilds which included all persons with common commercial interests. These guilds had aims and regulations similar to those of the craft guilds. Overlords had generally encouraged them in their early beginning, and the guilds had been largely responsible for obtaining the town charter and special privileges from the lord. The merchant guilds rose to great prominence in the town government, for they usually had a dominant share in the magistracy. Often they were guilty of furthering only their own interests. Later, with the rise of craft guilds, the merchants had many difficulties in keeping the new class from town rule.

TOWN GOVERNMENT

The typical medieval town was ruled by a council of magistrates who were elected either by the people, or by means of some complicated system. The magistrates had both administrative and judicial duties. Medieval town government was generally of a very democratic nature, especially in the earlier stages, and it has been often looked upon as the first representative government in Western civilization. In many cities, however, the magistracy dwindled into a handful of moneyed aristocrats. Venice is the outstanding example of this dominance of the merchants. Towns conferred citizenship upon burghers only after they had met a number of property and character qualifications. Usually outsiders were excluded from citizenship, but there were numerous

Receiver of Taxes in his office. As the feudal system was broken up, the dues which had been paid to the lord were supplanted by governmental taxes

Tradesmen Pay Toll to cross a bridge. Such tolls were designed to protect the local tradesmen and to maintain the bridge; the revenue was often misused

exceptions. There was evidence of a local patriotic spirit similar to that which is exemplified in modern times by such slogans as "Trade at Home!", "Buy British!" or "Buy American!" The privilege of citizenship was highly prized by the burgher and in return he promised to conform to the laws of the city and to fulfill his military duties.

Siege of a Town. The besieging forces are issuing a summons for the inhabitants of the town to lay down their arms and open the gates

MEDIEVAL COMMERCE

The smallest trading centers in the Middle Ages were the markets. These were of a distinctly local character, the exchange of goods being confined largely to the neighboring regions. Of much greater and even international significance were the fairs which developed along with improvements in the systems of communication. Originally merely incidental to religious pilgrimages, they subsequently developed into regular seasonal occurrences to which flocked merchants from all parts of Europe. With the revival of oversea trade, mainly because of the activities of the Italian cities, goods from the Orient, from Africa, and from Scandinavia were represented at these fairs.

What the robber Vikings destroyed in commercial intercourse in the early Middle Ages, they made up for by stimulating and establishing new trade centers. Despite their activities as pirates, they had opened up trade relations in the Baltic region and with Russia. Because of the extensive domination of the Mediterranean coasts by the Moslems, some oriental products found their way into Europe by way of Russia. During the time of the Crusades, the Italian cities were opened to a lively commerce with the East. Constantinople had largely dominated the oriental trade, but this monopoly was seized by Venice when this city, in conjunction with a Crusade, sacked Constantinople in the opening of the thirteenth century. Between the Italian cities themselves there existed a bitter rivalry, but Venice and Genoa were able to maintain their prominent positions. In northern Europe the commercial towns united into powerful leagues, thus enabling themselves to present a united front against rival nations as well as maintaining their independence against imperial authority. The most famous of these, the Hanseatic League, comprised a number of flourishing cities, with trading posts in London and central Russia.

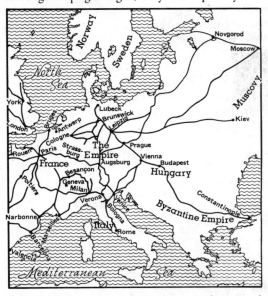

Important Towns and Trade Routes of medieval Europe. Commerce influenced the location of castles. Towns were an integral part of feudal society

Dues on Wines were often collected by religious orders through the right granted to them by a king

With the increase of commercial activity there arose a definite need for a larger banking system. The banks that sprang up were a contribution to our modern civilization. Successful banking families, like the Medici and the Peruzzi, became prominent in politics as well as in business. There was a tendency to devise more satisfactory systems of coinage, and attempts were made to standardize the currency.

LIFE IN A MEDIEVAL TOWN

Although each medieval town experienced its own characteristic history, it had a few factors in common with the other towns. It was encircled by a strong wall with dozens of fortified towers, pierced by four or five large gates providing the only means of entrance. For further protection there was usually a moat outside the wall. The gates were locked up in the evening, by which time peddlers, and usual-ly the Jews, had to leave the city.

The walls naturally restricted the ground for building, and as a consequence many peculiar forms of houses developed. Lack of space was pitifully apparent in the narrow streets scarcely wide enough to permit a small cart to be driven through them. Many houses, in in order to obtain more floor space, were built with protruding upper stories so that from the street the sky was hardly visible. The streets were constructed to fit the unevenness of the landscape and there was no semblance of regularity. The cathedral and the city hall, located in a large, central square, dominated the town.

The houses of the well-to-do were often of imposing dimensions and beauty. The lower floor was usually occupied by business quarters. Homes of the common people were less pretentious and suffered from lack of light and fresh air, a condition which favored disease and pestilence.

Medieval towns with their narrow, crooked streets and houses crowded together, knew little of sanitation. Heaps of refuse littered the streets, a method of garbage disposal which must have pleased the pigs wandering about in search of food. A housewife used the nearest window for getting rid of dirty water, much to the annoyance of whatever unfortunate pedestrian might be in the way. Conditions of this sort continued to exist for several centuries. In spite of its picturesque features, the medieval town would hardly be attractive to the citizen of a modern community with its means of sanitation.

Mountebank's Stage was one of the sources of entertainment for people in medieval times. The mountebank used a simple stage illuminated by torches for the performance to promote the sale of his quack medicine

28. European States in Transition

THE DECAY OF FEUDALISM

As WE STUDY THE RISE and fall of political and social orders, we come to the conclusion that forces of change, either growth or retrogression, are bred within each system. No mode of life tends to perpetuate itself; as it develops, it produces the forces which will bring about its dissolution or upon which a new order will be built. The feudal system gives us one of our best examples of this historical evolution.

Feudalism was an attempt to bring order out of the chaos in Europe following the end of the Roman Empire and the Roman Peace. It set up a large number of self-sufficient states based on an agricultural society. But the very success of the feudal system prepared the way for something new. Its perfection spelled its doom. For when feudalism succeeded in restoring order, and when it brought a small measure of culture and prosperity, Europe was ready for a revival of trade and town life. The towns, natural enemies of the feudal overlords from whom they struggled to gain their freedom, became supporters of the kings. The townspeople stood to gain by the development of national states, for trade, the lifeblood of the towns, was better able to develop in a strong national state than in a heterogeneous collection of warring duchies.

So, side by side with the decline of the power of the feudal barons and the rise of the towns, went the growth of national power. As we shall see, strong kings arose in England and France, and they gradually expanded their power at the expense of the nobles. A money revenue was necessary to the establishment of a strong royal power, and the beginning of wealth in the form of goods and money, rather than in land alone, gave the kings a more available source of revenue.

The introduction of the cannon ended walled castles as a means of defense, and the long bow made foot soldiers, recruited from the ranks of the common people, more serviceable in warfare than the heavily armored knight.

The power and influence of the Church declined hand in hand with feudalism. The national states became powerful enough to defy the papacy, and improvement in the material comforts of many people caused their interest to shift from the life after death to life in this world. Thus, in the cultural and religious sphere, the way was paved for Humanism, the Renaissance, and Reformation.

FRANCE FINDS A KING

France, the most highly developed of the feudal nations, was the first of the continental countries to develop a centralized government. By the twelfth century royal power was definitely in the ascendancy. France was fortunate in having an unbroken line of monarchs which produced several energetic, able rulers. The royal administration was characterized by more intelligent and better trained men, drawn from the ranks of the clergy in large part, than was the case with the courts of the feudal barons. A characteristic of all the developing national states was the growth of the power of the king in the administration of justice. This factor is discernible in twelfth-century France, where traveling judges of the king's court brought royal justice to scattered parts of the realm.

Silhouetted against this background of increasing monarchical power, stands the figure of Philip II, known as Philip Augustus, who ruled from 1180 to 1223. To him, more than to any other French monarch, is due the

Medieval Siege Artillery, left, from a 16th century engraving. French archers, right. The introduction of cannon reduced the power of castles; the long bow helped remove armored knights from the scene

credit for the growth in power and prestige of the kingship. Philip was successful in the fields of administration, war, and diplomacy. He gave the townspeople a place in the administration of Paris, and their representatives met with the nobles and clergy. Philip, among all the kings of medieval France, was alone in his aid to the townspeople in establishing new communes, and the rents he derived from them increased his revenue. Royal finances improved under Philip. He levied heavy taxes, forced the feudal nobles to pay him fees, and resorted to borrowing from the Templars and the Jewish bankers.

The great accomplishment of Philip was the increase in the royal domain. For years Philip struggled to gain the French holdings of Henry II of England, but not until the reign of John was he successful in defeating his greatest vassals. Thus he acquired Normandy, Maine, Anjou, and Touraine, but the struggle with England was to go on intermittently for many decades.

Although many of the great lords continued to keep their holdings under Philip, he made them feel the force of his power, and invaded their once supreme rights in their own territories. Part of this influence was gained by interference with marriages and part by skillful diplomacy. Philip acquired something of a half-interest in many fiefs; he dictated appointments and received part of the revenue, which he demanded be paid in currency. As time went on, the royal interest in these great holdings became more and more dominant.

Great public improvements were initiated. The streets of Paris were paved and its walls were enlarged. Thus Paris has been spoken of as the first city to exhibit the characteristics of a great European capital.

King Louis VIII and the papal legate entering Avignon during the crusade against the Albigensians

ROYAL POWER MOVES SOUTH

When Philip died after his long reign of forty-three years, he left to his son, Louis VIII, a France wealthier and more powerful than it had been since the days of Charlemagne. While Louis was not as capable as his father, the kingdom went forward in his reign. During his father's lifetime, Louis joined the crusade against the Albigensian heretics in southern France, and when he came to the throne in 1223 he continued the Holy War. Finally, at a great cost in human blood, the heresy was stamped out. From this time forward the power of the king was paramount in southern France.

SAINT LOUIS

The untimely death of Louis in 1226 seemed a likely moment for England and the French nobles to regain the territories and prerogatives lost to Philip II, for the crown of France rested on the head of twelve-year-old Louis IX. But

St. Louis and his Brothers taken prisoners by the Saracens in 1250; they were soon released

these plans were thwarted by a strong regency under the control of the widowed queen, Blanche. She was a pious and able woman who left the stamp of her character upon Louis. Because of his religious life and good works, he was canonized and is known to history as St. Louis, diverging far from the general run of medieval monarchs.

Despite his piety, Louis gave France a strong government. When the nobles of southwestern France revolted against him in 1242, Louis was brought into conflict with their ally, Henry III of England. But his armies soon put down the revolt, and from 1243 to the end of the reign France was free from internal strife.

The spread of royal power was accompanied again by a broadening of jurisdiction of the king's courts. The king's coinage was made sole currency in the royal domain, and Louis forced the nobles to allow its circulation in their realms. The improvement of the royal coinage soon made it more acceptable to the people than that produced by the local lords.

To the reign of Louis IX may be traced the development of the French judiciary and treasury. Louis broadened the sphere of the royal courts, and became famed throughout Europe as a dispenser of justice. With increase of the number of cases appealed to the king's

St. Louis Serving the Poor. This French king built hospitals and visited and tended the sick

courts, a special group of members of the Great Council was set up to hear such cases. Likewise, another group of members of the Great Council was detailed to care for the financial transactions of the king's household.

COMPLETION OF FRENCH TERRITORIAL EXPANSION

Philip the Bold (Philip III), king of France, 1270-1285

The reign following that of Louis was of distinctly less importance, for Philip III (1270-1285) did not possess the great ability or outstanding character of his father. But he inherited a strong kingdom, and little initiative was needed to complete the work which had been carried so far. When the heiress of the county of Champagne was married to his son, that district came under the control of the crown. And the final territorial acquisition of the medieval French kings came when Poitu escheated to the king. Thus the boundaries were rounded out, and they remained substantially the same until the advent of the modern period.

With the reign of Philip IV, or Philip the Fair, the transitional stage of the French kingdom may be said to be concluded. The centralized state was brought into a form which we should today recognize as a nation. Let us see what some of these characteristics were.

Philip gave France a national standing army, supported by the king's treasury. Thus the old feudal levy disappeared in favor of a trained body of soldiers. A large body of administrators was needed to look after the various affairs of the kingdom, and control of these officials was centralized under the king. They were required to submit to him reports of the progress of their work.

And finally, the reign of Philip marks the end of papal power within the nation. Philip engaged in a long conflict with the pope over the

Siege of the Fortress Gerberoi. William the Conqueror being rescued after he was wounded by his eldest son, Robert. Defeated, William soon gave up the siege of Robert's castle, and, shortly afterward, father and son were reconciled for a brief time

right to tax the clergy, and in the end the king won out. He refused to permit the export of bullion, and thus a great part of the revenue of the pope was cut off. Another conflict arose over the arrest and trial of a representative of the pope. In a papal bull, which marked the highest claim of the papacy to authority, Boniface VIII stated that "submission to the bishop of Rome on the part of everyone is altogether necessary to salvation." Philip was excommunicated, but he appealed to the people and clergy of France to vindicate him. He received their support and then went on to invade the papal states in Italy. The pope was taken prisoner and treated with great disrespect. Thus did the emergent national state triumph over the most powerful institution of the medieval world.

SONS OF WILLIAM THE CONQUEROR

After William the Conqueror died, his son William Rufus, or William the Red, ruled England from 1087 to 1100. His exactions of money, his unfair use of church revenues, and the cruel, unjust treatment of his subjects, made him very unpopular. His most serious trouble was the result of a quarrel with Anselm, Archbishop of Canterbury, who wished to go to Rome to receive the emblems of his

Death of William Rufus. While hunting, he was shot by an arrow from an unknown hand. His brother, Henry, rode away to claim the throne

office from the pope. William objected because there were two claimants for the papal office and the archbishop's journey would make it necessary to recognize one or the other as the true pope. For political reasons William was unwilling to do this. Moreover, he was unwilling to make certain reforms desired by the archbishop, for they would have deprived him of some of the revenue which he was unfairly receiving. The quarrel was something of a draw; after long friction Anselm won the right to make his journey, but, discouraged in his efforts at reform, he went into voluntary exile.

In 1100 the king was accidentally killed, and the crown passed to his younger brother Henry. His first act was to bid for popularity by granting a charter promising to reform all the abuses of his brother's reign. Soon, however, he took up the quarrel with Anselm. This struggle was far more fundamental than a mere difference between two men; the real question was whether the Church or the State should be supreme, a problem which agitated all Europe during the Middle Ages.

The particular issue upon which Anselm and Henry differed, was lay investiture. Lay investiture owed its importance to the fact that those who gave church officials the symbols of their office could in reality veto church elections. The quarrel was settled by a compromise: the king could not invest churchmen with their symbols of office, but he would receive homage from them for the land they held as feudal vassals. This looked like a victory for the Church, but in reality the king was strong enough to continue influencing church elections.

Some of Henry I's principal difficulties during the early part of his reign were with his eldest brother, Robert. In dividing his holdings among his sons, William the Conqueror favored his third son, William Rufus, by giving him England; Robert, whom he regarded as weak and irresolute, and who had engaged in several revolts against his father, was given the dukedom of Normandy. Richard, the second son, had been killed earlier, while hunting, and Henry, the youngest, was given only a monetary grant. Robert remained duke of Normandy throughout William Rufus' reign, though he pledged the lands to raise funds to go on the First Crusade. On his return in 1100, he found his youngest brother Henry on the English throne. In 1101 Robert invaded England, but Henry met him and their difficulties were temporarily settled without battle. But the peace did not last. Henry regarded Robert as a threat to his own security, and in 1106 he crossed into Normandy, and at the Battle of Tinchebrai took his brother prisoner. Robert was well treated, but remained a prisoner until his death in 1134.

On the whole, Henry was a good king. He maintained order and preserved justice. In fact, so great was his reputation for protecting the weak against the strong, that he was called "the lion of justice." He was a good financial manager and efficiently organized the exchequer, or treasury department. He strengthened his control over the country by sending royal judges, called itinerant justices, over the land to hear cases. Finally, he waged no major wars, although he did take an active part in international affairs.

Unfortunately, the next reign undid much of Henry's work. As he lay dying, in 1135, leaving no sons, he wanted his daughter Mathilda to rule. But a woman ruler was not welcomed by the barons and Mathilda's husband, Geoffrey of Anjou, was not popular. Thus it was fairly easy for Stephen, the son of the Conqueror's daughter, to win the crown. Yet, he was never able to wear it securely. In order to gain support he was forced to weaken the monarchy by making concessions to the great nobles who soon indulged in private warfare, discovering that Stephen could not preserve order. In 1138, a rebellion in favor of Mathilda broke out, lasting until 1153, when a peace was arranged providing that Stephen should continue to be king during his lifetime, but that Mathilda's son, Henry, should succeed him. The next year Stephen died.

LIKE GRANDFATHER, LIKE GRANDSON

Henry II, king of England, 1153-89

When Henry II came to the throne, his one aim was to restore the country to its condition under his grandfather. Not only was he successful in this, but he also left the monarchy much stronger than it had been under Henry I. He preserved law and order, further centralized the government, codified the law, and curtailed the rights of the private courts which feudal lords held, though these courts remained strong.

Like his grandfather he became involved in a quarrel with the archbishop, Thomas à Becket. The quarrel was over the right of the royal courts to punish criminal clergymen. At a great council at Clarendon in 1164, the king produced the Constitutions of Clarendon, a written statement of the laws he wished the clergy to observe in this matter, based on the settlement of William the Conqueror. The archbishop said that church law was superior to national law and refused to give way. After long friction, the king in a fit of rage spoke words which led four of his knights to seek out Becket, now returned from a period of exile, and to murder him in his cathedral (1170).

Murder of Thomas à Becket in the cathedral at Canterbury. Becket was later buried in the cathedral, and his shrine was long a favorite object of pilgrimage, as described in Chaucer

Public opinion was scandalized, and Henry was forced to make peace with the pope by surrendering the right to punish criminal clergymen, though he held out on some other points.

Under Henry II, Wales, which had never been thoroughly conquered, came more definitely under the control of the English kings. The Scottish king, who was helping Henry's rebellious subjects, was captured, and Henry forced him to do homage for Scotland as a dependency of England. Ireland, too, came partly under his control through the efforts of a small group of nobles, who founded the Irish Pale and paved the way for the future hatred and friction between the two countries. Finally, Henry had great trouble because of his sons, Henry, Richard, Geoffrey, and John. Eager for power, they grew dissatisfied and, with the encouragement of their mother, who had quarreled with Henry, they rebelled one by one. Henry's enemies, particularly Philip Augustus of France, used them as pawns against their father. After varying success he was at length humiliated, for, shortly before his death in 1189, he was defeated by Philip together with Geoffrey and Richard.

Richard the Lionhearted watching the massacre by his order of Saracen prisoners captured at Acre in 1191, during the Third Crusade. This was the chief blot on Richard's often-storied career

Death of Richard while he was besieging Chalus. The picture has two scenes. At lower left, Richard and his force depart for Normandy. At upper right, the English king has been mortally wounded by an arrow

THE LION-HEARTED KING AND HIS SUCCESSOR

Richard, the oldest surviving son of Henry II, succeeded to the throne. His reign (1189-1199) is important chiefly for the part which he played in the Third Crusade. His deeds of valor won him the leadership of the Crusade and a lasting fame, but did not recover the Holy City. On the way home he was captured by the Duke of Austria, and English subjects were forced to pay huge sums to ransom him. After a brief visit to England for money, he collected an army for war against Philip Augustus and his brother John, who were striving for Normandy, but he died from a battle-wound while the result of the war was still undecided.

John, with some justice, has been called the worst of the Plantagenet line of kings. He carried on the war against his late ally, Philip, who was striving for the English possessions in France; but through mismanagement he lost all of his French holdings except the larger part of the province of Acquitaine. Next, he became involved in a quarrel with Pope Innocent III over the election of the Archbishop of Canterbury. When John refused to accept the papal candidate, Stephen Langton, the pope replied first with an interdict and then with a sentence of excommunication. John might have held out, had he not been ruling his kingdom so badly that his subjects were thinking of revolt. So, when the pope declared him deposed and told Philip Augustus to carry out the sentence, John was forced to give in to all the papal demands.

MAGNA CARTA

Soon afterward John returned from an unsuccessful war with Philip to find his barons demanding reforms based on the charter of Henry I. On June 15, 1215, the barons met him at Runnymede and made him sign the document known as the Great Charter, or Magna Carta, generally considered to be the basis of the English constitution. There were many provisions remedying the worst evils of his reign, depriving him of certain rights, and safeguarding law and order. Most important of all was the provision that the king was bound to rule by the well-established laws of

The Magna Carta. Here King John is shown being confronted by the leaders of the revolt against his arbitrary rule. Their demands for reform were later ratified as the Great Charter

the kingdom, and giving his subjects the right to revolt if he should not.

John's son, Henry III (1216-1272), was to know the meaning of that last provision. Since he was a boy of nine when he inherited the throne, there was a long regency, during which he was under the protection of the papacy for the most part and a papal legate ruled. For a time Hubert de Burgh, who was hostile to the papacy, controlled affairs; but when Henry took over the government he soon (1232) dismissed him.

TROUBLE WITH THE BARONS

The next forty years were troubled ones. The king, who was weak and willful, tried to rule with personal favorites whom he brought over from the Continent. He was extravagant and exacted high taxes and otherwise mismanaged affairs. He was always under the domination of the pope and allowed him to take large amounts of money out of England in the form of taxes on the English clergy. For all these reasons he was very unpopular, and the barons at length decided to take matters into their own hands. They forced the king to submit to the Provisions of Oxford (1258) which provided that all royal officials be re-

The Provisions of Oxford, resulting from demands made upon Henry III by the council, made all royal officials responsible to a council of barons

sponsible, not to the king but to a council of fifteen which represented the barons. The new government worked badly, however, for the barons could not agree upon what they wanted done. There was great confusion and finally war.

By this time the leader of the barons was Simon de Montfort, a French and English noble who had very liberal ideas about reform and the rights of the middle class. In 1264 he forced Henry to agree to the *mise of Lewes* which put the government in a council of nine dominated by Simon. He called a great council which was notable for the fact that representa-

tives of both towns and rural districts were called to sit with the barons. But some of the barons were alarmed at this liberalism and the next year Simon was killed in battle. Thus the movement failed and the kingdom was at peace until Henry's death in 1272.

CONSTITUTIONAL MONARCHY

Edward I (1272-1307) as a boy learned many lessons from the troubles of his father, and his reign was, for the development of the English constitution, the most important of any in the Middle Ages. He codified the law more systematically than it had ever been done before and made many new laws. He deprived the feudal lords of some of their most important privileges, including the right to hold private courts for their tenants, and made their military duties less important by requiring others as well to be fully equipped and ready to serve the king in battle. He reorganized the central administration of the government very thoroughly by making officers of his personal household or wardrobe, into government officials and placing members of the middle class, who would be loyal, in such positions. The government financial system was also improved and the courts were made more accessible to the people.

One of the most important of the changes under Edward was the fact that he summoned representatives of the towns and rural districts to consult with the great council. They had been summoned before on certain occasions, especially by Simon de Montfort, but Edward was the first to call them regularly, and thus make their presence a normal part of the government. The parliament, as it was now getting to be called, which he summoned in 1295 came to be known as the Model Parliament, because later ones were formed on the same plan. In 1297 the king confirmed the various charters of liberties that had been granted before him, and at that time was established the principle that the king could not impose nonfeudal taxes without the consent of the commons, the name given to the new representatives of the towns and country districts. This was the foundation of the later, well-known principle of "no taxation without representation."

On the whole, Edward got along very well with the papacy, and co-operated with the pope to tax the clergy. He did oppose successfully the papal bull, *Clericis laicos*, which forbade clergy to pay taxes to the king without the consent of the pope. The Parliament of Carlisle in 1307 restricted the papal power to collect taxes from the English clergy.

Edward undertook campaigns against the Welsh, whose princes were becoming too strong and getting out of hand. He conquered the country completely, and by the Statute of Wales in 1284 organized it as it was to remain for centuries. He also took advantage of a disputed succession in Scotland to insist upon his claim as overlord of the country; but the people resisted his claim and set aside the king who had done homage to him. Edward, therefore, invaded and conquered Scotland. But the Scotch under William Wallace, and later under Robert Bruce, successfully rebelled and when Edward died in 1307, a haphazard war was still going on between the two countries.

Edward II, unlike his father, was a weak king with little ability. He carried on the war against Scotland, but was so badly defeated at the Battle of Bannockburn (1314) that Scottish independence for the rest of the Middle Ages was assured. Worse yet, he was in constant

The Coronation Chair in Westminster Abbey. On the sacred Stone of Scone embedded in it, all English kings since Edward I have been crowned

The Message of the Spurs. Robert Bruce being given the spurs sent him by his friend De Clare, to warn him of the approach of the English

Robert Bruce at Bannockburn. He is showing his followers the battleaxe with which he killed Henry de Bohun in single combat before the battle

trouble with the barons. They had objected to his father's policy of taking away their influence in the government and had tried to remedy the situation in 1311. Against Edward II they had more success, and a conspiracy led by the queen and her lover, Roger Mortimer, finally forced the king to abdicate in favor of his son, Edward III (1327). Shortly afterward Edward II was murdered. The English monarchy was so strong, however, that even the reign of a weak king did not lessen the authority or power of the crown.

THE HOLY ROMAN EMPIRE

Under Otto the Great, as we have seen, the Empire had risen to be the most powerful force in Europe. But it did not tend toward the formation of a nation. The very forces which contributed to its influential position in the feudal world delayed the unification of Germany and Italy into national states. The emperors relied on the support of a political clergy to strengthen their power. The policy of gaining the support of the lesser nobles by granting them portions of larger fiefs, and making these grants hereditary, also delayed German nationalism. Eventually the result was the division of Germany into literally hundreds of semiautonomous states.

Another cause for the failure of Germany to develop into a nation was the Italian policy of the emperors. Instead of concerning themselves with Germany's internal affairs, they consistently went off on futile expeditions south of the Alps. Thus they wasted their resources in fruitless friction with the Italian states, while the unruly nobles were given every opportunity to assert their own power.

On the death of Henry V in 1225, three years after the Council of Worms, the nobles once again seized the right to choose the emperor by election, for Henry died without heirs. They chose the Duke of Saxony, Lothair II. Lothair's reign is not outstanding; he followed the practice of interfering in Italian affairs, this time at the invitation of St. Bernard. His successor, also chosen by the nobles, was Conrad III, the nephew of Henry V. He, like his successor, did little to strengthen the power of the king within Germany; the distraction in his reign was the Second Crusade, of which he was made leader.

FREDERICK BARBAROSSA

The successor of Conrad III, Frederick Barbarossa, (1152-1190) was one of the remarkable figures of the medieval period. He was fortunate in his birth, for in him were combined the two rival houses of Guelphs and Ghibellines. These two great families were engaged in a feud which rent Germany and Italy for many years. But Frederick was able

King Edward II in the hands of his jailers after he was forced to give up the throne early in 1327. He was murdered a few months later

Queen Philippa at the feet of her husband, King Edward III, begging him to spare the lives of six hostages taken after the English capture of Calais

to bring temporary peace to the two warring factions by his descent from both families and by diplomatic handling of his cousin, Henry the Lion, the leader of the Guelphs. The freedom which he delegated to Henry was put to safe use: Henry carried on warfare against the Slavs in the East, and established towns and bishoprics in the newly acquired lands. Under Henry's rule Saxony became the center of German commercial life.

But while he established peace at home, Frederick was unable to avoid the pitfall which made the Holy Roman Empire a "brilliant failure." Like his predecessors, he saw himself as heir to the Caesars. Through men from the great University of Bologna he be-

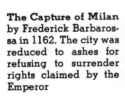

The Capture of Milan by Frederick Barbarossa in 1162. The city was reduced to ashes for refusing to surrender rights claimed by the Emperor

came acquainted with Roman law and imagined himself wielding the despotic power which it granted to the rulers of Rome in her period of glory. But, with all these grand illusions, Frederick was no mere dreamer. He combined a propensity toward religion and grand ideas with the ability to act quickly and shrewdly.

When he had consolidated his position at home, Frederick went off to Italy, where he was crowned king of Lombardy and Holy Roman Emperor. Three years later, Frederick was in Lombardy seeking to assert his imperial prerogatives over the developing commercial cities. To meet his demands would mean surrendering the cities' right of self-government. Milan, which had refused to do homage to Frederick as king in 1158, held out against his demands. So Frederick proceeded to besiege, capture, and destroy the recalcitrant city. The Lombard cities, realizing that their independence was at stake, banded together to form the Lombard League and secured the aid of the pope against the emperor. Distracted by political troubles in Germany, Frederick went to meet the forces of the coalition, and at the Battle of Legnano in 1176, he was decisively defeated. In 1177 he concluded a six-year truce with the Lombards, by then at war among themselves, and composed his differences with the pope. By the Peace of Constance in 1183 Frederick made a final settlement with the Lombards. Their towns recovered full control within their walls, but outside the walls retained only rights already granted. Their position was that of semi-independence under the emperor's loose feudal control.

Frederick now turned his attention to Henry the Lion. The disaster at Legnano was due in part to Henry's lack of support. So Henry's lands were seized and divided among supporters of Frederick, furthering the tendency of feudal Germany to subdivide herself into ever-smaller parts. Once more supreme at home, Frederick added to his power by acquiring Naples and Sicily through the marriage of his son Henry. In this way the Italian kingdom of the Normans was prevented from falling into the control of the enemies of Frederick on the peninsula.

Frederick, greatest of the Ghibelline (Ho-

The Holy Roman Empire under the Hohenstaufens, 1138-1254. The emperors' claims in northern Italy were often challenged by the papacy and the cities of the Lombard League

henstaufen) rulers of Germany, offers a marked contrast to the other monarchs whose methods of creating national states we have observed. While they introduced governmental reforms, Frederick became involved in the tangled affairs of Italy and the papacy. While they gathered more land and power to themselves, Frederick furthered the feudal disintegration of his realm. Nevertheless, under him the empire reached a peak of power. After the fall of the Hohenstaufens, Frederick became a legendary figure—*der alte Kaiser*—who would someday emerge from his centuries-long enchanted sleep in a hidden mountain cavern, and bring peace and unity to Germany.

29. France and England in the Hundred Years' War

NATURE OF THE HUNDRED YEARS' WAR

DURING THE TWELFTH AND THIRTEENTH CENTURIES, the existence of French feudal territories held by the English kings in nominal vassalage from the French rulers, was a constant source of conflict between those monarchs. France, as an expanding, growing nation, looked with envy upon territories so near at hand and seemingly belonging within her own natural boundaries. National consciousness was growing and the French felt that areas in which their own language was spoken should belong to France. A large enough part of France was now ruled directly by the king to enable him to dominate most of the great feudal principalities that were still outside of the royal domain.

On the other hand, the English kings were of the opinion that they had legitimate title to their French possessions. The revenue derived from them made the English kings more independent in their own country. For various reasons they were bent upon extending their influence and power on the continent, but because of the growth of French royal power they had not been successful. British troops usually had to be transported across the channel, while French troops could operate close to their home base and were more easily furnished with supplies and reinforcements. However, at the beginning of the fourteenth century, the duchy of Brittany in the northwest of France, and Guienne and Gascony in the southwest, were the only territories on the continent remaining in English control.

Historical language has given the name of "Hundred Years' War " to the series of intermittent wars which raged between England and France from about 1337 to 1461. Strictly speaking, the term is hardly correct, since it would seem to indicate a century of continual warfare. Rather, wars and battles were fought during certain years, interspersed with long periods of exhaustion and peace.

ECONOMIC AND SOCIAL CAUSES

The causes of the wars were varied and complex. While formerly the rivalries and wars between the monarchs of the two countries had been chiefly a matter of feudal power politics, profound economic and social factors played an important role in the events precipitating the Hundred Years' War. Most of these centered around the interests of the French and English kings in Flanders and Gascony.

Without hesitancy one may say that at the time Flanders was the richest country in Europe. The main source of its wealth was the manufacturing of wool cloth. Such cities as Ghent, Bruges, Ypres, and many others, had an enormous trade in finished wool products. Much of Europe and Asia was dependent on Flanders for these articles. Ypres alone made more than 800,000 pieces of cloth a year.

Politically, the Flemish cities were practically independent, a natural result of their power and glory; but the Count of Flanders owed feudal allegiance to the King of France. French influence and culture were also great in Flanders. As royal power expanded, the French kings looked with longing eyes at Flemish wealth which they regarded as a potential source of taxation. Hence, their policies were designed to extend their political control and influence over these cities. The ruling merchant oligarchies in Flanders usually looked to the French king; the smaller merchants sought help from England. At Courtrai in 1302 the French knights were defeated by the Flemings, but in 1328 the French won at Cassel.

On the other hand, Flanders had closer trade relations with England. The wool for the manufactures of Flanders came from the backs of English sheep. The process of enclosure was already in full swing in the England of that day. Large areas of pasture land were fenced in by the nobility and rich monasteries for the grazing of sheep. In return for wool the English obtained finished cloth, also iron, copper, and other goods from the low countries.

It was thus of vital concern for England that

King Edward III of England, whose claim to France was a cause of the Hundred Years' War

Burgess of Ghent and his wife in church

its sea communications with Flanders remain open. Yet, often English vessels were harassed by French pirates and freebooters. Already at that early date a rivalry for mastery of the sea between the two countries developed. The ensuing war was as much a struggle for commercial supremacy and control of the sea as similar wars in succeeding centuries.

In Gascony, in southern France, a somewhat similar situation prevailed. Gascony was the best wool-growing section on the continent. Its fisheries on the Gulf of Biscay were of great value. The trade of its fine commercial port, Bordeaux, with England was large. It supplied all of England with wine. The duties on these imports from Bordeaux were a great,

independent source of income for the English kings. The latter did not intend to witness calmly French intrigue for the acquisition of Gascony. Since the English king held Gascony in fief from the French king, it was humiliating for the former to pay homage to the latter.

IMMEDIATE CAUSES

An event occurred in France which was to be the immediate cause of the war. The last male heir of the French royal house died in

Ghent, trade center of medieval Flanders, was a powerful city state with more than 200,000 inhabitants

1328 and according to Salic law no women might ascend the throne. Edward III, king of England, a grandson of the deceased French king, now claimed the French crown. Instead, the French barons chose Philip of Valois, or Philip VI, as their king. For the moment Edward III yielded, later to revive his claim for strategic reasons.

Edward III, who ruled from 1327 to 1377, was a man of considerable ability. He realized that war with France was inevitable. Therefore he set out to organize a system of alliances with the purpose of isolating Philip VI. This proved to be an expensive procedure, straining English financial resources to the utmost. The Emperor alone received 400,000 florins in return for his promise to aid Edward.

In Flanders, also, events were leading to a crisis. The new Count of Flanders, related to the French king, inaugurated a pro-French policy. This was more than Edward could bear. Astutely he took advantage of the critical political conditions in Flanders. He supported the working classes, artisans, and peasants in their century-old struggle with the patrician merchant class and the court. If a rebellion were successful, Flanders' pro-French policies might be altered. By placing an embargo on all wool destined for Flanders, thereby stopping Flemish industry, Edward hoped to make the Flemish people realize that only an alliance with England would give them work and prosperity. Since Flanders owed nominal allegiance to the French king, Edward claimed that he was the legitimate heir to the French throne, thereby satisfying the feudal conscience of the Flemish peoples. This declaration meant the same as a declaration of war to Philip VI of France.

Meanwhile, Jacob van Artevelde, capable Flemish citizen-leader, rallied the artisans and workers around him. He heartily denounced the pro-French policy of the nobility and the count. "No wool—no work," proved itself a powerful slogan. In 1340 Edward III received the oath of allegiance of the people of the three largest cities in Flanders. In return, Edward pledged his protection of Flemish trade, privileges, and liberties, and promised return of lost territory.

Jacob van Artevelde, shown here standing in his doorway, roused Flanders against French domination

EARLY PROGRESS OF THE WAR

A naval engagement near the Flemish coast at Sluys in 1340 opened the war. The English and Flemish forces defeated a French fleet of two hundred vessels and as a result established the supremacy of their sea power. In spite of a truce which was observed until 1345, the English and French kings supported opposing sides in a dispute about the duchy of Brittany. The French king by his cruel methods alienated

Sluys, the harbor of Bruges, from an old engraving. Here the English fleet defeated the French in 1340

English capture of Caen in 1346

The Battle of Crécy

The English siege of Calais, captured in 1347

the people of Brittany, who now supported the English more heartily.

In 1346 the English king landed in Normandy with a small but efficient army. This expeditionary force devastated the country around La Hogue but seemed to have no definite aim in mind. Typically of the times, Philip invited Edward to a personal duel. But nothing came of it, since Edward, as the price of defeat, merely wanted to give up his claim to the French throne, while he demanded that Philip put up the throne of France, which the latter actually held, as his stake.

ENGLISH VICTORY AT CRÉCY

Edward now retired into Flanders and took up a position near the village of Crécy. Here the French attacked but were thoroughly defeated. The importance of Crécy in history lay in the fact that, apart from the skillful generalship of Edward, this great triumph was due to English archery and the use of the longbow instead of the old-fashioned crossbow formerly used. Long, steel-tipped shafts were shot from powerful bows carried by English yeomen. The Genoese crossbowmen of the French army were outranged, and their rout impeded the charges of the French mounted knights. The English knights and men-at-arms were dismounted in three divisions, each flanked by lines of bowmen. The triumph of the archery-fire and the dismounted, defensive dispositions of the English force marked the beginning of the eventual doom of the heavily armored feudal knight. Edward the Black Prince, eldest son of Edward III, commanded the English right wing at Crécy, and here established his military reputation.

The victorious English army marched to Calais, the French port on the Straits of Dover, and encamped before the city. To relieve this danger, Philip urged the Scotch to invade England, but the Scotch army was defeated by the English. Since the citizens of Calais stoutly defended their city, and its position was nearly impregnable, Edward decided to starve it out. Because of his control of the sea, he was able to keep all supplies from entering. After a long siege the city was finally forced to surrender. The burghers were treated well, but were told to leave the city. Calais was soon filled with English citizens and for centuries remained a strategic stronghold of British power on the continent.

In 1347 a truce was made which lasted, except for skirmishes in Brittany and Gascony, for a period of eight years. In the meantime the Count of Flanders, with the aid of French troops, had reconquered his territory from his rebellious subjects. The English, however, did nothing to aid the Flemish people. The former had obtained Calais and through their control of the sea were no longer as dependent on the Flemish as formerly.

THE "BLACK DEATH"

From 1348-1349 a new and strange disaster swept through Europe. The "Black Death," a form of bubonic plague, had been brought from Asia by the caravans, and in 1348 decimated the population of the European continent. The disease was so called from the fact that one of the chief symptoms was a discoloring of the skin. A person stricken by it died within three days. The mortality was greatest among the poor and for the entire continent of Europe might have been anywhere from 30 to 50 per cent of the population, although accurate statistics are not obtainable.

The effect of the plague in England was to raise the rate of wages paid by landowners, who now tilled their fields mostly by hired labor, and to cause legislation to compel the peasants to work at fixed wages in their own localities. Much of the land ceased, from lack of laborers, to be tilled for grain, and became pasture for the raising of wool, a great source of profit for landowners and exporters who supplied the looms of the low countries. The plague was thus a factor in the elimination of the yeoman from the English countryside.

RESUMPTION OF THE WAR

John the Good became king of France in 1350, and in 1355 the war was resumed. Edward, Prince of Wales, also called the Black Prince, set out on a plundering expedition and laid waste all Languedoc. King John, pressed for finances, was forced to seek aid from the Estates General, which reluctantly agreed to

The Battle of Poitiers. Fighting desperately, King John of France and his young son are surrounded and forced to surrender to the Black Prince

levy a general tax, on condition that the administration of both collection and disbursement would be in its hands. John had to yield to these demands which he regarded as humiliating; but later the French kings were able to do away with these annoying financial hindrances.

In 1356 John marched south and met the Black Prince at Poitiers. Here the story of Crécy was repeated. Although the French outnumbered the English three to one, the superiority of the English tactics and archery was again demonstrated. John the Good and his son were among the prisoners and were taken to England in captivity. For a time the war ended with the Peace of Brétigny in 1360, by which Edward renounced his claim to the French crown, and received in return the territories of Poitou, Gascony, and Guienne in full sovereignty, not merely as feudal fiefs. These treaties' terms, however, were only of temporary significance since they were soon violated.

INFLUENCE OF WAR ON CONSTITUTIONAL GOVERNMENT IN ENGLAND

The wars did much to break down the internal independence of the king, and brought about certain changes in the relation of sovereign and Parliament. For the continuance of the war he was forced at times to go to Parliament to ask for financial support. Parliament thus came to hold the power of taxation. In exchange for the voting of money, Parliament in the course of time often wrung liberties and privileges from the king.

Parliament often stepped in when kings were unwilling or unable to act. Edward III, at the close of his reign, greatly relaxed his capable vigilance over the country, and it was necessary for Parliament to interfere. The legislation of that period included statutes to prevent appointments by the pope to Church livings in England, and the famous law forbidding suits to be carried or appealed from the king's courts to that of Rome. England already was showing her independence in religious affairs, later to culminate in the various acts of Henry VIII.

INTERNAL EVENTS IN FRANCE

In France, almost a complete breakdown took place after the Treaty of Brétigny. Roving bands of mercenaries, on which both sides had depended during the course of the war, roamed through the country and lived by pillage and plunder. The fact that King John for some time was held as a hostage in England undermined the prestige and power of the central government. The dauphin, or the heir apparent, who ruled in his place, proved himself incapable and flouted the wishes of the Estates General, and this led to serious rioting in Paris. A revolt of the peasantry broke out, called the Jacquerie rebellion, from the term Jacques Bonhomme, referring to the peasant. The peasant had suffered much because of the English devastation of the country, and the heavy tax burden in support of the wars became almost unbearable. Quite naturally he blamed the feudal lords for his misfortunes. The rebellion, which for a time took the proportions of a general revolution, was finally put down by the dauphin, and about twenty thousand peasants were slaughtered in punishment. The Estates General lost in prestige, since the belief was that its attitude had done much to encourage the discontent.

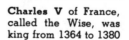

Charles V of France, called the Wise, was king from 1364 to 1380

FRANCE UNDER CHARLES THE WISE (1364-1380)

When Charles V came to the throne of France, he at once began a policy of reform. Both the country's finances and armies were reorganized. The Estates General was placed in the background, since at the beginning of his rule the king had succeeded in inducing the Estates to vote permanent taxes. Since the tax burden was to fall mainly on the common people, the Estates, chiefly representative of the nobility and clergy, readily consented.

Charles V found a

Bertrand du Guesclin, c.1320–80, chief French soldier of his period

The Jacquerie, a French peasant revolt in 1358, was crushed in a battle fought near the city of Meaux

Sea Fight off La Rochelle, 1372. English fleet, carrying men to France, was destroyed by Castilians

John Ball preaching to peasants. He denounced social inequality and helped organize revolt of 1381

capable general in Bertrand du Guesclin, and in 1369 he set out to reorganize and reconquer the territories lost to France. Gradually, the English were driven back, partly because they had lost the capable leadership of the Black Prince, who in ill health had returned to England. On the sea, too, France was more successful and in 1372 the English fleet was defeated at La Rochelle.

The French king was thus able to restore confidence, and because of his efficiency and success the French people rallied to his support. War practically ceased and was not resumed till after the year 1400.

In England, meanwhile, royal power witnessed a temporary decline of popularity. Confidence in royalty was lacking because of the reverses in the war. In 1376 the so-called "Good Parliament" was summoned in order to vote funds for the war. The Parliament reacted

in much the same way as the Estates General of France had previously behaved on a similar occasion. Parliament demanded an audit of all of the public accounts. Two of the king's chief officials, Latimer and Lyons, were impeached by Parliament; it was the first time in history that such procedure was employed.

The conflict of other social forces and interests also made itself felt. Feudalism was declining rapidly, a social change which was accompanied by unrest and discontent. During the reign of Richard II (1377-1399) the end of serfdom was hastened by the famous peasant rising of the men of Kent and Essex in 1381. It has been noted that Parliament after the Black Prince had passed labor laws, ordering that wages be the same as before the plague, though living costs had risen. In addition, Parliament had passed a poll tax, thereby shifting taxes from the merchants and landowners to the common people.

An armed mob of peasants and artisans, several thousand strong, incited by John Ball, a Kentish priest, and led by Wat Tyler, made its way into London. Palaces were burned and the Archbishop of Canterbury and the Chancellor, who were responsible for the taxes, were seized and beheaded. The rebels were finally induced to disperse as the result of lavish promises made by the young king at the suggestion of his advisers. These promises included pardon for the violence done, low rents and the abolition of serfdom, of tolls, and of market dues. Once the trouble was over, the king collected his troops, and Ball and thou-

Richard II meeting leaders of the Peasants' Revolt. King's men killed Wat Tyler, rebel leader

Visit of Richard II to his uncle, John of Gaunt, Duke of Lancaster, at his castle at Pleshy

Richard II giving up his crown to his cousin, the Duke of Hereford, who became Henry IV

sands of peasants were hanged for treason.

During the early years of Richard's minority, Parliament exercised much control over the royal administration. At this time, Parliament was largely representative of the commercial classes and large landholders. On the one hand, it was interested in checking the power of the king; on the other hand, like the other educated and ruling elements of society in that time, it did not even consider the possibility of giving ignorant workingmen and landless farmers a voice in the government.

In 1388, after several attempts by Richard to carry on personal rule, Parliament regained control of the royal administration. Eight years of constitutional rule followed. Then, in 1397, Richard struck back, gained control of Parliament, and established absolute rule. His arbitrary actions alienated all support, and his cousin, Henry of Lancaster, whom he had exiled, organized a plot to overthrow the king. Henry landed in England in 1399, people rallied to his cause, and Richard II, deserted by nearly everyone, was compelled to abdicate. Parliament ratified the abdication and declared Lancaster king as Henry IV; he ruled till 1413. The first years of his reign were marked by numerous revolts. Henry crushed them and was succeeded by his son, Henry V.

WAR WITH FRANCE RESUMED

Meanwhile, in France, a civil war flared up over a disputed succession to the throne. Henry V took advantage of the situation and, like Edward III, acted on the pretext that he had a claim to the French throne. War was resumed and the English invaded France at different times and won some brilliant victories, particularly in the Battle of Agincourt. This brilliant victory over five times the number of Frenchmen, was due, as at Crécy and Poitiers, to the English bowmen. In 1417 Normandy was invaded, and the country ravaged up to the gates of Paris. France, helpless from civil war, was forced to terms in the Treaty of Troyes, whereby Henry V married the French king's daughter Katherine, and it was arranged that on the death of Charles VI, he was to become king of France. The son of Charles VI, however, soon resumed the war, and when Henry V was about to conquer France once more, he suddenly died at Vincennes in 1522. The crown then passed to Henry VI, but the

King Henry IV receiving homage from the nobles after Parliament ratified his overthrow of Richard

French people never acquiesced in English rule. A continued guerrilla warfare was kept up against the foreign conquerors.

In 1429 the youthful King Charles VII lived in southeastern France, where he still retained some territory south of the Loire River. The English, in alliance with Burgundy, controlled the northern part of France and also Gascony, their old possession in the southwest. In order to unite these territories the English decided to capture the city of Orleans, a French stronghold lying between their possessions. In the siege of Orleans, by Henry VI, cannons were used for the first time in history.

JOAN OF ARC

At this junction, while things looked darkest for France, the country was saved from foreign aggression in a most unusual manner. Salvation came in the person of Joan of Arc, the daughter of a small farmer in Champagne. Since her thirteenth year she had heard "voices from heaven" and had seen visions. She brooded over her country's miserable condition. She succeeded in making her way, clad in soldier's garb, to the king, Charles VII, and at last induced him to believe it was her mission to save France from the English. He gave her some troops so that she might try to break the siege of Orleans. On the way to this city her ranks swelled with newcomers. In April, 1429, she took the field clad in a suit of white armor, mounted on a black horse, and

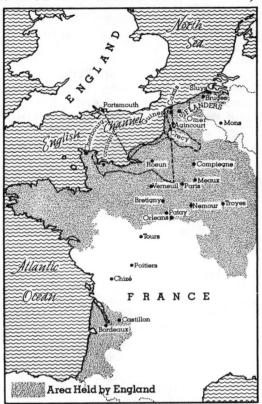

The Hundred Years' War. Broken lines show routes followed by Edward III (1346) and Henry V (1415)

carrying a lance. One English stronghold after another fell to the invincible maid.

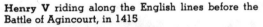

Henry V riding along the English lines before the Battle of Agincourt, in 1415

Burgundians entering Paris during the French civil wars which followed the death of Charles V

In order to understand the success now achieved by Frenchmen against the victors of Crécy, Poitiers, and Agincourt, we must remember the immense power of faith, or credulity of that age. The followers of Joan firmly believed her to be the chosen instrument of heaven. Her enemies, on the other hand, believed she was aided by the dark powers of evil and the devil. All the rest was due to the skill of the new French leaders, the personal courage of Joan, and the restoration of strict discipline in the French army. At Orleans she led the attack against the besiegers, while the inhabitants of the city, encouraged by her advent, took an active part in the battle. The enemy was soon put to flight. Joan then led the triumphant French army to Reims, where Charles VII was formally crowned king in July, 1429.

Her final fate was tragic. In May, 1430, she was captured by the Burgundians, and in the following year she was tried by a court strongly influenced by the English, and found guilty of witchcraft. On the fourteenth of May, 1431, she was burned at the stake in the market place of Rouen.

Following her death, however, the English were no longer successful. Gradually their power in France dwindled. In 1435 the Duke of Burgundy made an alliance with Charles VII, who entered Paris the following year. A period of inaction followed, used by the king to carry out internal reforms. In 1449 the war was renewed, and three years later Bordeaux, the last fortress in English hands except Calais, was taken. The dream of the conquest of France thus came to an end. Succeeding attempts of Edward IV and Henry VII were equally futile.

RESULTS OF THE CENTURY OF CONFLICT

The continual wars had left France in an unfortunate state, and her people had suffered much. A great nation's progress had been retarded for many years. Yet a national feeling and national unity had developed as the result of foreign aggression. In subsequent centuries France was to rise to the rank of the foremost nation in Europe. In the internal struggle for power, both the feudal princes and the Estates General were left behind, and France succumbed to a royal *absolutism*.

The social effects of the war were somewhat different in England. During the conflict the yeoman demonstrated his superiority in battle over the mailed knight. Royal strength was further developed by replacing the old feudal armies with forces of hired commoners and mercenaries. The British Parliament also established traditions which, although temporarily destroyed during the reigns of the Tudors, were later to form the basis of modern English constitutional government.

Joan of Arc telling Charles VII of her mission to help him regain his kingdom and drive out the English

"Joan of Arc, at Domrémy," by Henri Chapu (1833–91). Original in the Louvre

30. The Changing Church

ASSERTION OF WORLDLY AUTHORITY

SINCE THE DISSOLUTION of the Roman Empire the Roman Catholic Church had dominated the Western world. Her severe discipline had kept the half-barbaric successors to the Romans from slipping into paganism and a lower order of society; her authority served to check, in a measure, the destruction brought by brutal and powerful warrior-leaders; and she united, in the face of foes, the strength of Western civilization. Powerful and strict, the Church had controlled Europe for centuries, and with the beginning of the fourteenth century, appeared well able to hold her position. But change, no less effective than it had been in Roman times, was operating to bring about a new social order. The Church, having had to dogmatize her doctrine and concentrate her force, was in a period of stagnation.

The Church had reached a point beyond which it could not go—beyond which it was impossible to go. Having evolved the Medieval System, the Church intended to run it: to care not only for the souls of men, but also for their bodies and their temporal affairs. The whole world was to be ruled by the Church, since the saving of men's souls was dependent to a large extent upon caring for their bodies. It was not pure religious fervor which motivated their will to stewardship, it is regrettable to state, but an altogether worldly desire for money, increased power, and "a place in the sun." The Church had changed in its spiritual and mundane activities from the institution which had repelled the Vikings.

NATIONALISM—THE FOE OF A TEMPORAL CHURCH

Ambitions for increased temporal power met with opposition from unexpected quarters. The princes and the people, instead of aiding the plan, refused to cooperate. They had business of their own. And this fact, the growth of private interest, with a consequent disregard for cosmic affairs or the ramifications of a universal state—the very notion of the "Good Neighbor" attitude advocated in the Sermon on the Mount—is called, summarily, nationalism.

Being nationalistic, England and France flouted the Church. Names were called, and conflict, largely verbal, took place. The Church arose to crush another foe, this time within her own ranks. But she had stagnated too much and, the old methods failing her, was unable to meet the situation. Thus the history of the period is largely the story of how the Church was buffeted first one way and then another; of how she failed to react; and of the social and religious innovations which naturally arose.

Nationalism developed rapidly in England, a country which was never under Charlemagne and which was unified in the struggle with the Northmen. The Norman Conquest, instead of establishing complete feudalism, took such a turn that the king was relatively powerful. The Norman kings, because of their enforced absence, had developed a body of laws which to a great extent governed for them. England was far removed from Rome, and Catholicism never attained a full hold upon the English people. For these and other reasons, chiefly economic, England resented the papal assumption of temporal power.

France was in much the same circumstances. She too had a system of laws and a king who was almost supreme. Her feudal lords were powerful, but were not individually superior to the king, and the number of factors preventing their union rendered their single strength futile. France had a parliament, too, the Estates General, which showed the nobles that national power was necessary, for a time, before a quarrel over spoils could arise. These two nations, therefore, felt imposed upon when the Church attempted to wreck their system.

In the closing years of the thirteenth century, France and England both asserted their right to tax the clergy and proceeded to do so. Edward I of England demanded a fifth from the clergy who possessed goods or property. Philip IV of France, more moderate, asked at first only one-hundredth, then later raised his assessment to one-fiftieth. The outraged clergy protested. Pope Boniface VIII was overwhelmed and also protested. Not content with refusal, he insisted that both kings allow him to arbitrate their quarrel over the possession of Aquitaine. Papal arbitration usually had been used in the past on invitation only; therefore, Boniface's demand would lead to a precedent and, in effect, legalize his claim to supreme temporal power. The kings refused the offer for good and sufficient reasons.

CORRUPTION WITHIN THE CHURCH

The Church had become, over the centuries, very corrupt, and likewise very rich. All the offices in the Church were for sale. The pope, having the appointive power, quickly developed a monopoly of the higher places, and those who received these offices from him paid for them, a practice known as simony. These officers, upon obtaining their positions, frequently repeated the process with the subordinates they appointed, and so on down to the lowest parish priest.

Naturally there was bidding for positions, and the victor looked to his office for remuneration. The people were the ones who supplied this and other compensations. The sale of indulgences, best known through Luther's attack much later, was one sure way of raising money. Plain asking was another. By various means churchmen extorted money from the laity, and in many cases they purchased land which was a source of income.

The pope had his own methods. The annual contribution or tax, called Peter's Pence, furnished him with plenty of money. These sums, in addition to the revenue from simony, made each pope a rich man. Practices like these could not be expected to increase respect for the medieval papacy. It was to be expected that Edward and Philip, both of whom were serious and practical, should refuse to accept the domination of men who had the temerity to drain their kingdoms of gold at a time when each was desperately pressed.

FRENCH CHALLENGE TO PAPAL POWER

Philip of France carried the war to the enemy by forbidding church revenues to leave the country. The revenues of France amounted to a sufficient sum to cause Boniface to execute a partial retreat. Relinquishing his large claims, he declared that he had not meant to weaken temporal vows, or the "Loaning of money to kings by the clergy." But the contest, thus opened, was not to be given up by Boniface.

In 1301 he issued a bull against Philip which plainly asserted papal supremacy in the temporal realm. Philip burned it, with the approval of the Estates General. Undaunted, Boniface issued another bull in 1302, which elaborated on the doctrine. By ingenious logic he declared that the Church was the only means of salvation, and that nonmembers were definitely proscribed by the Bible. This theory was broad enough to include the unpropagandized heathen, as well as Europeans, and implied papal temporal power as an adjunct to spiritual power, with damnation as the penalty for nonconformists in either realm. This second bull brought forth a counter-claim, or claims by the Estates General. It accused Boniface of unchastity, heresy, and tyranny, effectually answering his claims.

The popes at this time held three positions: bishop of Rome, head of the Roman state, and head of the Church. Since they were local officials in Rome, the Italians demanded the privilege of electing them, a demand which made their other positions somewhat complicated. As Italians they were uninterested in universal affairs, and as heads of the Church they were little interested in Italian affairs. Papal duties required the larger share of their time, and Italian affairs were ill-conducted. In fact, Italian politics were neglected so much that Clement V, who followed Boniface's short-lived successor, moved to France in 1309, partly to escape the turmoil. Local politics interfered too much with his other duties, and he and his College of Cardinals were fearful of violence if they stayed longer in Rome.

Boniface had been injured in an attack by one of the local men whom he had exiled. This man, in the pay of Philip, struck the pope in the face, partly for personal reasons, and partly to satisfy Philip, who had been excommunicated by Boniface because of his disobedience. Thus Philip, on the removal of Clement V to France, had reason to keep him there until the ban was lifted, and a few other adjustments made.

BABYLONIAN CAPTIVITY

Clement never ventured to Rome, and, with only one exception, neither did his successors. From 1309 until 1377 the popes lived in Avignon, and because of their manner of living, this interval is called the "Babylonian Captivity."

There were good reasons for their staying. They were safe in France while on their good behavior. They would not have enjoyed similar security in Rome; but since they were

Avignon, the French city where the popes lived during the "Babylonian Captivity," 1309 to 1377

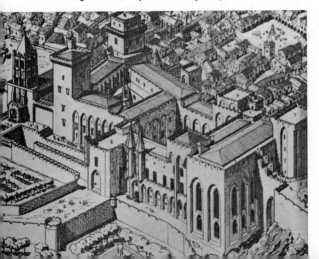

all Frenchmen, Rome was not especially attractive to them. The College of Cardinals, which quickly became Gallicized, preferred to stay where they were safe and in a position to prosper; in Rome they would have been supplanted by Italians. The French kings also preferred that the popes stay in France, and, though the popes were not subservient to French policies, they stayed. For these reasons the popes remained in Avignon, though complaints and accusations, embarrassing in the extreme, were directed to and at them by Italians and Englishmen.

The papal possessions, especially Rome, were difficult to govern in the best of circumstances. Hampered by distance and a lack of respect, the Babylonian popes had little success in attempting to restrain the warring parties. Their presence was needed in Rome. They lost more prestige by refusing to go; and still more from the way they lived. Always magnificent, the court of the Avignon popes was the most splendid in Europe, inclined to condone an indulgence in worldly pleasures.

The need for money led to simony in its worst form. Offices were sold at higher prices, and Church fees were increased throughout Europe. For the Babylonian popes, having no revenues from Rome, were forced into increasing their demands on the clergy. There was an increase in "reservatives," or offices held open by the pope at the death of the incumbent. These offices could be purchased by the highest bidder. The price of benefices, which rose to one-half of the year's income, was made standard and called "annates." Communicants were urged to "contribute" by buying indulgences, dispensations, and pardons. The court resembled a market, and had the same spiritual effect on pilgrims.

Inevitably an outcry arose at this exploitation of religion. It came from all over Europe, but most loudly from France's rival, England. The corruption in the Church was universal, and apparent to the lowest peasant as well as to the more interested lord. In the literature of the time this shame received much mention, though usually the attacks were accompanied by a profession of faith

John Wyclif

the Church return to its task, and give up the wealth which hampered the execution of that task. Like Luther, Wyclif translated the Bible into the vernacular, with much the same purpose and motive as the later reformer. Wyclif believed that papal supremacy was a falsification of doctrine; that, although the Church was infallible, it was composed of all its communicants.

Paralleling Luther's career in other respects, Wyclif's life was distracted by a peasants' revolt, which cost him much of his aristocratic support. Though not punished for heresy, Wyclif was partially silenced, and many of his followers were alienated in England by a later development of his theology. But in Bohemia, John Huss, a follower of Wyclif, succeeded in establishing a strong reform movement.

Huss was excommunicated in 1411, but he refused to recant. At a trial for heresy, he was convicted and burned at the stake. He became a martyr through the manner of his death and his fortitude in meeting it; and his doctrines, instead of disappearing, had more influence than ever. When a new king, who had concurred in Huss's death, attempted to ascend the Bohemian throne, the people resisted him, thus leaving the way open for the pope to suppress the Hussites.

in the real principles of the Church. Dante and Petrarch in Italy, and Langland (if he was the author of *Piers Plowman*) and Chaucer in England condemned the debauchery in works that are classics.

WYCLIF AND HUSS

But a radical reformer, whose theology rested upon several assumptions which were then heretical, also appeared. John Wyclif, a clergyman and scholar, was the founder of this new theology, and his followers were known as "Lollards." Wyclif represented many of the English ideas, and for a period received the protection and support of the English ruling classes.

Wyclif, basing his criticism on an almost Lutheran theology, attacked the symbols which the Church misused: relics, indulgences, pilgrimages, and the like. He advocated that

John Huss

St. Catherine of Siena. (Kress Collection, National Gallery of Art)

This suppression was possible because by 1376 the Babylonian Captivity was ended, and the papacy returned to Rome. This migration was effected by a girl known as St. Catherine of Siena. An Italian, she desired the pope to live in Rome, where she believed he would be able to accomplish more in the way of religious reforms. She succeeded in persuading the incumbent pope to return. Gregory XI died soon after his return, and in the election of a new pope in 1378 a situation arose which is called the Great Schism.

THE GREAT SCHISM

The populace of Rome besieged the Vatican, and their demand that an Italian be elected was so threatening that the College of Cardinals quickly agreed upon a Neapolitan, who then became Pope Urban VI. As soon as he was crowned, Urban began to reprove and censure the Church, the clergy, and the College. His manner was overbearing, and, at that time, his attitude was insupportable. Urban had been elected, it was said, under compulsion; and the French cardinals, who did not receive any part of the papal revenues and were allowed no place in the direction of papal policy, soon left Rome and held another election.

This time, they were sure, there would be no mistake about revenues and power. They declared that the election of Urban was not canonical since it had been forced, and that the new pope would be the genuine one. It is not difficult to note the power of French nationalism in this election. At any rate another pope was elected, who took the name of Clement VII, and went to Avignon to live. Thus there were two popes ruling the same territory at the same time, and, in line with national interests, the clergy of various countries held loyalty one way or another. Germany and Italy gave strong support to Urban, the Italian pope, as did England, Flanders, Portugal, Hungary, and Poland; while France, Scotland, Aragon, Navarre and Castile recognized Clement, the French pope, as the rightful one.

Thus Europe was split into factions in line with national interests, while the Church fought internally and religious observance declined. Each pope augmented the number of cardinals, so there were soon two rival electoral bodies, with power to make new popes and continue the schism. In the struggle to achieve power each group made concessions to nationalism.

THE COUNCILS

The sight of two popes, each claiming to be the direct descendent of Peter and head of the true Church, annoyed Christian people in all Europe. Several plans were suggested to end the schism, but none met with the approval of both popes. Heresy flourished while the exponents of the true religion debated, and levies on the clergy increased. Finally, the Sorbonne (the university at Paris) proposed a council of the two bodies of cardinals, and the first council, or Council of Pisa, took place in 1409.

The idea of a council was repugnant to the popes for several reasons. The most important one was the fact that a council definitely made the College (or Colleges) superior to the pope. The idea was that the *Church*, a term including the laity as well as the clergy, was the institution founded and headed by Christ, that the pope was merely second in command and subservient to the Church, which was directed by Christ. In practice this theory meant that the pope was no longer supreme, that his revenues and levies would pass into the hands of the cardinals, who represented the Church. The conception of the Church was sound doctrine, and the popes were helpless to fight it openly; but nevertheless they opposed it until the Council of Trent, after the Reformation, in which papal

supremacy was established by political maneuvering.

Neither of the popes appeared at the Council of Pisa, so the Council called both of them heretics and elected a new pope, who assumed the name of Alexander V. As the former popes refused to abdicate there were now three popes! Because of the great tasks which it assumed, the council made no progress in Church reform. Heresy, or illegal differences of opinion, still had reason to arise and outlaw sects increased. Therefore, a second council met in 1414 at Constance to deal with these matters. Summoning the Lollard, John Huss, before it on a safe-conduct, the Council tried him and, finding him persistent in error, burned him in 1415. The work of the Council was but begun, however, for there were

Sigismund I being crowned Holy Roman Emperor by Pope Eugenius IV at Rome, in 1433. As "King of the Romans," Sigismund had actually been Emperor from 1410. The Council of Constance was largely due to him

present three sets of papal representatives.

One of the popes, Gregory, resigned. The Council of Pisa's pope, John XIII, was removed as easily; but the other, Benedict XIII, elected by the French cardinals refused to resign. By political means his support was won away from him, and he was deposed. In 1417 the Council ended the schism with the election of Martin V. The way was thus cleared for more pressing business.

SUPPRESSION OF HERESY

Sigismund, king of Bohemia, on whose land the Council was held, had been one of the men who had martyred Huss. Huss's followers, therefore, refused to let him ascend the throne when he came due. To oblige Sigismund, as well as to restore a measure of the Church's old power, Martin preached a crusade against the various Bohemian sects. Crusaders, especially Germans, flocked to the cross to put down heresy and win a share of Bohemian land for themselves. There were several rival sects, and it was thought that it would be easy to conquer them one by one. But, under their leader, John Ziska, the heretics proved superior to their foes. Using firearms and other new methods of warfare, they had no trouble in defeating the Crusaders whenever they met.

Arms proving of no avail, a new council was called in 1431, to treat with the heretics. Partial success was achieved in a battle which was fought while negotiations went ahead, and the Crusaders were able to effect more advantageous terms. But not until almost the sixteenth century were the heretics eliminated and then more by their own efforts than by external opposition.

The Council of 1431 also saw the settling for the time of the conciliar theory. The Council had been called by the cardinals, but Eugenius had refused to attend, and had gone so far as to call a rival assembly together while the other one sat. Through negotiations with the head of the Eastern Church, a quasi-union was formed; and in the meantime public opinion had swung around to favor Eugenius. Thus by his dilatory tactics Eugenius quashed the idea of conciliar supremacy.

Eugenius IV, pope from 1431 to 1447

The waning spiritual and temporal power of the papacy forced it to resort to subterfuge and tortuous policies in order to retain a vestige of power and a stream of revenue. Instead of attempting to seize temporal power in their own names, the popes used the princes as their pawns, often with little success, since the pawns had ideas of their own. The checking of heresy was absolutely essential to the continued power of the popes, and the only method they had was the support of the princes. Thus, some time later, Luther escaped persecution because of his political connections, just as Wyclif had done before him. Princes frequently refused to cooperate with the popes in checking the growth of heresy.

THE INQUISITION

The most important instrument the popes had in fighting heresy was the Inquisition of Spain, support of which soon became a part of the foreign policy of the Spanish rulers. The Inquisition had been in operation for some time and had proved effective but it was not

Expulsion of the Moriscos (Christian Moors) from Granada

definitely used as an instrument of papal dominion until the time of Philip II of Spain, during the period of the Reformation. Thus, in order to increase his power, the pope had to work for the power of the Spanish kings, and at the same time keep them submissive to his own schemes. The task was impossible, and illustrates the decay of the pope's position. Where he had been supreme, the pope became a politician, a player in the world arena.

The nature of the pope's ambitions and gradual obsession with temporal power were the chief causes of the Reformation. In seeking temporal power through political means, the pope yielded the last vestige of dignity and, in point of fact, behaved in a manner altogether unworthy of his high office. Church reform and moral reform were neglected, making it possible for Luther and Protestantism to develop.

A Tribunal of the Inquisition

31. Essential Features of the Renaissance

WHAT WAS THE RENAISSANCE?

UNTIL RECENTLY the Renaissance has been looked upon as a period of sudden reawakening from the "dark" Middle Ages. Renaissance, meaning rebirth, is a term used to describe the spectacular advance of culture in the fifteenth century. Principal causes for the Renaissance were held to be the revelation of ancient classical monuments in Italy, and a westward movement of numerous Greek scholars from Constantinople. These scholars, it was supposed, brought with them a knowledge of Greek literature and philosophy, and aroused a new interest in classical culture. This apparently accidental stimulus from the East was thought to have been one of the principal causes of that magnificent outburst of cultural endeavor which characterized the fifteenth and sixteenth centuries.

Some recent scholarship, however, rejects the view of a "dark" period in the Middle Ages. It regards the Renaissance as a natural consequence of gradual cultural movement that began as far back as the eleventh century with the evolution of the Romanesque style in architecture. The Renaissance, then, constitutes not only a transition, but also an inevitable stage in the growth of Western civilization.

It is a characteristic feature of culture to make its appearance where there are aggregations of people. The rise of towns in western Europe, therefore, marks the beginning of new cultural expression. The development of urban centers did not take place simultaneously all over Europe; rather, it was conditioned by various political, social, economic, geographic, and climatic factors.

Northern Italy seems to have been most favorable to the development of towns. Here we find, in the fourteenth century, a number of flourishing, independent cities, controlling certain rural territories around them, which hence are called city-states. The paralyzing struggles between the papacy and the Holy Roman Emperors, temporary confinement of the papacy to France in the fourteenth century, the schisms that followed, and the resultant decline in the authority of the Church, all proved favorable for the independent political development of the Italian cities. Following the Crusades there arose a lively Eastern trade in spices and luxuries which brought wealth to the cities. Wealth made the brilliant achievements of the Renaissance possible; and the money economy, by now in use everywhere, facilitated intercourse between people.

VENICE—LEADER OF ITALIAN CITY-STATES

The leading city-state in northern Italy was Venice. This city was very advantageously located for commerce with the luxurious Orient, and was also sufficiently isolated to be inaccessible to invaders. During the course of the fifteenth century Venice annexed a large portion of the surrounding territory, thereby safeguarding her access to the Alpine

Grand stairs of the ducal palace at Venice, one of the earliest centers of the Italian Renaissance

passes which were vital to her trade with the north. The government of Venice was essentially an aristocratic one, although a republic in theory. The nominal head of the government was called the doge. He performed the duties of government with the aid of the Council of Ten, while both were subordinate to the Grand Council. This Council was supposed to represent the people at large; but actually it consisted only of members of noble families, and by 1300 all townsmen were excluded from it. In spite of the aristocratic rule, or perhaps because of it, Venice was free from popular criticism and rebellions, in contrast to Florence where all classes claimed themselves entitled to a share in the government. Venetian merchants were so absorbed in their profitable enterprises that they were very willing to leave the business of government to those competent to rule.

MILAN AND FLORENCE

The city-state of Milan displayed the principle of despotism. Under the rule of the Visconti in the fourteenth century, Milan conquered several neighboring towns until it included almost all of Lombardy. The most able ruler of the House of Visconti was Gian Galeazzo (1351-1402), who secured the title of duke of Milan from the Holy Roman Emperor. Upon the death of the last Visconti, the government was seized by Francesco Sforza, a common-born condottiere, but a vigorous and skillful ruler and a patron of the arts.

The city which exhibited the most beautiful and most versatile cultural development was Florence. Under the rule of the Medici, a wealthy banking family whose supremacy began in 1434, Florence became a powerful and prosperous state, which reached its greatest height under Lorenzo the Magnificent. This remarkable man was perhaps the most brilliant ruler of the Renaissance. He exemplified the typical Renaissance personality in versatility as well as refinement of tastes. An outstanding ruler, he was a poet of note, as well as a highly educated patron of the arts.

The Medici ruled Florence in the manner of the modern political boss, craftily controlling the supposedly republican governmental machinery without an official title. It is surprising that, despite the unusually large number of intelligent and talented men that Florence produced, the people never succeeded in developing an efficient democratic government. On the other hand, the despotism of the Medici was not inimical to the city's welfare, since for the

Lorenzo the Magnificent, Medici ruler of Florence, 1469 to 1492

most part the Medici combined political craft with generosity and intellectual and cultural refinement.

THE PAPACY AND MINOR CITY-STATES

Of somewhat lesser importance were the States of the Church, theoretically under the authority of the pope. During and after the "Babylonian Captivity" of the popes (1309-1377) however, nearly every city succumbed to petty adventurer-despots. Upon the return of the popes to Rome, they became involved in worldly politics. In their endeavor to regain control of their territories, the ecclesiastical princes differed little from the contemporary lay princes. But the popes of the Renaissance were highly educated men and generous patrons of the arts. The papal court attracted many of the most gifted sculptors, painters, and architects; and Florence surrendered its leadership in Italian art to Rome after Leo X, a member of the Medici family, became pope in 1513.

There were many other flourishing cities in Italy, vying with one another for supremacy, and each with a history of its own. The most important of these cities were the kingdom of Naples, for a long period under French rule; Siena, which lost its independence to Florence after three centuries of bitter rivalry; and finally, Genoa and Pisa.

PROMINENT CITIES OF NORTHERN EUROPE

While northern Italy was particularly outstanding with its large number of towns, we must not forget that in other parts of Europe there were many prosperous cities. After gaining their charters and therewith their independence from the neighboring nobles, a movement which was made possible through the increase in commerce and wealth, these cities organized democratic governments and rapidly developed into powerful commercial centers. Their positions were further strengthened by the organization of leagues, such as the Hanseatic, the Rhenish, and Swabian leagues, which enabled the cities to resist ambitious rulers as well as rival nations.

ITALY—CRADLE OF THE RENAISSANCE

It is difficult to explain why Renaissance culture should have its beginning in the Italian city-states. The Baltic cities had a profitable trade with Scandinavia and Russia; Bruges, Ghent, Amsterdam, and a host of Flemish cities prospered in their textile industry and extensive commerce. But why were they not the cradle of the Renaissance?

The greatest advantage which Italy possessed was a certain atmosphere of freedom of thought. Scholasticism had never really taken root in Italy. This is evident in the different trends in Bologna, site of the leading university of Italy. The study of logic, so doggedly pursued in French and German universities, was unpopular in the University of Bologna. The Italian mind simply was unwilling and unsuited for the study of logic as an end in itself. Realities dealing with everyday life were of more interest to them than abstract mental acrobatics. Law was the main curriculum at Bologna, and this is an indication of the habit of calm, practical reasoning, peculiar to Italians at this time.

Furthermore, Italy enjoyed a lively contact with the Byzantine Empire in the East, an empire which still had immense wealth and prestige. The Moslem civilization, too, was bound to exert an influence on its immediate northern neighbors. Climatically, northern Italy is favored by nature with a climate very conducive to a moderate balance between activity and leisure. The northern countries were subject to a more rigorous climate, which forced people to spend more time on the mere struggle for existence. Development in northern countries was, therefore, more retarded, and even the spread of the spirit of the Renaissance from Italy continued at a much slower pace. For these reasons, we find certain phases of the Renaissance manifested one or even two centuries later in Germany, England, and Scandinavia than in Italy.

The influx of wealth into the towns naturally revolutionized the social life of the citizens. Their interests were diverted from

Dante Alighieri, whose "Divine Comedy" was one of the first great literary works written in Italian

Francesco Petrarch, whose sonnets and canzoni set a pattern for Renaissance love poetry

Giovanni Boccaccio, whose racy "Decameron" tales are important in Renaissance literature

things religious and mystical to things in this present life, earthly and real. Men began to find delight in occupations and diversions outside the realm of the Church. Commerce and the accompanying development of finance demanded a sense of objectivity, a hard, matter-of-fact common sense, as contrasted to the previous preoccupation with the hereafter. The dominance of feudal lords and that of the Church was loosening, and a new spirit of individualism arose among the people. This individualism first became apparent in the fields of learning and art; later it appeared also in the realm of religion, and led in the fifteenth and sixteenth centuries to a religious renaissance—the Reformation.

BIRTH OF NATIONAL LITERATURE IN ITALY

The new spirit appeared markedly in learning. There had been an unconditional reverence for Aristotelian logic and a blind adherence to scholastic dogmas as laid down by the medieval scholars. Toward the end of the thirteenth century there was a new tendency to study the wealth of unused sources which became available. New Greek works were found through contact with Moslem scholars; many Latin works of the Roman period, hitherto unknown, were discovered. Greek and Latin were considered the basis of a liberal education in the universities.

Dante already showed a great reverence for classical writers, and a generation later Petrarch represents the first modern personality in his enthusiasm for classical literature and in his denouncement of the customary scholastic studies of his day.

It is significant too, that with Dante and Petrarch there appeared the first important literature in the Italian language. The Italian vernacular, like other dialects, was not con-

Scene from Boccaccio's "Decameron," a collection of 100 entertaining tales of 13th century Italy

Geoffrey Chaucer. His "Canterbury Tales" show Italian influences

sidered sufficiently dignified by writers of the Middle Ages; but Dante loved his native dialect and had confidence in its capacity for beautiful expression. Petrarch felt disdain toward the Italian dialect, in which he wrote a few sonnets; but he wished to be remembered mainly for his Latin histories and essays. He is far better known for his Italian sonnets, although they were scorned by him. The fourteenth century also produced Boccaccio, a friend of Petrarch and a biographer of Dante. His *Decameron*, a collection of racy, bold love stories, has been a source of enjoyment to a steady, appreciative public, and has experienced a revival in recent years.

CHAUCER AND SHAKESPEARE

Geoffrey Chaucer, after a visit to Italy, used his native English enthusiastically in the *Canterbury Tales*. Thus Chaucer did for the English language what Dante and Petrarch did for the Italian. In all countries in Europe there were a vigorous assertion and development of the language of the people. In France the popular enjoyment of mystery and miracle plays, the farces, and entertainment by traveling songsters called troubadours, helped to establish the mother tongue. German *Meistersinger* and popular comedians delighted the burghers and peasantry alike; yet even Luther's translation of the Bible in the sixteenth century had a profound influence on the formation of the German language. Thus, we find local dialects forming everywhere; local forces once liberated asserted themselves boldly.

The literature of the common people that had arisen during the later Middle Ages was for a time superseded by Latin literature of the early Renaissance. But in the sixteenth century a national literature arose in the different countries. The brilliant reign of Queen Elizabeth was accompanied by a manifestation in English literature of the new national pride. Edmund Spenser's *Faerie Queene* is classical in its form and allusions, while its theme is the praise of England's greatest queen. English drama during this period rose to a height which has not been reached for three centuries. The towering figure of this school was William Shakespeare, a dramatic genius of great versatility with an outlook on life that was universal.

There were a great number of lesser dramatists, such as Marlowe and Ben Jonson, who wrote during the Shakespearian age. Although we cannot mention all of them here, we must not forget the significance of their

Shakespeare directing a rehearsal of one of his plays. The stage is typical of the Elizabethan age, when English drama reached its greatest height

The Renaissance was an era of rich and varied creativeness during which man's physical, spiritual, and intellectual life was broadened immeasurably. Hans Holbein the Younger's painting, "The Ambassadors," upper left, illustrates the establishment during the Renaissance of regular political relations among nations. Upper right is a 16th century war vessel. Above are two pictures of Italian scholars during this period, which saw the rise of Humanism. Below is represented a session of the Council of Trent. Below right, an author presents a copy of his book to Henry II of France

Life in the Renaissance. Above, a torch dance, from an engraving by Albrecht Dürer (1471–1528). Above right, German street musicians of the 16th century. Below, a fashionable pastime—ladies hunting. Below right, an interior scene in a Renaissance inn, from an early 16th century woodcut

Agriculture during the early Renaissance. Farming techniques differed little from those of medieval times. Below left, harvesting grapes for wine-making. Below right, sheep shearing in the 15th century

The King James Bible, shown here being presented to King James I by its compilers, was a landmark in the literary development of the English language

ought to be lived according to the law of nature, and man's reasoning power is strong enough to control all of his passions—this forms the kernel of Montaigne's philosophy which he expressed in the inimitable *Essays*. As an essayist he may be regarded the earliest, and his style exerted a strong influence on the writings of subsequent centuries.

contributions to English drama. Aside from the Latin work *Utopia* by Sir Thomas More, and the treatises of Sir Philip Sidney, there is one other outstanding work of the period. This is the King James version of the Bible.

Written during the reign of James I, it had great influence on subsequent English prose style, and it is still in use in the entire English-speaking world.

GROWTH OF NATIONAL LITERATURE IN FRANCE AND GERMANY

French literature, too, was temporarily checked by the polished Latin of the Humanists. But in the sixteenth century, the chapter of French literature opened with the works of two great writers. François Rabelais, although a profound classical scholar, wrote for the common people rather than for the exclusive circle of scholars. One of the greatest satirists of all time, he ridiculed the follies

François Rabelais, famous French satirist

of men in his tales of *Gargantua and Pantagruel*, a work which found wide popular appeal. The other great writer, Montaigne, was typical of the revivifying force of the Renaissance movement. He was the first great champion of free thought and individualism. Life

Rabelais' satirical theme in his tale of Gargantua was taken over by Fischart in Germany, who wrote a German version of the work. The prodigious dramatic productivity of Hans Sachs, a shoemaker and *Meistersinger* of Nuremberg, was only one aspect of an already vigorous folk literature in Germany. Folk songs and tales were popular everywhere. They flowed from rich sources of popular themes, centering in the endless fooleries of the incorrigible Till Eulenspiegel, or the tragic fate of the heretic Dr. Faustus. The days of the Thirty Years' War were brought back to life in the realistic narrative of Grimmelshausen's *Simplicissimus*.

Catholic literature was represented in the profound poetry of Angelus Silesius, while Paul Gerhardt contributed his unforgettable church songs to Protestant literature. The country was alive with drama; Shakespeare's influence and wandering English comedians had imparted an impetus to the drama, and the dramatic works of Gryphius were among the best of the time. German writers were emphasizing the use of the German language, national subjects took precedence over religious ones, and in general the growing nationalizing tendency was manifested in all European literature during this century.

THE PRINTING PRESS

In this connection it is desirable to discuss an invention which was beyond doubt the most important agent in the dissemination of knowledge and opinions. Printed books are a relatively recent achievement, since until about 1400 all books had to be written and copied by hand. Books were consequently few and expensive, and could be purchased only by aristocrats or other wealthy citizens. It is clear that culture was thereby restricted to a small circle, while the large mass of people were kept in utter ignorance.

Johann Gutenberg examining the first proofs from his printing press. He is usually credited with the invention of printing. (Am. Inst. of Graphic Arts)

We do not know the exact origin of the printing press; but it is certain that a system of movable type was used by Johann Gutenberg in his printing shop in Germany about the year 1450. The principle of movable type was preceded by the use of wooden blocks with reversed letters carved on them. Kings and nobles used such devices for their seals or signatures; but, of course, large-scale printing was impossible with such an awkward system. The new process made use of individual letters cast in metal and arranged in the desired sequence. The very easy setting and resetting of letters enabled an unlimited variety of printing.

The new invention spread with amazing rapidity throughout the European world. Scholars and popes welcomed the improvement, and printing presses were built everywhere. Instead of the two books which the most skillful copyist could complete in a year, it was soon possible to produce some 2,500 volumes with one printing press in the same amount of time.

The effect of such prodigious output of books is obvious. It is impossible to overestimate the importance of the printing press in the development of modern civilization. Books and pamphlets were poured out among the people who were now financially able to buy them. Members of the middle class, in particular, assimilated the new available information, and gradually developed into the most powerful and most influential class in the nations. Not only did the ready access to knowledge create the modern intelligent public, but it also produced considerable intellectual unrest. The dissemination of knowledge aided the secularization of literature and art, the breaking down of time-proved traditions, and particularly, the democratization of culture.

HUMANISM

The great intellectual development was inaugurated by a movement called Humanism. In the fourteenth century there had been a marked interest in the study of classical literature. The Turkish conquest of Constantinople, a city which possessed a Greek culture, drove many Greek scholars to Italy. Thus they gave impetus to a movement that was already well under way. It is true that classical texts were difficult to find, and even the available ones were poor translations. The influx of Greek scholars into Italy partially remedied this lack of reliable classical texts, and exerted a refreshing and invigorating influence on Western thought.

Humanism, the study of Greek and Roman culture, is a word derived from *humanitas*, which means culture. But the word Humanism also has come to imply that new interest in man and his earthly destiny, as expressed previously by the Greeks. The main motive for Italian Humanists was a search and appreciation for beauty, and it mattered little

Sir Thomas More (1478-1535), English Humanist wrote "Utopia"   **Michel Montaigne (1533-1592),** French writer of famous essays   **Desiderius Erasmus (1466?-1536),** Renaissance scholar and reformer

to them whether this beauty were expressed in religious or pagan themes. Due to the renewed acquaintance with classical art and literature, there was a decided leaning toward pagan subjects, such as themes dealing with Greek and Roman mythology. This tendency was not strong in Germany, where people were more serious, and there Humanism took on a religious note. Scholars were concerned with discovering the real truth of the Bible, and with overcoming some of the shallow and corrupt practices of the Church.

The two most interesting figures involved in the religious movement were Martin Luther, the great reformer, and Erasmus of Rotterdam. The influence of these two men on the Reformation will be treated in greater length in the following chapter, but their importance as intellectual figures must be brought out here. Luther was the sturdy, bold, and stubborn rebel type in spite of caution and self-discipline in his attitude toward the Church, but Luther knew no limit in asserting his own ideas after he broke with the Church. He had no equal in courage, outspoken earnestness, and power of language.

Erasmus was a very different person. His sincere aim, too, was to reform the corrupt Church; but he was by temperament cautious to the point of timidity, diplomatic, always neutral, and extremely anxious to preserve peace. Luther was the man of action; Erasmus was hesitant, and contented himself with directing witty and stinging satires against his opponents. He did not desire to break away from the Church, but wanted to reform it from within. Erasmus was cool and calm in his reasoning, totally free from passion of any sort. He was naturally a pacifist, and much of the conflict which appeared in succeeding years might have been avoided had there been more men like Erasmus.

As a literary figure Erasmus enjoyed an enviable, widespread reputation. He was looked upon as a universal authority in intellectual matters; his judgment was final. He wrote and spoke in excellent Latin, and felt at home in any country where he could find learned men with whom to converse. Never before had there been such universal admiration for a scholar, and he was beyond doubt the "Prince of the Humanists."

The humanistic movement contained a large number of scholars in all countries. Among the German Humanists, John Reuchlin, and the passionate knight and poet, Ulrich von Hutten, were both ardent supporters of the Reformation. In England, Sir Thomas More, not a supporter of the Reformation as Henry VIII interpreted it, is best known for his idealistic work, *Utopia*. In France, we may think of Montaigne, the skeptic philosopher, as a Humanist. The movement had a widespread effect on the intellectual development of subsequent times, and many great writers and philosophers even up to the end of the seventeenth century, can be said to be a product of Humanism.

32. Renaissance Arts and Science

ARCHITECTURE AND SCULPTURE

ART IS ALWAYS the first medium of expression which reflects the changes and new tendencies of an age. During the Middle Ages, the arts and crafts were largely in the service of the Church, or at least under its guidance. The individual artist and craftsman was but a small link, a subordinated part of an organization, and his individual personality was almost completely obscured in the interest of the whole work. This practice had some advantages. Work was of a generally uniform high quality, and such structures as cathedrals showed a unified purpose and strength.

The whole period of Gothic art was subject to these conditions. The architect and sculptor alike did their work anonymously, and there can be little doubt that these artists were happy in their simplicity and modesty. But the consequence was a formal, stereotyped art, unsusceptible to the realities of its environment. This reality gradually penetrated the realm of art during the fourteenth century under the secularizing influence of commerce and wealth. Artists became conscious of their personalities; they found that their work was highly desired by worldly and ecclesiastical princes who offered attractive remuneration for their creations. The history of Renaissance art, therefore, becomes a history of artists.

The Gothic style of architecture predominated in northern Europe until the end of the fifteenth century. Italy never really adopted this style, but continued to build in a modified Romanesque form. During the fourteenth century architects began to study and experiment with the remains of classical architecture, and a new style, simplified and well balanced, emerged. Brunelleschi in Florence was a successful pioneer, and the new style found its highest expression in the works of Bramante and Palladio and, most of all, Michelangelo.

While sculpture was only a part of the architecture of the Middle Ages, it asserted itself as an independent art in the Renaissance under its resourceful artists. They prepared the world for an appreciation of the classical conception of beauty. Laws of perspective were studied, and the beauty of the human figure was boldly revealed and emphasized. Pioneers in this field were the Pisanos, who had experimented with these forms at the close of the thirteenth century. Under the encouragement of the Medici family, Florence produced a number of brilliant sculptors, among whom Lorenzo Ghiberti was the first really great master. His exquisite figures on the doors of the baptistery in Florence are still a wonder of the art world. Donatello and Verrocchio made imposing equestrian statues for their patrons, who desired to immortalize their personalities. A unique and refined art was developed by Luca della Robbia who, in addition to being an excellent marbleworker, specialized on glazed enamel and ceramics. The dominant figure in sculpture was Michelangelo. His powerful, restless figures constitute a style unique among Renaissance artists. Sculpture was his natural medium, and a sculptural element is definitely revealed also in his painting.

GREAT ITALIAN PAINTERS

The most highly developed art of the period was painting. We find the first attempt to break away from the lifeless, prescribed style of the day in the youthful, refreshing pictures of Giotto, a Florentine who was a close friend of Dante. Passion, instead of sentiment, was expressed in Giotto's painting. A delightfully fresh and joyful soul himself, he was first to

Bronze Panels by Ghiberti on a door of the baptistery in Florence

Piero de Medici, bronze statue by Andrea del Verrochio

"Madonna," a relief in glazed terra cotta by Andrea della Robbia

emphasize expression of the human soul.

Giotto's example in painting was enthusiastically pursued by the humble Dominican monk, Fra Angelico, and by the unusually gifted Masaccio, whose technique was far in advance of his time. Sandro Botticelli represented the graceful, aristocratic ladies of Florence in his pagan themes. The enthusiasm for paganism went so far that it produced a popular, democratic reaction under the leadership of the fanatic monk, Savonarola. It was aimed against the ruling Medici family, who patronized the classical art. Penitent, Botticelli burned his exquisite nude figures and resolved to abandon profane subjects. Nevertheless, his subsequent Madonnas continued to be elegant ladies of his refined surroundings; the new style had already taken root too deeply to be

suppressed by a temporary reaction.

The papal court was far from being backward in the movement toward worldliness. The popes vied with the lay princes in securing for themselves the best artistic talents of the age. Raphael, a brilliant and prolific genius, produced his technically unsurpassed works under the patronage of Julius II and Leo X. For these popes, too, Michelangelo spent his best energy in decorating the Sistine Chapel with monumental frescoes.

Painting during the Renaissance was regional. Each community had its own peculiar school of artists, for the influences of landscape and economic pursuits made themselves felt on the style of the local masters. Venice was a wealthy commercial city with wide international relations and the Venetians were

"Presentation of Mary in the Temple," from the Life of Mary by Giotto di Bondone (1266–1337)

Pope Sixtus II creating St. Lawrence archdeacon of Rome, from a fresco by Fra Angelico (1387–1455)

"Creation of Adam," from Michelangelo's frescoes on the ceiling of the Sistine Chapel

consequently less intellectual than they were sensuous and emotional. The paintings of Giovanni Bellini show a marked Byzantine influ-

Leonardo da Vinci's famous painting of "The Last Supper"

ence. Later, the Venetian love for color and magnificence found its fullest expression in the famous works of Giorgione and Titian.

become proficient in several of them. Leonardo da Vinci was an accomplished painter, sculptor, and architect; but his indefatigable search for the secret of life led him farther into almost all vocations of his time. He was an ingenious inventor, a mathematician, and musician; and his observations and sketches in anatomy are still among the most accurate up to this day. Benvenuto Cellini was a goldsmith as well as a sculptor and a clever writer. Michelangelo's and Lorenzo de' Medici's versatilities have already been mentioned. Sonnet writing became the pastime of everyone as

DA VINCI

Probably the most striking personality of this period was Leonardo da Vinci. In connection with Lorenzo de' Medici, reference has already been made to the great versatility of the Renaissance genius. It was the aim of artists, not only to master one art, but also to

"Primavera," or "The Allegory of Spring," one of Botticelli's masterpieces

Rembrandt, greatest Dutch painter of the Renaissance, painted this picture of "Abraham's Sacrifice"

"Self Portrait," 1498, one of several by Albrecht Dürer (1471–1528), German painter and engraver

music became everybody's hobby a century later. But no one man had combined so many fields of knowledge in one personality as did Leonardo.

RENAISSANCE PAINTERS IN NORTHERN EUROPE

While Renaissance art in Italy took on a distinctly classical note, in northern Europe it served to give expression to the innate Germanic spirit. There were neither Byzantine traditions nor classical influences in the north. France and Spain accepted the Italian style; but Germany, Scandinavia, and the Low Countries show surprisingly few effects of the classical tradition.

In Holland and Flanders painting began in the fifteenth century with the exquisite works of the Van Eyck brothers. They were followed by a number of different local schools, of which the virile, colorful peasant pictures by Pieter Bruegel are perhaps the most interesting. Dutch and Flemish painting did not come to a climax until the seventeenth century in the baroque style. This style is a continuation of classical forms, but it is characterized by a love for movement, splendor, and ornaments.

The Low Countries had many really great painters. The voluptuous, earthly women in the pictures of Rubens express a reaction with a vengeance against the rigid Catholicism of the Spanish rule. The realistic paintings of Frans Hals show no longer any pretense of restraint and idealization. Van Dyck's style reflects the cool, aristocratic air of his refined environment. Here the artisan ceases; a worldly, elegant, and highly respected artist-personality appears—a polished gentleman, at ease with kings and nobles. The towering figure among the great number of Flemish and Dutch painters was Rembrandt van Rijn. A deeply religious man, he was misunderstood by his contemporaries. His art is lofty and noble, superior to contemporary artists in both craft and content. His etchings and paintings, largely scorned in his time, now command fabulous prices.

The art of the Low Countries was characterized by a love for subjects concerning the experiences of everyday life. It was a skillful expression of a local, national feeling; always real, vivid, and vigorous, it was unconcerned with abstractions about the hereafter.

Germany possessed very few painters in the Renaissance and almost no baroque painters.

"Fray Felix," by El Greco (1541–1614), greatest Spanish painter of the Renaissance

The etchings of Dürer and the marvelous English portraits of Holbein the Younger are the most famous works that Germany produced during this period.

French and Spanish artists imitated the Italian style. But it was especially in Spain that Renaissance painting culminated in a flourishing baroque style. El Greco, the chief representative, produced weird color and light effects which suggest visions of a dreamer. In the refined atmosphere of the Spanish court, Velasquez produced a number of magnificent royal portraits and classical subjects among which the decidedly pagan theme of Venus in the mirror is the best known. There is one other great painter to be noted in the Spanish baroque, Bartolomé Murillo, whose portraits of madonnas and saints reflect a deeper religious mind than any of his contemporaries, with the possible exception of Rembrandt.

Renaissance art decayed in a further outgrowth of the baroque into the rococo style. The art of this period lost its balance of form and content in a wholesale application of ornaments. The rococo style still has a great appeal for modern generations for its grace and childlike beauty; but it led in a direction of little further development.

The devastating religious wars of the seventeenth century almost completely stifled any artistic endeavor. Architecture, which had experienced an encouraging revival at the beginning of the century, sank into complete stagnation during the Thirty Years' War. The condition of painting was even more depressing. Only music gave a delightful evidence of vigorous activity, and before long it became the dominant art in Germany and in parts of the Austrian (Holy Roman) Empire.

MUSIC

Up to the fourteenth century music consisted of simple chants, used only in connection with the Catholic services. From the existing Greek modes there now emerged the minor and major scales of today, and a strict polyphonic style developed. In Italy this style found its highest expression in the works of Palestrina. In the north, especially in the Low Countries, it culminated in the magnificent choral works of Orlando di Lasso, Josquin Des Prés, known as the "king of music," and William Dufay.

A significant change came about with the development of musical instruments. Up to this time musical artistry had been expressed in vocal works. There were a few string and wind instruments in existence, such as the guitar, lute, and harp, and the bagpipe, oboe, and a simple type of organ. Aside from church music, the improvised songs of the wandering minstrels in the thirteenth and fourteenth centuries flourished in early Renaissance music. Gradually, with the development of the organ, the violin, and the flute, there arose a popular desire for instrumental music. Not only professional musicians, but also the whole enthusiastic laity participated in small orchestral ensembles, as well as madrigals (short secular choral works) and religious music. The sixteenth century marks the zenith of musical activity from the point of view of popular participation, an art which was completely driven out by the brilliant performances of professional musicians. The new musical artist was now ascending from a mere craftsman to a

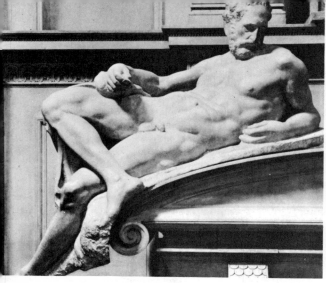

"Evening," by Michelangelo (1475–1564)

"Antoine de Granvelle," by Titian (1477–1576)

"Portrait of a Genoese Lady," by Anthony Van Dyck (1599–1641)

"Doge Lorendano," by Giovanni Bellini (1430?–1516)

"Poetry," a mosiac painting by Raphael, in the Vatican, Rome

"Apollo and Daphne," by Giovanni Bernini (1598–1680)

"Head of Cyrus, Brought to Queen Tomyris," by Peter Paul Rubens

Decorative Art of the Renaissance. Above left is a gilded German wrought silver standing cup or chalice, made in Augsburg in 1550. Farthest above, center, is a French chasse, or reliquary, of enamel on copper. Below it is the Rospigliosi Cup, by the famous Italian goldsmith, Benvenuto Cellini (1500–1571). Above right is the astronomical clock of the Cathedral of Strasbourg, made in 1573

Renaissance Architecture. Right, the Chateau de Chambord, in Touraine, begun in 1526, is typical of early French Renaissance chateaux. Below, the Castle of Frederiksborg, near Copenhagen, Denmark. In Dutch Renaissance style, with some Gothic detail, nearly all of it was built in 1602–20

The Villa Medici in Rome, begun in 1550 and completed in 1590, has the extensive ornamentation characteristic of the later Italian Renaissance

George F. Handel
(1685-1759)

position as protégé of the aristocracy.

In England, Purcell and Handel were developing a magnificent instrumental style, while also toying with the opera, which was then a musical innovation. This type of musical composition attempted to fuse dramatic art and music in one form, to enlarge and intensify the scope of artistic expression. It originated with Monteverdi in Italy about 1600, and was eagerly taken up by Heinrich Schütz in Germany. Schütz also developed a form of religious opera, the oratorio. This religious opera without action culminated in the works of Johann Sebastian Bach, the great exponent of Protestant church music. An extraordinary organist, he was the most versatile and prolific composer of his day. Bach and Handel are well named "baroque musicians" and they brought music to a height during this period of development.

Johann S. Bach
(1685-1750)

ASTRONOMY

During the Renaissance the rise of individualism, the great sea voyages and discoveries, the relaxing of the ancient doctrine, and the growth of free thought combined to encourage scientific development. There still persisted numerous superstitions and a belief in magic, notwithstanding the bold strides taken in the direction of scientific thought by the scientists of the fifteenth and sixteenth centuries.

Perhaps the study of astronomy exercised little direct influence on the development of practical, applied science; but it completely revolutionized man's conception of the universe and of himself. The Ptolemaic theory originated by the Greek philosopher Ptolemy in the second century A.D., dominated throughout the Middle Ages. Ptolemy held that the earth was the center of the universe, with the sun, moon, and planets revolving around it.

Notwithstanding the staunch belief in the Ptolemaic system, or the geocentric theory, there had been other conceptions of the universe. The Pythagoreans believed in a heliocentric world, the idea that the sun is the center of the system. This theory was revived by early Italian astronomers when classical culture was rediscovered.

The founder of modern astronomy was a Polish priest, Copernicus. A champion of the Pythagorean theory, he published his computations and observations in a work called *On the Revolutions of the Celestial Bodies*, and dedicated the volume to Pope Paul III. The "Copernican system," as it came to be known, displaced man's superior position in the world and placed the earth on the same level with any other planet. It is conceivable that such a revolutionary doctrine aroused widespread interest and curiosity, as well as indignation.

During the course of the sixteenth century, astronomers were busily improving their instruments for observing the skies. The most outstanding astronomical observer to test the Copernican theory was the Danish astronomer, Tycho Brahe. He set up an elaborate observatory, a veritable "Castle of the Heavens," as he called it, on a small island in the Baltic Sea. Here he diligently and systematically collected scientific data under the patronage of his king, until, falling into disrepute, he became official astronomer to the Holy Roman Emperor.

Kepler, who succeeded Tycho Brahe, continued the studies of his predecessor. His main contribution to the new theory was his establishment of the elliptical path of the planets

Tycho Brahe
(1546-1601)

around the sun, in contrast to the notion of a circular movement of the planets. Kepler witnessed the trial of his mother for witchcraft, and it was popularly believed that Kepler was not free from the inspiration of Satan. It is not surprising, therefore, that Kepler catered to the superstitions of people by casting horoscopes for his customers, among whom the eminent Wallenstein was the most frequent caller.

The Copernican hypothesis was brilliantly expounded and popularized by the gifted Italian scientist, Galileo. A true Renaissance mind in his diverse talents, he was a classical scholar, an able musician, and an eloquent writer as well. Galileo made permanent contributions to physics and celestial mechanics. He discovered the equal velocities of falling bodies subject to gravity, and the oscillations of a pendulum. Mechanics, existing up to this time only as a diffuse collection of a few laws and theorems, was definitely established as a science by Galileo. He invented a telescope, which is similar to the modern opera glass, but with it he discovered the satellites of Jupiter, the sunspots, and the substance of the Milky Way. His publications evoked the suspicion of the Inquisition, an ecclesiastical court devised to suppress heresy. Found guilty by the tribunal, he was forced to abjure the heliocentric theory.

Copernicus instructing his students in his theories of astronomy. This drawing shows Copernicus holding a model of the sun and the earth

Galileo Galilei
(1564–1642)

Nevertheless, Galileo's work survived the fanatic persecutions of the Inquisition, and his discoveries in mechanics and dynamics furnished a basis for the work of Newton.

MATHEMATICS, PHYSICS, AND METALLURGY

While modern astronomy received inspiration from classical theories, the science of mathematics developed on European ground from the crude beginnings of medieval science. A stimulus was provided by the current happenings in navigation, in warfare, and, most of all, by the needs of commerce. The use of Arabic numerals and elementary algebra had been taken over from the Moslems; geometry and arithmetic had been inherited from the Greeks; but on these elementary foundations, European scholars built the magnificent structure of modern mathematics.

Under the pressure of commerce and finance, mathematicians labored to devise accurate and efficient methods for calculating prices, weights and measures, wages, and coinage. Treatises were written on military science, on bookkeeping, and a somewhat roguish physician named Cardan even reckoned the calculus of possibilities in gambling.

In the field of physics, the name of Galileo again appears as a leading figure. He had made studies of motion and sound phenomena. As an inventor, he contributed the air thermometer and the architect's level. The first microscope was probably devised by the Dutch inventor, Janssen, and the invention was of utmost significance for the development of biological sciences. At this point we might also take note of the experiments of William Gilbert, who observed certain "electrical" phenomena in magnetic bodies, a discovery which ultimately led to the electro-magnetic motor.

Zacharias Janssen
(c. 1560–c. 1610)

The growth of mining enterprises, made possible through the rise of capitalism, created a need for the study of minerals and metals. A German student of natural sciences, George Agricola, made a beginning in this field by his visits to mines in Bohemia and Bavaria. He summed up his observations in his *Twelve Books on Metals*, and with this work became the founder of the sciences of mineralogy and metallurgy.

PAPER AND GUNPOWDER

In addition to the inventions already named there were two others of epoch-making consequences, paper and gunpowder. Modern paper has been in use for not more than five centuries. Books and manuscripts had been written largely on papyrus rolls in Egypt, on parchment or vellum in Europe. A type of linen paper was in use in the thirteenth century, but parchment was preferred because of its greater durability. With the invention of printing in the middle of the fifteenth century, it was necessary to manufacture a type of paper which was cheap enough for large-scale printing. Cotton and linen were previously used in the making of paper; but, with the shifting of the industry to

northern countries, woolen rags were used in a synthetic process. The problem of a cheap paper having been solved, printing was enabled to embark on a mass publication of writings.

Of tremendous importance was the invention of gunpowder. Crossbows, longbows, and pikes had been the main weapons of infantry. In a manuscript dated 1220, gunpowder had been mentioned. Roger Bacon gave a detailed description of it, after studying various forms. But it was not until the invention of the cannon that the explosion of gunpowder could be controlled. Cannons throwing iron projectiles were mounted on wheels and were used by the end of the fourteenth century. Smaller guns fired by powder were beginning to displace the longbows and crossbows. These guns were relatively crude and the method of ignition was inefficient, so that the bow and arrow was still in use in Cromwell's army. Military tactics were revolutionized considerably with the use of firearms, although, in comparison with the mass slaughter of modern times, wars up to the nineteenth century were still rather mild affairs.

NATURAL SCIENCES

The name Paracelsus is a symbol for natural sciences in the sixteenth century. He was a remarkable man—a versatile student of nature, a musician, physician, and mystic philosopher. A restless and quarrelsome soul, he spent most of his life denouncing the prevailing notions of Aristotle and the Roman physician Galen, and demanded recognition of individual contemporary research. He visited mining families in the Fugger mines in Tyrol, and studied the diseases to which they were subject. Most important of all, he insisted that functions in the human body are chemical in nature, and can be treated with chemical processes. During his time, Paracelsus was considered a "quack," but modern science gives recognition to many of his revolutionary beliefs.

Another noted physician to break away from the Galen tradition, which dominated medical science in the Middle Ages was the eminent Netherlander, Vesalius. Up to his time surgery had been performed by barbers. Nev-

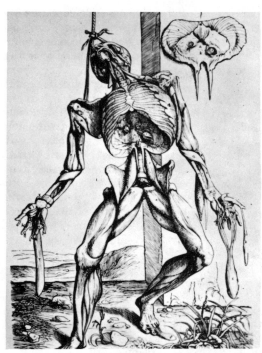

Anatomical Drawing from Andreas Vesalius' "De humani corporis fabrica," the first complete and exact treatise on human anatomy based on actual observation. It was illustrated by woodcuts like this

ertheless, barbers were not always incompetent, and valuable contributions had been made by barber-surgeons in wars when devising artificial limbs for injured soldiers. Vesalius denounced surgery performed by inexperienced barbers, and advocated the thorough study of anatomy as a basis for training surgeons and physicians. His long treatise on anatomy was a study on the digestive and circulatory systems, the muscles, lungs, and brain. It constitutes an important stepping stone in the history of medical science. However, the actual processes of the circulatory system were not known until William Harvey published,

in the beginning of the seventeenth century, his learned work, a discovery of prime significance to medicine.

RENAISSANCE PHILOSOPHY

It was natural that, with such revolutionizing discoveries in all fields of science, there should emerge new systems of philosophy. Men like Galileo and Kepler were philosophers as well as scientists. The Italian philosopher, Tommaso Campanella, developed a philosophy of nature with which he combined social and political ideas. In his *City of the Sun* he visualized a socialistic Utopia, for which he was persecuted by the Church and imprisoned for twenty-five years. The most interesting and first "modern" philosopher, however, was the Neapolitan, Giordano Bruno.

Beginning his interesting career in a Dominican monastery and brought up in the time-honored Aristotelian tradition, he soon came under the influence of Neo-Platonism. He became thoroughly imbued with the scientific spirit of his day and gradually became an enthusiastic supporter of the Copernican system. Realizing that conflicts with the Church were imminent, he threw off his ecclesiastic robe and undertook the endless wanderings that led him through France, Switzerland, Germany, and even far-off England. He sought the company of broad-minded scientists and scholars, conversed with Sidney and Shakespeare, and won the admiration of kings and princes. But he possessed a rash, irritable temper that led him into frequent troubles. Bruno was the first prophet of pantheism, the philosophy which

Circulation of the Blood being demonstrated to King Charles I by Sir William Harvey, who discovered this phenomenon in the early 17th century

conceives God to be embodied in nature. Naturally, such a philosophy was regarded by the Church as "heretical," and upon Bruno's return to Italy he was imprisoned and committed to the flames. Besides possessing all the qualities that characterize the modern intellectual man, Bruno is significant for being the first monistic philosopher and a predecessor to Spinoza.

Sir Francis Bacon (1561–1626)

Contemporary with Giordano Bruno, but living under more favorable circumstances, Francis Bacon was philosophizing about natural science. A student of law at the University of Cambridge, he embarked on a brilliant political career and finally became lord chancellor to King James I. He was an ambitious man, striving for wealth and fame, and he spent most of his life in the company of nobles and royal personages. Bacon, like so many of his contemporaries, definitely broke away from Aristotle and Scholasticism, and devoted most of his time to the study of the physical sciences and to the writing of philosophical works. Divorcing belief from science, he founded empirical philosophy, that is, philosophy based on experience. Yet, in spite of the work of mathematicians like Galileo and Kepler, Bacon failed to apply mathematics to philosophy. This step was finally taken by the great Frenchman, René Descartes.

THE DECLINE OF THE RENAISSANCE

When did the Renaissance finally end? There are those who believe that its continuity has never been broken, that historical periods must be measured by centuries rather than decades. It may further be argued that the main cultural characteristics which distinguished the Renaissance from the Middle Ages have been sustained in modern times: nationalism over clerical universalism, commercial urbanism over agricultural regionalism, democratic centripetal authority over feudal centrifugal authority, individual over the collective group, science over superstition, the here over the hereafter, and all the rest. The 19th century, with its republicanism, freedom of conscience, progressivism, and scientific and empirical spirit, was probably more of a culmination of the Renaissance than the 20th century, with its state control of thought and absorption of the individual into the mass. Yet it is doubtful whether one could consider that the Renaissance lasted so late.

René Descartes (1596–1650)

The Renaissance began its true decline in the third quarter of the 16th century, before the great accomplishments of Shakespeare, Camoens, Tasso, or Cervantes. For Italy, the seat of the Third Classicism, the sustaining influence of the Revival of Learning, the nation whose arts and sciences had swayed the thoughts and activities of Renaissance men everywhere, fell into a decline. What caused the decline in Italy? Reasons may be adduced by the economic positivists (the great trade routes shifted from the Mediterranean to the Atlantic), by the political scientists (invading armies made a vast battleground of the peninsula), and by the Protestant historians (the Counterreformation suppressed intellectual and creative energies). Or the decline may be explained as a combined result of these and other factors. Whatever the cause, the inspirational springs on the Italian peninsula ran dry, and the resulting siccity in Western Europe lasted just long enough to mark the close of an historical era, one of those rare phenomena men have come to call a golden age. Perhaps other golden ages in the future may match the accomplishments of the Renaissance, but probably none will ever match its enthusiastic belief in the inevitable progress of mankind.

33. Martin Luther and the Protestant Reformation

SCANDALS WITHIN THE CHURCH

THE PROTESTANT REFORMATION has been looked upon as the northern version of the Renaissance. Protestants, in the eyes of the Church, were no more and no less than heretics. The word heresy, meaning "choosing for one's self," gives us an admirable suggestion as to what characterized the spirit of the Protestant. Here again, the innate drive for individual assertion, the same force that gave impetus to the Renaissance, manifested itself in the northern countries.

The story of the Reformation is a dynamic drama. We can definitely recognize feeble beginnings many centuries before the actual issue came to a climax, and it took many years before the opposing factions settled their difficulties in a compromise.

The thirteenth century, which produced a Dante, also carried the germs of religious differences and opposition to the Church. The resentment of heretics was founded particularly on the appalling abuses and scandals within the Church. The clergy were forsaking more and more the religious and social virtues that were requisites for their sacred profession. They were giving free rein to selfish and greedy motives, shocking to the laity. High officers of the Church, bishops, cardinals, and popes alike, no longer made pretenses about their worldly ambitions and desire for luxury. We find the reaction of the common people to the state of affairs in the Church vividly reflected in many medieval literary works.

HERESY AND THE GREAT SCHISM

Heresy was manifested in various religious sects that were particularly prominent in the twelfth and thirteenth centuries. The Waldensians and Albigensians in southern France took some of their doctrines from mystic cults of eastern Europe and the Orient. Although most members of these sects were massacred or scattered by cruel persecutions, they are important because of their stubborn persistence even up to the nineteenth century. They are of even greater immediate significance due to their influence on such early reformers as Wyclif and Huss.

The Church met these infidels in two ways. There was the possibility of remedying the chief abuses by reform within the Church. The establishment of the Dominican and Franciscan orders revived what once were the monastic ideals of Christian poverty and humility, while the various councils of the fifteenth century had attempted to alleviate the worst evils. Another method of suppressing heresy was the resort to plain force and persecution. The Inquisition, an efficient institution for persecution, was devised to eradicate heresy by persuasion or brute strength. Finally, the notorious crusades against the Albigensians and Waldensians, being nothing but wholesale slaughter, were far from successful. They injured the reputation of the Church, and in the end were instrumental in renewing the vigor and resistance of the heretics.

Nothing contributed more to the loss of prestige by the Church than the Great Schism, created by the double papal elections in the fourteenth century. A council held in Pisa in 1409, intended to clarify the situation, only added insult to injury by adding a third pope. The consequent indignation of the whole Christian world demanded an instant settlement of the issue; and the resultant Council of Constance, while it healed the Schism, only succeeded in further stirring the passion of the opponents, by its burning of Huss.

The Burning of John Huss by order of the Council of Constance stirred the Bohemians to revolt against the Church and the authority of the Empire

In connection with the Council of Constance, there was a point of great significance to be noted. The main issue involved in the meetings of the council was whether or not a council's decision was superior to that of the pope. The council's superiority would have meant representative government in the Catholic Church. But the national rivalry and differences among the members of the council effected the triumphant emergence of the pope. The pope had therefore retained his absolute authority, a victory of tremendous consequence throughout the following centuries. After the adjournment of the Council of Constance, the papacy consolidated its worldly possessions and proceeded to extract all possible revenue from its subjects.

Meanwhile, the martyrdom of Huss had aroused violent resentment among the Bohemians. A revolt broke out in Prague, and the imperial troops were driven back by the Hussites. Emperor Sigismund was ignominiously defeated and the surrounding territory plundered. At the Council of Basel peace was made with the moderate faction of the Hussites, while the more radical groups were suppressed.

These various happenings illustrate the decline of the authority of the Church between the eleventh and sixteenth centuries. And yet, despite all these attacks on the Church, despite the heretical movements, despite schisms and scandals—at the close of the fifteenth century the Church still dominated the life of the people. Religion was the unifying force, the one

common interest which had an intensity totally foreign to the present generation.

The Catholic Church at that time practically determined the course of a person's social and spiritual life. Children of Christian parents were born into the Church, as they are born into the state today. The state assumed the enforcement of the people's adherence to the rules and doctrines of the Church. Support of the Church was effected by taxes on individuals, taxes which were compulsory, not optional. In short, it was through the Church alone that man could organize his life in this world and attain eternal happiness hereafter.

RESENTMENT AGAINST PAPAL POLICIES

In the meantime, abuses and scandals were increasing. Pope Alexander VI shocked the whole Christian world with his immoral life and his equally immoral daughter, Lucrezia Borgia. His successor, Julius II, was concerned primarily with the centralization of the

Sigismund II, Holy Roman Emperor, who was defeated by the Hussites

papal states in central Italy. The highly educated Medici pope, Leo X, who embodied the artistic traditions of his famous family, was nevertheless guilty of gross malpractices in his efforts to finance extravagant projects. He was a generous patron of the arts—the greatest artists, including Michelangelo, were in his employ—and he was imbued with the Renaissance desire for art and learning. His ambitious project, the building of St. Peter's in Rome, was a heavy burden on his resources. Funds were procured through loans, through sale of ecclesiastical offices and worst of all, through sales of "indulgences."

The indulgences were an innovation of the sixteenth century. In consideration for a sum of money, an individual was granted an indulgence, which promised to remit all or part of the punishments which were dealt out to a sinner after his death. Indulgences did not forgive nor permit sins, and they were granted by the pope only on the assumption that the transgressor in question had sincerely shown penitence for his sin. True penitence was shown by doing good works, and good works were primarily those which involved money payment to the pope.

The church controlled various other methods of obtaining money. Besides the ordinary revenues, such as Peter's Pence, feudal dues, and court expenses, there were "annates" from the subordinate clergy. It had been customary for every clergyman to derive his support from the proceeds of a tract of land, called the "benefice." After receiving the benefice, the clergyman—priest, abbot, or bishop—usually paid the first year's revenue, the annate, to his ecclesiastical superior. But a vicious practice developed when the pope handed out benefices in all parts of the Christian world to Italian favorites, who drew the revenues from far-off lands and remained in their luxurious homes as absentee landlords. Germany was particularly exploited by the papacy and absentees, and the German people were loath to see so much money flow out of their country into Italy. It aroused an actual nationalistic resentment in Germany and served to put the papacy further into disgrace.

"Pope Leo X and Cardinals," painted by Raphael. The "Medici pope" was a patron of many Renaissance artists, including Michelangelo and Raphael

THE RISING TIDE OF CRITICISM

While the Catholic Church had been able to resist criticisms and suppress heretics for so many centuries, by the opening of the sixteenth century new forces had appeared which were too strong to be dealt with easily. The vice and weakness of the clergy came to popular attention, particularly through the writings of humanist scholars. Erasmus and Reuchlin made profound studies of the Bible and early Christian documents. Emphasis was laid on a purer Christian organization, on the true message of the Gospel, and on a humble clergy. The works of these writers were popularized by various pamphleteers who ridiculed the Church in more coarse and drastic terms.

More radical in their effects were the changes that took place in the economic world. Commerce had increased the supply of money; industries and crafts were freeing themselves from ecclesiastical dominance; a general shift of emphasis from agriculture to urban life and urban occupation was apparent. People became money-minded, and followed pursuits that promised pecuniary enrichment. They cast envious looks on the wealth which the Church possessed, and they were easily won to a movement which promised eventual gains in lands and money. These capitalistic burghers showed great interest in a scheme which entailed the confiscation of Church property, and gladly cooperated with princes to bring about such seizures.

Not only did growing capitalism stir the greed of merchants and manufacturers, but also it further accentuated their comparative freedom of movement and individual strength. They became largely indifferent to their churches, and grew aggressive, vigorous, and assertive.

CONFLICT WITH NATIONALISM

Along with economic and social changes, there came considerable transformation on the political horizon as well. For centuries the Church had been a political power of strong caliber. Its clergy claimed immunity from civil duties, and in spiritual matters held themselves superior to the government. Church property was exempt from civil taxation, while the Church itself levied taxes on all its subjects without interference by the state. All cases involving clergymen, and a few special cases involving outsiders, were tried by the Church's own courts. While such political jurisdiction by the Church proved a blessing in the days of feudalism, it was bound to conflict with the ambitions of worldly rulers when feudalism disintegrated. The growth of national pride and the emergence of nations were accompanied by a desire for absolutism on the part of kings and princes. The Church proved to be the great rival to and hindrance from complete national sovereignty, and rulers realized that not until they had succeeded in subordinating the Church to the state would they be sole heads of their nations.

Under Emperor Maximilian I, the Holy Roman Empire had become particularly strong. Because of significant concentration of power in the Hapsburg family, and due to some very marked territorial additions made by Maximilian, the Hapsburgs were established as sole and undisputed rulers. The days of rivalry among princes for the imperial throne were definitely over. On the other hand, an important counterpart appeared with the development of the imperial diet into a real representative body. Not only the princes but the cities, too, now obtained a vote in the diet, and all important imperial issues were fought in this new and strong assembly. No longer was the Emperor awarded the imperial crown by the pope; he was now *elected* by seven high princes, the Electors. With Maximilian the old dualism, the opposition between nobles and the crown, became especially marked. The Emperor's position was materially and politically strengthened by the addition of Bohemia and Hungary through shrewd marriage arrangements. The inheritance of the duchy of Burgundy and the Netherlands provided the Empire with two buffer states against France, a situation which determined the political history of Europe for the next three centuries. A more doubtful blessing was the joining of Spain to the Empire under Charles V, for it decentralized the imperial power, and became of considerable consequence in determining the course of the Reformation.

Thus we notice radical changes in the religious, social, economic, and political atmosphere of Europe. The ground was prepared for a movement that would give prominent expression to indignation and discontent, sentiments which previously had been hidden and suppressed. It would give vent to ambitions,

Maximilian I receiving a delegation from Vienna

Martin Luther (1483–1546), the great German leader of the Protestant Reformation

LUTHER

There was nothing unusual about the fact that Luther showed disobedience to his father when he sought admittance to the Augustinian order in Erfurt. The following years in the monastery gave the young and serious monk the usual theology and philosophy taught throughout Europe in his day. In these early years, Luther was driven to search for the real meaning of the Gospel, the real message of God, and his longing for clarity was so great that he felt himself drawing away from the clergy around him. He became convinced of the permanence of his own sinful nature through Adam and Eve, and he felt that his penitence, however sincere, was hopelessly inadequate to receive God's grace. He drew on the mystics for inspiration, and suddenly it became clear to him: only by faith, by blindly believing, could man win the grace of God. Desperate had been the struggles before he arrived at this conclusion; joyful was the message of the Gospel, now that the divine light had shown him the true meaning.

greed, and envy—finally to break forth in an immeasurable and uncontrollable movement which shook the Christian world to its core. It would become an organized protest as soon as there would appear one man, sufficiently convinced, able, and courageous—a vigorous leader. At the end of the sixteenth century such a leader appeared in the person of Martin Luther. He was soon to lead the army of *protesters* into a general *protestant revolution*.

THE NINETY-FIVE THESES

This was Luther's mental and spiritual state when the issue of indulgences came up.

Martin Luther nailing his 95 theses to the church door at Wittenberg. In these theses, which opposed the sale of indulgences, Luther made his first break with the church. The theses were widely copied

He had already become a reformer from within, so it is erroneous to believe that the arrogant sale of indulgences—an external factor—led Luther to oppose the church. But the effrontery of the salesmen shocked Luther. He believed that the pope was unaware of the corruption of these clerical vendors, and he was resolved to draw the Holy Father's attention to this lamentable state of affairs. He did not know the financial crookedness involved in the sales—the personal enrichment of the archbishop of Mainz, his bribing of the papal officers, and his loans from the Fuggers—his only concern was the corruption of the clergy and the blessing of Jesus.

It was not so much the idea of "selling" indulgences which Luther resented, but rather the conception that pardon or grace could be obtained for any good deeds whatsoever, without having complete faith, was the intrinsic objection. Firm in the belief that it could not possibly be the pope's intent to offer indulgences so promiscuously, and determined to bring the truth of "indulgences" to public attention, on October 31, 1517, he posted the famous ninety-five theses on the door of the court church in Wittenberg.

The theses, or assertions, were written in Latin and signified a challenge to a theological debate. Being translated into German, they were widely read and aroused great popular interest. Luther still had no intentions of breaking from the Church; he would have been deeply insulted to be termed a heretic in the sense in which John Huss had been condemned. When the news of Luther's action reached Rome, Pope Leo X summoned the monk to appear before his judges in Rome. However, the pope was prevailed upon by Luther's protector, Frederick of Saxony, to transfer the trial to Germany.

LUTHER'S BREAK WITH ROME

A year after the theses had been posted in Wittenberg, Luther, in his indigent monk's attire, undertook his pilgrimage to Augsburg where the trial was scheduled to take place. He appeared before the papal legate, a cardinal imbued with enough Erasmian learning to be a broad-minded and modern prelate. The legate found Luther to be a far more learned and profound theologian than he had expected, but between the two men there was an unbridgeable gap in their respective doctrines. Luther refused to recant, and fled into seclusion.

Following his trial in Augsburg, Luther went one step further in his new theology. In a debate with the celebrated Catholic theologian, John Eck, he admitted openly that certain points of his doctrine coincided with those of John Huss, and expressed his doubt as to the infallibility of the pope and of the Church councils. Having thus identified himself with a notorious heretic, Luther had definitely broken his connection with the Church.

Now Luther was convinced that open revolt, not by force but by preaching and writing, was the only way of succeeding in a reform of the Church. He penned a series of vigorous attacks on the Church, pamphlets persuading the nobles to revolt, and other works expounding the new belief. Leo X promptly excommunicated him, and a summons was sent to him by the Emperor commanding his presence at the Diet of Worms. Luther, armed with a writ of protection from Charles V, presented himself to the assembly of all ecclesiastical and lay princes of the Empire. And here too, in his bold, stubborn, German manner, he refused to recant, and consequently was pronounced an outlaw. Luther then retired to the Wartburg, the castle of the elector of Saxony. There he undertook a new translation of the Bible, a work which exerted profound influence on the new High German language.

THE REFORMATION AND GERMAN ECONOMICS

The next few decades witnessed the development of Luther's rebellion into a national movement. We must bear in mind that the new Emperor, Charles V, had his hands full in disciplining his many distant lands. He was kept occupied in the Netherlands, in Spain, and in Italy, and thus could not easily carry out a concentrated suppression of the German heretics. The ranks of the latter swelled with the new support of men from all classes and regions, but especially from the urban centers in the north. The prospect of taking over Church

Luther under Examination at the Diet of Worms in 1521. Here, Luther, who had been excommunicated and was pressed by demands to recant, made a forthright refusal. A month later a papal ban was put on him

properties appealed to nobles, merchants, and peasants alike. It was relatively easy for powerful princes to lend protection to the movement, since the imperial government was weak and inefficient. Peasants who felt oppressed were eager to gain improvement of their lot by joining a promising movement.

A contributory cause was the nationalistic feeling that became apparent among the German people during the sixteenth century. Not only was there resentment that so much money flowed into Italy, but Germans actually felt that they were being tyrannized by a foreign power. Slogans were coined which reminded the people of the victory of the German armies under the heroic Arminius against the Roman oppressors. The time had come for the descendants of Arminius again to repel the dominance of the descendants of Varus, the commander of the legion of Rome.

Before long the Reformation seemed to be taking on a distinctly revolutionary character, and the various uprisings that occurred in southern and western Germany did not exactly contribute to the prestige of the movement

among the upper classes. One of the most ardent supporters was the poet-knight, Ulrich von Hutten, who wrote a number of pamphlets and poems against the Catholic Church. He was a prophet of the new nationalism, but not in favor of using force.

Quite different was the temperament of Franz von Sickingen, an adventurous army leader equal to the most unscrupulous, bold condottiere of the fourteenth century. He laid siege to the city of Trier with the largest army he ever had; but here was a case where the ecclesiastical power, the archbishop of Trier, was fully equal to the worldly knight. Sickingen was forced to leave Trier, was pursued by the armies of the warlike bishop, and finally defeated and killed in his fortress in 1523.

THE PEASANTS' REVOLT

Of much greater magnitude and of a grave nature was the Peasants' Revolt that came in the next year. Most important among the motives of the uprising were economic grievances. The dominant cause was the encroachment upon their old rights by petty nobles, rights which the peasants were determined to defend. They justified their action on grounds of the new teachings of Luther; the divine justice, promised in the Gospel, they chose to take into their own hands. Even the Twelve Articles which they published did not express their real grievances, and were only a "party program" under which they could organize.

The revolt spread through Swabia and Franconia, and was characterized by barbarous roughness. Luther was indignant. He went south to preach obedience and nonviolence. But he was shouted down and almost attacked by the wild mobs, whereupon he encouraged the nobility to "smite, strangle, or stab" the rebels. His words were hardly necessary, for the revolt was crushed with the utmost cruelty in 1525. As many as fifty thousand people were slaughtered in the war, and the nobles emerged stronger than ever.

PROTESTANTISM TRIUMPHANT

Philip Melanchthon (1497–1560)

Meanwhile, another imperial diet at Speyer, while not recognizing the legal status of the new faith, had declared that "each prince should so conduct himself as he could answer for his behavior to God and to the Emperor," a vague declaration but rather favorable to the reformers. When a subsequent diet revoked this declaration by the decision that laws against heretics should be enforced, the Lutherans presented a formal protest. The name Protestant was derived from this protest.

Conciliation between the Catholic and Lutheran princes becoming impossible, Philip Melanchthon, humanist and close friend of Luther, drew up and presented a statement of the Lutheran principles to the diet at Augsburg in 1530. The "Augsburg Confession," as it was called, was rejected by the diet, and conciliation was henceforth out of the question.

The Emperor, becoming vexed by the disobedience of his subjects, planned to exterminate heresy by military force. The Protestant princes responded by uniting in the Schmalkaldic League for effective resistance. A series of conflicts, known as the Schmalkaldic Wars, ensued during which neither the imperial forces nor the Protestants achieved any decisive results. The Peace of Augsburg which followed granted to the Lutheran princes freedom of worship and the right to introduce their own faith within their territories.

Thus, the treaty of Augsburg marked the actual establishment of the Protestant faith. The new church ignored all papal authority, as well as any worship of saints, the Virgin, or relics. Services were now in German, while belief in purgatory, indulgences, and pilgrimages was rejected. In general, it was decided to retain everything in the church organization and services that was not, in their judgment, forbidden by the Bible.

The Reformation did not confine itself to Germany alone. Conditions which favored the Reformation in that country were also largely present in other countries, and the movement spread very rapidly into all parts of northern and central Europe. Due to the varying local conditions, it took on a different character in different countries. Furthermore, the new faith was often used for political purposes. In Denmark, Frederick I and Christian III introduced Lutheranism because it broke the authority of the Catholic Church which rivaled the royal power. The sympathy of Swedish Catholics for union with Denmark moved the king, Gustavus Vasa, to introduce Protestantism into Sweden. The Protestants embodied the national cause, and it was not long until the new faith pushed out the old. In western European countries the Reformation evolved a new type of Protestantism, which, taken as a whole, is known as Calvinism.

King Gustavus I Vasa (1496–1560)

34. Protestant Sects and Counter-Reformation

ZWINGLI AND RELIGIOUS WAR IN SWITZERLAND

THE FORERUNNER of the Reformation in Switzerland was Ulrich Zwingli, a contemporary of Luther, and a Catholic priest in the small town of Einsiedeln. His early opposition to the papacy was confined to criticism on certain political abuses in which the papacy was involved. Upon his appointment as a preacher in the Zurich Cathedral, he came out boldly with a denial of papal supremacy, advocating the Bible as the sole source for guidance. The canton of Zurich supported its preacher and declared complete independence from the Catholic Church. Other cantons followed rapidly in the acceptance of the new doctrines held by Zwingli.

Attempts were made to cooperate with the parallel movement led by Luther in Germany.

Ulrich Zwingli

But there existed some insurmountable differences between the doctrines of the two men. Zwingli urged far more radical reforms: he insisted on the reform of the government as well as of the Church. His aim was an ideal state, in which democratic practices in politics and religion would prevail. In 1524 five of the "forest" cantons banded together against Zurich and the Reformation movement; five other cantons accepted it; while the other two remained Catholic. In 1531, war broke out between the Catholic cantons and Zurich. The Protestant canton was defeated in the Battle of Kappel, and Zwingli was killed. The peace that followed provided that each canton could determine its own religion. Switzerland has remained partly Protestant, partly Catholic to this day. Throughout the rest of the century, however, there were conflicts.

JOHN CALVIN

Deprived of its founder, the movement was continued under the Frenchman John Calvin, after whom the Swiss reform movement was named. He had been "converted" in a vague way in his early years, and desired to organize a purer Christian church. There had been no formal revolt away from the Church; but France, like other countries, was filled with

John Calvin

humanists and religious critics. Lutheran doctrines had penetrated into the country and there was a widespread discontent with the Church.

When it became known that Francis I, king of France, intended to persecute the religious dissenters in his kingdom, Calvin thought it expedient to leave the country. He went to Geneva and aided the citizens in their struggle for liberty against the Catholic Duke of Savoy. As a reward he was given the post of chief pastor of the city, a position which came to be a high civil and religious office.

Calvin came to be the head of a theocracy, a government by religious leaders, that exerted a rigid rule on the city of Geneva. Radical reforms were inaugurated under Calvin's despotism, and Geneva became famous throughout Europe. Worldly amusements, such as dances, theaters, music, and, to some extent, art were looked upon as works of the devil, and were banned from the life of the people. A cloud of austerity hung over the community, while Calvin was busy issuing numerous treatises, as well as a French translation of the Bible. He founded the University of Geneva which soon enrolled students from France, the Netherlands, Germany and Scotland, and was responsible for the diffusion of Calvinism to many foreign countries.

Calvinists in France came to be known as Huguenots. Although Protestant doctrines did not have nearly as many supporters in France as in Germany, large numbers of middle-class people embraced Calvinism. Here too, it appealed to the moneyed classes and to a large portion of the lower nobility. The civil law courts contained a particularly large element of Protestants, and it was here that royal power was most effectively opposed.

RELIGIOUS WARS IN FRANCE

A period of religious wars began in the middle of the sixteenth century when Catherine de' Medici became regent of France. It was a long internal struggle, interspersed with sporadic attempts at conciliation. Powerful nobles, among them the Bourbons, had taken up the Huguenot cause. On August 24, 1572, there began a series of massacres, initiated by Catherine de' Medici, and aimed toward the annihilation of the Huguenots. The first of these massacres is known as the St. Bartholomew's Day Massacre. It is estimated that perhaps 10,000 were killed during the frightful period.

Catherine de' Medici

War continued with Henry of Navarre leading the Huguenot cause. Henry aspired to become king. Realizing that being a Protestant would prevent the achievement of his ambition, he abjured Protestantism. In 1594, he ascended the throne as Henry IV, although he had actually ruled since 1589. In spite of his defection, Henry came to the aid of the Huguenots.

In the Edict of Nantes (1598) he granted them toleration and a degree of self-government.

SPREAD OF CALVINISM ON THE CONTINENT

The Swiss reform movement radiated from Geneva to all adjoining territories. In the southern states of Germany, where Luther's opposition to the Peasants' Revolt had already alienated large numbers from Lutheranism, Calvinism permeated the middle classes. The Treaty of Augsburg, which recognized only the Catholic and Lutheran churches, prevented the spread of Calvinistic doctrines. In Germany they did not attain toleration until the end of the Thirty Years' War.

The Netherlands, due to their proximity to Germany, were naturally exposed to the reform movement. But Charles V tried energetically to stamp out the Lutheran heresy, and he largely succeeded. Yet in the end it was succeeded by another form of Protestantism, for Calvinism was descending from Geneva along the Rhine provinces. In the southern provinces—Spanish Netherlands—the Catholic Church persisted, but the northern part of the country in its fight for independence from Spain emerged dominantly Calvinistic.

POLITICAL NATURE OF THE ENGLISH REFORMATION

The English Reformation was mainly a political movement clothed with religious phrases. Prior to the Reformation a strong anticlerical and antipapal movement had arisen. There had been constant antagonism between the clergy and some other elements, for it was felt that the clergy formed a state within a state, subject not to English control but to that of Rome.

England had never been one of the strongest pillars of the Catholic Church. From the days of William the Conqueror there had been a dislike of the interference of Rome in English affairs. John Wyclif had fulminated against the interference of the Church in secular affairs. He wished church property to be confiscated, and his ideas on this point had been very well received at the time. After the establishment of Tudor supremacy (1485), Eng-

Johannes Gutenberg's Movable Type, invented about the middle of the 15th century. Cheaper printing processes resulted and printing spread through Europe.

Mona Lisa (La Gioconda), painted by Leonardo da Vinci from 1503 to 1506. This exquisite portrait is a fine example of Renaissance art. It now hangs in the Louvre.

The Edict of Worms, 1521. Martin Luther had been excommunicated. He refused to recant when summoned by Charles V to Worms to present his case to the Diet of the Holy Roman Empire. Charles issued the Edict of Worms, which condemned Luther and his works. He was pronounced a heretic, and his works were proscribed.

Mary, Queen of Scots on the eve of her execution. When Elizabeth I of England suspected that her cousin Mary had conspired against her to become queen of England, she imprisoned her. Eighteen years later (1587), Elizabeth ordered her execution. The night before her death she gave her jewels to friends and servants.

Henry VIII Chartering a Barber-Surgeons' Guild. Once two separate guilds, the barbers and surgeons in London united but kept their separate functions. In Tudor England many guilds were amalgamated under one head. The state also increased the regulation of their activities. Henry VIII granted his charter to many guilds.

ROBERT FLEURY: Three Lions

Galileo Before the Inquisition, 1633. The great astronomer and physicist refused to retract his doctrines concerning the universe. He believed that the earth was not the center of the universe but revolved around the sun. He finally recanted; however, on rising he is said to have murmured to himself, "Yet it moves!"

After painting by ARTHUR A. HUNT: Three Lions

Elizabeth I and William Gilbert, the "father of electricity." His experiments with magnetism led him to discover the connection between electricity and magnetism. The electro-magnetic motor is the outgrowth of this observation. He was the queen's physician, as well as England's leading physical scientist.

Molière and his Company of Actors. Jean Baptiste Poquelin, known as Molière, was the greatest French dramatist of the 17th century. He found favor with King Louis XIV and rose to great success. His comedies ridiculed the morals and manners of his age. His company of actors was known as the "King's Company."

Louis XIV, the Sun King, King of France from 1643 to 1715. His despotic rule and his desire for French colonial supremacy kept Europe in continual turmoil.

Peter the Great, Czar of Russia 1689-1725. He introduced western culture into Russia, established absolutism, and raised Russia to the rank of a great power.

First Meeting of Henry VIII and Anne of Cleves.
Henry thought his new queen looked like a "Flanders
mare." The marriage was soon annulled. It had been
contracted to ally Henry with German Protestants

lish nationalism had grown even stronger and
with it the hatred of Rome.

The marital affairs of Henry VIII (1509-
1547) brought the issue of England versus the
Roman Church to the fore. Henry cared little
if anything about religion. At the appearance of
Lutheranism he wrote a pamphlet in defense of
the Catholic doctrines for which he received
the title, Defender of the Faith, from the pope.
Later he took the opposite view. His main concern was the perpetuation of his rule.

Henry's wife, Catherine of Aragon, was the
widow of his younger brother, Arthur. This
marriage, although against church law, had
been permitted by the pope. Catherine gave
birth to many children, but only one, the sick-
ly Mary, survived. Some feared that Catherine
had become barren because of the breaking of
the church law. Above all, Henry wanted a
legitimate male heir in order to insure the continuity of his line. To make matters worse he
fell in love with the pretty Anne Boleyn. Soon
he turned to the pope, Clement VII, for an annulment of his marriage; but Charles V, the
nephew of Catherine, used his influence to
prevent Clement from granting the decree.

The king became impatient, especially because Anne was awaiting the birth of a child
who, Henry hoped, would be a boy. Henry
put a series of acts through Parliament (1529-
1534) establishing the Church of England,
with the king as its head. The king was di-
vorced from Catherine and soon married Anne
who bore him a daughter, Elizabeth.

SUPREMACY OF THE CHURCH OF ENGLAND

The formulation of a religious doctrine
for the new church was conditioned by political considerations. At the prospect of an
alliance with the German princes, Henry
leaned toward Lutheranism. As the pros-
pects faded, his Lutheran feelings did likewise. Toward the end of his reign many
Catholic doctrines were restored. However,
both Catholics and Protestants were burned
for nonconformity to Henry's changing beliefs. Confiscation of monasteries and other
church property proceeded all through Henry's
reign. The immorality of the clergy had been
the excuse for having Parliament pass successive acts confiscating the extensive property of the church. Part of the revenue was
devoted to the king's own uses, and the rest
was parceled out among the nobles who were
most in need of persuasion.

At Henry's death he was succeeded by Edward VI (1547-1553), a son by his third
wife, Jane Seymour. Extreme Protestantism
flourished for a while, but the early death of
the frail king brought Mary (1553-1558) to
the throne. Being the daughter of Catherine,
she had been brought up a Catholic. In her
short reign she incurred the lasting enmity of
all England. The Catholic religion was restored and many dissenters were burned.
The populace called her "Bloody Mary."
Her marriage to the hated Philip II of Spain
did not add to her popularity. Mary's efforts
to restore Catholicism failed, for she soon
died without leaving an heir.

Her successor, Elizabeth (1558-1603), had
no other choice but Protestantism. The Catholics regarded Henry's marriage with Anne
Boleyn as void. Hence they looked upon
Mary, Queen of Scots, the great-grand-

Queen Mary and Philip II plighting their troth. The marriage was extremely unpopular in England

daughter of Henry VII, as the legitimate queen. Under Elizabeth the Anglican Church took its final shape. Doctrine was of minor importance to Elizabeth: she was interested in securing conformity and loyalty. The Anglican doctrine, as stated in the Thirty-nine Articles (1563), was most nearly Catholic of all the Protestant creeds.

Elizabeth felt that loyalty to her was synonymous with loyalty to the Church of England. Therefore neither Catholics nor dissenting Protestants were tolerated. A Court of High Commission was established to deal with heresy, be it Protestant or Catholic.

Nevertheless, large sections of the English people were not good Anglicans. Within the church a group known as Puritans demanded that Anglicanism be cleansed of its Catholic elements. Outside of the church, Presbyterians, Independents, and other Protestant sects were growing apace. There was also a considerable Catholic minority.

REFORMATION IN SCOTLAND

North of England, in Scotland, events were unfolding rapidly. The Church was in a deplorable condition. The clergy was licentious, turbulent, and much too wealthy for its own good. The Church owned half the wealth of Scotland. The government was in a chaotic condition. The nobles were in a constant state of war, either with the English, or uniting against a weak king or regent.

In 1525 the first Lutheran influence was felt in Scotland. One of the first converts, a noble by the name of Patrick Hamilton, was executed in 1528. The king, James V, attempted to suppress Lutheranism, but he died in 1542, and Cardinal Beaton carried forward the persecution until a few incensed Protestants stopped his activities forever in 1546, by murdering the Cardinal in his castle.

The name which dominates the Scotch Reformation is that of John Knox. Knox had felt the "call" of the Reformation at an early age. Within a short time he was arrested and committed to the galleys. After his release he went to England where his religious convictions became stronger. For a time he was the royal chaplain, but after the accession of "Bloody Mary" he fled to the Continent. Knox soon turned up at Geneva where he was greatly affected by Calvin. From Geneva he became the counselor of the ever-growing Scotch Reform party.

Mary Queen of Scots (1542–87)

John Knox (1505–72), leader of the Reformation in Scotland

At the insistence of the Scotch lords, Knox returned to Scotland where the Protestants already had a pre-eminent position. This fact, together with the support of England, placed power in the hands of the Protestant lords. The return of the fiery Knox fanned the flame. As he thundered against idolatry and popery, the reform movement grew swiftly.

Mary, Queen of Scots, who had ascended the throne, was compelled to summon a parliament. Here the burghers and small lords assumed control and effected a religious revolution. The new faith was called Presbyterianism, an extreme form of Calvinism and destined to become very influential.

The new faith was accompanied by a new regime, a partly democratic, puritanical theocracy in which the ministers and elders of the church were in control. As in Geneva, the life, manners, and thoughts of the people were subjected to narrow and rigid supervision. In theory, church and state were to work hand in hand. In fact, the "kirk" was the state.

MINOR SECTS—THE RADICAL PROTESTANTS

The Reformation was not only the revolt of Lutheranism and Calvinism against the Catholic Church, but there were also many diverse, opposing factions. It was a thorough religious revolution; a dozen new sects were formed, most of which had an individualistic tendency and failed to cooperate with the leading Protestant faiths.

Most of these minor sects can be classified as radical Protestants. They generally relied on the Scriptures for their beliefs, rejected all those religious usages that were not expressly commanded by the Bible, and usually opposed any form of church organization. What made these radical sects really dangerous, however, was their view of government. They were ardent advocates of a general overthrow of the governments and the establishment of some form of communism or even complete anarchy. It is understandable, therefore, why their members were ruthlessly persecuted by political authorities, as well as by Lutherans, Calvinists, and Catholics.

The Anabaptists were a curious sect, exemplifying the principles of Evangelicalism, a system in which the emotional element predominated. It insisted on an individual, spiritual intimacy with Christ, a relationship which was totally divested of theological doctrine. Evangelicalists believed that the Scriptures, word for word, were divinely inspired. Besides these evangelicalistic principles, Anabaptism believed in baptism for adults, since only the conscious and mature decision of an adult could effect conversion and salvation. The foremost preacher and leader of the Anabaptists was Thomas Münzer. After failing to win Luther's sympathy, he wandered through Germany, preaching political and religious anarchy. He was finally executed after passionately supporting the peasants in their revolt.

A very strange form of Anabaptism existed temporarily in the Westphalian city of Munster. Here a communistic group was organized under John of Leiden, a Dutch tailor. He believed himself to be the successor of King David, and he followed his prototype in everything including the sanction of polygamy. But after a short-lived existence of two years, the city was reoccupied by the Catholics, and "King David's successor" was beheaded.

Anabaptism had many recruits from the lower classes, miners, peasants, and crude craftsmen. It appealed generally to people who wished to live a humble life. There existed several versions of this faith, and among these the tenets of the Mennonites from Holland were prominent. In later times Anabaptists have been called simply Baptists.

Congregationalism did more perhaps than any other faith to cause the creation of numerous sects. Its intrinsic principle is an emphasis on independent "congregations"

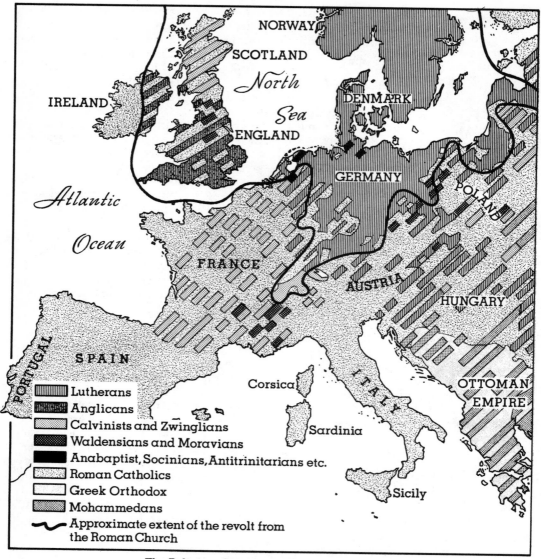

The Religious Situation in Europe about 1560

free from the influence of an institution or even from outsiders. These bodies consisted of lay members who elected their own officers, and who were subject only to the rules of their own congregation. From this tendency toward local freedom there arose various similar sects whose very names indicate their nature: Separatists, Independents, Puritans.

In contrast to the Evangelicalists, there were radical Protestants who rejected the mystical elements of Christianity and sought an intellectual interpretation of religion. These radical groups, which were violently opposed by the Catholic and Protestant churches, later formed the Unitarian sect.

While most of the radical Protestant sects were comparatively unimportant in the beginning, it is certain that they considerably influenced the further development of Protestantism. The critical tendencies of Unitarians gave rise in the eighteenth century to Deism and the modern "Liberal Christianity" which has become the religious attitude of most Protestants in recent times. Evangelicalism, on the other hand, was instrumental in the development of Puritanism and Methodism in England.

THE CATHOLIC REFORMATION

The great upheaval that was caused by the Protestant Reformation was bound to give rise to a reaction on the part of the Catholic Church. Far from being indifferent, the Church was well aware of the criticism advanced by the rebels, and it made an honest effort to remove the main grounds for discontent. It is difficult to determine whether the Catholic Church would have undergone an inner reform regardless of the Protestant revolt, or whether it reacted to the revolt with a "counter-reformation" to safeguard its existence. In either case, the seriousness of the Protestant revolt certainly gave further impetus to the Catholic Reformation. It is significant that the Church possessed so much flexibility of action despite the hardened dogmatism of its teachings. It was just such flexibility as this that has enabled the Catholic Church to overcome all crises and to maintain its position to this day.

The foremost defender of the Catholic Church during the sixteenth century was the former Spanish soldier, Ignatius of Loyola. Realizing the danger that threatened the Church, he resolved to organize an order which would assist in the fight against the rebels. Insisting on absolute obedience, poverty, and chastity, the Jesuits, by educating children and by carrying Catholicism to natives in America, Africa, and Asia, succeeded in winning back many members. The Jesuits used every possible device to reestablish the authority of the pope; the powers of rulers and traditions of literature, art, and science were enlisted to reinforce the Catholic Church.

Complementary to the aggressive actions of the Jesuits, the Church attempted to fight

"Miracle of St. Ignatius of Loyola," a painting by Peter Paul Rubens

heresy by reviving an old, but rather ineffective, institution of the thirteenth century, the Inquisition. Adhering rigidly to the "Index," a list containing a series of proscriptions of heretical books, the Inquisition proceeded to punish any possible offenders. It was especially active in Spain and Italy, but as a measure for opposing the Protestants it was decidedly less effective than other more enlightened methods taken by the Church.

Of great importance in stimulating further reforms was the meeting of the Council of Trent in the middle of the sixteenth century. Although Protestants had been invited to attend, no Protestant was present. The council remedied most of the abuses and clearly defined certain doctrines. All of the principles of the Church, like the sacraments and indulgences, were retained, and Protestantism was completely rejected. This position, while it purified and clarified the Church as an institution, utterly prevented reconciliation with the rebels.

35. The Thirty Years' War

THE GATHERING STORM

THE TREATY OF AUGSBURG in 1555, while it offered a temporary truce between Catholics and Protestants, contained one vexatious and unsettled issue, the so-called Ecclesiastical Reservation. At the time of the treaty, no agreement could be reached on this provision, which prohibited further secularization of Church lands. Since land is, after all, of singular importance because of the wealth that is produced, and since land was owned and ruled by princes, it is easily conceivable why the powerful princes were primarily interested in the provisions of the Treaty of Augsburg. For the Catholic princes it had already meant the loss of a great deal of property; for the Protestant, "territorial" princes it meant a good possibility of making additional territorial gains. The series of wars which followed more than half a century after the Augsburg peace was fought by and in the interest of princes. The Thirty Years' War was, therefore, predominantly a political war.

As a result of the persistent efforts of the Catholic Reformation, the Catholic party had succeeded in regaining a large number of territories from the Protestants. In order to retain these gains and definitely to check any further spread of Protestantism, the Catholic princes formed a league under the leadership of Duke Maximilian of Bavaria. Likewise, the Protestants were preparing for effective opposition by means of the Protestant Union, headed by the ambitious Frederick, Elector of the Palatinate. But it was not only an issue involving Catholic and Protestant princes; the danger of Hapsburg absolutism was equally apparent to both parties. Emperor Matthias had made some attempt to centralize Hapsburg power, and there was strong possibility that, being childless, he would be succeeded by the far more ambitious and fanatic Ferdinand of Bohemia.

Because he was a man of iron determination, cool-headed even in the most trying difficulties, and bearing a passionate hatred for anything non-Catholic, the accession of Ferdinand was certain to result in a formidable advance against all Protestant factions. Emperor Matthias had been forced frequently enough, under the pressure of the threatening Turkish peril, and the dangerous Protestant alliances, to make concessions to the latter in regard to the religious and secular provisions of the Augsburg Treaty.

By the opening of the seventeenth century there had developed an unbearable tension between all political and religious factions in the Holy Roman Empire. While political greed was the main issue, religious sympathies added new vitality to the alliances, and religious motives furnished a convenient guise for more material ambitions. Sweden's part in the war is a good example of this dual motivation, while the case of France plainly reveals the political considerations, since that country disregarded religious sympathies altogether.

BOHEMIAN PHASE OF THE THIRTY YEARS' WAR

In 1618 an event occurred which gave the signal for belligerent action. Bohemian nobles, who feared the election of Ferdinand to the imperial throne, forced their way into a conference of imperial representatives in the castle of Prague, and threw them out of the window into a moat which surrounded it. Following this "defenestration," which was a

Count Ernst Mansfeld, from a Van Dyck painting

Ferdinand II (1578–1637)

gross insult to imperial prestige, the Bohemian nobles deposed Ferdinand from the throne of Bohemia and elected the head of the Protestant Union, the Calvinistic Frederick, elector palatine, as the king of Bohemia.

To the great distress of the Bohemian nobles, Matthias I died in the same year and Ferdinand of Bohemia was elected Holy Roman Emperor. Ferdinand presently proceeded to oust Frederick from the Bohemian throne. Under the command of Count Thurn the Bohemian army staged a revolt in Prague. The Protestant Union joined the Bohemians by sending them the adventurous and hotheaded Count Mansfeld with an army. The new Emperor, Ferdinand II, having now allied himself with the Duke of Bavaria, as well as with Spain and the Elector of Saxony, was able to inflict a disastrous defeat on the Protestant forces. Frederick lost his Bohemian crown, his lands in the Palatinate were confiscated, and he himself was compelled to seek refuge in Holland. As a consequence of the defeat of Frederick, now called the "Winter King" because of his short-lived kingship, the Catholic armies, with the help

of the Spanish, conquered the Palatinate. Protestantism was outlawed in Bohemia, and the Protestant Union was dissolved.

For the Protestants the future looked sinister. The dominance of the Hapsburg crown, with its powerful allies, seemed definitely assured. The Protestants, moreover, were badly weakened, and lack of mutual agreement made cooperative action impossible. The hopes that were pinned on the Elector Palatine were shattered since his ignominious defeat, and the expected aid from his father-in-law, James I of England, was not forthcoming.

DANISH INTERVENTION

At this point, the Protestant future was brightened temporarily by the intervention of Christian IV of Denmark. Christian was anxious to increase his control over the Baltic Sea, and as Duke of Holstein he was opposed to the encroaching authority of the Hapsburgs. Liberally subsidized by the English, and furnished with troops by numerous German princes, he invaded Germany. He was met by the imperial troops under Tilly

The Count of Tilly (1559–1632)

Albrecht von Wallenstein (1583–1632)

and the extraordinary general, Albert of Wallenstein. The latter was a Bohemian noble who had reaped an immense fortune out of the confiscated property of rebels. Prompted by boundless ambition for power and wealth, he organized a private army and offered his services to the Emperor. Faced with a new enemy in the person of Christian IV, Ferdinand was only too glad to accept the services of Wallenstein, and appointed him chief commander of the imperial army. The combined forces of Tilly and Wallenstein were able to defeat the Danish king and drive him out of German territory. Hostilities ceased with the signing of the Treaty of Lubeck in 1629, which permitted Christian to keep all of his possessions with the exception of a few German bishoprics.

In the same year, the Catholic party followed up its successes by persuading the Emperor to issue the Edict of Restitution, which provided for the restoration to the Catholic party of all property illegally confiscated by the Protestants since the Treaty of Augsburg in 1555. The Emperor was also persuaded to dismiss the all too powerful General Wallenstein on the grounds that his

armies supported themselves by robbing and plundering the German population.

The third phase of the war was characterized by the appearance of a new power on the Protestant side. Gustavus Adolphus, king of

King Gustavus Adolphus (1594–1632)

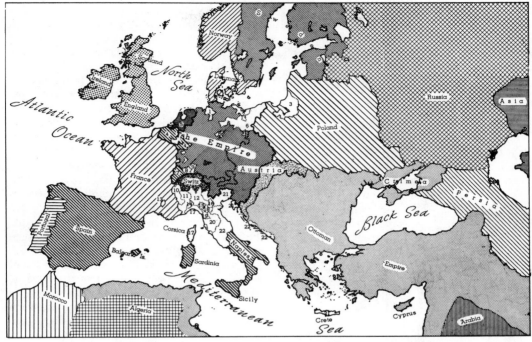

Map of Europe after the Treaty of Westphalia in 1648

1. Bremen	8. Sundgau	16. Mantua
2. Hither Pomerania	9. Breisach (Austria)	17. Genoa and holdings
3. Prussia	10. Savoy	18. Modena
4. Spanish Netherlands	11. Piedmont	19. Florence
5. United Netherlands	12. Milan	20. Tuscany
6. Brandenburg	13. Orange	21. Venice and holdings
7. Franche Comte	14. Montferrat	22. Papal States
	15. Parma	

Sweden, led by similar political and religious motives as Christian of Denmark, decided to oppose Hapsburg power by aiding the Protestant forces. He was an ambitious monarch who had dreams of extending his influence on the Baltic by a possible acquisition of Pomerania and Prussia, which would raise Sweden to the status of the leading power of northern Europe. He was also convinced that he was the divinely appointed champion of the Protestant cause, just as Ferdinand felt himself to be the ordained protector of the Catholic Church. Gustavus Adolphus landed in Pomerania with a powerful army, the best disciplined and most modern of this time, drove out the imperial forces, and succeeded in gaining the support of the Elector of Saxony and the Elector of

Brandenburg. Leading his armies to southern Germany, at the Battle of Lützen he was able to defeat the imperial army under the command of Wallenstein, who had been hastily reinstated as commander in chief. At this battle, however, the great protector of Lutheranism in the north was mortally wounded.

Following the death of Gustavus Adolphus, the government of Sweden passed into the hands of the king's loyal adviser and tutor, Oxenstierna, who decided to continue the war with the Hapsburgs. The German princes reaffirmed their support of Sweden in the alliance formed by the League of Heilbronn.

In the succeeding battles no decisive advantage was gained by either side until, in the

Battle of Nördlingen, the Swedish army was practically destroyed. In the same year, Brandenburg and Saxony withdrew from the war and peace was made with the Emperor at Prague in 1635.

FRENCH INTERVENTION AND END OF THE THIRTY YEARS' WAR

France, under the dictatorship of the shrewd Cardinal Richelieu, had given little actual support to the Protestants up to this time. Richelieu, although a Catholic, was moved by other than religious considerations. His main fear was the threatening absolutism and hegemony of the Hapsburg family, and

"The Great Condé"

Marshal Turenne

he was determined to oppose them by fair means or foul. Negotiations had already resulted in subsidies for Gustavus Adolphus, and now, after his death, there was strong possibility of Sweden's withdrawal from the war. The ambitious cardinal now openly declared war against the Empire and sent his ablest generals, Condé and Turenne, to reconquer the Palatinate of the Rhine and to oppose the Spanish forces in the Netherlands. In 1636 the war lost much of its meaning and vitality due to the sudden death of Ferdinand II. The new monarch, Ferdinand III, was desirous of peace, and, because of the general exhaustion of most of the participants, negotiations for peace were begun. Finally, after several years of indecision and disagreement, the Peace of Westphalia was signed in 1648.

Under the terms of the Peace of Westphalia, Sweden received as a fief of the Empire, Pomerania and various German cities on the Baltic coast, as well as a few bishoprics and a large sum of money. France was given the important cities of Metz, Verdun, and Toul. Brandenburg was compensated for the loss of Pomerania by the gain of the city of Magdeburg and three other bishoprics in central Germany. In this treaty also, the United Netherlands and Switzerland were finally recognized as independent republics. In general, there was an attempt to return to the status quo before 1618. The religious conflicts were settled in a compromise giving recognition to Lutherans and Calvinists on an equal footing with Catholics. Württemberg, Baden, and the lower Palatinate were permitted to exercise their new religion, while the rebels of Austria and Bohemia were given no additional rights. The ecclesiastical reservation was to be enforced in the future, while all territories secularized before January 1, 1624, were to remain as such.

Thus ended the great conflict between Catholics and Protestants, between the Hapsburgs and their enemies, between the old time and the new. Protestantism was able to gain complete recognition, but it was not able to eliminate Catholicism. It is erroneous to think that, with this recognition, the principle of religious freedom and toleration was completely achieved; religious freedom is a very recent achievement, and is only indirectly due to the efforts of Protestantism. It is often believed also that Protestantism furthered the democratic principle; this was true at first chiefly of the Calvinists with the system of self-government in their organization. It is also interesting to note the opinion of some scholars that modern capitalism was in part derived from the Reformation. Here too, the Calvinists may be regarded as largely responsible for the ethics of work and thrift which were advocated in Calvinistic teachings, and which were favorable to the accumulation of capital. In summary, it can be said that the Reformation, by gaining recognition that man's beliefs could operate through new channels and organizations, gave great impetus to individualism, the basic factor in modern religious freedom and forms of self-government.

36. The Age of Charles V

CHRISTIAN RECONQUEST OF SPAIN AND PORTUGAL

DURING THE MIDDLE AGES the Moors conquered nearly all of the Iberian peninsula. As time went on, however, a group of Christian feudal principalities managed to establish themselves in the north, while the Moors were continually pushed southward. The Christian states gradually united into a few large political units, so that about 1300 there existed three large Christian kingdoms in the peninsula: Aragon, Castile, and Portugal, in addition to the smaller states of Moorish Granada and Christian Navarre.

Portugal was on the verge of becoming a flourishing nation in the fifteenth century. This alluring prospect was largely the result of the courageous efforts of Portuguese explorers and traders, and the achievements of many capable kings. The discoveries and adventures of the Portuguese sailors will be discussed in a succeeding section. It suffices to mention here that Prince Henry the Navigator is a famous figure in Portuguese history, and that his name indicates the sponsorship of numerous discoveries and explorations. The beginnings of a large Portuguese empire were laid by Prince Henry and his intrepid seamen.

The monarchy in Portugal, like that in many other countries of that day, was absolute. After 1521, the Portuguese Cortes, or parliament, ceased to meet regularly and exerted little political influence.

In 1580 the Portuguese king died and left no immediate heir. Consequently, the Portuguese throne was won by Philip II of Spain, who was a close relative of the deceased Portuguese king. Thus two large colonial empires were united under one head, and for over sixty years Spanish and Portuguese colonial expansion and exploration in the New World went hand in hand.

The history of Spain as a modern state begins with the marriage of Ferdinand of Aragon and Isabella of Castile in 1469, thereby unifying the largest two Christian kingdoms in the Iberian Peninsula under one head. After their marriage, Ferdinand and Isabella set out to conquer the rest of the peninsula excepting that part held by Portugal, and in 1492, Granada, the last Moorish stronghold, was captured. The surviving Mohammedans were promised liberty of religion, but this promise was broken and persecutions took place. Finally, in 1610, all the Mohammedan survivors, numbering over half a million, were exiled from Spain into North Africa. This expulsion, as well as the persecution of the Jews, greatly weakened the commerce and industries of the country, which previously had been limited almost solely to these two non-Christian peoples.

NATIONAL CONSOLIDATION

The methods of internal consolidation employed by Ferdinand and Isabella in Spain were much like those used by monarchs of the other rising states of Europe. In order to secure cooperation of the middle class against the ambitions of the nobility, the former were given extensive protection and privileges. Trade and commerce were fostered everywhere.

Also, Isabella and Ferdinand established the infamous Inquisition as a state institution. The Inquisition originated in the attempt of the Church to ferret out all unbelievers such as Jews, heretics, and others. Pope Sixtus IV turned the control of the Inquisition over to the Spanish state in 1478. It soon became a state tribunal, entirely under the control of the sovereign. Nonconformists in religion were regarded as dangerous to the security of the state. It is asserted that between 1401 and 1492, two thousand Jews were burned alive in Andalusia. The methods of the Inquisition were extremely cruel, and no attempts were made to give fair trials. The introduction of the Inquisition into the Spanish Netherlands proved to be a boomerang to the Spanish monarchs.

For a time, however, Spain was destined to become the greatest nation in Europe. Several factors contributed to this phenomenon. In the long struggle with the Moors the Spanish armies gained much experience, and were considered the best and bravest in Europe. Spain was also one of the richest countries in Europe. Wealth flowed in from the West Indies, Mexico, and Peru. The discovery of America had been sponsored by Isabella and Ferdinand, and Spain became a great empire builder. In addition, the Spanish kings by advantageous marriages and clever intrigue were able to add to their territory, power, and glory.

ATTEMPTS TO UNIFY THE HOLY ROMAN EMPIRE

We must now turn our attention to the Holy Roman Empire, which had been grad- ually decreased in territory and influence. By the fifteenth century the development of independent states, such as France, Spain, and England, had deprived the Emperor of all allegiance from these countries. The Empire from now on was to include primarily the German-speaking countries. Its internal weakness was proverbial; decentralization and confusion were its characteristics. Duchies, baronies, counties, and free cities continually asserted their independence and acknowledged only nominal allegiance to the Emperor. They were involved in continual warfare with one another, and at times even took the field against the Emperor himself. It was only the fear of Slavic and Turkish invasions that gave the Empire some cohesion.

By 1400 it had become the custom of the German princes called Electors to select a member of the house of the Austrian Hapsburgs as Holy Roman Emperor. One of the Hapsburgs, Maximilian I, Emperor from 1493 to 1519, is known for his military campaigns into Italy, his hostility to France, and his attempt to bring unity to the Empire. He gathered the Diet of German princes at Worms in 1495, and put an end to the pernicious warfare between petty princes and nobles by compelling them to bring their quarrels before a new supreme court, the Imperial Chamber. He also established a regular postal system, and divided the Empire into ten districts for the better maintenance of public order.

A series of significant matrimonial alliances, of great importance to the reigning Austrian family and to Spain, was arranged during this period. The marriage of Maximilian with Mary of Burgundy gave control of the Netherlands to the Hapsburgs. Maximilian's heir

Early quick-firing guns used in the military campaigns of Maximilian I, Holy Roman Emperor from 1493 to 1519

Maximilian of Austria (later Emperor Maximilian I) with his wife, Mary of Burgundy, and his young son Philip, afterward king of Castile

Ferdinand I, Holy Roman Emperor, 1556-64

was Philip who married Joanna, the daughter of Ferdinand and Isabella of Spain. Philip and Joanna had two sons who became prominent in European politics. The elder of these sons was Charles, who inherited the Austrian possessions from his father and the Spanish possessions from his mother. The younger son was Ferdinand, founder of the German Hapsburgs, who married the sister of the last king of Bohemia and Hungary. This union brought the crowns of those countries to the house of Hapsburg.

After the death of Philip in 1506, Charles became king of Spain and lord of the Netherlands when he was only six years old. In 1519, on the death of his grandfather, Maximilian, Charles inherited the Austrian possessions of the Hapsburgs. The German princes elected Charles as Holy Roman Emperor in 1519. His activities as Emperor were largely determined by events which had been taking place in eastern Europe.

TURKISH THREAT TO EUROPE

In the late Middle Ages, Mongol pressure forced the Turks westward in Asia and finally brought them into Europe. Earlier it was the Seljuk Turks who were warring with the Byzantine emperors in Syria and Asia Minor. Presently the Ottoman Turks took their place, and founded the great Ottoman empire. They made the Black Sea a Turkish lake, and held all the territory on the east and south of the Mediterranean. They ruled at Bagdad, Alexandria, Cairo, Tunis, Tripoli, and Algiers, as well as at Smyrna, and later at Constantinople.

Between 1350 and 1400 the Turks transferred their military activities to eastern Europe and crossed the Bosporus. The Byzantine emperors, who from the west were harassed by the Slavs, could offer little resistance. By 1400 the Turks had conquered the entire Balkan Peninsula except Constantinople. That city fell in 1453 after a long siege by the Turks under Mohammed II. All Europe became alarmed at the advance of the infidels, as the Turks were called; but, because of internal dissensions, little was done about it.

Sultan Suleiman II (1520-1566) intended to extend his empire still farther. He conquered all of present Rumania and Hungary, and finally laid siege to Vienna in 1529; but here the Turkish avalanche was finally stopped, although the Emperors and the Polish kings failed in several attempts to drive the Turks from Rumania and Hungary.

The Ottoman Empire by its nature was not a homogeneous political unit. It was inhabited by hundreds of different peoples, belonging to various races, speaking different languages, and professing different religions. What held this empire together was the military prowess of the Turks and the administrative ability of their sultans. The latter were not always the intolerant tyrants often pictured. Their Christian and Jewish subjects were usually granted religious liberty under special edicts of toleration.

However, the advance of the Turks into Europe was a great danger to the development of the Western world. It explains partly why the German princes selected the strongest one among their number as leader—the man who must meet this invader.

CHARLES V AND HIS DIFFICULTIES

The empire of Charles V did not constitute a unified, central state, but it was a group of states, brought together by marriage and inheritance under the House of Hapsburg. This fact made the tasks of Charles V almost overwhelming. Each of the political units under his control had to be ruled according to its own administrative system, its own laws and customs, and in its own language. Conflicting interests had to be reconciled and some sort of unity had to be achieved in order to present a united front to foreign foes. While Charles V thus headed an aggregation of many countries, their lack of unity detracted greatly from the total strength one might have expected them to possess. Charles

V had an unusual quota of administrative ability, a quality which enabled him to overcome many seemingly insurmountable obstacles.

During most of his reign, Charles was forced to oppose the ambitious French king, Francis I. France was almost surrounded by Hapsburg territories, a situation which was far from pleasing. Francis and Charles had been rival claimants for the crown of the Holy Roman Empire; but the latter's bribes proved more decisive than those of Francis in the election of the emperor in 1519. The two monarchs also had designs on territories in other parts of Europe, especially Italy, Flanders, and Navarre. The outcome of these struggles usually favored Charles V, but Francis I and his successors were by no means inclined to renounce their plans to weaken the Hapsburgs.

Charles V was also bothered by many internal problems. He was a devout Catholic, and for both religious and political reasons he watched with alarm the growth of Protestantism and dissension in the various parts of his huge empire. His failure to deal with and

Fortifications overlooking the Bosporus, the important strait that separates southeastern Europe from Asia Minor. These walls and towers were built before the Turkish capture of Constantinople in 1453

THE AGE OF CHARLES V

to suppress these irresistible religious developments has been dealt with in the discussion of the Reformation.

Charles V, Holy Roman Emperor, 1520–56

Although born in the Netherlands, which Charles continued to regard as his native land, he spent most of his time in Spain. The latter country during his reign was easily the predominant nation in Europe, and Charles gained the loyalty of the Spanish by making them feel that he regarded their country as the most important part of the empire. His persecution and extermination of the Moors received hearty approval. Also, at this time, a wonderful colonial expansion was taking place and Spain was building a great empire in the Americas. In his various wars Charles relied greatly on aid from the Iberian Peninsula. Without the abundance of gold, resources, and the superior soldiers and ships of Spain, Charles could not have been successful in war.

The people of the Netherlands were personally loyal to Charles, whom they regarded as one of themselves. But the increasing foreign and Spanish influence was greatly resented. They also felt that the growing wealth of the Netherlands, which was heavily taxed, was used chiefly to advance imperial interests rather than for their own benefit. Heresy also grew by leaps and bounds, especially in the north. Lutheran, Anabaptist, and, later, Calvinist doctrines were widely accepted. The persecution of these heretics by Charles V was resented, even by non-Protestants. The Dutch revolt against Spain did not take place, however, until the rule of Charles's son, Philip II of Spain.

Philip II of Spain

CHARLES'S POLICIES IN THE HOLY ROMAN EMPIRE

The attempts of Charles V at reform in the Germanies proved to be a total failure. The German peoples at the time had some vague feeling that they really belonged to one race and nation; but the conflicting interests and ambitions of princes, dukes, kings, and free cities were too great to be overcome by this still hardly conscious feeling of national unity. A German national state was to be achieved much later and as the culmination of an entirely different process (described in Part X, Chapter 63).

At the Diet of Worms in 1521, Charles outlined plans for the political consolidation of the Empire. A Council of Regency was created, representing the interests of twenty-three German princes. This council was intended to bring stability and uniformity to the Empire, so that continuity might be secured in case of the absence or death of the Emperor. The Council, however, found itself powerless to overcome dissension. It had no administrative and judicial branches and no military power to carry out its decisions, which were simply ignored or badly enforced by the various rulers. Many princes had developed Lutheran sympathies. The attempts of the Council to put down two rebellions, one in 1522 and the other, the so-called Peasants' Revolt in 1524, were only partially successful. The German princes themselves stepped in to deal with these rebellions, which clearly showed the growing economic discontent of the time.

THE STRUGGLE WITH THE TURKS

When Charles V became Emperor, the Ottoman Empire included what formerly had been the Byzantine Empire. During his

Suleiman the Magnificent (1496?–1566), Turkish sultan who gained control of most of Hungary

reign, Ottoman encroachments on Hungary and Bohemia were the order of the day. Charles's brother, Ferdinand, held the throne of these two countries during the Turkish advances. The Moslem danger became so great that Ferdinand was forced to make concessions to the Protestant heretics in his territories. Charles also temporarily had to come to terms with the Protestants in the Empire, in order to give more effective aid to Ferdinand in his struggle with the Turks.

The siege of Vienna by the Turks failed in 1529, but their advance into Austria was resumed in 1532. Charles's preoccupation with his other possessions left Ferdinand to carry on the struggle alone. In 1547 he and the Emperor were forced to sign a treaty of peace with Sultan Suleiman the Magnificent, leaving most of Hungary in the possession of the latter. Hungary agreed to pay the sultan an annual tribute of thirty thousand ducats.

RELIGIOUS ISSUE TEMPORARILY SOLVED

Meanwhile, religious strife tore the Empire asunder. Charles at times was able to subdue the various princes, but could not check the spread of the Protestant faith among the German people. In 1552 a revolt of the German princes, aided by Henry II of France, forced the Emperor to compromise. A religious truce was arranged at the Diet of Augsburg in 1555, referred to as the Religious Peace of Augsburg. It was agreed that each German prince was to choose the state religion for his own territory. The religion of each state thus became that of its ruler. The choice lay only between Lutheranism and Catholicism, however; nothing was said about Calvinism. It was decided that the Protestant princes could retain the lands confiscated by them prior to 1552.

Charles V abdicated in 1556, shortly after the Peace of Augsburg. He experienced one more disappointment when the German Electors refused to choose his son Philip as their Emperor. Philip therefore became king of Spain and Italy and lord of the Netherlands, while Ferdinand, by Charles's will, inherited Austria and was elected Emperor of the Holy Roman Empire.

37. Consolidation of Royal Power in France

THE BARONS SUBDUED

THE DEVELOPMENT OF FRANCE as a national unit illustrates how the multitudes of feudal fiefs in Europe were consolidated into various larger areas, each with its own language, common culture, common national feeling, and political organization. It answers the questions which no doubt have often arisen in the reader's mind: How did nations arise? How did it happen that the anarchic, feudal arrangement of thousands of more or less independent political units was finally replaced by relatively few and larger units—the European countries as we know them today?

We have already seen how the decline of feudalism was accompanied by such factors as the rise of towns, the growth of trade, and the ascendancy of the middle class. While formerly there had been only the simple rural economy of serfs and nobles, the burghers in the towns now became a powerful influence. Later we shall see how the kings, in order to consolidate their position, used the new middle class as an ally in their struggle against the nobles who were envious of the growing power of the king.

Philip II (1180-1223) was the first king of France who, by a series of successful wars, was able to subdue the recalcitrant barons in his own territory. By conquest and by the inheritance of Artois he also enlarged the scope of his domain. For more than forty years in the thirteenth century, Louis IX furthered centralization of power in the reigning house. He inaugurated internal reforms and deprived the feudal lords of absolute judicial authority over their serfs by permitting appeal to the royal courts.

The kings now strengthened their position by doing away with the civil and military services of the barons. Civil servants were recruited from the middle class and the groundwork was laid for a faithful royal bureaucracy on which the king could depend in the administration of the country. Mercenary troops and hired fleets replaced the intermittent aid of the undependable military bands formerly supplied by the feudal barons. It is easy to surmise that the latter measure especially added to royal independence and power. Great sums of money were required to support the operations of these royal armies, and it was not strange that the people failed to enjoy the game of hide-and-seek they were compelled to play with tax collectors.

The invention and use of gunpowder and cannons also weakened the position of the barons. Hitherto, it was possible for a feudal lord to wage war or go out on a plundering expedition, and, when danger arose, to retreat into his castle. The mercenary armies of the king, equipped with primitive artillery, were now able to break down the once impregnable castle walls.

To gain the favor and financial support of the middle class, or *bourgeoisie*, Philip IV established the French parliament, or Estates General. Its importance lay in the fact that not only the representatives of the clergy and nobility were summoned, but also that the middle class was asked to send its representatives. The latter were called the "third estate."

The French parliament, however, did not gain the power and prominence of its British counterpart. Under more powerful kings the French Estates General was never able to wring liberties and privileges from the king. The French people never had a Magna Carta. The English people were gradually able to

Pope Julius II, who regained control of the Papal States and helped drive the French from Italy

Edward IV of England and Louis XI of France meeting at Pecquigny in 1475

abolish royal absolutism through the growing dependence of the king on Parliament for money. In France royal power, which had served to weld a great people into one nation, and which retained control of its own purse, later became oppressive and led inevitably to one of the greatest social upheavals of all time —the French Revolution.

BURGUNDIAN AMBITIONS

The largest independent fief that challenged the power of kings was the duchy of Burgundy.

Charles the Bold presiding over a chapter meeting of the Order of the Golden Fleece, instituted by his father. Under Charles, Burgundy was a strong, independent dukedom, but its power was broken in 1477

We have seen how the Duke of Burgundy aided the English in their invasion of France during the Hundred Years' War by attacking the French from the east. The dukes of Burgundy aspired to a powerful independent kingdom of their own. Already by conquest, inheritance, and marriage they had greatly extended their territories, which for a long time included the entire Netherlands. Finally, Charles the Bold (1467-1477) nearly succeeded in defeating France, but by arousing the ill-will of his warlike neighbors, the Swiss, he soon faced enemies on all sides and was killed in battle. The clever intrigue of Louis XI of France contributed much to this result.

Mary of Burgundy, who succeeded Charles the Bold, was aided in her struggle with France by her husband, Maximilian of Hapsburg. Upon her death Maximilian was forced to surrender the duchy of Burgundy to France. The remainder of his holdings, including the Netherlands, was incorporated into the territories of the Austrian Hapsburgs.

TRIUMPH OVER CHURCH AND NOBLES

Louis XI (1461-1483) was one of the most crafty of the Bourbon kings. Under him France was strengthened and more closely unified. Clerical privileges were curtailed, judicial appeals to Rome were forbidden, and the rights

Anne of Brittany, whose marriage with Charles VIII of France united Brittany with France

Francis I of France, who campaigned against Charles V and tried to gain part of northern Italy

of the French church were emphasized. The extinction of the House of Anjou in 1480 added Anjou, Provence, Maine, and Lorraine to the royal domains of Louis XI. Several powerful nobles were executed on various charges. Internal order was restored and the king thereby gained the favor of the middle class, which desired peace and security for its trading activities. The *bourgeoisie* were given further privileges, such as the election of their own magistrates. Industry and trade were greatly encouraged, and with Louis XI the medieval system in France almost came to an end.

His son Charles VIII (1483-1498) was able to suppress a serious rebellion led by the duke of Orleans and Brittany. The marriage of the king and Anne, the duchess of Brittany, in 1491 added this last great feudal territory to his dominions. The boundaries of France at the end of the fifteenth century were thus very much like those of the France we know today.

FAILURE IN ITALY

In 1494, Charles VIII decided to press a distant claim to the kingdom of Naples, and crossed the Alps into Italy. His expedition was at first successful: Naples was reached and occupied. But the Italians combined against the French king; his conquests were lost; and he escaped with difficulty from Italy.

Louis XII succeeded to the throne in 1498.

Italian wars occupied his chief attention. He claimed both Naples and Milan and occupied the latter in 1500. With Spain, Louis then attacked Naples. It was conquered, but the victors soon quarreled, and in the war that followed the Spaniards expelled the French.

In 1508, as a member of the League of Cambrai, formed to attack Venice, Louis XII again invaded Italy. The expedition followed the usual pattern: Initial victory; a rearrangement of alliances; then, in spite of Gaston de Foix' brilliant victory at Ravenna in 1512, defeat, and expulsion from Italy (1513).

RIVALRY BETWEEN FRANCE AND SPAIN

Louis' cousin, Francis I, succeeded him in 1515. France and Spain were already jealous rivals, but in this reign they entered on a struggle which was a feature of European war and diplomacy for nearly 200 years. Young and ambitious, Francis at once took up the Italian venture. He crossed the Alps in 1515 and gained a great victory over the Swiss and Milanese at Marignano. The pope, who had been one of Francis' enemies, came to terms in the Concordat of Bologna (1516), which left ecclesiastical appointments in France in the hands of the king. Francis granted the pope certain revenues and recognized his supremacy over church councils.

349

In 1519 Emperor Maximilian died, and both Francis and the Spanish king, Charles, became candidates for the imperial crown. France was already partly enclosed by Hapsburg territories, and when Charles was elected emperor, the breach between the two rivals was complete. Charles insisted that Milan was a fief of the Holy Roman Empire, which he was bound to recover, while Francis had designs in the Low Countries and asserted the claims of a kinsman to Navarre. War broke out in 1522, and with a few breaks lasted beyond the lives of both rulers.

In the first stage of the struggle, the French, under Lautrec, were driven from Milan, which was granted to the Sforza family as a fief of the Empire. Francis was further troubled by the defection to his enemies of the duke of Bourbon, constable of France. Once high in the favor of the king, the duke had lost his influence at court, and Francis' mother, Louise of Savoy, using an ancient, weak claim to the Bourbon domain, had urged the king to seize the duke's lands. Before the parlement of France could make a decision, Francis actually took possession of some of the disputed territory and gave it to his mother. This plus the duke's fear that his life was in danger from the king, led Bourbon to flee from France with a small band of followers. A French invasion of Italy in 1523–24, was repelled, and the Imperial forces thereupon invaded southern France. Francis raised the siege of Marseilles and then recaptured Milan. However, in the Battle of Pavia (1525), the Spanish commanders, one of whom was the duke of Bourbon, inflicted a complete defeat on the French. Francis himself was taken prisoner and sent to Madrid. There he signed the Treaty of Madrid, by which he promised to give up his Italian claims, cede Burgundy, and renounce his overlordship of Artois and Flanders. On his return to France, however, Francis immediately repudiated the Treaty terms as having been forced, and war was resumed. In 1527 Charles's forces sacked Rome (the pope was an ally of the French), and peace was made at Cambrai in 1529. By 1530 Charles was virtual master of all Italy. There were three more French

campaigns in Italy in the succeeding decades, but by the peace of Cateau-Cambrésis, (1559) France gave up the Italian struggle in return for three bishoprics on her eastern frontier.

HENRY IV AND THE DUKE OF SULLY

As we have seen in a previous section, the internal history of France during the sixteenth century was characterized by bloody religious conflict. In the latter part of the century political and religious motives became mixed in

Henry IV of France

the civil struggle, which was not always beneficial to the Protestant cause. Henry IV, who ascended the throne in 1589, increased his political power by instituting religious reforms. Although the religious problem was of great importance, Henry's most

The Duke of Sully

difficult tasks were to restore prosperity to a country devastated and disordered by civil war, and to restore the prestige of the monarchy. He began a series of political and economic reforms which were continued in part by his successors and which made France the greatest and strongest nation in Europe.

Henry IV, like most French kings, lived a life of personal pleasure and extravagance; and, like his successors, he knew how to select capable civil servants. The most noted of these was his chief adviser and minister, the duke of Sully. The latter strictly controlled the landed gentry and provincial governors. He fostered agriculture, which he believed to be the foun-

Cardinal Richelieu at the Siege of La Rochelle. (Ewing Galloway)

dation of the nation's prosperity. A beginning was made with the building of roads and canals, which until then had scarcely existed. France soon had the best roads in Europe. Commerce was stimulated thereby, but the political significance of a good system of highways should not be forgotten. It enabled the kings to move their troops swiftly and economically.

Sully's contribution to the financial administration of France is of importance. Within ten years the national debt was reduced eighty-five per cent. Between 1596 and 1609 the revenue was more than doubled; still later the treasury showed a large surplus, the arsenals were prepared for war, and the fleet was well equipped. This new emphasis on national efficiency and capable administration was something new in the history of Europe. It was a factor of primary importance in the building of the new national state. It aided the king in consolidating his power, both internally and externally.

RICHELIEU—CARDINAL AND STATESMAN

When Henry IV was assassinated in 1610, Louis XIII ascended the throne. During his reign the Estates General, or national parliament, was summoned for the last time before the French Revolution. Its powers were so limited that it exercised little real authority. The centuries before the Revolution in France were characterized by absolute royal power with little or no popular control.

France was actually ruled by Cardinal Richelieu, one of the greatest of modern statesmen, diplomats, and administrators, for nearly twenty years during the reign of Louis XIII. He was a capable and resolute ruler, unscrupulous as to means and clear-headed about his aims. He crushed all plots against his power and overcame the resistance of the nobles. The Huguenots, suppressed primarily for political reasons, were finally mastered in the capture of their chief stronghold, La Rochelle, in 1629. The final outcome of the Thirty Years' War was greatly influenced by his policy and his success. France at his death in 1642 succeeded Spain as the foremost nation in Europe. Richelieu thus laid the foundations, both at home and abroad, for the power and influence exercised by Louis XIV.

Cardinal Richelieu

351

38. The Age of Louis XIV

MAZARIN AND THE FRONDE

THE REIGN OF LOUIS XIV (1643–1715) ushered in a period of warfare which continued, with intervals of peace, from about 1650 to 1815. These wars centered largely around the struggle of France and Great Britain for colonial supremacy, and the desire of France to become the foremost power on the European continent. These struggles far exceeded previous wars in importance if we judge by the number of combatants engaged, the power and resources of the belligerents, the skill of the commanders, and the interest attached to the chief battles fought on land and sea.

Louis XIV was but five years of age at the death of his father, Louis XIII, and the regency was held by his mother Anne. Fortunately, the young king was aided in his early years by the capable advice of his chief minister, Mazarin. The latter was a political and diplomatic pupil of the great Richelieu. It was he who continued Richelieu's policy of interference in the Thirty Years' War, and gained Alsace for France by the Treaty of Westphalia in 1648. He also succeeded in defeating the Hapsburg king of Spain, and by the Treaty of the Pyrenees France gained Roussillon and a part of the Spanish Netherlands.

A civil uprising, called the Fronde, occupied the attention of Mazarin from 1648 to 1652. It was the last effort on the part of the nobility to regain their lost authority. They were joined by some groups of the middle class, which had become alarmed at the rise of royal absolutism. Mazarin had abolished the weak Paris *parlement*, or supreme court, and this action had been a cause for alarm. In addition to its judicial powers, the *parlement* had obtained the right to "register" the royal decrees: it formerly promulgated the king's orders as laws to the country. At times the *parlement* had shown a desire to refuse to promulgate these decrees.

The *parlement* defied the young king and his minister in 1648, and claimed that its consent was necessary to any kind of taxation. The mob in the street supported these demands by active street fighting. For the moment Mazarin had to give in; but, once the troops were recalled from Germany, he annulled his concession and deprived the *parlement* of all its political and financial powers. The nobility's power was broken, and except for minor uprisings royal absolutism went unchallenged until the final reckoning—the French Revolution.

"MASTER OF KINGCRAFT"

Louis personally assumed direction of state affairs when Mazarin died in 1661. At once he showed himself a master of his position. Macaulay describes him as "a consummate master of kingcraft—of all the arts which most advantageously display the merits of a prince and best hide his defects." At all times he was in full command of the situation. Never did a European sovereign demand and receive a submission so closely resembling that given to an oriental sultan. He wielded despotic power. Although he seldom employed force in internal affairs, he always kept it in the background.

Louis XIV

Anne of Austria and Cardinal Mazarin. Anne was regent for her son, Louis XIV, until 1651, but the government of France was conducted by Mazarin

Louis, like James I of England, thoroughly believed in the divine and absolute right of kings. But unlike James he did not have to deal with deep-rooted traditions of popular representation and liberty which greatly modified the Stuart's claim to absolutism.

Louis XIV, though somewhat pompous, was dignified and graceful in his manners. He promoted French culture, art, and the sciences. His name is closely associated with those of Corneille, Racine, and Molière. The court at Versailles became a symbol for sparkling fountains, beautiful women, and luxury.

COLBERT AND LOUVOIS

Louis possessed a remarkable talent for choosing as ministers, diplomats, administrators, and generals, capable men from all ranks of life who were the ablest of their day. Foremost in this distinguished company was Colbert, the financial adviser and administrator. He somewhat lightened the financial burden of the peasants by substituting general taxes for their special burdens. He encouraged agriculture, manufacture, and commerce, and developed France by the building of roads and canals. The Languedoc Canal, which joins the Mediterranean and the Atlantic, was constructed by him. Under his guidance France for the first time emerged as a great naval power, and various colonies were acquired. Louvois was Louis' great war minister. Under his supervision France evolved the efficient military machine which Louis used to keep Europe in turmoil for nearly fifty years.

DUTCH OPPOSITION TO THE GRAND MONARCH

It was the ambition of Louis to extend the frontiers of France to the Alps, the Pyrenees, and the Rhine, and ultimately to gain European predominance through the annexation, by alliance with the House of Bourbon, of all the Spanish dominions. No sacrifices of blood and resources by the French people were considered too large to achieve these grand designs. Little respect was shown either to obligations of public faith or to foreign treaties. Wars were begun whenever opportunity presented itself.

When the French king's father-in-law, Philip IV of Spain, died in 1665, Louis claimed the Spanish Netherlands, and in 1667 Turenne marched into Flanders at the head of fifty

The Fronde (1648–53). Parisians being urged to join the Fronde, a revolt of the great nobles and the parlement of Paris against Mazarin and young Louis

Molière and his friends at dinner. Molière was a great actor and playwright of Louis XIV's time. Right, Pierre Corneille (1606–84), another great French playwright of the time. He is best known for tragedies

thousand French troops. The Flemish fortresses were soon conquered, and so was the territory called Franche-Comté. Holland and England now became alarmed and feared a disturbance of the balance of power in Europe. Under the leadership of the capable Dutch statesman, Jan De Witt, the famous Triple Alliance was formed between England, Holland, and Sweden. This combination was too much for Louis, and in the Treaty of Aix-la-Chapelle he was forced to give up Franche-Comté, but retained the fortresses of Flanders.

Bent on revenge, Louis bought the neutrality of England by the secret Treaty of Dover with Charles II. A great French army under Condé

William III (previously William of Orange)

and Turenne poured into Holland. Louis accompanied this army in person. He was opposed by the young and apparently feeble William of Orange, who afterward became William III of England.

The French soon overran most of Holland and all seemed lost for the Dutch cause. But the French forces were driven from much of the country when William ordered the dikes to be cut, and so turned Holland into a sea out of which Amsterdam stood up like a vast fortress.

William, by capable statesmanship, formed a new coalition against the French, composed

Jan De Witt

of the Emperor, the Elector of Brandenburg, and the Spanish Netherlands. De Ruyter fought effectively on the sea against combined French and English fleets. In the end the French were forced to leave the Netherlands, and the Rhine countries became the new battlefields. The outcome of the war was indecisive and the Peace of Nimwegen in 1678 left France in possession of many of the Flanders fortresses and, in addition, of Franche-Comté.

Louis did not disband his army, however. His troops took part in numerous wars and campaigns. More territory was gained for

France in the Rhineland, including the city of Strassburg. Louis aided Austria in its struggle against the Turks, and in order to weaken Spain he worked to sustain Portugal's independence. Quarrels with the pope were settled in Louis' favor and he exerted influence in Italy.

BALANCE OF POWER RESTORED

In 1686, French aggression again led William of Orange to rouse Europe against Louis, by forming the League of Augsburg which included the Emperor, several German princes, Sweden, Spain, and the Netherlands. In retaliation the French invaded Germany, devastated the Rhenish Palatinate, and sacked Mannheim and Heidelberg.

Three years later, William of Orange, now king of England, succeeded in forming the "Grand Alliance" by adding England to the League of Augsburg. The French fleet was defeated at La Hogue when it was about to transport James II and a French army into England to regain the throne for the House of Stuart. The French armies won many brilliant victories, but William never permitted the French to take full advantage of them. The wars were costly to France, which could not

forever stand the strain on its men and resources. But with the Peace of Ryswick in 1697, the French king's acquisitions in Spain and Flanders were restored, and Alsace and Strassburg remained in his possession.

WAR OF THE SPANISH SUCCESSION

Louis' desire for power and territory, however, was not yet satisfied. It now drew France into the War of the Spanish Succession which ended less fortunately for her, practically bringing to a close the period of French dominance in Europe. In his will in 1700, Charles II of Spain had left all his dominions to Philip of Anjou, grandson of Louis. The latter exultantly exclaimed: "There are no longer any Pyrenees!" This indicated that he intended to unite France and Spain under one crown. But the Emperor Leopold claimed the Spanish throne for his son; and England and Holland, to maintain the balance of power, opposed this latest piece of French diplomacy.

The "Grand Alliance" was instantly reorganized by William III, whose death in 1702 was a great blow to the Dutch and English. Louis recognized James Stuart as William's successor. In the naval engagement which

Louis XIV entering Dunkirk. From a Gobelin tapestry

opened the war, the allies were able to defeat the French and Spanish fleets. It was at this time that the fortress of Gibraltar fell to Sir George Rooke, an acquisition which was never relinquished by England.

On land Louis was not as successful as in his previous wars. The French people had sacrificed much and were exhausted. Louis was driven out of Italy by the Emperor, and the combined forces of the Dutch and English under Marlborough defeated the French in Flanders. In 1704, Marlborough and Eugene of Austria defeated the French at Blenheim.

TREATY OF UTRECHT

The war was concluded in 1713 with the Treaty of Utrecht. The Dutch Republic received security by gaining the right to occupy a series of fortresses along the French frontier. Savoy and Prussia also received more territory. The Spanish Netherlands (modern Belgium) were turned over to the Emperor and thus became the Austrian Netherlands. Philip V, however, retained the crown of Spain, with the stipulation that the crowns of Spain and France were to be kept separate, a decision which settled the original matter in dispute.

From the viewpoint of international diplomacy the treaty marks an important epoch in European history. While Spain had been predominant in the sixteenth century, and the Dutch had been the foremost nation in Europe during the early part of the seventeenth, in the latter half of that age France had been decidedly the foremost nation of the world. France, upon the death of Louis XIV in 1715, entered upon a period of decline and internal weakness. The primary role in Europe was now assumed by Great Britain.

TRIUMPH OF MERCANTILISM

Since the record of early modern European history is marked by wars, fought on a greater scale than ever before, the reader may well wonder what type of economic organization made such costly ventures possible. The simple feudal economy never could have supported the extensive and intensive military operations of this period, which involved expensive army equipment and naval vessels, and tens of thousands of trained soldiers instead of the thousands in the temporary feudal levies.

A new system of economic production and distribution arose. The beginnings of modern capitalism occurred at this time, replacing the simple feudal and handicraft economy. The new national states fostered these beginnings. This early form of state-supported and state-regulated capitalism is called mercantilism. France, better than any other European country at the time, illustrates mercantilism as an instrument of national and royal policy. In Spain, Holland, and England mercantilism was more closely related to colonial expansion, and therefore will be discussed again in the treatment of that subject.

CAPITALISTIC PRODUCTION

Hobson, the English economist, defines capitalism as "the organization of business upon a large scale by an employer or company of employers possessing an accumulated stock of wealth wherewith to acquire raw materials and tools, and hire labor, so as to produce an increased quantity of wealth which shall constitute a profit." Production in feudal times was much simpler in its operation than the new capitalism. Agricultural products were produced cooperatively on large estates and consumed locally, and no attempts were made to accumulate large savings. The same was true of the manufacturing of goods, in which the craft guild played the important role.

At the beginning of the sixteenth century a noticeable change took place. Landlords began to rent their lands to tenants instead of exacting services from serfs. On the lands managed by the owners themselves, hired laborers replaced the serfs. The craft guilds were gradually superseded by manufacturers who hired labor and produced goods for a large market. To fill the need for capital, modern banking emerged.

The new economic order, as compared with the old, is characterized by the free flow and mobility of labor and capital, thus making large scale production possible; by a desire to make a profit; by the production for a large market and unknown consumers; by the rise of the middle class, or employer group, which re-

The town crier, a scene in 17th century France. Right, cavalry and artillery, showing military uniforms of the time

Signing a marriage contract during the age of Louis XIV. Left, a garden scene, showing dress worn by the upper classes

Popular entertainers in France during the 17th century. Many such troupes of entertainers toured the provinces

Grand staircase at Versailles

gards itself as socially superior to the workers it employs; and by the splitting up of ownership into stocks or shares, making possible the concentration of capital from various sources in single large scale enterprises.

The new national states soon took a hand in stimulating and regulating capitalism. The idea became prevalent that a country in order to be wealthy and powerful should have in its possession a large supply of money, and large stocks of silver and gold. This was one of the central ideas of mercantilism. Colbert, minister of Louis XIV, stated, "I believe . . . it is only the abundance of money in a state that determines its greatness and power." As a result of this widely-held view, national policy was aimed at securing and keeping as much gold and silver as possible within the national domain. Spanish and Portuguese ships and colonies were raided by the Dutch, French, and English in a mad scramble for the possession of precious metals.

TARIFFS, REGULATIONS, MONOPOLIES

King Henry IV in 1603 forbade the exportation of gold and silver from France. Heavy duties were laid on the importation of manufactured goods, and the export of raw mate-

Jean Baptiste Colbert (1619–83)

rials, such as wool, was forbidden. A complete system of protective tariffs was gradually developed, which in France, reaching its height under Colbert, was called Colbertism. Internal tariff boundaries on the other hand were eliminated, thus making the country one great economic unit.

Another aspect of mercantilism was the giving of economic privileges by the king to individuals or companies. These often took the form of monopolies. Outstanding examples were the great trading companies of France, England, and Holland, which were given monopolies in certain geographical areas. The British East India Company was one of the greatest of these companies.

Regulation of economic life in its minutest detail was the order of the day and often took ridiculous forms. In France the size of weaving tools was prescribed and the use of certain colors and kinds of dyes forbidden. An elaborate system of bounties and premiums was organized to stimulate capitalistic enterprise and exports. Colbert alone handed out five and a half million francs in bounties.

The prestige and power of the state was greatly increased by this emphasis on a national economy. The new merchant and manufacturing class looked to the king for help and support. Local thought and feeling were supplanted by a national outlook. Thus feudal localism and the ambitions of the nobility were gradually eliminated and supplanted by royal absolutism. Royal revenues increased greatly. The annual income of the French kings increased from ten million livres in 1600, to nearly five hundred million livres a hundred years later.

However, in the growth of royal power and the process of state unification, the wishes of the common people and working classes were not consulted. The mass of people lived in ignorance and misery, had few privileges and liberties. They were required to make great sacrifices to support royal wars, royal court life and extravagance, and royal bureaucracy, which became more oppressive and exploitative as time went on. Eventually royal power was destroyed, but the national state remained as the permanent political unit in the world.

39. Two Centuries of English Development

HENRY VII—FIRST OF THE TUDORS

WHILE THE KINGS OF FRANCE were consolidating their power and attempting to become the masters of Europe, England was passing through a series of crises. During the period from 1485 to 1713, the Reformation swept over England; significant constitutional changes occurred; the sea power of Spain was humbled; an English empire was built abroad; and England challenged France for supremacy in the international arena.

The Wars of the Roses, waged between the houses of Lancaster and York for control of the crown, so weakened and exhausted the English nobility that it became easy for a strong king to assert his authority. The people generally were tired of continual civil war and wanted someone who would be a king for all of England. This national feeling was strengthened by the policies of Henry VII who, in 1485, became the first Tudor king after defeating the treacherous Richard III in the Battle of Bosworth.

By his marriage to Elizabeth of York shortly after coming to the throne, Henry united the White and Red Roses and embarked upon a long and peaceful reign. He carefully limited the power and number of the nobles, and encouraged the rising middle class by fostering commerce and business. He governed efficiently, and levied his taxes lightly upon the mass of the people. By the end of Henry's quarter-century reign the new line of monarchs had become firmly established. He had averted war, checked rival claimants to the throne, and left to his son a more united nation and increased royal power.

HENRY VIII AND THE BREAK WITH ROME

Henry VIII, one of the most colorful of English kings, succeeded his father in 1509. Young, handsome, and intelligent, he was already popular. The first part of Henry's reign was featured by the brilliant if not lasting diplomatic ventures of his great adviser, Cardinal Wolsey. The cardinal by taking advantage of the rivalry between Emperor Charles V and the French king, gave England the balance of power; but no lasting gains were obtained, and the result of his policy was that Charles obtained control of the papacy just before Henry wanted the pope to annul his marriage to Catherine of Aragon, the Emperor's aunt.

When Henry had reigned twenty years without having a son, he convinced himself that his marriage to his brother's widow was unlawful. This, with a passion for young Anne Boleyn, drove him to press the pope for a divorce. The pope, influenced by Charles V, refused, and Henry began the separation of the English church from Rome. The process was completed by the Acts of Annates, Appeals, and Supremacy, which set up a national church with the king at its head.

Desire for Anne Boleyn and a son to succeed him was not the most important cause of Henry's break with Rome. Deeper causes, long rooted in English history, were at work; and the break was really the religious aspect of the growth of nationalism and independent spirit in England. People did not want the Church to be ruled by a foreign head, and the Renaissance, by fostering the spread of knowledge, made some laymen grope for a religion more personal and not dominated by the clergy.

Henry rudely put down those who refused to see in him the supreme head of the Church, and in 1536 began to seize and abolish the monasteries. The great wealth of these religious homes Henry took for himself; he also

Henry VII being acclaimed king of England after his victory over Richard III at Bosworth Field

rewarded private families friendly to the Crown. The king, however, departed but little from traditional Catholic doctrine, and maintained many of the ceremonies of the old church.

By the end of Henry's reign England had moved far toward a permanent national unity. The king had advanced the work, not only by aiding the formation of a state church, but also by maintaining the absolute sovereignty of the Crown in Parliament. He consolidated England's boundaries, began to reorganize Ireland, and incorporated Wales into the English state.

RISING DISCONTENT

Edward VI, who came to the throne in 1547, was the son of Henry VIII by Jane Seymour, the third of his six wives. Since Ed-

ward was but ten years old at his accession, his uncle, Edward Seymour, was named Protector, and made duke of Somerset. Even in his youth the king was learned and religious, and like his uncle, was markedly Protestant. Their haste in pressing advanced Reformation ideas upon the country led to a minor revolt; but this was put down, and the religious changes continued. Images in the churches were done away with, Henry's six articles of faith repealed, and a new service book, the Book of Common Prayer, was compiled and ordered to be used in the churches.

Somerset was faced, however, with increasing social and religious resentment throughout the nation. Competition was beginning to be substituted for custom as the dominant economic principle, and land was coming to be

Anne Boleyn

regarded as a source of money. With the amassing of large estates and the change from corn growing to sheep grazing, small tenants were evicted; there was more profit in large scale wool growing than in small scale farming. Thousands of countrymen became hired laborers or were thrown out of work. This new vagrant class began to drift to the cities and

Henry VIII, king of England, 1509–47

Cardinal Wolsey and his friends

seaports, there to aid in the growth of industries and shipping.

MARY, SPAIN, AND CATHOLICISM

The end of the Somerset regime came in 1552. John Dudley, earl of Warwick, excited the nation against the Protector, and the latter was deposed and executed. Dudley, created duke of Northumberland, now became Protector. Learning that Edward was not likely to live, he defied the will of Henry VIII by persuading Edward to name Lady Jane Grey, the Protector's daughter-in-law, as the next ruler, But with Edward's death in 1553, the country reacted against the extreme Protestantism of his reign. Nobles and commoners joined to bring Mary, Catholic daughter of Henry VIII, to the throne, and Lady

Lady Jane Grey

Jane Grey's career as queen lasted but nine days. It was with almost universal joy that she was deposed and Mary named Queen of England.

Mary soon lost her initial popularity. By putting England under the influence of Spain, whose king she married, and by restoring the authority of the pope, she alienated English national spirit. Those who advocated Protes-

tantism and England's independence of the papacy, were severely persecuted, hundreds being burned at the stake. In aiding Spain, Mary lost Calais by warring with France, and offended the spirit of expansion in English nationalism by prohibiting Englishmen from competing with the Spanish in the New World. The news of Mary's death, in 1558, was received joyously by the nation. Henceforth, it would be impossible for any ruler to subjugate England to Spain or to renew the influence of Rome in English religion.

GOOD QUEEN BESS

With the accession of Elizabeth, Mary's Protestant half-sister, England was to enter upon one of the most glorious periods of her history, a period in which her ardent nationalism was to start the country on a career of growing influence in European affairs. Elizabeth opened her long reign by restoring England's independence. All connection with the papacy was abolished, and the state church set up once more. Typically English, the queen stood for compromise in religious affairs. Although the Catholic connection was severed, she offended the early Puritans by retaining some Catholic practices. Elizabeth, however, showed marked Protestant tendencies. She drew the fire of Catholic Europe by helping to expel the French from Scotland, and showed her independence of Spain by aiding the Dutch against Philip II, her brother-in-law. Subtle

Edward VI, king of England, 1547–53

Elizabeth, queen of England, 1558–1603

Queen Elizabeth knighting Francis Drake after his voyage around the world, 1577-80

Mary Queen of Scots as she received the news that she was to be executed the following morning

and wise in her diplomacy, Elizabeth, aided by such gifted advisers as Cecil and Walsingham, started England on a rapid road to success in rivalry with other nations.

Two factors entered into England's rise: the genuine national feelings of the people; and an aptitude for seafaring. Aiding in the rise of nationalism was the flexibility of English character and society. The people readily adapted themselves to changes. The growth of the middle class was stimulated by the fact that there was no rigid line between it and the nobility. Younger sons of noble families often went into trade and business, and commoners frequently rose to the rank of the nobility. Justices of the peace, heavily relied upon by the Tudors, were often descended from successful city men who had established themselves in the country. Elizabeth herself was the great-great-granddaughter of a London mayor. All in all, one of the important factors in England's rise to power was the fact that the government was responsive to the commercial classes, important in the expansion of any nation. There never existed in England that scorn of commerce which was characteristic of the Continental rulers and nobility.

Likewise, the English readily took to the sea, and the pope's prohibition of English expansion in the New World had the effect of arousing the strongly Protestant feeling of English seamen, as had Mary's refusal to allow them to compete with Spanish colonizers. The English sailors, therefore, began to prey on Spanish and Portuguese shipping and raided the Spanish New World colonies. When

Elizabeth came to the throne, this became a national sport, and such sea dogs as Drake and Hawkins became the terror of the Spanish colonies and shipping lanes.

STRUGGLE WITH SPAIN

The depredations of these gay, devil-may-care English sailors widened the already broad rift between England and Spain. Philip had never given up his hopes of making England Catholic, even after Mary's death. In 1569 the northern English earls had risen in favor of Mary Queen of Scots, a Catholic, but had been easily suppressed by Cecil, one of Elizabeth's ministers. This defeat and the pope's excommunication of Elizabeth in 1570 shattered the Catholic party, and the majority of Catholics accepted the state religion; but a number fled to foreign courts, there to conspire with Spain to recover England for Catholicism.

Gradually the two countries drifted apart, although a truce existed for several years. But there could not be compromise between Spanish and English desires in the New World, and between Protestant English nationalism and Spain's desire to reconquer England for the Catholic Church. The Spanish acquisition of Portugal, the assassination of William of Orange, Dutch Protestant leader of the revolt against Spain, and Spanish victories in the Netherlands led Elizabeth to act. She aided the Dutch, executed the Queen of Scots, sent Drake to raid the Spanish West Indies in 1585, and destroyed Philip's fleet at Cadiz in 1587.

Philip finally retaliated in 1588 with the Spanish Armada. Under the delusion that the

362

The Spanish Armada coming up the English Channel, from a tapestry in the British House of Lords

majority of the English people would rise against Elizabeth if given the chance, he sent an immense fleet to aid them. But England arose as one man to repel the invader. Her prowess on the sea served her in good stead, and English seamanship and gunnery, plus the effects of a Channel storm, forever destroyed Spanish hopes of conquest. Her continuance of the war was merely based on the hope of getting guarantees against English interference in the New World. To this end, Philip incited the Irish to revolt, but England easily suppressed them, and embarked upon the first real conquest of Ireland.

GOLDEN AGE OF ENGLAND

Elizabeth's reign was one in which all fields of English endeavor began to express the national feelings of the people. Particularly after the defeat of the Armada, when the fear of foreign intervention had passed, English nationalism began to express itself in many new ways. Spenser, Sidney, Shakespeare, and Marlowe developed a truly great English literature, relatively free from foreign influences and models.

In domestic politics Parliament, after years of being overshadowed by the Tudor rulers, began to assert itself. The old alliance of Crown and Parliament against the Church and foreign interference was being changed. More democratic ideas of government in Church and state led Parliament to challenge the Crown's right to establish monopolies, to levy indirect taxes without its consent, and to imprison subjects arbitrarily. Now that the nation was strong and independent, the people, too, no longer favored a powerful monarchy. Gradually the nation began to demand more self-government, even before Elizabeth's death in 1603 ended the sway of the Tudor family. England was now truly a national state.

KINGS BY DIVINE RIGHT

James I, who now ascended the throne, was the first of the Stuart family of kings. He was the son of Mary, Queen of Scots, and had long been king of Scotland. James, who was a political theorist, ardently believed in the divine right of kings, and forgot that heredity had not been the only means of succession. Parliament lost no time in telling him that it would not let him have the power that Elizabeth had wielded. James's stubbornness and their feeling that he was using selfishly authority that had been wielded by the Tudors for the good of the nation, widened the breach between the king and Parliament. There was no desire for democracy, but a general feeling that parliamentary legislation should be supreme.

The dispute over religion, Parliament's rights, and foreign affairs made the House of Commons reluctant to levy taxes for James's treasury. In 1606 the king levied additional

Edmund Spenser, Sir Philip Sidney, and King James I

customs duties; they were legal, but increased James's unpopularity. Various other levies, and arbitrary interference with the decisions of the judges, enlivened the closing years of his reign, and maintained the breach between king and Parliament.

With the accession of Charles I, son of James, in 1625, the dispute over taxation came to a head when the sturdy country gentlemen and merchants of the House of Commons refused to vote certain lifetime grants to the king. Charles claimed that Parliament had lost the right to refuse them. He levied them on his own authority, and demanded a forced loan from part of the people. When five knights refused to pay it they were sent to prison. In retaliation, Parliament passed the Petition of Right in 1628, protesting against such forced loans, imprisonment without due process of law, billeting of soldiers in private homes, and martial law in time of peace.

In 1629 the quarrel between king and Parliament broke out again over Charles's right to levy certain duties. In anger he dissolved Parliament, and for eleven years ruled without one. During this time he obtained money by reviving old forms of taxation, which he levied on his own authority. Those who were provoked to resist, suffered prison for their pains. But by 1639 Charles had tapped dry these tax

Thomas Wentworth, Earl of Strafford, going to his execution after he was convicted by Parliament

Battle of Marston Moor, July 2, 1644, in which Northern Royalist army was defeated

sources, and needed sums which only Parliament could raise.

RELIGIOUS DIFFICULTIES

Another important factor was creating discord between the king and part of his people. The growing strength of the Puritans, despite the opposition of James and Charles, led them to dare to join those who stood against the illegal political acts of the king. James had frowned upon Puritanism, and Charles's adviser, Archbishop Laud, was following a steady policy of forcing everyone to conform to the practices of the state Church. But Puritan sentiment grew, for punishment could not alter men's consciences. Thousands of the Puritans, who stood for high personal morality and the elimination of certain practices from the Established Church, went to America; but the vast majority remained to add religious discontent to the grievances against Charles.

In 1638 Charles attempted to pattern the Scottish church after the English state church, but the Scots revolted and set up Presbyterianism. Charles went to war to enforce his will, but needed Parliament to levy taxes to pay his expenses. Called in 1639, Parliament was dissolved because it refused to give the king any money unless he consented to redress their grievances. But Charles still needed money, and in 1640 called the Long Parliament, which

Battle of Naseby, June 14, 1645. Here the Parliamentary forces destroyed the last Royalist army

Charles I just before his execution, ordered by the Rump Parliament on charges of treason

realized that it was now master of the king. It demanded that a Parliament be called every three years at least, and that the king choose ministers whom Parliament approved. To show how insistent it was upon the responsibility of the king's advisers to Parliament, Strafford and Laud, two of Charles's chief ministers, were executed.

THE ROUNDHEAD REVOLUTION

When Parliament, leaning toward Presbyterianism, began to attack the state church, Charles fled to Oxford, set up the royal flag, and gathered his supporters about him. With this began the civil war. The Royalists were successful at first, but eventually Oliver Cromwell led his hard fighting, deeply religious Roundheads to victory in the battles of Marston Moor and Naseby, and in 1646 the king surrendered himself. The Roundheads were Independents, that is, they stood for religious tolerance, and Charles tried to regain his authority by playing them against the Presbyterians, who were for a state church. But Charles's crafty plan fell through and led to a second civil war, his execution in 1649, and the abolition of the monarchy and the House of Lords.

Cromwell had now crushed Catholic Ireland and Presbyterian Scotland, and turned to the problem of governing England. Religious tolerance was established, but his new Commonwealth government soon became a military despotism. Cromwell himself was practically a monarch, with the title of Protector. In 1657 he attempted to reestablish a Parliament, but his death the following year threw the country into anarchy, which ended by the recall in 1660 of Charles II. Curiously enough, divided internally though England was during the Commonwealth period, she presented a united front in foreign affairs. Cromwell was really the founder of the modern English navy, and his captains swept the seas clear of Spanish and Dutch ships. During this period England began her long dominance in the Mediterranean. Foreign nations recognized the Protector and English trade began to expand rapidly.

THE RESTORATION

Charles II, handsome, able, unscrupulous, and popular, returned to England and entered upon his reign with one main objective: to avoid having to "set out on his travels again." He had two secondary hopes: to secure the Crown from outside control, and to emancipate Catholics from their position of restricted political power. But he could not do both, for he needed the help of the established church to increase the power of the Crown, and the church was not willing to relax the decrees against Roman Catholics.

Oliver Cromwell, "the Great Protector," refusing the offer of a Commonwealth parliament in 1656 to make him king of England

with the Dutch in return for subsidies from France. The war was not entirely unpopular, since England had twice warred with the Dutch over trade during the previous decade; but the discovery of the secret treaty made the nation reluctant to fight their fellow-Protestants. The Church led resistance against the now unpopular war, and Charles saw the danger of a new period of exile, so he disbanded the Cabal and permitted the passage of the Test Act which put the Catholics in a worse position than before.

Charles first was led by his chief adviser, Clarendon, to support the church; but in 1667 he replaced his veteran aide by the "Cabal," no member of which was a good Anglican churchman. With its aid he issued his "Proclamation of Indulgence" for Roman Catholics and Dissenters and tried to secure help against Parliament by signing a secret agreement, the Treaty of Dover, with Louis XIV of France. In 1672 Charles plunged the nation into war

Earl of Clarendon, left, Charles II's chief adviser to 1667; right, Charles's mother, Henrietta

Charles II, of the Stuart family, was king of England, from 1660 to 1685. (Ewing Galloway)

Convinced of the failure of his Catholic policy, Charles discarded it, and began to concentrate on making the Crown independent of Parliament. But the nation was still alarmed over the Catholic danger. The opposition party, who came to be called Whigs, took advantage of a fictitious "Popish Plot" to strike hard at the Tories, who upheld the king. Panic followed, but after a period of disorder, during which the Habeas Corpus Act was passed, Charles turned the national reaction to his own advantage. The Whig leaders were silenced, Tories put in control, and for the last four years of his reign Charles ruled as an absolute mon-

James II, king of England, 1685–88

arch, without Parliament, but with the support of the English church and the Tory party.

THE GLORIOUS REVOLUTION

Charles was succeeded, in 1685, by his brother, James II, an avowed Catholic. Things looked well for James at the beginning of his reign, despite two rebellions against him. These were suppressed without much difficulty. He had a Tory Parliament, and by the nation he was respected for his honesty. Unwisely, however, James deviated from his brother's later policy and began to revive the earlier Roman Catholic program, thereby cutting off the important support of the church. Laws were suspended and dispensed with, Catholics placed in the army, the universities, and the privy council, and a large standing army was raised. In attempting to secure his control of municipal governments, he met the opposition of seven bishops whom he prosecuted for seditious libel. This was the last straw. Men of all parties invited the Protestant William III, king of the Netherlands and husband of James's daughter, Mary, to replace James on the throne. James fled at the deliverer's approach; unlike his father, Charles I, he had no group to aid him in his hour of trial.

The peaceful change of rulers, called the "Glorious Revolution," was culminated by a series of acts which established the firm basis of the modern English nation. By the Act of Succession, William and Mary were conjoined as co-rulers, James was excluded from the throne, no Catholic was henceforth to rule England, and Parliament firmly established itself as the deciding voice in regulating the succession.

The Bill of Rights established political liberty by declaring unconstitutional James's arbitrary acts of royal power—the suspension of laws by the royal prerogative, levying of taxes without parliamentary consent, the maintenance of a standing army in time of peace, interference with justice, the exaction of excessive bail, and the denial of the right of petition. It further upheld freedom of debate in Parliament, freedom of elections, and freedom of petition. Religious toleration, freedom of speech, and freedom of the press were guaranteed by other acts.

William III, intent on his wars with Louis XIV, gave Parliament an opportunity to establish itself in its new position. Political parties came into active existence as the Whigs and Tories, descendants of the old groups of the time of Charles II, scrambled for influence in the government. William preferred the Whigs because they favored his war policy,

William and Mary

Death of James II. Louis XIV is shown as he visited the dying exiled king of England

but the country frequently selected Tories. Internal developments were of little interest to William III, although in 1691 he suppressed an uprising in Ireland led by the former king, James II. At the time of his death, he was still ardently defending Holland and England against the aggressive policy of Louis XIV.

ANNE AND ENGLISH SUPREMACY

Anne, a daughter of James II, succeeded William III in 1702. At this time England was deeply involved in the War of the Spanish Succession, and a ministry from all parties was formed to secure united parliamentary support. But the country was saved from its danger by the military genius of the duke of Marlborough. By a series of victories initiated by the smashing defeat of the French and Bavarians at Blenheim, the duke destroyed both the armies and prestige of Louis XIV and raised England to the most influential position in the

politics of the European nations.

At home, the wing of the Tory party which favored peace split with the war-favoring minority, and the latter became purely Whig in 1708. Two years later, however, the cabinet fell, and was replaced by one exclusively Tory. Anne, a quiet woman of average intelligence, acquiesced in this growth of the responsibility of ministers to Parliament. The Tory majority forced the withdrawal of England from the war in 1711, but so potent had been Marlborough's earlier victories that at the peace settlement England emerged as the dominant power of the world. By the Peace of Utrecht, in 1713, she secured favorable trade rights from Spain and Portugal, and was given a large part of Canada.

Queen Anne, the last Stuart. (Brown Bros.)

With the signing of the treaties which made up the Peace of Utrecht, England completed a significant step in her development as a nation. Disorganized and weakened by the Wars of the Roses in 1485, she had been united internally by the Tudors. Under the Stuarts occurred the transition from a strong monarchy to a limited one, in which Parliament, representative of the whole nation, constituted the fundamental power.

Duke of Marlborough

England was now fully prepared to take the position of the world's leading power. Not even a change of dynasty in 1714, when Anne, last of the Stuarts, died, could alter her status. The relative flexibility of her social system, the advanced degree of freedom existing within her borders, and the sensational growth of English commerce were to maintain the position attained in 1713.

40. Prussia as a National State

DECLINE OF THE EMPIRE

THE INTERNAL WEAKNESS of the Holy Roman Empire during the sixteenth century has been discussed. As a result of the Thirty Years' War (1618–1648) which left the population decimated and impoverished, this weakness became more accentuated in the next century. Over three hundred separate political units existed at the time. Causes contributing to this result were: the mutual jealousies among the various rulers; the inability of the Emperor to establish his power absolutely, and at the expense of the lesser princes, as had been done in other countries; the conflict of authority between the emperors and the popes; and the religious struggles and dissensions within the Empire.

Although the Holy Roman Empire was little more than an aggregation of petty, quarreling states, a centralizing force made itself felt in the Germanies during the seventeenth century. The agent of this force was the smaller but dynamic principality of Brandenburg, later called Prussia, which grew in power and extent until Germany emerged as a strong national state in the nineteenth century.

INCREASING IMPORTANCE OF BRANDENBURG

An event of great importance in later German history occurred in 1415. In that year the Emperor vested the House of Hohenzollern with the electorate of the border province called Brandenburg. Until that time the Hohenzollerns had been an unimportant family in southern Germany, but they shifted their residence to the north when they became members of the German Electoral College.

The Hohenzollerns accepted Lutheranism in the sixteenth century, and so were able to strengthen their position by the seizure of all the church lands, and by freeing themselves of all papal and religious restrictions on their political power. Soon Prussia was recognized as the leading Protestant state of Germany, just as Austria in the south was recognized as the principal Catholic state.

The Thirty Years' War played havoc in the Brandenburg territories; but for various reasons Brandenburg benefited from this struggle. As a result of matrimonial arrangements, the duchy of Cleves and the duchy of East Prussia were acquired. The latter was located near the Baltic and north of Poland. At the end of the war still other territories were gained and imperial influence over this region greatly decreased. Though nominally still a vassal of the Emperor, in fact, the Hohenzollerns were becoming independent.

THE GREAT ELECTOR AND HIS SUCCESSORS

Frederick William (1640-1688), also known as the Great Elector, has a historical reputation which extends far beyond the borders of Germany. He realized that vigorous measures were necessary in order to rehabilitate his country, which had been laid waste by war and which was poor in natural resources. A firm believer in absolutist government, he was an extremely capable administrator. Previous to his accession to power, various parts of the Great Elector's realm possessed their own separate political institutions. There were three different diets or parliaments, armies, and administrations. After a severe struggle with various vested interests, Frederick William succeeded in unifying the various military units into one national army, in bringing all financial administration under his personal

Frederick I, first king of Prussia, was previously Frederick III, Elector of Brandenburg

control, and in depriving the diets of their political power. The new state was to be characterized by highly centralized, efficient administration and royal absolutism.

Frederick also greatly improved the internal economy of Brandenburg. Industry and agriculture were aided, and several marshes were drained. The Frederick William Canal, joining the Oder and Elbe rivers, was built under his direction. With the revocation of the Edict of Nantes by Louis XIV in 1685, nearly twenty thousand Huguenots fled to Brandenburg. They were highly industrious and taught their trade skills to the Germans. Berlin, the capital, in a short time grew from a town of eight thousand inhabitants to a city of twenty thousand.

The Great Elector was also successful in foreign affairs. At the Treaty of Westphalia, by skillful diplomacy, he obtained important territories. He used the war between Sweden and Poland (1655-1660) to his advantage. Later he defeated the Swedes and thereby established the reputation of his army in Europe.

The son of the Great Elector, Frederick III, did not exhibit the same capacity for administration. He was more extravagant and somewhat frivolous, showing a strange contrast to his father. His interest in the arts, sciences, and learning was great, however. Under his patronage the University of Halle was founded and so were the Academy of Arts and Academy of Sciences at Berlin.

By bargaining with the Emperor, Frederick III obtained the latter's consent to change his title from the simple "Elector of Brandenburg" to "King of Prussia." This consent was purchased by the sending of eight thousand troops to aid the Emperor in the War of the Spanish Succession. The title of king of Prussia had considerable prestige and gave Prussia a new vantage point on the chessboard of European diplomacy.

KING FREDERICK WILLIAM

Under the rule of King Frederick William I (1713-1740), Prussia rose to the rank of a first-rate power in Europe. In every respect this king displayed the same characteristics of

Revocation of the Edict of Nantes by Louis XIV in 1685 drove many Huguenots from France

austerity and efficiency as his grandfather, the Elector Frederick William. He realized that his country was poor in resources and his methods were designed to make up for this deficiency. By rigid economies and by the introduction of a scientific system of budgeting, the treasury was soon well filled. His army became the best trained and best equipped in Europe, which gave much weight to his position in continental affairs. He was the first king in Europe to make free, elementary education compulsory for the people.

Frederick William I was able to carry government to previously unattained heights of efficiency and responsibility. He made a distinct contribution to the art of government by introducing merit as the basis for selection of government officials. Positions were nearly all given to recruits of the middle class, in sharp contrast with the usual practice of the day when sons of the nobility were usually placed in government service.

The new class of officials was industrious, incorruptible, and took great pride in its position. Its loyalty to state and king went unquestioned. Many aims were secured at once by these methods. On the one hand, government was made efficient and financial resources were released for military purposes and internal improvements. On the other hand, the development of a professional group of government officials, recruited from the middle class and absolutely loyal to the king, completely broke all power of the nobility. Prussian history does not record strong resistance by the aristocracy to royal authority.

Frederick II, known to history as Frederick the Great, ascended the throne when his father died in 1740. The new king was greatly tempted to employ the fully trained and well equipped army his father left him. Since his foreign diplomacy and wars have much to do with Austria of that time, it is well to retrace our steps and discuss shortly the historical developments within that country.

AUSTRIA AFTER CHARLES V

From the thirteenth century, the electors usually chose as Emperor the head of the House of Hapsburg. This powerful family had

Frederick the Great, king of Prussia, 1740–86. Under him, Prussia became a major European power

ruled Austria and the neighboring provinces since 1268. The rule of this latter region was hereditary and the title "Archduke of Austria" was kept distinct and separate from that of "Emperor of the Holy Roman Empire," bestowed by election, even though the same individual usually held both titles. His power as Emperor was not great, especially after the Thirty Years' War, but in his own hereditary domain of Austria an opposite trend appeared. Here royal power was consolidated and Hapsburg rule became absolute. The territories of Austria were also expanded. Ferdinand I, brother of Charles V, also became king of Bohemia and Hungary by marriage, and the succeeding Hapsburgs retained these thrones. They ruled over a combination of various races and peoples, and the Austrian empire lacked internal cohesion. Revolts often took place, especially on the outskirts of Hungary, where the Croats, Rumanians, and the Slovaks often were a cause of disturbance. A revolt of the Czechs of Bohemia against Ferdinand II inaugurated the Thirty Years' War.

In the seventeenth century the Hapsburgs once more had to deal with the Turks who, bent on conquest, again conquered all of Hungary, and the legions of Mohammed IV soon appeared before the walls of Vienna. Leopold I (1658-1705), the ruling Hapsburg at the time, found himself in a desperate situation. At the critical moment the brave king of Poland, John III, came to his rescue, defeated the Turks, and saved Vienna. The pope also became aroused and issued a call to all of Christendom to drive back the infidel. What has been called the Last Crusade was organized, and the combined resources and men of Austria, Poland, Venice, and Papal States, Russia, and even France, after a long struggle, drove back the Turks. Most of the fruits of this religious fervor were reaped by Austria, which regained all of Hungary and the territories north of the Danube when the Treaty of Karlowitz was signed in 1699.

The fortunes of Austria in the War of the Spanish Succession have been discussed. At the treaty of Utrecht in 1713, the Belgian Netherlands, the duchy of Milan, and the kingdom of the two Sicilies came under the rule of the Hapsburgs. Thus Austria, though lacking internal unity, grew in territory and prestige. It soon was engaged in rivalry with rising Prussia for the dominant position in Germany.

Charles VI (1711-1740) of Austria had no sons or brothers, and long custom dictated that only male heirs could inherit the throne. The break-up of the Austrian domain seemed imminent. But in a document, since called the Pragmatic Sanction, Charles declared that, in the absence of a male heir, a female heir might inherit the throne. During his reign he succeeded in obtaining assent to this new ruling, not only from his own dominions, but also from the great foreign powers of Europe, including France, Great Britain, Russia, and even Prussia. When Charles died in 1740, his only daughter, Maria Theresa, came to the throne of a large domain, which, however, was financially poor and equipped with only a small army. That same year Frederick II became king of Prussia.

FREDERICK THE GREAT AND HIS ROLE ON THE CONTINENT

Frederick II came to the throne at the age of twenty-eight. Because of his interest in art

and science he had been harshly treated by his father, who had a thorough contempt for learning. Frederick also forsook the orthodox religion of his father and became an adherent of the rationalism prevalent in his day. His intellectual activities as an enlightened despot will be described elsewhere.

Upon his accession to power, Frederick im-

Maria Theresa

mediately disregarded the Prussian promise given to Charles VI, concerning the Pragmatic Sanction. The internally weak Austrian Empire seemed a fair prey to his ambitions. At once he disputed Maria's right to her throne, and made agreements with France and Bavaria for the spoliation of Austria. The Elector of Bavaria was to be made Holy Roman Emperor, France desired the Austrian Netherlands, and Frederick wanted to add Silesia to his realm. The latter was a rich country and inhabited chiefly by Germans.

Frederick promptly seized Silesia, while Bavaria and France attacked Austria from the west. Maria fled to Hungary, but soon the Magyars, Austrians, and Bohemians rallied to her banner. There ensued a long war, called the War of the Austrian Succession. Spain and England also joined, but on opposite sides. England, because of her rivalry with France, sent money and troops to defend the Netherlands against France and Hanover against Prussia. Spain, which was then ruled by a Bourbon relative of the French king, aided France and Prussia in order to regain the possessions in Italy which had been lost at the Treaty of Utrecht in 1713. Holland, fearing

Austria had been strongly aroused by Prussian success, and Maria Theresa was brooding over the loss of Silesia. Frederick used the following eleven years of peace to inaugurate internal improvements of Silesian resources, and to maintain his splendid army in the highest state of efficiency. There were other European powers which regarded Prussia

Madame Pompadour

Empress Elizabeth I of Russia

French aggression in the Netherlands, also joined England and Austria.

FREDERICK VICTORIOUS

The fortunes of war wavered and numerous bloody battles were fought. Maria Theresa, however, was unable to dislodge Frederick from Silesia, and at the Treaty of Dresden, in 1745, she was forced to cede this territory to Prussia. A general peace was made at Aix-la-Chapelle in 1748, which left the map of Europe as it had been before the war, except for Silesia. Maria was recognized as the legitimate ruler of the Austrian domains. Thus ended the first phase of the struggle between Prussia and Austria for supremacy in the Germanies.

Frederick was well aware that the Peace of Dresden was only a truce. The jealousy of

with envy, and Maria, preparing for revenge, had no difficulty in finding allies. Both the Russian Czarina Elizabeth and Madame de Pompadour, the mistress of Louis XV, had been greatly offended by Frederick's sarcastic poetry, and this resentment was a factor in leading both Russia and France to come to Austria's aid. France was offered the Austrian Netherlands as a reward for its help.

Britain, meanwhile, interested in the breakdown of French colonial power, supported Prussia. Thus a complete realignment of forces took place in Europe. This shift of forces preceding the Seven Years' War is officially called the "Diplomatic Revolution."

THE SEVEN YEARS' WAR

Frederick the Great, supported by British gold, was now completely surrounded by enemies. In the final analysis it was his military genius which saved Prussia from complete extinction. In 1756 he invaded Saxony, which sided with Austria, and held it during the entire period of the war. The Austrians suffered a series of severe defeats at his hands. But Frederick failed to capture Prague and was forced to fall back into his own country to meet invading French and Russian armies. With a small force he completely defeated the French, then suddenly turned upon and defeated the Austrians gathered in Silesia at the Battle of Leuthen in 1757. Napoleon later extolled this battle as a masterpiece of tactical skill.

Frederick's resources, however, were small compared to the combined forces of his enemies. Only British money saved him from complete financial ruin. His armies were shattered and his country had too small a population to fill the ranks again. Russian troops from the east overran the country, and twice Berlin was captured. The death of Pitt in England also meant disaster, since his successor made peace with France.

By a stroke of luck, Prussia's fortunes changed suddenly with the death of Czarina Elizabeth of Russia. The new Russian Czar, Peter III, was a friend and personal admirer of Frederick the Great. The former's wife, later known as Czarina Catherine II, was a German princess, who knew Frederick well. The Russian troops were ordered to desert Austria and to side with Frederick. Silesia was regained. A combination of luck and military genius had saved Prussia from utter destruction. The Seven Years' War finally came to an end with the Treaty of Hubertsburg in 1763. Maria Theresa failed in her reconquest of Silesia, and Prussia emerged as a leading power in Europe. The predominance of Great Britain over France was secured by victories at sea and abroad.

FIRST PARTITION OF POLAND

Frederick the Great's ambitions were not yet satisfied. He was fully aware of Catherine the Great's designs upon Poland, and so he made an alliance with her in order to share in the booty. In 1772 the first partition of Poland took place. Prussia obtained West Prussia, thereby connecting Brandenburg and East Prussia, which formerly had been separated by Polish territory. Catherine II annexed the lands east of the Duna and Dnieper rivers. Maria Theresa, though verbally professing her opposition to the shady transaction, annexed Galicia. Of her, Frederick said: "She wept, but kept on taking." Poland lost one fourth of its territory.

Prussia definitely became the leader of the northern Protestant princes and gradually weakened Austria's influence. When Austria claimed part of Bavaria in 1778, during a dispute as to the succession of its elector, Frederick frustrated Austrian designs by diplomatic maneuvering and threats of force. As Austria's sun was slowly setting, Prussia rose in power and influence. In the nineteenth century this development became more clearly evident, but, for the present, Austria was still a world power, whose wish must be given full consideration in any continental affair.

FREDERICK'S INTERNAL POLICY

The efforts and capacities of Frederick the Great, however, were not entirely directed toward war and destruction. He spent considerable energy on the internal development of the country. He loved his people much and styled himself "their first servant." Every day he worked hard from morning till night and expected his officials to do the same. During his reign, canals and roads were constructed, over fifteen hundred square miles of marsh and wasteland were redeemed, and even new villages were built to attract settlers from all Europe. His economic policy was mercantilistic in the attempts to keep money and wealth within the borders of the country. Taxes were heavy, but the people felt their money was well spent.

Frederick was a great king in many ways. In addition to political achievements, his intellectual and artistic pursuits must be mentioned. His writings fill over thirty volumes. In religious tolerance he was far advanced for the age. It is safe to say that he may be characterized as the most remarkable enlightened despot in history.

41. Russia Becomes a European Power

RISE OF MUSCOVY

BEFORE AND DURING THE MIDDLE AGES, what we now know as Russia was occupied by numerous tribes of Slavic peoples. They were subjected to attacks of the Mongolian tribes and the Tartars from the east, to the influence of Byzantine culture from the south, and to the pressure of Scandinavia from the west. By the ninth century, a group of eastern Slavs formed a small state called Kiev. This civilization, however, was broken up by more Mongolian raids two hundred years later. Although the Slavs continued to found additional settlements in the north, they were disorganized until the fifteenth century because of these oriental invasions, Scandinavian interference, and internal disagreements.

During this time the grand duchy of Muscovy grew in importance, and one of its rulers, Ivan the Great (1462-1505), took the first steps toward making Russia a great nation. One of his most outstanding acts was to end the Tartar control of the Russians. Moreover, through the influence of his wife, Sophia Paleologus, niece of the last Byzantine emperor, he assumed the position of successor to the Byzantine emperors and ruler of Russia, instead of Muscovy only.

His grandson, Ivan IV, (1533-1584) called the Terrible because of his cruelty, further extended Russian power. He assumed the title of Czar of all Russia, and during his reign the Russian church, which was Greek Orthodox, was freed from the control of the bishops at Constantinople.

During the next two centuries, some progress was made in expansion. The Slavic peoples migrated and settled along the many rivers of Russia. Many dangers were encountered, and bands of bold Cossacks were organized to act both as a spearhead of the expansion and as a military guard for the new settlements. These Cossacks were to be important in later Russian history. The Russians also expanded into Asia, settling in many places now included in Siberia. But Russia did not develop rapidly as a strong national state. Its predominantly agricultural organization, its large territory with poor communication and transportation, and its lack of outlets to the western seas combined to prevent the rise of a national spirit. Long contact with Byzantine and oriental culture made it difficult to introduce Western customs.

Furthermore, the Russian people suffered a lack of good rulers. With the death of Ivan the Terrible, the old Rurik line of rulers came to an end, and the succeeding struggle for the throne caused this period to be known as the "Troublous Times." Not only did the Russians themselves disagree, but Sweden, Poland, and the Ottoman Empire, profiting from the confusion, acquired territory and power at Muscovy's expense. Finally in 1613, a national assembly of nobles met to elect a czar, and chose Michael Romanov who was distantly connected with the family of the Ivans. His government gradually restored order and stopped the incursion of the militant neighbors.

RUSSIA FACES WEST

It was Michael's grandson, Peter the Great, who first made Russia an important nation. Peter began ruling with his imbecile brother Ivan in 1682, but in 1696 Ivan died, leaving Peter sole ruler. The young czar was intensely interested in mechanical things and in

Ivan IV, "the Terrible," 1530–84

One of his first projects was to replace the rebellious *streltsi* by a powerful and well-disciplined army formed on the Prussian model and completely subordinate to his will. He next obtained control over the church, which might otherwise have opposed him. By transferring the power of the Moscow patriarch to a body called the Holy Synod, whose members he himself selected, Peter made himself supreme in ecclesiastical affairs. He realized the importance of the church in the lives of the people, who retained the Orthodox faith wherever they went; therefore, he rigorously persecuted all nonconformers.

Another of Peter's accomplishments was the centralization of government. By abolishing the existing local governments and dividing the country into districts, with his army officers in charge, he increased royal power. These officers ruthlessly extracted money from the peasants, thus providing the funds needed for his reforms. He also made the Duma, or nobles' council, practically powerless by transferring their work to himself and his personally chosen aides.

all phases of the culture of Western Europe. He was determined to westernize Russia as well as to increase her power. To do this he needed both a knowledge of Western affairs and outlets to the Western world.

In a war against the Turks, Peter captured the port of Azov, but could make no further progress without European support. Therefore, he traveled through continental Europe and England. Although he failed to get support, since Europe at that time was about to go to war over the Spanish succession, he acquired much information and sent many experts and workmen back to Russia. These foreigners were to be used only until such time as native Russians were able and willing to assume their duties.

While Peter was abroad, he learned that the *streltsi*, the royal military guard, had revolted. He hurried back to Russia, mercilessly annihilated the *streltsi*, and began the reorganization of the country. An autocrat by nature, he was convinced by his observation of European governments, particularly that of Louis XIV, that absolutism was the best form of rule.

The Intercession Cathedral, Moscow, built in the 16th century on orders of Czar Ivan IV. It was modified in the 19th century but later restored

Peter I, "the Great," 1672–1725

SOCIAL AND ECONOMIC CHANGES

The rigid class system, which existed into the twentieth century, was largely the result of Peter's work. He raised many of his supporters to the rank of nobles, simultaneously rewarding them and weakening the power of the old nobility who were not his enthusiastic admirers. At the same time the lower classes were further regimented, and the institution of serfdom was extended and more firmly established.

Peter's attempts to improve agriculture were only partially successful; but he did succeed to some degree in promoting trades and industries which Russia so woefully lacked. So thorough was his attempt to westernize Russia that he even forced the people to wear Western dress, the men to shave their beards, and the women to emerge from their traditional seclusion. As might be expected, many of these changes affected the upper class only, while the lower classes lived much as before. More momentous was the construction of his new capital, called St. Petersburg, which was built upon land re-claimed from marshes. Symbolically, the young city was known as "Peter's Window into Europe."

SUPREMACY OVER SWEDEN

Peter's foreign policy was to gain territory and to win satisfactory outlets to the seas. The Ottoman Empire, to the south, and Sweden, to the west, were to feel the force of these Russian ambitions.

Since the days of Gustavus Adolphus, Sweden had been regarded as the leader of northern Europe; so vast was her territory around the Baltic Sea. The opposition of France, Denmark, Brandenburg, and Poland failed, and the treaties in 1660 confirmed Sweden's holdings. However, her strength was less than it seemed, because her borders included many nationalities so restless that an armed force was needed to keep them in subjection. Further weakness was caused by the belligerent disposition of the Swedish rulers whose wars exhausted the wealth, manpower, and enthusiasm of the nation.

Charles XII

When Charles XII, only fifteen years old, came to the Swedish throne in 1697, his foreign rivals saw an opportunity to strike and to divide his possessions among them. Prussia refused to take advantage of the king's youth, but Saxony, Russia, and Denmark formed an alliance and prepared to fight what is known as the Great Northern War. To their surprise, Charles, who loved a fight as much as his predecessors, caught them unprepared and defeated them. He then turned south, defeated the Poles, and forced them to dethrone their king, Augustus, and accept his candidate, Stanislaus Leszczynski. Charles was not satisfied with these victories, and, while he delayed making peace in hope of getting more than the allies offered, Peter the Great reorganized his army, renewed the war, and overwhelmed the Swedish at Poltava

Catherine II, empress of Russia, 1762-96

Russian capital. In 1762 Catherine disposed of her half-mad husband, and from then on ruled alone for thirty-four years. Desiring to appear an enlightened despot, concerned only with the welfare of her people, she made some pretenses in that direction, such as encouraging learning among the upper classes, corresponding with the French philosophers, and showing interest in science.

At heart, however, Catherine was an autocrat of the first order. Dominating, passionate, and utterly without moral scruples, she opposed real enlightenment because it would decrease her power. She was undisturbed by the sufferings of the masses and made the central government stronger than ever. By transferring church property to state control, she put the church entirely at her mercy.

However grim a picture her internal policy presents, her foreign activities did add to the glory of Russia.

WAR AGAINST THE TURKS

One part of her program was directed south against the Ottoman Empire, for she realized its weakness and degeneracy. In Turkey, the government's corruption and inefficiency were revealed by the fact that buying and selling all offices from the lowest to the highest was an established practice. Confusion increased, because the many nationalities included in the empire required a powerful army if order were to be maintained; this the Turks lacked, for corruption had also demoralized the army. Discipline was lax, and equipment and tactics were behind the times. It was indeed an excellent time for Catherine to intervene.

The opportunity came in 1768 when a border incident caused war with the Turks. The French, wishing to see Russia weakened, encouraged Turkey, but the inferiority of the Ottomans was quickly revealed in battle, and Russia recaptured the port of Azov, which Peter had won and lost. The Russians went on to greater victories, conquering most of the Rumanian section, and threatening to go farther south into the Balkans.

Finally, in 1774, peace was made. By the Treaty of Kuchuk Kainarji, Russia received

(1709). Charles then sought Turkish aid against Russia, which Peter prevented by returning the port of Azov to the Ottoman Empire. Charles still persisted in his opposition, and Great Britain, Hanover, and Prussia joined the coalition against him.

Not until his death in 1718 was peace restored. By the treaties of Stockholm in 1719 and 1720, Sweden lost nearly all of her German holdings to Hanover and Prussia. Poland was allowed to re-establish Augustus as king. The next year, by the Treaty of Nystad, Russia took from Sweden the Baltic provinces of Latvia and Esthonia and other territories as well. Peter had acquired his opening to the Baltic and became a leader of Europe.

CATHERINE EXTENDS RUSSIA

The immediate successors of Peter were an undistinguished lot who did little to change the status of Russia; but, with the accession of Catherine the Great, Russia made another great advance. She was a German princess, and her marriage to Czar Peter III of Russia had been arranged by Frederick the Great, who thereby increased his influence in the

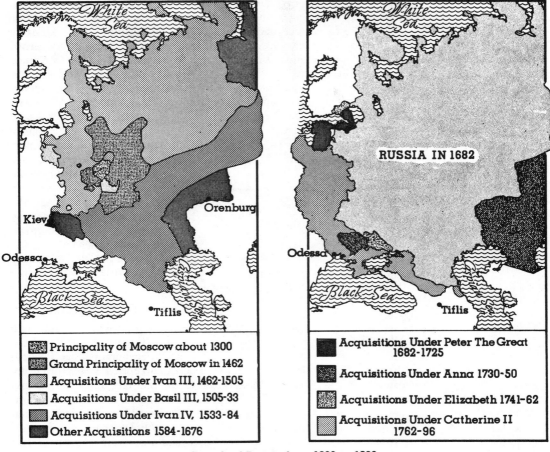

White Sea
Kiev
Orenburg
Odessa
Black Sea
Tiflis
Principality of Moscow about 1300
Grand Principality of Moscow in 1462
Acquisitions Under Ivan III, 1462-1505
Acquisitions Under Basil III, 1505-33
Acquisitions Under Ivan IV, 1533-84
Other Acquisitions 1584-1676
White Sea
RUSSIA IN 1682
Odessa
Black Sea
Tiflis
Acquisitions Under Peter The Great 1682-1725
Acquisitions Under Anna 1730-50
Acquisitions Under Elizabeth 1741-62
Acquisitions Under Catherine II 1762-96

Growth of Russia from 1300 to 1800

the port of Azov and surrounding country; the Turks retained the Rumanian provinces, on condition that the government be reformed; and Russia obtained free navigation in Ottoman waters for her merchant ships and was recognized as protector of certain Christian churches in Constantinople.

By a treaty in 1792 Russian territory was further extended at Turkey's expense. The practical results of these treaties were that Russia now had an outlet to the southern waters and thereby to western Europe, better opportunities to develop her commerce, and the possibility of future intervention and expansion on the pretext of protecting the Christians in the Balkans and in Constantinople.

POLAND FALLS BEFORE RUSSIA'S ADVANCE

Catherine's expansion was also directed westward against Poland, and she had intervened there even before she embarked on the war against Turkey. Here again was a tempting field of activity, for throughout the eighteenth century Poland had been torn by dissension and weakness. The kingdom was a conglomeration of Poles (who predominated), Lithuanians, Latvians, Ukrainians, Cossacks, and Germans. Of these, the first three groups were fairly well united, and in the seventeenth century cooperated in opposing the Swedes in the Baltic and helping

Austria against the Turks, thereby acquiring territory. The others, however, were distinctly minority groups, whose eyes turned toward Russia and Germany. In addition, these many nationalities were of several religions. The majority—Poles and Lithuanians—were Catholics; the Germans were Lutherans; the various Russians were Greek Orthodox; and there were many Jews. The confusion was increased by class difference between the group of selfish, bickering nobles and the mass of mistreated, underprivileged peasants.

Only a strong government could control and remedy such a situation, and, like Turkey, Poland had none. One weakness was the choice of king by election, which caused serious quarrels and enabled the noble electors to collect immense bribes from the candidates. In 1733, this problem led to the War of the Polish Election. Stanislaus Leszczynski, who had been the candidate of Charles XII for the throne, was now supported by his son-in-law, Louis XV. Austria and Russia favored Augustus, the Elector of Saxony, and only a five years' war settled the problem. France was defeated, Augustus III ascended the throne, and most important, Poland was further weakened.

Not only was the kingship weak, but legislative action was practically impossible because, by the freedom of veto, the opposition of one member of the Diet could defeat any proposal.

The incident which actually afforded an opportunity for Russian intervention was the death of Augustus III in 1763. Catherine had her favorite, Stanislaus Poniatowski, made king, theoretically independent, but actually at her command. Frederick the Great and Maria Theresa cooperated with Catherine to prevent the now aroused Polish people from making any governmental reforms which would strengthen Poland. Finally in 1772 the three rulers united in the first partition of Poland, which has already been noted.

This wholesale robbery aroused even the hitherto indifferent Polish nobles, but, because of the losses of the first partition, Poland was far too weak to make any progress. It was merely a matter of time until fresh depredations would be made. Although Frederick and Maria Theresa died in the eighties, their successors were willing to carry on the partition. In 1793 and 1795, therefore, they joined Catherine in the second and third partitions of Poland. The Poles under the valiant Kosciuszko resisted desperately, but they were easily defeated by their powerful enemies. King Stanislaus II resigned and moved to Russia, and Poland ceased to be.

Kosciuszko

By the partitions of Poland, Catherine had extended Russia's boundaries westward until they adjoined Austria and Prussia. By Catherine's effective, if unethical, methods, Russia had become an important part of western Europe.

Battle of Raclawice (1794), in which Kosciuszko defeated the Russians

42. An All-Water Route to India

EUROPE LOOKS BEYOND

SINCE THE BEGINNING OF recorded history, civilization has been moving westward. As the peoples of the Tigris and Euphrates valleys reached the height of their cultures, they lived to see their western neighbors of the "fertile crescent" region adopt their civilization and adapt it to the new and different requirements of their environment. Later the Greeks took the torch of civilization, then the Romans. Each time culture traveled, some of its characteristics were retained; but the acquirement of the new frontier caused changes and variations in the old order. This influence of the frontier has been one of the most important factors in the development of civilization.

This process of movement and change was about to make its most spectacular westward leap at the opening of the modern era. At the same time that kings were centralizing their power and modern nations were making their appearance, Europe was looking beyond its borders.

Part of this enlarged point of view was a result of the Crusades. Knights, on returning from the Holy Land, brought with them strange tales of stranger lands. They aroused interest and curiosity about what existed beyond the knowledge of those who stayed at home. Their awakened imagination demanded more information of the East.

The returning Crusaders brought with them something of even greater importance—spices! The value of this eastern product was obvious to a Europe which had no refrigeration, and was accustomed to food of uncertain age. With this oriental luxury, dining became more enjoyable; in fact, so accustomed did the noble and middle-class families become to these condiments that, lacking spices, the food formerly eaten without question became almost inedible. Spices from the East had become necessities.

IMPORTANCE OF THE RENAISSANCE

Two centuries earlier this interest in the East and the demand for an eastern product would have gone largely unsatisfied. Now, however, there were those who were ready to meet the need. This was a result of the great change, known as the Renaissance, which had swept over southern Europe by the middle of the fifteenth century.

No longer were the most intelligent and best educated minds restricted to supernatural matters. An interest in things worldly was no longer condemned. The attitude of the church toward business and commerce was relaxed, as can be seen in the Catholic theologians' arguments that the taking of interest on money loaned was no longer a sin, and in the beginnings of the Medici banking facilities in Italy. Throughout Europe trade was awakening and commerce was developing under a crude capitalistic system. This commercial revolution, which has been described in a previous section, was part of the general awakening which was affecting every phase of European life.

Marco Polo and his father and uncle on their arrival at the court of Kublai Khan

The Renaissance, however, did not change the attitude of Europe merely toward trade and commerce. The new interest in history, literature, and the humanities seemed to increase the thirst for knowledge of things beyond the limited confines of the European world. An appreciative audience was found by travelers and merchants who told of their visits to India, China, or Japan.

MARCO POLO

The most famous of the men who recounted what had been seen in the East was Marco

Marco Polo (1254?–?1324)

Polo, a Venetian merchant. His father, Nicolo Polo, and his uncle, Maffeo Polo, had made extensive travels through the Far East in the course of their trading ventures, and had visited the magnificent court of the Tartar emperor, Kublai Khan. In 1271 Marco Polo accompanied them on another long trading journey, and in 1275 they arrived in Peking. Marco quickly became a favorite of the Khan, and was entrusted with several official missions for the government. Wherever he went, Marco Polo was impressed by the splendor and riches of the Orient. This wealth, accumulated over centuries by Oriental despots, was a source of amazement to a man of 13th-century Europe, where there was no over-all ruler, and conflicts among small states and feudal principalities had helped prevent such great magnificence and display of riches. The Venetian travelers remained in China for 17 years. Finally given permission to leave, they sailed along the Chinese, Malayan, and Indian coasts to Persia, and then traveled overland to the Mediterranean. They arrived in Venice in 1295.

A few years later, while he was fighting for the Venetians in one of the numerous wars between Italian city-states, Marco Polo was captured in a naval encounter with the Genoese, and was thrown into prison. There he dictated an account of his travels to a fellow captive. Published as *The Book of Marco Polo*, his book showed him to be a keen, entertaining observer. Its descriptions of Oriental wealth and magnificence stirred European interest in the Far East and encouraged attempts to find a more direct route to it. It undoubtedly had a great influence on subsequent European exploration.

NEW INVENTIONS

Great inventions and discoveries in the field of science made it possible to spread information about lands beyond Europe. To Johann Gutenberg of Mainz is usually given the credit for the invention, about 1447, of printing by means of movable type although the use of movable initial letters, certainly a forerunner of the invention, was in use previously. This epoch-making invention's effect on the spread of knowledge can hardly be over-emphasized. Information regarding dis-

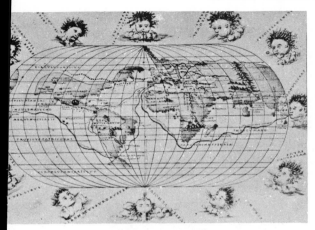

Map of the World, made by Battista Agnese in the 16th century. Agnese, a Genoese, is supposed to have made his maps in Venice, about 1536-64

coveries or explorations would henceforth be rapidly diffused over broad areas. As each new seeker of knowledge set out, he had at hand the combined information gained by all of his predecessors.

About the same time more accurate maps and charts were introduced. Earlier, the compass and astrolabe had come into use. These new aids permitted the navigator to make longer voyages. No more must the mariner hug the coast and follow each irregularity of the shore line. Finally the invention of the telescope, though it occurred much later (1609), freed the sailor from much of the uncertainty of sea travel.

TRADE ROUTES OF VENICE AND GENOA

The first European traders to profit as a result of the demand for products of the East were those of the Italian city-states. Making their way through the Mediterranean to Asia, these Italians were met by Arab traders, who had carried goods from such centers as Calicut and Malacca. These products were then distributed in Europe by the Italians themselves or passed on to merchants from the countries of northern Europe. The Asiatic routes were either overland, across deserts and mountains, or else by a long sea route around the eastern and southern coasts,

then through the Red Sea or Persian Gulf, and finally by land to the cities of the Black and Mediterranean seas.

Either by land or by sea, this means of transporting goods was uncertain and very expensive. Not only was the route long, and the mountains, deserts, and seas dangerous, but the threat of bandits and pirates was always present.

In spite of the tremendous risks involved, Venice, Genoa, and the other Italian cities profited because of their geographical position. The position of Italy made it the logical center of Mediterranean shipping, and trade bound for the German rivers of northern Europe found it convenient to use Venice or Genoa as southern terminals. It was partly an accident of geography that gave Italy a virtual monopoly of intercontinental trade.

This monopoly depended upon two conditions: the eastern end of the Mediterranean, the gateway to the Orient, must remain open; and this gateway must be the only one into Asia. The Portuguese and the Ottoman Turks threatened to remove these requirements for monopoly. Portuguese navigators, directed by Prince Henry, began cautiously to advance along the unknown African coast in an attempt to find an all-water route to India. If they succeeded, not only would transportation costs be lowered significantly, but also

Levant Traders, from a 15th-century MS. The Levant was the eastern Mediterranean region

the bulk of the trade from the Orient would avoid the Mediterranean and Italy entirely by following the Atlantic coast to the northern European market.

The idea that the Turks closed the trade routes, and so caused the discovery of America and the all-water route to India, persists in spite of revelations which modify that interpretation. Traders from Italian city-states enjoyed favored positions in important Near Eastern cities. Their privileges were threatened by the expansion of the Ottoman Turks, and considerable friction resulted. Mohammed II began in 1452 to levy tariff duties, or tribute, on trading vessels passing through the Bosporous. Constantinople fell in 1453, and ten years later the Turks and the Venetians began a war which lasted until 1479. During this period there were clashes in Syria, Asia Minor, Greece, and the Mediterranean islands. By 1500, Genoa as well as Venice lost important colonies in the Near East.

The northern trade route from the Orient was threatened by warfare between the Turks; but Damascus, Beirut, Aleppo, and Alexandria grew in importance while the middle and northern routes were practically closed. The Turks continued their advance. Damascus fell in 1516, and in the following year Cairo was added to the Ottoman possessions. So it was that by 1520 the old routes between Orient and Occident were under Ottoman control.

PRINCE HENRY THE NAVIGATOR

Significant events were happening in the West while the Ottoman Turks were successfully challenging Italian preeminence in the Near East. Prince Henry, a younger son of King John I of Portugal, was directing the Portuguese search for an all-water route to India. The Navigator, as he is known to history, had taken part in the conquest of Ceuta and was inspired with the hope of finding the rumored kingdom of Prester John. Henry possessed an independent income and was keenly interested in geography and navigation. The astronomical laboratory which he built on the promontory of Sagres in south-

Prince Henry the Navigator (1394–1460)

western Portugal, became the gathering place of those daring navigators who were advancing down the African coast. As these voyages continued, Henry apparently lost much of his desire to effect an alliance with Prester John to attack the Ottomans from the rear, and concentrated his attention on discovery.

Trained in the school conducted at the laboratory, financed by the prince, encouraged and aided by new charts and maps, daring mariners made important progress. The Madeira Islands were reached by 1420, and then in time the whole western coast of Africa became known to Europeans. Cape Verde was reached in 1445, the mouth of the Gambia River in 1455, and, when Henry died in 1462, his navigators had advanced to a point within twelve degrees of the equator.

Tracing the African coast line was only one of the contributions made by Prince Henry and his associates. An even more important result was the training given to navigators and the development of navigation. It can be said that the science of navigation originated with Prince Henry, since it scarcely existed before his day. A large number of the early explorers and discoverers of the New World were trained by Henry, and they all profited from his efforts.

DOWN AND AROUND AFRICA

Moreover, the attempts to encircle Africa did not die with the prince. Portuguese captains continued their efforts. When Cape Palmas was discovered and it was found that the coast bent eastward, there was great rejoicing. Now the sea route to India had been found! The southern coast of Africa had been reached! Hopes were dashed the following year when they discovered that, after twelve hundred miles, the coast again swung southward. The slow, progressive, stage-by-stage following of the coast line had to be continued. In 1471 the equator was crossed, and thereafter progress was more rapid.

Vasco da Gama (1469?–1524)

Bartholomew Diaz (1450?–1500), Portuguese mariner who discovered the Cape of Good Hope

In 1486, Diaz encountered a storm off the coast and for thirteen days was blown southward, out of sight of shore. When he saw land again, he found he was two hundred miles east of the southern tip of Africa. Upon his return, Diaz named this point the Cape of Storms; but soon afterward King John II changed the name to Cape of Good Hope, because it gave promise of a sea route to India and great profits.

Both of these hopes were realized in 1498 when Vasco da Gama reached India and on his return brought back a cargo worth sixty times the cost of his expedition. This discovery of a sea route to India was the finishing blow to Italian trade supremacy. The Asiatic land routes were almost wholly discarded and the Atlantic superseded the Mediterranean as the center of European sea trade. World economic leadership moved westward from Italy to Portugal and her neighbor in the Iberian peninsula, Spain.

Christopher Columbus at the Royal Court of Spain

Departure of Columbus' Expedition from Palos, Spain, in August, 1492

Columbus' Landing on San Salvador, from a copper engraving by Theodore de Bry, 1590

Columbus in Cuba, left; center, discovery of San Domingo, from a sketch attributed to Columbus, in "Epistola Christofori Colom", published about 1494; right, one of Columbus' vessels, from the same book

43. The Search for "El Dorado"

COLUMBUS

THE ENTERPRISING Spanish monarchs, having expelled the Moors from Spain, were free to turn their attention to the pleas of Columbus, a Genoese seafarer, who had lived for several years in the Madeira Islands. Here he had listened eagerly to his fellow sailors discussing stories and legends of the uncharted lands to the west. He had early accepted the views of the new scientific school: that the world was spherical in shape and that but a short stretch of water lay between western Europe and the Orient. He was fired with the desire to be the first to find a western route to the rich spice markets.

Repeated discouragement and failure met his efforts to gain royal aid in both Portugal and England. Queen Isabella of Spain, however, was finally won over by his enthusiasm and persistence. Thus, but for the shortsightedness of John II of Portugal and Henry VII of England, those countries might have had the honor of discovering the new world.

Three small vessels, well fitted out and manned by crews of capable young sailors, set sail from Palos on August 3, 1492. The little fleet first made the Canary Islands, and then sailed westward September 6 on the real voyage of discovery. After five weeks, Columbus' expedition sighted land on October 12, 1492. It was probably the island known now as Watling Island in the Bahama group. The natives found there were called "Indians" by Columbus, because he believed he had reached a part of the Indies.

After sailing along the coast of Cuba and exploring the island of Haiti in a fruitless search for gold and spices, Columbus left for Spain with two vessels of the fleet. The wreckage of the third, which had run aground on the shores of the island of Haiti, was used to construct a fort for the forty-four Spaniards who remained and founded the first colony in the New World.

Columbus was received by Ferdinand and Isabella with great honor and was granted the titles of admiral, and viceroy of all the lands he had discovered. He made three other western voyages, in which he touched various islands of the Caribbean, the northern coast of South America, and what is now British Honduras. He died in 1506, probably not knowing that instead of discovering a new route to the Indies, he had found a New World.

There is fairly valid evidence to show that Leif Ericsson discovered America in the year 1000, and gave the name Vinland to the

Landing of Lief Ericsson in the New World, from an original painting by Edward Moran

Americus Vespucius

region he visited. No permanent results came from this discovery, and so far as the European world is concerned, Columbus was the discoverer of America. Although Columbus made one of the greatest discoveries in history, the New World was named for Americus Vespucius. Without any basis of fact, Vespucius claimed to have made a voyage to the New World before Columbus' voyage of 1498, and geographers called the new lands America.

Spain and Portugal divided the newly discovered lands between them by the Treaty of Tordesillas in 1494. This treaty took the place of the papal bull of 1493, and gave to Portugal those areas which lay east of a line drawn 370 leagues west of the Cape Verde Islands, while Spain was to have those areas which lay west of the line.

MAGELLAN

Various Spanish expeditions between 1493 and about 1530, traced the American coast line from what became New England to the Straits of Magellan. Greatest of all Spanish explorers was Magellan, a native of Portugal who entered Spanish service.

Ferdinand Magellan

On September 10, 1519, Magellan's little fleet of five vessels and some 250 men set sail from Spain. Only one of the five was to complete the first voyage around the world. After spending the winter on the shores of Patagonia in southern Argentina, quelling innumerable mutinies among his crew, and suffering terrible physical hardships, Magellan reached the Philippine Islands early in the spring of 1521. Here he lost his life in a native uprising. In spite of the loss of leader, vessels, and crew, one ship of the original fleet, the *Victoria*, persevered and cast anchor in Seville on September 8, 1522, just three years after it had left Spain.

This voyage, supplemented by earlier ones, gave the Spaniards a limited idea, at least, of the Atlantic coast line of the New World and definitely proved that the Spice Islands could be reached by sailing west. Spanish interest in the lucrative spice trade was reawakened, and stately galleons soon appeared in the regions visited by Magellan and his companions.

CORTÉS—GREATEST OF THE CONQUISTADORES

Balboa, a bankrupt stowaway on an expedition to Central America, led an expedition across the Isthmus of Panama in 1513 and discovered the Pacific Ocean, which he called the South Sea. Unfortunately, Balboa was executed by the treacherous Pedrarias Dávila, the governor who was sent by Charles V to take charge of affairs on the Isthmus.

Great as were the achievements of Balboa, another explorer was to surpass them within a few years. This man was Hernando Cortés, who possessed remarkable military and executive ability. After distinguishing himself in the conquest of Cuba, Cortés won greater glory in Mexico. The governor of Cuba gave him command of an expedition to Mexico in

Balboa claiming the Pacific Ocean for Spain

1519, a command which Cortés retained in spite of later efforts to remove him. Equipped with eleven vessels, four hundred soldiers, two hundred Indians, thirty-two horses, and ten cannon, Cortés set out for the mainland and disembarked at what is now Vera Cruz.

In Mexico he found the Aztecs, a powerful and highly civilized people who had migrated from the north early in the fourteenth century. They had quickly conquered the natives and set up a harsh rule over them. The subjugated tribes saw in Cortés and his army a way to avenge themselves and were eager to join forces against their hated rulers. Montezuma, the Aztec king, feared that these white strangers were the supernatural beings for whom his subject people had been waiting to free them from oppression. He hastened to send gifts to the Spaniards rather than attacking them. Cortés, fired with the zeal of conquest, proceeded on his way to the Aztec capital, Mexico City, or Tenochtitlán, as it was then called.

The magnificence of this city, with its great stone buildings and its vast stores of precious metals, exceeded even the most extravagant hopes of Cortés and his followers. The daring Spanish leader immediately strengthened his position by seizing the person of Montezuma and assuming virtual charge of the government. His successful conquest, however, was interrupted by a recall expedition sent out by Velásquez, governor of Cuba. Cortés ignored the governor's command, defeated his forces, and incorporated them into his own troops.

Upon returning to the Aztec capital, the Spanish conqueror found the city and countryside in a state of insurrection. He released Montezuma, hoping that his influence would quiet the frenzied condition of the Aztecs. This stratagem was of no avail, for the native ruler was fatally wounded by one of his own race when he urged obedience to the Spaniards.

Attacked by Indian hordes, Cortés' army suffered severely, losing most of its horses, cannon, and treasure, although a few soldiers survived and escaped to friendly near-by tribes. Sufficient reinforcements arrived from Cuba late in 1520, however, so that by the summer of the next year, Cortés recaptured Mexico City and proceeded to consolidate the conquest of the rest of Mexico. Not content with this, he organized new expeditions to explore the territory south of Mexico, and to voyage along the Pacific coast in an attempt to find a strait through the continent.

CONQUEST OF THE INCAS

Similar activity was going on in South America with Panama as a base. The most spectacular of these expeditions and conquests was that of Pizarro in Peru, which parallels the earlier Mexican conquest in many instances. The natives of Peru, the Incas, were as far advanced in government and civilization as the Aztecs in Mexico. By conquest and amalgamation, the Inca

Cortés and Montezuma

Execution of the Inca by Pizarro

An Inca Dwelling

empire had acquired great wealth and political efficiency.

Pizarro, the Spanish conqueror of Peru, was of humble origin. His was a striking military character, with tremendous capacity for work, and indomitable perseverance. Though less brilliant and attractive than Cortés, Pizarro gained the confidence and obedience of his subordinates. Associated with him were an adventurous soldier named Almagro and a renegade priest known as De Luque. This priest had gained a considerable fortune and served as financier of the Pizarro expeditions.

After several perilous attempts, Pizarro sailed for Peru in January, 1531, with an army of less than two hundred men, and twenty-seven horses. He established his headquarters near the present Tumbez. Here he learned of civil war caused by the jealousy of two Inca brothers, Huascar and Atahualpa. The latter had succeeded in establishing his authority in Cuzco, and like Montezuma, was inclined to believe the white intruders were supernatural beings and sought to placate them with gifts.

The Spaniards, in the meantime, moved into the interior toward Caxamarca, which they found deserted. Outside the city, Atahualpa and the Inca army of forty thousand drew up ready to annihilate the tiny Spanish force. Pizarro stationed his forces in strategic positions, seized the Inca, and slaughtered great numbers of the over-confident natives. Atahualpa hoped to secure his release by assembling a dazzling store of treasure; but the Spaniards took the treasure and then executed the Inca because of his complicity in the death of Huascar.

Pizarro entered Cuzco in November, 1533, and began to consolidate his victories. Details of government, allotment of lands and Indian laborers, management of mines, and the organization of new expeditions occupied the efforts of Pizarro for the next few years. Civil wars and rebellion disturbed the peace of Peru until the Pizarros and the Almagros were eliminated, but the conquest of South America continued.

EXTENSION OF SPANISH CONTROL

Tales of mines of fabulous wealth, rich cities, and incredible buried treasure kept these eager conquerors in constant search of "El Dorado." Hostile natives, swamps, rivers, pathless mountains, deserts, disease, and jealousy did not daunt them. Always just beyond, they expected to find the veritable pot of gold. Although Cortés and Pizarro present the most fascinating and picturesque figures among them, many others in a lesser degree carried on similar conquests in Ecuador, Colombia, the Amazon basin, and Chile.

Spanish conquest of the central portion of the continent, now occupied largely by Argentina and Paraguay, began with the expedition of Mendoza to the Plata basin in 1536. An early attempt to found Buenos Aires failed, but control over the great river system which converges into the estuary known as La Plata, was secured after 1537. In that year a fort was built at the site of Asunción, now the capital of Paraguay. Martínez de Irala governed Asunción with more than usual skill, and sent exploring expeditions into the Gran Chaco west of the Paraguay River. Buenos Aires was finally founded in 1580 by Garay; but by that time the western portion of modern Argentina was being settled from Chile and Peru.

SPANISH CONQUESTS NORTH OF THE GULF AND THE RIO GRANDE

Spanish efforts in the New World were by no means confined to Mexico and South America during the era of the *conquistadores*. Florida, the northern Gulf coast, and the

De Soto's Discovery of the Mississippi in 1541, from a painting by W. H. Powell. (Three Lions)

great southwest were traversed by Spanish forces before 1550.

The first Spanish adventurer to visit what is now the United States, was Juan Ponce de León who sought in vain for the Fountain of Youth in Florida. Many attempts to colonize Florida failed. An expedition led by Narvaez in 1528 was almost completely destroyed. Hernando de Soto landed at Tampa Bay in 1539 with more than five hundred men. For three years De Soto led his men through the wilderness in an irregular march which crossed most of what is now the southern part of the United States east of the Mississippi River. De Soto himself was buried in the Mississippi when he died in 1542, and the remnants of the expedition returned to Mexico.

Ponce de León

Francisco Vásquez de Coronado led another expedition into the great southwest while De Soto was on his odyssey. Coronado was seeking the Seven Cities of Cibola, supposedly rich in gold and other treasures. The exploration took Coronado as far as modern Kansas, but no wealthy cities were found. A party from this expedition discovered the Grand Canyon of the Colorado and added much to knowledge of the regions visited.

In the same year that Coronado returned to Mexico, 1542, explorations were made by sea northward along the California coast by Cabrillo and Ferrelo. Sixty years later Vizcaíno sailed along the same route.

Successful Spanish colonies were established by 1609 at two points in what is now the United States. The first was that of St. Augustine, Florida, which Menéndez de Avilés founded in 1565 to defeat French efforts to gain a foothold. The second was Santa Fe, New Mexico, which Juan de Oñate placed on a permanent basis between 1598 and 1609. It has been a capital ever since.

Coronado leading his men across New Mexico in their search for the Seven Cities of Cibola

Spain was less successful in her colonizing efforts in continental North America than in the southern continent. This situation is partially explained by the wide area over which Spanish efforts were scattered, and by the small population of Spain itself. Then, too, the northern wilderness was far less attractive than the more southern regions where Indian tribes were usually more docile, and where there were rich civilizations to conquer.

POLITICAL ADMINISTRATION IN SPANISH COLONIES

The whole Spanish colonial policy was dictated by royal authority. The Spanish possessions in the New World were considered as belonging personally to the sovereigns of Castile. With the rapid growth of colonial territory, it was necessary in 1524 to organize a special advisory committee. This royal body, the Council of the Indies, was the final legislative and judicial authority of Spanish America. It organized territorial units, and filled political and religious offices.

At first the king had allowed private adventurers to organize and subsidize their own expeditions, and rule and dispose of the territory they had conquered, with certain royal restrictions. It was found, however, that frequently the "conqueror" was tempted to ignore superior authority. Thus the king decided to send a royal appointee, known as a viceroy, to represent him personally in the New World. The territory over which he had charge was known as a viceroyalty.

The *audiencia*, in reality an administrative court system, grew up as a check on the viceroy. This body acted as the supreme judicial authority in the colonies, and had original jurisdiction over matters concerning the crown and the Indians. It came to act in a supervisory capacity over trade and finance, as well as over general preservation of law and order.

In the colonial towns, some degree of self-government manifested itself. The function of the *cabildo*, or municipal council, was similar to that of the New England town meeting. The tendency in Spanish America, however, was

Latin America about 1700

away from municipal democratic political organization, due largely to royal hostility and local corruption. Spain made an effort to maintain an honest and efficient colonial administration, which resulted in a system of checks on all officials. The viceroy was watched by the *audiencia*, which in turn was spied upon by the lower officials. Later on, a *residencia*, or royal visitor, was sent over to look into the conduct of all the officials, large and small, in a given political unit.

Since corruption, however, was a chronic malady in Spanish America, the wonder is not that the governmental structure finally weakened, but that it survived as long as it did.

ECONOMIC ORGANIZATION IN SOUTH AMERICA

The economic life of the Spanish colonies was also closely supervised by government officials. Spain, as well as the other nations, held mercantilist views of commerce. The welfare of the state, so the theory proposed, required a full treasury of gold, a large consuming and producing population, and an extensive merchant marine. A favorable balance of trade must be always maintained; therefore, exports must exceed imports so that specie may come into the country. To accomplish this, raw materials must be brought in, manufactured, exported, and sold.

Colonies, it was held, should furnish raw materials and markets for the mother country, but must not be competitors. It was the policy of each European state to monopolize and control the trade of its colonies.

As early as 1503, Spain organized the *Casa de Contratación* or House of Trade, for the purpose of controlling colonial commerce. Certain ports, such as Seville in Spain and Vera Cruz and Porto Bello in America, were opened for colonial trade. To protect and supervise this commerce, a fleet system was established. Land commerce in America had to be carried on by pack trains and river boats, while wholesale and retail trade was conducted in markets and fairs, the most famous of which was held in Porto Bello in Panama.

In spite of her efforts, Spain was not able to maintain her trade monopoly, for Dutch, English, and French freebooters and pirates captured her treasure fleets, and smuggled great quantities of goods into Spanish colonial ports.

The labor supply in Spanish America came largely from the native population. The first "conquerors" were given the right to the labor of the Indians living within their royal grant. This plan was known as the *encomienda* system and aimed to protect and civilize the native, as

Mission San Diego de Alcala

well as to exploit him. Among those who early opposed this virtual enslavement of the Indian population was Father Las Casas. He used his influence against the continuance of this system, but, strange to say, favored Negro slavery in its place.

The principal occupations in Spanish America were agriculture and stock raising, although mining attracted the attention of the more adventurous and was heavily subsidized by the home government.

SOCIAL LIFE IN THE SPANISH COLONIES

Spanish American civilization became a composite of Spanish and native culture, based on a fairly rigid caste system. Most of the high political offices were held by native born Spaniards, while next in the social scale were the Creoles, who were American born. Below them came the *mestizo*, half Spanish and half Indian, who made up the larger part of the army. The two lowest classes, the Indians and the Negroes, had no social or political privileges and were held in slavery.

Education was by no means neglected, but it too was based on the caste system. Only the sons of government officials, wealthy merchants, and professional men attended the colonial universities. The scholarly qualities of the universities of Mexico and Lima, established by royal decree in 1553, were recognized by contemporary European institutions of higher learning. Many of the clergy were devotees of intellectual pursuits, and books were written on scholarly and popular subjects.

Las Casas protecting Indians from soldiers

393

Instruction and curriculum in the universities, as well as in the mission school, were supervised closely by the Church. Only the most elementary educational institutions were opened to the *mestizos*.

The influence of the Church, however, was perhaps felt most in the frontier Indian mission, where the *encomienda* system failed or proved unprofitable. Members of the Jesuit, Dominican, and Franciscan orders were especially zealous in carrying Christianity and European civilization to the frontier natives. The aim of these missionaries was not only to gain religious converts, but to give industrial and agricultural training.

Each mission had its grain fields, ranges, vegetable gardens, orchards, and vineyards, which were cared for by the Indians. The men were given instruction in carpentry and winemaking, while the native women learned spinning, weaving, sewing, and cooking. The intention was to train the natives to support themselves, and eventually to give them the mission lands and transfer their religious care to the parish priest.

By continuing this process, the Spanish missionaries gradually carried Christianity north of the Rio Grande into Texas, and by 1776 they had gone as far north as the present San Francisco. Prominent among these zealous *padres* were Kino and Serra who planted missions in the southwest and in California.

Frequently military posts, *presidios*, were found necessary to protect the mission outposts. Thus the *padre* and the soldier became the two civilizing forces on the frontier. In spite of these military and religious efforts, however, the Spaniards were unable to gain more than a feeble political hold on what is now southwestern United States.

Whatever the shortcomings of the Spanish treatment of the native population, it does not compare unfavorably with that of other European powers. Spain aimed at racial, religious, and cultural assimilation rather than annihilation as England did. This practice resulted in a large population of mixed blood and the removal of racial antipathies. Today there are in Spanish America relatively few families of pure European blood.

CONTRIBUTION OF SPAIN TO THE AMERICAS

Historians in the past have unjustly minimized Spanish contributions to the Americas. The "conquerors" bore not only the sword, but also Christianity to the New World. They brought with them such plants as the citrus fruits, sugar and cotton; and such animals as cattle, sheep, horses, and mules.

From Mexico to Chile, the Spanish language and institutions are still dominant. Some of the United States have Spanish names, namely, California, Florida, Colorado, and Nevada. Innumerable rivers, mountains, towns, and cities north of the Río Grande bear Spanish names, while the southwestern Indian tribes in the United States still speak Spanish in preference to English. In many of the cities in the same region, there is a Spanish quarter in which life goes on much as it has done for generations past. Spanish architecture is still popular, and in Florida and the southwestern states are interesting old missions and government buildings erected by the early Spaniards.

The southern and western festival, rodeo, and mission plays are carried over from colonial days. Even the American cowboy has inherited his trade, his horse, his outfit, vocabulary, and methods from his earlier Spanish prototype. Bells in numerous belfries of mission churches and cathedrals from Florida to California bear the Spanish royal coat of arms; while land surveys in many of the southwestern states still rest on early Spanish grants, whose original records are now in Mexico City or Madrid. In fact, the literature, history, and life of this whole region of the United States is distinctly colored by its early background. Thus in spite of the fact that Spain was eventually pushed out of the limits of the United States, she has left us a rich heritage.

Her greatest contribution, however, was made to the present Latin-American nations. Today the Spanish blood, language, religion, and culture are the dominant forces in the republics to the south. Spain no longer controls the political destiny of any area of the New World, but she still wields immeasurable influence in her gift of Hispanic civilization.